The Greenwood Encyclopedia of
Global Medieval
Life and Culture

The Greenwood Encyclopedia of
Global Medieval
Life and Culture

Volume 3
ASIA AND OCEANIA

Joyce E. Salisbury, General Editor

Raman N. Seylon, South Asia
William B. Ashbaugh, East Asia
Nancy Sullivan, Oceania

GREENWOOD PRESS
Westport, Connecticut · London

Library of Congress Cataloging-in-Publication Data

The Greenwood encyclopedia of global Medieval life and culture / Joyce E. Salisbury, general editor.
    p. cm.
  Includes bibliographical references and index.
   ISBN 978-0-313-33801-4 ((set) : alk. paper) — ISBN 978-0-313-33802-1 ((vol. 1) : alk. paper) — ISBN 978-0-313-33803-8 ((vol. 2) : alk. paper) — ISBN 978-0-313-33804-5 ((vol. 3) : alk. paper)
   1. Civilization, Medieval.   I. Salisbury, Joyce E.
CB351.G743   2009
940.1 — dc22   2008036709

British Library Cataloguing in Publication Data is available.

Library of Congress Catalog Card Number: 2008036709
ISBN: 978-0-313-33801-4 (set)
      978-0-313-33802-1 (vol. 1)
      978-0-313-33803-8 (vol. 2)
      978-0-313-33804-5 (vol. 3)

First published in 2009

Greenwood Press, 88 Post Road West, Westport, CT 06881
An imprint of Greenwood Publishing Group, Inc.
www.greenwood.com

Printed in the United States of America

The paper used in this book complies with the
Permanent Paper Standard issued by the National
Information Standards Organization (Z39.48–1984).

10 9 8 7 6 5 4 3 2 1

The publisher has done its best to make sure the instructions and/or recipes in this book are correct. However, users should apply judgment and experience when preparing recipes, especially parents and teachers working with young people. The publisher accepts no responsibility for the outcome of any recipe included in this volume.

Contents

Preface for Users of Global Medieval Life and Culture ix

VOLUME 1

EUROPE *by Joyce E. Salisbury* 1

Chronology 3
Maps 7
Overview and Topical Essays 15
 1. Historical Overview 15
 2. Religion 24
 3. Economy 33
 4. The Arts 42
 5. Society 51
 6. Science and Technology 60
 7. Global Ties 69
Short Entries: People, Ideas, Events, and Terms 79
Primary Documents 149
Appendix: Dynasties of Medieval Europe 177

THE AMERICAS *by James L. Fitzsimmons* 179

Chronology 181
Maps 185
Overview and Topical Essays 189
 1. Historical Overview 189
 2. Religion 196
 3. Economy 204
 4. The Arts 213
 5. Society 224
 6. Science and Technology 238
 7. Global Ties 251
Short Entries: People, Ideas, Events, and Terms 259
Primary Documents 341
Appendix: Mesoamérican Rulers and Historical Periods 355

VOLUME 2

AFRICA *by Victoria B. Tashjian*   357

Chronology   359
Maps   363
Overview and Topical Essays   367
    1. Historical Overview   367
    2. Religion   377
    3. Economy   386
    4. The Arts   395
    5. Society   405
    6. Science and Technology   415
    7. Global Ties   425
Short Entries: People, Ideas, Events, and Terms   435
Primary Documents   497
Appendix: Dynasties of Medieval Africa   513

NORTH AFRICA AND THE MIDDLE EAST *by James E. Lindsay*   515

Chronology   517
Maps   519
Overview and Topical Essays   525
    1. Historical Overview   525
    2. Religion   533
    3. Economy   541
    4. The Arts   549
    5. Society   556
    6. Science and Technology   566
    7. Global Ties   573
Short Entries: People, Ideas, Events, and Terms   581
Primary Documents   641
Appendix: Medieval Islamic Caliphs   657

VOLUME 3

SOUTH ASIA *by Raman N. Seylon, with the assistance of Joyce E. Salisbury and John A. Wagner*   659

Chronology   661
Maps   665
Overview and Topical Essays   671
    1. Historical Overview   671
    2. Religion   688
    3. Economy   702
    4. The Arts   719
    5. Society   736
    6. Science and Technology   752
    7. Global Ties   766
Short Entries: People, Ideas, Events, and Terms   775
Primary Documents   837
Appendix: Dynasties of Medieval India   859

EAST ASIA *by William B. Ashbaugh* 861

Chronology 863
Maps 865
Overview and Topical Essays 871
    1. Historical Overview 871
    2. Religion 885
    3. Economy 895
    4. The Arts 903
    5. Society 911
    6. Science and Technology 918
    7. Global Ties 925
Short Entries: People, Ideas, Events, and Terms 935
Primary Documents 1009
Appendix: Dynasties of Medieval China, Rulers of Medieval Japan,
and Chinese Inventions 1021

OCEANIA *by Nancy Sullivan, with the assistance of Robert D. Craig* 1025

Chronology 1027
Map 1029
Overview and Topical Essays 1031
    1. Historical Overview 1031
    2. Religion 1040
    3. Economy 1046
    4. The Arts 1050
    5. Society 1054
    6. Science and Technology 1058
    7. Global Ties 1062
Short Entries: People, Ideas, Events, and Terms 1067
Primary Documents 1137
Appendix: Major Island Groups of Oceania 1151

Index 1153
About the Editor, Authors, and Contributors 1173

Preface for Users of Global Medieval Life and Culture

Two concepts have dominated the twenty-first century: globalization and the information explosion facilitated by the Internet. When we decided to present a new history of the medieval world—also called the Middle Ages—we knew these modern principles could help guide us to new insights into the past. In these volumes, globalization shapes the content that we have chosen to cover, and the electronic age has guided our organization. In addition, the features are carefully considered to make these volumes engaging and pedagogically useful.

Global Content

The medieval age was a European concept. From about the fourteenth century, Europeans defined the 1,000 years from the fall of the Roman Empire to the Renaissance as the "middle," separating the classical world from the "modern" one. Practically from the time of this designation, scholars have argued about whether this periodization makes sense, but scholarly arguments have not substantially changed the designation. Textbooks and curricula have kept the period as a separate entity, and we study the medieval world that extends from about 400 to 1400 C.E. with undiminished fascination.

Scholars of medieval Europe have shown that, during this formative period, many of the ideas and institutions developed that shape our modern world. The rise of democratic institutions, a prosperous middle class, and a vibrant Christianity are just a few of the developments that marked medieval Europe. These are some of the reasons that have kept the field of study vibrant. But what of the world?

Scholarship has disproved the Eurocentric analysis that defined the period of the Middle Ages. Exciting innovations took place all over the world during this pivotal millennium. Religious movements such as the rise of Islam and the spread of Buddhism irrevocably shaped much of the world, innovations in transportation allowed people to settle islands throughout the Pacific, and agricultural improvements stimulated empires in South America.

Furthermore, these societies did not develop in isolation. Most people remember Marco Polo's visit to the China of the Yuan Dynasty, but his voyage was not an exception. People, goods, and ideas spread all across the Eurasian land mass and down into Africa. This encyclopedia traces the global connections that fueled the worldwide developments of the Middle Ages.

To emphasize the global quality of this reference work, we have organized the volumes by regions. Volume 1 covers Europe and the Americas. We begin with Europe because this was the region that first defined the medieval world. At first glance, linking Europe with the Americas (which were not colonized until after the Middle Ages) might seem to join the most disparate of regions. However, we do so to remind us that Vikings crossed the North Atlantic in the Middle Ages to discover this rich new land, which was already inhabited by prosperous indigenous peoples. The organization of this first volume demonstrates that Europe never developed in isolation!

Volume 2 considers the Middle East and Africa. These regions saw the growth of Islam and the vibrant interactions that took place in the diverse continent of Africa. Volume 3 takes on the enormous task of focusing on South Asia, East Asia, and Oceania.

This organization forces us to compromise on some content. Because we are not taking a chronological approach, we must collapse 1,000 years of history in regions that had many diverse developments. We partially address this issue in the Historical Overviews at the beginning of each section. These essays will point readers to the varied historical events of the regions.

However, we gain modern insights through our on Global Ties essays within each section. These essays offer a great contrast with other medieval works because they show the significance of global connections throughout this millennium. Readers will learn that globalization was not invented in the twenty-first century. Indeed, the great developments of the past flourished because people from diverse cultures communicated with each other. Perhaps this was the greatest contribution of the Middle Ages, and this encyclopedia highlights it.

Organization for the Internet Age

The Internet brings an astonishing amount of information to us with a quick search. If we Google Marco Polo, castles, or windmills, we are given an immediate array of information more quickly than we could have imagined a mere decade ago. However, as teachers too readily realize when reading the results of such searches, this is not enough. The very volume of information sometimes makes it hard to see how these disparate elements of the past fit together and how they compare with other elements. We have organized this encyclopedia to address these issues.

Each volume contains two or three regions of the world, and each region includes seven in-depth essays that cover the following topics:

1. Historical Overview
2. Religion
3. Economy
4. The Arts
5. Society
6. Science and Technology
7. Global Ties

These essays provide coherent descriptions of each part of the world. They allow readers readily to compare developments in different regions, so one can really understand how the economy in Africa differed from mercantile patterns in China. In-depth essays like this not only provide clear information but model historical writing. But there is more.

Like other good encyclopedias, we have A–Z entries offering in-depth information on many topics—from the general (food, money, law) to the specific (people, events, and places). All the essays indicate the A–Z entries in bold, much as an online essay might have hyperlinks to more detailed information, so readers can immediately see what topics offer more in-depth information and how each fits in with the larger narrative. In the same way, readers who begin with the A–Z entries know that they can see how their topic fits in a larger picture by consulting the in-depth essays. Finally, this integration of essays with A–Z entries provides an easy way to do crosscultural comparisons. Readers can compare roles of women in Islam and Asia, then see how women fit in the larger context of society by consulting the two larger essays.

This is a reference work that builds on the rapid information accessible online while doing what books do best: offer a thoughtful integration of knowledge. We have enhanced what we hope is a useful organization by adding a number of special features designed to help the readers learn as much as possible about the medieval millennium.

Features

- *Primary Documents*. In this information age it is easy to forget that historians find out about the past primarily by reading the written voices left by the ancients. To keep this recognition of the interpretive nature of the past, we have included primary documents for all regions of the world. These short works are designed to engage readers by bringing the past to life, and all have head notes and cross-references to help readers put the documents in context.
- *Chronologies*. The chronologies will help readers quickly identify key events in a particular region during the medieval period.
- *Maps*. History and geography are inextricably linked, and no more so than in a global encyclopedia. The maps throughout the text will help readers locate the medieval world in space as well as time.
- *Illustrations*. All the illustrations are chosen to be historical evidence not ornamentation. All are drawn from medieval sources to show the Middle Ages as the people at the time saw themselves. The captions encourage readers to analyze the content of the images.
- *Complete Index*. The key to gathering information in the twenty-first century is the ability to rapidly locate topics of interest. We have recognized this with the A–Z entries linked to the essays and the extensive cross-referencing. However, nothing can replace a good index, so we have made sure there is a complete and cumulative index that links the information among the volumes.
- *Bibliographies*. Each of the long essays contains a list of recommended readings. These readings will not only offer more information to those interested in following up on the topic but also will serve as further information for the A–Z entries highlighted within the essays. This approach furthers our desire to integrate the information we are presenting.
- *Appendixes*. The appendixes provide basic factual information, such as important regional dynasties or time period designations.

The Greenwood Encyclopedia of Global Medieval Life and Culture has been a satisfying project to present. In over 30 years of research and study of the Middle Ages, we have never lost the thrill of exploring a culture that's so different from our own, yet was formative in creating who we have become. Furthermore, we are delighted to present this age in its global context, because then as now (indeed throughout history) globalization has shaped the growth of culture. In this information age, it is good to remember that we have always lived linked together on spaceship earth. We all hope readers will share our enthusiasm for this millennium.

SOUTH ASIA

Raman N. Seylon, with the assistance of Joyce E. Salisbury and John A. Wagner

Chronology

c. 100 B.C.E.–100 C.E.	Composition of *Bhagavad Gita*
c. 100–200 C.E.	Compilation of the early law code of Yajnavalkya
c. 200–400	Composition of Bharata's *Treatise on Dramaturgy*
c. 300	*Mahabharata* brought to its final written form
c. 300–500	A sect of Nestorian (Syrian) Christians is in existence at Cochin in South India
c. 300–888	Hindu Pallava dynasty rules at Kanchi in south India
c. 320–335	Reign of Chandra Gupta I, who begins expansion of the Gupta Empire across North India
c. 335–375	Reign of Samudra Gupta, son and successor of Chandra Gupta, who extended Gupta dominance to the south and west
c. 375–415	Reign of Chandra Gupta II, who extended the Gupta Empire westward to the coast of the Arabian Sea; the reign is also noted for the flourishing of Hindu culture, particularly in art, literature, and science
c. 380–450	Life of medieval India's greatest poet, Kalidasa
c. 399–412	Faxian, a Chinese Buddhist monk, visits China to collect samples of Buddhist literature; he leaves a detailed account of his sojourn in Gupta India
c. 400–500	Composition of Vatsyayana's *Aphorisms of Love*
c. 415–455	Reign of Kumara Gupta is a period of peace and political stability known today as India's "Golden Age"
c. 454	First Hun (Huna) invasion of northern India is largely repelled by the Guptas
c. 455–487	Reign of Skanda Gupta, who is generally considered the last of the great Gupta rulers; his reign was marked by attacks by outside invaders, especially the Huns, which greatly weakened the Gupta state militarily and financially
c. 477	Guptas repel another Hun attack
c. 484	Huns conquer Persia under the leadership of Toramana
c. 495	Huns invade North India overrunning much of the Gupta Empire
528	Yasodharman, king of the central Indian state of Mawa, defeated the Huns, thereby checking Hun expansion and beginning the process of driving them back into the Punjab by the early 540s

c. 540	End of the Gupta dynasty
c. 550–753	Rule of the Hindu Western Chalukya dynasty in the Deccan
606–647	Rule of Harsha at Kanauj in North India reconstitutes some of the Gupta state; Banabhatta (Bana), a Sanskrit scholar who was court poet, leaves a biography of Harsha (*Harsha Carita*), which is an important source for the early part of the reign
c. 629–645	Xuanzang, a Chinese Buddhist scholar, visits India and writes an account of India during the reign of Harsha
c. 630–970	Rule of Hindu Eastern Chalukya dynasty in the Deccan
644	Arabs conquer Balochistan
c. 647–700	Disintegration of Harsha's kingdom into various smaller Hindu states
711–715	Muslims under Muhammad ibn Qasim conquer Sind
c. 760–1142	Hindu Pala dynasty rules in Bihar and Bengal
c. 907–1310	Hindu Chola Empire is ruled from Tanjore in South India
962	Foundation of the Turkish Muslim principality of Ghaznin in western Afghanistan
c. 973–1189	Second Hindu Chalukya dynasty rules western and central Deccan
988	Capture of Kabul by Sabuktgin of Ghaznin
999–1026	Mahmud of Ghazni raids India
c. 1000–1100	Rise of Hindu Tantrism
1021	Foundation of Ghaznavid principality at Lahore
1040	Ghaznavids defeated at the Battle of Dandanqan by the Seljuks, who seize control of the bulk of the Ghaznavid territories
c. 1097–1223	Sena dynasty rules in Bengal
1151	Ghazni is burned by the ruler of the rising Muslim principality of Ghor in central Afghanistan
1170s–1206	Muhammad of Ghor, governor and general of the Ghorid dynasty, captures Lahore and destroys the Ghaznavid state
1192	Muhammad of Ghor defeats the Hindu ruler Prithviraj Chauhan at the Second Battle of Tarain, thus extending Muslim Ghorid rule into North India, with headquarters at Delhi
1192–1206	Ghorid conquest of North India
c. 1200–1300	Composition of Sharngadeva's treatise on music, *Sangitaratnakara*
1206	Upon the death of Muhammad of Ghor, Ghorid general Qutb-ud-din Aybak declares his independence as Sultan of Delhi, thereby establishing the Delhi Sultanate, which rules in North India under various dynasties until 1526
1211–1236	Rule of Iltutmish as sultan of Delhi
1223–1224	First Mongol invasion of South Asia
1236–1240	Rule in Delhi of Razia Sultana, one of the few female rulers of medieval India

1266–1287	Sultan Balban consolidates the power of the Delhi sultanate
1296–1316	Reign of Sultan Allauddin Khilji, who extends the dominion of the Delhi sultanate into South India and checks Mongol invasions of North India
1306–1310	Conquest of much of South India by Delhi sultanate; foundation of independent Muslim Bahmani sultanate in the Deccan
1325–1351	Rule in Delhi of Sultan Muhammad bin Tughluq
1336–1565	Vijayanagara, the last great Hindu kingdom, flourishes in South India
1351–1388	Rule in Delhi of Sultan Firuz Shah Tughluq, whose reign marks the end of the Delhi sultanate's imperial expansion
1398–1399	Timur (Timur the Lame or Tamerlane), a Turkish-Mongol invader, captures and sacks Delhi, killing or enslaving almost the entire population
c. 1399–1450	Rise of various independent regional Muslim sultanates in North India
1451–1526	Revival of the Delhi sultanate under the Lodi dynasty
1469	Birth of Guru Nanak, the founder of Sikhism
1504	Babur, a descendent of Timur and Chinggis (Genghis) Khan, captures Kabul in Afghanistan
1526	Babur defeats the Lodi sultan of Delhi at the Battle of Panipat and seizes control of Delhi and Agra, thereby ending the Delhi sultanate and establishing the Muslim Mughal Empire in North India
c. 1542	Francis Xavier, a Catholic missionary from Spain, arrives in India

Gupta Empire under Chandra Gupta II, c. 375–415

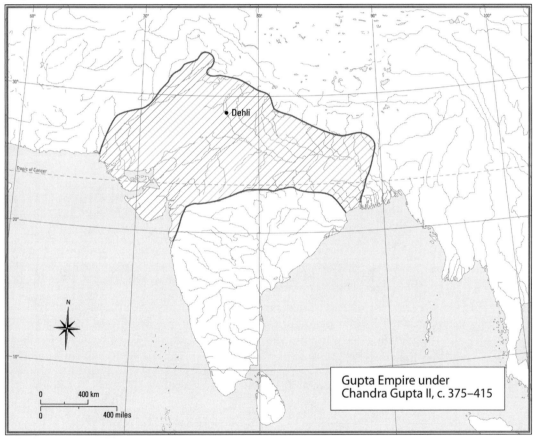

Gupta Empire under
Chandra Gupta II, c. 375–415

Pre-Muslim India, c. 1200

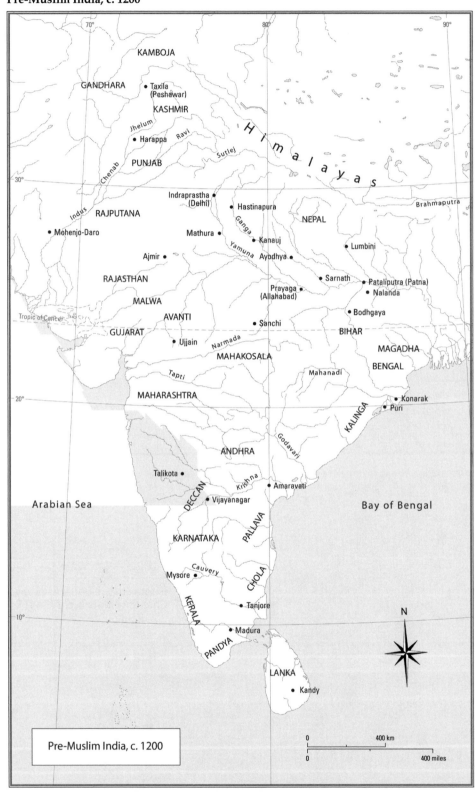

Pre-Muslim India, c. 1200

Delhi Sultanate, 1236

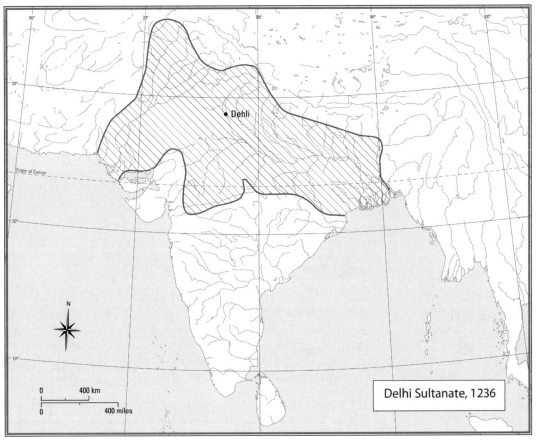

Delhi Sultanate, 1236

Delhi Sultanate, 1325

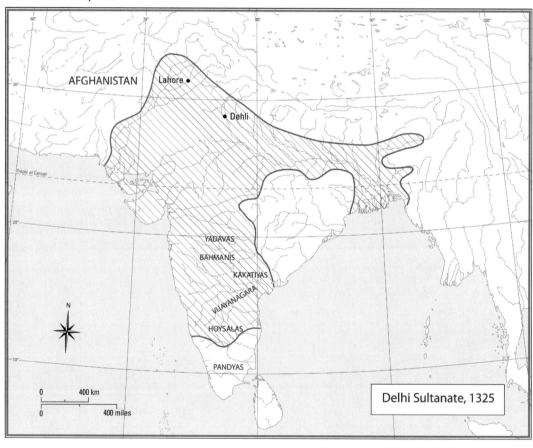

Delhi Sultanate, 1325

India, c. 1500

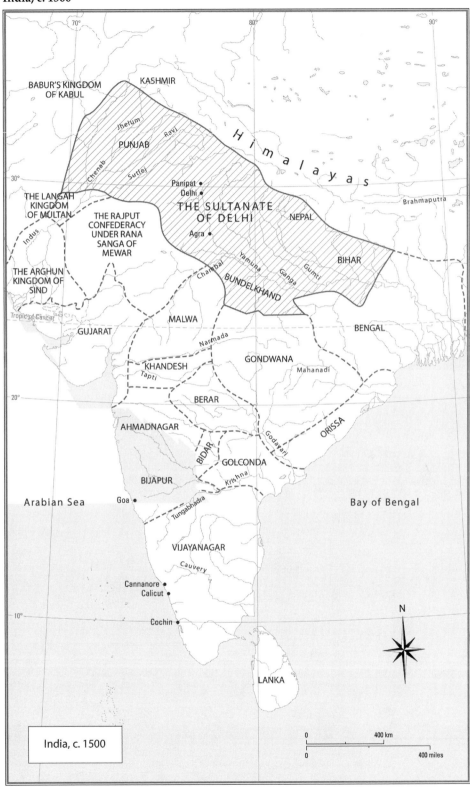

India, c. 1500

Overview and Topical Essays

1. HISTORICAL OVERVIEW

The Imperial Guptas

By the start of the third century C.E., India was entering a period of political disunity, with northern India ruled by various local rulers and chieftains. The reunification of northern India occurred with the formation of the **Gupta Empire** (c. 320–550 C.E.). The Gupta ruling house was centered in the Magada region of the Ganges Valley, which had been the center of North Indian political culture since the time of Alexander the Great's invasion in the fourth century B.C.E. Little is known about the origins of the Guptas, but, according to inscriptional evidence, the earliest Gupta rulers were Sri Gupta and Ghatotkacha Gupta (Keay, 134), who may have been minor princes in the area. The *Puranas* tell us that the early Gupta rulers dominated the area from the ancient city of Prayag (present-day Allahabad) to territories in Magada, but they do not seem to have controlled the capital of Magada, the city of Pataliputra, which was the cultural capital of this period. Commercial dominance, not military prowess, may have led to the political rise of the Guptas, because they were considered members of the merchant or Vaishya caste, which may have been the dominant caste of this region (Keay, 134).

In February 320 C.E., the accession of the first major Gupta monarch, Chandra Gupta, laid the foundation for the most splendid era of Indian history since the demise of the Mauryan dynasty in the second century B.C.E. (Basham, 1951, 63). Chandra Gupta made the year of his accession the year 1 of a new calendar system and took the lofty Sanskrit title *maha-raja-adhi-raja*, meaning "supreme ruler of the great kings," which was used previously by the Kushana dynasty, rulers of northwestern India and Afghanistan. Under Chandra, Magada and the city of Pataliputra, which had been the capital of the first India-wide state, the Mauryan Empire (320–200 B.C.E.), again became the cultural and political capital of northern India. Chadra's regional dominance rested in large part upon a favorable marriage alliance with the ancient and prestigious Lichavi clan, which had long ruled neighboring north Indian territories that extended to the foothills of the Himalayas. The Gupta–Lichavi marriage alliance may have united both families and their neighboring kingdoms (Wolpert, 86). The importance of this marriage alliance is illustrated by the minting of special commemorative coins that bear images of Chandra Gupta and his Lichavi queen, Kumara Devi, on one side, and a goddess seated on a lion with the inscription "Lichavi" on the reverse side. On his coins, Samudra Gupta

(335–375 c.e.), the son of Chandra Gupta, emphasized his maternal lineage, rather than his descent from a Gupta ruler. Such practices bear testimony to the high prestige of the Lichavi name during this period (Kulke and Rothermund, 80).

Samudra Gupta expanded the boundaries of the kingdom to include Punjab in the west, Assam in the east, Kashmir to the north, and the Northern **Tamil country** to the south. Called by some historians the "Napoleon of India," Samudra Gupta recreated the territorial extent of the Mauryan Empire. An inscription placed during the Gupta Period on a preexisting iron pillar built by the Mauryan ruler Asoka in the city of Allahabad strongly suggests Samudra Gupta's ambition to mimic his Mauryan predecessors and establish an India-wide empire. Although the Mauryan state had strived for a more centralized, direct rule than the Guptas loose tributary alliance, the Gupta state was the major power center in most of northern India in the early part of the first millennium c.e.

Samudra Gupta's political successors continued his policy of territorial expansion with mixed success, as confirmed by a Sanskrit play composed in the sixth century by Visakhadatta. Titled *Devi Chandra Gupta*, the "Queen of Chandra Gupta," the play tells of a ruler named Rama Gupta, who briefly succeeded Samudra Gupta. Most historians had doubted the existence of Rama Gupta, but discoveries of copper coins bearing his name confirm his reign. According to the play, when Rama Gupta attacked the kingdom of the Shakas to the west, he was defeated. Seeking to prevent his own capture, Rama Gupta was forced to give serious consideration to the Shaka ruler's demand for the surrender of Rama Gupta's chief queen, Dhruva Devi. This humiliating option was unacceptable to the king's younger brother, Chandra, who undertook a daring plot to assassinate the Shaka ruler. Chandra disguised himself as the beautiful Dhruva Devi and was escorted into the enemy camp, where he slew the Shaka ruler when he embraced his much desired price. In the resulting confusion, Chandra made his escape. Disgraced by his attempted dishonorable, Rama Gupta was soon replaced by his brother, who assumed the dynastic title **Chandra Gupta II** (Keay, 141). It is impossible to verify whether such an event is historically accurate, or whether it is what one historian calls a formulaic narrative that both obscures and legitimates an internal palace coup.

Chandra Gupta II (c. 375–415 c.e.) conquered large areas and forced the Shaka rulers to pay homage, though they were not overthrown and continued to control vast areas of western India from their capital at Ujjayini (modern Ujjain). The Shakas ruled over the western coastal area that included what is today the state of Gujarat, as well as the rich ports along the Arabian Sea, which had facilitated long-distance oceanic trade for over 2,000 years. Their fortuitous geographical location of these ports allowed them to benefit not only from the Indian Ocean trade but also from the overland trade routes of the Silk Road that passed through India.

Chandra Gupta II, like earlier Gupta rulers, also expanded his power through matrimonial alliances, in this case, by marrying his daughter to the powerful rulers of central India. He also issued special gold commemorative coinage to celebrate his military victories and assumed the title of Vikramadita ("one whose splendor equals one thousand suns"), which was the name of a legendary ruler who founded the Vikrama era, an important Hindu dating system begun in 58 b.c.e. and still used in North India. The fifth major Gupta ruler was Kumara Gupta (c. 415–455 C.E.), whose reign marked a period of peace and tranquility in north India. During this period, other great empires, such as the Roman Empire in Europe and the Han Empire in China, were facing nomadic invasions and political turmoil. The sociopolitical tranquility and cultural and scientific creativity that defines this period in Indian history have led historians to characterize it as the "Golden Era," when the cultural fruits of Gupta peace spread to wider areas in western, central, and eastern Asia through trade routes.

The Guptas ruled during a period when there was a revival of Sanskrit scholarship in the fields of literature and philosophy. This was the era of **Kalidasa**, who is considered the Shakespeare of Sanskrit literature. Kalidasa is known today for two epic lyrical works that have survived to our time. One is a poem titled *Meghaduta* or *Cloud Messenger*, and the other a drama titled *Abhijnana-Sakuntala* or *The Recognition of Sakuntala*, which is considered his masterpiece. Other lesser known pieces that have survived include *Malavikagnimitram* (Malavika and Agnimitra), a comedy set in the palace harem, and *Vikramorvasi* or *Urvasi*, a love story. During the Gupta Period, much of the great epic poetry that had been hitherto transmitted orally was written down, including the great epics **Ramayana** and **Mahabharata**. These two epics grew from simpler origins to poems of great length by picking up various additions, and verses were added in their surviving modern form. They have been the major sources of Indian high culture ever since.

Apart from Sanskrit literature, the Gupta Period was also noted for the development of the Sanskrit language. Official Gupta correspondence employed Sanskrit, which was as anachronistic in India as was Latin during the European Middle Ages; everyday use of both languages has long since faded away. Even the Mauryan dynasty, which ruled some 500 years earlier, used Prakrit, a derivation of Sanskrit, in its official inscriptions. Prakrit may have been closer to the common language spoken by the people. During the Gupta era, Sanskrit **law** codes called *Dhramasastra* and the manuals of statecraft called *Arthasastra* were revised and codified. These texts are ideal descriptive manuals rather than actual rules to be enforced. Gupta rulers and elite patronized scholars and artists and set aside funds for maintaining higher centers of learning, such as the prestigious Buddhist University at Taxila in northwest India and another at Nalinda in the Gangatic Valley. These institutions were visited and attended by Chinese scholar-monks, including **Faxian** and **Xuanzang**, both of whom have left valuable descriptions. Xuan Tang's description is much more vivid and comprehensive and, therefore, is of greater value to historians. He left us detailed eyewitness accounts of the people, the land, and the kingdoms of India in his travelogue "Records of the western regions" (Si-Yu-Ki). It provides a valuable source for seventh-century India and chronicles the decline of Buddhism in India and Indonesia before the advent of Islam (*see* "Religion" section).

As under the Mauryan Empire, most trade was regulated and undertaken by the state. The Gupta rulers made private fortunes from their control of mines and their commercial activities. The private sector also played a vital role and was regulated by great caste guilds. Evidence suggests that a cash-based economy was in operation since the second century B.C.E., when copper and gold coinage may have been introduced from the Middle East. But for everyday trading, barter was the norm, because there seemed to be insufficient coinage for free circulation. Generally speaking, ancient and medieval Indian coinage is crude and unattractive when compared to that issued by the Bactrian Greek rulers of Northwest India, whose coinage is among the finest in the ancient world (*see* **Money and Exchange Systems**). The Gupta coinage remains an exception; it is far clearer in its fine details and more attractive than any issued in India. After the Guptas, the numismatic standards declined quickly until the days of the Moghul Empire when portraits of the rulers again became reasonably recognizable. It has been suggested that coins issued by the Guptas were not actual tokens of exchange but rather commemorative issues. As noted by Xuanzang, even as late as the seventh century, most local commerce was conducted by barter.

In a strict sense, the Gupta rule did not politically unify the territories it covered, but it did so ideologically in terms of the Hindu ideals of *chakravatin*, or universal ruler. Samudra Gupta, being faithful to this Hindu Imperial ideology, performed the great horse sacrifice, *Ashwa Metha*, and proclaimed himself the universal ruler (Wolpert, 87). Recent scholarship sees this more as a case of political propaganda than as actual reality. According to this view, not even the central core of the Guptas' realm was fully under their rule. Various unsubdued wild tribes still held their autonomy, though the Guptas' political muscle probably did prevent these tribes from making raids into settled areas. This core area was surrounded by a concentric ring of frontier kingdoms, whose rulers were expected to pay tribute and to act as vassals of Samudra Gupta, which included attending his court for important functions. The early Indian form of vassalage differered from the European concept of vassalage; in Europe, vassals were expected to supply provisions and troops during military conflict. In later times in India, a class of tributary princes called *samantas* (relations) rose to high positions in the court and came closer to the Western type of feudal vassal (Kulke and Rothermund, 88).

Gupta Society and Religion

Much of what we know about life in medieval India comes from two early Chinese scholar-pilgrims, Faxian and Xuanzang. The Buddhist scholar, Faxian, who spent several years in India during the reign of Chandra Gupta II in the fifth century C.E., has left the following description of Gupta society:

> The people are very well off, without the poll tax or official restrictions. The kings govern without corporal punishment, and criminals are fined according to circumstances either lightly or heavily. Even in cases of repeated rebellion, they only cut off the right hand. The king's personal attendants who guard him on the right and left have fixed salaries. Throughout the country, the people kill no living thing, nor drink wine, nor do they eat garlic or onions, with the exception of *chandalas* only. These *chandalas* are named "evil man" and dwelt apart from others. If they entered a town, or a village, or a market, they make a sound with a piece of wood to announce their presence and to themselves separate themselves, then men not knowing who they are avoid coming in contact with them. In this country they do not keep swine or fowl, and do not deal in cattle. They have no slaughter house or wine shop in their market places. In selling, they use *cowrie* shells (as small demotional currency). The *chandalas* only hunt and sell flesh.

Like traders before him, Faxian came to India using branches of the Silk Road: a major overland trade route to India. He entered India by the Kara

Koram mountain trails, traveled along the Gangatic basin, and visited in safety all the major holy sites associated with the Buddha's life. His mention of the *chandalas*, whose treatment he found degrading, is one of the earliest references to a segment of Indian society later referred to as the "untouchables."

The *chandalas* were outcasts by reason of their degrading occupation: They were removers of human and animal carrion. This polluting task done made *chandalas* agents of contamination, or pollution, and, as a result, they were ostracized by the rest of society, which, paradoxically, needed this essential service provided by the *chandalas*. The *chandalas* had to make warning sounds so that caste-conscious shoppers and sellers could take necessary precautions to avoid them by diverting their gaze, which was believed to secure them from being contaminated. Curiously, Faxian himself failed to criticize this practice, which seems to us as a blatant violation of human dignity. But Faxian was certainly impressed by the peace and tranquility that India enjoyed under Gupta rule, and his glowing description of Indian society can possibly be read as a critique of the political disunion and social turmoil that had afflicted his Chinese homeland since the fall of the Han dynasty in the early third century C.E.

Others sources also indicate that Gupta society was industrious and contented. Highly influential guilds or *sreni* regulated an elaborate system of quality control, pricing, distribution, and training for every craft. They also acted in the capacity of bankers, even to the royal court. Their governing body, or *Sriesthem*, met regularly in a joint council that was much like a chamber of commerce. Trading was extensive, by land and sea, inside and outside India (*see* "Economy" section).

When Faxian returned to China, he did not use the long overland route but took an Indian sailing vessel that was involved in trade with Southeast Asia, and possibly with China. These vessels were also notoriously unreliable. From the Bengali port of Tamralipi, Faxian was almost shipwrecked off the coast of Burma, and the later Chinese traveler Xuanzang reached one of the major Indonesian islands (either Java or Sumatra), or part of Western Malaysia, which he called Ye-poti. Here, just as in other ports of Indo China, Faxian noted the overwhelming presence of a Brahmin community, which indicates Hinduism as the dominant faith, and he notes that the laws of the Buddhists were less well known. After more mishaps, Faxian returned to China, again in the company of the Brahmins, and possibly in Indian sailing vessels.

From Faxian's writings, we find that urban life in Magada was very impressive; the towns of Magada were the largest and its people, according to Faxian, were prosperous and virtuous. We also see the return of Brahminical Hinduism to the center of religious life and learn that the historic sites associated with Buddhism, such as the city of Kapilavasta, the birthplace of the historic Buddha, look somewhat dilapidated. Faxian found Kapilavasta a great desert without a king or people, and the impressive palace of Ashoka was in ruins. However, thousands of Buddhist *stupas* still dotted the countryside (just as they do in present-day Burma or Thailand) (*see* **Temples, Buddhist: Stupas**). So, despite a decline in popularity from the time of Megasthenes' visit to India in the third century B.C.E., Buddhism still enjoyed a wide following in large sections of the country, where Buddhist monasteries still housed thousands of monks.

Faxian was not at all concerned with contemporary political affairs and says nothing about Chandra Gupta II or his court. But the Chinese traveler, like a present-day tourist, was greatly impressed by spectacular religious ceremonies, such as the annual cast or *ratha* festival in the city of Pataliputra. This occasion was marked by a magnificent procession of some 20-wheeled juggernauts in the form of *stupas*. These had sharp bristling towers with the images of the deities decorated in gold and silver, including seated figures of the Buddha attended by standing *Bodhisattvas*. As this procession approached the city, Faxian watched the *Bramacharias,* or Brahmin students, come forth and offer their invitation for the procession to enter the *Bodhisattvas* in their giant carts; then, one after another, the carts entered the city of Pataliputra.

According to Mahayana belief, *Bodhisattvas* were individuals who attained enlightenment and were eligible to enter the state of *nirvana* after death but, due to their great compassion, chose instead to remain on earth in spirit form to help all human beings achieve relief from the cycle of life. For the Orthodox, or Theraveda Buddhism, the concept of *Bodhisattvas* only applied to Siddhartha Gautama himself, and they denounced the teachings of the Mahayana as being inspired by demons. But to the proponents of Mahayana, such ideas extended the hope of salvation to the masses. Mahayana Buddhists revered saintly individuals who, according to the tradition, had become *Bodhisattva* at death, and erected temples in their honor so that the whole population could pray and make ritual offerings. The most popular *Bodhisattva* is Bodhisattvas Avalokitesvara, whose name, in Sanskrit, means "lord of compassion." Perhaps due to this identification of Avalokitesvara with the concept of mercy, in China where he was transformed in China into a female goddess known as Gwan Yin, the goddess of mercy.

Here, perhaps, is an example of religious ecumenism that was practiced in Gupta India, which witnessed a resurgence of the Hindu religious authority. Major systems of Brahminical post-Vedic and pre-Bhakti or devotional Hindu philosophy were being articulated and expanded from the earlier teachings of the Upanishads. The Vedanta philosophy posed a powerful alternate version to Buddhism and Brahminical Hinduism began to regain its ascendancy over Buddhism in India.

Caste rules were elaborated and enforced with greater vigor. The high-level Gupta administrators and wealthy landlords gave patronage to Brahmins in the form of land grants or court positions. The Brahmin priests also asserted their role in ritual performance. Buddhism, which had flourished through the patronage of earlier empires, and had the support of the business classes, let the Brahmin priests handle many of the ritual performances and thus began to decline as the basis for everyday forms of devotion. Although the Gupta rulers had adopted the Brahminical Hindu faith, identifying themselves with the Hindu god Vishnu and performing ancient Vedic sacrifices, they granted endowments to Buddhist and Brahmin establishments in an even-handed manner (*see* **Caste System**).

Yet the physical separation between the Buddhist and Brahminical establishments implied by Faxian may be significant. Buddhist monasteries are usually located near enough to the main centers of population to collect alms and instruct the laity, but far enough from urban centers for peace and seclusion. The term "Brahmacharia," on the other hand, which technically means unmarried Brahmin students, is here employed to mean the entire Brahmin educational establishment. It was located within the city, close to the court and the wealthier segment of the population. So what Faxian was witnessing, as he watched the religious procession of the giant *stupa* carts, is a clear example of Buddhist rituals being absorbed by Brahminical Hinduism. Major Buddhist rituals had become a Brahmin monopoly and were undertaken under Brahmin supervision. These interactions often led to some mutual hostility between Brahmins and Buddhists.

During the early Gupta Period, at least for a while, Buddhism was able to counter Brahminical Hinduism with its own salvationist creed of Mahayana, which also emphasized devotion. But the role of Buddhism as a popular faith in India was coming to a conclusion during the Gupta Period.

India after the Guptas

By the late fifth century C.E., the Gupta Empire was coming under pressure from the **Huns**, or Hunas, as they are referred to in Indian records. Called *xiongnu* in Chinese chronicles, these nomadic invaders from the Central Asian steppes attacked India through the northwest corridor. One of the last great Gupta emperors Skanda Gupta (455–467 C.E.) repulsed the first major Hun invasion. He mentions the victory in an inscription that refers to the Huns as *mlecchas*, or "foreign barbarians." But the continuing Hun presence on the northwest frontier disrupted international trade along the Silk Road and reduced Gupta wealth.

Skanda Gupta's successors apparently could not hold the empire together, and regional strongmen began to achieve autonomy. The Huns invaded again around 500, and for the next half-century controlled much of Central India from their political centre at Bamiyan in Afghanistan. The Huns in India earned a reputation for acts of great cruelty, which were reported not only by the Indians, but also, in 520, by the Chinese ambassador to the Hun court at Gandara and, some 20 years later, by the Greek sea traveler Cosmos. Though brutal, Hun rule was mercifully brief; by 528 a coalition of Indian princes drove the Huns northwest, as far as Kashmir. About a generation later, Turkish and Persian armies defeated the main Hun concentration (Kulke and Rohermund, 91), thereby removing them as a threat to India.

The social impact of Hun rule was traumatic and long-lasting. As recorded by the Chinese scholar-monk, Fa Hsiun, the tranquil nature of North Indian society was forever lost. The Hun invasion rippled an already enfeeble Gupta state, and the defense of distant frontiers exhausted the imperial treasury; the empire collapsed by the year 550 as regional princes openly declared their independence and carved out territories. Pataliputra, the cultural capital of North India for nearly 1,000 years, was replaced by the city of Kanya Kubja, or **Kanauj**, which remained the cultural capital for the next 500 years. In 606, a 16-year-old prince named Harsha-Vardana, or **Harsha** as he is popularly known, was offered the crown by the magnates of Kanya Kubja. Although not strictly of Gupta lineage, Harsha restored the better days of Gupta rule during his 40-year reign.

Harsha is the best-known Indian ruler of this period because his biography was recorded by his court poet **Banabhatta** (known as Bana), who was a somewhat rakish Brahmin with a shady past. Bana's *Harsha Carita*, a prose account of Harsha's rise to power, is the first historical biography in Sanskrit, as well as a masterpiece of medieval Indian literature.

Bana's work records only the early years of Harsha. For the later years of Harsha's life, we have an eyewitness account by the Chinese scholar-monk Xuanzang (596–664), who, like Faxian 200 years earlier, described his travels through India. Xuanzang stayed in India from 630 to 644. He was from a privileged background, a member of the Sui-Tang gentry from the city of Luoyang. Early in his life, he and his older brother developed a deep appreciation for Buddhism, which he embraced, and, by his late teens, he had established himself as an authority in the Theravada and Mahayana branches of Buddhism in China. He also gained a reputation as a Confucian scholar and as a learned and eloquent monk.

Dissatisfied with the existing translations of Buddhist doctrines, which contained contradictions and errors, he sought to study the original Pali cannons in India. In 629, Xuanzang left for India in great secrecy against the wishes of the reigning Tang emperor Tang Tai zong. Traveling by the northern route through Central Asia, he crossed high mountain passes and bleak deserts, barely escaping bandits. Xuanzang was considered charming and courtly and was honored by the great monarchs of Northern India, including Harsha and Baskara Varman of Kama Rupa or Assam. Xuanzang also stayed at the Buddhist center of learning at **Nalanda** for 5 years, while studying Buddhist philosophy with the great scholar of the age, Silabhadra.

It was customary for the Buddhist monasteries to honor learned and visiting monks with a presentation of a precious book. Xuanzang is said to have collected some 657 volumes, many of them rare texts. These collected volumes were so bulky that they had to be carried by a pack of twenty horses along the Silk Road back to China. Xuanzang came to India when Buddhism was in a state of deep decline; he made it possible for texts on Buddhist philosophy to survive in their Chinese versions after the Pali and Sanskrit originals were long lost in India.

For the next 19 years, until his death, Xuanzang worked at translating his large collection of Sanskrit texts brought from India. Altogether he translated some seventy-five books, including sixty-five biographies of Chinese monks who visited India. The most important ones being his own and those of Faxian and I Shang. For modern secular historians, Xuanzang's account provides valuable information about India in this period; he took meticulous notes about his personal experiences and all aspects of the societies he encountered during his travels. Largely because of this we have first-hand detailed accounts of North Indian society and cultural practices in the midseventh century and of the decayed state of central Asian Buddhism just before the advent of Islam.

Fortunately, Xuanzang's description, unlike the earlier account of Mauryan India by the Greek traveler Megasthenes (350–290 B.C.E.), has survived intact. Although, like all Chinese Buddhist scholar-monks, Xuanzang's main goals were to obtain primary documents of rare Buddhist texts, he was also an astute observer and had a sharp eye for local customs. He had the foresight to record much of the secular lifestyle that he witnessed.

Most popular history texts portray Harsha as the last great Buddhist ruler of India, but this is erroneous. Harsha's enthusiasm for Buddhism may have been stimulated by his meeting with Xuanzang, who had an honored place at Harsha's court. Evidence indicates that Harsha, although actively sponsoring Buddhism, was not a Buddhist ruler, but a Hindu. In *Harsha Charita*, Bana claims that Harsha belonged to the Saivaite sect of Hinduism. Harsha's interest in Buddhism likely came quite late and largely as a result of the influence of

Kandariya Mahadeva temple, sculptures. Khajuraho, Madhya Pradesh, India. c. 1050 C.E.
DeA Picture Library / Art Resource, NY.

Xuanzang; there is no definitive indication that he actually embraced Buddhism. But he practiced extreme tolerance toward all faiths in his realm, building monasteries for the Buddhists and temples for the Hindus. For the
Buddhists, Harsha built a *vihara* and a temple at Nalanda, the Buddhist center
of higher learning, and 1,000 *stupas* along the banks of the Ganges, which paralleled the actions of the great Mauryan ruler Ashoka (r. 269–232 B.C.E.). Harsha also undertook a variety of humanitarian and public welfare activities.

Xuanzang's records also indicate that Buddhism in India was losing its appeal in favor of devotional Hinduism, most especially in the Deep South and
in Tamil country, where Buddhism had ceased to exist as a living faith. In
spite of Harsha's patronage, theistic Hinduism advanced all across India at the
expense of Buddhism. We also see the developments of *puja* as the standard
Hindu form of worship, which required devotees to bring fresh fruits, seeds,
sweets, and other accepted offerings to the sacred icons of Hindu deities,
which were worshipped with deep devotion or *bhakti*.

The period also saw the development of nontraditional forms of Hinduism,
which may be deemed occult or magical in form. These forms developed during the latter days of Gupta Period and include the worship of feminine deities in manners that may seem shocking or polluting to the orthodox and that
fall under the category of Tantrism.

Harsha's Administration

Although Harsha seems to have controlled most of North India (from Kathi-
war to Bengal), his empire was decentralized and feudal in structure. Outside
the immediate domain of his capital, Kanya Kubja, many vanquished rulers of

neighboring kingdoms retained their thrones. It is unclear how Harsha's kingdom differed from that of the Guptas. According to most historians, centralized rule existed under powerful Gupta monarchs, such as Chandra Gupta II and his son, Samudra Gupta, but was restricted to the central part of the Gangatic Plain that lay between the capital of Pataliputra and the city of Madhura, near present-day Delhi. Beyond this area, there was no centralized rule. But, unlike the great Gupta monarchs, Harsha never controlled the trade routes in northwest India. As a result, he lacked the financial resources of the Guptas.

Thus, Harsha did not have ready sources of revenue to pay his officials, who were instead granted land. These grants to officials and donations to Hindus and Buddhist institutions further depleted his central treasury. Because Harsha could not afford a large bureaucracy to run territories under his control, he had to set up an alternate system of government called the *Samantha* system, where rulers of recently subjugated territories were left in place if they swore allegiance and loyalty to Harsha. This indirect and semiautonomous rule of large territories contributed to Indian regionalism.

Also promoting regionalism was the westward shift of capital from Pataliputra to Kanauj, which encouraged the growth of autonomous kingdoms around the Gangatic delta during periods of weakening central authority. Under Harsha's successors, this eastern area was permanently lost to his kingdom. Another and more definitive contrast between Harsha's empire and that of the early Guptas was that the founders of the Gupta dynasty had few formidable rivals within India. Harsha's southern boundary was under the control of the powerful Chalukya ruler of the **Deccan** kingdom, Pulukasin II, who surprised and humbled Harsha when he sought to extend his authority southward.

Harsha stayed in touch with public opinion and maintained control over his vast domain by constantly traveling from province to province. By Harsha's reign, the centralized administrative system devised by the Mauriyans was unworkable in the context of the prevailing socioeconomic conditions. Harsha's extensive tours were attempts to hold together his domain by sheer force of personality. Xuanzang portrayed him as a man of intense energy and dedication. He is said to have heard the complaints of his humbler subjects with great patience in a roadside traveling pavilion. Harsha, like all medieval Indian monarchs, was also well aware of how the trappings of political power could help maintain his authority and was accompanied by a large train of attendants, including courtiers, officials, Buddhist monks, Brahmins, and a retinue of court drummers who gave weight to the king's public actions. The literary sources also inform us that he was a loyal friend to those who knew him and was generous financially to those he favored. Harsha also loved philosophy and literature and in his leisure found time to write three competent Sanskrit dramas and three comedies, one with a religious theme.

The Last Years of Harsha's Rule

Under Harsha, law and order were not as well maintained as under the early Gupta monarchs. In contrast to the account of Faxian, who was highly impressed by the general peaceful state of the country, Xuanzang, 200 years later, was robbed twice by bandits within Harsha's domain. On one occasion, he is said to have narrowly escaped being sacrificed to Goddess Kali by highwaymen, who, like the later thugs, murdered their victims after robbing them.

Crime was a serious problem in medieval India, and local officials and military commanders tried to counteract it by maintaining large numbers of informants or "spies" and special watchmen to keep guard throughout the night in cities and villages. In some medieval kingdoms, special officers were given the task of hunting down criminals. Apart from the high crime rate, we also find unrest among Orthodox Hindus, who were enraged by Harsha's generosity and partiality toward Buddhists, which led to a plot to assassinate him. Harsha was fortunate to escape one such attempt; the plot leaders were executed, and five hundred Orthodox Brahmins were exiled.

Under Gupta rule, the humanitarian ideals of Buddhist doctrine led to the abolition of capital and corporal punishment. But under Harsha, torture and long-term imprisonment were common forms of punishment (Auboyer, 59). Despite Harsha's lifetime efforts to forge one large imperial structure, his empire collapsed after his death in 647. How Harsha died is not exactly clear, but assassination is suspected by some historians, who also see Harsha becoming more paranoid and ruthless toward his opponents in later years. Chinese chronicles indicate the throne was usurped by Harsha's Brahmin minister. The Chinese Tang emperor, Tai Tsung, with whom Harsha cultivated good relations and had exchanged an earlier diplomatic mission in 643, sent another ambassador to his court in 647. This time, the Chinese arrived in the midst of a political and sectarian conflict; they were ill treated, robbed, and held captive by the usurper. The Chinese ambassador barely escaped, fleeing to Tibet. From there, acting in concert with Harsha's allies in Nepal and Assam, he defeated the usurper, who was taken to China, where he died in captivity as a personal attendant to the Tang emperor. Upon the disintegration of Harsha's empire, local rulers once again turned North India into a battleground as they sought to enlarge their realms at the expense of their immediate neighbors.

Dynastic Turmoil

Following Harsha's death, India entered a period of political instability and chronic **warfare** between rival dynasties. The five major Indian dynasties of the period were the Gurjara Pritihara from the western region of Rajasthan; the Palas from Bengal in the east; the Chalukyas, whose capital was at Badami in the southwest; the Cholas, whose capital was at Tanjore in the far southeast; and the Pallavas who were centered at Kanchipuram, a city north of Tanjore in southeastern India. In the north, the Gurjara Pritihara and the Palas fought for regional dominance, especially for control Harsha's capital Kanauj. Further south, the Chalukyas and Pallavas raided each other's territories and sacked their rival's capital. Eventually vassals won dominance other their former overlords, as occurred when the Rashtrakutas, a dynasty that ruled a large swath of western India from the seventh to the thirteenth centuries, absorbed the Chalukyas, and the Cholas absorbed the Pallavas in the southeast.

North India

In North India, the Gangatic heartland of Harsha's empire, the major political conflict was between the Palas of Bengal and the Gurjara-Pritihara from Rajasthanire. By the ninth century, the Palas from eastern India had gained ascendency and become rulers of the city of Kanauj. The Pala dynasty was closely linked to the Indian Ocean trade and had commercial and political relations with the Sailandra dynasty kings of Srivijaya from Sumatra. The Pala kings patronized Buddhism, which had, by this period, had taken an unorthodox tantric form in Bengal. From the Pala Empire, Buddhism was introduced to Tibet that, in combination with local beliefs, became the basis of modern Tibetan Buddhism.

The early sixth-century invasions by nomadic groups such as the Huns, which had dealt a deathblow to the Gupta Empire, also destroyed or dispersed the original warrior castes of Rajasthan. The migrating Turks Hinduized themselves and assumed the role of Ksatriyas, and from them arose most of the warrior castes of North India, such as the Rajputs.

Also around the time of the Hun invasion, a nomadic group called Gujars emerged as one of the most powerful North Indian dynasties of the Indian Middle Ages. In the ninth and tenth centuries, the descendants of this nomadic tribe, now joined with another and calling themselves Gurjara-Pritiharas, migrated from their base in Rajasthan and became masters of Kanauj, which they seized from the Palas to become the most powerful kings of North India. They had also successfully resisted the Arabs, stopping the Abbasid dynasty when it tried to expand eastward from its base in Sind province, which had been occupied by Arabs in 712. However, the Gurjara-Pritihara kings were themselves weakened by the repeated attacks from the powerful Rashtrakuta dynasty of Deccan in central India, who temporarily occupied Kanauj in the early tenth century (Basham, 1967, 74).

These continuous raids and threats from the southern frontiers turned the attention of Gurjara-Pritihara kings away from Northwest India, where was gathering a new and more formidable foe, who would ultimately seal the fate of many of the Hindu dynasties and end Hindu political power in northern India for a thousand years. This was the arrival of Islamized Turks, who established their center of power in Afghanistan.

Although the Gurjara-Pritihara eventually regained their capital from the Rashtrakutas, they never regained their earlier dominance. As a result, throughout the tenth century, the Gurjara-Pritihara vassals grew powerful at the expense of their former masters. Around this time in Afghanistan, a powerful line of Turkish chieftains established a powerful kingdom at Ghazni and began to look eagerly at the rich plains of India, which lacked a strong political center and seemed ripe for plunder.

South India

In the south, despite recurrent and mutually destructive warfare between the rival Pallava and Chalukya dynasties, there was a revival of Hindu culture. Following the fall of Harsha's kingdom, contact between Indo-European speakers of the north and the Dravidian-speaking south produced a lively hybrid. This cultural synthesis was to influence not only the south, but the entire Indian civilization.

Political power in the south was centered on two areas. One was western Deccan in central India, and the other was in southeast India, along the Coromandel Coast, where were located the Chola capital of Tanjore and the Pallava capital of Kanchipuram. The political history of Deccan was largely concerned with the struggle between the dynasties that controlled these two centers.

Around the time of Harsha, central India came under the control of the Chalukya dynasty, ruling from Vatapi (now called Badami) in Andra, near the western coast of India. Southeast of the Chalukya kingdom was Kanchipuram, or Kanchi, capital of the Pallava dynasty. The Pallava kingdom, which was known to Roman and Chinese traders, owed its existence to the prosperous irrigation and dense agricultural settlement around Kanchi as well as to the Indian Ocean trade.

The origins of the Pallava dynasty remain a mystery. Some historians maintain that their origins could be traced to Pallava (or Parthian Persian) of northwest India. But it is more likely the Sanskrit equivalent of the Tamil word *Tondai*, or *Tondai Mandalam*, describes the area of southern India from where they originated. Other lineage legends claim that the first Pallava ruler was an adventurous outsider who married a local Naga princess (the Nagas, or snakes, were symbols of fertility and also a local tribal power). Similar lineage histories are also found in Southeast Asia concerning the rise of Hindu dynasties there.

What seems to be clear about the Pallavas is that they did not belong to any of the ancient south Indian dynasties such as the Cholas, Cheras, and Pandiyas. They owed their rise to the defeat of the Kalabhras, who, in the first centuries C.E., were a Tamil country regional power that patronized the Jains and Buddhists. The Kalabhras had defeated the three traditional Tamil country dynasties. By the late seventh century, however, the Pallava had extended their power into the heart of Tamil country, overthrowing the Kalabhras and creating the largest kingdom in south India until that time.

The Pallavas also confronted the Chalukyas in the north, under the powerful Pallava rulers Mahendra Varman and Narashima Varman. Mahendra Varman had a reputation as a talented ruler and constructed the first Hindu cave temples of south India. According to Hindu sacred history, Mahendra Varman had been converted from **Jainism** by the Hindu saint Appar, one of the charismatic Bhakti saints of devotional Hinduism. The Pallava rulers also constructed ports for the Indian Ocean trade, with bonfire lighthouses, as well as some of the most beautiful rock-carved temples of south India (*see* **Temples, Hindu**). The southern architectural style, which portrays the temple tower as a steep mountain, was perfected under the Pallavas and was later transmitted to Southeast Asia, especially to Java.

The city of Kanchi flourished as a royal capital, and the Pallavas, although they were Hindus, extended their patronage to Buddhists. Xuanzang visited the Pallava kingdom in the reign of Narashima Varman and reported that there were about one hundred Buddhist monasteries with ten thousand monks studying the doctrines of Mahayana Buddhism. To the south of the Pallava country was the Chola kingdom where Xuanzang reported that Buddhism had become extinct.

The northwest of the Pallava country was under the rule of the Chalukya dynasty, whose kings were known to be patrons of art and architecture. Earlier scholars regarded the Chalukyas as mere transmitters of preexisting copies of Gupta art and architecture, but recent, more detailed studies show that the Chalukyas were creative in their own right. According to some art critics, the Chalukya sculptures are among the greatest of Hindu iconography. Many of the major figures of Hindu mythology are portrayed in beautiful stone sculptures.

Politically, the Chalukyas reached their zenith under King Pulakasin II (609–642), the ruler who had defeated Harsha and thereby ended his southward expansion. But Pulakasin was himself soon killed by the Pallava ruler Narashima Varman. As the Pallavas fought with such north Indian powers such as Chalukyas and the Rashtrakutas, who were themselves one-time vassals of the Chalukyas, Pallava vassals, such as the Cholas, began asserting their independence. In spite of their declining political fortunes, the Pallavas of Kanchi survived until the end of the eighth century, when their territories were annexed by the Cholas of Tanjore.

The Cholas of Tanjore

The Chola kingdom was one of the three great kingdoms of Tamil culture. Emerging in the eighth century from centuries of dominance by the Pallavas, the Cholas so dominated the southeastern coast of India for the next 300 years that the entire area is still called Coromandel, or Chola Mandal — the domain of the Cholas. Chola domination gave security to the people of southern India, and supported a flourishing social and cultural life.

The most notable Chola ruler was Raja Raja Chola I (r. 985–1014), under whom Chola power reached its zenith. Raja Raja conquered Sri Lanka, and his son, Rajandra Chola, extended his power into the Gangatic basin. Rajandra Chola also conducted punitive naval expeditions to various parts of Southeast Asia, including Burma, Malaya, and Sumatra. These expeditions were perhaps undertaken with the intention of ending the piratical activities of the Sumatran kings of Srivijaya, who were interfering with Indian merchant guilds conducting the flourishing trade between India and China.

The Chola hold on Southeast Asia did not last long, but, in spite of this, Raja Raja's naval expeditions were unique to the history of India. The Cholas ruled over Sri Lanka until 1070, when they were expelled by the local Singalese princes. From then on, Chola power declined due to military pressure from the Chalukyas of Deccan and unrest among the vassals, especially among the Pandia princes, who sought to regain their autonomy and independence.

In spite of their declining power, the Cholas maintained their hold over the central part of their empire: the Tamil country from Kanchi to Tanjore. The political stability and freedom from external attack that strong Chola rulers provided in the tenth and eleventh centuries encouraged the development of Tamil culture, which thrived under a stable and flourishing economy and entered a period of artistic and architectural achievement (Basham, 1967, 74–75).

Like other medieval Indian polities, the Chola state was decentralized. At the local level, administration was in the hands of autonomous village councils. Chola power collapses in the midthirteenth century, and their territory was shared by their former vassals the Pandiyas, who were centered in the city of Madurai.

The Coming of Islam

In the twelfth century in the region of Afghanistan, a Muslim dynasty called the Ghaurids arose to influence the whole region. In the thirteenth and fourteenth centuries, a new religious force, Islam, entered India in full strength. Northern and western Deccan fell to Islamic invaders (*see* **Balban**). Eastern Deccan and even the heartland of Chola country was raided by Muslim generals such as Malik **Kafur**, a former captive and converted Hindu who became general of the army of **Allauddin Khilji** (r. 1296–1316), second Khilji ruler of the **Delhi sultanate**. The Khilij dynasty was the first major Islamic dynasty on Indian soil. Under Malik Kafur's leadership, the Turkish Muslims army toppled all local Hindu states throughout the entire subcontinent, compelling them to become vassals. Their treasures were carted off to Delhi to finance the foundation of the Delhi sultanate.

Allauddin's political and administrative reforms were as comprehensive as his military exploits. He decided to tackle the irregularities of tax and tribute payment right at its root. He first undertook a survey of the entire agricultural resources of his kingdom and then imposed a fixed standardized tax on all agricultural landholders, which was half their crop. A similar tax was also imposed on pastoralists. The revenue was collected by military officials and deposited into the central treasury. By this act, Allauddin was able to increase his land revenue and make it more reliable while reducing the powers of his courtiers and of local magistrates, such as petty rajahs and village chiefs. These Hindu chieftains were seen as the major source of conspiracies and rebellion against his rule. Therefore, according to Islamic chronicles, Allauddin believed that if everyone was busy earning a living to pay for his taxes, nobody could ever have time to think about rebellion.

Allauddin felt that the feasts and excessive drinking of his Muslim officials were also a source of plots against him. Therefore, alcohol, which was in any case forbidden under Islam, was now prohibited by the state, along with feasts and private meetings. Spies watched for transgressions of these orders. Allauddin, despite the unpopularity by these harsh methods, was able to control his ambitious courtier officials and rebellious local chieftains.

To maintain his authority, Allauddin required a large standing army. To hire more troops with the same budget, Allauddin lowered his soldiers' pay but, to prevent unrest in the army, also issued an edict fixing the prices of basic necessities so that they remained affordable for soldiers. To provide subsidized grain for his soldiers, Allauddin's state granaries provided the necessary grain stocks to military garrisons from grain previously collected as tax. To eliminate the occurrence of any future uprising against Muslim rule by Hindus, Allauddin closely regulated the power of Hindu chieftains, who were thus unable to effectively raise rebellion. It is also difficult to judge how effective Allauddin was in implementing these measures. According to Muslim chronicles his prohibitive measures were flaunted and the official prohibition of alcohol led to distilling of illicit liquor, which was sold in Delhi in the spirit of prohibition-era Chicago. Bazaar traders also violated the fixed price rules by using smaller measures. Further away from Delhi many of these measures had no significant impact and, as a general rule, before the British Period, no Indian ruler had any direct authority outside a radius of 100 miles from his capital.

Allauddin's most notable deed for the history of India was his ability to withstand **Mongol** assaults on his capital and keep India from the Mongol yoke. When he died in 1316, his general and supposed lover Malik Kafur tried to control the Muslim Turkish court and the army, but he was murdered by his own men. One of Allauddin's sons, Qutb-ud-din Mubarak, survived as ruler for 4 years by undoing some of his father's draconian measures. Tughluq, a former slave soldier in Allauddin's service, overthrew Qutb-ud-din Mubarak in 1320. In 1324, Tughluq's son, **Muhammad bin Tughluq**, deposed his father and ruled the Delhi sultanate until 1351.

Allauddin conquered and looted but preferred to leave the old Hindu ruling families as his vassals. However, Muhammad bin Tughluq dreamed of making the entire Indian subcontinent his realm. To this end, he built a new capital at a more central location 700 miles to the south at Dalutabad, to which he forced the inhabitants of Delhi to move. Although, in theory, this venture made sense; in practice, it failed and, perhaps, led to the downfall of the sultanate.

After moving his capital to Dalutabad, Mohammad lost control over North India and failed to consolidate his hold on the South. When he returned to Delhi 2 years later, the return was seen as a weakness by his vassals, Hindu and Muslim, and many broke away to form independent states in southern and eastern India. In 1334, the governor of Madurai, deep in Tamil country, declared his independence and called himself the sultan of Mabar, and, 4 years later, Bengal followed suit. In 1336, the Hindu Empire of **Vijayanagar**, the last and largest Hindu state in terms of area, was founded in South India. In Central India, the **Bahmani kingdom** was founded in 1347.

To revitalize the economy and support his policy of expansion, Muhammad bin Tughluq had introduced economic and administrative reforms. He extended the system of direct administration to all the provinces, but it could only be implemented at the core region of the Sultanate. Whereas Allauddin collected a great deal of revenue in kind from the core region to secure a reliable supply system to Delhi, Muhammad Tughluq insisted on tax in cash to transfer the anticipated revenues from the far-flung provinces to his capital. When Muhammad Tughluq discovered that the stock of coins and mintable silver was inadequate for such an extensive monetization, instead of abandoning the scheme, he issued token currency in copper, an idea that was foreign to India, where the nominal value of coins never deviated from their intrinsic value.

Perhaps with the hope of imitating China's successful use of paper currency, Muhammad bin Tughluq issued his token brass and copper-based currency with the equivalent value of the rare silver tanka (140 grams of silver). Indians were also permitted to turn in their copper tokens at the royal mint for silver and gold. And, with this policy, according to the chronicles, every house became a mint producing copper tokens, and the entire currency system of the sultanate collapsed. This novel economic experiment thus ended in financial disaster. Muhammad bin Tughluq was forced to withdraw his token currency barely 3 years after its launch. To direct attention away from this monetary fiasco, he launched two major military campaigns against Persia and Central Asia, which were unsuccessful.

After the failure of this ambitious plan, Muhammad bin Tughluq's rule disintegrated into a reign of terror, of which the fourteenth-century Moroccan traveler **Ibn Battuta** gives us a vivid account. Although the rural Hindu population also suffered oppression and exploitation, the main targets of Muhammad bin Tughluq's reign of terror were Muslims living in the urban areas, where even learned Islamic scholars were swiftly eliminated if their views displeased the sultan.

Despite the tyranny of his later years, and his failed monetary innovations, Muhammad bin Tughluq tried to fashion a form of kingship that could win the allegiance of Hindus and Muslims. To this end, he adapted some of the familiar symbols of Indian kingship, such as processions on richly decorated elephants on special days. He also attempted to lend legitimacy to his rule by obtaining a document of authorization, or investiture, from the puppet Abbasid caliph of Cairo.

The last important sultan of Delhi was **Firuz Shah Tughluq**, who succeeded his cousin Muhammad bin Tughluq in 1351 and enjoyed 37-year reign. Firuz Shah consolidated his power in North India and made a few unsuccessful attempts to win back lost territory in Bengal and Sind. The latter ended in military disaster. After this, he suspended any further military campaigns. On the cultural front, Firuz Shah added to the archaeological splendor of Delhi by building new mosques, forts, and waterways.

A multistoried structure known as the Firuz Shah Kotala (citadel) was built in Delhi and adorned with two Ashoka columns transported from distant provinces. Firuz Shah is said to have consulted the learned Brahmins in an attempt to decipher the inscription on these pillars, but no one was able to decipher them because the Brahmi script had long fallen into disuse (it was only decoded in the nineteenth century by an East India Company official). These polished sandstone Ashokan pillars posed a psychological challenge for later rulers, due to the artistic merits of their carving and the techniques and methods used in transporting and erecting them. They, therefore, challenged the very authority of the new Islamic states, which is perhaps why such a great deal of effort was spent on transporting them by Firuz Shah, who reerected them in Delhi with a great public celebration.

Like his predecessors, Firuz Shah also introduced reforms. He abolished judicial torture and extended the Islamic *zhyza* or poll tax on non-Muslims, to the previously exempt Brahmins, possibly in an effort to convert them to Islam. He also rewarded new Hindu converts. Enslaved Indians from the provinces were converted and sent to the capital, perhaps to augment the number of Islamic residents who would support the sultanate against any potential rebellions by the Hindu majority.

When Firuz Shah died in 1388, the Delhi sultanate disintegrated with a succession struggle. With weakness at the center, provincial governors declared their autonomy and reigned as independent sovereigns. In 1398, another new Turkish invader swept into the plains of North India. This was **Timur** the Lame, or Timurlane, as he is known to Europeans.

Fresh from the victories in Western Asia, where he conquered Persia and captured the city of Baghdad, then one of the biggest metropolises in the Islamic world, Timur sacked the city of Delhi. For 3 days, Timur's soldiers indulged in an orgy of murder and plunder. The entire Hindu population in the city was massacred. The Muslims were spared their lives, but their movable properties were confiscated. The deeds of the Turkish warriors shocked even Timur who wrote in his autobiography that he was not responsible for these terrible events, and only his soldiers should be blamed.

After Timur left the city, Delhi remained desolate for years, and the first epoch of Muslim political power in India came to an end. A new period of Afghan rule in North India commenced in 1451 when the Afghan clan of Lodis established a new dynasty in North India centered in Delhi (*see* **Babur**). To their credit, the Lodi sultans established an efficient administrative system that later provided a good foundation for Mughal rule after 1526.

Further Reading

Auboyer, Jeannine. *Daily Life in Ancient India: From Approximately 200 BC to 700 AD.* New York: Macmillan, 1975.

Basham, A. L. *The Wonder that Was India.* London: Sidgwick & Jackson, 1982.

Basham, A. L., ed. *A Cultural History of India*. Delhi: New York: Oxford University Press, 1983.

Coedes, G. *The Indianized States of South East Asia*. Honolulu: East-West Center, University of Hawai'i, 1968.

Elliot, H. M., and John Dowson. *The History of India: As Told by Its Own Historians*. Calcutta: Susil Gupta, 1963.

Khan, Iqtidar Alam. *Historical Dictionary of Medieval India*. Lanham, MD: Scarecrow Press, 2008.

Kulke, Hermann, and Dietmar Rothermund. *A History of India*. New York: Rutledge, 1998.

Spear, Percival. *A History of India*. Vol. 2. London: Penguin Books, 1990.

Thapar, Romila. *A History of India*. Vol. 1. London: Penguin Books, 1982.

Wolpert, Stanley. *A New History of India*. New York: Oxford University Press, 2000.

Raman N. Seylon

2. RELIGION

Buddhism

That Indian Buddhism grew and thrived between 200 B.C.E. and 200 C.E. is confirmed by the numerous Buddhist sites and archaeological remains from the period.

From India, Buddhism was spread to Sri Lanka, East and Southeast Asia, and parts of Central Asia by traders, envoys, immigrants, and missionary monks. The sacred Buddhist sites, such as where the Buddha was born, got his enlightenment, preached his first sermon, and died, became centers of pilgrimage for Indian and foreign monks. With the patronage of wealthy merchant communities and pious donors, Buddhist centers were stylishly rebuilt, and rulers gave away the entire revenues of prosperous villages to support large monastic organizations. Buddhism, like all major religions, split into two (later three) divisions as the great vehicle and lesser vehicle.

As Buddhism began to expand during this period, changes occurred within the old Vedic or Brahminical Hinduism (see below), which strengthened that tradition. The earlier sacrifice-centered religion with its pantheon of nature deities gave way to new deities who sought great devotion more than sacrificial offerings. By the time of the Emperor **Harsha**, who ascended the throne in 606 C.E. and ruled northern India for 41 years, the lesser vehicle Buddhism had vanished from India, and Buddhism itself was slowly disappearing. The Chinese scholar-monk, **Xuanzang**, who

Seated Buddha with Dharmachakra Mudra hand position. 10th century. Pala. East India. Bildarchiv Preussischer Kulturbesitz/Art Resource.

visited India during the time of Harsha, noted that Buddhism seemed to lack the emotional pull of reinvigorated Hinduism. Xuanzang observed that many former centers of pilgrimage were deserted, though a few major ones, such as the Buddhist University of Nalanda, were still active. Nalanda was a major center of Buddhist scholarship where thousands of novice monks were taught by noted Buddhist scholars. It attracted foreign students from all over India and also from East and Southeast Asia (Basham, 1967, 265).

Eastern India, around the early medieval period, saw a growth in interest in Tantric or magical, mystical rites that also involved the breaking of social or sexual mores, and these ideas affected Hinduism and Buddhism. In Buddhism, this development gave rise to a third path, *Vajrayana* (meaning "vehicle of the thunderbolt"). Xuanzang viewed these new developments unfavorably, as doctrinal corruption. This form of Buddhism grew in popularity in Bengal and Bihar in northeastern India, and it was this form of Buddhism that was to become the basis of Tibetan Buddhism. With the death of Harsha in 647 C.E., eastern India came under the rule of the Palas, a dynasty centered in Bihar, whose kings patronized Buddhism for the next three centuries. Under the Palas, Tantric Buddhism became part of the mainstream and Tantric literature was widely available (Wayman, 318).

Xuanzang had also noted that in Tamil Nadu in the far south Sivaism and Vaisnavaism were gaining popularity at the expense of more monastic-centered Buddhism. In Karnataka in southwestern India, Buddhism lost its appeal to Jainism, and later, to a new form of Sivaism called Lingayat, which may have been influenced by the ideals of Islam. Also at this time, Indian Buddhist scholars began migrating to Tibet, then a new and promising religious frontier where the popularity of Buddhism was growing. The Buddhism they brought with them had elements of Tantric rituals and beliefs.

The decline of Buddhism in India was due to a number of factors, external and internal. According to Columbia University Buddhist scholar and historian Alex Wayman, the chief internal reasons for Buddhism's demise were the following:

1. Buddhist strength lay in monasteries and was not deeply embedded in the village life of the people.
2. Buddhist prosperity depended on steady patronage from royalty and rich merchants.
3. Although Buddhism did not embark on any active campaign against India's caste-based social system, its egalitarian message offended and challenged the powerful upper castes, especially the Brahmins.
4. Buddhist sectarian divisions and rivalry wastefully drained the powers of its institutions.
5. Buddhism, in its Indian form, was non-violent, and had no defense against a determined and organized aggressor motivated by plunder and ideology.
6 Buddhist doctrine was too profound for the masses.

Wayman lists the external reasons for Buddhism's decline as follows:

1. Hinduism had adapted many of the strong points of Buddhism.
2. Hostile kings, plundering invaders, and, sometimes, fanatical mobs destroyed Buddhist monasteries and monuments and murdered monks.

3. Hinduism, now revived and invigorated by a new devotional ideology, challenged Buddhism and squeezed it out of its sacred centers by deliberately placing Hindu icons or shrines in them.
4. The works of Sankara (788–820), who debated with Buddhists and set up four Hindu holy sees or "maths" at four corners of India, greatly strengthened Hinduism. Most important, he systematized and unified the Hindu great and little traditions, and established a new form of devotional "monistic" Hinduism that spread to all corners of India (Wayman, 381; Basham, 265).

Although Buddhists faced persecution, the more formidable challenge came from the revived and reformed Hinduism that spread west from **Tamil country** from the ninth century onwards. This new form of Hinduism, with its emphasis on a personal god, had a profound appeal to ordinary folks. Also, the Hindu tendency to assimilate caused Buddha to be seen as the ninth incarnation of Vishnu and, with that, Buddhism began to lose its individuality and special appeal.

A more fatal blow to Buddhism came with the Turkish Muslim invasion of India that began in the early eleventh century. Buddhist monasteries, with their libraries and rare collections, were obvious targets for the Muslim Turks, who sacked many, forcing surviving monks to migrate to functioning Buddhist centers outside India, in Tibet and Nepal. With this migration, Indian Buddhism ceased to be a functioning faith (Basham, 1967, 265).

Jainism

Jainism was another major Indian religion that coevolved with Buddhism but has survived in India to the present day. Like Buddhism, Jainism also thrived during periods of state patronage and, like Buddhism, split into two sects in its early history. The major schism among the two branches of Indian Judaism focused primarily on dress code. The monks of the south, from whom originated the *Digambar* ("sky clad") sect, insisted on an orthodox dress code of total nudity whereas the north Indian Jains, from whom derived the Svetambar sect, wore white garments. This division was established early in the history of Jainism, during the first century C.E. Unlike the schism among the Buddhists, there were no doctrinal differences between the Jain sects. In the Middle Ages, the Jain monks spent time, as religious merit, in writing commentaries on sacred and secular literature of the period. It was largely through their efforts that many rare and almost unknown texts of non-Jain origins have survived to the present. By the medieval period, the white-clad sect was centered in the northwest at Kathiawar in Rajesthan, whereas the sky-clad sect was based in Andhra and Karnataka in the southwest, all of which places were also home to large concentrations of Jews.

The influence and popularity of the Jain sects among the Indian populace depended upon charismatic Jain teachers and pious Jain rulers. The loss of imperial patronage also meant loss of prestige and influence, and such loss often occurred as a result of the revival of devotional Hinduism. Just as it was with Buddhism, Jainism became the target of persecution instigated by *bhakti* saints and rulers who were recent converts to Hinduism. We have few references of

Jain monks accompanying trade and diplomatic delegations sent abroad. But, unlike Buddhism, Jainism never gained any appeal outside India. However, the Jains left a lasting memory among the ancient Greeks and Romans, especially the Jain practice of self-immolation as a way to end their lives. In spite of this, Jainism survives today in India, where it has millions of followers, including wealthy merchants.

Jainism shares many fundamental ideas with Buddhism. Like Buddhism, it was basically an atheistic faith, which sees the universe functioning according to an impersonal law of cause and effect. Unlike the Hindus, the Jain cosmology has no universal deluge, or destruction; the Jain universe is eternal, although within it there are a number of micro cycles with their periods of improvements and decline. The process of decline continues some 40,000 years until civilization returns to barbarism, and then the cycle improves and reaches another high crest, and then yet another decline, a cycle that goes on forever. Unlike Buddhism, Jainism offers no course for salvation for ordinary laypeople. Nirvana or salvation in Jainism is only possible for a monk. To attain nirvana, a Jain devotee must abandon all material earthly possessions, including clothes, and undertake long periods of fasting and self-mortification, meditation, and study. Thus, only Jain monks could ever hope to gain salvation. Unlike Hinduism, Jainism does not permit spectacular penances but seeks only quiet fasting. It was common for a Jain monk to fast himself to death. Jainism totally renounces all forms of violence and even the lives of insects are spared. Jains take special care not to harm even the tiniest forms of life. They strain water before drinking and sweep the path with a feather duster to brush away any small insects and thus prevent them from being trampled under their feet. They also mask their mouths, like surgeons, to prevent any living form from being inhaled or killed accidentally.

The Ajivakas

The third major non-Hindu sect that coevolved with the Buddhists but survived only till about the fourteenth century was the Ajivakas, a group of ascetics who followed a rigorous spiritual discipline similar to that of the Jains. They too, like the sky-clad sect of Jains, went about in total nudity. The founder of this sect was Gosala Makkhaliputra, a former friend of Mahavira, the founder of Jainism. Like Mahavira, he took preexisting teachings of local ascetic groups and further developed them. Unlike Buddha and Mahavira, Gosala Makkhaliputra, who died around 484 B.C.E., was of humble birth; his followers combined the teachings of Gosala with other teachers and founded a synchronic sect.

The Ajivakas were never as popular as the Buddhists or Jains and remained only the south, in eastern Karnataka and Tamil Nadu until the fourteenth century, when all records of them cease. Unfortunately, we also don't have any sacred texts of the Ajivakas; these must be reconstructed from the surviving criticisms of them by their rivals, the Buddhists and Jains. From these it seems that the Ajivakas, like the Buddhists and Jains, were atheistic but had a central doctrine of strict determinism, which was very different from the karma, or cause and effect doctrine common to the Buddhists, Jains, and Hindus (Basham, 296). The doctrine of karma believes that a person's present condition was determined by his or her past actions and therefore influences future fate in this life and in future life. Likewise, individuals could influence their destiny by choosing right actions and conduct. Such a dynamic view of fate was rejected by Ajivakas. They saw their entire universe as conditioned by an impersonal law called Niyati, (rule or destiny). Niyati controls and determines every single detail of the material universe, and it was impossible to influence future states in any way. It also saw the world of movement as illusory, and that reality is fixed and unchanging. The real world is forever at rest.

In spite of their belief in the fixity of each person's predestination, Ajivaka monks practiced rather severe forms of asceticism. They explained this seeming contradiction not in terms of an attempt to gain merits to alter their karmaic fate, which they believed impossible, but rather as a result of that very destiny. In latter periods, Ajivakas survived in small pockets in south India and resembled the Mahayana, or great vehicle, Buddhism, with Gosala taking the central role of a Buddha. Although the Ajivakas, like Buddhists and Jains, paid no attention to supernatural beings or gods, they were not true atheists; they accepted the existence of supernatural beings, though these had no real bearing on human affairs.

School of Ajita

Some Indian scholars of philosophy were totally atheistic. The earliest known of these atheistic schools was found by Ajita Kesakambali (Ajita of the hair blanket), who wore only a piece of blanket fashioned out of human hair and lived in the sixth century B.C.E. about the time of the Buddha. According to this atheistic school, man "is formed out of four elements. When he dies the earth returns to earth, water to water and fire to fire, air to air and the senses vanish into space. . . . They are fools who preach almsgiving and those who maintain the categories of immaterial speak in vain and lying nonsense. When the body dies, fools and wise alike are cut off and perish for they do not survive after death" (Basham, 1967, 296).

According to Buddhist scripture, Ajita founded a sect that was condemned by the historical Buddha as having no real reason for performing asceticism. It is also possible that this particular school was not an order of monks, but a brotherhood that, at least from the writings of their adversaries, declared all religious observances and morality to be futile. The ultimate purpose of life was to derive the greatest happiness. In this sense, they were similar to the Greek School of Epicureans. They also rejected the virtues and morality preached by the Jains and Buddhists. Perhaps in response to the self-denying dictums of their rivals, they subscribed to the following general motto: "Those who shy away from pleasure and joy that is freely available for various metaphysical reasons are fools no better than dumb animals." Because our sources for the Ajita and all other heterodox atheistic schools come from the writings of Buddhists, they are not impartial observations or devoid of polemics (Basham, 296–297).

Hinduism

The early Vedic Hinduism brought to India by Indo-European Aryan tribes was seriously undermined during the time of Alexander the Great's invasion of India in the second century C.E. by various popular cults. New deities emerged and became the focus of popular veneration. One of these new gods that was popular in western India during the Greek invasion was a deity named Vasudeva. A stone column in Besnagar erected by one of the Greek rulers of northwest India (the descendents of Alexander's generals) in honor of Vasudeva informs us that the cult of Vasudeva had royal sanction and was popular among the ruling elite. We also find the link between the cult of Vasudeva and a minor Vedic deity named Vishnu, an equally minor deity called Narayana, and a flute-playing pastoral hero god Krishna (who also appears in the epic *Mahabharata*). A number of regional gods were also associated with the composite Vasudeva/Vishnu/Narayana/Krishna cult, such as the cult of the divine boar, which was gaining popularity in the Gupta Period (fourth to sixth centuries C.E.). Later the hero of the second major epic *Ramayana* was also associated with this composite, which became the core of what came to be known as the Vishnavite traditions. The hero of the great epic, along with the divine boar, came to be seen as various incarnations of the composite deity now known as the "Supreme Vishnu"—or Mahavishnu. To a member of the Vishnavite tradition, Mahavishnu is the universal god, the source of all things in the universe; all other gods are but manifestations of Vishnu in other forms. Vishnu is seen as a compassionate deity who takes on various incarnations to serve humanity and save it from all forms of danger. Traditionally, there are ten incarnations of Vishnu in human and supernatural forms, including a divine gigantic boar incarnation, to save humankind. Nine of these incarnations, including the historic Buddha, have already taken place, with the final incarnation yet to appear.

The second major cult to emerge during this period was the worship of Siva, whose origin may have been as a non-Aryan fertility deity popular among the Dravidian-speaking people. This deity probably emerged among the Harrapan people of the Indus Valley civilization prior to the Aryan invasion. This god was known as "Proto-Siva" and appears in Harrapan artifacts as a deity in meditation (possibly having three faces), who had the power to attract wild animals and who may have been worshipped as a phallic symbol. This non-Aryan deity was associated with the Aryan god of storms called Rudhra. In later times, known popularly as Siva and seen as a father god in high heaven, he was just as popular as Vishnu and thus became the second major sect of popular Hinduism. Other popular regional deities also became associated with the cult of Siva; these included Ganesha, the elephant-faced lord of (or remover of) material and spiritual obstacles, and Skanda or Murugan, the lord of war, who were seen as two of his sons. Whereas Vishnu was generally benevolent, Siva could, at times, be ferocious. In popular imagery, he is shown as wearing a garland of skulls and does a spectacular awe-inspiring dance in the company of goblins, ghosts, and demons. But Siva is also a great yogi, the perfect ascetic often seen deep in meditation and perfect stillness. He is also the god of all motion as Nataraja—the lord of dances. In Hindu religious iconography, nothing can rival the bronze imaging of Nataraja, where Siva becomes the cosmic dancer, with four hands and flying locks he dances on a prostrated dwarf (*apasmara purusa*) who symbolizes human ignorance. The Siva's left back hand holds an hour glass–shaped drum (*damaru*) symbolizing the sound of creation, while the front hand has a "fear-not" gesture made by holding the arm upward, which also symbolizes the act of preservation or protection. Siva's right back hand holds flames (*agni*) in his hands, the fire signifying destruction. The front left hand is held across the chest in the elephant trunk pose, with fingers pointing downwards toward an uplifted left foot, which symbolizes release. The dancing figure of Siva is encircled by a ring of flames or *prabha mandala* symbolizing the entire visible universe. The form of the dance is called the tandava dance.

The significance of this dance is that Siva is the source of all movement. The purpose of the dance is to release humans from illusion, and it takes place at Chidambaram, the center of the universe, which is also considered the center of one's heart. Other dances of Siva, seen in bronze, are the terrible, wild tandava dance, which is performed at the time of the dissolution of the universe and destroys the world, thus ending a cosmic cycle. In the sacred puranic stories, this dance is performed in auspicious places, like cremation grounds, with his fierce dwarf attendants (*gana*) and his consort Devi (*see* **Puranas**).

Siva, like Vishnu, manifests himself from time to time in temporary incarnations either to destroy the wicked and to test the faith of his devotees or to uphold virtue in an exemplary fashion. Since the early part of the first millennium C.E., most educated Hindus were either Vishnavites (worshippers of Vishnu) or Saivaites (worshippers of Siva). All other deities are seen as holding secondary positions as manifestations of the supreme godhead. In this sense, a Vishnavite does not deny the existence of Siva but sees Siva as one of the many secondary creations of Maha-Vishnu and vice versa.

Many devout Vishnavites and Saivaites see the gods they worship as different aspects of the same ultimate godhead. Attempts had been made to harmonize Vaisnavism and Saivism. A Hindu trinity or *trimurti*, a composite figure combining the Brahma, the creator; Vishnu, the preserver; and Siva, the destroyer, evolved during the Gupta Period; this figure strongly resembles the three-faced Harrapan deity called the "Proto-Siva" and thus points to the deeper roots of popular Hindu traditions. In central India there developed during the middle ages a fusion of Siva and Vishnu as Hari Hara (*Hari* is another name for Vishnu and *Hara* an alternate name of Siva), which combined the attributes of both deities.

Goddess Worship

Apart from Siva and Vishnu, the worship of goddesses became a major focus of Hindu devotion in the Middle Ages. Images of goddesses are found in Harrapan sites, but in early Vedic Hinduism goddesses were rarely the source of popular veneration. The worship of goddesses reemerged in the Gupta Period from the fourth to sixth centuries C.E. and has gained popularity ever since. Today, all Hindu classes and castes worship powerful female deities in their own accord and as consorts to major deities associated with either the Saivaite or Vaisnavite traditions. The goddess is seen as *shakti* or the strength of her male consort and the potent force behind static transcendent male deities. The most popular pan-Indian mother goddesses are Parvati, the consort of Siva, who is also seen in an autonomous malevolent form as Durga, and as the terrifying Kali. Durga is a fierce goddess who rides a lion and battles a buffalo-headed demon. The repulsive Kali is a jet black or purple-colored female figure, with bloody tongue sticking out and wearing a garland of freshly decapitated hands and amputated limbs, and dances on the body of her husband Siva. There is also a fusion of Siva and Parvati, an androgynous deity combining the masculine and feminine energies of godhead known as

Aradanarisvara. It is commonly depicted in sculptures as a half male and female figure fused as one. It is an imagery found in Chola bronzes or carved in the cave temples of Ellora and Elephanta.

Hindu Religious Change in Medieval India

Between the thirteenth and seventeenth centuries, Hinduism underwent a dramatic transformation, so profound that it basically altered the very nature of the faith. The primary focus of worship moved from the polytheistic Vedic deities to a supreme, paramount deity, and his manifestations and incarnations.

A new emotional attitude towards the deity became the core of a passionate religion of self-abandonment; called *bhakti* (devotion), this religion began to supersede the older sacrifice-based Vedic religion with its meditations and mystical techniques, and one that exemplified the ascetic virtues and renunciation. Now, the new ascetic mysticism replaced the older philosophical mysticism of the Upanishads. Devotional love songs, sung in groups called *kirtans*, became the dominant mode of popular religious expression, pushing the esoteric Sanskrit Vedic chanting and Brahmanical Hindu rituals into the inner sanctuaries of temples. Because these *kirtans* were sung in local vernaculars, they also gave a boost to regional literature. These changes in the very fabric of everyday Hinduism altered the essential role of the Brahmins, who, as a caste, lost much of their prestige and authority. The leadership of popular Hinduism passed to *bhakti* saints and gurus whose songs and sacred inspirational and miracle stories became the new Vedas, accessible to everyone. Although this new devotional form of worship did not destroy the older Hindu socioritual order, it made it less significant. The new devotional religion fostered a sense of equality before a loving god. Most *bhakti* saints were non-Brahmins, who also included untouchables and women in their ranks.

The Development of Devotional Hinduism

Around the first century B.C.E., the earliest devotional form of Hindu worship emerged among the sect of Bhagavatas, who worshipped Vasudeva, a god associated with the pastoral deity Krishna and the Vedic deity Vishnu. Some time later, a similar mode of worship appeared among a sect known as the Pasupathas, who worshipped Siva. The early histories of these devotional sects are still murky but both stressed worship rather than sacrifice. By the Middle Ages, they had also developed their own religious doctrines and philosophy (Basham 1967, 328–29).

These earlier forms of devotional worship were more restrained than the later full-fledged *bhakti* mode of worship. The earlier godhead had been seen as a benevolent but distant father and king to be worshipped and venerated from afar, while the ever-present imminent deity of *bhakti* tradition was worshipped with deep, uncontrolled passion. These new modes of devotional worship may have been influenced by the earlier Mahayana Buddhist cult of Buddhisattava, which presented a compassionate being deeply concerned with the plight of ordinary mortals (Basham, 1967, 329).

The *bhakti* form of intense devotional worship first developed in the Tamil country of southern India. Here was the first development of a godhead that had deep love for humanity and whose devotees were expected to express a similar passionate devotion. Early devotional hymns by Saivaite saints, called Nayanmar, and Vaisnavite saints, called Alwars, originated in Tamil country and facilitated the full development of this intense devotional form of worship.

This new emotionally charged Hinduism moved north from Tamil country by about the ninth century. According to Hindu tradition, this devotional mode of new worship was spread by charismatic and articulate theologians, such as Sankara, who travelled the length and breadth of India debating and defeating Buddhists and Jains in public and setting up Hindu monastic centers to carry out further dissemination of this new form of Hinduism (the Jains also have their alternate versions where Jain monks triumph in public debates). This devotional *bhakti* tradition became the basis of modern Hindu tradition. Early Hindu sacred literature, such as the Vedas and Upanishads, had been the total monopoly of the literate Brahminical class, but now sacred literature, such as the epics of *Mahabharata* and *Ramayana* and the sacred devotional hymns (*tevaram*) and stories (*puranas*), became available to all.

At this period, the two great epics of India, the *Mahabharata* and *Ramayana*, which are often comparable to the Greek *Iliad* and *Odyssey*, began to be interpreted as devotional texts from which inspiration could be drawn. These texts were enlarged with additional legend stories, moral tales, and sacred laws. The mystical and philosophical texts of the *Bhagavad Gita*, which was independently composed, was fused to the main body of the *Mahabharata*. The *Ramayana*, which perhaps began as two separate secular tales (one about a prince who rescued his wife with an army of monkeys and another about a righteous prince who abdicated his right to rule to fulfill his father's vows) was fused as a single continuous epic and enlarged after the Gupta Period (*see* **Gupta Empire**).

During the Gupta Period, the eighteen chief sacred stories, or *puranas* — stories on god's grace, miracles, and religious teachings — came to include the additional Vishnu purana, Agni purana, and Bhagavala purana. These contained many earlier religious stories but were now put in a more polished form. Between the seventh and tenth centuries, these devotional Saivaite saints composed twelve devotional books (Tirumurai); the main ones, a collection of deep devotional hymns by four Saivaite Bhakti saints called Tevaram, are still sung as a popular mode of worship. The Tamil Vishnavite *bhakti* saints, called Alwars, also produced hymns — four thousand (nalayiram) stanzas were composed by the twelve Alwars. Similar devotional poems were also produced in other Dravidian vernaculars, such as Kannada and Telugu. In the thirteenth century Vaisnavite *bhakti* saints composed hymns in North Indian languages, such as Marathi. This passionate form of devotional songs affected the entire religious world of Tamil country and was also loosely associated with the philosophical teachingts of the Upanishads, by a number of eminent southern theologians (Basham, 1967, 332).

The best known among of these Bhakti theologians was Adi Shankara (or Adi Sankaracarya), a Brahmin scholar from the great Vishnu Temple of Sri Rangam, called Ramanuja. Just like his Shaivite predecessor, Adi Shankara, the Vishnavite theologian Ramanuja also travelled the length and breadth of India and wrote long commentaries on cardinal Hindu scriptures, such as the *Bhagavad Gita* and the Upanishads. Like all *bhakti* saints, Ramanuja also prescribed intense devotion to his deity Vishnu as the best means for salvation — far superior to salvation by knowledge (as proposed by Adi Shankara) or by ritual observances. Ramanuja believed that those who totally abandoned their entire being to the service of god and totally trusted divine grace would find themselves in the superior state of bliss. The devotional path carved out by Ramanuja was popular and spread throughout India; it became the source of all subsequent devotional movements (Basham, 1967, 333).

Another Vishnavite teacher who developed Ramanuja's doctrines was Madhava, who lived in the thirteenth century. Madhava interpreted the monastic doctrines of the Upanishad concerning the unity of god as figurative and subscribed to a form of dualism. According to this view, individual soul and matter are totally separate. Vishnu has sole power over both and saves the deserving souls by his divine grace while the evil souls are sent to eternal damnation. Perpetual rebirths (a Hindu version of purgatory) were reserved for the average that blends both characters. Some historians believe Madhava's teachings were inspired by the Syrian Christian community in Malabar. They point to the important part played by the wind god Vayu, who was Vishnu's agent in this world, whose role seems to closely resemble the idea of the Holy Ghost in Christianity. In Syriac, the meaning of the term *Holy Ghost* is divine wind or breath. This idea, along with the sharp division between god and the human spirit, the idea of eternal damnation, the essential role played by Vayu, and the numerous miracle stories surrounding Madva that seem to parallel the stories of Christ, suggesting probable influences from Eastern of Syrian Christianity of the Malabar coast (Basham, 1967, 333).

In Kashmir in northern India, another school of Shaivism, known as Trika, or triad, emerged. This doctrine, unlike the South Indian variety, shared the philosophical outlook of Sankara. Here the general outlook is that the phenomenal world, as we know it, is unreal and its existence is due to the failure of the souls to understand its true nature. The sect teaches that salvation comes of sudden enlightenment. The best-known philosopher of this text is the tenth-century teacher Abhinava Gupta.

The third important Saivaite sect was the Lingayat or Virasaiva sect. This sect of Savism was founded in the tenth century by Basava (1134–1196), who was a royal minister. Basava opposed image worship, and his sect worshipped the gods in the form of a miniature linga, a symbol of the god carried by the faithful. Basava also rejected the teachings of the Vedas, and the social status of the Brahmins. The Virasaivas have their own order of priests, called the Jangamas, and all believers are considered equal. Unlike many Hindu castes, they also permitted widow remarriage. Basava opposed religious pilgrimages, sacrifices, and the cremation of the dead (Virasaivas bury their dead). It is highly plausible that lingayats were influenced by what Basava may have heard about the essential ideals of Islam.

The Lingayats of today are concentrated in the South Indian states of Andhra and Karnataka. Although they keep separate from other Hindus, their religious scriptures are in the local vernaculars of Telegu and Kanada. Many have adapted the customs of the orthodox Hindus around them.

Hindu Ritual Changes in the Middle Ages

In Vedic Hinduism, the main mode of worship was sacrifice, whereas in devotional Bhakti Hinduism it was puja or worship with deep emotionally charged devotion. In Bhakti Hinduism the deity is worshipped in the form of an icon as opposed to the un-iconic Vedic rituals. It is believed that god is present or occupies the sacred icons for the devotion of the ritual (Basham, 335). Puja is more than quiet prayer. It is also paying homage to the deity and also to amuse him in the form of entertainment. The deity is treated as a king or honored guest, and in major temples, devadasi dancing girls perform dances on special occasions. Also on such occasions, the deity tours the area around the shrine in a special car pulled by devotees and led by musicians and accompanied by Brahmin attendants with parasols and fly whisks.

Another new development was the building of temples, which was not part of Vedic Hinduism. The Hindu temple building tradition became well-established by the end of the Gupta Period in 600. We also see the disappearance of animal sacrifice, which was a high point in Vedic ritual; it is replaced by devotional offerings of fruits, flowers, or specially cooked consecrated food, which is later shared among the worshippers. Although the major form of worship in modern Hinduism was puja or devotional ritual, animal sacrifices did not entirely disappear but remained a part of folk or village Hindu tradition.

In the Gupta Period, magical practices and secretive occultist rituals were often associated in the worship of female deities by small states mainly in Eastern India. These secretive sects are called Tantrics, and their scriptures *tantras*. The members of these sects believe that the usual Hindu practices are only for ordinary folk, but specially initiated followers of the goddess can choose the tantric rituals, which are far more potent. These rituals involved breaking the cardinal taboos and pollution rules of Hindu life and took place in secret in the dead of night, often in auspicious spaces, such as cremation grounds or in houses of members. The initiates sat in a circle around a magical diagram or yantra drawn on the floor. These rituals break the caste rules by including all castes. Brahmins may sit next to untouchables, and there is no ritual pollution associated in mutually taking part in all rituals. After performing the necessary rites to placate the spirits, the participants take part in a ritual that breaks all major food and social taboos, which include consumption of alcohol, eating meat and fish, and orgiastic dancing and group sex. In these cases of tantric ritualized sexual intercourse, the sex may involve either a physical partner or partners or be symbolic, with the participants mentally performing the sexual union (Basham, 1967, 344).

Non-Indian Religions: Christians, Jews, and Zoroastrians

According to popular Christian tradition, the Apostle St. Thomas is believed to have made the first Christian converts in India and said to have died a martyr's death in Mylapore, South India. But most historians consider these accounts unreliable. The first certifiable evidence of Christianity in medieval India is found in a text titled *The Christian Topography*, by Cosmos Indicopleustes, a sixth-century Greek monk from Alexandria, who has left us interesting accounts of his travels. He writes of Christian churches in Malabar and Sri Lanka, run by Iranian Christian priests and under the control of the Iranian bishop of Cochin. Iranian Christianity belongs to the Nestorian branch of the Christian faith, which, in the eyes of the Catholic and Orthodox Churches, is a heresy. Before the coming of Islam, Iranian Nestorian Christianity was gaining a strong following in Sassanian Iran, which was officially and predominantly Zoroastrian. The Nestorians were active missionaries who spread their branch of Christianity as far as China along the Silk Road. The legend of St. Paul may well be based on the Nestorian missionary activities in parts of India.

When Islam became the dominant faith in Iran, it also completely wiped out Iranian Christianity; as a result, Indian Christians looked upon the patriarch of Antioch, in Syria, as their spiritual head and therefore came to be known as "Syrian Christians." Over the ages, the Indian Christians, isolated from their first Asian roots, began to adapt Hindu customs, and would have eventually become a heterodox Hindu sect, like the Buddhists before them. This Hinduization process came to a sudden halt with the arrival of European Christian missionaries, especially the Portuguese Jesuits in the sixteenth century. This European intervention also led to a split in the Church; one section accepted the authority of Rome, while the other continued to maintain its link with Antioch. Most of the Hindu customs were eradicated as the Christian groups attempted to unify their rituals in conformity with their respective mother churches.

There was also a small community of Jews in Malabar. The earliest reference to the Indian Jewish communities was the tenth-century Charter by Bhaskara RaviVarman II, the Chera ruler of Kerala in southwestern India. The Chera king is said to have granted land and rights to a Yemani Jew by the name of Joseph Rabban. There may also have been a large community of Jews at Cochin, a major trading center in southwestern Malabar since around the first century C.E. Known as Beni Israel (or sons of Israel), the members of this colony were descended from Middle Eastern Jewish expatriate merchants who married local women. In appearance, they look no different from the Hindus of their neighborhoods. Although other Indian Jews, such as the Baghdadi Jews, migrants from Iraq and other parts of the Middle East who married other migrant Jews, looked very "Semitic" in appearance.

Another known Indian ex-patriot community that made significant impact on Indian history was the Zoroastrians, who are referred to as the Parsis. The name originates from a province in Iran, Pars, which is the heartland of ancient Iranian civilization. Before the seventh century, when Iran was under Sassanian rule (224–642 C.E.), Zoroastrianism was the state religion. Iranian trading communities that had established themselves in India were largely Zoroastrians in faith. Little remains of this community; and, as a result, we have little information, either oral or textual, about the medieval Iranian mercantile community in India. Zoroastrian refugees from Iran came to seek sanctuary in India in large numbers only after the Arab conquest of Iran. They settled in the western ports of India near Bombay in the eighth century and established a lasting foothold in western India from where they played key roles in politics and the economic life of pre- and postindependent India.

Islam

The largest communities of non-Hindus in medieval India were Muslim. Arab merchants had visited India long before Islam became the religion of Arabia in the seventh century C.E. There were Arab, Persian, and Jewish settlements in the coastal towns of India. Once such community is the Mappila in Malabar, where Arab sailors and merchants who cohabited with the local women and adopted India as their home. There is no evidence of Indian Islamic communities existing before the first Islamic invasions.

The first Islamic invasion occurred in 711, when Arab armies sent by the governor of Baghdad invaded the Indus Valley and annexed portions of northwest India to the Islamic Umayyad Empire. Two other waves of Islamic invasions followed the Arabs—the eleventh-century Turkish invasion and the sixteenth-century Turkish-Afghan invasion. All three invasions placed large parts of northern India under the control of invaders whose religious heritage was totally different from the traditional Indian faiths. Very early on Islamic rulers also

Timur's invasion of India, from Zafar Nama. Life of Timur or Tamerlaine, 1336–1405, Turkic conqueror of Islamic faith. The Art Archive/ Victoria and Albert Museum London/Eileen Tweedy.

realized that they were a tiny minority in an ancient and confident civilization, and they could hope to govern the territories they had conquered only with the cooperation and consent of the Hindus, who could not, therefore, be treated as polytheistic pagans fit for religious conversion. Early Arab conquerors and later Turkish dynasties had to be pragmatic and maintain the legal fiction that Hindus were people of the book and thus entitled to the privilege of being protected people or *zimmi*, analogous to Christian and Jewish communities in the Middle East. The early Arab rulers of Sind in northwestern India were careful not to violate the caste hierarchy, allowing Brahmins to maintain their high status and at times exempting them from special discriminatory head taxes (*jiziya*) imposed on non-Muslims. Arabs also adapted Indian modes of kinship rituals and maintained themselves as Arab maharajahs of Sind.

Under the subsequent **Delhi sultanate** (1206–1526), Islam became the religion of the ruling Turkish elite and assumed the role of state religion. The court culture of the Turkish ruling class was Persian, and this was to become the dominant expression of Islamic high culture. The Turks also adapted Persian forms of statecraft, court rituals, literature, and arts. A separate Islamic cultural identity was also strengthened by the infusion of large number of Iranian and central Asian migrants fleeing the political turmoil created by the **Mongol** invasions under Genghis Khan and his immediate successors. Although Islam forbids racial discrimination, the new central Asian and Persian migrants saw themselves as the Ashraf community, that is, one that is socially distinct and superior to the rest of Indians, whether Hindus or new Muslim converts. Members of the Ashraf community held the highest civil, military, commercial, or scholarly positions.

Few Hindus converted to Islam during the earlier period of the Arab conquest. Later, under the Turkish Delhi sultanate, when Islam was the state religion and enjoyed official patronage, conversion rates increased and separate Indian Muslim communities began to form. Most of the early converts may have been disaffected Indian Buddhists. Hindu conversion to Islam was a relatively slow and lengthy process taking many centuries. Hindus converted for many reasons, including personal ambition; the promise of material rewards, such as top positions in the state bureaucracy; the prospect of war booty, or the fear of enslavement or death. Some converts sought to escape the stigma of low social status within the Hindu **caste system**, or the prospect of becoming outcastes through their close dealings with Muslims; in either case, conversion seemed a better alternative. But most religious conversions of Hindus to Islam came through the efforts of Islamic ascetics like the Sufis, who spread Islam at local levels through their social work, healing skills, and popular, synchronic blend of

Hindu and Islamic mysticism. Sufis lived either by themselves or among disciples in the manner of the Hindu swamis or sadus. The prestige of these Islamic mystics was a major source of influence that no Islamic ruler could afford to ignore. A medieval Islamic ruler's authority rested on three bases of support: (1) the noble and military class, (2) the Islamic scholars trained at madrasas, who staffed government offices and had the power to issue fatwas, or legal opinions, and (3) the Sufis. No sultan could maintain himself in power long without the active cooperation and tacit consensus of these three power groups.

Unlike the *ulama*, legal scholars who specialized in Islamic law that dealt with practical matters, the Sufis were members of mystical brotherhoods. In India, Sufis borrowed Hindu and Buddhist monastic practices and philosophical ideas and incorporated them into an Islamic framework. By the time of the Delhi sultanate in the thirteenth century, the Sufis were divided into fourteen brotherhoods, or orders, with each under its *shaikh* or *pir*, a spiritual guide who alone can initiate disciples. The center of any Sufi order was the hospice, which is where the novice went to seek guidance in the spiritual life from a Sufi master. The first major Sufi auspice was established in the northwestern town of Multan (present-day Pakistan) by the Sufi Shaikh Bahaud-din Zakariyya (1182–1262), a member of the Suhrawardiyya Order, which was established in Punjab, Sind, and Bengal, all major centers of Islamic activity. Eager for the conversion of Hindus to Islam, the Subrawardiyya were aided in this by their wealth, which was derived from gifts from pious merchants and state officials, and by their links with the centers of Islamic power.

The second most important Sufi auspice established in urban India under the Delhi sultanate was the Chishtyya, or the Chisti Order. This particular order was brought to India by a Persian mystic, Khwaja Muinud-din Chishti (1142–1236), who made his final home in the town of Ajmir in 1206. By the time of his death, the Chishti auspices were established in many parts of the Delhi sultanate. The Chishti Sufis led a life of poverty and asceticism that was devoted to their single universal deity, Allah. Although they were dependent on public charity, their distribution of wealth and feeding stations for the poor made a favorable impression even among the Hindus. The shine of Muinud-din Chishti in Ajmir is still a center of pilgrimage for Muslims and Hindus.

The Chishti Sufis, like the Hindu yogis, practiced breath control and meditation and were influenced by the ascetic exercises (*see* **Yoga**). They also composed Hindi poetry with Vishnavite and Saivaite overtones, which was seen as far more suited to elevate them to a higher status of mystical ecstasy than the earlier Persian mystical poetry. Such activities and a spirit of tolerant ecumenism were frowned upon by the more orthodox *ullama*, who urged the state to end these un-Islamic practices. These efforts failed largely due to the great influence wielded by the Sufi masters. However, the ullama were sometimes able to convince the more orthodox sultans to publicly execute a few Sufis in an effort to stamp out what they saw as deviant practices, but these were rare exceptions. Certain Sufi philosophies concerning the nature of reality and god were remarkably similar to the teachings of Hindu mystics or yogis, who played a vital role in popular Hinduism. On an intellectual level, the Sufis were also influenced by Hindu yogic texts such as *Amrita Kunda*, a Hatha yogic text that was translated into Persian or Arabic. Such texts were instrumental in teaching the Sufis their meditation techniques and in providing information about Hindu healing arts, such as the medicinal or chemical properties of herbs.

After nearly 600 years of political domination and proselytizing, Islam chose to coexist with Hinduism in India. Although the central tenets of the two religious traditions seem diametrically opposite, Hindus and Muslims interacted to produce areas of commonality. Once again, Hinduism was able to face a major challenge, like that of Buddhism some 2,550 years earlier, without altering its basic form, but, unlike it did with Buddhism, Hinduism could not overwhelm, absorb, and redefine Indian Islam as a heterodox sect within the fabric of an inclusive Hindu tradition. *See also* Document 10.

Further Reading

Basham, A. L. *The Wonder that Was India*. London: Sidgwick & Jackson, 1982.
Beal, Samuel. *Buddhist Records of the Western World*. Reprint ed. Delhi, India: Oriental Books Reprint Corporation, 2004.
Goyal, S. R. *History of Indian Buddhism*. Meerut, India: Kusumanjali Prakashan, 1987.
Warder, A. K. *Indian Buddhism*. Delhi, India: Motilal Banarsidass, 1970.
Wayman, Alex. *Buddhism in Historia Religionum: Handbook for the History of Religions*. Volume II: *Religions of the Present*. Edited by C. Jouco Bleeker and Geo Windengren. Leiden, The Netherlands: E.J. Brill, 1971.

Raman N. Seylon

3. ECONOMY

The Hun invasions of the fifth and sixth centuries C.E. and the subsequent collapse of the centralized Gupta rule had its impact on long-distance trade and the North Indian economy. We find less evidence of the minting of new coins during the period, which is one indication of a downturn in trade, especially international trade. But, in medieval India, the state's minted coins were only one medium of exchange; there was a multiplicity of currencies and other mediums of exchange, which varied from region to region (*see* **Money and Exchange Systems**). These other mediums of exchange included gold bullion, sliver rods and bars, and even iron needles or cowry shells as small denominations. And in many cases transactions did not involve any money. In premodern times, taxes were paid in kind, such as paddy (un-husked rice). An inscription in the Chola capital of Tanjore dated to the early eleventh century mentions that in rural areas paddy served as a form of currency to pay for many everyday **food** items, such as dhal (lentils), curds, ghee (clarified butter), tamarind, salt, pulse, and betel leaves (Appadurai, vol. II, 703). The latter, a mild peppery tasting leaf, was chewed along with quick-lime and areca palm nuts and served as a stimulant and a breath freshener. It also had a variety of ritual and social uses and is still central to traditional Indian hospitality. It was also a major trade article as well as an item of everyday consumption.

The political fragmentation of the **Gupta Empire** meant that regional states became the norm in early medieval India. In northern India, **Rajput** dynasties, such as the Pritiharas from Rajasthan, dominated the region from the eighth century and fought the Pala dynasty of Bengal and Bihar for control of **Kanauj** and the central Gangatic region. By the eleventh century, the Palas were overtaken by the Sena dynasty. The western and central **Deccan** was under the control of the Chalukyas (973–1189) and the south was under the Cholas, who waged frequent war against the Chalukyas. The Cholas, at the height of their power in the tenth and eleventh centuries established firm bureaucratic control over the core riverside areas through their ability to dominate local chieftains and assemblies.

Agrarian Base of the Medieval Indian State

As is the case today, the majority of the population in medieval India lived in small villages and was involved in **agriculture**. The ownership of land conferred a great deal of prestige, and everyone, regardless of their main profession, aimed to have their own personal plots of land. A large class of landless laborers assisted in the agricultural operation and shared in a portion of the final harvest. Along with seasonal monsoon, irrigation, whether based on river-fed canals or on man-made dams, played a major part in the cultivation of crops, and great importance was attached to its upkeep. The state encouraged the reclamation and cultivation of new lands by granting special tax concessions for frontier cultivators. The prosperity of any cultivator depended not only on the availability of water and the nature of his tenure but also on the revenue demands of the state (Nilakanta Sastri, 326).

Land revenue, the most important revenue source for all premodern Indian states, was collected in kind. The gross revenue of any great or small landowner was divided into a number of separate categories, such as state dues, village dues, community dues, and temple dues. The rate of tax was determined by the state revenue department, which standardized rates according to the type of land, type of crops, and the actual harvest. Collection in kind was done by state officials but also through lineage heads, who managed the river valley, or through the assembly of *nadu* heads, who managed the dry lands. There is considerable difference in opinion as to the exact portion of the gross produce that was the king's share or *kadamai*. According to the Brahmin legalist Manu in his first-century C.E. compendium within a larger collection of Hindu legal texts collectively known as the Dhramasastra, the king's share should be anywhere from one-sixth to one-fourth. But this legal ideal fails to consider other forms of dues, such as funds for the maintenance of irrigation canals, funds to support local village officials, and funds for the maintenance of local temples and Brahmin settlements. The proceeds of these dues did not reach the coffers of the state but nevertheless were demands upon the land revenue collected on the authority of the state (Appadurai, vol. II, 681). Some historians of medieval India, such as Richard Sewell, author of *A Forgotten Empire: Vijayanagar*, are convinced that the dues collected as land tax by Hindu and Islamic powers were one-half the gross harvest of a cultivator (Appadurai, vol. II, 674). Throughout the Middle Ages, Indian states carried out careful surveys to estimate the revenue potential of the land under their jurisdiction, and payment was both in cash and kind, either directly collected by the state or by its intermediaries (Appadurai, vol. II, 685, 691).

Aspects of Crafts and Small-Scale Industry in Early Medieval India

The basic unit of production in medieval India was the individual craftsman who worked from his own home and would have been aided by members of his extended household. In premodern India, the type of craft that could be undertaken was circumscribed by the **caste system** and by community norms, and was linked to Hindu ideas concerning purity and pollution. The most common form of village industry was the manufacturing of textiles, which employed large numbers of workers. Most were manufactured for the local market, but the export of finer varieties of textiles to other parts of India and to overseas markets was made possible by the movements of individual merchants and by a highly developed and organized network of mercantile corporations (Nilakanta Sastri, 329).

There is also evidence of large-scale manufacturing by entrepreneurs who hired pools of workers and fleets of transport boats to distribute their products. Although such large-scale productions were rare, ancient Buddhist Jataka tales refer to wealthy manufacturers, such as Saddala Puta, who had five-hundred workshops of pottery manufacturing. The Jataka stories also mention what could be considered workers' cooperatives, which undertook the building of large enterprises such temples or large private houses. The nature of their work led to a division of labor. The employer and the workers safeguarded their part of the agreement by contracts with clauses and penalties outlining the punishments for breaking the contract by any member of the cooperative.

By far the largest industrial or trade organization was the "guild" or *sreni*, which included the individual craftsman, and the cooperative group belonging to that trade. Of the craft guilds, medieval inscriptions list goldsmiths, coiners, blacksmiths, carpenters and masons, weavers, oil mongers, gardeners, stonecutters, braziers, rope makers, jewellers, potters, basket weavers, mat makers, toddy (palm beer) drawers, and tailors. In some respects, medieval Indian guilds functioned like modern-day trade unions; they had clearly established the rules for work and wages and accepted standards and prices for commodities. Its rules and regulations had the authority of **law** and were respected even by the local ruler. All conflicts concerning its members were resolved in the guild trade court, which functioned much like a traditional village panchayat or caste council. The court had the power to expel errant or refractory members, a punishment equal to the social outcasting imposed by a caste council. Labor outcasting forbade the condemned to continue to practice his profession, making the laborer unemployable. Also like the caste council, the guild had influence over the social life of its members; it settled domestic disputes and took care of orphans and widows, thus providing a form of basic social insurance for its members. It was possible to have two or more guilds for a single profession or trade, which indicates that guilds may have split whenever the need arose. The head of a guild, called *jetthaka*, or "elder," in Buddhist texts, was assisted by a council of respected senior members. The office of elder was hereditary and held by the most influential and wealthy householders. Guilds also functioned in the capacity of major financial donors to local and regional temples and funded ritual functions. The fund acquired for such pious deeds came from membership dues and from criminal fines on those violating guild rules. Guilds also functioned in other capacities, such as acting as lending institutions or "banks" that lent money to merchants at interest, trustees of religious organizations, and the funders and maintainers of perpetual lamps at particular shrines.

The regulations and the cooperative spirit of guilds gave medieval India a better qualified and organized labor force, as well as the capacity to safeguard the collective interests of all workmen. But the guilds also had shortcomings.

Like feuding castes, they had the capacity to create public disorder or riots against their rivals. This was more common in the Deccan region, where guild members and caste groups were often the same (Basham, 1967, 224).

Apart from the trade guilds, kings and large temples also functioned as lending institutions and financed large undertakings. Kings or officials made loans to peasants to encourage the clearing and cultivation of wastelands and the development of irrigation canals and ditches. Large temples also lent money to villages in their neighborhood. In South India, professional money lending and commercial castes, called Chetty or Chettyar (also spelled as Shetty), functioned as moneylenders and merchants. Members of the wealthy south Indian castes were also leading guild members. By medieval times, these castes settled in other parts of South Asia and there developed wider networks of commercial ties.

Medieval India also had guilds of sellers or merchants, which were called *vira valanjiar* or "company of valiant merchants." These merchant guilds undertook major commercial ventures, such as outfitting and providing security for trade caravans, outfitting commercial ocean voyages, building warehouses, and maintaining agents in foreign ports and cities to assist members. They may also have participated in joint ventures with craft guilds. But the main function of merchant guilds was not to function as a trading body, but to protect and regulate the activities of its members and further their common interests. Just like craft or manufacturing guilds, the merchant guild also had social responsibilities. They aided families of members who met financial misfortunes or personal loss. They kept strict watch over the quality of products and business practices, preventing any unethical malpractice among members. The also undertook the role of spokesman for their members at the king's court. Their influence was such that even kings sought their counsel and advice. The Indian guilds, like their medieval European counterparts, had their own banners and emblems granted to them by the king, which were similar to those of the local nobility, and were carried in local religious processions. They also had their own mercenary armies, which may also served with the king's army in critical times.

Trade in Early Medieval India

Since the time of the prehistoric Indus Valley civilization, Indian merchants participated in overseas trade. But we have far more evidence from the medieval period, including local records left by merchants. Perhaps the most interesting is one that came from the outside—a series of tall tales left by a fictious merchant adventurer named Sinbad. Often overlooked as fantasy fiction or an Arabian adventure story, the story of the merchant Sinbad from Basra contains elements of actual accounts of Indian Ocean trade during the Middle Ages. It also gives a rare glimpse into the ideas, worldviews, spirit, and attitudes of Indian Ocean traders of the ninth and tenth centuries.

The primary Indian export of the period was "spices," a broad term that includes food flavorings, medicines, and raw material for making perfumes. In food flavoring, Indian spices had the reputation of making even the coarsest dishes palatable. The most highly sought after flavor spice was pepper—this is reflected in the a pepper shaker which is still a standard fixture on every Western dinner table. Most pepper in India is grown along the southwestern coast of Malabar. In the story of Sinbad, his fourth voyage is to gather pepper in Malabar. Another important spice, cloves, was imported to South India from the Indonesian island of Java and reexported to the Middle Eastern or Mediterranean markets. Cloves are used to flavor food and drinks and also as medicine. Ginger, another highly valued spice in the Middle Ages, was also both a flavor agent and a medicinal drug.

Among Indian medicines, the most important were aloes (used for everything from burns, coughs, and headaches to arthritis and constipation), rhubarb (a reexported item from Sumatra used to treat eye diseases), balsam resin (for making medicines and perfumes), gum, benzoin resin (a fragrant resin from Java and Sumatra used for making incense and believed to have antiseptic properties), cardamom, and camphor (Appadurai, vol. II, 534). Wood was also exported to the tree-scarce Persian Gulf and the Arabian coastal cities. Most important was teak wood, which was used for construction and shipbuilding because it was not affected by saltwater. Most of the teak wood came from the Konkon forests on the east coast of India. Bamboo, from the west coast, had a variety of usages, such as scaffolding for buildings, thanks to its lightness and strength. Luxury wood exports included ebony for furniture and sandalwood for medicine, perfume, and dye. The most important textile dye was indigo (the source of the blue dye used in the original blue jeans). India was also a major source of precious stones, including diamonds, the trade of which was in the hands of south Indian merchants and mariners (Appadurai, vol. II, 492). Among the food products exported, the most sought after was sugar. Ancient India pioneered the manufacture of this universal sweetener from the treated and boiled juice of sugar-cane plants, which crystallizes as it cools. In medieval times, sugar was exported from Bengal in northeastern India in a powder wrapped in small dried leaf packets. The English terms *sugar* and *candy* (solid pieces of sugar) have Sanskrit roots. The modern term English *sugar* comes from the Sanskrit term *shakara*, through the Persian and Arabic *shakar* and the Spanish *azucar*. Another Indian foodstuff that had a prominent place in medieval Arabic cuisine was the coconut, which was used as a sweetener. But India also produced and traded various important byproducts of the coconut palm, such as coconut oil, used for cooking; palm sugar or jaggery, used in traditional Indian medicine; and, most important, the "coir" rope, which was in heavy demand in shipping because it was light, highly durable, elastic, and impervious to saltwater. For the late Indian Middle Ages, Portuguese accounts tell of Indian-dyed cotton textiles and food grains such as wheat, millet, and rice, being exported to the Swahili coast of East Africa. An early-sixteenth-century Italian traveller noted that an immense quantity of cotton was produced near Cambay (near present-day Mumbai), and every year forty or fifty vassals filled with cotton and silk textiles came to Cambay and from there these textiles were shipped overseas (Nilakanda Sastri, 336). The importance of this Arabian Sea commerce is underlined by the large amount of revenue extracted from it in the form of custom duties. According to one Arabic source, the custom toll from three major Persian Gulf and South Arabian ports in the twelfth century was well over 2.5 million gold dinars (Appadurai, vol. II, 512).

In South India, there were two different merchant circuits. Those who operated locally, called *Svadeshi*, and those who took part in international trade, called *Nana-deshi* (Kulke and Rothermund, 125). These merchants lived in their own settlement areas. Although autonomous, their activities in port areas fell under state supervision. Long before the time of the Chola Empire (eighth to thirteenth centuries), the network of South Indian guild merchants linked various towns and became a powerful and influential body. In their multiple roles, they functioned as bankers and financiers of kings and funding agencies for local development projects and temple constructions; the economic benefits provided by these guilds made them vital institutions in any kingdom. Their multiregional role and their ability to employ mercenary armies ensured that the state recognized their exclusive sphere of activity and did not interfere in their affairs. All south Indian rulers respected the authority and wishes of their local guild and gave it autonomy, allowing the guilds to act much like a state within a state. In this sense, the Indian guilds were analogous to the European warrior-merchant companies of the seventeenth and eighteenth centuries, which also functioned as autonomous trading bodies outside the jurisdiction of the local land powers (Kulke and Rothermund, 125).

Three of the most powerful guilds in medieval India were the Ayyavole, Anjuvaranam, and Manigramam. The Ayyavole guild, from the Deccan near modern Aihole in Karnataka State, had branches in every major Indian city and controlled the West Asian trade. Members were identified by their flag, which had a symbol of a seated bull and was carried in procession in temple rituals. Confident in their overseas ventures, they claimed to be known "all over the world" for their daring trading activities and to have travelled land and water routes penetrating all the countries of the six continents (Nilakanta Sastri, 331). The Manigramam guild from South India focused on the South East Asian trade, though this was, by no means, its exclusive domain. Inscriptions at Takuapa, in Southern Thailand, and another in Sumatra dated 1088 testify the Manigramam guild's overseas ventures. Not much is known about Anjuvaranam (meaning "fire colors") guild except that it often shared duties such as the collection of customs in Trivancore along with the Manigramam guild. Both had complete control over these duties without the interference by the state. Anjuvaranam may have been primarily based in Trivancore (Appadurai, vol. 1, 413).

Apart from commercial links, the South Indian states, notably the Pallavas and Cholas, were engaged in military actions against powerful Indonesian states such as Srivijaya and its vassals centered on the Isthmus of Siam. The Pallavas and Cholas undermined the political power of the Srivijaya state. These overseas conflicts arose from local disputes, struggles over markets, the need to support the South Indian merchant guilds and their mercenary armies, or simply long-distance looting expeditions. Inscriptional evidence indicates that under the Pallava ruler Nandivarman III (844–866) a ritual water tank was constructed and handed over to expatriate merchants of the South Indian merchant guilds in the island of Sumatra. The merchants were living in an armed camp, probably engaged in a power struggle with the regional Srivijaya rulers, and had sought the aid from the powerful fleet of the Pallavas, who were then the paramount power in southeast India (Nilakanda Sastri, 160, 331)

The Cholas, who followed the Pallavas, also sent naval fleets — first in 1025 and again after 1069. The precise reasons why the south Indian monarchs sent out these naval expeditions is not known. However, one thing is clear; the south Indian states actively supported their merchant guilds in conducting their overseas business, and occasionally resorted to the use of force (Kulke and Rothermund, 123–125). Inscriptional evidence also indicates that the merchant guild of Manigramam, which had branches in Sri Lanka, also got involved in local power struggles by lending its own mercenary armies at a price to local Singhalese princes during succession struggles.

Major Trade Rules in Early Medieval Period

Since antiquity, the major artery of trade routes covered most of northern India. The largest route (the predecessor of what later became the grand trunk road in the colonial era) ran from what is present-day Calcutta through the ancient town of Pataliputra to Delhi, then crossed the three rivers of the Punjab to Taksasila, and continued to the Kabul Valley and Central Asia. The great cities north of the Ganges were linked to this major trade route by secondary roads. Earlier, during the height of India's first political union under the Mauryan dynasty in the second century B.C.E. the main trade routes that crossed through Mauryan territories are said to have had milestone markers and traveller inns at regular intervals (Basham, 224). Another long-distance trade route was located further south; it went from the city of Ujjayini in northwest Deccan to the city of Kanchi (capital of the Pallavas) and Madurai (capital of the Pandiyas). A vast network of secondary routes had developed by the first century linking all-important cities of the peninsula. The breath of a major trade road was about 24 feet and well suited for wheeled transport. There were also numerous tracks only slightly better than footpaths that were unsuited for wheeled transport (Nilakanta Sastri, 330).

With the fall of the Gupta Empire, the roads were not maintained, and the encroaching jungles with their large predators, wild elephants, and poisonous reptiles, as well as hostile tribes, further discouraged long-distance travel. Further disruption of travel was caused by seasonal flooding during monsoons, which shut down ferry service across major rivers. Indian states left the maintenance of roads to local authorities, and neighboring villagers were expected to provide free labor to maintain them. The state also did not attempt to bridge major rivers but depended on private ferry services at all important crossing points along major travel routes. Thus, the absence of a strong central authority meant serious disruption of the transport system; regional travel became more difficult during periods of political crisis, which provided more opportunities for hostile tribes and castes of professional thieves to plunder any traveller, merchant, or pilgrim.

When central authority reestablished its control over trade routes, professional guides and hired guards led large merchant caravans of pack animals loaded with luxury goods westward toward the Silk Road, from where they travelled to the market towns of Central Asia and the ports of the Mediterranean Basin. These large caravan trains had about five-hundred handlers, a caravan leader (*sarthavaha*), and an experienced land pilot (*thalaniyyamaka*), who could guide it through unmarked routes and deserts by using the stars. The major articles of this long-distance trade were luxury fabrics, masks, gemstones, and spices. The major rivers, such as the Ganges and Indus, were also used to transport goods, but these, apart from navigational hazards such as hidden rocks or sand banks, were plagued, especially in unsettled times, by professional bands of river pirates (Basham, 225).

Apart from the land routes linking India to the Silk Road, which stretched from China to the Mediterranean Basin, a parallel sea route also linked India to western Asia, southeastern, and eastern Asia. These routes were well established before the Gupta Empire (320–600 C.E.), and most certainly as early as the first century C.E. The wind patterns of the monsoon were used for deep ocean sailing, and knowledge of these seasonal wind currents was essential for a safe voyage. Summer monsoon winds blew from the southeast and winter monsoon winds from the northwest. Indian Ocean merchants learned to plan their trading schedules around these changes in wind patterns. During winter months, merchants from western India sailed the Persian Gulf to the Red Sea and then used the summer monsoons to sail back to India. Shipbuilding flourished in Calicut on the Malabar coast, which had large forests of teak wood particularly suited for ship construction. The the high demand of Indian goods, led to the construction of keeled ships, which could carry goods weighing 1,200 bahares (about 480,000 pounds), were built. To carry maximum cargo, Indian merchant ships were built without decks. Their construction did not use nails, and the entire hull was sewn with coir rope and waterproofed with bitumen. These stitched ships had a number of advantages over nailed ships: they were more resilient, could better withstand the fierce storms of the monsoon season, and could better navigate over coral reefs (Basham, 1967, 227). They were all conditioned for Indian Ocean trade, being able to dock in shallow ocean and river ports without danger of serious structural damage, and needed a thorough overhaul only every 5 years as opposed to annual maintenance required by a nailed ship. Their shortcomings included the need for continuous bailing—they were not as leakproof as nailed ships—and, as revealed later with the coming of the Portuguese, their unsuitability for gunpowder-based warfare. A sixteenth-century Portuguese traveller named Duarte Barbosa noted that every monsoon these stitched merchant vassals left Calicut laden with goods gathered from various parts of India and journeyed to the Red Sea ports from where they shipped their goods through intermediaries to Venice (Nilakanda Sastri, 335).

In the Middle Ages, the island of Socotra, strategically located near the mouth of the Red Sea and East Africa (its original name may have come from the Sanskrit word for "blissful island"), had a large Indian merchant settlement and was a major landfall for merchant ships crossing the Indian Ocean (Basham, 218). Indian merchants also made regular trip to Alexandria, then the major trade emporium on the desert crossing of Egypt from the Red Sea to the Nile and then to the Mediterranean. Before steamships, sailing the full length of the Red Sea was extremely hazardous. The northern part of the Red Sea was swept year round by northwest winds while the rest of the sea was subject to reversible seasonal wind patterns. Along the Red Sea shore, treacherous rocks reached right to the water's edge, and the entire coast was uninhabited and unprotected. Therefore, travelling was only possible during daytime; at nights, ships had to find a safe shelter to lay anchor. The sea is also subject to heavy fog cover and violent gale force winds. For this reason, Indian merchants disembarked at the port of Jeddah on the Arabian Peninsula and transshipped their goods through local Arab ships, which were familiar with this difficult waterway, or carried their goods overland by caravan, crossing the desert to a Nile port. One merchant who made this trip left evidence of his presence in the form of graffiti at the ancient shrine of the Min, an Egyptian deity of travellers later identified with the Greek god Pan, at Wadi Mia, a major land link between the Red Sea and the Nile River. It states "Sophon the Indian pays homage to Pan for good journey." *Sophon* may well have been the Hellenized version of the Indian name *Subhanu*. The pastoral Greek deity Pan may well have been the Indian counterpart of the Hindu deity Krishna. Like Pan, Krishna played a small flute to his flocks. One thing is certain: unknown Indian merchant on route to the Mediterranean port city of Alexandria was highly Hellenized (Basham, 228).

In late antiquity, the net balance of trade in this Indo-Mediterranean exchange was unfavorable to Rome. In return for its exports to the Roman world, Indian merchants mainly wanted precious metals in the form of gold coins. Although there was a limited Indian demand for wine, slave girls, industrial metals such as tin and lead, and semiprecious corals from the Mediterranean, the Indian appetite for Roman coin led to a serious drainage of gold from the Roman Treasury. This unfavorable balance of trade concerned the Roman government and Roman citizens, such as Pliny, who calculated the annual gold drain as 100 million sesterces. This drain was an important cause of Roman financial difficulties since the time of Nero (r. 54–68 C.E.), who took economic measures to reduce the gold content of Roman coinage, thus frustrating Indian merchants who had appreciated the formerly high gold content and standardized weight of Roman coins. In Medieval India, except in port cities, Roman coins were not used as a medium of exchange, but as the monetary reserves of princes. For this reason, Roman coins in India are often found in hordes.

By the time of the Gupta Empire, the collapse of the Western Roman Empire also led to the demise of the Mediterranean trade, which probably prompted Indian merchants to seek other sources of gold and trade opportunities. Roman trade was replaced by increasing trade with Southeast Asia and China. According to the Chinese pilgrim-scholar **Faxian**, by the Gupta Period, Indian merchant ships had the capacity to carry two-hundred sailors and passengers (Basham, 1967, 226).

Indian trade with China began during the Gupta Empire, when the Chinese demanded similar trade items to that of the Romans. Imports to China included manufactured textiles, mostly of cotton, medicinal drugs, and spices, but the most valuable exports were jewels and semiprecious items such as ivory, rhinoceros horn, ebony, amber, coral, and perfumes. This trade was welcomed by the Chinese state, which in return offered silk and porcelain, both of which found ready markets in India and throughout the entire Indian Ocean Basin. The local Indian silk industry probably felt the adverse impact of cheaper and better quality Chinese silk. By late ninth century, political troubles made China unsafe for foreigners, but Chinese ships still came regularly to ports on the Malay Peninsula and Sumatra to buy Indian and other foreign goods. These voyages were the beginning of Chinese navigation deeper into the Indian Ocean. From the twelfth to the fourteenth centuries, Chinese vassals frequently visited the west coast of India. But in the twelfth century, the drain of currency and precious metals resulting from this expansion of trade in luxuries caused serious concern for the Chinese, who banned the export of precious metals and coined money and put restrictions on trade with India. (Nilakanda Sastri, 333). However, trade continued uninterrupted until the end of the thirteenth century, when China again faced political turmoil, this time due to the **Mongol** invasion.

In the early fifteenth century, the third Ming Emperor Yongle (1405–1425) sent a large fleet under Admiral Zheng He to intimidate India and Sri Lanka. The fleet included sixty-two giant nine-masted "treasure" ships and over three-hundred support vessels, including water tankers, as well as an army of over twenty-seven thousand men. Zheng He made seven epic voyages and visited ports in western India. He sought, through military means, to establish Ming hegemony over the Indian Ocean trade, and interfered in the internal political affairs of a number of Southeast Asian states and Sri Lanka. But after 1433, China's overseas naval ventures ended as abruptly and completely as they had begun.

In the late medieval period, the shipping of Indian products was increasingly undertaken by foreign merchants in foreign vessels. This was because advances in nautical engineering among the Arab, the Persians, and, especially, the Chinese, gave them vessels that were more seaworthy than those available to Indian shipping. Indian merchants found that it made more economic sense to sell their products to foreign middlemen and to use foreign vessels for shipping (Basham 1967, 231). Waves of foreign invasions since the eleventh century also created a sense of xenophobia in Hindu India. The earlier zeal for establishing merchant guilds overseas to conduct all aspects of trade gave way in later times to religious sanctions against ocean travel; the sea came to be seen as dark and forbidding, the very embodiment of pollution.

The Integration of South Indian Trade Guilds with the Local Agrarian Economy

During the height of Chola rule in South India from the eleventh to the thirteenth centuries, inscriptions show that trade guilds played an influential role in South Indian society. Although the guilds lingered on until the sixteenth century, they were by then largely marginal. In trying to understand the function of these guilds, we must see them as intimately integrated with the rural-based agrarian social and economic order and not with the towns of medieval India.

The agrarian system of the Eastern or Coromandel coast of South India was a combination of two types of settlements and cultivation. The core areas had settled villages where cultivation was based on irrigation from rivers or dammed water reservoirs called tanks. These core agricultural areas were under the control of the two dominant castes, the Brahmin and the Vellala peasantry and their assemblies, which also included some artisan castes. These agricultural settlements that spread along the fertile river basins were well integrated into these trade networks (Stein, 233).

The second type of settlement was located in the peripheral hilly and forested areas. These settlements were inhabited by hostile tribal groups that practiced shifting **agriculture** and engaged in predatory activities such as cattle theft. This is also a frontier area of conflict. As the land-hungry Vellala peasantry expanded into this frontier zone, cutting down forests to bring more land under cultivation, they also pushed many of these tribal people further away from their traditional homes. This led to tensions and open hostility between the expanding migrant peasantry and the local tribal population, but it also slowly assimilated the tribal people into a more developed form of peasant economy.

The Brahmin-controlled villages (or *brahmdeyas*) had been earlier donated to Brahmin families by pious Hindu rulers to support the essebtial role of Brahmin as teachers and ritual specialists. Brahmin families were given the right to collect the surplus of village produce, and the right to manage all aspects of village life through their own caste assembly, the Brahmin-mahasabha, the grand assembly of Brahmins.

The Vellalas, the dominant agrarian peasant caste, governed their areas of settled agriculture through assemblies called ur, which included the vast majority of settled villages in the core areas as well as the peripheral areas of agricultural development. The network of peasant settlements in these core areas were at the heart of the medieval Southeast Indian society. They were self-governing and were loosely linked in a variety of ways with other areas in the region and were also instrumental in maintaining the state's political hold over the entire region.

As governing bodies, the supraregional assembly representing all communities within the core area met occasionally met to act as a single unit. These multicaste assemblies of the dominant Vellala and Brahmin castes were called *periya-nadu* ("supra region") or *chitrameli* ("sign of the ploughshare")—inscriptional records are often adorned with a picture of a ploughshare. The *chitrameli* formed an overarching umbrella association linking various smaller associations within the irrigated core agricultural areas. During the Chola Period, inscriptional evidence indicates a close relationship between the agriculturalists and the merchant classes. Trade items included such commodities as grain, salt, iron, horses, and elephants, with the last two mainly used for the armies of local princes.

According to inscriptional evidence, overseas trade organizations (*nana desi*), such as Ayyavole, Manigramum, and Anjuranam, were active from the eighth to the seventeenth centuries, but their period of importance in the local South Indian economy did not go beyond the thirteenth century. The inscriptions also make clear that these merchant guilds were well integrated and subordinate to the assemblies representing the major interest groups in the developed parts of Coromandal.

The supraregional assemblies or *chitrameli* were made up of agriculturalists, who produced many of the commodities that were later sold by the merchants involved in local and multiregional trade. Both types of trade were essential and well integrated into the fabric of this predominantly agricultural society. It is, therefore, understandable that the fate of these large merchant guilds was closely linked to development of the agrarian order of the medieval Coromandal coast.

The decline of Chola military power in the thirteenth century meant the core areas were increasing vulnerable to predatory attacks by outside warrior groups. After the demise of the Cholas, attacks by Turkish horseman from the Islamic states to the north; Hindu raiders from neighboring kingdoms, such as the Hosalas and Pandiayas; migrant Telugu warrior castes from the northeast (acting as vanguard of the **Vijayanagar Empire**), and Tamil warrior castes such as Maravar and Kallar permanently altered the earlier social and political order (Stein, 239). After a period of political turmoil lasing more than a century, a new political order, the Hindu agrarian regime of the Vijayanagar Empire, filled the power vacuum in South India. In the Vijayanagar state, political organization was subordinated to and dictated by military needs (Stein, 239). The writings of foreign visitors describe the large standing armies of the Vijayanagar rulers, and the division of much of South India into a patchwork of two-hundred military fiefs under households of various sizes. This system of military households was based on the one already in practice in the **Delhi sultanate** of North India, and its origins could be traced to the Turkish heartland in Central Asia. This new military revenue requirement could only be met by altering the earlier agrarian setup of South India. The formerly autonomous local caste assemblies of the Vellala and Brahmin castes now became subordinate to the new demands of the powerful military households of the Telugu and Tamil warrior castes (Stein, 239) (*see* **Tamil Country**). Many of the Telugu-speaking warrior groups came south either as vanguards of the Vijayanagar armies or were driven from their northern homelands by expanding Islamic power.

Each military household was assigned or controlled a fief (*amaram*), which was composed of a number of revenue-bearing villages. Each household closely guarded the resources within its territory and made its fief into a self-sufficient economic unit that was relatively isolated from any major trans-regional economic network. The households also encouraged internal development of their fiefs by establishing towns with their capital, for fortified citadels and garrisons, and for pilgrim centers and temple sites within their territories. These new towns became the new focus of local trade groups, the development of which led to the narrowing of trading activities and the demise of the former great network of itinerant trade.

Warrior control of southern India increased the colonization and settlement of previously marginal areas. This process involved cutting down forest areas and reclaiming it for agricultural purposes, primarily to meet the military needs of the new warrior-based polity. The fourteenth through the seventeenth centuries saw large-scale settlement and expansion of agricultural villages that were not integrated organizationally with the larger economy and lacked the self-government of earlier times.

This tendency toward more localized military households that exerted maximum control over all the resources within its territory also led to the shrinking of the number of commodities that were now traded. As regional trade became limited, the focus was more on essentials and luxuries. The more extensive overseas trade of textiles and food grains fell into the hands of foreign West Asian merchants, who now had colonies in every major Indian port. This domination of the agrarian order by warrior-based states weakened the South Indian-based trade guilds that earlier had played such a key social and economic role locally and regionally.

These military households, whether great or small, sought to reduce the power of the trade groups. As mentioned earlier, under the Cholas, the multiregional and overseas trade networks of Ayyavole and Manigramam functioned as an autonomous state within a state. They were self-governing and autonomous bodies whose interests were motivated largely by economic factors. They also safeguarded their interests by hiring bodies of mercenaries and private militias. In the Vijayanager Period, the military households viewed these private militias as a threat to their power. The isolation and self-sufficiency sought by these new military households benefited locally based merchant groups at the expense of large trade guilds. Advantages were also gained by the migrant Telugu merchant classes that belonged to the home territories of the new Telugu military households. Telugu migrant castes, such as the

Komatis, who were patronized and supported by their fellow Telugu Poligars, became the new powerful trade cliques of South India.

The older trade guilds faced a slow but steady road to extinction, and all epigraphic records of the great merchant guilds ceased by the seventeenth century, when they were mere shadow of their former selves. By the time European traders arrived in force, these trade groups were gone; nothing was ever mentioned about them in the copious records of the Portuguese.

Aspects of Craft and Small-Scale Industry in North India during the Later Middle Ages

Despite all the chaos and social displacement that resulted from the Turkish invasions of North India, archaeological evidence suggests urban growth. In 1330, the Moroccan traveller Ibn Battuta wrote that Delhi, the capital of the Delhi sultanate, and Daulalabad, where much of the population had shifted under the eccentric reign of Muhammad Tughluq, were two of the largest cities in the entire Islamic world.

The growth in craft production that accompanied this urban growth was a result of a number of technical developments. One of the biggest craft industries in medieval India was the manufacture of textiles. The antiquity of Indian domination of the textile trade can be illustrated by modern English terminology for various everyday fabrics, such as calico (from Calicut, a port in Malabar), chintz (from the Hindi word *chitra* or "design"), dungarees (named for a place near Mumbai where this heavy denim fabric, so favored by seafarers, was sold), seersucker (from the Hindi word *shir shakkar*), cashmere wool (from a goat indigenous to Kashmir), pashmina (a high-luxury shawl made from the wool of a high-altitude Himalayan mountain goat), bandana (from the Hindi word "to tie"), jute (from the Bengali word *jhuto*), gunny (from the Hindi word *ghoni*), and khaki (from the Hindustani term meaning "dust colored"). However, India's greatest textile contribution was the manufacture of cotton, a cheap and durable fabric that is universally preferred for everyday wear. The history of cotton manufacture is goes back over 4,000 years and predates Indian's first urban civilization (Harappan). The cotton plant is native to India, and Indian cotton textiles were in demand throughout the medieval world. For over a millennia, the production of the cotton textiles was based on a simple and labor-intensive manufacturing technique. The most important contribution of the medieval period to the manufacturing of cotton was the spinning wheel, or *charkha*, which increased the production of cotton yarn. This device, along with the threader, probably originated in China and spread quickly once it arrived in India via the Silk Road. The spinning wheel and the weaver's threader were essential for the subsequent expansion of the Indian cotton textile industry, which made cotton textiles readily available and more affordable. Similar innovations also took place in the manufacture of silk production, yet another development from China. Before this, any large demand for good quality silk could only be satisfied by Chinese imports. Now, as a result of improvements and innovation in silk weaving, the Indian silk industry took off, making the price of silk more affordable, though it is unclear whether Indian silk matched the quality of the Chinese import.

A craft industry that arrived from Persia with the Turkish invasions was carpet weaving. The use of vertical beams for carpet weaving dates from the time of the Delhi sultanate. Another Chinese invention that revolutionized all aspects of storing and disseminating information was paper. Paper mills in India developed in Gujarat, and by the thirteenth century paper production was ample enough to allow the use of paper for packing popular delicacies, such as sweet meats, another foreign import (Habib, 372). Both paper and carpet making are also associated with Islamic religious usages in the form of Qur'anic texts and prayer rugs.

In the production of metals, the incorporation of Chinese techniques of zinc production through distillation was to revolutionize the Indian brass industry. Commercial production of zinc from mines in Rajasthan was important in the manufacture of brass utensils and weapons. In construction, lime began to be used as cement, and vaulted rooms were introduced. The use of Mediterranean architectural techniques, such as the true arch, as opposed to the Indian corbel or false arch, and the use of domes, allowed for larger interiors in the building of mosques and palaces.

The Economy of the Delhi Sultanate

The development and introduction of new techniques, and the spread of new technologies, resulted from two major factors. First is the development of a large pool of skilled Muslim urban dwellers, including the integration into Indian society of artisans and merchants migrating from the Islamic world and bringing with them new methods and tools. Second, during the Delhi sultanate, there a pool of cheap and able-bodied laborers who could be made to do complex tasks. These laborers included a large enslaved population and prisoners of war. Related to this was an improved system for using the rural agricultural surplus to feed the urban labor force.

The enslaved population was a cheap source of labor that arose from the human military booty of the Dehli sultans. Estimates of the size of this population, which also included people enslaved as a result of debt bondage, range from twenty thousand to fifty thousand. Slaves provided the largest supply of manpower during the expansion phase of the Delhi sultanate but became a dwindling resource as slaves died and their descendents bought their freedom within a few generations. Slave labor is also less efficient and skillful than free labor, and slaves lacked the incentive for creativity and had no motivational drive other than fear. As the period of conquest ended so did the source of fresh slaves to replace declining stock; and, by the sixteenth century, it had shrunk to insignificant levels that are not mentioned by European sources.

The methods of revenue collection changed significantly during the Delhi sultanate period. The two major means of revenue extraction were the *iqta* and the *Kharaj*. The *iqta*, which was brought to India by the Central Asian Turks, significantly increased revenue extraction from the countryside. The *iqta* was a temporary revenue assignment on particular lands—usually non-Muslims—made to nobles and military commanders in lieu of a salary. Use of the *iqta* allowed the central administration to effectively control rural surpluses without the need for an extensive and costly administrative setup, and the regular payments *iqta* holders made out of their revenue to the sultan's treasury funded military forces for local defense in emergencies and the maintenance of order in the countryside. The *iqta* enabled the Delhi sultanate to maintain its large cavalry force and feed a large urban-based, nonagricultural population.

The *Kharaj* was a new form of land tax introduced during the reign of Sultan **Allaudin Khilji** (1296–1316). Imposed on territories under the control of the Delhi sultanate, the *Kharaj* consisted of half the total produce from a given piece of land paid in both cash and kind. With an additional house and cattle tax, imposition of the *Kharaj* meant that a large portion of peasant production was sent to urban areas, which lowered grain prices in Delhi and other large towns. Lower grain prices meant the sultanate could afford to maintain a larger standing army in urban centers. The *Kharaj* also significantly reduced the power of rural Hindu magistrates by depriving them of much of the peasant surplus. However, this sharp increase in the amount of direct taxes extracted from the rural peasantry, especially under Sultan **Muhammad bin Tughluq** (1325–1351), triggered peasant uprisings. Nonetheless, this new augmented land tax was the major source of state revenue until the end of colonial rule, and from this point on the state functioned as the dominant or even the sole proprietor of all land within its realm.

A number of key technological innovations that spread during the Delhi sultanate period aided agricultural production and small-scale manufacturing. The introduction of the Persian wheel, a geared water wheel run by animal power, allowed for extensive irrigation from deep wells. This system was primarily used in Punjab, India's wheat basket, which was close to Delhi. In textile manufacturing, the use of lime and gypsum-based waterproof cement allowed for the construction of larger indigo vats replacing the smaller stone vats. This innovation allowed for large-scale dying of textiles because indigo is a natural dye extensively used in textile manufacturing. Another new technology the liquor still, originated in Central Asia; the still was used to distil alcohol from fermented sugar syrup, thus increasing production of distilled alcohol.

Trade in Later Medieval India

The large amounts of late medieval gold and silver coins that have been found testify to the growth of trade in this period. Whereas earlier gold coins were rare and silver was often debased, the increased amount of gold in this period and the fact that gold coins were also used as a medium of exchange indicate an increase in trade with the Middle East and in the flow of gold from Sub-Saharan Africa to India.

The expanded trade included increasing import of high-spirited cavalry horses. The military demand for cavalry horses among Indian rulers grew with the success of Turkish horsemen in conquering vast stretches of Northern India. No Indian ruler could defend his kingdom against the Turks or rival princes unless he adopted the new form of mounted warfare. Unfortunately, most of the horses imported to India succumbed to poor maintenance. Lacking any local horse culture, most Indians were not familiar with the proper care and feeding of horses. Some were even said to have been fed with a specially cooked rich human diet, including roasted barley, boiled rice, boiled meat, or grains boiled in milk. As a result of this bad feeding and bad training, most of the high-strung imports either died prematurely or grew fat and sluggish, losing all their vigor and vitality. Because the Indian climate was generally unsuitable for breeding cavalry mounts, little breeding of warhorses occurred in India. It was therefore more practical to import cavalry mounts from the Persian Gulf, Central Asia, or even the Ukraine and the Russian steppes.

Evidence of the latter sources for horses comes from the Moroccan traveller **Ibn Battuta**. Although constantly importing foreign horses was very costly, India's highly favorable balance of trade ensured a steady flow of gold for trade. To ensure that only the finest breeds were shipped, the rulers of powerful kingdoms paid for any horse that was injured or died en route, thus insuring against any hesitancy in shipping on the part of foreign horse traders. In exchange for horses, India sold textiles and indigo dye (Habib, 403).

One of the side benefits of greater numbers of mounted soldiers is that they could also double as effective tax collectors and regularly patrol trade routes. The increased commerce also led to the settling of new towns, which had garrisons of mounted soldiers, a treasury, and a market. The rise in international trade also led to greater monetization, which allowed tax collectors to receive their revenue more in cash than in produce.

Major Trade Routes during the Later Middle Ages

India's overland trade to the Mediterranean Basin went through the northwest mountain passes to Afghanistan and from there to Iran, Central Asia, and along the Silk Road to Antioch in Syria. Two other major sea routes also linked India with the Mediterranean, one ran through the Persian Gulf before linking up via the Silk Road to Antioch, and the other went through the Red Sea then overland to the Egyptian port of Alexandria. In Europe, Italian and Venetian merchants distributed Indian wares. Large communities of Indian merchants lived in the main Red Sea, such as Jeddah and Aden. The Arabian port of Dhofar, located in present-day southern Yemen, was a source of cavalry horses (Rizvi, 221).

In northwest India, the port of Debal (or Dewal) in Sind, which had been developed by the Arabs since their eighth-century conquest, had by the fifteenth century been eclipsed by Lahri Bandar in lower Sind (Rizvi, 221). Cambay in Gujarat was a major port along with Div, Surat, and Randar. Ships from these seaports were fully engaged in trade in the Arabian Sea, reaching the ports of the Red Sea and the Persian Gulf, and voyaging as far west as East Africa, and as far south as Kerala, the Malabar coast. The port of Bandar-e Sir-af (modern Taheri), located along the Iranian coast on the Persian Gulf, was a chief western emporium in the ninth and tenth centuries; its notoriously rich merchants invited merchants from China, Java, Malaya, and India to visit their city for a common feast. The caste taboos concerning commensality that prevailed in social relations among Indians were also faithfully duplicated abroad, and to the amazement of their Iranian hosts every Indian merchant at the feast insisted on having a separate plate exclusively reserved for his own use (Nilakanta Sastry, 333).

Ports in Kerala on the Malabar Coast of southwestern India were midway between Sri Lanka and Southeast Asia in the east, and the Persian Gulf, Red Sea, and East Africa in the west. As the result, these were the major ports in South India. Calicut and Quilon in Kerala were said to have rivalled Alexandria, then the largest Mediterranean port. Large Indian ports were also home for foreign expatriate merchant communities of Arabs, Persians, Jews, and Armenians who had the protection, patronage, and support of the local ruler.

Late medieval India exported precious stones, drugs, spices, sandalwood, saffron, aromatics, iron, sugar, rice, coconuts, textiles, beads, and seed pearls.

In return, India imported Arabian horses, gold, silver, lead, mercury, coral, vermilion, rosewater, and opium. Trade between the port of Calicut and ports along the Arabian Sea was dominated in the late medieval period by Arab and Persian merchants who were based in Calicut and travelled twice a year to the Persian Gulf and Red Sea. Along with Persians and Turks, Gujarati merchants, Hindu and Muslim, handled the other great trade routes. Arab settlements along the Swahili coast in East Africa, such as Mombasa, Mogadiscio, and Kiwa promoted trade between East Africa and Gujarat. Ships carried rice, cloth, beads, and spices in exchange for African ivory, wax, gold, and slaves (Rizvi, 221).

The sailors were Muslims, but ship owners were Hindus and Muslims. Indian ports also functioned as convenient staging areas and depots for trade between the western and eastern fringes of the Indian Ocean Basin. In the East Indian Ocean, Gujarati merchants controlled the trade from Malacca, which is situated between the Malay Peninsula and the island of Sumatra. There was a large Gujarati settlement in Malacca, composed of Muslims and Hindus. The port at Malacca was the source for many of that region's commodities, including gold from Sumatra, cloves from the Moluccas, sandalwood from Timor, mace and nutmeg from Banda, camphor from Borneo, and aloe wood from China. These items were exchanged for Indian textiles, spices, drugs, and goods obtained through West Asian trade (Rizvi, 221–222).

Before the development of Malacca as a major commercial center, Chinese ships had to travel as far as the Red Sea to tap the vast Asian trade. They had to make frequent stops at ports in South India that catered exclusively to Southeast Asian trade. However, after the fourteenth century, Indian merchants established a large trading emporium at Malacca. Because most of the Indian products were now readily available in this emporium, Chinese ships rarely ventured farther west because there was now no strong economic reason to do so. This had serious economic implications for Indian ports, which specialized in the China and Southeast Asian trade.

The Islamic conquest of North India and the Arab, Iranian, and Gujarati Muslim domination of shipping also led to the Islamization of much of the Malay Peninsula and the islands of Indonesia. One notable sea-faring tradition resulting from this was the development of an Islamic patron saint of seafarers. In the thirteenth and fourteenth centuries, Muslim sailors and merchants were deeply devoted to an Iranian Sufi saint, Shaykh Abu Ishaq Gaziruni (d. 1035) (Rizvi, 322). A chain of Abu Ishaq hospices was started which offered free hospitality to merchants from the Persian Gulf to the South China Sea. These hospices were financed by contributions made by grateful merchants who made wows to the saint in return for a safe passage. Muslim merchants made interest-free loans to the hospices to sustain them. Communities of independent merchants that lacked the local integration or the grand organization of earlier guilds now oversaw Indian Ocean trade. Indian rulers heavily depended on these foreign and local Muslim and Hindu merchants to get luxury goods from overseas as well as cavalry horses and slaves. This prompted rulers, including the sultan of Delhi, to grant a great deal of autonomy to these merchants in their port cities, allowing them to act independently in their own self-interest. Even Hindu merchants enjoyed considerable autonomy in the field of banking, which they dominated largely due Qur'anic injunctions against usury. As a result, Hindus were medieval India's chief bankers and moneylenders. The moneylenders, called *Sarraf*, dominated all monetary trans-actions; they acted as bankers, issued bills of exchange, and organized insurance of goods. The risk-sharing insurance setup, or *bina*, was another by-product of the long-distance trade that developed in India, and had no parallel system in the Islamic commercial network (Habib, 402–403).

Further Reading

Appadurai, A. *Economic Conditions in Southern India*. Vols. 1 and 2. Madras, India: University of Madras, 1990.

Basham, A. L. *The Wonder that Was India*. London: Sidgwick & Jackson, 1982.

Habib, Irfan. *Essays in Indian History: Towards a Marxist Perception with the Economic History of Medieval India: A Survey*. London: Anthem Press, 2002.

Kulke, Hermann, and Dietmar Rothermund. *A History of India*. New York: Rutledge, 1998.

Sastri, Nilakanta. *Colas*. Madras, India: University of Madras Press, 1984.

Sastri, Nilakanta. *A History of South India*. 4th ed. Madres, India: Oxford University Press, 1984.

Sewell, Richard. *A Forgotten Empire: Vijayanagar*. New Delhi, India: National Book Trust, 1962.

Stein, Berton. "Coromandel Trade in Medieval India." In John Parker, ed., *Merchants and Scholars*. Minneapolis: University of Minnesota Press, 1965.

Stein, Berton. *Peasant State and Society in Medieval India*. New Delhi, India: Oxford University Press, 1980.

Raman N. Seylon

4. THE ARTS

The Indian medieval period is generally assumed to have come after the fall of the **Gupta Empire**. However, the usage of the term *medieval* in the Indian context is somewhat problematic, because it invites a comparison with the European medieval period. In Europe, the medieval period lies between two high points of European civilization: the high civilization of classical Greece and Rome and the rebirth of high culture during the European Renaissance. However, in India, it represents the further refinement of developments of the Gupta era, such as its artistic maturation; according to one historian, a better term than "medieval" in the Indian context would be "Baroque" (Lannoy, 57).

However, we cannot isolate India from the rest of the Eurasian landmass; the developments that occurred elsewhere in the Near East or in Europe had their consequences and parallels in India. This is especially true with the advent of Islam. A faith with followers in the Middle East and India, Islam acted as a culture bearer between India and the rest of Eurasia. Ideas and events that touched the medieval Middle East, or even originated in medieval Europe, had their effects in medieval India through Islamic-Turkish or Arab intermediaries (Lannoy, 57).

Hindu Architecture

Religious architecture is an area where India differs from the rest of Eurasia in the early Middle Ages. Whereas the rest of Eurasia was building its finest monumental places of worship above ground, Indians were building their finest religious edifices below ground, or quarrying them out of cliff faces. This had been the case since the time of the Mauryan Empire (322–185 B.C.E.); and, for a thousand years, the most important cultural monuments were inside these man-made caves (*see* **Temples, Hindu**). Although this is a key distinguishing factor of early medieval Indian religious architecture, there were Buddhist and Hindu places of worship built out of stone, brick, or wood above ground. The writings of the seventh-century Chinese traveler **Xuanzang** mention what seem like fortified sangharamas or monasteries with multistory turrets of various sizes and three-story towers on all four sides; Xuanzang praises the extraordinary skillful architecture of these structures. These monasteries had a large central hall for communal prayers and profusely painted and ornamented monks' quarters (Beal, 74). They also may have served as caravansaries for travelling merchants, who may have provided the funds for their upkeep and may have commissioned the beautiful murals on their walls. Because these were constructed with perishable bricks and wood, they have long vanished. They never exhibited the same aesthetic perfection attained in the underground cave centers, which often imitated and sculptured the finer points of the above-ground wooden monastic architecture in stone. More than twelve hundred such man-made caves at some twenty major sites were quarried between the third and the tenth centuries. The earliest example of this rock-cut architecture, the Lomasa Rishi Caves at the Barabar Hills in Gaya, was constructed for the ascetic monks of the atheistic Ajivaka sect by Emperor Ashoka (273–232 B.C.E.) of the Mauryan dynasty. Its entrance way is carved to imitate a bamboo, wood, and thatched roof hut with a pottery top finial—the illusion of its perishable materials faithfully carved in solid granite.

Some of these cave centers even had cells for monks, spacious assembly halls, shrines, and galleries quarried from sheer cliff faces to a depth of 100 feet or more. The tools used for these excavations were rather basic; the two main ones were a ¾-inch wide iron chisel and a hammer, which were used for initial work and for chiselling the finer details. Studies in aborted cave projects inform us as to the techniques involved in quarrying the caves. The process of cutting began at the ceiling and then moved down. This method eliminated the need for any scaffolding during the early stages of work. Many types of workers were needed to complete such a project, including rock cutters who did the early work of splitting and removing the rocks. This task was accomplished by inserting wooden pegs into chiselled holes in the rock at close intervals along the line the cutters intended to split. When the pegs were soaked with water, the wood expanded and the rock fractured. By inserting the wooden pegs in a system of grids, the entire block could be dislodged. Next, masons did the more precise cutting, and then sculptors and polishers performed the final finishing. All the workers functioned as a team (Dehejia, 109). Some of the most spectacular man-made cave centers in the Indian tradition include the caves of Ajanta, Ellora, and Elephanta, and the rock-cut temples of Mamallapuram.

Early Indian architecture is closely related to changes in the religious sphere. Early Buddhist codes of behavior for monks demanded that they adhere to a life of wandering and be detached from anything that would affect their religious goals. The realities of India's weather led to monks setting up monasteries. Early *stupas* also had a large joining hall, which was used as a shelter to preach Buddhist teachings to the general public as early as the third century B.C.E. (*see* **Temples, Buddhist:** *Stupas*). Many of these early halls were built of wood, or had thatched rooftops, but from about 50 B.C.E in the Western **Deccan**, along the foothills of the Western Ghats, a number of man-made caves were quarried from softer volcanic rock, which reproduced these wooden teaching halls entirely in stone, with all their fine details, for example, roof ribs, windows, and porticos. The caves at Karle and Kancheri had life-sized couples on their facades, and others had attractive women sitting in balconies. Over time, the monks, who used these caves halls to preach, also began to live at the sites. This transformation of rudimentary cave shelters as preaching halls into cave quarters fit to house large groups of Buddhist monks can be clearly seen at Ajanta. Here, for eight centuries, beginning sometime around the third century B.C.E., twenty-six man-made caves were quarried, with four of them used as primarily as preaching caves while the rest were converted into living quarters to house a population of six hundred to seven hundred monks. Cave walls were plastered and painted several times over often with scenes from Buddhist legends. Few of the later paintings were done in more serious doctrinal themes, but the vast majority of the earlier ones may well have been painted by professional lay artists, because their imagery is very sensual and worldly. They seemingly sought to beautify and transform the bleak rocky interiors of these man-made caves so as to mirror murals from the palaces of the period's elite. In these majestic underground dwellings were created many great works of Buddhist scholarship in philosophy, psychology, and logic (Basham, 199–200).

To understand the need for the construction and functions of these man-made caves, we must define the word *monastic* in the Indian context. The Buddhist monastic tradition predated the Christian monastic tradition, which had first developed in the Egyptian desert under St. Anthony (251–356 C.E.) as a solitary retreat entirely cut off from the rest of society. The Indian monastic tradition, like its Christian counterpart, also served as a retreat for monks, but they also differed, in purpose and organization, from the Christian monastic tradition. The cave monasteries in the Indian context were not mere retreats, but places focused mainly on achieving nirvana, or union with the absolute. The sites themselves had been formally sacred spots and local places of veneration prior to becoming Buddhist monastic centers. In this capacity, they had always been places of pilgrimage, and never an exclusive domain of any monastic order (Lannoy, 33–34). Another major difference was that in spite of the respect in which they were held, these Buddhist monasteries never played an influential social role as it was the case with monasteries in medieval Europe (Dehejia, 112).

The construction of these cave monasteries was an expensive undertaking. Inscriptional evidence indicates that the earliest cave monasteries were funded by the collective donations of ordinary people of the community, including housewives, gardeners, fisherman, monks, and nuns, but there were also large individual donations from wealthy merchants, financiers, and guilds. For this reason, they were strategically located not too far from major trade routes, which would have brought wealthy merchants and distant pilgrims to the site as patrons and devotees able to provide a portion of the funds needed for the upkeep of the monastic centres (Dehejia, 109–110). The prosperity of the merchant classes in India during this period was due to the expanding trade network needed to satisfy Mediterranean markets; a great deal of wealth and prosperity was generated by the mercantile classes, and a portion of this wealth was given away as donations (Dehejia, 110–111). Although often located in difficult terrain, these monasteries were thus also well-known centers of pilgrimage, situated at strategic points along trade routes and providing access for all sections of society. In this sense, they were the opposite of the isolated and austere retreats of ascetic monks found in the Western Christian tradition. The worldly sensual art is a reflection of this attempt to appeal and cater to the interests of ordinary people outside the monastic setting.

Many of the early great Buddhist *stupas*—dome-shaped sacred mounts constructed out of wood and clay or bricks—have long vanished, but by studying their rock-carved replicas in caves modern researchers have a fair idea of what they looked like, and even some of the more practical details, such as the manner of preserving wooden columns that held the roof beams from termites and other wood-eating vermin. At a Buddhist cave site at Karle, about 100 miles from Mumbai, there are thirty-seven such columns with curious-looking vase-shaped bases, dating from late first and early second centuries C.E. They mimic the use of early earthen pots that once had protected the buried portions of the wooden columns from being eaten by vermin. Epigraphical evidence indicates that the seven of the interior pillars were gifts from by the Yavanas (Greek or foreign merchants), who presumably came here along the trade route that passed through this area. In its early days, Buddhism gained support from the general public and merchants, but around the fifth century C.E. this community base was being replaced by the patronage by royalty. The reasons for this shift are not clear, but the result was a flourishing of artistic endeavor. A good example of this is the monastic center at Ajanta, which was sponsored by the court of the Hindu ruler Harishena (r. 462–481 C.E.). It may seem odd that a Hindu monarch would sponsor construction of new Buddhist monasteries, but from the point of view of a medieval Indian ruler donations to any religious establishment brought good merit and perhaps more practical considerations as the encouragement and facilitation trade and the opening of new settlements throughout his territory.

Ajanta, perhaps the most well known of all cave monasteries of medieval India, is located in present-day state of Maharashtra. The site comprises a set of man-made caves in a horseshoe-shaped ravine, which was an escarpment rising from the riverbed. The caves in Ajanta were quarried and refashioned as Buddhist religious centers sometime between the fifth and eighth centuries C.E. They were conveniently located near the ancient trade routes that pass from the inland town of Ujjayani through the Western Ghats to the Western seaports. Previous to its receipt of royal patronage, Ajanta was an insignificant monastery. By the fifth century C.E., Ajanta had become a major Buddhist center of veneration that catered to increasing numbers of Buddhist pilgrims (Craven, 123). In Ajanta, as in other cave-quarried monasteries, the number of occupants increased, new excavations occurred, and the artificial caves grew in scale over the centuries (Basham, 352).

As centers of pilgrimage, these monasteries exhibit much secular art work by local artisans that captured domestic themes of everyday life in Buddhist India, which were blended with themes from the Buddhist moral Jataka tales and with religious iconography. These paintings were commissioned by wealthy patrons, who maintained a number of workshops of painters. These works allow us a glimpse of the complex art scene of post-Gupta India. The technique of making roughly hewn rock surfaces into large smooth canvasses took some effort but was rudimentary. First, the rough cave walls were plastered with a mixture of cow dung, mud, animal hair, and rice husk to give it strength and the necessary adhesive bond. This mixture was levelled and covered with lime plaster a half inch to 2 inches thick, which served as the painting surface. The plaster was first allowed to dry, then the artist outlined the scene in red paint, with details in gray paint. Colors made mainly from local minerals—lamp black, white lime, kaolin, mineral green, and imported blue Lapis Lazuli— were then added to the scene, and the whole composition was defined clearly with a black or brown line (Dehejia, 118). Then the entire work was either polished with a smooth stone or covered with stucco to give it the necessary luster and shine. Had these painters painted while the lime was wet, the work would have had the greater durability of a fresco, but by painting over the dried surface the work became a mural and as such was more delicate and water soluble. Such painting techniques allowed for the water damage that has subsequently affected these paintings. The rice husk in the original plaster was also affected by insect attacks, which weakened the planter foundation of the murals. Literary evidence suggests such types of mural art were common in the houses of the wealthy during this period; however, of the many galleries of paintings that may once have existed from this early period, only the ones in Ajanta have survived the ravages of time (Dehejia, 118).

Ajanta's murals may not have been intended only for the benefit of the resident monks but also for a diverse audience of pilgrims, though the paintings could have been only viewed by the use of oil lamps. This suggests that they may have functioned as touring art galleries to be viewed by outside patrons guided by monks, or been merely for the use of the monks to focus on their meditative practices (Dehejia, 122). The murals of Ajanta have greater numbers of Mahayana Buddhist imagery, especially the increasing number of Buddhist savior figures. This new group of Buddhist divine beings, known as Bodhisattva figures, were compassionate beings at the threshold of full Buddhahood who nevertheless chose to remain on earth to help others attain enlightenment (Dehejia, 114). The lotus-bearing Padmapani, also known as Avalokiteshvara (Bodhisattva of infinite compassion), is the best-known mural of Bodhisattva figures in Ajanta. The large scale of this mural is an indication of the significance the painters attached to this image, which they shaded and highlighted to create a sense of three-dimensionality (Dehejia, 114). In Ajanta, the fifth-century fresco of Padmapani is depicted with a pointed hair adornment and holding a blue lotus with serene expression; it is one of the great masterpieces of the post-Gupta murals. Other murals have more sensual or even erotic themes, such as two lovers engaged in a passionate courtship within an idealized architectural setting; this was to remain a common romantic motif even in later centuries, and could be seen in many of the **Rajput** miniatures of the nineteenth century. The concept of Avalokiteshwara, a popular Buddhist male savior figure, soon spread with Mahayana Buddhism to other parts of East Asia, where it curiously underwent something of a gender transformation into a popular female deity called *Guan yin* or "Goddess of Mercy" in China, *Kan on* in Japan, and *Gwan eum* in Korea. By the end of the first millennium C.E., Buddhism had lost much of its individuality and was being assimilated by theistic Hinduism and had vanished from India with the coming of the Muslim-Turkish invasions of the twelfth century.

The quarrying and painting in Ajanta began according to recent estimation about 462 C.E., when the Vakataka dynasty ruler Harishena came to throne; the work thrived during the lifetime of this monarch but seemed to stop abruptly with Harishena's death. The best most recent estimate is that the site was abandoned soon after 500 C.E. This is perhaps why Xuanzang failed to mention it and why the surviving paintings were preserved in such good condition. The caves themselves were abandoned and forgotten only to reemerge in the early days of the British rule.

In the early decades of the nineteenth century, the existence of a large cave complex at the frontiers of the Bombay presidency was part of the local lore known to British military personnel stationed in Bombay. In February 1824, a young British officer, James Alexander, who had taken leave from his regiment for some tiger hunting in the hills north of Aurangabad, decided to explore this local legend. This area was heavily forested, and Alexander was warned about the hostile aboriginal tribe living there. Undeterred, Alexander and his companions pressed on, following the river called Waghur into tiger-infested jungle country. Near its source, the river had, over the years, cut a deep horseshoe-shaped canyon out of the dark grey volcanic basalt rocks; high on this rock face Alexander spotted what seemed like a series of caves with the entrances flanked by elaborate stone pillars. As Alexander and his party hacked their way to the top, they realized that the site had previously served as a retreat for a large monastic community. But this site was different from other well-known cave retreats in that it had painted murals, well preserved in vivid color, that detailed the dress code, habits, and lifestyles of an ancient people now long forgotten (Allen, 129). The news of this discovery soon found its way into preeminent archaeological journals of the period. It first appeared in *The Transactions of the Royal Asiatic Society* in 1830 and then in the *Journal of the Asiatic Society of Bengal* in 1837. Under the full glare of the academic limelight, these long-forgotten medieval masterpieces again became the focus of popular attention.

About the same time as work ceased in Ajanta, cave quarrying was going on in the island of Elephanta off Mumbai Harbor. Unlike Ajanta, Elephanta was a Hindu sanctuary and, although the Hindus copied the quarrying techniques of the Buddhists, they redefined the rock-cut caves to meet their religious needs. As such, the Hindu caves in Elephanta have no living quarters for priests who may have resided in brick or wooden structures at the top. The caves reflect changes in Hindu religious faith, especially the path of devotion to a chosen deity known as Bhakti or devotional Hinduism. The preeminent deities Siva, Vishnu, and the Goddess Devi now began to dominate the Hindu religious sphere.

Dedicated to Siva, Cave I of Elephanta was 131 feet across and colonnaded; at one time it held a number of sculptures of Siva. Unfortunately, most of these sculptures were badly damaged by the artillery practice undertaken by the Portuguese garrison, which was stationed there (Craven, 123). One sculpture that escaped this fifteenth-century vandalism was the triple headed 18-foot-high sculpture of the triple form of Siva, which represents the fusion of attributes associated with Siva, fusing the three heads into one homogenous sculptural form. The serene, impassive central face of the sculpture is known as Sadyojata or Siva as absolute knowledge. The left face, with snakes as earrings, skulls rising out of matted hair, and an angry wrathful demeanor, is known as Aghora or Siva the destroyer of delusion. The right face with feminine features is known as Vamadava or Siva's beautiful consort the Goddess Parvati. There is also a large sculpture of a lingam or emblem of Siva, which is kept in a square chamber flanked by four guardians and purposely set off center of the cave complex. This was done to allow devotees entering though the north entrance to witness the full majesty of the triple form of Siva. Grouped around the cave are eight large sculptures that are from the sacred stories of Siva-purana, depicting the god's various forms to bestow grace upon his devotees and to delude, humble, or destroy the wicked. These stories of the eight large sculptures would have been familiar to all Shaivaite devotees. The imagery within Cave 1 depicts an even more profound philosophical concept of Sivaite Hinduism. According to the most recent interpretation, the Lingam, the triple form of Siva, and the eight figures are linked ideologically. The Lingam represents the un-manifest form of Siva. The triple form represents Sadashiva or the point where the formless begins to assume form. The eight sculptured forms from the Siva purana are the manifest forms through which Siva appears to his most ardent devotees (Dehejia, 126–127). The Elephanta sculptures may have been sponsored by the Kalachuri ruler Krishna Raja I (550–575 c.e.), who was a recent conqueror of this region and known for his deep devotion to Siva. The construction of this site is dated to 550, when it was undertaken to commemorate Krishna Raja's conquest of this territory.

Contemporaneously with this are the Pallava Period rock-sculptured temples at Mamallapuram, some 37 miles from the city of Chennai, Tamil Nadu, which had always had been a major tourist attraction. In medieval times, Mamallapuram was developed by the Pallava ruler Narashima Varman (630–668 c.e.), the forth ruler of the Pallava dynasty, as a major port with lighthouses to guide Coromandal Coast shipping. From these ports, the king sent naval vassals to engage in long distance commerce with states in Southeast Asia and to interfere in the domestic politics of Sri Lanka. Narashima, who was titled *mamalla* or great warrior (or great wrestler), also bequeathed his epithet to the town that was previously named Mamalai (or great hill) and turned this into a large open-air artistic center.

The most famous narrative relief sculpture at Mamallapuram is called the "Descent of the Ganges," which is 20 feet high and 80 feet long. Its theme is the Hindu religious story that honors the role played by Siva in cushioning the impact of the heavenly waters of the River Ganges by consenting to receive the river flow through the locks of his matted hair, thereby allowing it to fall gently to the ground. This new religious theistic Hindu devotion or *bhakti*, as opposed to the earlier contemplative Buddhist meditation or *dhayana*, demanded impressive narrative structures to focus the attention of worshippers. This was created by an emotive and colorful sacred story or *lila* from the Hindu sacred text Siva-purana, which seems to have functioned as "visual sermon," giving the devotees hope and optimism.

To emphasize that central cleft, the River Ganges, that area of the relief is filled with Nagas, mythological semidivine human snakes usually associated with water. Next is seen Siva granting a boon to an ascetic, who is identified either as the sage Bhagiratha, praying to Siva to bear the brunt of the torrential waters as the river makes its earthly descend, or the hero Arjuna, from the epic *Mahabharata*, praying to Siva to gain powerful magical weapons for the upcoming *Mahabharata* war (Dehejia, 190). Around Siva various ascetics perform rites of self-mortification. A comic relief involves a penance-performing cat, who, by standing on one paw, has cunningly attracted a crowd of pious mice with their front feet pressed together in prayer. In one of its side stories, the *Mahabharata* narrates this event as an allegorical moral story concerning the sad fate of gullible and trusting mice. There is strong evidence that there was once a storage water tank above this sculptured narrative relief with a pool below. It is, therefore, plausible that on special or ceremonial occasions the water from the pool could be let out to cascade down the cliff like a flowing river. By witnessing a reenactment of the central narrative of the purana, local devotees and visitors could experience the divine grace of Siva.

Another notable site at Mamallapuram is a group of small temples, most carved from a single granite boulder. Called the five rathas, or chariots, these might be replicas of five types of wooden temples with thatched roofs. Traditionally, they are identified with the five Pandava brothers, the heroes of the *Mahabharata*, although there is strong evidence that this was a later interpolation (Dehejia, 193). It is more likely that these are shrines for the three main traditional Hindu deities: Siva, Vishnu, and Devi (Dehejia, 193–194). This set of sculptured temples had been personally sponsored by Narashima Varman; the title *Mamalla* is prominently engraved in the site and indications are that work on the five rathas halted abruptly on that ruler's death in 668.

The Shore Temple is a stone Siva temple along the sea with a high conical tower. Many of the finer details of the temple's carvings and the rows of sculptured stone bulls that marked the temple's perimeter were eroded away by centuries of wave action as the sea expanded; the temple thus has a soft "melted look." According to local lore, four similar shore temples originally stood here in Pallava times but have now been swallowed up by the ocean. Recent archaeological surveys give some validity to these tales. These shore temples, with their pointed high towers, would have allowed Hindu sailors to pray from their boats to Siva for safe passage before undertaking long oceanic voyages or to give grateful thanks upon their safe arrival.

The design of these shores temples is important; they are perhaps the earliest stone-built temples in South India. The Mamallapuram shore temple, along with Kailasanatha temple at Kanchipuram (another stone-built temple by the Pallavas from around the same time), served as models for other stone temples, including those of the Cholas, who replaced the Pallavas as the preeminent dynasty of South India. They were also influenced Hindu architecture outside India, especially the Hindu temple architecture in the island of Java in the Indonesia, where Hinduism was once the dominant faith. Over one-half the monuments in the site remained unfinished, which was perhaps the result of a Pallava dynastic struggle. The new branch that came to power may have decided to focus their temple building near the Pallava capital at Kanchipuram, because the site at Mamallapuram had strong associations with the former ruling house (Dehejia, 137).

On par with Ajanta in grandeur were the rock-quarried Hindu cave temples constructed three centuries later at Ellora some 30 miles from Ajanta. Ellora, unlike Ajanta, is preeminently a Hindu site and was named after one of the hillside abodes of Siva, high in the Himalayas. Nevertheless, the Ellora site was ecumenical and had Buddhist and Jain meditation caves. This ecumenism reflected the changed religious landscape in this part of India where theistic Hinduism had now gained dominance at the expense of Buddhism and **Jainism**. Altogether, Ellora has some thirty-four caves, and its construction and quarrying work began ran from the fifth to the eighth centuries, which makes it contemporary with Ajanta, though its prominence outlasted Ajanta. The most important site in Ellora is the large late eighth-century monolithic Kailasanatha Temple (775 C.E.) built by the Rashtrakuta ruler Krishana I (757–873); its style also influences the Pallava art of the **Tamil country** in southeastern India. It was staggering in its dimensions. The entire rock face on a hillside was carved like a sculpture and an estimated million cubic feet of stone was quarried and excavated to construct a large temple with a shrine room, and a ground plan that equalled the size of the Parthenon in Greece (Basham, 354). One historian calls it the "most stupendous single work excavated in India." It differs form earlier cave temples in that its exterior and interior were excavated and then carved out of solid rock (Basham, 355; Dehejia, 131).

This Hindu architecture gets its inspiration from the Buddhist caves and monastic shrines in Ajanta and Hindu temples that were already coming into existence in South India. But unlike Ajanta's dark cave-like quarters, the temple at Ellora is open to the sky. It was also adorned with ornate pillars and painted with vivid colored frescos, differing from the average, plain-looking Hindu temples of earlier periods. The temple consists of three separate units and a gat house, a pavilion to house Siva's sacred bull vehicle Nandi, and a temple built in the South Indian pyramid-shaped temple style (discussed more below). Sacred climactic scenes from Hindu myths were used as a kind of theatrical effect to impose upon viewers the power of the divine and his mercy, for example, the image of ten-headed Ravana, the demon king of the epic *Ramayana*, trying to uproot and take to his kingdom at Lanka Mount Kailasa, the abode of Siva. According to this puranic story (*see* **Puranas**), as the demon king tried to uproot the mountain, the entire earth shook, and the alarmed goddess Parvati clutched her consort Siva. Calm and serene, Siva pressed his toe down thereby trapping the demon king under the crushing weight of the mountain. Fearing death, Ravana in desperation tears off one of his heads and an attached limb and used his tendons as the strings of a lyre to play a devotional ode to Siva, who in his benevolence takes pity upon the demon king and grants him freedom. Ravana in turn becomes an ardent devotee of Siva. This story and its various versions, which must have been familiar to every Hindu of this period, is an allegorical story about the divine grace of Siva and his infinite power, which is depicted here in three-dimensional dramatic sculptures. When these temples were new, they would have been coated outside and inside with a thin layer of plaster and painted with colorful murals. Sixteenth-century Islamic sources identify Kailasa temple as "Rang Mahal," or colored mansion. This name indicates that at one time it must have been richly decorated with colorful religious murals (just like modern-day Hindu temples), which had to be continuously repainted. Only traces of these paintings are now evident within the temple precinct (Dehejia, 134).

One of the advantages of the medieval Indian man-made caves is that they are easy to maintain and extremely durable habitats. They also had climatic advantages; they were cool during the hot season, dry during the torrential monsoon season, and could be easily heated during the cold season. They provided an ideal environment for contemplation for the layman and the monk to practice meditation. However, the increasing popularity of the Hindu Bhakti tradition called for a different kind of religious architecture, one that was open and spacious to accommodate large passionate crowds (Lannoy, 58). The resulting innovation was the stone-built Hindu temple. The surface-level Hindu temple had moved away architecturally from earlier simpler structures made of less durable wood with thatched roofs. It benefited from the experience Indian stone masons gained while working on rock quarried temples and monasteries. The early transitional forms were the ones at Mamallapuram, which stand midway between pure rock-carved cave halls and freestanding medieval temples (Lannoy, 59).

A comparison between the predominantly Buddhist cave temples and the Hindu temple underline the essential differences between these two religious ideologies. The Buddhist cave sanctuary is an enclosed space to which all monks had free access, one where they could stand face to face with the central Buddha imagery. The communal and fraternal relationship among monks and their brotherly bond with the historic Buddha is expressed in the layout of the cave sanctuary. Only in later caves, when Buddhism became incorporated with Hinduism, was the Buddha image kept in a separate cell and apart from the congregation of monks. However, in Hindu temples, the central image expresses a new theistic Hindu view; the devotees are distant from the deity and had the religious obligation to bridge this gap by their passionate devotion and service. The sanctum is accessible only to the ritually pure chief priest who conducted the *puja* (ritual); those in a ritually impure state were not permitted to enter the sanctum. It was also necessary for the lower castes to be kept at a distance from the holiest icon since they were also deemed ritually impure (Lannoy, 60).

As a reflection of changes in the theological landscape, temple construction in India also moved away from below-ground quarried artificial caves to above-ground constructions. From the eighth to the fifteenth centuries, there was a period of large above-ground construction of numerous large temples, often reaching great heights. The Hindu temples were constructed according to the strict cannons of architecture called *silpa-sastra* (Basham, 356). Underneath the towering pyramid-shaped structures was the main shrine hall for the presiding deity, surrounded by smaller shrines of various other deities, all of whose good will was essential for any successful undertaking. The sanctum or heart of the temple was the womb-like dark shrine called *garbha graha*, containing the stone image of the presiding deity. The *garbha graha* was adjoined by a hall for worshippers (*mandapa*), which was approached by a porch (*ardhamandapa*). The central pyramidal shaped tower above the *garbha graha* was complimented by lesser lower towers that adorned other parts of the temple complex.

Medieval Hindu society was dominated by an alliance of the Brahmin priests and the Kshatriya, the ruling elite of the court. Therefore, temple imagery and sacred scenery also tended to reflect the values, tastes, and lifestyles of the ruling elite, who funded and financed their undertaking. In these palaces of the gods the central temple imagery was modelled upon the court rituals of medieval Hindu kingship, where the presiding deity was clothed as a Hindu ruler surrounded by all the royal paraphernalia that accompanied a monarch (Lannoy, 62–63).

Two major temple styles emerged during this period; one was the North Indian Nagara style and the other was the South Indian Dravidian style. The Nagara style generally had a central tower or *sikhara* (mountain peak) with a rounded top and a plain curvilinear outline. The Dravidian *sikhara* (locally known as *vimana*) was shaped in the form of a rectangular truncated pyramid and tend to be highly ornate. South India contains a greater number of medieval temples; many northern temples were sacked and destroyed by the **Huns** and other Turkish invaders from Central Asia, while others were razed by the deliberate policies of the more zealous medieval Islamic rulers. In medieval South India, temple buildings developed further under the patronage of the Chola emperors. The Siva temple at Tanjore, built by the great Chola ruler Raja Raja the Great (r. 985–1014), was the largest temple *sikhara* built in India until that time. Like many other medieval monuments, it was built to commemorate Raja Raja's major victories over neighboring rulers. The base of the temple sanctum housed a giant stone linga, which symbolized the unmanifest and formless Siva; it was covered by a roof and topped by the central *sikhara*. The *sikhara* at Tanjore temple is far higher than its Pallava shore temple prototype, reaching nearly 200 feet tall. It is conical in shape with a hallow structure that is divided into thirteen horizontal stages. This tall Dravidian style *sikhara* set the standard for subsequent tall South Indian temples, and the modern variation of this temple style is still being built.

An elaborate temple architectural style also developed in Central India, under the rule of the Chaulokya, Rastrakuta, and Hoysala dynasties. Early Chaulokya temples resemble the style of the Guptas and later became increasingly elaborate and developed the distinct Central Indian or Vesara style *sikhara* that was a synthesis of both the Nagara and Dravidian styles. This synthesis had images and scenes from Hindu epics intermingled with repetitive sculptures of decorated stone elephants and armed horsemen from Indian royal pageantry. During this post-Gupta Period the fierce decorative motif known as "Kirttimuka" mask emerged as a commonly used decorative architectural feature in Hindu temples. Kirttimuka or "face of glory" is a grotesque face that was believed to be the remains of a demon created by Siva as the supreme destructive power in the universe, but whose uncontrollable hunger even consumed his own body. Kirttimuka is seen as a symbol of Siva's destructive powers and commonly placed over the entrances of Hindu Sivaite temples as an auspicious and protective symbol (Craven, 164). The Kirttimuka motif was also enthusiastically adapted by Southeast Asian Hindu artists and temple builders and became a standard feature of Indonesian and Cambodian architecture (Basham, 358).

A good example of North Indian medieval temple architecture is the temple of Khajuraho. The temple complex at Khajuraho may originally have housed some 85 temples, of which only 25 survive; the remains of another 25 can be traced. Most were built between 954 and 1035. Unlike their South Indian counterparts, these temples are not large, but they are certainly the most elegant examples of the North Indian style. The temples consist of three horizontal zones. First, a high solid basement rises above the terrace and requires a steep flight of stairs to enter. This is followed by the interior compartments of the temple, which contain the sanctum and various halls and are topped by a group of pyramidal *sikharas*. Each interior unit of the temple has its own successively taller *sikharas* rising toward the highest *sikhara* above the shrine. This design element was intentional; the imagery of the various smaller towers rising toward the main sikhara suggests a stylized version of the minor mountain ranges that surround Siva's Mount Kailasa, the most sacred mountain for Hindus. This style also makes the temple seem natural and organic and gives it a visual unity with its surroundings (Basham, 362). The best known of the Khajuraho temples is the Siva Temple of Kandariya-Mahadeo. This complex is only half the height of the Tanjore Siva temple and, like most northern temple towers, is curvilinear.

The midsection of the outer walls of the Khajuraho temples are made into a series of projections and recesses that provide space to carve a profusion of sculptured images in horizontal bands while still retaining the temple's sense of balance and proportion. The Kandariya-Mahadio has three such horizontal bands of sculpture that comprise about 650 half-life-size images. The deities and celestials are carved in deep relief giving a three-dimensional feeling. Originally, they would have been richly plastered and painted, giving them a life-like quality like some of the sculptures in modern Hindu temples. Some of the images, like some of their modern counterparts, had highly sensual and erotic poses that must have captured the attention of the most profane devotees. A combination of factors and ideas likely explain Khajuraho's erotic imagery, including the philosophical idea of a mystic union of the human soul with the Brahman (the infinite or the ultimate reality). The monistic Hindu doctrines of the Upanishads explain that the human soul emanates from the Brahman and is not a distinct entity; as the soul ends its earthly tenure, it returns and merges again with the Brahman. This doctrine stresses the unity of the apparent duality; the idea is sculpturally expressed with the graphic sexual symbolism of an orgasmic union, which medieval sculptors no doubt found a fitting and universal expression for depicting this profound philosophical principle. The profusion of sculptures on the exterior of the temple complex is a great medieval artistic innovation.

A second temple group illustrating the best of North Indian temple architecture is in Orissa, which may have the greatest concentration of temples in India. Many of these date to the tenth and thirteenth centuries and were built during the period of Islamic invasions from Central Asia. The two most important temples of the Orissan group are the temples of Vishnu Jagannatha (lord of the universe) at Puri, which is still an important functional temple famous for its annual *rath yatra* or towering temple cart-pulling festival, and the other is the great sun temple at Kanarak, built in the thirteenth century.

At Puri, the giant Jagannatha temple is a major Vishnavite center. Surrounded by an outer wall, this compound comprises a collection of over one hundred temple complexes and shrines. The rituals of this temple are quite spectacular and the size of the Jagannatha Temple cart must have amazed early British visitors. It is from Jagannatha that we get the English term *juggernaut*, which is today used as a general term for any unstoppable political force that crushes opponents. In medieval times, the piety of the devotees of the Jagannatha Shrine was of such fervor that many are said to have thrown themselves under the huge wheels of the cart to be crushed, a sacrifice they believed would ensure them a place in Vishnavite heaven (or Vaikuntam).

The Sun Temple located at Konarak, a small town in Orissa, is an unfinished temple built by Narasimhadeva (r. 1238–1264) of the Ganga dynasty. At the time of its construction, it was one of the largest temples in India, with its central *sikhara* reaching over 223 feet, making it the highest during the thirteenth century. This tall *sikhara* has long since collapsed, but its assembly hall remains. In Indo-Aryan mythology, the sun god Suriya rides across the heavens in a chariot drawn by seven horses bringing light and warmth. In Konarak, the sanctum and the hall of the temple represent a gigantic stone chariot, an earthly representation of the one driven across the sky by the sun god. The wheels of this giant chariot are beautifully carved along the sides; the entire monument includes twenty-four giant 10-foot wheels, perhaps in reference to the twelve months of the solar year. The entire cultural imagery is dominated by the erotic maithuna figures that may have been vividly painted. Depictions of couples embracing and performing various forms of sexual intercourse in a place of worship naturally shocked Victorian British visitors to the site and gave them a strongly unfavorable view of Hinduism in general.

Some later authors saw the imagery as being purely symbolic, expressing the aforementioned mystic union of the soul with the Brahman. Another theory contrasts the everyday world of flesh on the exterior of the temple with the structure's bare and austere interior, which symbolizes the deeper world of the spirit that the temple represents (Basham, 362). Other authors saw the figures as having something to do with sexual mysticism or the tantric cults that dominated this region and were patronized by local rulers. Another view sees the figures as simply images of fertility, which are appropriate for a temple dedicated to the sun god. If the recently discovered Baya Cakada manuscript is authentic, the Sun temple took 6 years to plan and hundreds of craftsmen working for 12 years to complete; its dedication ceremonies were held in 1258. The Sun temple at Konarak was the last of the major Hindu temple projects undertaken in North India. From the thirteenth century, political power in North India shifted to Islamic dynasties and henceforth until modern period, it was the minaret and not the *sikhara* that would occupy the prominent place in the skyline of medieval North India (Dehejia, 182).

The literary equivalent of this sculptural eroticism is the celebrated erotic poem *Gita Govinda*, a twelfth-century work by Jeyadeva, a well-known poet born in Puri who lived during the time of the Ganga dynasty. The Gangas controlled what is today Orisssa and are credited with building the large Jagannath Temple in Puri as well as the Konarak Sun Temple. The theme of *Gita Govinda* is the relationship between the god Krishna and his devoted paramour, a *gopi* (cowgirl) named Radha. The aim of this erotic poem is to show that a divinity such as Krishna transgresses all human rules of moral propriety or rules of human reason to achieve a blissful state of oneness and ecstatic unity with his beloved devotee (Lannoy, 64).

Likewise, the medieval tantric cults also saw that the surest way to achieve divine ecstasy was to get away from the normal sexual routine with one's spouse and go against the moral propriety of society. Because normal sexual union is often associated with procreation, a superior ecstatic transfiguring union could be attained easily by having abnormal sexual relations, which may be of an adulterous or incestuous nature. Because concern for the utility of intercourse is no longer present, the act itself becomes a purging catharsis to achieve pure ecstasy and a moment of union and oneness with the divine. For this reason, the erotic Hindu temple murals and sculptures portray what seems to us to be abnormal or unnatural acts of sex (Lannoy, 64).

A number of Hindu and Jain temples were built between the eleventh and thirteenth centuries in Gujarat. For religious reasons, Jains took mainly to trading rather than **agriculture** and benefited from the Indian Ocean trade that flowed through the ports of Gujarat (Dehejia, 172). The famous Jain temples at Mount Abu were built by Vimala, the devout Jain minister of the powerful

Solanki dynasty ruler Bhima I (r. 1022–1063). The Solanki dynasty was a branch of the Chalukya dynasty, which dominated this region from the sixth to the twelfth centuries. Bhima I was instrumental in defending this area against the armies of Sultan Muhmud of Gazani and also in reconstructing the Hindu temple of Somanath, which was destroyed by Sultan Muhmud in 1026. The Jain temple at Mount Abu sponsored by his minister Vimala was completed in 1032. In their style, Jain temples are similar to the Khajuraho Hindu temples but without the sexual allegories of intertwined couples. The central *sikhara* over the shrine also has a number of miniature towers. In Khajuraho, each major temple carried three distinctive ceilings; at Abu there are fifty-five ceilings. Three belong to the main temple unit while the others cover the roofs of the fifty-two small courtyard shrines, each with its own portico (Dehejia, 170).

Unlike the other rock-carved and stone and brick temple structures, the Jain shrines were built of pure white marble quarried and transported from nearby hills. Another thing that distinguishes this Jain temple at Mount Abu is the intricate details of its designs and carvings in the ceilings; each one is unique. The temple also includes a great variety of floral geometric designs with pillars decorated with stylized dancing celestials, large elephant sculptures, and intricately carved delicate marble garlands and festoons that extend from the pillars to the roof in its interior. The original temple was badly damaged by the armies of Sultan **Allauddin Khilji** of the **Delhi sultanate** and the new one was reconstructed as a faithful copy of the original around 1300. The steep wall that surrounds this temple is a testament to the constant danger posed by invasions during the medieval period.

South India, in late Chola and Pandya Periods during the twelfth and thirteenth centuries, saw newer forms of architectural innovation. One of the main changes was the shift of emphasis from the *sikhara* tower above the shrine to a tall tower above the entrance of the surrounding wall. The tall walls surrounding these South Indian temples may have been done in imitation of those surrounding the king's palaces, with gates on all four sides. The need to create large *sikhara* around the outer walls may have been necessitated by the need to expand the shrine to a large proportion, something required by changes in Hindu religious ideology concerning the expanded role of the presiding deity and how deity should be presented to its devotees. Earlier notions of a distant aloof temple divinity were replaced by one that parallels an earthly monarch. This idea included giving audiences, inspecting the temple premises, and taking a more active role in temple rituals, including celebrating birthdays and marriage anniversaries (Dehejia, 233). Tradition stated that it was improper to demolish an existing shrine so the only alternative was to encase it within large walls and add impressive *sikhara* to the entrance (Dehejia, 232).

One argument is that these new style *sikhara* may have been inspired by the existing watch towers and gatehouses characteristic of palace architecture of this period (Basham, 358). The resulting change in temple architecture resulted in the familiar oblong pyramid-shaped tower with a barrel vaulted roof crowned by a single tall or row of small multiple pot shaped finials, the entire structure is called a *gopuram* (or *vimana*), which is far taller than the smaller *sikhara* over the central shrine and that dominate the skylines of today's South Indian temple towns. A large temple complex may have more than one *gopuram*; often one stood over each of its main gateways and all being the same size. This tall oblong *gopuram* became a distinct feature of

Tamil country temple architecture, and currently its image is the state's official seal. The necessity of carrying the deity around the temple premises also led to the construction of portable bronze images of 2 or 3 feet in height that could be easily carried in procession. Each temple would commission up to seventy such bronzes because the appropriate form or manifestation of the deity was needed on each occasion, and most were used only once a year and stored in the temple complex. As temple rituals and celebrations were publicly enacted, there was also a need for larger halls within the temple complex, and each temple ritual needed a suitable hall for celebration where devotees assembled to witness the rituals and partake in the communal feasts cooked in the temple kitchen. This led to construction of large pillared halls and pavilions often done in a random manner within the temple complex (Dehejia, 234).

Except in cases of major temple ceremonies, the day-to-day Hindu mode of worship is an individual form of worship differing significantly from the Buddhist or Christian modes of communal worship. This fact can be seen in the nature of Hindu temple architecture built during this period. In spite of their major expansion in space, these large South Indian temples, with a number of minor shrines, was not one fully integrated place of worship but rather a collection of individual shrines patronized by various castes and classes and housed within a single sacred space. This lack of unity also mirrored the core values of the Hindu social order: separation and hierarchy. This hierarchically based interdependency in South Indian social spheres was architecturally reproduced by tall symmetrical temple *gopuram* and its collections of individual smaller shrines. Although they are architecturally enclosed within the sacred space of a single compound, they are nevertheless distinct, thereby symbolizing the prevailing social idea of hierarchy and interdependence, coexisting in harmony (Lannoy, 60).

The next phase of temple construction developed under the Rayas of the **Vijayanagar Empire** (1336–1565) and its secondary state under the Nayaks of Madura (1529–1736). They combined the Tamil country *gopuram* that evolved under Chola and Pandya rule with other regional styles, such as those of the vesara style *sikhara* of the Hosala kingdom of Karnatika. The elaborate carvings of the Hosalas were further developed and blended with the Chola-Pandya style *gopuram* and reached its present-day oblong-shaped tower in the form a multistoried structure with rows of detailed painted sculptures retelling sacred episodes from the Hindu *puranas*. These could be seen at the major temple complexes in Madurai and Srirangam built under the Nayaka kingdom during the seventeenth century (Basham, 358).

Every important temple in South India also had a shrine for the chief consort (or Amman-mother) of the presiding deity; by the sixteenth century the temple of the chief consort was as large as the temple of the presiding deity, again reflecting changes in the popular religious landscape. The icon of the god and goddess were being ceremonially united in a wedding ritual that became a major annual ceremonial event in the South Indian ritual calendar. This celestial wedding ritual was held in a large spacious pillared marriage hall, or *Kalyana Mandapam*. The pillars of this hall were profusely decorated with ornate carvings of racing horses, armed warriors, and other detailed sculptured figures and decorative motifs that have never been excelled architecturally wit in Hindu India (Basham, 359).

Islamic Architecture

Islam first arrived in India with the Arab invasion of 712 C.E. under Muhammad bin Qasim, a relatively minor incursion into Northwest India. The main thrust of Islamic armies into the plains of Northwest India, in the form of Turkish Afghan raiders, came many centuries later. A succession of Islamic polities that dominated North India became centered on the former Rajput citadel of Delhi, where a sultanate was formally established in 1206. The Islamic dominance of North India lasted until the late eighteenth century.

To commemorate his victory over the Hindus of North India, Sultan Muhammad of Ghor erected the first Islamic mosque on North Indian soil, which was built in Delhi by his general **Qutb al-Din Aybak**, in the late twelfth century. Built on a former Rajput fort, the mosque was named Quwwat ul Islam, or "the might of Islam." Mosque architecture is distinct from any previous India architectural tradition and is supposed to have taken its inspiration or model from the house of the prophet Muhammad in Medina, where the first Muslims met for prayer. The prophet's house was a rudimentary structure built of adobe bricks and had a colonnade of palm trunks holding a palm front for shade that also served as the prayer hall. The muezzin (announcer) called for prayer from the rooftop of the house and later a large tower was added to amplify this call to prayer (Dehejia, 252).

All future mosques were based on this model, with colonnades on three sides and a main courtyard open to the sky; the wall at the fourth side, the *qibla* or the front, marked the direction of Mecca. The center of this wall had a shallow empty niche called a *mihrab* to mark its distinction. The minaret, which was a later addition, came to symbolize an Islamic center (Craven, 252). In sticking to the idea that the victory was temporal as well as spiritual, Qutb al-Din Aybak is said to have pillaged twenty-seven Hindu temples to construct the mosque. It had pillared galleries, and its *qible* wall was built from stones and broken sculptures taken from Hindu and Jain temples. Because the Hindu pillars lacked the height needed for taller mosque pillars, they were stacked one on top of the other to meet the required height (Craven, 195). No two architectures could have been so diametrically opposite in their symbolic meanings as the Hindu temple and the Islamic mosque. The center of the Hindu temple complex, the sanctum, is an enclosed room with a single door; its interior is dark and mysterious, a restrictive space open only to the presiding ritually pure priest. Meanwhile, the mosque's well-lit interiors could be approached from any direction and were open to all believers (Dehejia, 353).

Aybak's mosque was built in 1192 to 1196 using local Hindu artisans. It had a 212-foot by 150-foot open courtyard used for communal prayer. The Mecca side of the courtyard was dominated by a hall with five arches; the central one was 45 feet high. These arches were meant to resemble Persian prototypes. But the Indian artisans who constructed them had not yet mastered the true arch, which was common to Middle Eastern and European architecture, so they used the traditional corbelling techniques of erecting from both sides of the gateway successive stones slightly projecting further then the previous one until they meet at the apex.

On the Southeast side of this courtyard was a tall minaret, the Qutb Minar, which was originally 238 feet high, one of the tallest brick minarets in the world. It was seen by its medieval builders as Islam's tower of victory over

Hindu India. As if to reinforce this message and to legitimize their rule in India, the inscription on the minaret proclaims, "To cast the long shadow of god over the conquered city of the Hindus." The architectural model for the Qutb Minar mosque comes from the mosque architecture of Ghazni, Afghanistan, but the building also has a number of distinctly Hindu elements because the builders were local Hindu craftsmen. They employed traditional Hindu building techniques and designs in constructing what must have been to them an entirely new style of architecture. Although decorated with bands of sacred Arabic calligraphy and leafy arabesques that were common design elements of Islamic architecture, the mosque also had carved Qur'anic verses intermingled with Hindu floral motifs creating a hybrid style that was to become the hallmark of Indian Islamic architecture. Another novel form of architecture was the Muslim tomb. Sultan Shams al-Din **Iltutmish** (1211–1236), the third Delhi sultan, built himself a magnificent tomb behind the mosque with a corbelled dome. The dome had a plain exterior but an interior richly caved with verses from the Qur'an. This is a deviation from early Islamic practice that reinvented the pre-Islamic tradition of glorifying the personage of the ruler (Dehejia, 258). Other Muslim rulers of India imitated this practice in building magnificent funerary architectures.

Sultan Allauddin Khilji (r. 1296–1316) further expanded the Qutb mosque adding a ceremonial gateway with a true arch form, indicating that by now local artisans had mastered the art of constructing the true arch and dome. Another decorative innovation in the façade of this gateway was the carved and decorated red sandstone intermixed with white marble; this was to develop into a major decorative art form in later Muslim times. Within the context of Islam, these design elements have a deeper spiritual meaning of the singleness of God and his presence everywhere as well a reaffirmation that God is the source of all matter (Dehejia, 259).

Between the coming of the first Islamic Turkish and Afghan rulers in the twelfth century and the arrival of the Mughuls in the sixteenth century, various Islamic dynasties ruled over North India and adapted various architectural styles from outside India. In the late thirteenth century, the Tughluqs built their buildings in Afghan style while the Lodhi sultans in Delhi brought Persian court culture and architecture to India (Craven, 197). The Persian architectural style was also influenced by the North Indian religious and secular architecture of the Great Mughals, who overthrew the Lodhi dynasty in 1526, and were to be the last and greatest Islamic dynasty to rule North India. Their hybrid style architecture became the symbol of the modern Indian state, such as the Delhi Red Fort and the Taj Mahal at Agra. *See also* Documents 1, 2, 5, 7, 8, and 16.

Further Reading

Allen, Charles. *The Search for the Buddha: The Men Who Discovered India's Lost Religion.* New York: Carroll & Graf, 2003.

Basham, A. L. *The Wonder that Was India.* London: Sidgwick & Jackson, 1982.

Beal, Samuel. *Buddhist Records of the Western World.* Reprint ed. Delhi, India: Oriental Books Reprint Corporation, 2004.

Craven, Roy C. *Indian Art: A Concise History.* London: Thames & Hudson, 1997.

Dehejia, Vidya. *Indian Art.* London: Phalidon Press Ltd., 1997.

Lannoy, Richard. *The Speaking Tree: A Study of Indian Culture and Society.* Oxford, UK: Oxford University Press, 1971.

Mookerji, Radha Kumud. *Ancient Indian Education: Brahmanical and Buddhist*. Delhi, India: Motilal Banarsidass, 1974.

Siddiqui, Iqtidar Husain. *Medieval India: Essays in Intellectual Thought and Culture*. Vol. 1. Delhi, India: Manohar, 2003.

Raman N. Seylon

5. SOCIETY

One of the most detailed and also earliest accounts of Indian society during the Middle Ages was written by the Chinese Buddhist scholar monk **Xuanzang** (602–664 C.E.), who came to India during the reign of Emperor **Harsha**, or Harsha Vardana (590–647 C.E.). Xuanzang stayed in India for nearly 13 years and visited many kingdoms, including Harsha's capital **Kanauj**, and returned to China in 645. Upon his return, he translated some seventy-three Buddhist works and, in addition, also produced a voluminous record of his travels in In-tu, or India, known as "the records of the western regions" or Su-Yu-Ki. This text gives us a vivid verbal portrait of India during the midseventh century. Xuanzang notes the following about Indian towns:

> The towns and villages of India have gates and surrounding walls that are broad and high; the streets and the lanes are narrow and crooked. The thoroughfares are dirty and stalls are managed on both sides of the road with appropriate signs. Butchers, fishermen, actors, executioners, scavengers and so on have their dwelling outside the city. Incoming and outgoing these persons are bound to keep on the left side of the road till they arrive at their homes (as the right side is used for relieving oneself, and as communal toilets. (Beal, 73–74)

Xuanzang's street-side details, such as why certain professionals are kept outside the city gates and in dirty surroundings, illustrate the underlying nature of Indian society, its customs, and taboos; especially those concerning notions of purity and pollution, which colored all aspects of Indian society.

Xuanzang also talks about clothing and the everyday fashions and customs of seventh-century India. Both sexes wore long unstitched plain rectangular garments wrapped around the body and made of cotton, silk, hemp, or fine goat-hair wool, depending on the status of the individual and the season of the year. White is the preferred color for clothing; brightly dyed or ornamental designs were inappropriate as public attire. Most males wound their garment through their midsection; it was then gathered under the armpits and loosely hung over their right shoulder leaving the left shoulder and lower calves exposed. During cold seasons, males wore a short close-fitting jacket, which may have been recently introduced from Central Asia. As head cover, men wore "hats" (possibly turbans) and adorned themselves with heavy jeweled necklaces as status markers. In public, most women completely covered their shoulders and their robes reached the ground. The female hair style then in vogue was tying a small circular bun at the crown with the rest of the hair let loose and adorned with fresh fragrant flowers. Most men wore their facial hair in the form mustaches; a few shaved or had styles that reflected individuals' status, personal taste, caste custom, or a denominational identity (Beal, 75).

The Indian propensity for personal cleanliness that is detailed by Xuanzang had as much do with prevailing ideas about purity and pollution as with hygiene. He states that "All wash themselves before eating and never use that had been left over (from a former meal): they do not pass the dishes. Wooden or stone vessels, when used, must be destroyed . . . After eating they cleanse their teeth with a willow stick (tooth brush) and wash their hands and mouth. Until these abolutions are finished they do not touch each other" (Beal, 77).

Another traveller who wrote extensively about India was Abu Raihan Muhammad ibn Ahmad Alberuni (973–1048), the great Persian-speaking scholar from Khwarezm (Uzbekistan), who travelled to India in the early tenth century, nearly five centuries after Xuanzang's epic pilgrimage. Alberuni has left us a monumental account of Indian culture in a work titled *Tahqiq ma lil-hind*, popularly known as *Alberuni's India*. It was written at a time of ruthless military campaigns by the Turkish Afghan monarch Sultan Mahmud of Ghazani. These conquests led to a still-resonant resentment toward the foreign Muslim invader and his faith among the Hindus of Northwest India. Alberuni wrote the following unique eyewitness account of the impact of the early invasions:

> Mahmud utterly ruined the prosperity of the country . . . and the Hindus became like atoms of dust scattered in all directions. They developed the most inveterate aversion towards all Muslims. This is also the reason why Hindu sciences have retired far away from these parts of the country conquered by us and have fled to places which our hand cannot yet reach, to Kashmir, Benaras, and other places. And the antagonism between them and all foreigners receive more and more nourishment both from political and religious sources. (Scahav, 22)

Commenting on the draped tradition of Indian male garments, Alberuni makes a rather surprising statement that Hindus use their turbans for their trousers (Robinson, 490). He describes Brahminical Hindu society as a self-assured, narrow-minded, and arrogant—a society smug in its self-centered worldview and its hostility toward foreigners. This worldview is perhaps a xenophobic reaction resulting from 30 years of Muslim raids. Alberuni elaborates as follows:

> Hindus believe that there is no country like theirs, no nation like theirs, no things like theirs, no religion like theirs, and no science like theirs. They are haughty, foolishly vain, self-conceited and stolid. They are, by nature, niggardly in communicating that which they know, and they take the greatest possible care to withhold it from men of another caste among their own people, still much more, of course, from any foreigner . . . . There haughtiness is such that, if you tell them of any science or scholar in Khurasam and Persis (Persia), they think you to be both an ignoramus and a liar. If they travelled and mixed with other nations, they could soon change their mind, for their ancestors were not as narrow-minded as the present generation is. (Scahav, 23–23)

Castes in Medieval India

Alberuni also gives a vivid picture of that quintessentially Indian social institution: the **caste system**. He notes that social hierarchy pervades all Hindu social institutions. Muslim society and religion stood entirely on the other side of such values, considering that all men are equal, and this, as Alberuni saw it, was the greatest obstacle that prevented any direct approach or understanding between Hindus and Muslims.

According to Alberuni, the "Hindus call their castes as *varnas*, (colours) and from a genealogical point of view they call them *jataka* (*jati*), i.e., births" (Scahav, v. 1, 100–101). Alberuni notes that the castes were four in number and then gives the rational behind the status of each of these four castes as narrated in the Hindu creation story:

1. The highest caste is the (priestly) Brahmana (Brahmin caste); of whom the sacred books of the Hindus tell they were created from the head of Brahman (i.e., the all-prevailing godhead). And as Brahman is only a name for the force called nature, and as the head is the highest part of the body, the Brahmana (Brahmin caste) are given the choice part of the entire community. Therefore, the Hindus venerate themselves as the very best of mankind.
2. The next caste is the Kshatriyas, who were created . . . from the shoulders and hands of Brahman. Their status is not much below that of the priestly Brahmin caste.
3. They are followed by the Vaisyas, who were created from the thigh of Brahman.
4. Finally the Sudras, who were created from his feet.
   Much, however, as these two later classes differ from each other, they lived together in the same houses and lodgings (Scahav, v. 1, 100–101).

The origins of this novel system, according to most historians, go back to the time of the early Indo-European nomads, called Aryans, who migrated to India some time around 1500 B.C.E. and established their cultural dominance over the indigenous populations. This four-fold division of society, called the *varna*, was sanctified by Aryan sacred texts and considered to be divinely ordained. Similar types of social divisions are also found in ancient Iran, from where the Aryans had migrated. As noted by Alberuni, the ancient four-fold social division that distinguished Indian society comprised the Brahmin, Kshatriya, Vaisya, and Sudra castes. According to the legal code of Ancient Hindu lawgiver Manu, the Brahmin's duty was priesthood and scholarship. The Brahmins are ritual specialists and revered as worthy teachers. The Kshatriya are warriors and administrators whose duty is to protect the common people. The Vaisya were cattle breeders and estate owners, and people involved in all forms of commercial activity. The Sudras were agricultural laborers or serfs.

There was no sharp social division between the Brahmin, Kshatriya, and Vaisya castes, which were considered the twice-born. These castes had an initiation ceremony, during which they received a sacred thread that marked them off as distinct from the lower Sudra castes. This sharp social division between the twice-born and the Sudra meant the latter was to serve the other three. According to the codes of Manu, it is better to do one's caste duty badly than to do another caste's duty well. Therefore, in an ideal sense, each individual is expected to fulfil only his assigned duty, and his place in society is fixed. This was a Brahmin-centric model, because nearly all early sacred texts were authored by Brahmins, who preferred to see the world around them ordered in this way. However, the Indian reality was far more complex, and this ideal precept of the four-fold caste was rarely ever fully carried out in practice.

These ideals were often seriously compromised in the ancient and medieval periods. For example, the law books do not favor the Brahmin caste engaging in **agriculture** because it inflicts injury on small life forms. But such prescriptive rules were widely ignored in practice. In reality, Brahmins, like other castes, pursued all manner of trade and professions, and several royal families and generals were members of the Brahmin caste.

Even Hindu sacred texts are not in accord concerning caste duties and roles. Although the *Bhagavad Gita*, one of the most authoritative and revered Hindu religious texts, seems to sanction the four-fold division of Hindu society and urges each caste to adhere to its allotted duties. However, it does so in an advisory, not a commanding tone; one should do so for the sake of one's own best interest, not to adhere to an inflexible socioreligious code. With respect to the *varna* categories, the *Gita* notes that the four-fold division of society was created by the creator, according to the distribution of the individual's own "gunas" (qualities or tendencies) and past actions (karma), but the creator is not responsible for the results derived from it (*Gita*, 4.13). The *Gita* also seems to reiterate Manu's legal dictum that a person should act in accordance with one's own nature, even if in doing so one may appear faulty: "It is better performing one's won duty than engaging in any other duties, however well you might attend to them. It is better to die engaging in accordance with one's own nature, for others' duties invite peril" (*Gita*, 3.35) (Swami B.T. Tripurari, 120, 145).

In medieval Hindu India, the Brahmin generally lived under the patronage of a king, often in segregated settlements, and were granted tax-free lands by the state. These lands were farmed by local peasants who paid taxes or portions of their harvest directly to the Brahmin. There were also large Brahmin estate holders who cultivated their tax-free land using hired laborers. The Brahmin also had a highly respected position at court or served and earned his livelihood as a teacher in all branches of medieval learning. The Brahmins of the period also founded Hindu monastic orders based on earlier Buddhist models.

The duty of the second class, the Kshatriya, was to defend and protect the Hindu social order. It was possible, in historic times, for a martial caste or tribe to claim Kshatriya status by the role they played, such as the ancestors of the present **Rajputs** of Rajasthan, who descended from Central Asian invaders.

The Vaisya *varna* included estate holders and cattle breeders but generally meant all commercial classes. Most were wealthy and organized into powerful merchant guilds (*sreni*). Wealthy Vaisyas were respected by kings, and many were also patrons of arts and sponsored large religious causes. In ancient India, a number of inscriptions record great donations made by Vaisya merchants to religious causes, especially to Buddhist monasteries. These merchant guilds were politically important and self-governing. They had their own laws, which the king was expected to recognize and respect. The guild acted as a social safety net for all members of the caste.

The Sudras or serfs were not twice-born and were treated as second-class citizens, being on the fringes of Indo-European-speaking society. Although, in practice, there was no bar to the free mobility of labor, there was also a strong stigma attached to certain professions, such as butchers, meat sellers, hunters, leather manufacturers, barbers, undertakers, hangmen, sweepers, and garbage collectors. Those who performed these professions were considered ritually polluted, because all these professions had to deal with handling articles that were deemed impure.

Alberuni notes that, after the Sudra *varna*, are people called Antyaja—those outside the *varna* system or outcastes—who rendered various kinds of menial services. During his visits, Alberuni found eight kinds of outcastes, as defined by their professions, within Indian society: fuller, shoemaker, juggler, basket and shield maker, sailor, fisherman, hunter, and the weaver. The four *varnas* do not live among the outcastes, which reside outside the villages or towns or the four *varna*. Other groups, called Doma and Chandala, were also not part of the four-fold division of the Hindu social order. The people did the dirtiest work, like cleaning the village latrines and getting rid of carcasses. They were considered a separate class and distinguished by their unclean occupations.

These people were the medieval equivalent to present-day outcastes, or untouchables. They were called the fifth class and were not allowed to live near the settlement of the four clean *varnas*, but in special quarters outside the towns and villages. The main task of the Chandala was the carrying and cremation of corpses; they also served as royal executioners. Any person of the upper caste who had any close relation with a Chandala was likely to lose his status.

At this period, the Chandalas, who may have accounted for a little over 6 percent of the Indian population, led a very demeaning life. Their presence, even the very sight of them, was considered inauspicious or polluting to members of other *varnas*. None of the other *varnas* would touch, let alone eat food either handled or prepared by the Chandala.

A major social change that took place in the medieval period was a shift in focus from the division of the four *varnas* to the development within them of a number of social groups or *jati*. The relations between the *jati* groups were governed by three basic rules: (1) rule of endogamy (marriage within the group), (2) commensality (food only received by members of the same or a higher group), and (3) craft exclusiveness (each man lives by the trade of his profession). It is the *jati* group that is known to outsiders as "caste." The word *caste* itself derived from the Portuguese term *casta* or something that is not mixed. It comes from the Latin root *castus* or chaste. This word was applied in India in the midfifteenth century by the Portuguese and may have been used by the Portuguese in the same sense as race, as they saw Indian society divided into a number of separate groups. Indian historian D. D. Kosombi, in his work *An Introduction to the Study of Indian History*, elaborates this view that castes did not arise out of the internal division in the original Vedic Aryan society but from an external process of coming together of various populations.

The entire course of Indian history shows tribal elements being fused to the dominant general society. This factor is the basis for the foundation of the most distinct feature of Indian society, the caste system. The term *jati* implies tribes. Tribes tend to be endogenous; and, as they entered the general society, they also carried their endogenous customs. And, if the tribe was already an agricultural community, once it became a *jati* group, it would become the peasant caste of that region. Over time, a number of small primitive hunter-gather groups, living in forest areas, would lose their traditional livelihood due to the relentless advance of the peasant community. If these hunter-gather groups were subjugated by the peasant agriculturalists, they might also be reduced to the status of the lowest *jatis* and outside the four *varnas* altogether.

One of the earliest accounts of Chandalas came from the Chinese scholar monk **Faxian**, who visited India during the early Gupta Period, some time between 399 and 414 C.E. (*see* **Gupta Empire**). As to the Chandalas, Faxian noted the following:

> Through the country the people kill no living thing nor drink wine, no do they eat garlic or onions, with the exception on Chandalas only. The Chandalas are named "evil men" and dwell apart form others; if they enter town or market, they sound a piece of wood to (announce their presence and to) separate themselves; then men, knowing who they are; avoid coming in to contact with then. . . . (Only the) Chandalas hunt and sell flesh. (Beal, 1969, xxxvii–xxxviii)

The Chandalas, a name that is synonymous with the earliest untouchable castes, were once categorized as hunter-gathers in ancient texts. Later, they were barred from becoming peasant cultivators and forced to be a part of a large pool of landless manual seasonal laborers. Historians also see the period between 500 B.C.E. to 400 C.E. as the period of the Indian caste system and its supporting ideology (Habib, 161–179).

Just as in the case with trade guilds, the existence of caste also emerged out of social necessity. This caste-based social organization gave its members a sense of mutual and collective security, a refuge for destitute members and orphans (a form of social safety net), and fostered a sense of order and control over their affairs and autonomy at a period that was often marked by political turmoil.

This system of separate, discrete social groups was to permeate South Asia with the spread of Brahminical Hindu ideology. In the **Tamil country** at the eastern tip of South India, we have no evidence of the four *varnas* and discrete social groups before the arrival of Brahminical Hinduism. By the tenth century, the Chola Period, the caste system, based on Brahminical ritual domination, was an integral part of the Tamil social landscape. Largely due to its late introduction, the *varnas* in Tamil country are mainly Brahmins, who were considered migrants from the north, and Sudras, or the agricultural Tamil castes and untouchables. Two rival confederacies called the "left hand" and "right hand" caste groups formed in Tamil country during the twelfth and thirteenth centuries. These new landholding castes may have emerged from such former martial and pastoral tribal groups, such as the Palli and Srigopala, who were either new migrants or had previously lived in peripheral areas. These new land holding castes were in direct competition with the older established landholding groups (Grewal, 209). The animosity and feuds between them lasted nearly 1,000 years. The majority of the cultivating and laboring castes, along with traders and weavers, belonged to the right-hand section while the left included a large number of craftsmen, but few agricultural castes, and thus are seen as recent migrants to Tamil country.

The organization of castes and the severe sanctions as well as the threat of social sanctions for violation of caste rules were instrumental in allowing Hindu India to preserve its core cultural traditions in the face of nearly 1,000 years of repeated conquests and long periods of foreign rule. Many medieval Indian reformist spiritual guides saw the hierarchical and inclusive nature of castes as morally repugnant to their inclusive egalitarian religious agendas of social equality and brotherhood. These reform movements belonging to either Hindu denominational (Saivaite or Vishnavite) Bhakti sects, such as that of Bhagat Ramanand (1366–1467), or those seeking interfaith unity, such that of Kibir (1398–1448), who sought Hindu Islamic synthesis and tried to abolish caste divisions among his followers, began over time to acquire the characteristics of a distinct new caste, and some even divided into separate hieratical castes, like social groupings, among themselves.

In many ways, the beginning of the thirteenth century marks a break in traditional Indian society, partly due to the intrusions of Islam and large-scale urbanization and craft specialization. The Islamic legal system did not recognize caste, but only the status differentiations between a free man and a slave. In spite of this, the general attitude of Muslims toward a caste-based social order was one of tolerant indifference. Muslim rulers allowed the continuation of earlier caste-based restrictions, and did not ideologically challenge it, as they had condemned Hindu polytheism and idol worship. The Indian Marxist historian Irfan Habib has suggested that "in so far as the caste system had helped to generate larger revenues from villages and lower the wages in the cities, the Indo-Muslim regime had every reason to protect it, however indifferent, if not hostile, they may have been for the Brahmin idol worshippers" (172–173).

Muslims also brought new technology and products, such as paper manufacturing, bitumen and lime cement, horseshoes, and the spinning wheel, and all these new products led to the creation of new professions, such as paper manufacturing, lime mixing, and the creation of new castes. Many groups that chose to take up these new occupations also converted to Islam, thereby over time creating a large Muslim population. In spite of such conversions, previous caste practices continued to influence these converted communities, which practiced endogenous marriage and segregated and looked down on untouchables. However, there were also sections of the Muslim population whose caste rules were weak and allowed for more flexible marriage patterns and occupational mobility (Habib, 172–174).

Religious prejudices and caste taboos were strong between Hindu and Muslim communities. Alberuni noted that all outsiders and non-Hindus were considered *mleccha* or unclean by the conventions of Hindu caste rules. **Ibn Battuta** (1304–1368), a fourteenth-century Berber traveller from Tangier, Morocco, who also briefly sought employment as a *quadi* (sharia judge) in Delhi under **Muhammad bin Tughluq** (1325–1351) gives us some insight into Hindu-Muslim relationships. He informs us that Muslims were not allowed into Hindu homes or to use Hindu utensils.

> The infidels of India would neither admit Muslims into their homes nor give food and water in their own utensils, although they will not hurt or insult them. Occasionally, we were compelled to ask some of the Hindus of India to cook meat for us. They used to bring it in their own cooking pots, and sit at a distance from us. They placed the food on a disposable banana leaf, and whatever remained was eaten by the dogs for birds. If any innocent child happened to pick anything from that remnant, they would beat him and compel him to eat cow dung which, according to their beliefs, purifies. [However] Muslims had no objection to accepting eatables made and offered by the Hindus. (Mahdi Husain, 34)

It may well be that the Muslims of this area took every opportunity to mingle with Hindus and did not like to be treated as untouchables by being socially ostracized. But for the Hindus, any close association with Muslims brought with it the danger of ritual pollution, and the threat of losing one's caste status. In spite of this uneasy relationship, the bitter communal tension and riots that became common in later colonial and postcolonial times was never a notable part of medieval urban life under Muslim rule. Hindus also showed devotion to Muslim saints, whose tombs were venerated by both committees.

Caste-based marriage taboos were another complication in the North Indian caste system. The institutions of *gotra* and *pravara* existed usually among the Brahmin castes but also among some of the twice-born castes. The term *gotra* means cowshed and roughly corresponds to the territory of a clan group that holds to the belief that all its members trace their descent from a legendary sage. All members of the *gotra* are forbidden to marry persons of the same *gotra*. The *pavara* refers to any other *gotra* that shares a remote relationship with another *gotra*'s founding sage ancestor; members of this *gotra* are also forbidden as marriage partners to the related *gotra*. By the early Middle Ages, this system had become rigid and castes had become fully endogenous.

The Indian Joint Family and the Four Stages of Hindu Life

Just below the caste is the family, and the Indian family was, and still is in rural India, a joint family. That is, members of a number of generations and, in its full sense, uncles, cousins, and brothers live under one roof with their aged parents. The senior active member is generally the head of the household. Within the joint family, there was no sense of individual property but the right of maintenance is granted to all male family heads and their families. All married women become members of their husband's household.

Left to itself, a joint family will increase in size until it becomes so large that it becomes unmanageable and breaks up. More commonly, such a partition takes place after the death of the head of the household, and his property is divided among his sons.

Just as the Hindu social order was divided into four *varnas*, the ideal life of an upper caste Hindu is likewise divided into four stages. For the twice-born, a ceremony marks the transition from childhood to studenthood (*brahmacarin*), where a twice-born individual leads a celibate life under the guidance of a teacher, often living with him as a junior member of the household. After getting his education, the individual returns to his family to lead the life of a householder (*grahasta*) after entering an arranged marriage. After having children, and in his late middle age, he becomes a forest hermit (*vanaprastha*) free from any material attachment and lives a life of reflection and meditation. At his ripe old age, he becomes a wandering mendicant, or *sannyasin*. These stages are only an ideal prescription, and few Hindus ever honor it to its full extent. Most genuine *sannyasins* in India are men who omitted the householder stage.

Modern Discourse Concerning the Caste System

No modern discourse about the Indian caste system is ever complete without looking at the major work of French structural anthropologist Louis Dumont (1911–1998) about the deeper underlying logic behind Indian castes. In the mid-1960s, as a novel way to explain this unique Indian social institution, Dumont contrasted the Indian caste-based system with the Western European social system. He noted that the Indian caste system is different from the European social system in its central ideology as the caste system is an extreme form of social stratification. In relation to its core ideology, the values of the Indian caste system could be directly contrasted with an egalitarian society, which at least in theory, the West holds. The two cardinal Western European ideals of liberty and equality follow from the conception that a human being is an individual, and all humans should be free and equal. The caste system, on the other hand, is centered on a system of hierarchy, which divides the entire society into large number of hereditary groups distinguished from one another and connected together by the following three principles:

1. Separation (in matters of marriage and contract).
2. Division of labor (where each group has, by theory or tradition, a profession from which their members come to depend only within certain limits).
3. Hierarchy (which ranks the groups as relatively superior or inferior to one another). This is the main characteristic of this system.

Dumont further noted that caste is also a "state of mind" and a pan-Indian institution of ideas and values. The three principles of separation, division of labor, and hierarchy rest on one fundamental concept, or one that is reducible to a single principle, which is the opposition of the pure to the impure.

As for the first principle of separation, it is the result of this opposition, or the idea that pure and impure must be separate. Castes separate themselves from one another by prohibiting marriage outside the group just as they prohibit contact and dining between persons belonging to different groups. For the second principle of division of labor the underlying idea is that pure and impure occupations must be kept apart and, likewise, the third principle of hierarchy is based on the same premise that pure is superior to impure. The entire system is founded on "the necessary and the hierarchical coexistence of the two opposites." Dumont further stated that this opposition between pure and impure as the basic foundation of the caste system is true only in an intellectual sense. It is by reference to this opposition that the entire society of castes appears consistent and rational to those who live by it (Dumont, 43–44).

The caste system, for Dumont, comprises specialization and interdependence of the groups of castes that constitute it. Specialization leads to separation between these groups, but it is also oriented toward the needs of the entire group. This relationship to the entire group must be emphasized, and it is this that links the division of labor with the hierarchy. It also distinguishes this Indian social division of labor from a modern economic division of labor, which is oriented mainly toward the individual's profit, subject to market forces, which is not so in the case of castes, where the majority of relationships are personal and are in reference to the hierarchical collectivity of the system.

In his book *Homo Hierarchicus: Essai sur le système des castes* (1966), Dumont saw the hierarchical principle as being at the very core of the caste system; without it there would be no caste. For Dumont, the caste system must be identified in terms of Hindu religious ideology and not as the result of economic or social forces. Other sociologists had long challenged this all-encompassing symmetrical model as too narrow, because it ignores crucial economic factors. They point out that Dumont's elegant interpretation and appealing theoretical framework is built on false premises to explain what India is, and Dumont's contrast between hierarchical India and egalitarian West is too simplistic and seriously flawed. Dumont's critics point out that he fails to see the economic forces that have radically altered the basis of the caste system in the last 100 years. The hereditary division of labor that was the system's foundation is now nearly gone, and what Dumont sees as primary, the religious or personal element, is only its surviving residue and not a crucial economic one (Habib, 161–164).

The Sacred Cows of Hindu India

An offshoot of Dumont's all-encompassing analysis of the Indian caste system is his explanation of Hindu dietary taboos. There is no Hindu dietary rule that evokes more wonder and puzzlement than the taboo against beef consumption. Even Alberuni commented on this taboo. He noted that cattle served humans by carrying loads, ploughing fields, and providing milk for **food** and dung for fuel. Therefore, the cow was worth far more alive than dead; this economic factor was, for Alberuni, the key behind the prohibition of killing and eating cattle.

For Dumont, this taboo could be logically explained by the Hindu ideas of purity and pollution. Since the time of the Vedic Aryans, some 3,500 years ago, cattle were storehouses of wealth and providers of ritually pure food. For other reasons, they were venerated and held sacred. But there was no taboo against cow sacrifice, which was often the high point of Aryan rituals, and the sacrificed cattle were consumed communally as concentrated food. So this taboo was a late development that must have arisen sometime during the late classical period. During the early part of the first millennium C.E., the formerly Jain and Buddhist ideology of not killing, or *ahminsa*, also became a core value of Hinduism (*see* **Jainism**). This meant that vegetarianism was considered superior to meat eating. Now, eating meat is not only a consumption of a less pure or polluting food but also a sinful food. The cow being the most venerated of all animals, it was also equated with the ritual purity of the Brahmin. With the taboo against consumption of beef, a dead cow is now the sole responsibility of an untouchable, who is the appointed remover of pollution. Because his ritual opposite the Brahmin was now being equated with the purity of a live cow, killing a cow is considered the moral equivalent of killing a Brahmin (Dumont, 146–151). This, according to Dumont, explains the killing of a cow, and the aversion toward eating it.

All products of a live cow are considered pure and are utilized, including its bodily waste. Alberuni and Xuanzang inform us that cow dung was used in various capacities in medieval Indian society, as is still done today in village India. Fresh cow dung is a mineral-rich slur with an earthy fragrance and has a number of practical usages, including as a floor coating. A floor coated with cow dung stays cooler and is water absorbent. Xuanzang reported that the floor of the average Indian home was regularly plastered with a cow dung and mud mixture to smoothen and harden it and then sprinkled with flowers. Sucha coating was also believed to possess insect repellent and antiseptic properties, which explains Alberuni's report that cow dung was used to cleanse and purify eating spaces: "Hindus eat singly, one by one on table cloth of dung" (eating space coated with fresh cow dung). He also described the everyday precautions taken to safeguard against food-related pollution: "They do not make use of the remainder of a meal, and the plates from which they have eaten are thrown away if they are earthen" (Sachau, vol. I, 180).

Sexual Relations in the Middle Ages

Despite the rather puritanical tone of Hindu public life and its sacred texts, having regular sexual relations with his wife was considered a husband's essential religious duty. The sexual relationship between couples was also considered the best among all available pleasures. The physical act of intercourse and its variations are celebrated in graphic detail in Hindu sacred iconography carved on some temple exteriors. The ideal of feminine beauty in India is a slim waist with large breasts and hips (Basham, 171). One of the earliest surviving guide-books for sex in world literature is the *Kamasutra*, composed by Mallanaga Vatsayana some time between fourth and sixth centuries C.E. during the Gupta era. It was based on earlier manuals that had long since vanished. Although, in modern times, the *Kamasutra* has become the most famous sex manual in history and is synonymous with various sexual positions during intercourse, this is a misunderstanding of the content and purpose of the text. It was writ-ten mainly to serve as a guidebook for refined living among upper-caste indi-viduals, where sex is only one among the various pleasures and activities for a complete life. A study of this text gives us an idea of the ideal prescriptive life-style of a medieval sophisticated urbanite.

Apart from art and literature, the use of sex for more profound and lofty needs also permeates Indian spirituality. During the late Middle Ages, espe-cially in Hinduism, we find the growth of heterodox tantric sects, which also use sexual intercourse as a means to achieve a higher level of spirituality and as an aid for spiritual salvation (Basham, 337).

The erotic life in ancient and medieval India was generally heterosexual. This does not rule out the presence of all other forms of sexual relations such as homosexuality. Still, anything other than heterosexual relations was not considered legitimate pleasure, and the *Kamasutra* treats homosexual acts more or less in a clinical fashion and not with genuine enthusiasm (Basham, 172).

Lives of Hindu Women in Medieval India

In relation to the early Vedic Period, the condition of Hindu upper caste woman in medieval India was one of subordination, with little personal free-dom either within or without the household. Women in medieval India lacked the right to make free choices about their personal life and were under the au-thority of their fathers during childhood, their husbands during adulthood, and their appointed guardians during widowhood. They did, however, have limited property rights, which, if they were widows, were not available dur-ing earlier periods. Movable property, such as cash, jewellery, and clothing, were given to a bride as her own share of the family fortune. A husband might exercise certain rights over his wife's property but it was considered as be-longing to her and was passed on to her daughters and not to her husband. In comparison to other medieval civilizations, Hindu women's property rights were far greater (Basham). As today, the intellectual life of medieval Indian women varied according to caste and class. Upper-class women took an active interest in arts and sciences; but for the vast majority in rural India, a woman's life revolved around household or farm work.

By the first century C.E., there is a gradual hardening of the role of women within the orthodox Hindu tradition. Although women were expected to be pious, they could not become priests nor were they encouraged to take the up the life of asceticism. However, in heterodox traditions, women still had im-portant roles. This is especially true in Hindu Tantric sects of this period, where female devotees played a major role and women had important places in the Tantric priesthood and Tantric orders of female ascetics.

The primary role of women within Hindu tradition was to marry—unlike men they could only marry once—and to take care of the family. Their duties were to wait on their husbands, to cook the family meals, and to produce male offspring. A virtuous woman was expected to put her husband's and her children's welfare before her own. Girls married at an early age, and the birth of a male child was one of the most important events in the life of a married woman. Members of a household were often married early by their parents and marriage was a family affair and not the concern of an individual couple (Grewal, 444). Affluent household members could have more than one wife, but, because the average Hindu could not afford to maintain more than one spouse, monogamy was the norm. The great model of femininity in medieval India, as today, was Princess Sita, the heroine of the grand epic *Ramayana*, who faithfully followed her hero husband Prince Rama into the wilderness to endure a life of exile and hardship without any remorse or regret.

Apart from religiously sanctioned norms and restrictions, women's own biological differences were used to maintain their subordinate status within a Hindu household. The Hindu obsession with purity and pollution created disabilities for a woman, who, during the time of menstruation, was regarded as impure and her husband was not allowed to come near her. Similarly, just after childbirth, women are not allowed to touch any vessels, and meals were consumed elsewhere and never within the house because it were considered a polluted area. The duration of this period of impurity varied form caste to caste—8 days for Brahmin households and 30 for those categorized as Sudra. But those outside the caste system had no fixed times for such social quarantine (Grewal, 448).

The right of a widow to inherit her husband's property was not recognized in Hindu legal texts until the third century B.C.E. Earlier, only males had the right to inherit family property, while the women were granted only maintenance. In medieval times, there was an increased recognition of the widow's right. The dictums of the Hindu law of inheritance, noted Alberuni, gave the daughter one-fourth of the family's wealth in relation to a son, and this was spent on her before her marriage and was also given as part of her dowry. After marriage, she received no income from her father's household. Alberuni based his information mainly on Hindu legal texts; but one of the dangers in using the ancient normative codes listed in Hindu legal texts is that there was great deal of regional variation within India. And these Hindu legal codes written by Brahmin jurists only had a prescriptive function; they were neglected altogether by most of the lower castes. The status of a Hindu widow varied not only over time but regionally and also from caste to caste as well as her position within the household. If the widow was young and childless she did not inherit any property of her husband, but the heirs of her deceased husband had the social obligation to provide her with basic sustenance and clothing as long as she lived. But the widow's rights over her husband's estate did grow over time and, by late middle ages, reformist Hindu jurists even gave widows a limited right to dispose of a husband's estate if a suitable heir was lacking, although in practice this right varied regionally. This represented a major expansion of the widow's right, because in earlier days the proceeds of the property in all such cases were given to charity or assumed by the state.

By the late Middle Ages, women also had a greater say in the disposal of family property. A temple inscription dated to the thirteenth century in Chidambaram, Tamil Nadu, records the sale of a property where a senior Brahmin widow and her daughter-in-laws had equal rights in the sale proceeds with her two sons and grandsons, and all the women had to give their consent for disposal of the family property, although the senior male members acted as signatories and as guardians who undertook the transactions (Nagaswami, 84–88). In spite of these reforms in widow's inheritance, in terms of customs and institutions, the late medieval period (1200–1800) was the most conservative time in Indian history, when Hindu widows had no right to remarry, and the wife was separated from her husband only by death, because Hindus have no divorce.

When North India fell under the rule of Islamic dynasties in the eleventh century, Hindu elites emulated the upper-class Muslim practice of female segregation or *purda* by instituting their own system of female seclusion, which shielded women of the household from the sight of any man, other than family members or close relatives. In later Hindu empires, such as **Vijayanagar**, royal women travelled in covered litters or palanquins in the manor of elite Muslim women of the **Delhi sultanate**. In spite of these restrictions, during the medieval period, aristocratic and upper-class Hindu women had freer mobility than women had in contemporary Islamic courts and the elaborate institutionalized *purdah* in India was mainly restricted to Muslim households in areas under direct Muslim rule (Grewal, 450). Hindu queens accompanied male rulers in temple rituals and on military campaigns. Medieval Arab travellers remarked in wondrous and disapproving tones about seeing queens in Hindu royal courts without veils (Basham, 179).

The only class of women outside such rules and restrictions comprised courtesans and temple dancers. Some royal courtesans were well accomplished, with great wealth and prestige; they even paid taxes to the state. These upper-crust courtesans were seen more as patrons of the arts and also resided in the most prestigious sections of the city, choosing the best accommodations available. Respected men could be seen in the company of such courtesans without facing social disapproval and visiting their homes regularly had no stigma attached to it. These women were also granted the rare privilege of being allowed to chew betel leaves with the queen (Grewal, 450). Their social position and fame is analogous to our modern-day mass media entertainers.

The practice of using professional dancers as an essential part of temple ritual was common in South India until the early twentieth century, and this was certainly a medieval social development (Basham, 185). In medieval period, most major Hindu temples had groups of temple dancers called *devadasis*. They were born and reared in the temple either as children of one of the temple dancers or were donated to the temple deity by their parents as a pious offering. They attended temple functions as dancers, performed other duties in the temple, and were paid from temple funds. Those among them who became courtesans to the wealthy and powerful were associated with the elite and some even had literary, poetic talents and were known for their scholarship as well as for being accomplished dancers. But they were still not as socially respected as married women of similar stature (Grewal, 450).

Colonial and medieval accounts give credence to the view that lower ranking *devadasis* functioned as ordinary prostitutes to support themselves and to provide funds for their temple. A fourteenth-century Arab source mentions a temple with sixty women who earned their money through prostitution and even offered services to travellers free of charge. Side-stepping the issue as whether such traveller's tales were of the same genre as the *Arabian Nights*, one thing seems clear: sex outside the conjugal setting was not viewed with disfavor in medieval Hindu society. The prostitute was recognized by the Hindu state, and to be regarded as a professional prostitute a woman had to be registered as such and only then had all the rights belonging to that profession. Prostitutes were said to be found in every town in medieval India, as Alberuni noted disapprovingly: "Hindus were not very severe in punishing whoredom (and) the fault laid with their kings." Alberuni also saw an economic incentive behind the toleration of the public sale of sex: "[Hindu] kings made them an attraction for their cities due to financial reasons [because] . . . they want to recover the expenditure on the army by the revenues that they derived from the business of temple girls both as fines and as taxes" (Grewal, 448). Outside this structured setting any women freelancing as a prostitute risked serious social sanctions; she would be forced to sever all ties with her household. In status, the freelancer was lower than the professional prostitute, who could even appear as a witness in a legal case. Professional prostitutes also were expected to abide by their own code of ethics and had to be seen as trustworthy in fulfilling their side of the agreement (Grewal, 453). In spite of this general tolerance toward courtesans and the prevalence of prostitution, adultery by women was not tolerated in Hindu India. Alberuni noted that an adulteress was driven from the husband's household and banished (Grewal, 448).

The Practice of Sati in Medieval India

In medieval India, if a Hindu wife lost her husband, she could not remarry. She had only two choices: perpetual widowhood or, as was the custom among certain castes, burning herself with honor. If a young upper-caste Hindu women chose widowhood she had to remain in the humiliating status of a widow as long as she lived. Under such status, she was expected to shave her hair; wear no jewellery or perfumes; eat one meal a day without meat, wine, or salt; and wear only white garments to mark her widowhood. Her days were passed in prayer and religious rituals, and she had to maintain an austere lifestyle until her death. Her only solace was the hope of being remarried to her husband in the next birth by her virtuous deeds. Alberuni noted that *sati* or self-immolation was preferable for many, because the widow was ill treated as long as she lived. They were considered inauspicious to everyone except their children. They were barred from attending any family festivals, and their presence was considered an ill omen to the household. As a result, a widow was shunned even by family servants and her life, if she was young; was a long period of continuous misery.

Sati was mainly practiced by the Brahmin or Kshatriya castes in Bengal or Rajesthan. This custom became common only in the Middle Ages. Some historians believe it received a boost after the early nomadic invasions because similar practices existed among the Sakas of Central Asia. There are numerous *sati* stones in Rajasthan and other parts of India commemorating wives who chose self-immolation upon the funeral pyre of their dead husbands. Among upper-caste women, the practice of *sati* was in theory a voluntary act, but it is possible that family pressure often drove a high-caste widow to self-immolation. But the act of *sati* is obligatory for the wives of Hindu Rajput royalty because it revolves around the notions of honor and virtue that are cardinal values for the martial Rajputs and other upper castes. For Rajputs, death is preferable to dishonor and humiliation at the hands of the victors. Alberuni noted "as regards the wives of kings, they are in the habit of burning themselves whether the woman wishes it or not. By which they desire to prevent any of them by chance, committing something unworthy of the illustrious husband. They made an exception only for women of advanced years and those who have children, for the son is the responsible protector of his mother" (Sachau, v. 2, 155).

Noclo dei Conti, a fifteenth-century Italian traveller, stated that as many as three-thousand wives and concubines of the king of Vijayanagar had pledged themselves to be burnt in the event of the ruler's death. Some South Indian kings were not only accompanied in death by their wives, but also by male courtiers, ministers, and palace servants. Criticism of the practice of *sati* appeared in medieval writings, especially among the Tantric schools of Hinduism. One Tantric writer wrote that a woman burning herself on her husband's pyre went straight to hell. But in spite of such heterodox views, the practice of female self-immolation received approval and support from orthodox medieval Hindu writers.

Lives of Muslim Women in Medieval India

We have little information about Islamic women during the early medieval period. Although there was no Muslim equal to the Hindu practice of *sati*, the Turkish Muslim invaders did bring with them similar notions of family honor. But the Muslims had different values concerning the idea of the family, and those pertaining to female inheritance and divorce. Because the Qur'an advocates the continuation of the family after the event of divorce or death, medieval Muslim women had a religious sanction to seek divorce and remarriage. Islamic religious codes also allow a divorced couple to seek reconciliation and remarriage. During the medieval period, Qur'anic statements concerning the position of women were far more advanced than those adhered to by any contemporary Hindu societies because they gave women better access to a religious life, property rights, and divorce. This does not necessarily mean that there was parity between males and females in medieval Islamic India, for the Qur'an also upholds many of the earlier patriarchical values and social structure and expects male members of the household to manage the social and economic affairs of women (Grewal, 454).

As regards family inheritance, the Qur'an emphasizes male child as equivalent to two females. The widow is given one-eighth of her husband's share of property if he has children and if not she receives one-fourth, whereas a widower gets nearly double in similar circumstances from his wife's property (Grewal, 454). These Qur'anic injunctions were only prescriptive and did not have legal sanctions. Within India, each Muslim community implemented its inheritance rules differently according to prevailing local customs, and there were wide variations. Among a few Muslim commercial families from India's west coast port city of Surat, female household heads did own and manage properties and directly managed their husband's business affairs after his death. And there are instances among the Muslim elites when the widow did gain control of the properties that were bequeathed to her late husband as trust. Many of the Islamic practices in India also have their roots in older pre-Islamic practices of

Persia and may have been adapted by the Persio-phile Muslim ruling elites in India to develop attitudes toward women that were highly prejudicial.

Muslim royalty in India did not neglect formal education for the female members of royal households; however, facilities for female education for commoners were generally lacking in Muslim religious schools or madrasas. But there were exceptions, as the Moroccan-born traveller Ibn Battuta recalled of the existence of thirteen schools for girls and nearly twice as many for boys at the commercial center of Hinawar in western India. However, he saw this as a local anomaly because he found no other schools for Muslim girls during his travels through India. This was probably due to prevailing Muslim attitudes concerning *purdah* and, as a result, the vast majority of Muslim women, like Hindu women, were illiterate. Among the Muslim upper classes, women played an important role in politics from behind the throne and even on occasion directly controlled the reins of power as in the case of Princess **Raziya** al Din (r. 1236–1240), who ruled as sultana in Delhi. She reportedly preferred to wear men's clothing and abandoned the dictates of *purdah* when conducting state affairs. But the conditions that led to her rule were exceptional, and her short reign ended tragically because she was seen as flaunting long-established customs and the ethnic and gender prejudices of the ruling Turkish elite.

The sultans maintained large numbers of wives and concubines within their harems, which also included all female members of their households. All female members of the harem were expected to rigidly maintain the laws of *purdah* when venturing outside and were thus shielded from public gaze. This rule of female seclusion was also followed by other member of the Muslim aristocracy. A respected aristocratic lady was expected to move in a covered litter while poor Muslim commoners wore a burqa (an all-enveloping garment that covered the entire body) (Grewal, 446). Living in *purdah* and inside harems was associated with wealth, good reputation, family honor, female virtue, and chastity.

Not surprisingly, these cherished notions of female chastity and modesty coexisted with the practice of prostitution and the culture of maintaining courtesans. Under the Muslim sultanates, the state's attitude toward the sale of sex was pragmatic, and no attempt was made to abolish houses of prostitution. The practice was perhaps seen as a safety valve to maintain public order and as an additional source of state revenue. Under the rule of **Allaudin Khalji**, one of the most powerful sultans of the Delhi sultanate, there were scheduled rates set for sexual services by prostitutes, whose houses became the favorite haunts of all classes of soldiers. Thus the city's commercial sale of sex was regulated for the service of the state (Grewal, 447). Courtesans, who were an essential part of royal celebrations even under Islamic rule, entertained the elite with songs and dances. Whole colonies of dancing girls and musicians, known as "tarabadad" (abode of pleasures), were present at city of Delhi during the time of Allaudin Khalji (Grewal, 456–457).

Domestic servitude and the institution of slavery were widely prevalent in the Muslim sultanates. Islam accepted the status of slavery as legally binding, and the master had rights of ownership. Most slaves were war captives and were seen as legitimate war booty, and the success of military campaigns was judged by how many captives it produced (at times as many fifty thousand were taken as slaves). With so many slaves available, even those with modest incomes could afford to keep slaves, and the number of slaves held by the nobles and sultans could be enormous. Sultan **Firuz Shah Tughluq** (1351–1388) is said to have owned as many as 180,000 slaves, with twelve thousand working in the craft industry. Apart from doing much of the domestic and craftwork, the slaves also engaged in commerce in the interest of their masters and functioned as agricultural laborers. (Grewal, 432–434). Female slaves were procured either as domestic help or as concubines. The price of an average Indian slave girl during this period varied, and those selected as domestics were generally considered cheap, but those with **education**, physical beauty, training, and charms attracted a great fortune as concubines. Slaves were also imported form East and Central Asia. The popular perceptions among the Muslim elite of the period vested the female slaves of different ethnic groups with different innate characters and abilities. Central Asian Turkish female slaves were usually preferred for hard outside work and obedience; Indian female slaves were employed as domestics and for wet-nursing, while Persian female slaves were chosen as companions. Both male and female slaves, whether foreign or domestic, were considered personal property of the master but did have certain basic rights granted by the Quran (Grewal, 447, 453). *See also* Documents 4 and 19.

Further Reading
Altekar, A. S. *Education in Ancient India*. Benares, India: The India Book Shop, 1934.
Altekar, A. S. *The Position of Women in Hindu Civilization*. New Delhi, India: Motilal Banarsidass, 1978.
Basham, A. L. *The Wonder that Was India*. London: Sidgwick & Jackson, 1982.
Beal, Samuel. *Buddhist Records of the Western World*. Reprint ed. Delhi, India: Oriental Books Reprint Corporation, 2004.
Dumont, Louis. *Homo Hierarchicus: The Caste System and Its Implications*. Chicago: University of Chicago Press, 1980.
Ghosh, Suresh Chandra. *History of Education in India*. Vol. 2: *Medieval India 1192 A.D.-1757 A.D.* New Delhi, India: Rawat Publishers, 2007.
Goyal, S. R. *History of Indian Buddhism*. Meerut, India: Kusumanjali Prakashan, 1987.
Grewal, J. S. *The State and Society in Medieval India*. Oxford, UK: Oxford University Press, 2005.
Habib, Irfan. *Essays in Indian History: Towards a Marxist Perception with the Economic History of Medieval India: A Survey*. London: Anthe Press, 2002.
Mookerji, Radha Kumud. *Ancient Indian Education: Brahmanical and Buddhist*. Delhi, India: Motilal Banarsidass, 1974.
Nagaswami, R. *Studies in Ancient Tamil Law and Society Institute of Epigraphy*. Tamil Nadu, India: The State Department of Archaeology Government of Tamil Nadu, 1978.
Ray, Krishnalal. *Education in Medieval India*. Delhi, India: B.R. Publishing Corporation, 1984.
Sachau Edward C., ed. *Alberuni's India*. New Delhi, India: Oriental Reprint, 1983.
Siddiqui, Iqtidar Husain. *Medieval India: Essays in Intellectual Thought and Culture*. Vol. 1. Delhi, India: Manohar, 2003.
Swami B. V. Tripurari. *Siksastakam of Sri Caitanya*. San Rafael, CA: Mandala Publishing, 2006.

Raman N. Seylon

6. SCIENCE AND TECHNOLOGY

Science, the historian David Pingree reminds us, is a product of culture and not a single unified entity: "Therefore, a historian of pre modern scientific texts—whether they be written in [Greek, Latin, Arabic, or Sanskrit] . . . must avoid the temptation to conceive of these sciences as more or less clumsy attempts to express scientific ideas. They must be undertaken and appreciated as what their practitioners believed them to be. The historian is interested in the truthfulness of this own understanding of the various sciences, not in the truth or falsehood of the science itself" (45). More or less in line with this ideal vision, this essay presents medieval Indian science as an aspect of Indian culture and not something outside it. Rather than just sampling key developments in various medieval Indian sciences, this essay points out how science was fostered by other facets of Indian culture.

Although medieval Indians may have lacked the precision, tools, and knowledge of the modern world, they did not lack imagination. In fact, some of their ultimate technological quests seem remarkably similar to our own. For instance, our modern quest for renewable sources of energy had a medieval counterpart—the idea of perpetual motion, which was said to have been originated in medieval India, and could be seen as a product of medieval Indian "scientific" imagination. It was certainly an appealing idea that spread to medieval Europe through Arab intermediaries. It set an ideal for the best European mechanical minds of the period. But the quest for perpetual motion proved just as illusive for medieval European thinkers as the attempt to turn base metals into gold for medieval alchemists. But other Indian discoveries did make profound and lasting contributions to the development of modern science.

The Indian Middle Ages begin with the **Gupta Empire** (c. 320–550). The Gupta era is considered the golden age of India in the development of Sanskrit literature and of ancient science, including early advances in Indian mathematics. Despite its lack of political unity, the post-Gupta Period was a time of tremendous advances in a number of fields; these revolutionary developments in the world of science and philosophy emerged out of a number of institutions of higher learning located in various parts of medieval India. Since the Gupta era, a primary center of higher learning existed in the city of Nalanda. During its peak, Nalanda University, which was reported to house three separate libraries with rare manuscripts, had several thousand students, some from such distant parts of Asia as Sri Lanka, Indonesia, Korea, and China. It is said that the demanding entrance exams eliminated two-thirds of the applicants. The university was supported by various private endowments, some from overseas Buddhist sources, and by grants from the state, including the revenue of two-hundred villages. The tuition was free for those who passed the entrance exam.

The standard subjects taught in Nalanda were geared toward Buddhist scholarship and included topics in philosophy, logic, and Sanskrit grammar. The university had a large faculty, numbering over 1,000 teachers, who gave lectures or conducted group discussions. Being a Buddhist institution, the majority of teachers were Buddhist monks, but there were also Hindu scholars, an indication of a broad, eclectic, and tolerant religious atmosphere. Nagarjuna (150–250 C.E.), one of the greatest Buddhist philosophers of ancient India, taught at Nalanda. Nagarjuna was the founder of the Madhyamika ("middle way") school, which differed from the mainstream Buddhist view of the cosmos. Most Buddhist schools believed that the entire universe was in a state of flux with momentary but interdependent events following one another in such a way as to evoke the illusion of stability and duration. Nagarjuna showed, by very subtle arguments, that in the final analysis this cosmic flux was illusory. To be real, a thing could have no predicate, something that Nagarjuna called *sunyatta* ("emptiness," or "void"); this early philosophical insight was also later to reemerge in the development of number theory in Indian mathematics (Basham, 278–279). For Nagarjuna's Madyamika school, true void was the foundation of all existence and lay at the end and beginning of all physical matter. All matter arises from emptiness and returns to it. The Madyamika school compared reality to the familiar long cotton garment worn by most Indians, which from a distance appeared seamless and solid but on closer inspection was nothing but a holey and loose assemblage of threads (Teresi, 217). In spite of this philosophical nihilism, the agnostic and skeptical Nagarjuna proposed that even though nothing is real in an absolute sense, we ought to conduct our lives as if the world had a qualified practical everyday reality.

Indian Mathematics

The Gupta era, which gave us such abstract philosophical thinking, also was a world of practical knowledge, such as mathematics. During the Gupta Period, India was at a higher level than was the study of mathematics in any other part of the world. At centers of high **education**, like Nalanda, Indian mathematics developed the early forms of algebra. This development facilitated more complex calculations than was possible for the ancient Greeks or Romans, who had used separate symbols for tens and hundreds and thousands (X, C, M), and had no symbol for zero. The Indians developed the modern decimal system of nine digits and zero. The Indian decimal system goes all the way back to the Indus Valley civilization (3000–1500 B.C.E.), some 4,000 years ago; its use could be deduced from the ratio of Indus weights that had been unearthed and identified by archaeologists. Were we to analyze the weights found in the Indus site at Harraspur their relation corresponds to our equivalent of 0.05, 0.1, 0.2, 0.5, 1, 2, 10, 20, 50, 100, 200, and 500 ratio scales.

The Vedic Period (1500–500 B.C.E.), which followed the demise of the Indus Valley civilization, also made its contribution to Indian mathematics. Of major importance to historians of mathematics are the ancient instructional texts called the *Sulva-Sutras* (800–500 B.C.E.), which deal with the construction of sacrificial altars in Vedic rituals. These also laid the foundation for the Indian geometry of later times by specifying correct geometric ratios for various parts of the altars and buildings in general. The texts state that to obtain a diagonal of a square (dvi-karani) we should "increase the measures by its third part, and again by the fourth part (of the third part) less the thirty-fourth part of itself (of the fourth part)." This will give you the approximation of the square root of 2 as in the formula $1 + 1/3 + 1/3.4 - 1/3.4.34$ or as 1.4142156, only differing from our modern calculations at the sixth decimal place (Basham, 147; Garratt, 34).

Equally interesting is the discussion on squaring a circle in the *Sulva-Sutra*, which states that, to square a circle, divide its diameter into eight parts, then divide one of these parts into twenty-nine parts and leave out twenty-eight of them, as well as the sixth part of the previous division less the eighth part of this last one. Formulas to calculate the relation between the radius of a circle and the two sides of an equivalent square were also given as $a = r - r/8 + r/8.29 - r/8.29.6$

+ r/8.29.6.8, where *r* equals the radius of the circle and 2 is the side of an equivalent square (Basham, 147).

The construction of altars for fire rituals, an essential part of early Vedic Hinduism, required a number of bricks of different sizes and shapes to construct complicated designs (such as the large falcon-shaped fire altar upon which the rituals were undertaken). The Vedic Aryans in their effort to fulfill their ritual demands (by constructing the perfect sacrificial platforms with all their geometric complexities to ensure success in their sacrifices) were also were laying the early foundations of modern mathematics.

What is widely recognized as the greatest contribution of India to the world of mathematics is the decimal system of numbers, which is the ancestor of our own number system. Historically, Indians were not the only people to invent and use the decimal system. But the Indian system was far more elegant and the first one to be widely used as well as having the abstraction needed for an accurate notational system (Basham, 495). According to mathematician George Joseph, the Indian system far surpassed those of the Babylonians, Mayans, and Chinese, because it is inextricably tied up with the Indian concept of zero. This idea of zero finds its origins in Indian philosophy. The Sanskrit word for zero is *sunya*, meaning "void" or "empty." It is related to the Indian spiritual practice of emptying the mind of all impressions as found in the Buddhist doctrine of emptiness called "sunyata" (Teresi, 308). Because system reached medieval Europe through the Arab middlemen, the modern decimal number system is called "Arabic numbers" in the West. But the Arabs themselves call "Hindisat," or Indian art (Basham, 496).

From the fifth century onward, a major mathematical revolution took place in India. One of the earliest documentary evidences to surface is the Bahkshali manuscript, currently stored at the University of Oxford. A farmer accidentally discovered this manuscript in 1881 while he was digging for treasure in a mound in the Peshawar district in Northwest India. He found some seventy leafs of birch bark manuscript written in the old Sarada characters in a dialect that combines Sanskrit and Prakrit. Although the manuscript had been seriously damaged by early careless handling, it retained sufficient data to suggest the earliest trends in Indian mathematical development. Although the manuscript itself is dated as late as the twelfth century, the mathematics it contains date to the third century. The manuscript covers such topics as fractions, square roots, simultaneous equations, and arithmetic and geometric progression; it is one of the few surviving manuscripts on medieval Indian science.

The earliest mention of zero, in the text *Chandahsutra* of Pingala, dates to the third century B.C.E. The earliest documented inscription of the decimal number system in India, which was found in Gwalior, dates to around 876. Most early developments may have been either transmitted orally or composed on perishable materials, such as palm leaves, and would have long ago turned to dust. The greatest medieval mathematical discovery, the number zero, was first noted down as a dot (bindu) and is also found in stone inscriptions in Southeast Asia (Cambodia [604 C.E.], Champa [609 C.E.], and Java [732 C.E.]); it was later depicted as a closed ring or "chidra" hole in an inscription on Banka Island in southern Sumatra and dated to be around 686. In all these places, there are clear indications of earlier Indian influences (Basham, 157). These developments spread further westward with the aid of the Arabs, and the Indian number system reached Baghdad, the capital of the Arab Abbasid dynasty, around 773 with the diplomatic mission from Sind in northwestern India (a present-day southern province of Pakistan), which had been under Arab rule since the early eighth century (Teresi, 381).

The mathematical developments in the Gupta Period won praise from the medieval Syrian writer, Severus Sebokht, who, writing around 662, noted the following:

> the subtle discoveries of the Hindus in astronomy, discoveries that are more ingenious than that of the Greeks and Babylonians, and of their invaluable methods of calculation which surpass description. I wish only to say computation is done by means of nine symbols. If those things were known by those who believe that they alone had mastered all the sciences because they speak Greek, and they had arrived at the limits of science then they would be convinced, though even at this late hour, that there are other folks, men of different tongue who also know something of value. (Garratt, 360)

This high acclaim from Sebokht, who was also the Christian bishop of Mesopotamia, was to underline the significance of this medieval Indian mathematical development, which, according to historian A. L. Basham, was the greatest contribution of medieval India to world civilization. In the West, the awkward Roman numbers posed serious obstacles for complex development in certain branches of mathematics, whereas in ancient India everything seemed to be in place for such a development. First, there was the use of versions of the decimal system since the time of the Indus culture. Second, there was the pioneering work of the ancient grammarian Panini (sixth century B.C.E.) in the field of Sanskrit grammar and linguistics. The text *Asthadhoyani* illustrates the algebraic origins of Indian mathematics arising from preexisting developments in the linguistic analysis of the Sanskrit language. In fact, Panini's grammatical work provided an example of a scientific notational model that could have influenced later mathematicians to use abstract notations in characterizing algebraic equations and algebraic theorems and their results. Whereas the mathematics of ancient Greece grew out of philosophy, in ancient India, it was partly an outcome of studies in linguistics. The developments in the Indian decimal system also gave rise to rapid progress in arithmetic and algebra. The decimal system and fractions were discovered and multiplication as well as square root ($\sqrt{\ }$), cube and cube root, and the tables of sine were formulated as well as the use of the letters of the alphabet to denote the unknown.

Simple multiplications and divisions that would have taken seconds for us to calculate using the Indian system would have posed a major challenge for any one using the cumbersome and painstaking methods employed by the Roman number system. In the Roman system, all multiplication involves a succession of doubling and adding the results (Teresi, 23–24). For example, using our modern number system, the answer to nine times by nine would be a simple operation. But using the Roman number system something as simple as finding the answer for nine multiplied by nine would have resulted in the following cumbersome steps:

9 times 1 = 9 (1X)
Double it = 18 (2X)
Double it = 36 (4X)
Double it = 72 (8X)

Now add up the combination of multiples in the right-hand column that add up to the correct multiplier. That is, by adding 8X with 1X we get 9 where 8X = 72 and 1X = 9 and adding these together we get the answer 81. Likewise, division involves the equally cumbersome process of halving the divisor until you arrive at the divider or one close approximation to it (Teresi, 24).

Another peculiarity of medieval Indian mathematics was a deep interest in immeasurably large units based on the decimal system and the smallest units or the minutest spans. The ancient Hindu epics *Ramayana* and *Mahabharata*, and other sacred texts, express these large powers as eons of time, a case where mystical insights formed in Hindu sacred texts seem to parallel Indian scientific thinking.

The two names that are usually associated with medieval Indian mathematics are **Brahmagupta** and Aryabhata I. Brahmagupta was the leading astronomer in the city of Ujjayini, which was the primary mathematical center of India. Brahmagupta wrote two major texts. The earlier text, composed around 628, was titled the *Brahmasphuta-Siddhata* ("the opening of the universe"). It had twenty-five chapters, of which two cover various aspects of mathematics; the rest deal with issues concerning astronomy, including lunar and solar eclipses, planetary conjunction, and methods to determine the position of a planet. The other text, composed 39 years later when Brahmagupta was nearly 67 years old, was titled *Khandakhakyaka*. Brahmagupta investigated the concept of zero in great detail and defined zero by the equation $x - x = 0$. And, as the first person to define zero mathematically, he also provided insights into the world of abstract numbers. In Brahmagupta's *Brahmagupta-Siddhata*, the number zero is treated as a separate entity having neither positive nor negative qualities. This treatment implies that *sunya*, or zero, is on the boundary line between two kinds of numbers. Brahmagupta had stated that a number, whether it is positive or negative, remains unchanged when zero is added, as in the case of $-x + x = 0$, $x + 0 = x$, and $0 + 0 = 0$. According to Brahmagupta, subtraction rules that involved zero worked as follows:

$0 - (-x) = x$ (a negative number subtracted from zero is positive)
$0 - (x) = -x$ (a positive number subtracted from zero is negative)
$-x - (0) = -x$ (zero subtracted from a positive number is positive)
$0 - 0 = 0$ (zero subtracted from zero is zero)

In multiplication, a number multiplied by zero is zero and, when zero is divided by zero or some other number, it is also zero. The square root of zero is zero and 0^2 is zero (Teresi, 83). Hence, the medieval Indians realized zero was more than just a placeholder or a sign, and the study of zero was conducted with great thoroughness.

Brahmagupta's work was preceded by the work of Aryabhata I (476–550). Born in what is today the South Indian state of Kerala, he presented his insights into the worlds of mathematics and astronomy in the treatise *Aryabhatiya* (499 C.E.). Aryabhata I is often seen as the greatest Indian mathematician of the middle ages. In his works, Aryabhata I dealt with such topics as square and cube roots, areas, volumes, properties of circles, and the basic foundations of algebra. Aryabhata I gave pi the modern approximation of 3.1416, and had expressed it in the form of a fraction as 62832/20000. This value was more accurate and precise than any earlier value for pi, including those by ancient

Greek mathematicians, who obviously lacked the advantage of a decimal system of numbers. Aryabhata I's calculation was further refined to nine decimal points by later Indian mathematicians.

Following the conventions of the time, the *Aryabhatiya* was written in verse couplets that cover aspects of astronomy, arithmetic, algebra and spherical trigonometry (which deals with triangles on the surface of a sphere—an essential for astronomical calculations), and plane trigonometry (which deals with triangles in a single plane). The thirty-three surviving verses of Aryabhata's work may well be only a small portion of his total work. In spite of this, Aryabhata I is more influential than any other medieval mathematician, and Indian astronomers were commenting on his work as late as 1430, nearly 1,000 years after his death. The condensed shorthand form he used for his formulas became the standard manner to transmit such formulas.

In the year 830, some two centuries after Brahmagupta's ground-breaking discoveries, the mathematician Mahavira composed a mathematical treatise *Ganita-Sara-Samgraha*, which updated Brahmagupta's pioneering work concerning the definition of zero. Mahavira noted that a number multiplied by zero is zero or $X \times 0 = 0$. The number remained the same if zero is subtracted from it or $X - 0 = 0$. But Brahmagupta also seems to have made a number of errors when he tried to divide by zero. He noted, as follows, that a positive or negative number divided by zero is a fraction with zero as the denominator:

$X/0 = X/0$ (what doesn't say much)
Or $0/0 = 0$ (which is erroneous by the standards of modern mathematics)

Mahavira, in his attempts to improve upon Brahmagupta's statement on dividing by zero also seems to have made an error when he states that a number remains unchanged when divided by zero as $X/0 = 0$ (which is also erroneous).

According to traditional Arabic accounts, an Indian scholar by the name of Kankah or Mankah had brought with him a major mathematical treatise in the year 773 to Bait al-Hikma or the "House of Wisdom," a library and a translation institute set up by the second Abbasid Caliph al-Mansur in Baghdad. The Arabs called this text *Sindhind*, which may be a corruption of the Sanskrit *Shddhana* and more likely *Surya-siddhana*, an early textbook on Indian astronomy written around 400 C.E. This and other translated Indian texts were further developed by Abbasid-era Arabic scholars such as al-Khwarizami, who died in 850; his work titled in English, *Arithmetic*, is the first Arab text to deal with these new Indian numerals. These Indian texts revolutionized Arab astronomy and mathematics, and the resulting Arab works were later translated into medieval Latin in Islamic Spain and from there spread to the rest of Europe (Garratt, 366–367, Teresi, 381).

The *Sindhind* text was to remain an important scientific work in medieval Arabic astronomy for many centuries as indicated by the fact that Arab astronomers measured their longitudinal from the meridian of Arin, which is a distortion of the Indian town Ujjayini, the math and astronomy capital of medieval India from whose meridian medieval Indians calculated their longitude. *Surya Siddhana* also contained other Indian ideas largely overlooked by medieval Arab translators, such as the view that "strings of air" either pushed or pulled the planets in their irregular motion. Some modern scholars saw this as an early pondering about the force of gravitation. The Sanskrit word for gravitation is *gurutvakarshan* (where *akarshan* means attracted), an indication the nature of this force was presumed to be similar to that of attraction (Teresi, 131)

Another noteworthy medieval Indian mathematician was Bhaskara Archaria or Bhaskara II (not to be confused with the seventh-century mathematician Bhaskara I). Bhaskara II (1114–1185), who was born in Karnataka in South India, became the head of the astronomical observatory at Ujjayini, where Brahamagupta and Varahamihira had earlier worked. Bhaskara's *Siddhanta-Siromani* ("Head Jewel of Accuracy") is perhaps last great work in Indian astronomy, detailing his astronomical observations and mathematics. As in modern algebra, Bhaskara II used letters to represent the unknown quantities and filled many gaps left in the earlier works by Brahmagupta. The Indian decimal number system reached its full maturity in the works of Bhaskara II. In spite of these developments, it should also be noted that between the time of Aryabhata in the fifth century and that of Bhaskara II in the twelfth century, there seems to be little in the way of theoretical development in Indian mathematics and methods of calculation remained much the same. Aryabhata's theory that the earth rotates on its own axis remained undeveloped by later mathematicians (Garrett, 350).

Medieval Indian Astronomy

By the early Common Era, Indian astronomers realized that the shape of the earth, as prescribed by earlier religious views, was false. But such views still colored the popular mythic and religious view. Indians, like the ancient Greeks, came to see the earth as spherical. Various estimates were made about the size of the globe, the most popular one being the one made by Brahmagupta (598–665), who gave the circumference of the earth as 500 yognas. One yogna is about 4.3 miles. Therefore, this estimate of the earth's circumference is 21,500 miles. The actual modern measurement of the earth's circumference is 22,901.5 miles, so Brahmagupta's calculation was not that far off. A more accurate measurement would be 533 yognas, which would have made it 22,919 miles.

Although Brahmagupta excelled as a mathematician, Aryabhata I had a greater influence on Indian astronomy. In his treatise, Aryabhata dealt with plane and spherical trigonometry, arithmetic, and astronomy. The major objective of his text was to simplify the mathematics involved in Indian astronomy to make the prediction and forecast of eclipses and the movements of planets needed in the Hindu ritual calendar.

On the basis of his observations, he offered a dramatic new interpretation of our solar system. He suggested that the earth was a giant sphere that revolved on its axis. This explained the apparent rotation of the heavens. These views seemed so blasphemous and so radically different from the then accepted wisdom that future commentators and editors changed the text of Aryabhata I to save him from making what they believed to be gross errors (Teresi, 133). Aryabhata's view was rediscovered only more than 1,000 years later in the sixteenth century by the European astronomer-monk Nicolaus Copernicus (1473–1543), who also challenged the accepted Biblically based cosmology that saw the earth as the center of the universe.

Aryabhata I also explained that the glow of the moon and the planets was the result of reflected sunlight. He was also the first to predict that the orbit of the planets was an ellipsis, 1,000 odd years before Johannes Kepler (1571–1630) came to the same conclusion (Teresi, 134). Aryabhata I also wrote that the cause of lunar eclipses was the shadow of the earth. This was contrary to the popular Hindu mythic version that eclipses were caused by a demon called Radhu trying to swallow the sun, a view that was rejected by medieval texts and scholars. Aryabhata's calculation for the length of a solar year was 365 days, 6 hours, 12 minutes, and 30 seconds, or 365.358680. But this is a slight overestimation by modern calculations; the true value is slightly lower than 365 days and 8 hours.

Aryabhata I was unique among medieval Indian astronomers because he did not compromise the scientific study of astronomy to the demands of religion and tradition. The key works of Aryabhata I were first translated into Latin only in the late thirteenth century. Through this translation, Western mathematicians found a means to calculate the volume of spheres and to calculate squares and square roots. But by the time Western astronomers had begun seriously to look at Aryabhata's explanations of such things as eclipses, his ideas had already been confirmed by Copernicus and Galileo. Therefore, Aryabhata's work failed to make a major impact on the European scientific community of that period, even though his discoveries were made in the fifth century, nearly 1,000 years earlier.

Fifty years after the completion Aryabhata's major treatise *Aryabhatiya*, another major philosopher-astronomer named Varahamihara wrote the text *Panca-Siddhantitaka*, or five treatises, which was a compendium of all the astronomical knowledge from various sources, including Egyptian, Greek, Roman, and Indian astronomy. Varahamihara, like Aryabhata I, conceptualized earth as a sphere with an attractive force keeping bodies stuck on earth, another early reflection on the idea of a gravitational force (Teresi, 134). But, unlike the more objective Aryabhata I, later astronomers, including Varahamihara, seem to have compromised their objective investigations to cater to the prevailing Hindu orthodox notions about astrology and horoscope. This compromise of the quest for scientific knowledge to the demands of popular tradition undermined later Indian astronomy (Garratt, 350).

A major impediment to Indian astronomy was the lack of precise measuring instruments other than the eyes of the astronomer (Basham, 491). Medieval astronomers seem to have perfected such instruments, which allowed for more accurate measurements and calculations. The Indian decimal system also aided the accuracy of measurement. Astronomical instruments from the Islamic world or even from ancient Ptolemic Egypt may have been introduced into India. These may well have been the predecessors of the five gigantic masonry observatories in Delhi, Jaipur, Ujjayini, Varanasi (Benares), and Mathura, which were constructed by the astronomer prince of Rajasthan, Maharaja Sawai Jai Singh II of Ambar (1686–1743) in the 1730s. These specially constructed astrological observatories used a measuring scale designed to maximize its accuracy, while their enormous scale was meant to minimize errors. But they were by the eighteenth century well behind the times in relation to Western European astronomical observatories.

Medieval Indian Physics

Among the early civilizations, the ideas developed in India come closest to our ideas of modern atomic theory and quantum physics. India developed its theory of atoms very early. An atomic theory was taught by Paukudha-Katayama, a contemporary of the Buddha (fifth century B.C.E.), who thus predated Democritus, the father of Greek atomic theory.

In spite of the fact that medieval Indians lacked the experimental sophistication of the ancient Chinese or medieval Arabs or Europeans since the Renaissance, they had reached new heights in scientific inquiry relying solely on logic and mathematics to devise novel theories of the basic nature of the visible universe. The ancient Indians explained the visible universe in terms of minute indivisible units called "anu" (i.e., atoms). In the Indian definition, an "anu" or atom is not only the smallest unit but also one that could not be created or destroyed (Teresi, 213). Although this is similar to the Greek notion, the India's logical arguments to come this conclusion seemed to differ. According to Democritus, a wedge of cheese cannot be cut into smaller and smaller pieces forever; eventually an undividable piece—the atom—will be reached. Indian scientific philosophers came to a similar understanding using a different logical route. Compare a mountain and a molehill they said, which has more particles? The answer: If the particle that makes them up is infinite, then the mountain has the same number as the molehill. This conclusion does not make any logical sense, which also proves the existence of a limit to the size a particle could attain and this is the atom. Most Indian philosophical schools also believed that the universe could be classified under five basic elements: earth, wind, fire, water, and space or *akasa* (which is also translated as ether). These schools also believed that four of these five elements could be composed of atoms. The Jains believed that all atoms, or "anu," were identical and the differences in the character of the elements is the way the atoms are combined. Other schools believed that each separate element is made up of a particular type of atom.

Many Indian philosophical schools believed atoms to be eternal and defined them as the tiniest objects occupying the tiniest space. Some schools of Buddhism believed that atoms not only occupy the minutest space but also the minutest time. In essence, they disappear the instant they are created only to be succeeded by another atom caused by the first, much like Max Planck's (1858–1947) early theories of quantum physics.

All these Indian philosophical schools shared a few common assumptions: that atoms are invisible and had no independent character; that they assumed a particular character; and that they assumed a particular character only when they combined with other atoms to form material objects in combinations of two or three. The school of Ajivakas, along with the Buddhists, believed that under normal conditions atoms did not exist in pure form, but only as mixtures or combinations of the four basic elements in different proportions. This meant that the characteristic of an atom is based on the predominance of the particular elements present and the property of matter is dependent on the type of atoms that made it up. Matter could also be composed of two or more kinds of atoms and thereby exhibit the characteristic of more than one element. Wax, for example, might melt and also burn because it contained proportions of the elements of water and fire. Mercury, which contained equal proportions of earth and water, was solid and liquid at the same time.

Indian atomic theories were accepted throughout the Middle Ages and were based on intuition or logic and never on any experiments. But, like Indian theories of cosmology, they were not universally shared by every Indian philosophical school. However, these theories developed in the ancient and medieval periods, and they offered imaginative explanations for understanding the basic properties that make up our natural world without resorting to the usual supernatural explanations. It is pure coincidence that there are instances in which they seem to agree with the insights derived from modern quantum physics.

Indian Cosmology

Just like ancient Indian theories concerning the atom, ancient Indian theories concerning the cosmos also endured and were accepted throughout the Middle Ages and were influenced by the Indian fascination with enormously large numbers. Indian theories saw the universe as an extremely vast space going through infinite cycles of evolution and dissolution. These ideas seem to be based purely on speculations and not on experimentation and were often colored by popular mythic views. Accordingly, the entire cosmos was believed to have passed through cycles for all eternity. The basic cycle was the Kalpa of 4.32 billion years (4,320 million years), which is one Brahma day. Within each of these Kalpa are secondary cycles (Manu-Antaras or Manuvantaras) each lasting 306,720,000 years with long intervals between them. After each interval, the earth was freshly re-created and a new Manu (father of humanity) was also created. According to this view, we are in the seventh Manuvantara of the present Kalpa. Each of these secondary cycles or Manuvantaras contains 71 Mahayuga or Aeons (1,000 Maha Yuga is one Kalpa).

Each of these yugas represents a progressive decline in morality, strength, longevity, and happiness. We, according to Hindu cosmology, the present era is Kaliyuga ("the chaotic dark age of Kali"), which, according to traditional accounts, began precisely at 3102 B.C.E., the year of traditional dating for the epic *Mahabharata* war. The end of the Kaliyuga is to be marked by confusion of classes, the overthrow of the established order, the cessation of ancient rituals, and domination by cruel alien rulers.

The largest cycle in the Indian cosmology is a Brahma century, which is 72,000 Kalpas or 311,040 billion years or 311 trillion years, when the entire cosmos collapses to a formless nothingness until it evolves again. The cosmology of the various Hindu and Buddhist philosophical schools could be summarized as follows:

1. The universe is unfathomably old.
2. Its evolution and decline are cyclical and repeated forever ad infinitum.
3. It is enormously large.
4. There are parallel universes and other universes beyond our own.

Although the cosmic schemes of the Buddhists differ from the Hindus in many details, the basic fundamentals are the same. A critical difference came from **Jainism**, at times a bitter rival to medieval devotional Hinduism, especially in Tamil-speaking South India (*see* **Tamil Country**). Jains rejected the idea of a cyclical created universe found in Hindu cosmology. The Jain monk Jinasena (ninth century C.E.) made the clearest rebuttal of the idea of a cyclical universe when he wrote the following:

> Some foolish men declare that Creator made the world. If god created the world, where was he before creation? If you say he was transcendent then, where is he

now? No single being had the skill to make the world—for how can an immaterial god create that which is material? How could god have made the world without any raw material? If you say he made this first, and then the world, you are face with an endless regression. If you declare that the raw material arose naturally you fall into another fallacy, for the whole universe might thus have been its own creator, and have risen equally naturally. (Teresi, 2003, 177–178)

And after making a logical argument refuting every notion that the world was created by god, Jinasena ended his discourse by stating that the world is uncreated and indestructible as time itself, without beginning or end and endures by the property of it own nature.

Medieval Indian Metallurgy

Metal casting and smelting technology reached a high point during Gupta and post-Gupta India, reaching a height never to be achieved until the modern period. Two major artifacts to be produced during the period are the iron pillar of Delhi and the copper colossus Buddha of Sultanganj. The iron pillar of Delhi is made of a rust resistant iron and measures 23 feet 8 inches. It has a bell-shaped capital. Its diameter varies from 16.4 to 12.5 inches and weighs nearly 6 tons.

An inscription commemorates the pillar as the lofty standard of the divine Vishnu. The pillar commemorates the military conquests of a ruler named Chandra, who is hailed as the "supreme world conqueror." But, unfortunately, the inscription offers no date, and most scholars assume the Chandra in this inscription to be **Chandra Gupta II** (c. 346–415 C.E.), one of the great Gupta kings who, like his predecessor, expanded Gupta rule. The pillar is remarkable for its technological achievement. It is cast from a single piece of iron. In an article written in 1881, "The Economic Geology of India," the writer declared that production of such a pillar would have been an impossibility before the nineteenth-century introduction of British industrial technology, and even then such a singularly large object could have been cast only in the largest foundries in the world. The pillar was obviously prepared with care and most authorities agree it was made by some form of welding process.

The Sultanganj copper icon of a colossal Buddha was accidentally unearthed in 1862 during railway construction at the town of Sultanganj in Bihar, which is a major center of Buddhism. The railways used stones from abandoned buildings as ballast (a common practice well into the twentieth century, which, unfortunately, led to the destruction of important archeological sites). This Buddha icon was dated to the sixth to eighth centuries C.E. and was the largest metal figure of its kind. It was found buried upside down, presumably to protect it from looters or vandals, by the monks when the monastery came under serious threat. The Sultanganj Buddha weighs 1,100 pounds and is about 7.5 feet high, cast by what is called a lost wax process; it is a good example of the classical Gupta style of sculpture. The monastic robe of this sculpture seems to cling tightly to the body as if the Buddha had been drenched by a downpour. The Buddha sculpture's raised right hand is a mark of offering of spiritual protection to the devotee, while his left hand makes a gesture granting the worshipper a special favor. Currently, the Sultanganj Buddha is housed in Birmingham Museum, where it occupies a special place as the largest metal standing Buddha sculpture from the Gupta Period.

Indian Medicine

The ancient and medieval science of Indian medicine is called Ayurveda. The term *ayur* could be translated as "life." It also implies that the role of a physician is not one of purely curing illness but also one of promoting a holistic and healthy lifestyle. The term *veda* could be translated as "knowledge." The foundation of this medieval system is the premise that the health of an individual lies in the balance of three primary fluids, or "dosas," in the body. These fluids are wind (*vata*), gall (*pitta*), and mucus (*kupha*). Furthermore, there are five separate breaths, or winds, which control bodily functions. When all these vital forces and the bodily fluids are within their correct proportion, the body is in a state of good health. Their imbalance, due to improper diet, leads to ill health and disease. Similar ideas also prevailed in European classical and medieval systems of medicine, but it is yet unclear whether the foundations of Indian medicine were from external influences or purely local independent developments.

The key point here is the underlying textual view that the functioning of the human body was a result of natural laws and that diseases were not due to supernatural forces, either evil demons or angry malevolent gods. Because humans are a microcosm of the universe, they too are subject to natural laws of cause and effect and disease is a by-product of such transactions. This is not to say, at the popular level down to the present day, major epidemic diseases, such as smallpox, were not seen as a visitation of a special pox goddess, but such folk ideas are rejected by the authors of authoritative ayurvedic medical texts such as Caraka, a first-century C.E. physician and author of the earliest medical text called *Caraka Samhita*. Caraka is believed to have been the court physician of King Kaniska of the Kusana dynasty of the first and second centuries C.E. The other major physicians are Susruta, Vagbhata, and Madhava. The ayurvedic system reached its classical form in the early centuries of the first millennium C.E. during the height of the Gupta Empire (Basham, 1975, 21).

The ayurvedic understanding that the environment had a major impact on the individual also led to the study of local pharmacopoeia to restore the bodily balance. The central purpose of this medical system is not only to cure illness but to preserve good health, which meant that proper diet played a major role in the ayurvedic system and how one should adapt to the climatic changes in the Indian environment. Emphasis on diet and physical exercise along with proper positive mental attitude are essential for the maintenance of good health. Although Ayurveda does not contradict the basic Hindu-Buddhist premise that the life and health of an individual is partly the result of good and evil deeds of this or past lives (karma), it also emphasizes that the health of an individual can be maintained by human actions and is not necessarily predetermined. The physician in the ayurvedic system is called the *vaidya*, which term also derives from the Sanskrit word for "knowledge" (the English word *doctor* is also semantically analogous as well as the Arabic word for physician, *hakim*, which is related to the term "hikma" or "knowledge"). In the ancient and medieval period, the *vaidya* were members of a practicing craft, and not a separate caste but generally tended to be members of the three clean castes: Brahmin, Kshatriya and Vaishyas (*see* **Caste System**). The training of a future physician was by apprenticeship, living at the home of a noted ayurvedic practitioner as a junior member of the household. This form of training could last up to 7 years. After this training, the *vaidya* was expected to increase his knowledge by his own personal observation, while treating his patients.

The omission of purification rituals in Indian medical texts also suggests that physicians took these Hindu religious taboos lightly. In the course of his practice, a physician may have to enter into the households of low castes and may touch excreta or sip a drop of urine for diagnostic purposes, practices that under normal circumstances would have brought forth strong ritual pollution. Taboos in dead animals were less than in humans, and a *vaidya*, as a student, may practice dentistry by extracting the teeth of dead animals, or learn to use a scalpel by making incisions on a dead animal (Basham, 1975, 27).

The medical profession promised rich material rewards and being such it was also filled with dangerous quacks and charlatans intent only on making money. During the Gupta Period, steps were also taken to prevent widespread quackery by a system of licensing, where a physician was sanctioned by the ruler. The state was considered responsible for maintaining competent physicians. Hindu legal texts prescribed that a competent doctor shall not be held responsible for the death of his patient, but an incompetent and negligent quack should be punished, perhaps even by death.

The earliest Indian medical text to be preserved was found in the wastes of Chinese Turkistan in 1890 and could be dated to be about fourth century C.E. This text was probably based on an earlier work, and its discovery suggests the existence of a well-developed Indian school of medicine during the late Gupta Period. The earliest preserved works belonged to Charaka and Susruta, who was another ancient legendary author whose name is attributed to many books. By late Gupta Period, the works of both these authors had become standards (Garrett, 352). These works were translated into Arabic around 800. About 16 other Indian works were known to the Arabs through translations. Because it was these Arabic texts that served as the chief guiding principles of European physicians as late as the seventeenth century, it could be said that the Indian medical texts also long indirectly influenced the practice of medicine in Europe (Garrett, 352).

Earliest ayurvedic medical texts make no mention of surgery. Ancient Indian ideas of physiology were thoroughly inaccurate by modern standards. This may be due to strong Hindu taboos on the handling of corpses. There were no clear ideas about the function of the brain, or the workings of the lungs, and it was believed that the seat of human consciousness was the human heart and not the brain. However, there seems to be a better understanding of the abdominal organs, perhaps due to the importance placed on proper dietary practices.

The strong taboo on contact with the dead prevented any clear anatomical knowledge well into modern times. The complete ignorance of the nature and functions of various organs of the human body, even among the best-educated Indian physicians, was a serious defect in ancient and medieval systems of Indian medicine.

In spite of these obvious shortcomings, a medieval Indian surgeon could remove calculi from the bladder and restitch exposed bowels as a result of wounds. The most brilliant aspect of Indian medical achievement was in the field of plastic surgery, and it was unsurpassed anywhere else until the eighteenth century, when European physicians, after studying the Indian technique of plastic surgery, began to apply it to their patients (Basham, 27). Another major development in medieval Indian medicine was the use of inoculation to prevent smallpox, notably in Bengal. It is not clear whether this was a result of local discovery or something that was borrowed from traditional Chinese medicine.

Indian hospitals, staffed by *vaidya*, were mentioned by the Chinese scholar-monk **Faxian**, who visited India during the Gupta era in the fifth century and saw hospitals in Pataliputra, the Gupta capital. Here physicians offered free treatment to the poor who were housed and fed until they recovered. These establishments were not funded by the state, but by wealthy private benefactors. There is no evidence of such free hospitals being found in smaller towns. The Chinese scholar-monk **Xuanzang**, who visited India during the reign of Emperor **Harsha** (590–647), does not mention free hospitals but does mention rest houses erected by Harsha along major highways. Here free meals and drinks were given to travelers, and physicians dispensed free medications to travelers and the poor.

Indian medicine was known in western Asia long before the Islamic Arab invasion in the eighth century. The Persian court physician of Emperor Knusrav Anusharvan of the pre-Islamic Sasassian dynasty of Iran had traveled to India in search of rare drugs and medical texts and tried to recruit famous Indian physicians as teachers for the medical schools of Gundi Shapur. After the Arab conquest of Northwest India, a number of major Indian medical manuals were translated into Arabic. There are also instances when Indian physicians, such as Manka, treated Arab rulers, such as the Abbasid Caliph Harun al-Rashid (763–809), and served as physician in major hospitals in Baghdad, the capital of the Arab Abbasid dynasty (750–1258) and one of the largest and most prosperous cities in the medieval world.

In spite of the fact that Islamic medicine was based on the early works of Galen and Avicenna and looked toward classical Europe, Muslim physicians (known as *hakim*, who practiced Unani or Greek medicine) did collaborate freely with ayurvedic physicians during the period of Islamic rule in medieval India. Because both were eager to learn from the other, their curiosity and mutual interest and respect overcame the bitter religious animosities and deep-rooted prejudices found among these two rival communities in their more mundane affairs. The medieval Indian ayurvedic medical system still has relevance in modern India as it is updated and offers an affordable and an alternate system of health care for certain types of common ailments in the general population.

Further Reading

Basham, A. L. *The Wonder that Was India.* London: Sidgwick & Jackson, 1975.
Garratt, G. T. *The Legacy of India.* Oxford, UK: Clarendon Press, 1962.
Siddiqui, Iqtidar Husain. *Medieval India: Essays in Intellectual Thought and Culture.* Vol. 1. Delhi, India: Manohar, 2003.
Teresi, Dick. *Lost Discoveries: The Ancient Roots of Modern Science.* NY: Simon and Schuster, 2003.

Raman N. Seylon

7. GLOBAL TIES

India and Southeast Asia

Religious and political ideologies found their way from India to Southeast Asia through the port cities and were transmitted by Indian traders and priests.

Religions, such as Hinduism, Buddhism, and even Islam, entered Southeast Asia with merchants and missionaries from India (*see* "Religion" section). While, at the same time, Indian political and cultural ideologies gradually influenced the civilizations of Southeast Asia. This was largely a product of the Indian Ocean trade (*see* "Economy" section).

Earlier increases in demand for spices from ancient Rome, which India was unable to supply, led Indian merchants to venture into Southeast Asia. India acted as the middleman for the spice trade from Southeast Asia to the very area that later came to be known as Spice Island, the present-day islands of Indonesia.

Just as geography facilitated trade, it also allowed for the spread of culture and religious ideology. In the eastern parts of the Indian Ocean, Indian culture and religious institutions created changes in Southeast Asian societies. Indian political ideology aided the formation of large empires such as the Mayapahit Empire in Central Java, the Sumatran kingdom of Sri Vijaya, and the Khamer kingdom in Cambodia by legitimizing the paramount position of former tribal chieftains as "divine kings." Indian architectural forms also gave inspiration for the construction of impressive monumental architecture, such as the temples and palaces of Angor Wat in Cambodia in the twelfth century and Barobadur in Java in the ninth century, which is the largest Buddhist Mandela-shaped structure and, according to one authority, "An expression in stone of the doctrines of Mahayana Buddhism."

The Southeast Asian states remained independent and were not provinces of an India-based empire, and the transmission of culture also preceded peacefully, largely spread by traders and priests. In fact, Indian Ocean traders and Sufi teachers, followers of a form of mystical Islam from India, spread Islam in Southeast Asia. The beginning of mass conversion came only in the fourteenth and fifteenth centuries by Sufi teachers just when the first traders arrived on the coast of Indonesia. As a result, Malaysia and Indonesia became overwhelmingly Muslim, except the island of Bali, which remained Hindu-Buddhist.

Land and People

The dominant ethnic groups in Southeast Asia originally migrated from mainland China before recorded history, either as refugees fleeing invasions or as migrants. But culturally all, except the Vietnamese, were influenced by aspects of Indian culture. Many terms, concepts, and ideologies of the Malays, Javanese, Thais, and Cambodians originated in India. Although the languages spoken by Thais, Cambodians, and Burmese belong to the Sino-Tibetan family of languages, their writing system was based on Indian-derived script. Only in Vietnam did Chinese models dominate. In spite of the continuing spread of Indian and Chinese influences, Southeast Asians also preserved their own clearly recognizable social and cultural forms. The Indian-derived epics, such as *Ramayana* and *Mahabharata*, are still popular in Java and Bali. They are retold through wayang puppet theatres and gamelan orchestras of gongs, drums, bamboo flutes, xylophones, and bells, which are pre-Indian aspects of Javanese culture.

Therefore, it is not correct to see the early Southeast Asian societies purely as an instance of cultural borrowing from various areas of India. Even in the case of architecture, which seems quintessentially Indian, there are no analogous Indian prototypes, so the architecture of the region is more than just copies of Indian originals. In fact, there is nothing in the Indian archaeological records that is similar to these monuments of Southeast Asia. They should be seen as structures in their own right based on selectively borrowed concepts that are peculiar to Southeast Asia.

Current evident indicates that contact between India and Southeast Asia is more than 2,000 years old. There is no evidence of a large-scale migration to Southeast Asia from India, but, by the fifth century C.E., Indian culture began to appear not only in areas of Cambodia, Vietnam, and Java, but also in remote, isolated, and sparsely settled areas. Indian prosperity, since the early centuries of C.E., sprang partly from the productivity of Indian society (*see* "Society" section). But it also depended on the vast wealth circulating in the commercial world of the Indian Ocean basin. The sea provided opportunities for commercial, religious, and political influences far beyond India, certainly since the time of Alexander the Great in the fourth century B.C.E.

By the first century B.C.E., sailors in the Indian Ocean began to exploit the seasonal shift in the direction of the monsoon wind pattern. According to tradition, this discovery was made by a single Greek captain named Happalus. This story is unlikely to be true. It is all the more likely that this seasonal shift of winds was known intuitively to inhabitants of the Indian Ocean basin. This practical knowledge was put to use in satisfying the economic demands of the Mediterranean basin centred in Rome and Alexandria for spices and medicine from India and Indonesia and silk and porcelain from China. The dangers and expense of the land route and better deep-water ship design were extra stimuli to the increase in oceanic shipping.

During the first millennia C.E., the Red Sea and Persian Gulf had become integrated with the commercial arteries of the Roman world. By the second century, merchants from the Mediterranean were also visiting the lands further east to the ports of India, Sri Lanka, and parts of mainland Southeast Asia. In this process, by the early Common Era, Southeast Asia was already part of the maritime luxury trade that linked the ports of the South China Sea and the Indian Ocean basin to the Mediterranean. India played a key role in this Eurasian trade. It is not clear if these trade routes to Southeast Asia existed prior to the Mediterranean and Middle Eastern demand for Southeast Asian and Chinese products, or whether it was this demand that brought Indian mariners to the shores of Southeast Asia.

The French historian George Coedes, whose influential book about the commercial and cultural link between India and Southeast Asia, *The Indianized States of South East Asia*, sees the reconstruction of Indian commercial interest eastward as due to changing political conditions in the Mediterranean basin and Central Asia. The Roman emperor Vespasian's prohibition (r. 69–79 C.E.) on exchanging gold for Eastern spices and luxury items in conjunction with nomadic disturbances in Central Asia cut India off both from African and Siberian gold. This situation led to a scarcity of gold in India and prompted Indian merchants to turn east to the legendary regions known as *Suvarnadvipa* (islands of gold) or *Suvannabhumi* (land of gold), India's El Dorado. Here legend has it that gold could be picked up from the ground, and luxury trade items such as rare spices and aromatics could be obtained.

Two major developments seemed to have gone hand in hand to stimulate this development. The first is technological, the other ideological. On the technological front was the innovation in ship construction that originated in the

Persian Gulf and spread to India. This innovation included the use of a rig that allowed the vessels to sail closer to the wind. The ships were also larger and could carry two-hundred men, as witnessed by the Chinese scholar-monk **Faxian**. Other ships were many times larger and alleged to have the capacity to carry 300 tons of cargo and transport some six-hundred to seven-hundred men at a travel time of 2 months from South China to Southeast Asia. The ideological development was the spread of Buddhism, which rejected Hindu ideas of pollution relating to foreign travel and did much to encourage Indian seamen to travel overseas. This greater freedom to travel to foreign lands is also illustrated by archaeological evidence in India, where has been excavated an image of Buddha as *Dipamkara*, or "calmer of waters," a favorite talisman of Indian seamen (Wheatley, 279).

During these early prehistoric periods, Southeast Asia had diverse cultures ranging from nomadic hunter-gathers to complex agrarian systems based on wet rice cultivation (*see* **Agriculture**). At the lower end were small bands of hunter-gathers made up of loosely linked families while at the higher end were tribes and political entities, nearly on the verge of true statehood, with a high degree of centralization and hereditary hierarchical status-based societies. The region had an economic system that extracted the surplus from the rice fields for the support of hereditary chieftains who were competing against each other for labor rights. According to Wheatley, by replacing the old tribal god with a new Indian-derived deity, and by exalting the power of this new deity with whom he was closely associated, the chief promoted his own kin group to the highest level in the control hierarchy of his chiefdom. Then, using this exalted position, the ruler was able to rearrange and fill the high positions of his chieftaincy with the members of other prominent kin groups. By this process, the chieftain's created a class-like stratum of court officials, while the chieftain took on the role of a theocratic ruler. The powerful integrative force that maintained this new reordering of society was the consensus among all groups within the population as to the validity of the chieftain's claims of his newly sanctified status and the attraction of an elaborate ritualized court life as well as the economic opportunities that the privileged nobles gained by the opportunity to siphon off the economic surplus at each successive level of the administrative hierarchy, along with the rewards and gifts from the paramount ruler in the form of land, commodities, status, privileges, and titles. The role of theocracies in Southeast Asia, in the development of state-like institutions and political centralization, is an attractive and compelling model for state formation due to the absence of any alternative, especially one that used coercive force (Wheatley, 325–326).

In this context, the transmission of Indian-derived political and social systems becomes significant. It came without military conquest and was entirely voluntary and peaceful, something which none of the other civilizations was able to achieve. As aspects of Indian political and social systems spread to various regions of Southeast Asia, it stimulated the reorganization of Southeast Asian societies as well as providing a market for Indian goods and a greater integration of Southeast Asia with the commercial world of the Indian Ocean basin.

Merchants, largely from the southern coast of India, supplied these Southeast Asian markets in return for gold, spices, and Chinese trade items that were in great demand in India. The following discussion of the mechanism of the transmission to and transformation of Southeast Asia by Indian cultural norms explains how, at the beginning of the Common Era, the only type of representative was the seasonal Indian merchant mariner but several centuries later there were divine kings in Southeast Asia claiming to reign over the four varnas, follow the Vedas, and observe the dharma (Wheatley, 273).

According to George Coedes, the Indianization of parts of Southeast Asia is essentially the continuation across the Bay of Bengal of the process of "Sanskritization," which had its beginnings in northwest India and spread eastward and southwards over centuries (Wheatley, 328). *Sanskritization*, a term coined by Indian sociologist M.N. Srinivas, is a process of adaptation of great traditions of Hinduism and its values that continues to this day.

Theories on the Transmission of Indian Culture to Southeast Asia

Modern historians have developed several competing theories regarding the transmission of Indian culture to South East Asia: Kshatriya theory, the Vaishya theory, and the Brahmana theory.

The Kshatriya Theory

The Kshatriya theory states that Indian warriors colonized parts of Southeast Asia. This view has now been rejected by most historians, but it was popular among the Indian Nationalist School of historians during the early and middle twentieth century. It owed its origins to the nationalist passions unleashed by the Indian Freedom Movement in the early twentieth century. Indian historians of this period were painfully aware of the stigma of their own colonial subjugation and tried to intellectually compensate for it by creating a parallel golden era of India's colonial heritage in ancient times. In 1926, "The Great India Society" was founded in Calcutta, the capital of British India until 1911. This school maintained the view that Indian kings and rulers had established colonies in Southeast Asia, and the Sanskrit names of ancient Southeast Asian rulers tend to support this evidence. The most influential proponent of this view was the Indian historian R.C. Majumdar, who published a series of scholarly articles titled *Ancient Indian Colonies in the Far East*. Such new interest in Southeast Asia, through the lens of Indian nationalism, did generate further research on the links between India and Southeast Asia. But this hypothesis also alienated scholars of Southeast Asia, who rejected the idea of being a colony of "Greater India."

As further archaeological research progressed, little evidence was found to support any direct Indian political control over any area of Southeast Asia. It was also demonstrated that the Southeast Asian rulers had adopted Sanskrit names voluntarily. Therefore, the mere presence of Sanskrit names could not be taken as evidence of the presence of Indian kings in a broad sense, although there may be a few rare exceptions to this rule.

Vaishya Theory

The Vaishya theory attributes the spread of Indian culture to Indian merchants. This theory is more solidly based on available evidence, because trade was the driving force behind many Indian-Southeast Asian contacts. Inscriptions also showed that Indian merchants had established outposts in many parts of Southeast Asia. Some of these inscriptions were written in major South Indian languages such as Tamil (Kulke and Rothermund, 144).

However, a number of problems raised serious doubts about the validity of the thesis that merchants were the major transmitters of Indian culture to Southeast Asia. First, if Indian merchants had been the chief agents of transmission of Indian culture, then all Indian regional languages should have also left their impact in Southeast Asian languages, not just Sanskrit. So, in spite of the fact that the Vaishya theory is more plausible than the Kshatriya theory, it fails to account for the large number of Sanskrit loan-words found in Southeast Asian languages. Although Indian merchants certainly played an important role in being a major vehicle for all kinds of cultural influences, they did not play the critical role. One of the important arguments against the Vaishya theory of cultural transmission is that some of the earliest traces of Indianized states are not found in the coastal areas usually frequented by Indian traders, but were located in out-of-the-way places, such as mountains in the interior.

Brahmin Theory

The Brahmin hypothesis credits Brahmins as playing a major role in the transmission of Indian culture. This theory is similar to the process that took place in South India, where Brahmins, Jains, and Buddhist were a critical factor in the spread of ideals and styles of the great tradition of Hindu kinship (*see* **Jainism**). Brahmins, unlike the Vaishyas and Kshatriyas, were well familiar with key Sanskrit texts concerning the law, such as *Dharmasastra*, or the art of statecraft, such as in *Arthasastra*, and the art of architecture as found in *Silpasastra*. Taking a modern analogy, we could say that the Brahmins may well have functioned in the role of development experts from abroad in different departments of the administration of Southeast Asian rulers, who were on the verge of becoming full-fledged states.

The question could be asked as to the role played by the local Southeast Asian population in this cultural borrowing. Are they passive recipients, or did they play an active role in this cultural transfer? The passive recipients theory was actively advanced by the "Greater India School" as well as by Western scholars belonging to the ruling European colonial powers of Southeast Asia. They saw the social reality of the times and projected it onto an earlier epoch. Their concept of the Indianization of Southeast Asia, therefore, closely parallels the Westernization under colonial rule. But recent research seems to validate the view that Indian influences alone could no longer be seen as the prime cause for cultural development in Southeast Asia. It is more likely to be a consequence, or by-product, of political and social development that was already taking place.

Epigraphical evidence from early Indonesia indicates that there was already considerable development of regional trade and social differentiation before the arrival of Indian influences. However, the local travel organization was egalitarian and stood in the way of the development of complex political organization or the idea that political organizations required a basic administrative set up, and the legitimating of the hierarchical, political organization, in the eyes of the local population. It is on this point that the local chieftain needed the assistance of Indian Brahmins.

Although Indian trade may have initially helped to provide the necessary information, the actual motives and initiatives came from the local Southeast Asian chieftain. The chieftain found a number of advantages in using an outsider such as the South Indian Brahmin. The invited Brahmin, being an outsider, was isolated from the local scene by culture and status and linked only to their patrons. In this manner, a "royal style" emerged just as it had occurred earlier in parts of South India. A good example of this kind of political development is provided in the earliest Sanskrit inscriptions in Indonesia from East Borneo, dating to around 400 C.E. Several inscriptions on a large megalith mention a local ruler named Kundunga. The name does not seem to have the slightest trace of Sanskrit influence (Kulke and Rothermund, 154).

The son of Kundunga assumes the Sanskrit name of Ashva Varman and founded a dynasty (Vamsa). A grandson of Kundunga, Mula Varman, who is the author of the inscription, celebrates a great Vedic sacrifice and gives valuable gifts to Brahmins. It is written on this megalith that the "Brahmin had come here," and the most likely place is from somewhere in India. It is further revealed, after performing this grand consecration of sacrificial rituals brought by Brahmins from India, that Mula Varman subjugated the neighboring rulers and made them tribute-bearing vassals in the manner of an Indian maharajah (Kulke and Rothermund, 154).

We could interpret this inscription as a history of an Indianized kingship in early Indonesia, and the foundation of a Sanskritized dynasty. The dynasty was founded by a son of a clan chief without the aid of Indian Brahmins. It is only in the third generation that Indian Brahmins are invited to aid in the celebration of the consecration sacrificial ritual. The presence of the Brahmin guests no doubt provided the necessary moral and scriptural support and the administrative know-how to create an Indian-style tributary relationship with his weaker neighbors. This kind of sociopolitical transformation also happened in parts of Central and South India.

What is important here is that in the early stages of development of the Indian-style kingship the initiative and intentions came as a result of local dynamics. The Brahminical presence only helped to legitimize and crystallize the sociopolitical process that had already been set in motion. It is likely that by the middle of the first millennium C.E. several such Indianized states in Southeast Asia had emerged in this fashion, and most were likely to have had a short life span. There must have been of great deal of competition among the many petty rajahs to be recognized as maharajah, with all its trappings of Sanskritic rituals, and the accompanying pageantry (Kulke and Rothermund, 146).

Indian influences increased in this way; and, by the second half of the first millennium C.E., we find hectic temple building in Java and Cambodia where these large Indian-style kingdoms emerged. But, as always, there are exceptions to such broad and sweeping theories. Although it is generally accepted that the Southeast Asian rulers played an active role in the process of state formation, we cannot rule out entirely the occasional direct input by Indian adventurers who may have come to Southeast Asia to seek their fortune.

The most important example of this kind of activity is found in the dynastic origin story of the Indianized state of Funan, at the mouth of the Mekong River in Vietnam. Origin stories, although their details are in formulaic composition and panegyric, cannot be entirely dismissed as fictions, because they do capture the historical realities in their broadest contours. According to Chinese sources, there was an Indian Brahmin named Kaundinya who was led to take a perilous journey to Funan in a dream. There he won the hand of the local Naga princess in a contest of archery and married her and founded the first Indianized political dynasty in Funan in the first century C.E.

This story is further confirmed by Chinese accounts that can be dated to the fourth century C.E., which describes the Indian dynasty of Funan as founded by an Indian usurper to the throne. The Chinese version lists the name as Chu-chan-tan. The term *Chu* is used to denote a person of Indian origin. According to the account found in the Chinese version, Chandana was a Brahmin who obeyed his inner voice and arrived at P'an-P'an, the southern part of Funan. The people of Funan enthusiastically chose him to be their king. He, accordingly, altered the laws of the land to conform to the norms existing in India. The story may well be an allegorical account about the sociocultural transformation that was already taking place in this part of Southeast Asia. It is during this period (fifth century C.E.) that we also note a major increase in Indian influence, including the earliest Sanskrit inscriptions in parts of Southeast Asia.

Here, again, we should note that there is no direct military involvement, but rather an invitation by the local population. The adventurer Kaundinya stayed at P'an-P'an, which is located on the isthmus of Siam, which was, at this period, under the control of Funan. Later, he was invited by nobles from the court of Funan to ascend the throne at a time of political upheaval to bring peace and stability. Whether the story is based on actual historical events, or a general sociological statement made using a familiar formulaic narrative, cannot be known with any certainty from the available evidence.

Finally, it must also be taken into consideration that Indian culture was changed or modified, as it was transferred to Southeast Asia. One of the most interesting examples of such modifications concerns the nature of kingship. The notion of the "god king" (*deva rajah*) was cultivated by rulers in parts of Southeast Asia. They may have been influenced by minor Sanskrit political tracts such as *Nandhismriti*. Southeast Asian rulers of the vast Khamer Empire, centered in what is present-day Cambodia, were able to construct vast palace-temple complexes, such as Angor Wat, using Indian norms and perhaps models. But nothing of this scale was ever attempted in India. Such a powerful interpretation of the role of kingship was something that was not adopted by medieval Indian rulers, but rather something more modest. The medieval Indian rulers considered themselves only as pious devotees of the dominant Hindu deities, such as Siva, Vishnu, or the goddess Durga.

Further Reading

Elliot, H. M., and John Dowson. *The History of India: As Told by Its Own Historians*. Calcutta: Susil Gupta, 1906.

Kulke, Hermann, and Dietmar Rothermund. *A History of India*. New York: Rutledge, 1998.

Raman N. Seylon

Short Entries: People, Ideas, Events, and Terms

Agriculture

In ancient and medieval times, wheat and barley were the staple crops in cooler North India, whereas rice prevailed in hotter and wetter South India. Millet was grown is the dryer lands of the **Deccan** plateau. In South India, rice was cooked by boiling it or it was ground and left to ferment overnight to make either *dosa*, a pancake-like crepe, or *idlis*, rice cakes that were eaten either for breakfast or dinner. Lentils, beans, and peas were widely grown and essential ingredients in Indian cooking. Sesame was indigenous to India and was widely cultivated for extraction of edible oil, which was used for cooking. Cotton, another indigenous crop cultivated primarily for textile production, became one of India's leading exports during the late Middle Ages.

Food is an essential component in Hindu rites of passage and other religious rituals. Auspicious rituals, such as birth and marriage ceremonies, call for elaborate feasts, whereas inauspicious rituals, such as funerals, call for prohibitions of certain foods. Marriage feasts reflect one's caste status, wealth, prestige, and family honor and thus are important and sensitive social affairs. Spices, herbs, and fruits constitute the heart of South Asian cooking. Such ingredients as turmeric, tamarind, coriander, fenugreek, cumin, ginger, cardamom, and pepper flavored Indian cuisine. Curiously, a few essential spices and vegetables in modern Indian dishes, such as red chili pepper, potato, tomato, or cauliflower were not present in India before the sixteenth century, hence the taste of medieval Indian food would have differed. Apart from these European introductions, the modern Indian dish also shows Persian and Central Asian influences. Each region in India specializes in dishes shaped by local ecology and culture. South India specializes in rice and lentil-based vegetarian dishes, such as *dosa*, *idlis*, *sambar*, and a great variety of curries; whereas eastern India specializes in rice and fish curry; Central Asian and Persian influences blended with Indian cooking in North India to develop naan, buriyani, tandoori, samosa, and halva.

When the Chinese Buddhist pilgrim **Faxian** visited India in the early fifth century, most members of the upper and middle castes were vegetarians; meat eating was confined to the lower castes. The seventh-century Chinese traveler **Xuanzang** reported that fish, mutton, gazelle, and deer were eaten and sometimes salted, but the flesh of oxen, asses, elephants, horses, pigs, dogs, and all manner of hairy beasts was forbidden as food and anyone who ate them was scorned and faced social sanctions. Such a person would be driven out of the city and forced to reside outside the city gates. Along with meat eating, some

Hindu texts list eating garlic and onions as polluting, although there was no religious sanction to back this up. Xuanzang noted that anyone caught using onion and garlic as food items within the city gates also faced severe social sanctions and was expelled from the city.

Meat and vegetables were seasoned in curried stews and eaten with rice. Fried flat unleavened wheat bread was eaten, and water, milk, buttermilk, and curd were drunk with meals. Cooking ingredients sometimes differed according to wealth; the rich fried their dishes with ghee or clarified butter while the poor substituted sesame seed oil. Xuanzang also noted that although the Indians had stew and saucepans, they cooked their rice by boiling it and (unlike the Chinese) had not learned how to use their pans as steamers for cooking rice. He also observed that the Indians used no spoons or chopsticks and ate with their hands from one vessel mixing all sorts of curries and condiments together. Indians also generally did not use their own cups for drinking water, which was poured directly into the mouth using a small copper pitcher or lota without the lips ever touching the surface of the vessel. The only time they used drinking cups made of copper was when they were sick. Most of these practices involved Hindu notions of purity and pollution and are still maintained by orthodox Hindu households.

The Islamic food system was ideologically different from the Hindu system. Unlike Hindus, most Muslims ate meat but also followed various food taboos, such as not eating pork, blood, and meat not slaughtered according to the strict Islamic ritual guidelines or *halal*. The absence of daytime food plays a major in Ramadan, which is a month-long fasting ritual practiced by devout Muslims the world over. The Muslim nighttime *iftar* meal, which ended the daytime Ramadan fast, was communally shared. In many ways, the Islamic communal eating practices were ideologically opposed to upper-caste Hindu food rituals.

Sugar was a major cash crop in ancient and medieval India; Indians had refined the techniques of making sugar from sugar cane juice, or jaggery, into a crystalline form. The very term *sugar* derived from the Sanskrit root *sharkara* and the term *candy* also derived from a Sanskrit root, *khandakati*, or pieces of hardened sugar. Xuanzang listed sugar and sugar candy as the most usual food items consumed in India. Sugar was also known to the Mediterranean basin since the time of Alexander's invasion of Northwest India in the fourth century B.C.E., and the ancient Greeks called it "solid honey" or "Indian salt." In the Middle Ages, India exported sugar to the Mediterranean basin, where it was something of a luxury item. Fruits, sweets, and sweet meats were popular, but many popular sweets eaten in North India today, such as *jelebi*, were brought originally from the Near East by Muslims. As for fruits, the fourteenth-century Moroccan traveler **Ibn Battuta** noted that mango was a highly prized fruit grown in orchards. Banana was grown in damper areas of India, from which it spread to the Middle East soon after the Arab conquest of the Sind. Currently, India produces nearly one-fourth of the world's bananas. The banana plant possibly originated in Southeast Asia as did the coconut palm, which may have been introduced to India during the first century C.E. In coastal South India, the common Palmyra palm provided India's staple writing material—Palmyra leaves; it was also used to produce a popular alcoholic drink known as toddy or arrack, which was frequently mentioned in early Tamil literature. Another valued palm plant was the areca or betel nut, which is used as a stimulant. The betel nut was dried, chopped, mixed with lime, wrapped in a leaf of the betel vine and then chewed; it was used for a variety of formal and informal social functions, including marriage ceremonies and various Hindu religious rituals.

Cattle were reared all across medieval India and used for plowing or transport; one's ownership of cattle was a measure of wealth. For plowing, a peasant used wooden plowshares (although iron plowshares were known) pulled by a pair of oxen, which were also used for thrashing the grain. Oxen also provided the milk need to produce to essentials of Indian diet — ghee (clarified butter) and yogurt. Other domestic animals included the water buffalo, which was second in importance to the ox. Water buffalo were also used for plowing and for pulling the large carts needed to haul heavy stone for building large temples or palace complexes. During the Middle Ages, when goddess worship became popular, water buffalo were the favorite sacrificial animals for the Goddess Durga. Goats and sheep were reared, the latter generally in cooler areas. Pigs were reared but did not play an important in the Hindu diet. Chicken was the most important fowl and was first known to have been domesticated in India. However, eggs played only a small part in the Indian diet. Peacocks were a favorite dish of the aristocracy and the wealthy.

As in modern India, drinking alcoholic beverages was taboo in Hinduism and Islam; today, those who drink regularly are either Westernized elites or members of low castes. Faxian tells wrote most respectable Indians did not drink, but drunkenness is mentioned in Tamil literature and depicted in sculptures, which indicates that this taboo was not particularly strong or uniform in medieval times (*see* **Tamil Country**). Xuanzang listed various kinds of wine and liquors and different kinds of alcoholic beverages consumed by different castes. The juice of the grape (wine) and sugar cane (rum) were drunk by the warrior caste. The merchant castes drank strong drinks; Brahmins and Jains drank syrup made from grapes or sugar cane juice but refrained from taking any fermented alcoholic drinks (*see* **Jainism**).

Managing meals and proper diet were important features of the ancient Indian ayurvedic medical system. A healthy body meant having a balance between the three *dosas* or bodily humors or vital fluids, such as the *vata* (wind), *pitta* (gall), and *kapha* (mucus). A careful regulation of diet sought balance between "hot," "neutral," and "cold" foods. If, for instance, a patient had a common cold, the ayurvedic prescription would be to avoid cold foods such as cheese, fruit juice, yogurt, radishes, or unboiled milk. The patient should instead take "hot" foods to aid in digestion. "Hot" foods included apples, hot soup, hot milk, herbal tea, or cooked rice or vegetables seasoned with hot spices, such as ginger or cumin to heat the body and regain its humoral equilibrium. An entire classificatory list of foods marking them as hot, cold, or neural existed in the ayurvedic health care system as guidelines for patients to maintain a balanced diet for better health.

Further Reading

Basham, A. L. *The Wonder that Was India*. London: Sidgwick & Jackson, 1982.

Beal, Samuel. *Buddhist Records of the Western World*. Reprint ed. Delhi, India: Oriental Books Reprint Corporation, 2004.

Raychaudhuri, Tapan, and Irfan Habib. *The Cambridge Economic History of India. Volume 1: c.1200–c.1750*. Cambridge, UK: Cambridge University Press, 1982.

Raman N. Seylon

Aybak, Qutb al-Din (d. 1210)

A former slave of the **Ghaurid** prince Mu'izz al-Din Muhammad, who conquered North India for the Muslim Ghaurid Empire of Afghanistan, Qutb al-Din Aibek is believed to have proclaimed himself independent as sultan of Delhi upon Muhammad Ghauri's death in 1206. Aibak's proclamation is usually considered by modern historians to be the beginning of the **Delhi sultanate**, which became the first significant Muslim kingdom on Indian soil and the dominant state of North India.

After his defeat of the Hindu ruler **Prithviraja** III at the Second Battle of Tarain in 1192, Muhammad Ghauri named Aibak governor of the newly conquered territories of North India. Headquartering himself in Delhi, which held out for some time against the Ghaurid forces, Aibak secured a letter of manumission from Muhammad Ghauri and written authority to govern the Indian provinces. Although there is no direct contemporary evidence that Aibak declared himself an independent ruler upon his former master's assassination, his actions in allying himself with other regional governors in the Ghaurid Empire suggest that he did so.

His marriage to the daughter of Taj al-Din Yildiz, who succeeded Muhammad Ghauri as governor at Ghazni in Afghanistan, looks like an attempt to forestall opposition within the empire to his acquisition of independent status. He married his own daughter and sister, respectively, to two other former slave officers—Shams al-Din **Iltutmish**, who was the Ghaurid command at Baran (modern Bulandshahr) and Nasir al-Din Qubacha, who was commander at Multan. He also forged an alliance with Ali bin Mardan, who took power in Bengal after Muhammad Ghauri's death. Although he ruled for only 4 years, dying in an accident at Lahore in 1210, Aibak was successful in imposing his authority over defeated Hindu rulers and in securing his effective independence from the Ghaurid state. He was succeeded by his son-in-law Shams al-Din Iltutmish.

Further Reading

Chandel, L. S. *Early Medieval State: A Study of Delhi Sultanate.* New Delhi, India: Commonwealth, 1989.

Habib, Muhammas, and Khaliq Ahmad Nizami, eds. *The Delhi Sultanate (A.D. 1206–1526): A Comprehensive History of India.* Vol. 5. New Delhi, India: Peoples Publishing House, 1982.

Jackson, Peter. *The Delhi Sultanate: A Political and Military History.* Cambridge, UK: Cambridge University Press, 1999.

John A. Wagner

Allauddin Khilji (d. 1316)

During the reign of Allauddin Khilji (1296–1316), second ruler of the Khilji dynasty, the **Delhi sultanate** reached the height of its political and military power and achieved its greatest geographic extent.

Allauddin served as a provincial governor under his uncle Jalal al-Din Firuz Shah, whom Allauddin overthrew in 1296. After 1298, Allauddin successfully foiled a series of **Mongol** invasions, which underscored the importance of maintaining the size and strength of the army. To afford a larger military establishment, Allauddin paid his men according to a prescribed wage scale, which barely met a solder's daily needs but that allowed for the hiring of more troops. To maintain morale, the sultan fixed prices for basic commodities at low rates. The *kharaj* (land tax) was set at one-half of a landholder's crop, which share was taken immediately upon harvest by government grain dealers who delivered what they collected to state granaries for sale to soldiers and others in urban centers at the fixed prices. Through this regulation of the market, Allauddin was able to increase and stabilize the revenue from land, upon which depended the supply of the army, as well as decrease the power of local Hindu chiefs and magistrates, who now had less control of the produce of their area and less scope for plotting rebellion.

To quell any possible disaffection within the Muslim nobility and the army, Allauddin ordered the creation and maintenance of rolls listing the military resources in horses and manpower of each province, and the occasional muster of local military contingents, practices aimed at limiting the opportunities of local magnates to report false returns and thereby build private military forces that could threaten the state. Allauddin also strictly enforced the Islamic prohibition against the use of alcohol and forbade private gatherings of court officials and military officers, restrictions that were unpopular but successfully overseen by spies.

In 1297, Allauddin annexed the Gujarat, and, by 1303, had extended his authority into eastern Rajasthan, where his forces captured the important strongholds of Ranthambhor and Chitor. By 1311, most of the **Deccan** had submitted to the sultan, whose power was now felt throughout much of southern India up to the area around Dorasamuda (the modern city of Mysore) and along the Coromandal coast in the southeast. The sultan entrusted leadership of his armies to Malik **Kafur**, an Indian eunuch who was originally a prisoner of war. However, upon his conversion to Islam, Malik Kafur, for whom the sultan supposedly felt a strong physical attraction, became the leader of several successful military campaigns into South India. Upon Allauddin's death in 1316, Malik Kafur tried unsuccessfully to seize power but was killed by his own men. The throne then passed to one of Allauddin's sons, Qutb-ud-din Mubarak, who sought to ameliorate some of his father's harsher restrictions. Qutb-ud-din Mubarak was overthrown in 1320 by the former slave Tughluq, founder of the Tughluq dynasty.

Further Reading

Barani, Ziyauddin. *Reign of Allauddin Khilji*. Translated by A. R. Fuller and A. Khalique. Calcutta, India: Pilgrim, 1967.

Jackson, Peter. *The Delhi Sultanate. A Political and Military History*. Cambridge, UK: Cambridge University Press, 1999.

Lal, K. S. *History of the Khaljis*. 3rd ed. New Delhi, India: Munshiram Manoharlal, 1980.

Pal, Dharam. "Ala'-ud-Din's Price Control System." *Islamic Culture* 18 (1944): 44–52.

Pal, Dharam. "Ala'-ud-Din Khilji's Mongol Policy." *Islamic Culture* 21 (1947): 255–263.

John A. Wagner

Babur (1483–1530)

At the end of the Middle Ages, Asia was dominated by three Turkish empires. The Ottomans conquered the Byzantine Empire, taking over the age-old city of Constantinople. The Safavids ruled in Persia, and the Mughals established their rule in India. All three were Islamic empires, and all three based their

Babur on his throne, surrounded by court and attendents. Miniature from the Baburnama. Fol. 247. Moghul dynasty, 1530. Scala/ Art Resource.

military success on the use of gunpowder, a technology that signaled the end of the medieval world. The Mughal Empire in India was founded by Zahir al-Din Muhammad, known as Babur ("the Tiger").

Babur claimed descent from Chinggis (Genghis) Khan and **Timur**, and like his forefathers, he dreamed of transforming his inherance of a small kingdom in Turkestan into an empire. He began by attacking Afghanistan and capturing Kabul in 1504, then he crossed the mountains into Hindustan and attacked the **Delhi sultanate**. Babur brought gunpowder weapons, including artillery and firearm, which gave him a large advantage over the more-numerous Indians. In 1526, at the Battle of Panipat, his small army of only twelve-thousand men defeated the sultan's forces. He captured Agra and Delhi and established himself as sultan. He founded a dynasty called the Mughal, which is a Persian term for "**Mongol**."

Babur seemed to care little for India. Many of his followers wanted to take their spoils of war and leave the hot, humid climate that ruined their bows and dampened their gunpowder, but the conqueror had decided to make India the center for a new empire. Babur was also unhappy to find no gardens in India like the ones he had known in Kabul, so he began construction of a magnificent Persian-style garden in Agra. Babur also had literary tastes and wrote an autobiography—the earliest Islamic autobiographical work—that is called in English, *The Baburnama*. This remains a fascinating glimpse into the life of this complex, influential man.

He was not content with the conquest of the north, and by the time of his death in 1530, Babur had built a loosely knit empire that stretched from Kabul through the Punjab to the borders of **Bengal**. The empire he founded was known for its interaction with the Portuguese and the British, and for creating magnificent artistic gems like the great Taj Mahal. But these events belong to the modern age; Babur was the medieval link between the old and the new. *See also* Document 22.

Further Reading

Richards, John F. *The Mughal Empire*. Cambridge, UK: Cambridge University Press, 1993.
Thackston, W. M. *The Baburnama: Memoirs of Babur, Prince and Emperor*. New York: Modern Library, 2002.

Joyce E. Salisbury

Bahmani Kingdom

The Bahmani kingdom was a Muslim sultanate centered on the northern **Deccan**. The kingdom was established in 1347, when Hasan Gangu, governor of the southern provinces of the **Delhi sultanate**, then ruled by Sultan

Muhammad bin Tughluq, declared his independence with the support of the southern nobility. Ruling as Ala al-Din Hasan Shah Bahmani, Hasan Gangu founded a dynasty that lasted until 1538.

Until 1425, when the capital was moved northward to Bidar by Ahmad Shah (r. 1422–1435), the Bahmanis ruled from the city of Gulbarga over a large territory that extended from the Arabian Sea in the west across the northern Deccan and ran from Berar in the north to the Krishna River in the south. For much of its existence the Bahmani kingdom was at war with the Hindu **Vijayanagar Empire** to the south, a conflict embittered by the clash of religions. The kingdom reached its height in the late fifteenth century, but thereafter the authority of the central government weakened; after 1518, various provincial governors declared their independence, causing the Bahmani state to break up into five successor states—Ahmednagar, Berar, Bidar, Bijapur, and Golconda—known collectively as the Deccan sultanates.

The Bahmani state was divided into four provinces governed by regional commanders who had extensive powers. Assisting in provincial administration were military officers who drew their revenues from lands assigned to them, similar to the *iqta* system employed in the Delhi sultanate. Indeed, the central administration of the Bahmani state tended to mirror that of the Delhi sultanate, except for a more highly developed financial department and a stronger wazir, the officer who headed the civil administration and who often tended to dominate the central government under a weak sultan. The Bahmani state also tended to employ large numbers of foreigners, especially Iranians, as local military officers and magistrates. Under the later sultans, Hindu Brahmans also frequently held important local positions, a practice that may have initially arisen from a popular tradition that a Brahman had prophesied Hasan Gangu's rise to power.

Further Reading

Qanungo, K. R. "Origin of the Bahamani Sultans of Deccan." *Dacca University Studies* 3 (1936): 137–144.

Sherwani, H. K. *The Bahmanis of the Deccan.* Hyderabad, India: Manager of Publications, 1955.

Sherwani, H. K. *The Great Bahmani Wazir Mahmud Gavan.* Allahabad, India: Kitabistan, 1942.

Sherwani, H. K. "The Independence of Bahmani Governors." *Proceedings of the Indian History Congress* (1944): 256–262.

Sinha, S. K. *Medieval History of the Deccan.* Edited by Muhammad Abdul Waheed Khan. Hyderabad, India: Andhra Pradesh Government, 1964.

John A. Wagner

Balban, Ghiyas al-Din (d. 1286)

A former slave of Sultan Shams al-Din **Iltutmish** (r. 1210–1236), Ghiyas al-Din Balban was sultan of Delhi from 1266 to 1286. During his reign, Balban strengthened the hold of the central government over the provincial governors of the **Delhi sultanate** and sought to restrict high position to persons of noble birth, a distinct change in policy for the Mamluk or Ghulam dynasty, whose members were mainly Turkish ex-slaves.

Balban was born into the Ilbaris tribe, a large Turkish clan of Central Asia over which his father was chief. As a youth, Balban was captured by the **Mongols** and sold into slavery, his first master being a rich merchant of Basra in what is now southern Iraq. His master took him to Delhi and sold him to Sultan Iltutmish, who made him a member of the *chihilganis*, the famous Corps of Forty, which consisted of Turkish slave military officers who each commanded a group of forty slave subordinates. Upon the sultan's death in 1236, Balban supported his daughter **Raziya Sultan**, who made him her Lord of the Hunt. However, Balban eventually turned against her and joined the conspiracy of nobles that overthrew her in 1240. Under Raziya's successors, Bahram Shah (r. 1240–1242) and Ala al-Din Mas'ud (r. 1242–1246), Balban served as commander of Rewari and Hansi and distinguished himself in campaigns against the Mongols.

During the reign of Nasir al-din Mahmud Shah (1246–1266), Balban served as *na'ib-i mamlikat*, or viceroy, running the central administration in the sultan's behalf. This position gave him great power but also made him enemies, and he was overthrown in 1252 by a palace coup led by Imad al-Din Rehan; however, because his supplanter was an Indian Muslim, most of the Turkish nobility rallied behind him and he was restored to his position in 1254. As *na'ib-i mamlikat*, Balban conducted several successful campaigns against the Mongols. Upon the sultan's death in 1266, Balban proclaimed himself sultan as Ghiyas al-Din.

Although he had risen from it, he considered the corps of Turkish slave offices to be the root cause of the political instability that had afflicted the Delhi sultanate since the death of Iltutmish. The *chihilganis* had displaced the nobility in the high offices of state and their intrigues and jealousies had disrupted the reigns of recent sultans. Balban thus eliminated the *chihilganis* and promoted men of noble birth. He continued to protect the northwest frontier from Mongol incursions and dealt harshly with any provincial governors, such as Toghril in **Bengal**, who opposed him. Balban died in 1266 and was succeeded by his grandson Muiz al-Din Qaiqabas (r. 1286–1290).

Further Reading

Chandel, L. S. *Early Medieval State: A Study of the Delhi Sultanate.* New Delhi, India: Commonwealth, 1989.

Hambly, Gavin R. G. "Who Were the Chihilgani, the Forty Slaves of Sultan Shams al-Din Iltutmish of Delhi?" *Iran* 10 (1972): 57–62.

Jackson, Peter. *The Delhi Sultanate. A Political and Military History.* Cambridge, UK: Cambridge University Press, 1999.

Nigam, S. B. P. *Nobility under the Sultans of Delhi A.D. 1260–1398.* Delhi, India: Munshiram Manoharlal, 1968.

John A. Wagner

Banabhatta (Bana) (fl. seventh century c.e.)

Recognized as one of the great Sanskrit literary figures of medieval India, Banabhatta (also known as Bana) was the *asthana kavi* or court poet to the seventh-century North Indian ruler **Harsha** of Kanauj (r. 606–647). Banabhatta's works were so well regarded that they gave rise to a famous Sanskrit pun, which states that while savoring his writing, readers "do not find interest in food."

Little is known of Banabhatta's life beyond what he says about himself in the opening chapters of the *Harsacarita* ("Deeds of Harsha"), his biography of

Harsha. Banabhatta was born in the village of Preetikoot into an important Brahmin family of the Vatsyayana clan. His mother died when he was very young and his father when he was about 14. He spent his youth traveling about North India with his half-brothers, visiting universities and royal courts and acquiring, through persistence and hard work, sufficient **education** to allow him to develop his skill at writing. Thanks to this skill, he was eventually called to the court of Harsha, who became his friend and patron.

Besides the *Harsacarita*, which is a valuable historical source, especially for the early years of Harsha's reign, and the finest example of medieval Sanskrit biography, Banabhatta wrote a prose romance titled *Kadambari*, which describes the adventures of two sets of lovers through a series of incarnations. Banabhatta's style is complex and elaborate, involving detailed descriptions, lengthy constructions, and many poetic devices. Both works were left unfinished, though *Kadambari* was completed by Banabhatta's son, Bhusanabhatta. *See also* Document 8.

Further Reading

Kadambari (of Banabhatta): A Classical Sanskrit Story of Magical Transformations. Translated with an Introduction by Gwendolyn Layne. Garland World Library of Literature in Translation, vol. 12. London: Garland Publishing, 1991.

Shastri, R. P., ed. *The Harsacharita of Banabhatta*. Translated by E. P. Cowell and P. W. Thomas. Global Sanskrit Literature Series in English, 12. Delhi, India: Global Vision Publishing House, 2004.

John A. Wagner

Bengal

Bengal is a historical and geographical region of northeastern India that today comprises the nation of Bangladesh and the Indian state of West Bengal, as well as portions of the states of Bihar, Orissa, and Tripura. During the life of Gautama Buddha in the sixth century B.C.E., Bengal was the center of the kingdom of Magadha, then one of the most important Indian states. In the early medieval period, Magadha formed the core of the North Indian Gupta Empire.

Shashanka, the first known king of an independent Bengal, ruled in the early seventh century. The accounts of **Banabhatta** (Bana), court poet of the Emperor **Harsha** (r. 606–647), and of the Chinese monk Xuanzang, seem to indicate that Shashanka, whom they also accuse of being anti-Buddhist, had some responsibility for the death of Harsha's elder brother Rajyavardhana, king of Thanesar, whose murder led to Harsha's accession to his brother's throne. Harsha, in alliance with other local rulers, launched a military campaign into Bengal, but the region does not appear to have come fully under Harsha's control until after Shashanka's death in about 625.

After a period of anarchy that followed the collapse of Harsha's empire, Gopala (r. c. 750–770) founded the Buddhist Pala dynasty, which ruled most of Bengal and Bihar until the late eleventh century. His successors Dharmapala (r. 770–810) and Devapala (r. 810–850) expanded the Pala Empire across northern and eastern India. The Pala state was overthrown by the Hindu Sena dynasty in about 1095. Buddhism, which had heretofore been a powerful influence in Bengal, declined under the Hindu Senas, who introduced the caste system into the region in the late twelfth century. The Sena dynasty lasted until about 1230, but parts of Bengal were conquered prior to that by the Muslim **Delhi sultanate**. The sultans of Delhi eventually controlled the entire region until the sultanate itself collapsed in the sixteenth century, when Bengal, like the rest of North India, was incorporated into the Muslim Mughal Empire.

Further Reading

Chowdhuri, Abdul Momin. *Dynastic History of Bengal (c. 750–1200 A.D.)*. Dacca, Bangladesh: Asiatic Society of Pakistan, 1967.

Husain, Sued Ejaz. *The Bengal Sultanate: Politics, Economy and Coins (A.D. 1205–1576)*. Delhi: Manohar, 2003.

Majumdar, R. C., ed. *History of Bengal*. Dacca, Bangladesh: University of Dacca, 1943.

Roy, Atul Chandra. *History of Bengal: Turko-Afghan Period*. New Delhi, India: Kalyani, 1987.

John A. Wagner

Brahmagupta (c. 598–c. 660)

Brahmagupta was an astronomer and mathematician who was born around 598 in the town of Bhillamala (modern Bhinnmal, near Mount Abu in Rajasthan). He moved to Ujjain, a town in the State of Gwalior in central India, which was then the center of Hindu mathematics and astronomy. It had the best observatory in India and also had a wonderful collection of the writings of ancient scientists, such as Hero of Alexandria (first century C.E.), Ptolemy (second century C.E.), and others from as far away as China. The young mathematician did more than study these ancients, he corrected their errors.

The Indian scientists in Ujjain wrote mathematical texts as poetry. Their view was that mathematical problems were undertaken for pleasure, so they were cloaked in poetry. Brahmagupta learned this style of writing and adopted it as his own. By the age of thirty, Brahmagupta had completed his masterwork, "The Improved Astronomical System of Brahma" (*Brahma sphuta siddhanta*). The first ten chapters of this work deal with various astronomical issues, including the true longitudes of the planets, lunar and solar eclipses, and the lunar crescent and its conjunctions with the planets. The following thirteen chapters consider an analysis of previous work on astronomy, and chapters on mathematics and geometry. All but two of the chapters deal with astronomy, but modern scholars focus on two chapters (12 and 18, which deal with algebra and mathematics.

Although Brahmagupta dismissed his own work on mathematics as incidental to the study of the heavens, modern scholars are particularly interested in his work on indeterminate equations and the geometry of quadrilaterals. Brahmagupta found the formulas for the diagonals of a quadrilateral. He provided fairly accurate figures for the circumference of the earth and the length of the calendar year. For all his advances, he refused to believe that the earth revolved around the sun and spun on its axis, both ideas that were under discussion at the time.

Probably his most influential contribution was the introduction of negative numbers. These negative numbers were especially useful to merchants in representing debts, so they came into wide use. By 700, Hindu merchants had introduced Brahmagupta's mathematics to the Arabs, and the entirety of his famous work was translated into Arabic by 775. Through these channels, the great mathematician's works influenced the history of mathematics through-out much of the world.

Further Reading
Prakash, Satya. *A Critical Study of Brahmagupta and His Works.* New Delhi: Indian Insti-tute of Astronomical and Sanskrit Research, 1968.

Joyce E. Salisbury

Caste System

The caste system was the traditional means of social organization in India. Its origins probably lay in ancient Indo-European settlements when invaders established rule over indigenous peoples and the rulers set themselves apart. The Indo-Europeans (also called Aryans) used the term *varna*, a Sanskrit word meaning "color," to refer to the major social classes. The term does not refer to skin color, but instead a system of color symbolism that reflects the qualities that were present in members of the castes.

By about 1000 B.C.E., the Aryans recognized four *varnas.* The highest *varna* is that of the Brahmans, the scholars and priests. Their obligations were to study and teach, to perform sacrifices to the deities, and to receive gifts. Brahmans were associated with white, the color of purity and lightness.

The second *varna* is that of the warriors and aristocrats, called *Kshatriya.* These were charged with protecting everyone in the kingdom, including the priestly Brahman, who in return performed the sacrifices necessary to bring blessings on the rulers. The *Kshatriya* were associated with red, the color of passion and energy. The ancient Hindu holy books always wrote of a power-struggle between these two top *varnas,* which paralleled the medieval struggle in the West between pope and emperor.

The third *varna* is that of the *Vaisya,* who made a living from the land. These included farmers, herders, artisans, and merchants. *Vaisyas* are associated with yellow, the color of the earth, reminding them of their duty to tend the land. Members of the lowest *varna* are the *shudras,* servants, landless serfs, and those who perform menial tasks. *Shudras* are associated with black, the color of dark-ness and inertia.

The first three *varnas* are called "twice-born," because the boys undergo an initiation ceremony: their "second birth." Only the twice-born castes were al-lowed to hear the sacred scriptures, the Vedas, and only the Brahmans could recite the scriptures during rituals.

These four groups made up traditional Indian society, but they were by no means the only inhabitants. One group was called the Untouchables. These were excluded from the caste system—literally "outcastes"—either because they were foreign, or more likely because they performed tasks that were consid-ered polluting, such as working with leather and sweeping excrement from the village. The untouchable classes certainly date from the first millennium B.C.E., and the medieval sources mention them as well. For example, the Chi-nese Buddhist pilgrim **Faxian** observed that untouchables had to strike a piece of wood before entering a town as a warning for people to avoid them (Giles, 21). Ascetics, Buddhists and Jains (*see* **Jainism**), may also be considered to be outside the *varna* system.

By the Middle Ages, the four *varnas* no longer adequately described society. As occupations became specialized and society more complex, a hierarchy of subcastes known as *jati* developed. The word *jati* means "birth," which emphasizes that one is born into one's status. Indeed one's caste is a property of the body and cannot be removed. Only in another life could one hope to rise in caste. The term *jati* refers to all categories of beings. Insects, plants, domestic animals, and wild animals are all *jatis* suggesting that the difference among castes is as great as a difference among species. Occupation largely determined an individual's *jati*, and to give a sense of the proliferation in complexity, by the eighteenth century, Brahmins divided themselves into some eighteen hundred *jati*.

The *jati* were supposed to keep the castes rigidly separate, with theoretical penalties imposed for crossing the caste barriers. However, the proliferation of *jatis* worked as a means of social mobility. Whole *jatis* might improve their status as a group, or a new one might develop. The whole caste system was so entrenched in the Middle Ages, that often individuals identified more closely with their *jati* than with their cities or states. Castes played a large role in maintaining social discipline in India. *See also* Document 4.

Further Reading

Flood, Gavin. *An Introduction to Hinduism.* Cambridge, UK: Cambridge University Press, 1996.

Giles, H. A. *The Travels of Fa-Hsien (399-415 AD).* Cambridge, UK: Cambridge University Press, 1923.

Thapar, Romila. *A History of India.* Harmondsworth, UK: Penguin, 1966.

Joyce E. Salisbury

Ganga, goddess personifying the river Ganges. Stone with architectural element, 5th–6th century, Gupta transition style, India. The Art Archive/Collection Antonovich/Gianni Dagli Orti.

Chandra Gupta II Vikramaditya (r. c. 375–c. 415)

Chandra Gupta II, often referred to as Vikramaditya, was the greatest ruler of the **Gupta Empire**. He expanded the empire by annexing neighboring kingdoms, so he ended up controlling a vast state extending from the mouth of the Ganges River to the mouth of the Indus River, and from what is now North Pakistan in the north to the mouth of the Narmada River in Central India.

Historians use coins as significant sources of information on a given period, as testimony to the wealth of the age and to see the iconography of the period. Chandra Gupta II's coins are particularly revealing. He issued a large number of gold coins showing the wealth of the Guptas during this period. However, he also started producing silver coins as well. Silver coins, worth less than gold, indicate that prosperity extended beyond the wealthiest rulers who could trade in gold. Silver exchange reveals the vibrant economy that marked the rule of the Gupta dynasty.

The Chinese pilgrim **Faxian** arrived in India during the reign of Chandra Gupta II, and his testimony reveals that the kingdom was prosperous and peaceful. Indeed, under Chandra Gupta II's reign the dynasty reached its height in wealth and cultural achievements.

In addition to supporting Buddhism, Chandra Gupta II was a patron of literature. He gathered a group of poets to his court. This group was known as the "Nine Gems," and the greatest among them was **Kalidasa**, who is often referred to as the Shakespeare of India. Kalidasa wrote three plays and four poems, which fuse together themes of nature and love within the framework of Hinduism. His works remain much read and reveal the courtly society of the times.

A tangible recollection of the greatness of Chandra Gupta's reign is an iron pillar in Delhi dating to the fourth century. This pillar bears an inscription saying it was erected in honor of the Hindu god Vishnu in memory of Chandra Gupta II. It is made of 98 percent wrought iron and has stood more than 1,600 years without rusting or decomposing. This pillar serves as eloquent remembrance of a king whose reign embodied greatness in religion, literature, and a science that could produce such a gem of metallurgy.

Further Reading
Hinds, Kathryn. *India's Gupta Dynasty*. New York: Benchmark Books, 1996.

Joyce E. Salisbury

Chaturanga

In the early sixth century C.E., Indians created a parlor game, called Chaturanga (four-fold division of the army), which mimicked the ancient Indian battlefield. It was a direct ancestor to the modern game of chess, but unlike chess it used chance (in the form of a dice throw) and skill. In the modern chess version of Chaturanga, the infantry is replaced by the pawn, the cavalry by the knight, the elephant by the bishop, the chariot by the rook, and the general by the queen. The original intention of the game as it related to the Indian battlefield could be seen by the manner in which each piece moved.

Further Reading
Hooper, David, and Kenneth Whyld. *The Oxford Companion to Chess*. 2nd ed. Oxford, UK: Oxford University Press, 1996.

Raman N. Seylon

Deccan

The term *Deccan* traditionally refers to an ill-defined region of South India extending roughly from the Namada River in central India to the land between the Krishna and Tungbhadra Rivers in southern India (the Krishna-Tungbhadra Doab) and encompassing mainly the hill country and central plateau of the southern subcontinent. Throughout the medieval period, the Deccan provided a tempting target for expansion to the Hindu and Muslim powers of the North, who sough frequently to push their authority beyond the Namada River, the traditional boundary between North and South India.

In the twelfth century, the northern Deccan came under the sway of the Yadavas, a Hindu dynasty that ruled from Deogir. The Yadavas were overthrown in 1307, when an invasion led by **Allauddin Khilji's** general Malik **Kafur** brought the region under the control of the **Delhi sultanate** and opened the Deccan to Islamic cultural influence. Sultan **Muhammad bin Tughluq** completed the Islamic conquest of the Deccan in the 1330s, but by 1347 a revolt of the local nobility ended Delhi's rule and resulted in the establishment of the **Bahmani kingdom**, an Islamic state that gradually expanded its authority across the Deccan at the expense of the Hindu states to the south. The Bahmani state lasted until the early sixteenth century, when it disintegrated into several smaller Muslim states that were gradually absorbed by the expanding Mughal Empire in the sixteenth and seventeenth centuries.

From the 1330s, the southern Deccan was largely controlled by the Hindu **Vijayanagar Empire**, with its capital at the newly built city of Vijayanagar on the southern bank of the Tungbhadra River. Until its collapse in the sixteenth century, Vijayanagar prevented the expansion of the Bahmani kingdom and its Muslim successor states into South India. However, the military and cultural influence of the Islamic powers to the north was made clear by one Vijayanagar king's assumption of the title "Sultan among Hindu Kings," and by the presence of Muslim cavalry in the kingdom's army.

Further Reading

Sherwani, H. K., and P. M. Joshi, eds. *History of Medieval Deccan, 1295–1724*. Hyderabad, India: Publications Bureau, Government of Maharashtra, 1973–74.

Sinha, S. K. *Medieval History of the Deccan*. Edited by Muhammad Abdul Waheed Khan. Hyderabad, India: Andhra Pradesh Government, 1964.

John A. Wagner

Delhi Sultanate

Ruled by a series of Turkish and Afghan dynasties from the thirteenth to the sixteenth centuries, the sultanate centered on the North Indian city of Delhi was the first major Islamic state on Indian soil.

The foundation of the sultanate and its first dynasty, known as the Mamluk dynasty, is usually dated to 1206. In that year, following the murder of the Afghan invader Muhammad Ghori, Qutb-ud-din **Aybak**, a Turkish ex-slave and one of the late sultan's commanders, is thought to have proclaimed himself first sultan of Delhi and ruler of Muhammad Ghauri's recently conquered North Indian territories. Qutb-ud-din Aibak died in 1210 and was succeeded by Shams al-Din **Iltutmish** (r. 1210–1236), another Turkish ex-slave who married his predecessor's daughter. He was succeeded by his daughter **Raziya**, who, as sultan from 1236 to 1240, was one of the few female rulers of medieval India. Iltutmish, who was formally recognized as sultan of Delhi in 1229 by the caliph of Baghdad, and Ghiyas al-Din **Balban** (r. 1266–1286), were the most capable of the Mamluk sultans.

In 1290, the Mamluks were overthrown by the Khilji dynasty, whose best-known member was Sultan **Allauddin Khilji** (r. 1296–1316). Allauddin extended his authority westward into Gujarat and southward into the **Deccan**, and during the course of the fourteenth century the sultanate came to control most of the Indian subcontinent. Under Allauddin, the armies of the sultanate drove back a series of **Mongol** invasions, thereby initiating a period of relative peace and order that allowed the development of an Indo-Muslim culture that achieved significant advances in music, architecture, literature, and religion.

In 1320, Ghiyas al-Din Tughluq, seized the throne and the dynasty he founded, the Tughluqs, ruled until the early fifteenth century. During the reigns of **Muhammad bin Tughluq** (1325–1351) and **Firuz Shah Tughluq** (1351–1388), attempts were made to strengthen the authority of the central government in the provinces and to stabilize the **food** supply by improving irrigation in the area around Delhi. Muhammad bin Tughluq extended state patronage to non-Muslim institutions and took Hindus into his service, but Firuz Shah Tughluq imposed the *jiziya* tax on Hindu Brahmins and more strictly enforced Islamic **law** throughout the sultanate. In 1398, 10 years after Firuz Shah's death, the Mongol-Turkish invader **Timur** captured and sacked Delhi, which event led to the fall of the Tughluq dynasty in 1412 and the fragmentation of the Tughluq state, with independent local sultanates being established in **Bengal**, Gujarat, and elsewhere. Although the sultanate revived briefly under the Lodi dynasty in the late fifteenth century, it was finally conquered by the first Mughal ruler, **Babur**, in 1526.

Further Reading

Chandel, L. S. *Early Medieval State: A Study of the Delhi Sultanate*. New Delhi, India: Commonwealth, 1989.

Husain, A. Madhi. *The Rise and Fall of Muhammad bin Tughluq*. Delhi, India: Idara-I Adbiyat, 1972.

Jackson, Peter. *The Delhi Sultanate. A Political and Military History*. Cambridge, UK: Cambridge University Press, 1999.

Lal, K. S. *History of the Khaljis*. 3rd ed. New Delhi, India: Munshiram Manoharlal, 1980.

John A. Wagner

Faxian (d. c. 422)

Buddhism had begun in India but had spread widely through Asia into China during the centuries after the death of the Buddha. In particular, the Emperor Ashoka of Mauryan dynasty in about 260 B.C.E. became a devout Buddhist. Under his patronage, missionaries began to spread throughout Asia. By the Middle Ages, there were Buddhist monks in China, and this tradition led to a remarkable account by Faxian, a Chinese Buddhist who traveled to India to learn more about Buddhism in the land of its birth. In the process, he left an account that is a valuable source of information about medieval India.

Faxian, whose name means "illustrious master of the law," had been orphaned at an early age. Instead of living with his uncle, he decided to follow the religious life. When he was age 25, Faxian wanted to learn about Buddhist traditions in India and to read authentic Buddhist writings, so he began an impressive pilgrimage. He made his way on foot across Xinjiang and the mountain passes, taking 6 years to reach India—from about 399–405 C.E. When he arrived at the capital of the **Gupta Empire**, he taught himself Sanskrit, procured texts, drawings, and relics, and then began his return journey by sea. He spent 2 years in Sri Lanka and also visited Java. Altogether, during the 15 years of his journey, he traveled a distance of some 8,000 miles. Once back in China, he devoted his life to translating the precious texts from Sanskrit. He died when he was about 88 years old.

Faxian's description of the Gupta Empire is colored by his piety and his Buddhism, but nevertheless it is a fascinating first-hand account of the golden age of the Guptas. He wrote that Buddhism was flourishing but noted that all the Hindu cults were tolerated and there was no animosity among them. Throughout his account, he described monastic rituals and the locations of the relics of Buddha.

He also described secular aspects of society. He described how roads were well maintained and safe. He commented that taxes were relatively light, and there was no capital punishment. (Such observations may say more by contrast about the state of things in the China he knew than in India.) He also described with praise the tradition of state-supported charities that provided free hospitalization to residents and visiting foreigners alike. No doubt overstating his observations, he claimed that all Indians were vegetarians and never drank intoxicating beverages. Finally, he described "untouchable" castes, people whose presence was so polluting that they could have no contact with others.

Faxian's travels were important for many reasons. Not only did he provide witness to medieval Indian society, but also he showed the enduring impact of cross-cultural contact between India and China. Furthermore, the texts he translated and preserved contributed to an invigorated Buddhist tradition in China. *See also* Documents 3 and 4.

Further Reading
Faxian. *A Record of the Buddhistic Kingdoms.* Translated by James Legge. Oxford, UK: Clarendon Press, 1886.

Joyce E. Salisbury

Firuz Shah Tughluq (d. 1388)

Firuz Shah succeeded his cousin, **Muhammad bin Tughluq**, as ruler of the **Dehli sultanate** in 1351, when he was proclaimed sultan by the nobles who had accompanied the army into Sind, where Muhammad Tughluq had been on campaign when he died.

Upon returning to Delhi, Firuz Shah's first act was the execution of his predecessor's wazir, Ahmad bin Ayaz Khwaja Jahan, who had attempted to place a young puppet sultan on the throne in the army's absence. Firuz Shah improved relations between the central government and the nobility by making the *iqta*, the assignment of revenue from a particular tract of land in lieu of a salary, hereditary, so that a son automatically inherited his father's financial resources and local influence. The sultan also ceased any further attempts to reestablish Delhi's control over the **Deccan**, **Bengal**, or Sind, thus reducing the pressure for men and supplies exerted by the central government on the magnates who administered the provinces.

In Delhi, Firuz Shah commenced an extensive building program, constructing new mosques, forts, dams, and canals. The latter constructions were an important part of the sultan's attempt to improve irrigation in the region around Delhi, where famines were a common occurrence. Adhering strictly to Islamic **law**, Firuz Shah abolished the harsh punishments imposed by his predecessors, especially on rebels, and eliminated various taxes not sanctioned by *shari'a*. However, he displayed little tolerance for Hinduism, extending the *jiziya*, a poll tax on non-Muslims, to the Brahmins, who had been exempt, and to Hindu residents of towns. He also demolished various Hindu temples, claiming that they had been constructed without permission in the reigns of previous sultans. The much more ancient Hindu temples at Puri and Kangra were destroyed during the course of a military campaign. Efforts were also made to encourage conversions to Islam. Voluntary Hindu converts received rich rewards, while enslaved Hindus from the provinces were forcibly converted and sent to Delhi, perhaps in an attempt to increase the city's Muslim population as well as its support for the Sultanate against the Hindu majority.

Firuz Shah was the last strong sultan of Delhi. Following his death in 1388, the Delhi sultanate was weakened by a succession struggle, which allowed local nobles to free themselves from the authority of Delhi and to govern their territories as independent rulers. In 1398, the army of the Central Asian invader **Timur** the Lame (Tamerlane) captured and sacked Delhi itself.

Further Reading

Bannerjee, Jamini Mohan. *History of Firoz Shah Tughluq*. Delhi, India: Munshiram Manoharlal, 1967.

Chandel, L. S. *Early Medieval State: A Study of the Delhi Sultanate*. New Delhi, India: Commonwealth, 1989.

Islam, Zafarul. "Firuz Shah's Attitude toward Non-Muslims." *Islamic Culture* 64, no. 4 (1990): 65–79.

Jackson, Peter. *The Delhi Sultanate. A Political and Military History*. Cambridge, UK: Cambridge University Press, 1999.

Wolpert, Stanley. *A New History of India*. 8th ed. Oxford, UK: Oxford University Press, 2008.

John A. Wagner

Food. *See* **Agriculture**

Ghaurids

Emerging as a power in the early twelfth century, the Muslim Ghaurid dynasty was the ruling family of Ghaur, a mountainous region in what is now Afghanistan. In the 1190s, the Ghaurids invaded and conquered much of North India, thereby creating a conglomeration of territories that after 1206 became the core of the **Delhi sultanate**, the first powerful Muslim state in India.

In the early twelfth century, the Ghaurids, who had their capital at Firuz Koh, experienced frequent raids on their territory by the rulers of Ghazni. In 1149, the Ghaurid ruler Eiz-ad Din Hosayn was slain during an abortive attack on Ghazni. However, in 1150, Eiz-ad Din Hosayn's son 'Ala al-Din (r. 1149–1161) captured Ghazni and sacked the city so ruthlessly that he acquired the sobriquet *Jahansoz* ("world incendiary"). In 1163, the Ghaurid throne passed to 'Ala al-Din's nephew Ghiyas al-Din Muhammad bin Sam, who, in 1175, installed his younger brother, Mu'izz al-Din Muhammad Ghauri, as sultan at Ghazni, while he continued to rule in Firuz Koh. Ghiyas al-Din extended Ghaurid authority westward into Iran, where he posed as the champion of Sunnis with the blessing of the Abbasid caliph in Baghdad. In the east, Muhammad Ghauri, leading an army comprising the hill people of Ghaur and Turkish and Khilji cavalry (the Khiljis were an Afghan nomadic people), captured Multan, in northwestern India, in 1176, and Lahore, in the Punjab, in 1186. To govern the conquered territories outside Ghaur, the two brothers recruited large numbers of Turkish slaves, who were given important administrative positions and military commands.

In 1191, Muhammad Ghauri, invaded North India, but was defeated by the Hindu ruler **Prithviraja III** at the First Battle of Tarain. In 1192, at the Second Battle of Tarain, Muhammad Ghauri defeated and killed Prithviraja, whose kingdom, which included Delhi, was largely overrun by the invaders. Administration of the new conquests was given to Muhammad Ghauri's former slave, **Qutb al-Din Aybak**, who established himself in Delhi. Upon Ghiyas al-din's death in 1203, Muhammad Ghauri ruled the vast Ghaurid Empire alone, until he was murdered in 1206, whereupon the Ghaurid state collapsed. In Delhi, Qutb al-Din Aybak declared himself independent, thereby establishing the Delhi Sultanate in the Ghaurid territories of North India, while Taj al-din Yildiz, another former slave of the Ghaurids, seized power in Ghazni.

Further Reading

Bosworth, C. E. "The Early Islamic History of Ghor." *Central Asiatic Journal* 6 (1961): 116–133.

Bosworth, C. E. "The Political and Dynastic History of the Iranian World (A.D. 1000–1200)." In P. Avery et al., eds., *The Cambridge History of Iran.* Volume 5. Cambridge, UK: Cambridge University Press, 1991, pp. 157–166.

Jackson, Peter. "The Fall of the Ghuarid Dynasty." In *Festschrift for Professor Edmund Bosworth.* Edited by Carloe Hillenbrand. Edinburgh, Scotland: n.p., n.d.

John A. Wagner

Gupta Empire (320–550)

Before the Middle Ages, northern India had been unified under the Mauryan dynasty. In 184 B.C.E., the last of the Mauryan kings was assassinated and northern India once again split into various kingdoms. Yet the Mauryan kingdom had left a legacy of the ideal of empire and a memory of how to administer an empire. Even as the subcontinent splintered into kingdoms that waged intermittent war among themselves, Indian society grew. The regional kingdoms provided stability within their realms, and commerce flourished. Merchants brought wealth into these kingdoms and periodically kings tried to emulate the Mauryans and create an empire. In 320 C.E., one king, Chandra Gupta I, succeeded. He strengthened his position by marriage with a neighboring dynasty.

Chandra Gupta's son, Samudragupta (c. 330–c. 375) completed the conquest of the north and claimed tribute from southeastern **Bengal** and as far away as Nepal and Sri Lanka. He was a patron of poetry and music, establishing the Gupta dynasty's continued patronage of the arts and culture. His grandson, Kumara Gupta (c. 415–455) probably founded the monastic community at Nalanda in the Ganges River valley near Pataliputra, the Gupta capital. At Nalanda, men could study not only Buddhism, but also the Vedas,

Hindu philosophy, logic, and medicine. People came from outside India to study at this famous center, which stood until it burned down in about 988.

Like the Mauryas, the center of Gupta power was Magadha, in the Ganges River valley. From there, they consolidated a kingdom over the eastern portion of northern India. They also established tributary alliances with others and ended up controlling much of the northern part of the subcontinent.

The Gupta emperors left local government and administration in the hands of local officials, creating a somewhat decentralized state, but they fostered economic policies that brought wealth into the royal coffers. The government controlled the working of precious metals and minting of coins, and had a monopoly on salt mining and weapons manufacture. Taxation included forced labor on public works and a fee for water used on irrigated lands. However, none of these impositions was so onerous that it interfered with the growth of **agriculture** and commerce.

The Guptas were also well placed to take advantage of international trade, and their empire became the center of exchange between China and the West through the important Silk Road that linked the Roman Empire with China. Through this prosperity, the Guptas introduced an era of relative peace that allowed Indian culture to flourish. The Gupta Period is regarded by many as the golden age of Indian culture.

The Gupta rulers served as patrons of magnificent architecture, sculpture, and painting. The wall paintings of Ajanta Cave, for example, are considered some of the most stunning of Indian art. They not only show the various lives of the Buddha, but also reveal elements of daily life in India at the time. This is only one of the architectural wonders built during the Gupta era.

The Mauryan rulers had fostered the spread of Buddhism, but the Guptas favored a reinvigorated Hinduism. Some of the great religious literature—for example, the *Puranas*—were written during the rule of this dynasty, and temples spread over the land. The Guptas and their successors bestowed grants of land on Hindu Brahmins and supported an educational system that promoted Hindu values. The Gupta educational establishments also fostered learning in mathematics, where scholars developed the concepts of zero and infinity (among other things). They also developed the numeric system that we use and call "Arabic numerals" in recollection of the fact that the West learned this system from Arabs who took it from the Guptas. Medicine was advanced by the establishment of free clinics. Outside the monastic schoolrooms, devotional Hinduism became more and more popular, becoming the dominant religion in India. By about 1000, Buddhism had noticeably declined in India; the Gupta patronage had effected a major shift in the land of the Buddha.

The Gupta Empire fell prey to invaders from the north. Beginning in the 400s, the **Huns**, a nomadic people from Central Asia, pushed across the Hindu Kush Mountains into India. For the first half of the fifth century, the Guptas repelled the Huns, but the effort weakened their resources. By 480, the Huns conquered the Guptas and took over northern India. Western India was overrun by 500, and the last of the Gupta kings, presiding over a diminished kingdom, died in 550. Not until the Mughal dynasty in the sixteenth century did any state rule as much of India as the Gupta Empire. Until then, medieval India remained made up of large regional kingdoms haunted by the memory of a united land. *See also* **Chandra Gupta II Vikramaditya** and Document 6.

Further Reading

Hinds, Kathryn. *India's Gupta Dynasty*. New York: Benchmark Books, 1996.

Raychaudhuri, Hemchandra. *Political History of Ancient India*. Oxford, UK: Oxford University Press, 1998.

Joyce E. Salisbury

Harsha (590–647)

Harsha-Vardana, younger son of Prabhakar Vardhan, was ruler of a seventh-century north Indian empire that at its height encompassed the entire Indo-Gangetic Plain, from Orissa and **Bengal** in the east to the Punjab in the west.

Upon the collapse of the Gupta Empire in the midsixth century, North India was divided among several small states and kingdoms, several of which were eventually brought under the control of the Vardhana dynasty by Harsha's father. In 606, following the death of his elder brother Rajyavardhan, Harsha, though only 16, was acclaimed king by an assembly of nobles from the city of Kanya Kubja, or **Kanauj**, successor to the old Gupta capital of Pataliputra, and now the cultural center of North India. An able military leader and capable administrator, Harsha united his father's kingdom with Kanya Kubja, to which he transferred his capital. He conquered Bengal, Bihar, and Orissa and extended his power in Gujarat, where he married his daughter to the local ruler. However, his attempts to push his kingdom to the south were defeated by the Chalukya ruler Pulakeshi II at a battle fought along the Narmada River in 620. The river thereafter marked the southern extent of Harsha's empire. In 641, Harsha dispatched a diplomatic mission to China, thereby establishing the first formal diplomatic relations between China and an Indian ruler.

Thanks to a Sanskrit prose biography written by his court poet, **Banabhatta** (Bana), Harsha is the best-known Indian ruler of the period. Besides being one of the most important works of medieval Indian literature, Banabhatta's *Harshacarita* is an important source for the period of Hasha's rise to power. Although his kingdom was the most powerful North Indian state since the fall of the Guptas, Harsha was never able to recreate the order and stability that the **Gupta Empire** had established in the region. Because, unlike the Guptas, Harsha did not control the major trade routes of the Northwest, he lacked the financial resources to refashion the more centralized Gupta state and his officers and officials were compensated with grants of land over which they exercised local authority. The travel accounts of the Chinese Buddhist monk **Xuanzang**, who visited Harsha's realm between 630 and 644, seem to indicate an increase in crime and political disorder in the last years of the reign, which also may have seen Harsha become more autocratic in his rule.

In religion, Harsha practiced broad tolerance for all faiths. He was so friendly to Buddhism, building many *stupas* and monasteries, that he is often claimed as a Buddhist, although, according to Bana, he was a Hindu of the Saivaite sect. Lasting more than 40 years, Harsha's reign ended in 647, perhaps with the emperor's assassination, although that is uncertain. Because Harsha apparently left no heir, his kingdom rapidly disintegrated into numerous successor states. *See also* Documents 8 and 9.

Further Reading

Mahajan, V. D. *Ancient India*. 8th ed. New Delhi, India: Chand & Company, 1978.

Wriggins, Sally Hovey. *The Silk Road Journey with Xuanzang*. Rev. ed. Boulder, CO: Westview Press, 2003.

John A. Wagner

Huns

The Huns (or Hunas) were a nomadic Central Asian people, possibly of Turkic origin, who invaded India in the fifth and sixth centuries. How these Huns may have been related to the people, also known as Huns, who invaded Europe in the fifth century is uncertain. The Hun invasion of India in the early sixth century led to the collapse of the **Gupta Empire**, the weakening of Indian Buddhism, and the political fragmentation of North India into numerous small states and kingdoms.

From the midfifth century, various Hun groups sought to enter India from the northwest via the Khyber Pass. They were held in check by the Gupta ruler Kumara Gupta (r. 415–455) and by his son Skanda Gupta (r. 455–487), but thereafter, under their leader Toramana, the Huns conquered Persia in 484 and invaded India in the 490s. By 500, they controlled the Punjab, and by 515 Toramana's son, Mihirakula, had overrun much of the Gangetic Plain, thereby virtually destroying the Guptan state. Mihirakula's reign is remembered in Indian and Chinese histories for its extreme cruelty, especially as regards the treatment of Indian Buddhists, whose monasteries and shrines were particularly marked for destruction. The decline in Buddhism noted in the midseventh century by the visiting Chinese monk **Xuanzang** was in part a legacy of the Hun conquest.

In 528, Yasodharman, king of the central Indian state of Malwi defeated the Huns and checked their expansion. By 542, shortly before his death, Mihirakula had been driven back into the Punjab by a coalition of princes allied with the fading Gupta state, which finally disappeared around 550. Thereafter, North India split into various Hindu kingdoms, which were temporarily reunited under the rule of **Harsha** in the early seventh century.

Further Reading

Mookerji, Radha K. *The Gupta Empire*. 3rd rev. ed. Delhi, India: Motilal Banarsidass, 1995.

Wolpert, Stanley. *A New History of India*. 8th ed. Oxford, UK: Oxford University Press, 2008.

John A. Wagner

Ibn Battuta (1304–1369/1377)

A Berber born in Tangier, Morocco, Abu 'Abdullah Muhammad Ibn Battuta was an Islamic scholar and jurist who is best known as a traveler and explorer who journeyed throughout almost the entire Muslim world in the fourteenth century. At the request of the sultan of Morocco, Ibn Battuta dictated a celebrated account of his travels entitled *A Gift to Those Who Contemplate the Wonders of the Cities and the Marvels of Traveling*, but popularly known simply as

Rihla or *Journey*. The *Rihla*, though appearing at times to be fictional, is virtually the only contemporary account available of life as it was in certain parts of the world in the fourteenth century, and is a valuable source for the history of the **Delhi sultanate** between 1333 and 1342.

Ibn Battuta's journeys lasted for almost 30 years and covered nearly 75,000 miles, taking him to regions that comprise 44 modern nations. Besides India, he visited East Africa, the Middle East, China, Southeast Asia, Spain, North Africa, Turkey, eastern Europe, and Mali and Timbuktu in West Africa. Ibn Battuta began his travels upon completion of his **education**, in about 1325 when he was 21. He went on pilgrimage to Mecca, but then, instead of returning home, he continued eastward, coming to India in 1333. In Delhi, Sultan **Muhammad bin Tughluq** appointed him a *qazi*, a judicial magistrate whole decided cases on the basis of Islamic **law**, a position he held for 7 years. He spent much time at court and accompanied the sultan on various trips and expeditions, including a prolonged stay at the Ganges River town of Swargadwari from 1339 to 1341.

Because of the sultan's erratic behavior, Ibn Battuta position at court was tenuous, alternating between periods of high favor and periods during which he was under suspicion for treason and other crimes. He sought to leave by expressing his desire to make another pilgrimage to Mecca, but, in 1342, Muhammad bin Tughluq opened another opportunity by sending him on embassy to the Yuan or **Mongol** dynasty emperor of China. Happy to resume his travels, Ibn Battuta used the trip to China to explore the Coromandel Coast of southeastern India, as well as Malabar and Sri Lanka. Upon the completion of his mission, instead of returning to India, Ibn Battuta simply journeyed westward, going eventually back to Tangier, from which he launched his later travels to other parts of the Islamic world. *See also* Documents 17 and 18.

Further Reading

Ibn Battuta. *The Travels of Ibn Battuta, A.D. 1325–1325.* Translated by A. R. Gibb. Vol. 3. Cambridge, UK: Cambridge University Press, 1971.
Mackintosh-Smith, Tim, ed. *The Travels of Ibn Battuta.* London: Macmillan, 2002.

John A. Wagner

Iltutmish, Shams al-Din (d. 1236)

A former slave of Sultan **Qutb al-Din Aybak**, Shams al-Din Iltutmish was sultan of Delhi from 1210 to 1236. During his reign, Iltutmish secured the independence of the **Delhi sultanate**, extended the authority of Delhi into the provinces, and avoided confrontation with the **Mongol** ruler Chinggis (Ghengis) Khan.

Born into a noble Turkish family of the Ilbari clan in Central Asia, Iltutmish, who was reportedly handsome and intelligent, excited the jealously of his brothers, who supposedly sold him to a slave trader. His new master than sold him to Qutb al-Din Aibak, himself a slave officer in the service of Mu'izz al-din Muhammad Ghauri, the **Ghaurid** ruler of Ghazni in Afghanistan. Distinguishing himself as a soldier, especially in a campaign against Khokhar tribesmen in the Punjab, Iltutmish was manumitted by his master and eventually married Aibak's daughter.

Upon the death of Mohammad Ghauri in 1206, Aibak proclaimed himself sultan of Delhi, making himself ruler of the Ghaurid territories in North India.

The new sultan appointed Iltutmish *muqti* of Baran (modern Bulandshahr); a *muqti* controlled a large territory as an ***iqta*** and was responsible for maintaining order in his holding. When Aibak died in 1210, the powerful corps of Turkish slave officers, the *chihilganis*, proclaimed Aram Shah as sultan, but his incompetence led to his rapid overthrow and replacement by Iltutmish.

The new sultan faced numerous challenges to his authority. In 1216, Illtutmish defeated Taj al-Din Yildiz, another former slave of Mohammad Ghauri, who proclaimed himself sultan at Ghazni on his master's death and who then sought to extend his rule into Mohammad Ghauri's former Indian territories. In 1227, Iltutmish defeated another claimant to his throne, Qubacha, the ruler of Sind in what is now southeastern Pakistan. In 1229, Iltutmish significantly bolstered his position by persuading the caliph of Baghdad to recognize him as sultan of Delhi.

In 1221, Iltutmish avoided a conflict with the Mongol conqueror Chinggis Khan, who had reached the banks of the Indus River in northwestern India while in pursuit of his defeated foe Jalal al-din Mingbarni. When Mingbarni crossed the river in hopes of finding refuge in the Delhi sultanate, Iltutmish refused to allow him to come to Delhi, thereby preventing a Mongol attack. Iltutmish also extended his authority in Hindu India, subjugating the rulers of Ranthambhor, Mandu, and Ujjain between 1226 and 1234. Iltutmish nominated his daughter **Raziya** as his successor, and, despite opposition from the nobility, she was able to assume the throne shortly after Iltutmish's death in 1236. *See also* Document 11.

Further Reading

Chandel, L. S. *Early Medieval State: A Study of the Delhi Sultanate*. New Delhi, India: Commonwealth, 1989.

Jackson, Peter. *The Delhi Sultanate. A Political and Military History*. Cambridge, UK: Cambridge University Press, 1999.

Wolpert, Stanley. *A New History of India*. 8th ed. Oxford, UK: Oxford University Press, 2008.

John A. Wagner

Iqta

In the **Delhi sultanate**, an *iqta* was a tract of land, varying in size from a single village to an entire province, that was granted by the sultan to nobles and military or civil officials in lieu of a cash salary. Unlike the feudal system in medieval Europe, under the *iqta* system, the land was not granted to the noble—ownership remained with its non-Muslim holder—only the revenue derived from the land. This revenue took the form of the *kharaj* or land tax on non-Muslims, collection of which was assigned to a particular individual in payment for his services to the state. The *iqta* system had developed in the Middle East in the ninth century as a method for paying military officers during periods between military campaigns when the amount of revenue flowing into the state treasury decreased.

The *iqta* system came to India via the Turks of Central Asia. It significantly increased revenue extraction from the Hindu countryside and allowed the central administration of the sultanate to effectively control rural surpluses without the need for an extensive and costly administrative structure. Because the *iqta* holders made regular payments to the government of the tithes they owed as Muslims out of the revenue they collected, the sultan's treasury funded military forces for local defense in emergencies and for the maintenance of order in the countryside. The *iqta* enabled the Delhi sultanate to maintain its large cavalry force during a period of threatened **Mongol** invasion and to feed a large urban-based, non-agricultural population.

A large *iqta* was held by a *muqti*, who maintained the cavalry forces paid for out of his revenue assignment and was responsible for **law** and order within the territories in his charge. A soldier who held only a small assignment, a village or part thereof, was called an *iqtadar*. Originally, *iqtas* were rotated among holders to prevent any individual from developing a strong interest in or claim to any particular territory. However, during the reign of Sultan **Firuz Shah Tughluq** (1351–1388) *iqtas* became hereditary, passing from father to son.

Further Reading

Habib, Irfan. "Economic History of the Delhi Sultanate: An Essay in Interpretation." *Indian Historical Review* 4 (1977): 287–303.

Qurieshi, I. H. *The Administration of the Sultanate of Delhi.* Lahore, India: Muhammad Ashraf, 1942.

Raychaudhury, Tapan, and Irfan Habib, eds. *The Cambridge Economic History of India.* Volume 1: *c. 1200–1750.* Cambridge, UK: Cambridge University Press, 1982.

John A. Wagner

Jainism

In about 540 B.C.E., a religion was founded in India that grew from the roots of Hinduism yet has been established as a separate religion on the subcontinent. The founder, Jnatrputra Vardhamana, who became known to his followers as Mahavira ("Great Hero"), was roughly a contemporary of the Buddha, and like him he was a member of the warrior caste.

Like Buddha, Mahavira was disillusioned with classical Hinduism and its pantheism of gods, and searched for enlightenment. Without clothes or a home, he wandered for 12 years and was often attacked by suspicious villagers. Eventually he experienced nirvana, a state of being free from ego and worldly attachments. After that, he was known as a "Jina" or conqueror. The word *Jain* means a follower of a Jina.

Once Mahavira achieved enlightenment, he spent his time in meditation, sitting in a crossed-legged lotus position. A Jain community consisting of monks, nuns, and laymen and **women** quickly rose up around him and numbered in the tens of thousands. When he died in about 527 B.C.E., a number of kings celebrated a festival of lights to mark the passing of his internal light, which had gone to nirvana. Jains believe that Mahavira is now in the blissful state of *ishatpragbhara*, beyond life, death, and reincarnation. After his death, his message was left in the care of eleven disciples, who collected and translated his scriptures into a canon known as the "Agamas."

Jains share with Hinduism a belief in reincarnation in a universe without beginning. Again, like Hinduism and Buddhism, Jains believe in karma, the belief that a person's thoughts and deeds are followed eventually by inevitable consequences. In Hinduism, karma is an explanation for the **caste system**; in Buddhism, karma is primarily psychological. In Jainism, however, it is understood in physical terms. Mahavira taught that individual souls are entrapped into matter perpetuated by successive births. Because every action produces karma and karma adds weight to the chains of physical bondage, the only route to escape is to avoid action altogether. In Mahavira's philosophy, an ideal life is one of extreme asceticism, culminating in death through self-starvation, a feat the master is alleged to have achieved.

Prominent in the Jain faith is the doctrine of *ahisma* or noninjury to living beings. Jains believe souls are entrapped in all living forms, from rats, to grasshoppers, to vegetables and weeds. In its extreme form of practice, holy men and women believe care should be taken to avoid taking life from any living thing. Water is strained to remove any creatures in it; masks are worn to avoid breathing small flies. Paths are swept before taking a step to clear insects, and the only acceptable **food** is that which does not cost a life. Therefore, holy people eat only fruit that has fallen naturally from trees.

Although Jainism does not acknowledge any deities, nevertheless it soon came to take on the trappings of other religions. Jains built temples for worshipers to meditate on the lives of "Tirthankaras" (pathfinders or ford builders), holy people like Mahavira, who have escaped the cycles of rebirth. Jains may also erect a Jina image and bathe it to demonstrate reverence. Some celebrate the birthday of Mahavira in the spring and his liberation in the fall.

Jainism has coexisted with Buddhism and Hinduism for millennia. The Jain view of life, with its respect for all creatures and its demand for nonviolence, has commanded much respect. It shares with Hinduism the **law** of karma and the cycle of rebirths. It shares with Buddhism the absence of deities, but, unlike the "middle way" of Buddhism, the renunciations of Jainism are more extreme.

Further Reading

Dundas, Paul. *The Jains*. New York: Routledge, 2002.

Ranking, Aidan. *The Jain Path: Ancient Wisdom for the West*. Berkeley, CA: O Books, 2006.

Joyce E. Salisbury

Jiziya

The *jiziya* was a poll tax imposed by Islamic states on their non-Muslim subjects. The tax was levied on all able-bodied non-Muslim men of military age, and thus was a payment in lieu of military service. The tax was not to be imposed on **women**, children, slaves, or those unfit for military service through age or illness, though these restrictions were often ignored in later centuries throughout the Islamic world. In the initial Muslim conquests, the *jiziya* was imposed mainly on Christians and Jews, people of a religious faith based on some type of scripture.

In India, the *jiziya* was imposed on Hindus and in Iran on Zoroastrians. For the conquered, the *jiziya* represented a continuation of the taxes they had paid to their former rulers; for the Muslims, it represented an acknowledgment of the taxpayer's subjugation to Islam. Although payment of the *jiziya* supposedly entitled non-Muslims to practice their faith, to some communal autonomy, to military protection, and to exemption from other taxes, these privileges were also often ignored, and many people converted to Islam to escape payment of the *jiziya*.

In the **Delhi sultanate**, there was initially little distinction between the *jiziya* and the land tax imposed on non-Muslims known as the *kharaj*. Under Sultan **Firuz Shah Tughluq** (r. 1351–1388), an attempt was made to extend imposition of the *jiziya* to Brahmins and to urban Hindus, but resistance was great and the tax was apparently dropped.

Further Reading

Goiten, S. D. "Evidence on the Muslim Poll Tax from Non-Muslim Sources." *Journal of the Economic and Social History of the Orient* 6 (1963): 278–279.

Habib, Irfan. "Economic History of the Delhi Sultanate: An Essay in Interpretation." *Indian Historical Review* 4 (1977): 287–303.

Islam, Riazul. "Some Aspects of the Economy of Northern South Asia during the Fourteenth Century. *Journal of Central Asia* 11, no. 2 (1988): 5–39.

Raychaudhury, Tapan, and Irfan Habib, eds. *The Cambridge Economic History of India.* Volume 1: *c. 1200–1750.* Cambridge, UK: Cambridge University Press, 1982.

John A. Wagner

Kafur Hazardinari, Malik (d. 1316)

As commander of the army of the **Delhi sultanate** under Sultan **Allauddin Khilji** (r. 1296–1316), Malik Kafur Hazardinari, an Indian slave and eunuch, launched various campaigns into South India that subjugated the Hindu states of the region to Delhi. In 1315 to 1316, during the sultan's final illness, Malik Kafur also directed the central administration as viceroy, a position that allowed him to make an ultimately unsuccessful attempt to control the succession to the throne.

How Malik Kafur became a slave of the sultan is unclear. Some sources indicate that he was taken prisoner when Allauddin Khilji conquered the city of Khambhat in Gujarat. Finding himself physically attracted to the Indian eunuch, the sultan took him to court. Other sources say the sultan found Malik Kafur in Gujarat and bought him as a slave for 1,000 dinars, hence his later use of the name "Hazardinari." After his conversion to Islam, Malik Kafur was appointed *barbeg*, or military chamberlain of the court. He commanded forces against the **Mongols** in 1306 and 1307 and in 1310 was given command of a campaign into South India. After successful sieges, he forced the Yadava king of Deogir and the Kakatiya king of Warangal to pay tribute to Delhi. In a second campaign in 1311, he pushed as far south as any Muslim army ever had, crossing the Krishna River and forcing the rulers of the Hoyasala and Pandya kingdoms to submit and pay tribute.

By 1315, Malik Kafur was viceroy and exercising a growing influence over the dying sultan. He obtained permission to imprison and blind Khizr Khan, Allauddin Khilji's eldest son and heir apparent, and procured the execution of his chief rival for power, Alp Khan. Upon the Allauddin Khilji's death in January 1316, Malik Kafur installed one of the late sultan's infant sons on the throne, intending to rule the Delhi sultanate in the child's name. The plan failed when Malik Kafur was assassinated by *paiks*, members of the sultan's elite bodyguard of Hindu warriors.

Further Reading

Chandel, L. S. *Early Medieval State: A Study of the Delhi Sultanate*. New Delhi, India: Commonwealth, 1989.

Husain, A. Madhi. *The Rise and Fall of Muhammad bin Tughluq*. Delhi, India: Idara-I Adbiyat, 1972.

Jackson, Peter. *The Delhi Sultanate. A Political and Military History*. Cambridge, UK: Cambridge University Press, 1999.

Lal, K. S. *History of the Khaljis*. 3rd ed. New Delhi, India: Munshiram Manoharlal, 1980.

John A. Wagner

Kalidasa (fl. fourth/fifth centuries c.e.)

The court of **Chandra Gupta II** provided a rich environment for cultural expressions, and most scholars place Kalidasa—the greatest Indian poet and dramatist—at his court. Although Kalidasa is recognized as the author of no more than three plays and four poems, he is regarded as the "Shakespeare of India."

Little is known of Kalidasa's life except hints within his works. He was identified in various stories as an orphan, idiot, laborer, and shepherd, yet his wide-ranging knowledge of Sanskrit, religion, and philosophy probably marks him as a Brahman and a follower of the cult of Siva. His name means "servant of Kali," one of the consorts of Siva. His familiarity with geography suggests that he was a traveler who may have served as an ambassador of his king. Although all these biographical notes are speculative, his writings stand on their own merits.

His greatest poem is the *Cloud Messenger* (The *Meghaduta*). The first part of the poem describes India from the view of a cloud. The poem then describes an earth spirit who, exiled from his wife, sends her a love message via the cloud traveling to the Himalayas. The poem plays on the intensity of love, and the travels of the cloud over Ujjain lends credence to the idea of Kalidasa as a traveler and diplomat. The poem is original and establishes the creative skill of the poet. This poem was translated in the nineteenth century, and influenced the German romantic poet Goethe.

Indian drama evolved out of a combination of religious instruction and entertainment. It combined dialogue in prose and poetry with dance and was performed by men and **women**. The plots dealt with romantic love and drew heavily on themes from the epics. The plays were never tragedies and resorted to magic or miracles to produce happy endings.

The most famous of all Sanskrit dramas is Kalidasa's masterpiece *Shakuntala*. This traces the fortunes of a woman deserted by her lover who has been robbed of his memory. The lover (who is a king) recognizes a ring recovered from the belly of fish as a token he had given to his beloved, and after a series of further misadventures the two are reunited to live happily ever after. Although the plot seems simple (and contrived), the play contrasts the demands of public life with the serenity of simple values to offer a complex portrait of courtly life. *Shakuntala* was translated into English in 1789, bringing this great dramatist to the attention of the West. Kalidasa was strikingly original in his own time, and his work has survived the test of time to bring the golden age of India into the modern world. *See also* Document 5.

Further Reading

Kalidasa. *Theater of Memory: The Plays of Kalidasa.* Translated by Edwin Gerow, David Gitomer, and Barbara Stoler Miller. New York: Columbia University Press, 1984.
Krishnamoorthy, K. *Kalidasa.* New York: Twayne Publishers, 1972.

Joyce E. Salisbury

Kanauj

Located in north central India, Kanauj was the sociopolitical center of North India for much of the pre-Muslim medieval period, from the height of the **Gupta Empire** in the fifth century to the Ghaurid invasion of the late twelfth century. The city was also an important religious center, being a noted site of Buddhist monasteries, especially during the Guptan and Harshan Periods, and a Hindu center of Brahmanical learning and influence in North India.

Kanauj was an important town, economically and religiously, under the Guptas. The town is frequently referred to in the epic *Mahabharata*. When the Chinese Buddhist monk **Faxian** visited the town in 405, it was not large and had only two Buddhist monasteries, but when **Xuanzang**, another Chinese pilgrim who visited India in the seventh century, came to the city in 636, he found a large and growing urban center with numerous Buddhist monasteries and shrines. Xuanzang chose to live in Kanauj for 7 years.

The city reached its height in the early seventh century, when it was the capital of the great North Indian empire ruled by **Harsha** (r. 606–647). Under Harsha, the city had a great population and was known for its grandeur and prosperity. The city was said to be strongly fortified and to have had many beautiful gardens and hundreds of Hindu and Buddhist temples and monasteries, which extended along the east bank of the Ganges River for almost 4 miles.

Harsha's empire collapsed shortly after his death, and, by the eighth century, control of Kanauj was contested by three dynasties, the **Rajput** Pratiharas of the kingdom of Malwa to the west, the Rashtrakutas of the **Deccan** to the south, and the Palas of Bengal to the east. In the late eighth century, the Pala king Dharmapal seized Kanauj and installed a puppet ruler in the city. In the ninth century, the Pratihara king Nagabhata II conquered Kanauj, which then served as the Pratihara capital for nearly 200 years. During the Pratihara Period, the city became known as a center of poetry and literature. In 916, the Rashtrakuta king Indra III captured Kanauj from the waning Pratihara kingdom.

In 1019, the Muslim invader Mahmud of Ghazni sacked Kanauj, and the city thereafter fell under the control of the Rajput Chandela clan and then, in 1085, to the Gahadvala dynasty, which, under its greatest ruler Govindachandra (r. 1112–1155), again made Kanauj the center of a great state. In 1193, the **Ghaurid** conqueror Mu'izz al-din Muhammad Ghauri defeated and killed the last Gahadvala king and annexed Kanauj to the Ghaurid Empire. The city then became part of the **Delhi sultanate** when that kingdom was formed out of the Ghaurids' Indian territories after 1206. Under the Delhi sultans, Kanauj was always a rich and important *iqta*, yielding significant revenues to its holder.

Further Reading

Tripathi, R. S. *History of Kanauj.* Delhi, India: Motilal Banarsidas, 1964.
Wolpert, Stanley. *A New History of India.* 8th ed. Oxford, UK: Oxford University Press, 2008.

John A. Wagner

Khara

The *kharaj* was the land tax collected in a Muslim state. In medieval India, it was introduced to the **Delhi sultanate** during the reign of Sultan **Allauddin Khilji** (1296–1316) and quickly became the most important source of state revenue.

The *kharaj* developed in the seventh century following the first Muslim conquests, when it was a tax, usually in the form of a lump-sum duty, levied on all *dhimmis*, or non-Muslim subjects living in the conquered territories. The *kharaj* was initially synonymous with the *jiziya*, which later developed into a poll tax imposed on *dhimmis*. Muslim landowners usually paid a *ushr*, a religious tithe, which was assessed at a much lower rate than the *kharaj*. As many *dhimmis* converted to Islam, tax revenues fell, and attempts to impose taxes at the full *kharaj* rate upon Muslims were fiercely resisted. Thus, in the eighth century, the Abbasid caliphs devised a compromise by forbidding the transfer of land subject to *kharaj* to Muslims and by decreeing that any Muslim who leased such land must paid *kharaj*. Over time, this compromise led to the imposition of *kharaj* on most lands, regardless of the owner's religion.

In fourteenth-century India, the *kharaj* collected in territories under the control of the Delhi sultanate, consisted of half the total produce from a given piece of land paid in cash and kind. The Delhi sultans did not appear to distinguish the *kharaj* land tax from the *jiziya*, which was elsewhere a poll tax on non-Muslims. Because Allauddin Khilji required large standing armies to resist the repeated incursions of the **Mongols**, the imposition of the *kharaj* and other taxes on Hindu peasants lowered grain prices in the cities, thus minimizing unrest in the urban centers and providing the government with greater revenues for maintaining and enlarging the army. The *kharaj* also significantly reduced the power of local Hindu magistrates by depriving them of control over any peasant surplus and it also helped to strengthen the central government in relation to provincial governors, who often took advantage of fiscal weakness in Delhi to increase their own authority in their territories. However, under Allauddin Khilji's successors, these high tax rates led to great unrest among the rural peasantry, and, especially under Sultan **Muhammad bin Tughluq** (r. 1325–1351), to peasant uprisings. Nonetheless, this augmented land tax remained the major source of state revenue far beyond the medieval period.

Further Reading

Habib, Irfan. "Economic History of the Delhi Sultanate: An Essay in Interpretation." *Indian Historical Review* 4 (1977): 287–303.

Islam, Riazul. "Some Aspects of the Economy of Northern South Asia during the Fourteenth Century. *Journal of Central Asia* 11, no. 2 (1988): 5–39.

Raychaudhury, Tapan, and Irfan Habib, eds. *The Cambridge Economic History of India.* Vol. 1: *c. 1200–1750*. Cambridge, UK: Cambridge University Press, 1982.

John A. Wagner

Law

Hindu Legal Texts

The Hindu jurisprudence or *Dhramasastra* (instructions of sacred laws) is not one single text but a collection of jural prescriptions, the most important of which were written down roughly between the second and twelfth centuries C.E.

before the advent of Muslim rule. They were composed in verse form and were often thought of, especially by British colonial jurists, as legal texts, which they are not. They are corpuses of jurisprudence or discourses on proper conduct of self for living a full moral life as a Hindu Brahmin. In ancient and medieval India, most legal disputes were determined locally within a village by customary laws, and only the most difficult civil disputes were brought to the attention to the ruler, who was morally bound to settle them. This was also the pattern under Muslim rule. In disputes brought to the king's court, each case was judged by its merits, and no reference was made to any legislative acts or recourse had to any binding legal procedures as is done in modern legal cases. Generally, the litigants were expected to plead their cases directly to the king; there were no professional lawyers in medieval India.

The Hindu legal system operated on broad principles sanctioned by the *Dhramasastra* texts, which offer prescriptive guidelines but no uniform binding set of rules. In the Middle Ages, the idea of litigation developed and the *Dhramasastra* texts began to give a number of procedural guidelines for the king and his legal officials to follow. Since the twelfth century, with the advent of Muslim rule in large parts of India, the development of Hindu jurisprudence seemed to stagnate, but the local customary law, by which cases were settled in villages and communities, continued to flourish.

There are a number of legal texts within the copus of *Dhramasastra*; the earliest, called *Manua Dhrama Sastra*, was written by Manu sometime during the second or third centuries C.E. Other important legal authors were Yājñvalkya, Nārada, and Vishnu. Manu was primarily concerned with human conduct while the writings of the later authorities look more like modern legal textbooks. Many medieval jurists also wrote long commentaries of *Dhramasastras*, most important being Vijnanesvara, who was a member of the court of the Chalukya ruler ruler Vikramaditya VI (1075–1127). Vijnanesvara's work, *Mitaksara*, a commentary of the legal texts of Vajnavalkya, has influenced modern Hindu civil law. Hemadri (c. 1300) and Jimutavahana (twelfth century) wrote works on property inheritance that have also influenced the civil laws of modern India.

Crime in Hindu States

Crime was a serious problem in medieval India, but apparently not so in ancient India. Early Greek travelers such as Megasthenis (350–290 B.C.E.), who was the Mauryan ambassador to the court of Chandra Gupta Maurya, wrote that Indians of his era were remarkably law abiding and serious crimes was rare. A similar impression is left by the writings of the Chinese traveler **Faxian**, who visited India during the early Gupta Period (*see* **Gupta Empire**). But during the time of **Harsha** in the seventh century C.E., serious crimes had increased many fold. The Chinese traveler **Xuanzang** wrote of hereditary bandits much like the nineteenth-century thugs, who robbed their victims and murdered them as religious sacrifices. Merchant caravans were plundered by organized highway robbers. To check this rampant increase in criminal behavior, kings used local officials, garrison commanders, and village and city watchmen. They also created a medieval version of detectives called *duhsadha sadhanika*, who had the role of tracking down and apprehending criminals.

Administration of Justice in Hindu States

According to ancient Hindu legal texts, the king was the sole source of justice. He had the role of chief judge and executioner and had the duty to strike criminals with his mace. But in reality, the administration of justice over vast territories was overwhelming for any single person, and the task of maintaining law and order was delegated to a number of lesser officials and courts. The king's court was reserved only for serious crimes, such as treason, and for appeals against the judgment of smaller courts or complaints about the actions of royal officials.

The composition of the court varied depending on the time and place, but evidence indicates that Indians seem to have preferred a group of three or five judges rather than a single judge. Literary evidence suggests a chief judge called *adhikaranika* presided over a case aided by two junior magistrates who were leading citizens of that community. The term *adhikara* means "government office," which suggests that the judge was a magistrate and also an administrator, very much like the district collector during British rule. There were also courts of appeals in towns and at the capital in the king's court.

Literary sources also tell of instances of judicial corruption, but the judges were expected to maintain high moral standards and character. To prevent bribery by the litigants, no private meetings were allowed between the judge and the litigants until the case was settled. The ancient text of statecraft *Arthasastra* prescribes that the honesty of the judge should be periodically tested by an ancient version of a sting operation. Certain of the *Dhramasastra* texts call for loss of property and banishment for a judge found guilty of either corruption or injustice, which are serious penalties for a member of the Brahmin caste. Many learned Brahmins could have used their legal knowledge from the *Dhramasastra* texts to achieve out-of-court settlements. There is also evidence in the late Middle Ages that some litigants employed learned Brahmin to support their case, and the Brahmin was rewarded by getting a share of the money awarded to the litigant as redress.

Giving false testimony was severely punished; the penalties were made all the more severe by religious sanctions providing for a number of miserable rebirths. In certain minor civil cases, only certain witnesses were admitted to give evidence in support of the litigants. Those who were rejected include learned Brahmins, women, government servants, debtors, people with criminal records, and people with physical defects—presumably people who could have prejudiced the outcome either by their personal status within the community, by self-interest, or by their general reputation or demeanor. Caste and status also influenced legal proceedings; the testimony of a low-caste or low-class person was not as valid as the testimony of higher caste members. In serious cases of litigation, evidence may be accepted from all sources. Several psychological tests were also given to ensure that the witness was mentally sound.

As for the use of judicial torture, Xuanzang flatly denied the use of corporal punishment to extract confessions even in serious criminal cases or those involving treason in the areas that he visited during the early seventh century. The guilty were simply given life sentences. But according to the Hindu legal text *Manua Dhrama Sastra*, the use of judicial torture to extract confessions was permitted (in the form of whipping) if there was overwhelming evidence that the accused was the culprit. Manu exempted from such judicial torture pregnant women, Brahmins, children, the sick, and lunatics. Xuanzang acknowledged common use of trial by ordeal for civil and criminal cases; he also stated that this procedure was used only when no other recourse was left to judge.

Trial by ordeal evolved only during the Middle Ages; ancient texts fail to mention it. Certain medieval legalists took a dim view of the entire notion of judicial torture and cautioned that the procedure should be employed only under the most exceptional circumstances. The logic behind trial by ordeal seemed straightforward to contemporaries. It called for supernatural interference in cases where there was no course left to find the guilty party. Divinity or the karmic law interceded to produce the unfavorable outcome and reveal the culprit. Xuanzang listed four kinds of trial by ordeal. In trial by water, the accused was placed into a burlap sack with weights attached and tossed into a deep pond; if they survived, they were deemed innocent. In trial by fire, the accused was asked to lift a scalding iron or to sit on a red hot plowshare; if there was no scarification or singed tongue, they were deemed innocent. In trial by weight, the accused was placed on a scale with a stone of equal weight; if the stone sank, it was judged as evidence of their guilt. In trial by poison, the thigh of a ram was slit open and the leftovers of the accused's meal were mixed with poison and placed in the incision; if the ram survived; the accused was judged innocent. If a person was judged unfit or unwilling to undergo these ordeals, then the judgment of the court was decided by proxy. Flower buds were tossed near the flame and if the buds opened then the party was judged innocent, but if the flower was scorched by the flames then the accused was judged guilty.

Nature of Punishments in Hindu States

In the ancient period, many crimes were punished by death; the *Arthasastra* prescribes hanging for burglary and being buried alive for plotting against the ruler. Death was also prescribed for forced entry into the king's harem; creating disaffection in the army; murder of one's own parents, siblings, or children; arson; committing willful murder; and stealing cattle. A person who deliberately broke a dam would be publicly drowned in it; a women who killed her own children would be publicly torn apart by a team of oxen; and civilians stealing military supplies would be killed by arrows. Most legalists, however, were surprisingly lenient toward sexual crimes. The most common form of execution was impalement. Literary evidence also suggests that there were questions raised as to the merits of condemning the guilty to death and this is discussed in a passage from the epic *Mahabharata*. The argument against capital punishment and heavy penalties was based on humanitarian grounds — the possibility that the innocent would suffer with the guilty and the suffering of the families of the condemned, who had to bear a large part of the burden. This case is however rejected on the basis of the greater good for society. The sprit of the law behind capital punishment argued in the passage from the *Mahabharata* was meant to avoid social anarchy by keeping the guilty away from the rest of the society so that the rest could conduct their lives in peace.

The medieval Indian state saw it self as a moral order and, by this time, the humanitarian ideal of Buddhism had sufficiently seeped in the society so that capital punishment was abolished by most rulers. This was confirmed by the Chinese traveler Faxian concerning North India. He noted most kings imposed fines for most crimes only in cases of serious revolt against the ruler an arm in amputated. The Chinese scholar-monk Xuanzang who visited early medieval India some 200 years later informs that death penalty was replaced by life sentences for serious crimes. In the opinion of Xuanzang, the criminal trial proceedings were conducted fairly as it gave the necessary consideration for the accused to defend them selves. And if the accused cooperated with the authorities then his punishments were also mitigated accordingly. He sees that the major factor that to prevent people from committing crimes was not so much the social sanctions or legal penalties but the far greater dread of violating the law of karma that would lead to unimaginable suffering in future lives. Ordinary people in India are easy going but are upright and honorable notes Xuanzang, and he has high regard as to the character of the average person who conducts himself with "much gentleness and sweetness." In financial dealings Xuanzang also find the Indians straight forward and good at keeping their oaths and promises.

From Chola country in South India inscriptional evidence indicates that for a case of the murder of an army officer the guilty party had to pay a fine of twenty-six sheep and endow funds to maintain a perpetual lamp in a temple. In cases of blood feuds if the guilty could appease the family of the victim he is then let off lightly. Others record murders who were freed after paying fines. Killing for self-defense was considered as a justified homicide in medieval South India, and the accused faced no legal sanction; and the stealing small quantities of food in the case of famine or to avoid starvation was also considered as a justified theft. It seems overall that the judicial norms and the criminal penalties in medieval India were relatively mild in relation to any other states of this period. For minor crimes there is always a chance of arbitration to settle the dispute. The minor crimes were also judged by the village council, caste guilds whose validity as jural bodies is recognized by the legal literature. They could punish the offender by their own customs either by making him pay a fine or in case of serious crimes by banishment. These local bodies played an important part in adjudicating everyday disputes as the king's court was for more serious crime. Xuanzang also mentions for serious civil cases mutilation was inflected. In exceptionally serious domestic spousal abuse or the neglect of the elderly, if the deeds of the accused seemed particularly repugnant to the moral code of the entire community then the offender will lose his limbs, either ear, nose, hand, or feet by amputation or will be forced in to exile to desolate areas.

In later times, many animals were protected by law, especially the cow. Wanton killing of a cow was a serious offense, and heavy fines were imposed for the cattle killer. The *Dhramasastras* were class biased and tended to be lenient toward upper class/caste violators. A Brahmin slandering a Kshatriya had to pay a fine of fifty pana, but slandering a Sudra cost him only half as much. An accused belonging to the Sudra caste had to pay a great deal more for slandering a Brahmin. But guilty Brahmins were not always let off easily for certain crimes, such as theft. If the Sudra criminal was caught stealing he had to make redress by paying eight times the value of the stolen item. Whereas the Brahmin caught stealing had to pay sixty times the value of the stolen item. These differences indicate that the upper castes were expected to follow higher standards of morality, and therefore the levels of their fines were also high.

Islamic Law

Muslim law or *shari'a* made an impact in Indian legal practice after the Islamic invasions of the tenth century. Muslim personal law also became important as the Muslim population continued to grow. Serious criminal cases were tried in the court of the sultan or by his appointed official at local and district level, and the sultans replaced the earlier Hindu criminal codes with Islamic criminal codes. Under Islamic rule, foreign-born Muslims who are well versed in *shari'a*, who were known a qadi (or magistrates), were offered attractive salaries to invite them to assume senior magistrate positions to settle legal cases involving Muslims. The most famous of these foreign magistrates was the Islamic scholar **Ibn Battuta**, who arrived in Delhi as a qadi in 1334. The qadi was expected to be guided as much by prevailing legal norms as by the legal injunctions prescribed by the Islamic *shari'a* code. As a result, pure *shari'a* injunctions were often modified and even superseded by local legal customs, especially those concerning inheritance, marriage, or adoption. The sultan's court also functioned as the court of last appeal, but most litigants in civil cases would have found it either difficult to access or far too intimidating to settle their disputes.

Further Reading
Basham, A. L. *The Wonder that Was India*. London: Sidgwick & Jackson, 1982.

Raman N. Seylon

Mahabharata

The early peoples of India produced stirring epic poetry commemorating their early history, portrayed as an heroic age of individual prowess. The longest of the epic poems is the *Mahabharata*, and it had a long history before it appeared in its final form in the Middle Ages.

Beginning in the middle of the first millennium B.C.E., the *Mahabharata* consisted of popular stories of gods and kings. Like heroic tales from all over the world, these were told and retold. After about 350 C.E., the tales were written down into what became a unified, sacred text of one-hundred thousand stanzas written in Sanskrit. Shortly after 1000, it began to be translated into vernacular languages of India that increased its influence and popularity.

The epic is a complex tale of the rivalry between two branches of the royal family of northern India. It tells of two sets of paternal first cousins, the five sons of the deceased king Pandu and the one-hundred sons of the blind King Khritarashtra who fought for the possession of the ancestral kingdom on the Ganga River. The account of the struggle is filled with exciting episodes including a rare example of polyandry: a princess agrees to marry all four brothers. It includes accounts of gambling as the brothers wage the kingdom on a throw of the dice.

An actual battle that was fought near Delhi around 1400 B.C.E. provides the climax of the story. Allegedly kings from Greece and China as well as from all over India joined in the fight, which lasted 18 days and ended with practically all the participants slain. The five brothers survived and recovered their kingdom with the aid of the god Krishna.

Much of the action is accompanied by a discussion and debate about the ethics of the decisions. The most famous sermon "The Song of the Blessed One" delivered during Krishna's revelation of his divinity just before the battle served as a powerful stimulus to the worship of Krishna and had a profound influence on the theology of Hinduism. Part of the power of the epic was that the victory in war did not eng the concern about the ethics of the battle. According to the epic, in the years that followed the war the king and queen retreated to a forest to live a life of asceticism and died with yogic calm in a forest fire. The other participants also completed their journey to their final test before entering heaven.

The *Mahabharata* grew to resemble an encyclopedia of early Indian mythology and history. It was chanted by priests performing sacrificial rites for royal courts, and it took on religious significance. Eventually the epics replaced the Vedas (restricted to the Brahmans) as the bible for common people because anyone could listen to them. The final form of the epics was one of the most significant contributions of medieval India. *See also* Document 1.

Further Reading

Buck, William. *Mahabhrata*. Berkeley: University of California Press, 2000.

Joyce E. Salisbury

Money and Exchange Systems

Pre-Islamic Currency

The exchange and currency system of early medieval South India, under the Cholas, can serve as general example of similar systems across the India. Two main exchange units were paddy rice (unhusked rice) and gold, which were used to buy regular food items, such as ghee (clarified butter). Imported long-distance trade items, such as cardamom seeds, were assigned in cash value. Livestock such as female sheep (ewes) were also used as a unit of barter, for example, a cow might be bartered for two ewes and a water buffalo cow for six ewes.

Battle between Babhruvahana, son of Arjuna the archer in Hinduism, fights against the snakes of the nether regions. Peacocks and other birds attack the snakes, some of which are hooded cobras. The men stand in chariots or ride horses with decorated cparisons, some use bows and arrows. From the Persian version of the *Mahabharata*, parvans XIV–XVIII. Erich Lessing/Art Resource.

In the Chola Period, a large piece of gold coin was called a *pon* or *kalanju*, with the latter term also referring to a unit of weight. Such coins were also referred to as *madhurantakan-madal* when not used as a medium of exchange but as gold endowments for temples. A smaller denomination, referred to as *kasu* (from which derives the modern term *cash*), was equal to one-half the weight of the *kalanju* and was issued for general circulation in the late tenth century. These issues of smaller denominations or gold *kasu* were possibly the direct result of expansion of maritime trade networks that stretched from the South India Sea to the Red Sea and were the standard gold currency used in trade. The ratio of *kasu* to *kalanju* fluctuated widely; one *kalanju* was equal to two *kasu* around 1050, but fetched one *kasu* and six *ma* (*mari*) in 1077.

By the twelfth century, minted coins of low exchange value appeared; these were composed of alloys of gold or silver mixed with copper. The term *fanam* was commonly used for the basic silver punch-marked coin that was present since antiquity. Great concentrations of low-value coins of alloy or copper have been found in port cities where there was a greater need for a standard unit of exchange.

It has been argued that a scarcity of minted coins in early medieval North India led to an exchange system that generally resorted to barter. This argument is supported by the Chinese scholar **Xuanzang** who stated: "They always barter their commercial transactions for they have no gold or silver coins (mother of pearls) or little pearls" (Beal, 89–90). However, archaeological evidence tends to undermine such sweeping statements; silver coins weighing 0.6 to 0.9 grams and dated from the seventh to the twelfth centuries were circulated in western and northwestern India.

Furthermore, due to a shortage of locally available minted coins, a single region may have used a variety of different coinage systems deriving from different geographical areas within India and abroad. However, this situation did not handicap the flow of local commerce because a vigorous exchange rate was created by fixing the range of minimum purity and the value of its weight to create a common currency system out of many separate coinage systems. Most of the foreign gold coins were hoarded as cash reserves by individuals and the state. These reserves were tapped during dire financial emergencies; for the state, this meant the salary for its soldiers during war — an unpaid medieval army often refused to fight or openly mutinied.

In premodern times, the value of a coin was directly proportional to the value of its metal content. Thus, coins were not only a facilitator of exchange of various goods and services, but also a commodity that had an intrinsic value independent of its monetary function. An uncoined, unstamped copper bar of silver or gold dust could also be used as a medium of exchange. In eastern India, cowry shells were used as small denominational currency. In Bengal, land rent was paid in cowry shells as late as the eighteenth century.

Islamic Currency

During the early days of Islamic conquest, the sultans of the Gangatic Plains used earlier Indian coins with the Hindu goddess of fortune on one side and the name of the ruler on the other. This meant that the entire process of coinage production was in the hands of local Indian moneyers. Hindu goldsmiths and money changers, known as *sarrafs*, were members of the Hindu Sonar caste and controlled the entire monetary policy of the sultanate, as they had done previously for Hindu dynasties. An important source of information on medieval Islamic coinage is *Drarya-Pariksha* (*An Examination of the Coins*), written in the fourteenth century by Thakkura Pheru, the son of the Hindu Master of Mint during the reign of **Allauddin Khilji.** The book deals with techniques for purifying gold and silver and making mixed metals and alloys and also discusses the weight and value of coins struck in different parts of India.

Gold was weighed by medieval jewellers and moneyers using the seeds of the *abrus precatorius* plant (or gunja seeds) as a standard in North India, and *molucca* beans (*caesalpinia crista*) as a standard in **Tamil country** in South India. The basic unit of gold by weight in Tamil country was called *kalanju*, which was equal to the weight of the *molucca* bean. The *kalanju* was divided into 20 *manjadis*, and each *manjadi* was further divided into two *kunari*. These weighing measures using either gunja seeds or *molucca* beans tended to fluctuate by area and over time.

Literary evidence is lacking for the early development of distinct Islamic gold and silver coinage that became the standard for much of India over the next seven centuries. One of the earliest specially minted coins were the "victory coins," which proclaimed the conquest of Hindu kingdoms by Moslem forces. The earliest of these coins, called a *tanka*, was specially minted for the **Delhi sultanate**; it had a galloping horseman with body armor holding a mace with his right hand. The coin's Arabic inscription dates it to 1205, while its Nagari inscription states "at the victory of Bengal."

These early coins, minted only in smaller denominations for wide circulation, seem to have been issued for the sole purpose of making a political statement to the masses about the transfer of political power. As the standard coin of the sultanate, the *tanka*, either in gold or silver, came in various denominations. Over time, it was replaced by two separate coins, the *diner*, which was the standard gold coin, and the *rupee* or *rupia*, the standard silver coin, which had a wider circulation. The exchange rate between gold and silver during the Delhi sultanate period was firmly fixed at 1:10. Most of precious metals were supplied by the plunder of Hindu kingdoms further south and east and the plunder of religious centers, such as monasteries and temples. The fourteenth-century historian Ziauddin Barani noted that the expedition to Pandian country in the deep south yielded 241 metric tons of gold (possibly an exaggeration). Despite the scarcity of silver in India—it came from mines in Afghanistan, Burma, and southwestern China—the rate of exchange remained constant. The value of gold in relation to silver did not depreciate considerably; rather silver disappeared from circulation as a currency.

Fractional coins were minted in larger quantities in gold and copper and their value ranged from 1/2 to 1/16 of a *tanka*. These coins were found in wider circulation, reaching the rich and the average through economic transactions; they also travelled outside the frontiers of the state through trade and pilgrimage. The language used on the coinage issued by the sultanate generally was Arabic, mixed with Persian and occasional was made of Nagari script. Modern coinage systems are used primarily to facilitate economic transactions, but, in medieval times, coins served a variety of noneconomic functions, such as legitimacy, propaganda, thanksgiving, and royal appeal.

Further Reading
Basham, A. L., ed. *A Cultural History of India*. New Delhi, India: Oxford University Press, 1983.
Beal, Samuel. *Buddhist Records of the Western World*. Reprint ed. Delhi, India: Oriental Books Reprint Corporation, 2004.
Ray, Himanshu Prabha. *Coins of Ancient India*. Mumbai, India: Marg Publication, 2006.
Raychaudhuri, Tapan, and Irfan Habib. *The Cambridge Economic History of India*. Volume 1: *c.1200–c.1750*. Cambridge, UK: Cambridge University Press, 1982.
Rizvi, S. A. A. *The Wonder that Was India*. Vol. II. London: Sidwick & Jackson, 1987.
Sastri, Nilakanta. *A History of South India*. 4th ed. Madras, India: Oxford University Press, 1984.

Raman N. Seylon

Mongols

The northwest edge of the Indian subcontinent (including modern Afghanistan) was always subject to invaders from Central Asia. In the thirteenth century, this region was controlled by the **Delhi sultanate**, a Muslim dynasty that was established in 1206. These rulers, however, had to contend with incursions by the Mongols, a fierce people who conquered all of northern Asia into Europe.

The great grasslands of Central Asia produced many nomadic peoples who herded grazing animals and moved as their animals thinned the vegetation. The Mongols were one more group of these nomads. The nomadic peoples were strongly linked to kinship groups, which made it difficult for them to join together into larger social entities. However, during the thirteenth century, the Mongols united and formed the largest empire the world had ever seen.

In the same year that the Delhi sultanate was established, a Mongol leader named Temujin brought all the tribes into a single confederation, and an assembly of Mongol leaders proclaimed him "Chinggis (Genghis) Khan," which means "universal ruler." Chinggis was an extraordinary figure, who is remembered for his appalling cruelty as well as for his wisdom and talent as a leader, for after the violence of his initial conquest, Chinggis established a peaceful, tolerant rule. He implemented the first Mongol written language and promulgated the first **law** code for his nomadic people.

Once he had united the Mongols, Chinggis Khan turned his formidable army against the settled societies of Central Asia. He conquered Tibet, northern China, Persia, and the Central Asian steppes. By 1215, the Mongols had captured the capital of China near modern Beijing. By the time of his death in 1227, Chinggis Khan had established a mighty empire centered in China and extending west to Persia and into Europe. His grandson, Kublai Khan, established the Yuan dynasty in China, and Kublai's brothers and cousins established Mongol kingdoms further west.

Kublai's brother Hulegu conquered the 'Abbasid empire in Persia and established the Mongol ilkhanate. In 1258, he captured the capital of Baghdad. It was this branch of the Mongol khans that swept into northwest India threatening the **sultanate of Delhi**. Even in areas where the ilkhanate of Persia was not able to exert direct control, the Mongol influence in India was felt. Groups of Mongols settled in northern India and adopted agricultural or industrial pursuits. So numerous were they in Delhi in the late thirteenth century that a section of the city was called "Mongol Town." The sultan employed Mongol troops as mercenaries, but that relationship was always tenuous. The sultans were often suspicious of their loyalty, and in one incident tens of thousands of Mongols were massacred.

The Mongols in China tried to stay aloof from their Chinese subjects and maintain their own separate identity. In Persia, on the other hand, the Mongols were more willing to assimilate. In 1295, Ilkhan Ghazan converted to Islam, and most of the Mongols in Persia followed his example. This allowed the Mongols who settled in Muslim India to adapt more easily to the local culture. The Mongol presence in the north contributed to the rich cultural mix that marked medieval Southeast Asia.

The various Mongol kingdoms facilitated trade throughout Asia. The most famous example of a traveler who benefited from the relative peace imposed by the Mongols was Marco **Polo** and his family. He was but one example of the globalization that marked the medieval world that was fostered by the Mongols.

Further Reading
Adshead, S. A. M. *Central Asia in World History*. New York: Palgrave Macmillan, 1993.
Morgan, D. *The Mongols*. Oxford, UK: Blackwell, 1986.

Joyce E. Salisbury

Muhammad bin Tughluq (d. 1351)

Muhammad bin Tughluq (known as Fakhr al-din Jauna prior to his accession) was the second sultan of Delhi from the Tughluq dynasty, ruling from 1325 to 1351. Although an intelligent and educated man, Muhammad bin Tughluq was also an unstable personality whose grand and visionary schemes often brought great physical suffering and economic hardship to his subjects.

In 1325, he succeeded his father Ghiyas al-Din Tughluq, whose death he was rumored to have arranged. The new sultan was a skilled writer and calligrapher and had an understanding of various branches of learning, including medicine, astronomy, logic, and philosophy. He was also a strict observer of Muslim religious rites and practices, abstaining from anything forbidden in the Qur'an, and attempting to enforce a similar discipline on his nobles.

In 1327, in an effort to improve administration in the southern provinces of the **Delhi sultanate**, the sultan ordered the removal of his capital from Delhi to Devagiri, which he renamed Daulatabad, a city lying 700 miles to the south in the Deccan. Not content with simply moving the royal administration to the new capital, he ordered the entire population of Delhi to be moved. Because of poor travel arrangements, many people died during the move, and because of an inadequate water supply at the new site, the capital had to be restored to Delhi in 1329, leading to further deaths during the return trip. When the traveler **Ibn Battuta** came to Delhi in the 1330s, he found the city was still a virtual ghost town.

Another of the sultan's failed schemes involved the introduction of a token currency of brass and copper to be backed by gold and silver held in the state treasury. Based on a Chinese model, the new currency failed to gain the support of the people, who refused to exchange their gold and silver coins for the new issue, and the confusion threw local markets into disorder, damaging the economy. Counterfeiting also became a problem, because the new currency was much easier to duplicate than the old. Other rumors claimed that the sultan intended to invade Persia and China, though neither campaign materialized. Ibn Battuta, whom Muhammad bin Tughluq appointed to a judicial position, found the sultan's behavior so erratic that he did not return to India after completing a diplomatic mission for him in China.

In the later years of the reign, Muhammad bin Tughluq's harsh treatment of his nobility encouraged frequent rebellions, one of which led in 1347 to the formation of the independent **Bahmani kingdom** out of sultanate territories in the **Deccan**. Although a devout Muslim, the sultan was tolerant of Hindu practices, allowing them to worship as they chose, participating in Hindu festivals, and permitting the building of various Hindu temples. The one exception to this tolerance was his discouragement of the practice of sati, which could only be performed with the sultan's permission. Muhammad bin Tughluq died in 1351 and was succeeded by his cousin **Firuz Shah Tughluq** (r. 1351–1388). *See also* Document 20.

Further Reading

Chandel, L. S. *Early Medieval State: A Study of the Delhi Sultanate.* New Delhi, India: Commonwealth, 1989.

Husain, A. Madhi. *The Rise and Fall of Muhammad bin Tughluq.* Delhi, India: Idara-I Adbiyat, 1972.

Jackson, Peter. *The Delhi Sultanate. A Political and Military History.* Cambridge, UK: Cambridge University Press, 1999.

Moinul, Haq S. "The Deccan Policy of Sultan Muhammad bin Tughluq." *Proceedings of the Indian History Congress* (1944): 269–276.

John A. Wagner

Muhammad Ghauri, Mu'izz al-Din. *See* Ghaurids

Nalanda

The University of Nalanda was one of the most important centers of higher learning in medieval India. Although a monastic Buddhist institution, its rise to prominence was largely due to the patronage of the Gupta rulers, who were Orthodox Hindus. Although a major monastic university was founded on the site by Kumara Gupta (414–454 C.E.), with other smaller monasteries added by later Gupta rulers, Nalanda may have originally existed as a minor Buddhist center called Nala. The Gupta rulers endowed the monasteries they founded with the revenue of a hundred villages. According to Chinese sources, the endowments allowed for free boarding, lodging, meals, clothing, and medical care for thousands of student monks. By the time of **Xuanzang**'s visit, the physical appearance of Nalanda was imposing; it was said to have had a large central college and seven halls with high turrets. Other sources tell of the deep ponds of blue lotus that surrounded it, adding to the allure of the place and providing fresh flowers and water for the institution. Excavations have revealed a thousand-room residence quarters for the monks with some double occupancy spaces providing two stone cots and two niches—one for lamps and another for storing manuscripts. Residence rooms were supposedly assigned to monks on the basis of seniority and redistributed each year. Recent estimates have suggested that the number of students attending the monastic college was about five thousand, with most of them possibly day students. Large hearths (*chullas*) unearthed on the site indicate that eating arrangements were communal. Large sundials noted the time, and resident monks carried their own miniature sundials to maintain punctuality. The entire monastic center was encircled by a wall with the main door on its southern side. Free boarding was not generally offered to lay students unless they agreed to perform manual work (*karmadana*) in exchange for board. Chinese sources say that Nalanda had eight big halls and three-hundred small classrooms. Authorities arranged for one hundred lectures daily. Learned monks who could teach well and elaborate on the Buddhist sutras were held in high esteem and provided with sedan chairs.

As a center for Buddhist scholarship, Nalanda was the home for numerous eminent Buddhist scholars, who had authored several treatises. There were about a thousand competent teachers and, on average, each teacher was in charge of no more than ten students. Personal attention was possible, and the student–teacher ratio was high. Due to its fame throughout Buddhist Asia, competition to secure a place in the monastic college was intense. Students from all parts of India and Southeast and East Asia competed through the demanding entry examination. The university also attracted such visiting Chinese scholars as **Faxian** (337–422), Xuanzang (602–664), and Yi Jing (635–713). Because the standard of admission was high, the majority of domestic and foreign applicants were rejected outright, and the ones selected had to have a good knowledge of old and modern Buddhist scholarship. Nalanda did not restrict itself to teaching Buddhist students but also students of other faiths. The courses taught included Hindu philosophy, the Vedas, literature, logic, Sanskrit grammar, law, medicine, and economics.

Nalanda was also known throughout Buddhist Asia for its excellent library facilities. It had three multistory library buildings called Ratna Sagara, Ratna Dadhi, and Ratna Ranjata, which were collectively known as Dhrama Ganja, or "mart of knowledge." The valuable and extensive manuscript collections contained within this library were one of the reasons for the succession of Chinese and other East Asian scholars who made an arduous land or sea journey to reach this monastery. Yi Jing copied over four-hundred Sanskrit works with about five million verses. The monastic college also benefited from foreign sponsorship, such as the ninth-century Sailendra ruler of Java and Sumatra, named Balaputradeva, who built a monastery here to serve as the residence for visiting Javanese monks and asked his friend, the last great Pala dynasty king of **Bengal**, Devapala (810–850), to grant the revenues of five villages for its upkeep and for copying books for the university library.

From Nalanda, Buddhism spread to Tibet. From the eighth century onwards, scholars of Nalanda, led by the missionary monk Padmasambhava (also called Guru Rinpoche in Tibet), played an active role in spreading Buddhist teachings to Tibet. The Tibetan language was taught at Nalanda, and monks from Nalanda were instrumental in building the first monastery in Tibet. Translations of manuscripts into Tibetan allowed for the preservation of many Buddhist texts for future generations.

From 1193 to 1205, all the universities of Bengal and Bihar in eastern India were systematically raided and looted by Muhammad Bakhiyar Khiji, a Muslim Afghan adventurer from Ghur, Afghanistan. Buddhist monks were massacred or forced to flee, and their buildings were burned. The brick and mortar wall of Nalanda and its temples were not obliterated due to their immense size, but the contents of the renowned library buildings were burned. According to the Tibetan Historian, 'Jo-nan Taranatha, the majority of Buddhist refugees went to Southeast Asia through Burma. Others went to Tibet or South India. Lacking guidance from the monks of the great monastic institutions, the Buddhist laity in India began to merge with the popular Hindu traditions that surrounded them, and Indian Buddhism ceased to exist.

Further Reading

Altekar, A. S. *Education in Ancient India*. Benares City, India: The India Book Shop, 1934.

Basham, A. L., ed. *A Cultural History of India*. New Delhi, India: Oxford University Press, 1983.

Mookerji, Radha Kumud. *Ancient Indian Education: Brahmanical and Buddhist*. Delhi, India: Motilal Banarsidass, 1974.

Raman N. Seylon

Polo, Marco (1254–c. 1324), in India

In the early fourteenth century, the great Mongol empires that extended from the Middle East to China fostered trade across its vast lands. Churchmen looking for new converts and merchants seeking vast wealth braved the long journeys from Europe to the court of the Great Khan in China. The most famous of these travelers were the Polos, an enterprising merchant family from Venice, Italy. Niccolo Polo and his brother Maffeo traveled to China. Between 1260 and 1269 they traded throughout Mongol lands, and they met Khubilai Khan as he was consolidating his power in Beijing. They returned to Venice and prepared for a longer trading journey. This time they took Niccolo's son, the 17-year-old Marco, with them.

The Great Khan, having recently established the **Mongol** Yuan dynasty, distrusted his Chinese subjects and relied heavily on foreigners to bring him information and conduct much of his business. Thus, he welcomed the Venetian merchants. He seems to have taken a special liking to young Marco, who had a talent for conversation and entertaining storytelling. The emperor sent him on numerous diplomatic missions during their stay. After 17 years in China, the Polos decided to return to Venice. They went back on the sea route by way of Sumatra, Sri Lanka, India, and Arabia, and arrived in Venice in 1295.

Their mission might have been forgotten, except that Marco had the bad luck to be captured and made a prisoner of war during a conflict between Venice and Genoa. While he was imprisoned, Marco told the tales of his travels to a fellow prisoner who recorded the adventures. This account circulated rapidly throughout Europe, and it served to stimulate interest in the lucrative trade networks. Hundreds of Italians traveled to China and India in the next century, and Christopher Columbus carried a well-marked copy of the book through his voyages. Although most of Marco's accounts refer to China, he nevertheless included some highly informative (and entertaining) tales of India that he visited on his way home.

All of Marco's observations were heavily influenced by his own interests. First and foremost, he was a merchant, so he noticed things to buy and sell and commented on the merchants who dealt in these items. In India, he was most impressed by the fabulous pearls that came from the surrounding seas. He described how divers harvested the oysters, and how carefully the king regulated the precious trade. He also commented on the rich diamonds from this land but strains credulity when he described how they were obtained: He claimed men took pieces of raw, bloody meat, tied them to ropes, and flung them down in the valley of diamonds. The gems would stick to the sticky flesh, which could then be pulled up. Sometimes eagles ate the flesh, so people had to gather diamonds from eagle droppings (Polo, 273). Marco probably gullibly listened to local accounts! His concern for commerce led him to talk about everything from pirates to pepper.

As a Christian, Marco was interested in religion, and he wrote of the great Christian shrine of St. Thomas the Apostle that still exists outside Chennai today. He also wrote of the beliefs and practices of Yogis, Hindus, and others. He loved superstitions and recounted how people could tell auspicious days by the behavior of tarantulas or shadows.

Finally as a youth, Marco was interested in **women** and sexuality. He described with fascination free expressions of sexuality and nudity, the many wives of kings, and women's clothing. His account of India offers the exciting narrative of an eyewitness, but it must be used with caution, for his reputation as a good storyteller led to much exaggeration. *See also* Documents 13, 14, and 15.

Further Reading
Polo, Marco. *The Travels*. London: Penguin, 1958.

Joyce E. Salisbury

Prithviraja III (d. 1192)

A member of the **Rajput** Chahaman dynasty, Prithviraja III ruled, from his capitals at Ajmer and Delhi, a large Hindu kingdom in North India in the late twelfth century. His defeat at the Second Battle of Tarain in 1192 by the Muslim invader Mu'izz al-Din Muhammad Ghauri opened North India to Muslim domination and led eventually to the establishment of the **Delhi Sultanate**.

Although still quite young when he came to the Chahaman throne around 1180, Prithviraja quickly conquered several neighboring Rajput kingdoms, including Delhi, making the Chahaman kingdom the dominant Hindu state in North India. His kingdom eventually encompassed most of the present-day Indian states of Rajasthan and Haryana, as well as portions of Uttar Pradesh and Punjab. Thanks to the writings of his friend and court poet Chandbardai, Prithviraja became a popular and romantic figure in Indian literature, his elopement with Samyukta (Sanyogita), the daughter of Jai Chandra, the king of **Kanauj**, is a well-known subject of Chandbardai's epic poem *Prithviraj Raso*.

When the Ghaurid commander Mu'izz al-Din Muhammad Ghauri, who had conquered the Punjab in 1186, attacked the Rajput kingdoms in 1191, Prithviraja led a Rajput coalition that defeated the invader at the First Battle of Tarain. However, in a second battle fought on the same field in 1192, the armies of Prithviraja were overwhelmed, and the king was taken prisoner and killed. Muhammad Ghauri occupied Ajmer and Delhi, forced Prithviraja's son to swear loyalty to the **Ghaurid** state, and, by 1206, had overthrown most of the other Rajput kingdoms in North India, consolidating a block of territory that became the basis of the future Muslim sultanate centered on Delhi.

Further Reading
Singh, R. B. *The History of the Chahamanas*. Varanasi, India: N. Kishore, 1964.
Vaidya, C. V. *Downfall of Hindu India*. Delhi, India: Gian Publishing House, 1986.

John A. Wagner

Puranas

Hinduism is an ancient set of beliefs that grew based upon sacred scriptures. Most were recorded long before the Middle Ages, but they had a continuing influence. The oldest were the Vedas, the ancient oral wisdom that was originally written in Sanskrit. There are four Vedic texts—*Rig, Sama, Yajur,* and *Atharva*. All were compiled between 1500 and 800 B.C.E., and they contain collections of hymns, spells, and cosmology. In the mid to late first millennium B.C.E., the *Upanishads* were added to sacred texts, and these revealed a trend toward inner contemplation rather than ritual activity as a path to salvation.

Two great epic poems joined the sacred Hindu texts probably during the early centuries C.E. These were the **Mahabharata** and the **Ramayana**. The first dealt with a massive war for the control of northern India between two groups of cousins. Although this may have begun as a historical account, priests credited the god Vishnu, the preserver of the world, with a prominent place in the resolution of the war.

The *Mahabharata* contains a short poetic work, the *Bhagavad Gita* ("song of the lord"), which is probably the most popular of the Hindu sacred texts. This work presents a dialogue between a warrior and his charioteer Krishna, who was a human incarnation of the god Vishnu. Through this dialogue, Krishna urges followers to fulfill their responsibilities as caste members.

The *Ramayana* was originally a love and adventure story about the legendary Prince Rama and his wife Sita, who experienced exciting adventures. Priests later made Rama an incarnation of Vishnu, once again using the romantic adventure as a vehicle for stimulating worship of the deity.

In the early Middle Ages at the same time that Buddhism spread, Vedic ritualism and Upanishadic contemplation there arose a spread of devotion (Bhakti) to individual deities. This trend was surely forwarded by local veneration to Buddha and the popularity of the epic literature that suggested that Vishnu and the other deities might actively participate in people's lives. This longing for a more personal relationship to deities was expressed in a new body of religious literature—the *Puranas*.

The *Puranas*—"stories of the ancient past"—are a vast body of complex narratives probably composed by 1000. These works contain genealogies of deities and kings (up to the Guptas), cosmologies, **law** codes, and descriptions of

ritual and pilgrimages to holy places, but the central theme of all the puranas is the powers and works of the gods. Some of the *Puranas* exhibit devotion to Siva, and others to Vishnu. These two cults became predominant in temple worship in India.

There are eighteen major *Puranas* and eighteen related subordinate texts known as *Upapuranas*. There are various ways these texts are classified. For example, one method might classify on the basis of qualities: impurity or purity, ignorance or knowledge. Another method might organize around whether Vishnu or Siva appears as the Supreme Being. This diversity of classification merely serves to show the richness of the material included. All the *Puranas* traditionally cover five topics: (1) the creation or manifestation of the universe; (2) the destruction and recreation of the universe; (3) the genealogies of gods and sages; (4) the reigns of the fourteen progenitors of humanity; and (5) history of the dynasties of kings.

The *Puranas* were highly instrumental in transforming the orthodox Brahminism of the Vedas into a Hinduism that was more receptive to popular forms of devotion and worship. Through the *Puranas*,

Siva Nataraja (Lord of the Dance). Hindu god dancing in ring of fire (the cosmos) and squashing a dwarf (representing ignorance). Bronze, 11th–12th century, Dravida style, Deccan, Tami Nadu, Southern India. Ferenc Cegledi/Shutterstock.

medieval Hinduism was marked by devotional cults to Vishnu and Siva that promised salvation for followers.

Further Reading

Doniger, Wendy, ed. *Purana Perennis: Reciprocity and Transformation in Hindu and Jaina Texts.* Albany: State University of New York Press, 1993.

Flood, Gavin. *An Introduction to Hinduism* Cambridge, UK: Cambridge University Press, 1996.

Joyce E. Salisbury

Rajputs

The Rajputs are medieval *Kshatriya* (warrior) clans originating in a region of northwestern India known as Rajputana and ruling over various Hindu kingdoms between the tenth and sixteenth centuries. Among the fiercest opponents of Muslim invasion and expansion in medieval times, the Rajputs have long had, and still have, a reputation as strong and skilled warriors.

Originally believed to be the descendents of migrants from Central Asia who were given *Kshatriya* status by Hindu priests, the Rajputs are now thought to have originated among those groups of people displaced from Rajputana by the **Hun** invasions of the sixth century. The term *Rajputra*, or "son of a king," first came into use during the reign of Harsha in the seventh century. *Rajput* is thought to be derived from "Rajputra" and may indicate the origins of the first clans among the younger sons and brothers of Indian rulers, who, despite being of royal blood, took up the profession of a warrior, because the Indian practice of primogeniture allowed only the eldest son of a king to succeed to the throne. Because, after the collapse of **Harsha**'s empire in the midseventh century, India was divided into many small kingdoms, such younger sons and brothers were plentiful.

As Rajput warriors began to establish themselves on various thrones, the ruling dynasties they founded began to be recognized in Brahmanical literature as belonging to the *kshatriya* class. Rajputs are mentioned in the *Puranas, **Ramayana, Mahabharata***, and other Hindu writings. Although the Rajputs came to be divided into many clans, the most significant medieval groups were the four *agnikula* or "Fire Family" clans, which are so named because they believe themselves descended from a mythical figure who arose out a great sacrificial fire pit near Mount Abu in ancient Rajputana. These clans are the Pratiharas, who ruled the kingdom of Malwa in the ninth and ten centuries; the Chahamans, who ruled a large kingdom based on Ajmer in the eleventh and twelfth centuries; the Chalukyas, who ruled parts of Gujarat and the **Deccan** from the eighth to eleventh centuries; and the Paramaras, who ruled in Rajputana from the tenth to twelfth centuries.

Further Reading

Prasad, Ishwari. *History of Medieval India.* Allahabad, India: Indian Press, 1966.

Pringle, V. *The Rajputs: The People, Their History and Culture.* 5 vols. New Delhi, India: Cosmo Publications, 2003.

Wolpert, Stanley. *A New History of India.* 8th ed. Oxford, UK: Oxford University Press, 2008.

John A. Wagner

Ramayana

Hindu culture and religion were dominated by two popular and significant epic poems: the *Ramayana* and the **Mahabhrata**. The *Ramayana* is the older and shorter of the two. Its origins in an oral tradition probably extend back to 1000 B.C.E., but it was probably written in Sanskrit in about the fourth century B.C.E. The core of the work is traditionally attributed to a single author named Valmiki, and some materials were added later by anonymous poets.

The story surrounds the adventures of Prince Rama, the eldest son of King Dasaratha and heir to the throne. However, a second queen contrives to have the prince sent into exile so her own son, Bharatha may become king. Prince Rama and his beautiful wife Sita go into exile and live in a forest where they have numerous adventures.

In the forest, Sita is abducted by Ravana, a demon-king of Sri Lanka. Rama searches for her aided by Hanuman, a monkey god, who in Indian lore exemplifies a loyal servant. The two rescue Sita, destroying Ravana and his entire force, and Rama returns in triumph, where he is restored to the throne.

Battle between the armies of Rama and Ravana. Moghul miniature, 16th century. Giraudon/Art ReBridgeman Art Library.

Sita is accused of having lost her purity while in captivity but is vindicated when Rama subjects her to a public test where she is to enter a fire. She is vindicated when the fire god refuses to harm her. In a supplement to the original text, Sita is sent to end her life at a hermitage. There she gives birth to twins and eventually pleads with the earth, from which she is descended to bear witness to her virtue. The earth swallows her up.

The Sanskrit contains nearly fifty-thousand lines of verse and is traditionally broken up into seven books:

1. Bala-kanda: the boyhood of Rama
2. Ayodhya-kanda: the court of Dasaratha and the exile of Rama
3. Aranya-kanda: forest life to the abduction of Sita
4. Kishkindhya-kanda: Rama's quest for Sita
5. Sundara-kanda: Rama and his allies arrive in Sri Lanka
6. Yuddha-kanda: the book of war revealing the defeat of Ravana and the rescue of Sita
7. Uttara-kanda: Rama's life in Ayodhya, Sita's death, and Rama's ascent into heaven.

The *Ramayana* came to be regarded as an exemplar of the ideal man and woman. Rama is an incarnation (avatar) of the god Vishnu, and the purpose of the incarnation was to demonstrate the righteous path (*dharma*) for all living creatures. These theological principles combined with the exciting narrative combine to make this an influential and much-loved work. *See also* Document 2.

Further Reading

Menon, Ramesh. *The Ramayana: A Modern Retelling of the Great Indian Epic.* Stanford, CA: North Point Press, 2004.

Joyce E. Salisbury

Raziya Sultan (d. 1240)

The daughter of Sultan Shams al-Din **Iltutmish** (r. 1211–1236), and chosen by him to succeed to the throne, Raziya was sultan of Delhi from 1236 to 1240. She was one of the few female rulers of medieval India.

Upon the death of Iltutmish, the Muslim nobility, being unwilling to be ruled by a woman, placed Rukn al-Din, one of the late sultan's sons, upon the throne. Dominated by his mother, and little interested in governing, Rukn al-Din proved thoroughly incompetent; and he and his mother were assassinated after only a few months in power. The nobility then reluctantly accepted Raziya as sultan, although they continued to oppose many of her proposals, including a plan to reduce or abolish some taxes on non-Muslims. Clever and popular, the sultan (she reportedly would not answer to the female title "sultana") was adept at playing off noble factions against each other and so was able to quickly secure her hold on the throne. However, the favor she showed to her Abyssinian master of horse, Malik Jalal al-din Yaqat, who was rumored to be her lover, offended the nobility and aroused great opposition within the court.

In 1239, the governor of Lahore rose in rebellion, which was suppressed, but not before a new revolt erupted under the leadership of Malik Altunia, governor of Sirhind. Betrayed by her Turkish guards, Raziya Sultan was handed over to the rebels, who killed Yaqat. While in the custody of Altunia, the sultan either agreed to marry her captor or persuaded him to accept a marriage alliance with her. With her new husband, Raziya then marched on Delhi, where the rebel nobility had placed her brother, Bahram, on the throne. Defeated in two battles near Kaithal, Raziya and Altunia fled but were captured and killed in October 1240 by local chiefs allied with her opponents. *See also* Document 12.

Further Reading

Chandel, L. S. *Early Medieval State: A Study of the Delhi Sultanate.* New Delhi, India: Commonwealth, 1989.

Jackson, Peter. *The Delhi Sultanate. A Political and Military History.* Cambridge, UK: Cambridge University Press, 1999.

Prasad, Ishwari. *History of Medieval India.* Allahabad, India: Indian Press, 1966.

John A. Wagner

Sati

Known in the West as "suttee," sati is a traditional Hindu funeral rite involving the voluntary self-immolation of a widow upon her husband's funeral pyre. Derived from Satī, the virtuous consort of the god Siva, who, in Hindu mythology, protested her father's disrespectful treatment of her husband by burning herself, the term *sati* refers also to any woman who distinguishes herself through her righteous and exemplary devotion to her spouse,

Funeral scene—on the death of the husband all his wives throw themselves into the fire, The Book of the Mogul, 17th century manuscript. The Art Archive/Biblioteca Nazionale Marciana Venice/Alfredo Dagli Orti.

especially by willingly following him into death.

Although the practice of sati is praised in the Vedic texts and may have been practiced as early as the fourth century B.C.E. among some warrior groups of North India, the first recorded instance dates to around 510 C.E., with the practice for long thereafter being a voluntary act confined largely to the wives of the *kshatriya* (warrior) caste. Although the exact origins of the rite of sati are unclear, the concept of eternal wifely devotion may be ancient. A series of double graves containing male and female skeletons and dating from before 1500 B.C.E. may indicate the existence at that time of a belief that wives should accompany their husbands from life into death.

Over time, sati came to be viewed as the greatest act of selfless love, and the act and those who undertook it became highly romanticized in Indian society. In 1303, Padmini, a princess of the **Rajputs**, led other Rajput wives in a *jauhur*, a mass sati, rather than submit to the invading armies of **Alauddin Khilji** (r. 1296–1316), sultan of Delhi. In the **Delhi sultanate**, sati was accepted as a Hindu cultural tradition that could be freely practiced as long as there was no coercion of the woman and the Muslim authorities were informed of its performance in advance.

The only evidence indicating an attempt to discourage the practice comes from the reign of **Muhammad bin Tughluq** (1325–1351), who declared that it could not be performed without his permission. However, the noted Muslim poet, Amir Khusrau (1254–1325), who was sympathetic to Hindu culture, declared sati a clear proof of the fidelity of Indian **women** to their men. In the Hindu empire of **Vijayanager**, the practice of sati was common, although voluntary, and practiced mostly among the upper classes. Sati continued to be practiced into modern times, although it was strongly discouraged during the period of British rule and was outlawed by the Indian Republic in the twentieth century.

Further Reading

Fisch, Jörg. *Burning Women: A Global History of Widow Sacrifice from Ancient Times to the Present*. London: Seagull, 2006.

Hawley, John Stratton, ed. *Sati, the Blessing and the Curse: The Burning of Wives in India*. New York: Oxford University Press, 1994.

Verghese, Amila. *Religious Traditions at Vijayanagar*. New Delhi, India: Manohar, 1995.

John A. Wagner

Tamil Country

In medieval Indian history, the term *Tamil country* refers to a region of extreme South India that includes the modern-day states of Tamil Nadu and Kerala, and portions of the neighboring states of Andhra Pradesh and Karnataka, as well as the island of Sri Lanka. The region was defined by the use there of the Tamil language, which is the earliest Dravidic language of South India. *Dravidian* is a term used to describe the peoples, cultures, and languages that existed in South India prior to the coming of the Aryans to India between about 1700 and 1300 B.C.E.

The Tamil language was first committed to writing in about the third century B.C.E., and the earliest period of Tamil literature encompassed the writing of the Sangam literature, the production of which extended well into the medieval period to about the tenth century C.E. Enriched by infusions from Sanskrit and by its employment in the literature of Hindu devotional cults between about 500 and 900, the Tamil language became fully developed during the rule of the Tamil Chola dynasty, which controlled portions of southern and eastern India from about 900 to 1300. The dynasty reached its peak during the reigns of Rajaraja Chola I (985–1014) and his son Rajendra Chola I (1014–1044), whose authority extended into Sri Lanka, the islands of Sumatra and Java, the Malay Peninsula, and portions of Southeast Asia. The Cholas' patronage resulted in the production of some of the greatest works of Tamil literature and some of the greatest achievements of Hindu religious architecture.

Two other important Tamil dynasties in the region were the Pandyas, who are mentioned in the Sangam literature and in Greek and Roman sources from the second and third centuries C.E. and who ruled until the sixteenth century, and the Chera, who ruled in extreme southwestern India until about the eighth century. In the fourteenth century, during the reigns of **Allauddin Khilji** (1296–1316) and **Muhammad bin Tughluq** (1325–1351), much of the Tamil region fell briefly under the domination of the Muslim **Delhi sultanate**.

Further Reading

Sastri, Nilakanta K. A. *Cholas*. Madras, India: University of Madras, 1955.

Sastri, Nilakanta K. A. *A History of South India*. London: Oxford University Press, 1955.

Shanmugam, P. *The Revenue System of the Cholas 850–1279*. Madras, India: New Era, 1987.

Srivastva, Balam. *Rajendra Chola*. New Delhi, India: National Book Trust, 1994.

Wolpert, Stanley. *A New History of India*. 8th ed. Oxford, UK: Oxford University Press, 2008.

John A. Wagner

Temples, Buddhist: *Stupas*

Stupas are religious buildings that were associated with Buddhism. Siddhartha Gautama (c. 563–c. 483 B.C.E.) was a prince who studied, meditated, and became known as "the enlightened one" — or "Buddha." Buddha had become enlightened while meditating under a large bodhi tree, which became associated with the temples that would be built in his honor. The religion he founded in India has been profoundly influential all over the world.

Lion capital, from Asoka or Ashoka pillar at Sarnath India. Erected by Ashoka, 273–232 B.C.E., Maurya Emperor and convert to Buddhism. The Art Archive.

At his death, his disciples wanted to be sure he would be remembered, so they established shrines to him. They divided his cremated remains and placed them in ten locations associated with his life and teachings. These early shrines were made up of a simple mound of rubble and earth, and these were known as *stupas*. These mounds served as the inspiration for later Buddhist architecture. In time, Buddhist monks settled around the *stupas*, which added to the temple design.

The Mauryan ruler Ashoka (268–232 B.C.E.) converted to Buddhism and added to the architectural design of the *stupa*. Ashoka was influenced by the Hellenistic and Persian cultures, and he brought builders proficient in stone construction to India. Under his patronage, the original simple *stupas* were enlarged, and many new shrines were created.

Under Ashoka, all *stupas* were built in hemispherical form covered by a dome. The dome represented the world mountain and the dome of the heavens. To indicate their sacred character, they were protected by a fence that marked the path for the faithful to walk around in ritual, meditative fashion. To be sure the temples would be permanent, the mounds were paved over with brick or stone. To remember Buddha, the temples were topped by a square railing (called *harmika*) and a three-tiered umbrella form (called *Chatra*) that represented the famous bodhi tree. The triple parasol represented royalty, and its supporting pole symbolized the axis of the world passing through the exact center of the hemispherical form of the *stupa*.

The *Great Stupa*, that was built between 250 B.C.E. and 250 C.E. at Sanchi, contained all these defining elements. It also has four gates opening to the four cardinal directions, and stairs at the south lead to the top. The shrine at Sanchi includes many buildings that were built over time, including three *stupas* along with monasteries for the monks, and other temples.

As Buddhism spread and came in contact with Hellenistic traditions, followers of Buddha began to revere their founder as a savior and included images of Buddha in their shrines. In the seventh century C.E., two colossal statues of Buddha were carved into the mountains of Bamiyan, Afghanistan, and these figures were replicated as far away as China. Sadly, these statues were destroyed by the Taliban in 2001.

Indian influence spread to Southeast Asia through merchants, and the *stupa* form of temple became even more elaborate. For example, the *stupa* shrine of Borobudur, on the island of Java, was built c. 800–850. It was built on a plain surrounded by mountains. A huge artificial hill covered in stone supports a *stupa* shrine that symbolizes the center of the universe. Visitors walk around the rising terraces in a pilgrimage that represents everyone's path to enlightenment. Along the way, they pass miniature *stupa* shrines holding images of the Buddha and of other *bodhisattvas* (individuals who achieved enlightenment but chose to remain in the world as a help to others). Over three miles of friezes along the path of the rising terraces portray events from the life of the Buddha.

The three-tiered parasol on top of the *stupas* had a far-reaching influence on Buddhist shrines outside of India. In China, images of the Buddha were placed inside "pagodas," multistoried buildings with layered roofs. The word *pagoda* is derived from the Sanskrit word for *stupa*, "*dagoba*." Many of these structures were built throughout medieval China. The oldest surviving brick structure in the country is the 130-foot-tall Saongyue Pagoda at Dengfeng, built in 523. At Yingxian, the Fogong Temple, built in 1056, includes the oldest surviving pagoda constructed entirely of wood. These are but a few examples of the highly influential *stupa* form of religious building that shows the spread of Buddhism throughout the Middle Ages.

Further Reading

Fisher, Robert W. *Buddhist Art and Architecture*. London: Thames & Hudson, 1993.

Joyce E. Salisbury

A statue of Tara, Bodhisattva of compassion. The most important of the female Bodhisattvas, she was created from the tear of Avalokitesvara and protects the human existence, 10th century C.E. Place of Origin: Eastern or Central India. Buff sandstone. Desiree Walstra/Shutterstock.

Temples, Hindu

In medieval India, Hinduism replaced Buddhism as the dominant religion, and Hindu temple building blossomed. The Hindu temple creates a link between humans and gods and served as a sacred space, just as the Buddhist *stupas* did. However, there were some striking differences.

Unlike Buddhism, which focuses on the life and teachings of one man, Hindus venerate many deities, and the temples reveal this multiplicity in complex, stunning architecture. The temples themselves serve many purposes. They are the dwelling of the gods, where worshipers may confront images of the deities' avatars (incarnated forms). These images are served by priests offering prayers, incense, and other offerings to the gods.

The buildings themselves, covered with sacred carvings, are objects of worship. Aspects of the universe are incorporated into the temple by the use of sculpture, sacred geometry, and axial alignments. Hindu religion recognizes several forms as sacred: a holy mountain, a sacred cave, and the cosmic axis, so temple architecture expresses these forms. Most have a womb-chamber (called a *garbhagriha*) at their center that radiates energy to the roof and the cardinal directions. A sacred mountain towers over the *garbhagriha*, and a passage for walking clockwise about the center is built to invite worshipers to contemplate the holy structure. Temple complexes are usually aligned on the cardinal points, representing the four corners of the earth, with the major entrances facing east to confront the sun's rise.

In the *garbhagriha* rests a sacred image or element as the symbol of the god's presence. If proper rituals are not performed, people believe that the god may choose to live somewhere else, so the job of the priests is to make the deity welcome and honored so he or she will continue to reside in and bless the temple. Rituals for the deity include ceremonies that honor the deity with music, **food**, dancing, the recital of religious texts, and the singing of hymns. Visitors count on the presence of the deity to bring them blessings as they visit the temple.

Priests perform sacred rites at regular times for the benefit of the entire community, but there is no congregational worship, so there is no need for a large enclosed gathering place. Instead, people come to offer private devotions at any time, taking their shoes off before they enter the sacred space of the temple complex. Western visitors are often bewildered by the various activities within the temple complex: people sell trinkets and flowers; others walk around admiring the carvings (many of which show explicit sexual activities) and talking; still others tend cattle, which are sacred and thus welcome in the temples. All these activities are manifestations of community veneration as much as the activities of those who silently meditate on the statues of the deities.

Throughout the Middle Ages there was a great deal of temple building, and many of the structures survive today. Some of the earliest surviving Hindu shrines are near Sanchi, the Buddhist shrine, and show clear influence from the Buddhist work. Temple 17 at Sanchi dates from the early fifth century. Hindu architects grew more skilled at working with stone and brick, and the towering mountain forms rose ever higher.

In northern India, the support of the rulers of the Gupta dynasty stimulated the building of temples, and this building expansion continued even with the political turmoil that marked northern India through the Middle Ages. For example, at Khajuraho there were at least twenty-five temples constructed over a 200-year period. The best preserved is the Lakshmana temple, built about 950, which has three huge halls each topped by a mountainous roof.

South India developed a distinctive style of temple that was as impressive as those built in the north. Under the patronage of the Cholo then the **Vijayanagar** rulers, temples began to dot the skylines and become centers for communities. One of the oldest surviving temples in the south is the stunning complex at Mahabalipuram, south of Chennai. This seaside temple was carved out of solid rock in the eighth century and still draws many awed tourists today. In the eleventh century, builders at Brihedesvara Temple at Tanjore built a 200-foot tower that was twice as high as anything else that had been built.

In southern India particularly, temples took on many public functions beyond religious celebrations. They served as economic and social centers as well. For example, priests coordinated work on irrigation systems and organized food supplies in times of famine. They also conducted schools for boys in the communities. Temple authorities served as bankers, made loans, and invested in business ventures. In these ways, temples remained crucial centers contributing to the economic health of southern India.

When Hinduism spread to other regions in Southeast Asia through the activities of Hindu merchants, temples architecture too moved out of the subcontinent. Unquestionably, the most famous temple outside of India is Angor Wat, which was begun c. 1120 in modern Cambodia. This magnificent temple complex represents a fusion of Hinduism with native Khmer tradition. The scale of the complex makes it one of the largest religious structures ever built, with a rectangular perimeter wall measuring 4,275 by 4,920 feet. If visitors were to follow the circumambulation of the temple in accordance with Hindu tradition, they would have to walk about 13 miles.

Angor Wat was begun in about 1120 as a shrine to the Hindu god Vishnu, then became the royal shrine of the Khmer dynasty. The Khmers abandoned Angkor in 1431 after the Thai people invaded. Once the complex was redis-covered by Westerners in the nineteenth century, it draws visitors from all over the world and remains a silent witness to the strength of medieval Hin-duism and the temples it spawned.

Further Reading

Anantharaman, Ambujam. *Temples of South India.* Chennai, India: East West Books, 2006.

Mannikka, Eleanor. *Angkor Wat: Time, Space, and Kingship.* Honolulu: University of Hawai'i Press, 1996.

Mitchell, George. *The Hindu Temple: An Introduction to Its Meaning and Forms.* Chicago: University of Chicago Press, 1988.

Joyce E. Salisbury

Timur/Tamerlane (1336–1405)

Throughout the Middle Ages, nomadic tribes originating in central Asia made an impact all over the Eurasian land mass. Whether **Huns** or **Mongols**, these warriors sent terror spreading before them whether they moved east or west. Another such group, the Turks began to take a prominent role in the eighth century with their conversion to Islam. Their embrace of Islam pro-vided a unifying force for the Turks and brought them into closer association with the civilizations of Persia, Iraq, and drew them into the Muslim lands of India.

In the fourteenth century, the great empires of the Mongols that had spanned Asia into Europe declined. As Mongol strength waned, Turkish peo-ples resumed their expansion that had been held at bay by the Mongols. During the late fourteenth and early fifteenth centuries, the Turkish conqueror Timur built an empire that rivaled that of Chinggis (Genghis) Khan.

Timur was born about 1336 near Samarkand and grew up influenced by the story of Chinggis Khan, who had also risen from a family of the minor no-bility. Timur had sustained an injury to his right leg and walked with a limp. Therefore his contempo-raries called him *Timur Lang*, or "Timur the Lame." This appellation made its way into English as Ta-merlane, by which he is known in most textbooks.

His limp did not keep Timur from becoming a brilliant horseman and warrior with a good deal of charisma. He attracted a loyal band of followers and by the 1360s had eliminated any rivals and was acknowledged leader of his tribe. By 1370 he had extended his authority throughout the old

Timur or Tamerlaine enthroned from Timur Nama by Hatifi, Persian, 1563–1565. Elliott 403 folio 120v. The Art Archive/Bodleian Library Oxford.

Khanate of Chaghatai in central Asia and built a magnificent capital in Samarkand. For the rest of his life, Timur led his armies to conquer an ever-greater empire, which extended from the Byzantine Empire in the west up to the Hindu Kush and the Indus River in the east.

Timur was a merciless follower of Islam, and he demonstrated this zeal when he drove into India. There, his troops slaughtered Hindus by the thousands and subjected Delhi to a ferocious sack. Contemporary chroniclers reported that for 2 months after the attack not even birds visited the devastated city. Later, Timur campaigned along the Ganga, although he never attempted to incorporate India into his empire.

Timur was a warrior more than an administrator. He ruled through tribal leaders, and even when he appointed overlords in the conquered territories, they relied on existing bureaucratic structures. This organization allowed continuity in local governments once the conqueror sped on to his next conquest.

In 1404, Timur began preparations for an invasion of China to complete his re-creation of the Mongol accomplishment. He was ill at that time, but that did not deter him from leading his armies. He was carried on a litter during his final campaign but died from his illness in 1405.

Timur's political accomplishments barely outlasted him. His sons and grandsons engaged in a long series of bitter conflicts that resulted in the contraction of his empire and its division into four main regions. For a century after his death, however, they maintained control over the region from Persia to Afghanistan.

Perhaps surprising for a warrior king, Timur's most longstanding accomplishments lay in the realm of culture. The conqueror served as patron for scholars and artists, and his capital at Samarkand was established as a cultural center for centuries. Great architectural monuments of the fourteenth and early fifteenth centuries still show his influence. He contracted great mosques in his birthplace, Kesh, and another, dedicated to his favorite wife, Bibi Khanum, in Samarkand. In literature, he fostered the use of the Turkic literary language called Chaghatay, which supplanted Persian. It survived as the primary language of the literary arts in Central Asia into the twentieth century. *See also* Document 21.

Further Reading

Gonzalez de Clavijo, Ruy. *Embassy to Tamerlane, 1403–1404*. Translated by Guy Le Strange. London: Routledge, 1928.

Manz, Beatrice Forbes. *The Rise and Rule of Tamerlane*. Cambridge, UK: Cambridge University Press, 1989.

Joyce E. Salisbury

Vijayanager Empire

The Vijayanagar Empire was a Hindu state of South India centered on the city of Vijayanagar on the Tungbhadra River; it controlled most of South India between the 1330s and 1560s. The empire was founded by the brothers Harihara I (r. 1336–1356) and Bukka Raya I (r. 1356–1377), who sought to create a Hindu state capable of warding off further Muslim invasions of South India from the **Delhi sultanate** and other Islamic kingdoms.

The origins of the founding brothers are uncertain. They claimed to be descendents of the Yadava kings of Deogir and were for a time in military service to Rudradeva, the Kakatiya ruler of Warangal, with whom they were carried to Delhi as prisoners in 1324 after the armies of the Delhi sultanate overran the Kakatiya kingdom. Upon their release, they returned to South India, where, by the mid-1330s, the repeated Islamic invasions of the region under the Sultans **Allauddin Khilji** (r. 1296–1316), and **Mohammad bin Tughluq** (r. 1325–1351) left the weakened Hoyasala kingdom as the only remaining independent Hindu state. Inspired to fight the Muslims by Vidyaranya, a Hindu holy man at the monastery of Sringeri, the brothers established a new state at the new city of Vijayanagar in about 1336. Upon the death in battle of King Veera Ballala III in 1343, the Hoyasala kingdom merged with the rapidly expanding Vijayanagar state, which over the next decades extended its control across South India.

Harihara I conquered most of the territory south of the Tungbhadra River, while Bukka Raya I absorbed most of the small states, Hindu and Muslim, of the central **Deccan**. Harihara II (1377–1404) pushed his authority well north of the Krishna River, bringing the whole of South India under his rule. For much of its existence, Vijayanager was at war with the **Bahmani kingdom**, its Islamic neighbor to the north. Although religious differences embittered this ongoing conflict, Islamic influence increased in Vijayanager, where the ruler called himself "Sultan among Hindu Kings" and employed significant numbers of Muslim cavalrymen. Beyond that the empire encouraged a flowering in the region of Hindu literature and arts, particularly in architecture.

The empire reached its height under Krisha Deva Raya (r. 1509–1529), who conquered territories in the northern Deccan formerly held by the Muslim Deccan sultanates, the successor states to the Bahmani kingdom, which broke up around 1518. In 1565, an alliance of Deccan sultanates killed King Aliya Rama Raya and crushed his army at the Battle of Talicota. This defeat began a period of decline that culminated with the breakup of the empire in the seventeenth century, with much of the north falling to the sultanates of Bijapur and Golkonda and much of the south being divided among various Hindu successor states.

Further Reading

Krishnaswami, A. *The Tamil Country under Vijayanagar*. Annamalainagar, India: Annamalai University, 1964.

Mahalingam, T. V. *Administration and Social Life under Vijayanagar*. 2nd ed. Madras, India: University of Madras, 1969.

Sadanandan, P. "Islamic Influence in Vijayangar Capital." *Journal of Andhra Historical Research Society* 30 (1964–65): 85–88.

Sewall, R. A. *A Forgotten Empire (Vijayanagar)*. New Delhi, India: National Book Trust, 1962.

John A. Wagner

Warfare

On medieval methods of military recruitment the Chinese monk **Xuanzang** noted that elite body soldiers were recruited from the bravest people, soldiering continued to be a hereditary profession, and the sons of soldiers learned the profession through a form of military apprenticeship. During peacetime, elite military forces were garrisoned around the royal palace; during war, they manned the front ranks in battle. The bulk of Hindu armies was infantry comprising members of the hereditary warrior caste, who were chosen for their reputation and loyalty. The Hindu infantryman was armed with a large pike and shield and sometimes a sword, the standard Indian infantry weaponry until the late eighteenth century. Other weapons included iron maces, iron battle axes, slings, long lances, javelins, and composite or bamboo bows; nearly all these weapons were said to be razor sharp and pointed. Hindu armies did not possess the necessary technology to make the advanced siege engines or flaming naphtha fire balls that were being used in the Mediterranean basin or in Europe during medieval times. This may well be due to the fact that although Indian rulers built large stone forts, most battles occurred in open plains with large standing armies. However, Indians were familiar with underground tunneling, something borrowed from the Greco-Bactrian kings (250–125 B.C.E.) who ruled Northwest India and Afghanistan.

Early medieval Hindu armies were also composed of units of cavalry, elephant corps, and war chariots, which, with infantry, made up the standard four-fold division of an army of the period. Commanders rode chariots that had two drivers or attendants and were pulled by a team of four horses. The commander's chariot was closely followed by a file of solders that stood near the wheels of the chariot. Cavalry was used in the front lines to harass the enemy and in case of retreat to send messages. Although the role of war chariots was largely replaced by cavalry and elephants by the fourth century B.C.E., chariots still served as command vehicles for officers and played a major role in Hindu royal and religious rituals.

Elephants and cavalry units began to come to service as the major offensive body of Indian army just as war chariots began to lose their prominence. As fast-moving attack vehicles, chariots were unsuited to jungle-covered uneven terrains or to the soft soils of the central Gangatic Plain. Elephants proved to be better suited as mobile platforms for carrying a body of soldiers. Elephants also terrified the untrained and unfamiliar horses of the enemy cavalry and were effective in breaking up enemy infantry formations. Also, most of India was unsuitable for breeding superior quality military horses; good cavalry mounts had to be imported from Arabia or Persia and were therefore expensive whereas elephants were plentiful in the jungles of eastern India. For this reason, Indian rulers, since antiquity, had maintained a large core of battle elephants. As a result of their strength and demeanor, elephants came to be associated with the pomp and pageantry of royalty and thus also became an integral part of royal ceremonial. War elephants acted like modern tanks, smashing fortress gates, palisades, and other wooden defenses; a line of elephants might act as a living bridge for crossing swollen rivers. Battle elephants were protected by leather armor and their tusks were tipped with metal spikes; the Chinese traveler Sung Yun (520–521 C.E.) reported seeing battle elephants with sharp swords fastened to their trunks. Elephants were guided by trained mahouts; carried soldiers armed with bows, long spears, and javelins; and were often accompanied by a small detachment of infantry. In the long run, however, heavy reliance on battle elephants proved to be a tactical error for Indian princes, for by the medieval period invading armies from Central Asia were well prepared to counter Indian battle elephants. Even the best trained elephants could be incapacitated or confused and panicked by battle wounds, sheer fatigue, or fire, and would inflect great damage as they fled the battle-field overthrowing riders and trampling its own support troops.

Thus, by the eleventh century large formations of battle elephants had become not only useless but also a serious liability against a well-disciplined cavalry. As early as the eighth century, the invading Umayyad Arab armies had used arrows and naphtha fireballs to cripple and immobilize the elephant corps. By the eleventh century, the Muslim Turks did much the same thing against battle elephants and the huge formations of infantry that accompanied them.

After the demise of the **Gupta Empire**, the warrior castes dominated Northwest India, the most prominent among them being the **Rajputs**. The ancestors of the Rajputs are believed to have migrated to India as part of early Central Asian invasions, such as those of the **Huns** in the sixth century. They then settled in India with the collapse of Gupta rule. The Rajputs considered them to be members of the ancient Kshatriya *varna* (*see* **Caste System**) and were known for their fanatical attempts to assert their Kshatriya status. This assertion distinguished the Rajputs from other similar castes who migrated from outside India. They were also known to be haughty and aristocratic and soon gained a reputation for suicidal bravery and chivalry, although their battle tactics eventually came to be old fashioned and cumbersome. **Babur**, the sixteenth-century founder of the Mughal Empire, reportedly declared that the Rajputs knew "how to die but did not know how to fight" (Lannoy, 69).

The brunt of the medieval Muslim Turkish invasions was borne by the Rajputs, but they wasted their energies in internecine quarrels instead of forming a joint confederacy to meet the common adversary. The Muslim invasions of the Middle Ages made cavalry warfare supreme. Rajput cavalry techniques were by then antiquated and clumsy, and they were outmaneuvered by the superior cavalry techniques of the Muslims. The Rajputs were also hampered by their notions of warfare, which were based on individual valor, and thus unsuited to the effective coordination of effort needed to counter the strategy and tactics of Muslim Turkish horsemen. The Rajput cavalry also consisted of freemen, who were poor in obeying orders, whereas the Muslim Turkish cavalry was composed of specially trained slaves who obeyed all orders without question. The Turks also practically grew up on horseback and went through constant battle drills to sharpen their cavalry skills. Among the superior cavalry techniques employed by the Muslim Turks was the seemingly suicidal charge, which was halted at the last minute so the horses could be turned to allow their riders to launch a deadly volley of arrows at the onrushing enemy at virtually point-blank range. Used repeatedly, his tactic confused and demoralized the Rajput cavalry, which suffered heavy casualties while inflicting few losses on the Muslim horsemen.

The Indians were also unfamiliar with the kind of religious-based zealotry and religiously motivated warfare with which the Muslims confronted them. War among the Rajputs was only a royal pastime, more like a ritual, and the men recruited for it were either kinsmen or mercenaries whose primary aim was to loot. This traditional mode of warfare led to frequent defeats at the hands of the dangerous Muslim Turks, who were better led and had superior battle tactics. The Turks were also fired up by religious zeal to fight the infidels, while the Indians lacked similar religious and ideological motivations.

Caste divisions amongst the Indians also separated Hindu rulers from the ruled and discouraged the communal solidarity needed to put up an effective resistance or defense against such a formidable adversary. Muslim society was egalitarian, and anyone who wanted to join the army could; a talented soldier could quickly rise up the ranks. In the rigid caste-based Hindu society, the rank of an officer did not necessarily correspond to their military competence. A form of "military Darwinian," or survival of the fittest, existed among the Muslim Turkish military class. Evan a sultan may be replaced by a slave turned general if the former could not maintain his position.

The Battle of Peshawar, fought on November 28, 1001, was the first major encounter between the army of Muhmud of Ghori and the local Indian Raja Jaipal. The Muslim chronicles report that an Indian army of 12,000 cavalry, 30,000 infantry, and 300 battle elephants was defeated by a smaller army of irregular infantry and 15,000 select cavalry. But the Rajputs, by their sheer obstinacy and valor, proved to be a formidable enemy in resisting the Muslin invaders. However, the superior cavalry techniques of the Turks even allowed them to thwart Mongol incursions into India by the armies of Genghis Khan and his successors.

In 1526, Babur, the young ruler of Kabul in Afghanistan, brought with him field artillery pieces and muskets to defeat the one-hundred-thousand-man cavalry formation of the last ruler of **Delhi sultanate**, Ibrahim Lodhi. Curiously, the Muslim Turkish rulers of the Delhi sultanate, who had earlier defeated Hindu Rajput armies equipped with battle elephants, themselves succumbed to the lore of the elephant and saw it as having military potential. Ibrahim Lodhi had a corps of one thousand battle elephants in his fateful encounter with Babur. Babur's field artillery put an end to the use of battle elephants in Indian warfare.

Further Reading

Barua, Pradeep P. *The State at War in South Asia*. Lincoln: University of Nebraska Press, 2005.

Basham, A. L. *The Wonder that Was India*. London: Sidgwick & Jackson, 1982.

Beal, Samuel. *Buddhist Records of the Western World*. Reprint ed. Delhi, India: Oriental Books Reprint Corporation, 2004.

Kulke, Hermann, and Dietmar Rothermund. *A History of India*. New York: Rutledge, 1998.

Lannoy, Richard. *The Speaking Tree: A Study of Indian Culture and Society*. Oxford, UK: Oxford University Press, 1971.

Raman N. Seylon

Women. *See* "Society" section

Xuanzang (602–664)

Since the fall of the Gupta Empire in northern India in 550, there had been decentralization and petty **warfare**. In 606, however, a brilliant 16-year-old king, **Harsha**, was able to reunite much of northern India. Harsha's ruled his kingdom until 648, establishing a reign that fostered scholarship, Buddhism, and piety. His kingdom served as a welcoming place for Xuanzang, a Chinese pilgrim who came to study Buddhism in India.

Xuanzang was the youngest of four children who amazed his father with his early grasp on Confucian rituals. After his father died in 611, his older brother, Changjie, who was a Buddhist monk came to be his greatest influence. Xuanzang visited his brother, studied the texts, and became a zealous new convert. He took his vows as a monk at the age of 13. In 618, China was engaged in violent civil wars, and the brothers sought refuge in the mountains of Sichuan to pursue their studies. Young Xuanzang was bothered by seeming contradictions in the texts, so he decided to go to India to study in the birthplace of Buddhism. The Emperor Taizong forbade travel outside China to preserve national security, but the young monk defied the decree. In 629, he secretly set out on his journey.

His journeys were arduous. His guide abandoned him in the Gobi Desert, where he lost his water bag and almost succumbed to the heat before he luckily made his was to the oasis town of Turpan on the Silk Road. The Buddhist ruler of Turpan gave him supplies, gifts, and twenty-four letters of introduction to rulers of lands along the way. Thus supplied, the monk continued on his way, crossing three of the world's highest mountain ranges: the Tian Shan, Hindu Kush, and Pamir ranges. He lost one-third of his party to cold and starvation and faced numerous attacks from bandits.

He finally arrived in India in 630 where he lived for more than 12 years, visiting the holy sites of Buddhism and studying languages and Buddhist texts. He spent most of his time at Nalanda, the famous monastery, where he became the special student of the abbot Silabhadra. His intellectual skills soon brought him to the attention of King Harsha, who called a conference in 643 on religion and philosophy. Purportedly, Xuanzang defeated five hundred Brahmins, Jains, and Buddhist in a spirited debate.

Finally the monk was ready to return to China. He brought a huge collection of relics and images, as well as 657 books, which he packed into 527 crates. He was fortunate that by the time of his return in 645, China had come under the rule of the Tang dynasty, which fostered trade and presided over an era of peace and economic prosperity. In spite of having violated the travel ban, Xuanzang was received as a hero by the Emperor Taizong.

Xuanzang declined an offer of an official position with the emperor and entered the Temple of Great Happiness. There, assisted by a staff of more than twenty translators, he translated the texts he had brought from India. He was engaged in this task until his death in 664. His efforts helped popularize Buddhism, reconciling it with Confucianism, and bringing about the almost universal acceptance of Buddhism in China. *See also* Document 9.

Further Reading

Bernstein, Richard. *Ultimate Journey: Retracing the Path of an Ancient Buddhist Monk Who Crossed Asia in Search of Enlightenment.* New York: Alfred A. Knopf, 2001.

Wriggins, Sally Hovey. *Xuanzang: A Buddhist Pilgrim on the Silk Road.* Boulder, CO: Westview Press, 1996.

Joyce E. Salisbury

Yoga

The goal of Hindus is to achieve salvation through detachment from the body and its concerns in this world, and a desire to join with the divine, or universal spirit. The path to salvation is generally called *yoga*, which in Sanskrit means "yoke," or joining oneself to the divine. Medieval travelers from the West and from Muslim lands wrote of their encounters with holy people, "yogis" who could do remarkable feats of physical activity and endure physical deprivation. These travelers joined the Hindus who recognized these people as particularly holy. The practice of yoga in India is very old and was well established by the Middle Ages. Although the goal of yoga is to connect with divinity, there are various kinds of yoga, each emphasizing different paths to God.

In the modern United States, we are most familiar with "hatha yoga." In this form of yoga, a practitioner believes that the path to God is through the body itself, so he or she practices various postures (called "asanas") of increasing difficulty. While performing these asanas, the yogi focuses on breathing deeply and consciously, joining mind, body, and breath into a harmonious whole. Hatha yoga practitioners use this focused integration to bring their whole body into meditation, which represents the distancing from the concerns of this world and focus on the divinity. Medieval travelers commented with wonder at the physical prowess of the practitioners of hatha yoga as they were able to place their bodies into challenging poses.

Karma yoga means the "Way of Works" and was praised by the god Krishna in the *Bhagavad Gita*. This form of practice requires one to perform the proper rituals every day and at turning points in life. This is not the highest road to salvation (i.e., not as difficult as other forms, nor as certain), but nevertheless it can lead to salvation, or release from the cycle of rebirth. In Karmic yoga, men and **women** had distinctive ritual duties. Men were primarily responsible for offerings for their ancestors to try to keep them from the wheel of rebirth. Women earned release through service in the home and preparing **food**s in ritual ways. As Hindus practice karma yoga, their daily lives become an attempt to connect to the divine.

Jnana yoga is the "Way of Knowledge." In this practice, believers see ignorance as the main reason for the alienation of the human from God. The ignorant do not know that the human soul is ultimately of the same essence as the ultimate reality (Brahma) but instead thinks it is identified with the world. It is this misconception that draws the soul into a series of rebirths. Through study and training the mind, individuals can learn their true identity and earn the release from rebirth.

Bhakti yoga is the "Way of Devotion." Like the Karma yoga, this path was also emphasized in the *Bhagavad Gita*. In this path, practitioners embrace God through passionate love. Bhakti was widespread among Hindus during the reign of the Gupta emperors, and this practice was written down in many devotional works like the Puranas. Those who want to commit to the Way of Devotion focus their devotion on one of the major deities. Brahma is the creator. His responsibilities are shared with Vishnu, the preserver, and Siva, the destroyer. Vishnu is worshiped in his incarnation as Krishna, as the personification of divine love. In popular Hinduism, most people usually choose to serve Siva or Vishnu, and the temples are filled with devotees bringing offerings of love as they follow the Way of Devotion.

Raja yoga, the "Way of Physical Discipline," is often identified with the Yoga Sutra, attributed to Patanjali in about the second century C.E. The goal of raja yoga is training the physical body with a special emphasis on meditation. It is this emphasis that separates raja yoga from hatha yoga. Raja yoga requires such long meditation that its practice is usually restricted to monks. The practitioner tries to focus so intently on one object that it fills his or her whole mind. In the next step, they withdraw the object until the person is no longer conscious of it. The final step extinguishes all consciousness of the world, which prepares the adept to escape the cycle of rebirth.

Tantric yoga explores the idea of release through embracing the body in a ritual way. Practitioners — often worshippers of Siva — embrace sexual intercourse as a ritual to generate the power of the spirit. The embrace of sexuality has led many in the West to explore this form of yoga, however, in its Hindu context it remains one more path to escaping the attachments of this world.

Vishnu sleeping on many-headed world snake Ananta or Sesha. Black basalt, late Dravida style, Southern Indian. The Art Archive/Musée Guimet Paris/Gianni Dagli Orti.

All these pathways recognize the diversity of Hinduism. Through all of them, however, the goal remains to escape the cycle of rebirth and to escape this world into union with the divine principle. *See also* Document 15.

Further Reading

Feuerstein, Georg. *The Yoga Tradition: Its History, Literature, Philosophy and Practice.* Prescott, AZ: Hohm Press, 2001.

Kaminoff, Leslie. *Yoga Anatomy.* Champaign, IL: Human Kinetics, 2007.

Joyce E. Salisbury

Primary Documents

1. Excerpt for the *Bhagavad Gita:* The Nature of Brahman

The *Bhagavad Gita* is a long poem of metrical verse that is part of an even longer epic poem titled the *Mahabharata*, which, at some ten-thousand verses, is one of the longest poems in the world. Parts of the *Mahabharata* date back to the fifth century B.C.E., but the *Bhagavad Gita* may have been composed as late as 200 C.E. The *Mahabharata* tells the story of an 18-day battle fought between two factions of a warring family. Describing one episode during that 18-day period, the *Bhagavad Gita* is the record of a conversation between Arjuna, a member of one of the factions, and his charioteer, Krishna, the head of the related Yadava clan, as they wait in their chariot between the two armies on the field of battle. Responding to Arjuna's doubts and moral confusion regarding the war, Krishna explains to Arjuna his duties as a prince and as a good Ksatriya or warrior and also elaborates on different yogic and Vedantic philosophies. In the course of this discussion, it becomes clear that Krishna is no mere mortal, but an incarnation of the god Vishnu, who is to Hindus the Preserver of the World. Because of the arguments Krishna uses to ultimately convince Arjuna to fight, the *Bhagavad Gita* is often described as a concise guide to Hindu philosophy and as a practical guide to life. During the discourse, Krishna reveals his divine identity and favors Arjuna with an awe-inspiring glimpse of his divine image. In the following excerpt from the *Bhagavad Gita*, Krishna answers Arjuna's questions about the form and nature of the deity.

Chapter VIII
Arjuna asked:

1. What is Brahman?, what is Atman, and what is karma?, Oh Best of Men. What is your material nature, and what is your divine nature?
2. What is your sacrificial nature in this body, and how does it operate, Oh Madhusudana? How again, are you to be known at the time of death by those with their minds in yoga?

The Blessed Lord answered:

3. Brahman is the indestructible, the supreme, whose essential nature is called Atman. Karma is the name for the creative power which causes the births of beings.
4. The foundation of all existence is My material nature, the basis of all Spirit is My divine nature. The basis of all sacrifices is My sacrificial nature; I am here, in the body, Oh Greatest of Embodied Ones.

5. And that one who at the hour of his death, thinking on Me alone as he casts off his body, he enters into My nature. Of this there is no doubt.

6. On whatever state of being a man thinks when at the end he gives up his body, to that state of being he goes, Oh Son of Kunti, having been totally absorbed in the thoughts of that state.

7. Therefore think upon Me at all times and fight. When your mind and reason are fixed on Me, then, without doubt, you shall come to Me.

8. With the Mind not wandering after anything else, with the mind yoked by yoga and practice, meditating on the highest divine Spirit, to that Spirit you will go.

9. He who meditates on the ancient Seer, the World Controller, Who is smaller than the smallest, the Establisher of all, of form unfathomable, sun-colored, beyond the darkness;

10. He who does this, at the time of his death, by an unswerving mind fixed in devotion, and by the power of yoga drawing the life breath to the center of the eyebrows, he goes to this Spirit, supreme and divine.

11. Now I will tell you about That state which the knowers of the Veda call Indestructible; That which those who are controlled and free from passion enter, and That desiring which they lead a life of bramacarya.

12. With all the gates of the body closed, confining the mind within the heart and his own breath in his head, using the concentration of yoga;

13. Then he who recited the singly syllable Aum!, which is Brahman, and meditating on Me as he dies, giving up his body, he goes to the highest goal.

14. That man who constantly meditates on Me, thinking of no other, who is a yogi truly disciplined, by him I am easily obtained.

Source: Herman, A. L., ed. *The Bhagavad Gita: A Translation and Critical Commentary.* Springfield, IL: Charles C. Thomas, Publisher, 1973, pp. 70–71.

2. The *Ramayana*: The Story of Ahalya and the God Indra

One of the most important literary works of ancient India, the *Ramayana* is a Sanskrit epic comprising some twenty-four-thousand verses divided into seven books and telling the story of Rama, a Hindu prince who is an incarnation of the god Vishnu. Authorship of the work is traditionally attributed to Valmiki, who is revered as the first poet in Hinduism. Although most scholars accept that the original kernel of the *Ramayana* may have been written by one person between about 750 and 500 B.C.E., making it somewhat older than the *Mahabharata* (*see* Document 1), the epic as it exists today is the result of centuries of revisions and interpolations by others and may not have reached its final form until India's medieval period. The oldest existing manuscript dates from the eleventh century C.E. The following prose excerpt, which tells the story of the beautiful woman Ahalya, is drawn from a version of the *Ramayana* crafted by the Tamil poet Kamban in the thirteenth century.

Brahma once created, out of the ingredients of absolute beauty, a woman, and she was called Ahalya. . . . God Indra, being the highest god among the gods, was attracted by her beauty and was convinced that he alone was worthy of claiming her hand. Brahma, noticing the conceit and presumptuousness of

Indra, ignored him, sought out Sage Gautama and left him in charge of the girl. She grew up in his custody, and when the time came the sage took her back to Brahma and handed her over to him.

Brahma appreciated Gautama's purity of mind and heart (never once had any carnal thought crossed his mind), and said, "Marry her, she is fit to be your wife, or rather you alone deserve to be her husband." Accordingly, she was married, blessed by Brahma and other gods. . . .

Indra, however, never got over his infatuation for Ahalya, and often came in different guises near to Gautama's ashram, waiting for every chance to gaze and feast on ahalya's form and figure . . . One day . . . Indra assumed the voice of a rooster, and woke up the sage, who, thinking the morning had come, left for the river. Now Indra assumed the sage's form, entered the hut, and made love to Ahalya. She surrendered herself, but at some stage realized that the man enjoying her was an imposter; but she could do nothing about it. Gautama came back at this moment, and surprised the couple in bed. Ahalya stood aside filled with shame and remorse; Indra assumed the form of a cat (the most facile form for sneaking in or out) and tried to slip away. The sage . . . was not to be deceived. He arrested the cat where he was with these words:

"Cat, I know you; your obsession with the female is your undoing. May your body be covered with a thousand female marks, so that in all the worlds, people may understand what reales on in your mind all the time." Hardly had these words left his lips when every inch of Indra's body displayed the female organ. There could be no greater shame for the proud and self-preening Indra.

After Indra slunk away, back to his world, Gautama looked at his wife and said, "You have sinned with your body. May that body Harden into a shapeless piece of granite . . .

Indra's predicament became a joke in all the worlds. . . . He stayed in darkness and seclusion and could never appear before men or women. This caused much concern to all the gods, as his multifarious duties in various worlds remained suspended, and they . . . requested [Brahma] to intercede with Gautama. By this time, the sage's resentment had vanished. And he said in response to Brahma's appeal, "May the thousand additions to Indra's features become eyes." Indra thereafter came to be known as the "thousand-eyed god."

Source: Narayan, R. K., ed. *The Ramayana: A Shortened Modern Prose Version of the Indian Epic.* New York: Penguin Books, 1977, pp. 20–22.

3. Excerpt from the Travel Account of Faxian: A Cremation in Ceylon, c. 400

Faxian (c. 337–c. 422) was a Chinese Buddhist monk who traveled through India between about 399 and 412, during the reign of Chandra Gupta II. Faxian's mission was to find and acquire works of Buddhist literature and to bring them to China for translation. While in India, Faxian visited many Buddhist sites, including the birthplace of Lord Buddha at Lumbini. Faxian's account of his travels *Record of the Buddhistic Kingdoms* is one of the world's great travel books and a valuable source of information on Gupta India and on early Buddhism. In the following excerpt, Faxian describes a cremation he witnessed in Ceylon. *See also* Document 4, for another except from the writings of Faxian.

Seven *li* to the south of the city there is a shrine called the Great Shrine, with three thousand resident priests. Among them was one reverend Shaman, so pure in his conduct as regards the Disciples that all suspected him of being a Lo-han [i.e., one who has followed the eight-fold path and has achieved deliverance from earthly existence]. When he was at the point of death, the king came to look into the matter; and when, in accordance with the rules of the Faith, he had assembled the priests, he asked, "Has this religious mendicant become a Lo-han?" The priests at once told the truth and replied, "He is a Lo-han." When he was dead the king accordingly buried him with the ceremonial due to a Lo-han, as laid down in the Canons.

Four or five *li* to the east of the shrine a great pile of wood was collected, over thirty feet square and of about the same height. Sandalwood, garoo wood (lign-aloes), and all kinds of scented woods were laced on the top, and at the four sides steps were made. Over it was spread clean white cashmere which surrounded and quite covered the pyre; and again on the top of this was placed a car, in form like the hearses of China, but without the dragon. At the time of the cremation the king and his subjects collected together from all quarters, and with offerings of flowers and incense followed the car to the burial-ground, the king himself making personal offerings of flowers and incense. When these ceremonies were finished, the car was placed on the top of the pyre, oil of sweet basil was poured all over it, and a light was applied. While the fire was blazing, every one was moved with a feeling of reverence, and each took off his upper garment, and together with feather-fan and umbrella, threw it from a distance into the midst of the flames, so as to help on the cremation. When it was all over, the bones were collected and a pagoda raised over them. Fa-hsien did not arrive while the deceased was yet alive, but only in time to see his funeral.

Source: Giles, M. A., trans. *The Travels of Fa-hsien (399–414 A.D.), or Record of the Buddhistic Kingdoms*. London: Routledge & Kegan Paul, 1959, pp. 72–73.

4. Excerpt from the Travel Account of Faxian: The Chandalas, c. 400

In this excerpt from Faxian's *Record of the Buddhistic Kingdoms*, the Chinese scholar-monk makes reference to the Chandalas, members of the lowest Hindu caste, who must separate themselves from the rest of Gupta society. Faxian also describes the esteem with which Indian rulers regard Buddhist holy men and the rewards such men receive for their pure way of life. *See also* Document 3, for another excerpt from the writings of Faxian.

All south from this is named the Middle Kingdom [central India, the northern Deccan]. In it the cold and heat are finely tempered, and there is neither hoarfrost nor snow. The people are numerous and happy; they have not to register their households, or attend to any magistrates and their rules; only those who cultivate the royal land have to pay (a portion of) the gain from it. If they want to go, they go; if they want to stay on, they stay. The king governs without decapitation or (other) corporal punishments. Criminals are simply fined, lightly or heavily, according to the circumstances (of each case). Even in cases of repeated attempts at wicked rebellion, they only have their right hands cut off. The king's body-guards and attendants all have salaries. Throughout the whole country the people do not kill any living creature, nor drink intoxicating liquor, nor eat onions or garlic. The only exception is that of the Chandalas [Untouchables]. That is the name for those who are (held to be) wicked men, and live apart from others. When they enter the gate of a city or a market-place, they strike a piece of wood to make themselves known, so that men know and avoid them. and do not come into contact with them. In that country they do not keep pigs or fowls, and do not sell live cattle; in the markets there are no butchers' shops and no dealers in intoxicating drink. In buying and selling commodities they use cowries. Only the Chandalas are fishermen and hunters, and sell flesh meat.

After Buddha attained to pari-nirvâna [i.e., when Buddha died] the kings of the various countries and the heads of the Vaisyas built vihâras for the priests, and endowed them with fields, houses, gardens, and orchards, along with the resident populations and their cattle, the grants being engraved on plates of metal, so that afterwards they were handed down from king to king, without any one daring to annul them, and they remain even to the present time.

Source: Legge, James, ed. and trans. *A Record of the Buddhistic Kingdoms: Being an Account by the Chinese Monk Fâ Hien of His Travels in India and Ceylon (A.D. 399–414) in Search of the Buddhist Books of Discipline.* New York: Dover Publications, 1965, pp. 42–43.

5. Excerpt from the Poem "The Birth of the War-God" by Kalidasa, c. Fourth/Fifth Century C.E.

Kalidasa is the most renowned Sanskrit poet and playwright of medieval India. Although little is known about his life, the fame of his plays and poems, which are based mainly on Hindu mythology and philosophy, have earned him a place in Indian literature that is akin to that of William Shakespeare in English literature. Of his three known plays, the most acclaimed is *Abhijnanashakuntala*, which tells the story of the mishaps that befall King Dushyanta and his wife Shakuntala. Also attributed to him are two epic poems and several long lyric poems. Scholars are uncertain as to just when Kalidasa lived and wrote, though most place his life between 300 and 470 C.E., with many narrowing it to sometime during the reign of Chandra Gupta II in the early fifth century. The following excerpt is taken from Kalidasa'a poem, "The Birth of the War-God."

Canto Second

The Address to Brahma
While impious Tarak in resistless might
Was troubling heaven and earth with wild affright,
To Brahma's high abode, by Indra led,
The mournful deities for refuge fled.
As when the Day-God's loving beams awake
The lotus slumbering on the silver lake,
So Brahma deigned his glorious face to show,
And poured sweet comfort on their looks of woe.

Then nearer came the suppliant Gods to pay
Honour to him whose face turns every way.
They bowed them low before the Lord of Speech,
And sought with truthful words his heart to reach:
"Glory to Thee! before the world was made,
One single form thy Majesty displayed.
Next Thou, to body forth the mystic Three,
Didst fill three Persons: Glory, Lord, to Thee!
Unborn and unbegotten! from thy hand
The fruitful seed rained down; at thy command
From that small germ o'er quickening waters thrown
All things that move not, all that move have grown.
Before thy triple form in awe they bow:
Maker, preserver, and destroyer, Thou!
Thou, when a longing urged thee to create,
Thy single form in twain didst separate.
The Sire, the Mother that made all things be
By their first union were but parts of Thee.
From them the life that fills this earthly frame,
And fruitful Nature, self-renewing, came.
Thous countest not thy time by mortals' light;
With thee there is but one vast day and night.
When Brahma slumbers fainting Nature dies,
When Brahma wakens all again arise.
Creator of the world, and uncreate!
Endless! all things from Thee their end await.
Before the world wast Thou! each Lord shall fall
Before Thee, mightiest, highest, Lord of all.
The self-taught soul thine own deep spirit knows;
Made by thyself they mighty form arose;
Into the same, when all things have their end,
Shall thy great self, absorbed in Thee, descend.
Lord, who may hope thy essence to declare?
Firm, yet subtle as the yielding air:
Fixt, all-pervading; ponderous, yet light,
Patent to all, yet hidden from the sight.
Thine are the sacred hymns which mortals raise,
Commencing ever with the word of praise,
With three-toned chant the sacrifice to grace,
And win at last in heaven a blissful place.
They hail Thee Nature labouring to free
The Immortal Soul from low humanity;
Hail Thee the stranger Spirit, unimpressed,
Gazing on Nature from thy lofty rest.
Father of fathers, God of gods art thou,
Creator, highest, hearer of the vow!
Thou art the sacrifice, and Thou the priest,
Thou, he that eateth; Thou the holy feast.
Thou art the knowledge which by thee is taught,
The mighty thinker, and the highest thought!"

Source: Griffith, Ralph T. H., trans. *The Birth of the War-God: A Poem by Kalidasa.* 2nd ed. London: Trübner & Company, 1879, pp. 17–19.

6. Inscriptions of the Gupta Kings, Fourth and Fifth Centuries c.e.

Reproduced below are three inscriptions from the Gupta Period in which the Gupta monarchs and other rulers celebrate their achievements and lineage. The first refers, probably posthumously, to Samudra Gupta, who reigned from about 335 to 375; it was carved on a stone pillar near what is today the North Indian city of Allahabad. The second inscription is from the reign of Chandra Gupta II (c. 375–415) and mentions the *asvamedha* or horse sacrifice, a ritual that gave great power and prestige to whomever carried it out. As it is here, this ritual, which did not always include the actual immolation of a horse, is always associated with Samudra Gupta, who is said to have "displayed prowess by a horse-sacrifice." The third inscription refers to Yasodharman, a sixth-century king of Malwi, a Hindu kingdom of central India.

Inscription of Samuda Gupta

This lofty column [is] as it were an arm of the earth, proclaiming the fame, — which, having pervaded the entire surface of the earth with [its] development that was caused by [his] conquest of the whole world, [has departed] hence [and now] experiences the sweet happiness attained by [his] having gone to the abode of [Indra] the lord of the gods, — of the Maharajadhiraja, the glorious Samudragupta, . . . Whose happy mind was accustomed to associate with learned people; — who was the supporter of the real truth of scriptures . . . who, having overwhelmed, with the [fore of the] commands of the collective merits of [his] learned men, those things which obstruct the beauty of excellent poetry, [still] enjoys, in the world of the wise, the sovereignty of the fame [produced] by much poetry. . . .

Inscription of Chandra Gupta II

By him who is the son, — accepted by him, [and] begotten on the Mahadevi Dattadevi, — of the Maharajadhiraja, [the glorious] Samudragupta, — [Who was the exterminator of all kings; who had no antagonist [of equal power] in the word; [whose fame was] tasted]by the waters of the four oceans]; who was equal to [the gods]; who was [the very axe] of [the god] Kritanta; who was the giver of [many] millions of]lawfully acquired cows] and gold; [who was the restorer of the asvamedha-sacrifice, that had been long in abeyance, — Who was the son of the son's son of the Maharaja, the illustrious Gupta; the son's son of [the Maharaja, the illustrious] Ghatotkacha; [and] the son of the Maharajadhiraja [the glorious Chandragupta [I], [and] the daughter's son oif Lichchhavi, begotten on the Mahadevi Kumaradevi; — By him, the most devout worshipper of the Divine One, the Maharajadhiraja, the glorious Chandragupta [II]. . . .

Inscription of Yasodharman

Perfection has been attained! Victorious is he, [the god] Pinakin, the lord of [all] worlds, — in whose songs, hummed with smiles, the splendour of [his] teeth, like the luster of lightning sparkling in the night, envelops and brings into full view all this universe! . . . Now, victorious is that tribal ruler, having the name of the glorious Yasodharman, who, having plunged into the army of [his enemies, as if into a grove of thornapple-trees, [and] having bent down the reputations of heroes like the tender creepers of trees, effects the adornment of [his] body with the fragments of young sprouts which are the wounds [inflicted on him].

Source: Fleet, John Faithfull, ed. *Corpus Inscriptionum Indicarum.* Volume III: *Inscriptions of the Early Gupta Kings and Their Successors.* Varanasi, India: Indological Book House, 1963, pp. 10–11, 27–28, 154–155.

7. Except from *The Minister's Seal*, a Work by the Gupta Playwright Visakhadatta, Early Fifth Century c.e.

Little is known about Visakhadatta beyond what the playwright says of himself in the following excerpt from the prologue to his play, *The Minister's Seal*. Given that his grandfather was a governor and that he is sometimes referred to as Visakhadeva—*deva* being a royal appellation—it seems likely that he was a member of the Gupta nobility. His life dates are uncertain, but, because the final benediction of the play mentions King Chandra Gupta, it is likely that he lived during the Reign of Chandra Gupta II (c. 375–415). *The Minister's Seal* is semihistorical in that the king whose throne is in jeopardy in the play is an historical figure, known from Greek sources for having defeated Alexander the Great's commander Seleucus Nicator in 305 b.c.e. The circumstances of the play, however, appear to be entirely fictional. The excerpt below is from the prologue, wherein the director sets the stage for the coming performance.

After the blessing has been said, enter the Director.

Director: This will do. I have been instructed by the audience to stage a new play today, a play by the poet Visakhadatta, the son of Maharaja Bhaskara and the grandson of governor Vatesvaradatta. The play is a heroic drama, entitled The Minister's Seal. In fact, I am extremely happy to stage a play for an audience like this that is so appreciative of good literature. For even a fool can reap a rich harvest, if his seed falls on good soil; the abundance of his crop does not depend on the sower's skill. So I had better get home and call my wife, so that we can begin the performance with our troupe. . . . Here we are. Well, well, what is going on here? It looks as if we are having a celebration. All the servants are unusually busy at their jobs. One is carrying buckets full of water, another is mixing incense, a third is fashioning garlands of all kinds of flowers, and still another is humming while she pounds with her pestle. All right, then, I'll call my wife and ask what is happening. [*He looks toward the backstage.*]

Enter an Actress

Actress: Here I am, my Lord. Be good enough to grace me with your orders.

Director: My orders can wait. Tell me, have you invited these reverend Brahmins to grace our house, or have they come by themselves as welcome guests, since there is such a variety of dishes being prepared?

Actress: No, I invited the reverend Brahmins myself.

Director: Why?

Actress: We must worship the moon today. There is an eclipse.

Director: Whoever told you that?

Actress: someone from the City.

Director: Madam, I have made an elaborate study of all sixty-four chapters of astrology. By all means, carry on your cooking for the Brahmins, but we are not going to have an eclipse today. Somebody has played a trick on you! Look, . . . a Cruel Grasper wants to violate the Moon's Immaculate Realm . . .

Voice Offstage: Who dares, while I am here!

Director: . . . but the Conjunction of Mercury will save the day!

Actress: Who was that man who, safely on earth, wants to save the moon and stave off its attackers?

Director: I could not quite catch it myself. Let me try again [*repeats the phrase:* "A Cruel Grasper . . . "]

Voice Offstage: Who dares violate my Lord the Moon while I am here? Speak up!

Director [listening]: Ah, I have got it! Kautilya! [*Actress shrinks with fear.*] Yes, Kautilya of the crooked mind, who burnt the house of the Nandas in the fire of his fury. He heard that someone tried to grasp the Moon and thought that his lord Chandragupta was threatened. Let us get away from here! [*Exeunt.*].

Source: Van Buitenen, J. A. B., trans. *Two Plays of Ancient India.* New York: Columbia University Press, 1968, pp. 185–187.

8. Banabhatta's Account of How the Newly Crowned Harsha Turned a Bad Omen to His Advantage, c. 606

Banabhatta (known as Bana) was court poet to the seventh-century North Indian ruler Harsha, whose life and deeds were recorded by Bana in his Sanskrit biography of the king, the *Harshacharita*. Although written in florid and poetic prose, the *Harshacharita* is the first historical biography in Sanskrit and appears to be based on accurate and detailed observation of the people and events it depicts. It also has an element of autobiography, telling us something about the thought and personality of Bana himself. The following excerpt describes an incident that occurred when Harsha first came to the throne in difficult circumstances following the murder of his older brother. *See also* Document 9, for another description of the start of Harsha's reign.

On the outskirts of the city of Sthanesvara, the local notary came "with his whole retinue of clerks" to pay homage to the newly crowned an consecrated Harsha, saying "'Let his majesty, whose edicts are never void, even now bestow upon us his commands for the day,' so [he] presented a newly made golden seal with a bull for its emblem. The king took it. As soon, however, as a ball of earth was produced, the seal slipped from the king's hand and fell face downwards upon the ground, and the lines of the letters were distinctly marked upon the nearly dry mud and soft earth of Saravati's bank. Apprehensive of an evil omen, the courtiers were depressed, but the king thought in his heart: 'The minds of the dull are indeed blind to reality. The omen signifies that the earth shall be stamped with the single seal of my sole command: but the rustics interpret otherwise.' Having thus mentally welcomed the omen, he bestowed upon the Brahmanas a hundred villages delimited by a thousand ploughs. That day he spent in the same place, and when night arrived, complimented all the kings and retired to rest."

Source: Quoted in Srivastava, Bireshwar Nath. *Harsha and His Times: A Glimpse of Political History during the Seventh Century* A.D. The Chowkhamba Sanskrit Studies Vol. LXXXVI. Varanasi, India: The Chowkhamba Sanskrit Series Office, 1979, pp. 25–26, n. 1.

9. Xuanzang's Account of Harsha's Accession to the Throne, c. 606

Xuanzang (c. 602–654), like that earlier Chinese visitor to India, Faxian (*see* Documents 3 and 4), was a Buddhist monk. Xuanzang traveled through India in the early seventh century visiting Buddhist sites and studying with Buddhist scholars. He spent several years studying Sanskrit, logic, and grammar at Nalanda, the great Buddhist center of learning in early medieval India. When he returned to China in the 640s, he brought back many Buddhist texts, for which he established a translation bureau with the permission of the Chinese emperor. Also at the emperor's request, he wrote an autobiography, which includes detailed descriptions of his experiences in India during the reign of Harsha. The following excerpt describes the circumstances surrounding Harsha's accession to the throne. *See also* Document 8, for another account of the start of Harsha's reign.

The great minister Po-ni whose office/wisdom, and reputation were high and of much weight, addressing the assembled ministers and officials said, "The destiny of the nation is to be fixed today. The old king's son [Rajyavardhana] is dead; the brother of the prince [Harsha-vardhana], however, is humane and affectionate, and his disposition, heaven conferred, is filial and respectful. Because he is strongly attached to his family, the people will trust in him. I propose that he assume royal authority. Let each one give his opinion on this matter, whatever he thinks." There was no dissention and they all admired his virtue.

On this the ministers and officials all exhorted him to take authority saying: "Let the royal prince attend! The accumulated merit and the conspicuous virtue of the former king were so illustrious as to cause this kingdom to be most happily governed. When he was followed by Rajya-vardhana we thought he would end his years [as king]; but, owing to the badness of his ministers, he was led to subject his person to the hand of the enemy, and the kingdom has suffered great affliction; but it is because he lacked good ministers. the opinion of the people, as shown in their songs, proves their real submission to your eminent qualities. Reign, then, with glory over the land; conquer the enemies of your family; wash out the insult laid on your kingdom and glorify the deeds of your illustrious father. Great will your merit be in such a case. We pray you reject not our prayer."

The prince replied: ". . . Setting up a ruler on the throne—this should be done with great circumspection. I am indeed of little virtue and my father and brother have orphaned me. . . . Although public opinion thinks me fit for the throne, how dare I forget my insufficiency. Now, on the banks of the Ganga there is a statue of the Avalokitesvara Bodhi-sattva which has witnessed many spiritual wonders. I will go and request a response."

Forthwith coming to the spot where the figure of the Bodhi-sattva was, he remained before it fasting and praying. The Boshi-sattva was moved by his sincerity and appeared in bodily form and enquired, "What do you seek that you are so earnest in your supplications?" the prince answered, "I have suffered under a load of affliction. My kindly father indeed is dead and to add to this cruel punishment my good brother has been murdered. I am aware that I am lacking in virtue, nevertheless the people would exalt me to royal dignity, to glorify my illustrious father. Yet, I am indeed but ignorant and foolish. In my trouble I ask for holy direction."

The Bodhi-sattva replied, . . . The Law of Buddha having been destroyed by the king of Kanrna-suvarna, you, when you become king, should revive it. If you be compassionate to the distressed and cherish them, then before long you shall rule over the five Indias."

Source: Quoted in Devahuti, D. *Harsha: A Political Study.* Oxford, UK: Clarendon Press, 1970, pp. 80–81.

10. A Muslim Account of Hindu Devotions, 1041

Muhammad Kasim Firishta (c. 1560–c. 1620) was an Indian Muslim historian, who, under the patronage of the shah of Bijapur, wrote a history of the Muslims in India since the tenth century. His work, which was translated in 1829, is a landmark in Indian historiography because it provides detailed information on the history of medieval India. The following excerpt is a less-than-flattering account of Hinduism and its followers in eleventh-century India.

In the year 435 [1041 C.E.], the prince of Delhi in alliance with others, raising an army, took Hassi, Tannasar, and their dependencies, from the governors to whom Modood [Sultan Manmood] had entrusted them. The Hindoos from thence marched towards the fort of Nagracut, which they besieged for four months, and the garrison being distressed for provisions, and no succours coming from Lahore, were under the necessity of capitulating. The Hindoos, according to the ancient form, erected new idols, and recommenced the rites of idolatry. We are told that the prince of Delhi, observing a weakness in the empire of Ghizni, pretended to have seen a vision, in which the great idol of Nagracut told him, that having now revenged himself upon the Ghizni, he would meet him at Nagracut in his former temple. This story being propagated by the Brahmins, who probably were in the secret, it gained faith among the superstitious, by which means the Raja was joined by zealots from all parts, and soon saw himself at the head of a very numerous army. With this army as we have already mentioned, he besieged Nargacut, and when the place surrendered, he took care to have an idol, of the same shape and size with the former, which he had caused to be made at Delhi, introduced, in the night, into a garden in the center of the place. This image being discovered in the morning, there was a prodigious rejoicing among his deluded votaries, who exclaimed, that their God was returned from Ghizni. The Raja, and the Brahmins, taking the advantage of the credulity of the populace, with great pomp and festivity, carried him into the temple, where he received the worship and congratulations of his people. This story raised so much the fame of the idol, that thousands came daily to worship from all parts of Hindostan, as also to consult him as an oracle, upon all important occasions. The manner of consultation was this: The person who came to inquire into futurity, slept on the floor of the temple before him, after drinking a dose of something which the Brahmins prescribed to create dreams, from which they predicted their fortune, in the morning, according to their own fancy.

Source: Firishta, Muhammad Kasim. *The History of Hindostan.* Translated by Alexander Dow. Vol. 1. London: Printed for J. Walker, 1812, p. 8.

11. A Description of the City of Delhi at the End of the Reign of Sultan Shams al-Din Iltutmish, 1236

The following excerpt from the writings of the thirteenth-century Indian historian Al Minhaj Bin Siraj (*see also* Document 12) is a laudatory description of the power and prestige of the city of Delhi at the end of the reign of Sultan Shams al-Din Iltutmish (d. 1236). Although born into a noble Central Asian family, Iltutmish was a former slave who was proclaimed sultan of Delhi in 1210 in succession to his former master, Sultan Qutb al-Din Aibek.

The capital city of Delhi . . . is the seat of the government of Hindustan, and the Centre of the circle of Islam, the sanctuary of the mandates and inhibitions of the law, the kernel of the Muhammadi religion, the marrow of the Ahmadi belief, and the tabernacle of the eastern parts of the universe—Guard it, O God, from calamities, and molestation! This city, through the number of the grants, and unbounded munificence of that pious monarch [Sultan Shams al-Din Iltutmish], became the retreat and resting-place for the learned, the virtuous, and the excellent of the various parts of the world; and those who, by the mercy of God, the most High, escaped from the toils of the calamities sustained by the provinces and cities of Ajam, and the misfortunes caused by the (irruption of the) infidel Mughals, made the capital—the asylum of the universe—of that sovereign their asylum, refuge, resting-place, and point of safety; and, up to the present day, those same rules are observed and remain unchanged, and such may they ever continue!

Source: Al Minhaj Bin Siraj. *Tabakat-i-Nasiri: A General History of the Muhammadan Dynasties of Asia.* Translated by H. G. Raverty. Vol. 1. Calcutta, India: Asiatic Society of Bengal, 1881, pp. 598–599.

12. Sultana Raziya and Nasiriah College, c. 1240

In this excerpt, the thirteenth-century historian Al Minhaj Bin Siraj (*see also* Document 11), describes how he was placed in charge of Nasiriah College. The appointment appears to have been made initially by Sultana Raziya, the daughter and successor of Sultan Shams al-Din Iltutmish and one of the few female rulers of medieval India. However, confirmation of the appointment seems to have been made some years later after Sultana Raziya had been overthrown and killed and the throne had come to Nasir al-Din Mahmud Shah.

[Sultana Raziya] issued commands for her troops to proceed to Gwaliyur, and bestowed rich and valuable presents. As disobedience was out of the questions, this servant of the victorious kingdom, Minhaj-i-Suraj, in conjunction with the Malik-ul Umra (the chief of theAmirs) Ziya-ud-Din, Junaidi, who was the Amir-I-Dad (chief magistrate) of Gwaliyur, and with other persons of note, came out of the preserved fortress of Gwaliyur on the 1st of the month of Sha'ban, 635 [1240] . . . and returned to Delhi, the capital; and, in this same month, Sultan Raziyyat committed to the charge of this servant . . . the Nasiriah College at the capital to which was added the Kazi-ship of Gwaliyur . . .

The writer of this book . . . reached the capital on Monday, the 14th of the month of Safar, 643 [1248] . . . and permission to pay homage at the sublime Court was obtained. On Thursday, the 17th of the month of Safar . . . the Nasiriah College, together with the superintendence of its endowments, the Kazi-ship of Gwaliyur, and the lecture-ship of Jami Masjid, all these, were confirmed to the author, according to the former grant, and that Malik (Ulugh Khan-i-Mu'azzam) conferred on the author a special honorary robe, and a caparisoned horse such as no other among his brethren of the same profession had ever obtained. God reward him for it!

Source: Al Minhaj Bin Siraj. *Tabakat-i-Nasiri: A General History of the Muhammadan Dynasties of Asia.* Translated by H. G. Raverty. Vol. 1. Calcutta, India: Asiatic Society of Bengal, 1881, pp. 643–644, 667.

13. Excerpt from the Account of Marco Polo: The Customs of Maabar, c. 1291

Marco Polo (1254–c. 1324) was a Venetian merchant and explorer who, with his father and uncle, traveled to Mongol China in the late thirteenth century. Polo's account of his travels, mainly in China, also through India and Southeast Asia, offers a European perspective of the peoples and places of East Asia. The following excerpt lists various customs of the people of Maabar, which appears to be the Coromandel Coast of southeastern coast of India. *See also* Document 14, for another selection from the writings of Marco Polo.

Another custom is this. when a man is dead and his body is being cremated, his wife flings herself into the same fire and lets herself be burnt with her husband. The ladies who do this are highly praised by all. And I assure you that there are many who do as I have told you. . . .

Here is yet another of their customs. The king and his barons and everyone else all sit on the earth. If you ask them why they do not seat themselves more honourably, they reply that to sit on the earth is honourable enough, because we were made from the earth and to the earth we must return, so that no one could honour the earth too highly and no one should slight it. . . .

This kingdom produces no grain excepting only rice. And here is a greater matter, well worth recounting: in this country if a stallion of noble breed covers a mare of the like mettle the offspring is a stunted colt with its feet awry. Horses so bed are worthless and cannot be ridden.

The people here go into battle with lance and shield and they go stark naked. They are not men of any valour or spirit, but paltry creatures and mean-spirited.

They kill no beasts or any living thing. When they have a mind to eat the flesh of a sheep or of any beast or bird, they employ a Saracen or some other who is not of their religion or rule to kill it for them. Another of their customs is that all of them, male or female, wash their whole body in cold water twice a day — that is, morning and evening. One who did not wash twice a day would be thought an ascetic. . . .

And you must know that in eating they use only the right hand; they would never touch food with their left. Whatever is clean and fair they do and touch with the right hand, believing that the function of the left hand is confined to such needful tasks as are unclean and foul, such as wiping the nose or the breach and suchlike. Likewise they drink only out of flasks, each one from his own; for no one would drink out of another's flask. When they are drinking, they do not set the flask to their lips, but hold it above and pour the fluid into their mouth. They would not on any account touch the flask with their lips nor pass it to a stranger to drink out of. If a stranger wants to drink and has not got his own flask with him, they will pour the wine or other fluid into his hands and he will drink out of them, so that his own hands will serve him for a cup.

Source: Latham, Ronald, ed. and trans. *The Travels of Marco Polo.* New York: Penguin Books, 1958, pp. 238–239.

14. Excerpt from the Account of Marco Polo: The Brahmins of Lar, c. 1291

Like Document 13, above, the following is a selection from the travel account of Venetian trader Marco Polo, who journeyed to China and other parts of East Asia in the late thirteenth century. This excerpt describes the merchants of the Indian province of Lar, which appears to be a district of southwestern India.

Leaving the place where rests the body of the glorious apostle Saint Thomas, and proceeding westward, you enter the province of Lar [probably the region around modern-day Mysore in southwestern India], from whence the Brahmins, who are spread over India, derive their origin. These are the best and most honorable merchants that can be found. No consideration whatever can induce them to speak an untruth, even though their lives should depend upon it. They have also an abhorrence of robbery or of purloining the goods of other persons. They are likewise remarkable for the virtue of continence, being satisfied with the possession of one wife. When any foreign merchant, unacquainted with the usages of the country, introduces himself to one of these, and commits to his hands the care of his adventure, this Brahmin undertakes the management of it, disposes of the goods, and renders a faithful account of the proceeds, attending scrupulously to the interests of the stranger, and not demanding any recompense for his trouble, should the owner uncourteously omit to make him the gratuitous offer. They eat meat, and drink the wine of the country. They do not, however, kill any animal themselves, but get it done by the Mahometans. The Brahmins are distinguished by a certain badge, consisting of a thick cotton thread, which passes over the shoulder and is tied under the arm, in such a manner that the thread appears upon the breast and behind the back.

The king is extremely rich and powerful, and has much delight in the possession of pearls and valuable stones. When the traders from Maabar [along the southeastern coast of India] present to him such as are of superior beauty, he trusts to their word with respect to the estimation of their value, and gives them double the sum that each is declared to have cost them. Under these circumstances, he has the offer of many fine jewels.

The people are gross idolaters, and much addicted to sorcery and divination. When they are about to make a purchase of goods, they immediately observe the shadow cast by their own bodies in the sunshine; and if the shadow be as large as it should be, they make the purchase that day. Moreover, when they are in any shop for the purpose of buying anything, if they see a tarantula, of which there are many there, they take notice from which side it comes, and regulate their business accordingly. Again, when they are going out of their houses, if they hear anyone sneeze, they return into the house, and stay at home. They are very abstemious in regard to eating, and live to any advanced age. Their teeth are preserved sound by the use of a certain vegetable which they are in the habit of masticating. It also promotes digestion, and conduces generally to the health of the body.

Source: Marsden, William, ed. and trans. *The Travels of Marco Polo: The Venetian.* Garden City, NY: Doubleday & Company, 1948, pp. 288–289.

15. Marco Polo Describes Yogis He Encounters in India, c. 1291

In this excerpt from the writings of the European traveler Marco Polo (*see* Documents 13 and 14), he describes Indian Yogis, with whom he is clearly fascinated.

Among them [Brahmans] are certain living under a rule who are called Yogis. They live even longer than the others, as much as 150 or 200 years. And their bodies remain so active that they can still come and go as they will and perform all the services required by their monastery and their idols and serve them just as well as if they were younger. This comes of their great abstinence and of eating very little food and only what is wholesome. For it is their practice to eat chiefly rice and milk. . . .

There is a regular religious order in this kingdom of Maabar, of those who are called by this name of Yogi, who carry abstinence to the extremes of which I will tell you and lead a harsh and austere life. You may take it for a fact that they go start naked, wearing not a stitch of clothing nor even covering their private parts or any bodily member. They worship the ox, and most of them carry a little ox made of gilt copper or bronze in the middle of the forehead. You must understand that they wear it tied on. Le me tell you further that they burn cow-dung and make a powder of it. With this they anoint various parts of their body with great reverence, no less than Christians display in the use of holy water. If anyone does reverence to them while they are passing in the street, they anoint him with this powder on the forehead in token of blessing. They do not eat out of platters or on trenchers; but they take their food on the leaves of apples of paradise or other big leaves — not green leaves, but dried ones; for they say that the green leaves have souls so that this would be a sin. For in their dealings with all living creatures they are at pains to do nothing that they believe to be a sin. Indeed they would sooner die than do anything that they deemed to be sinful. When other men ask them why they go naked and are not ashamed to show their sexual member, they say: "We go naked because we want nothing of this world. For we came into the world naked and unclothed. The reason why we are not ashamed to show our member is that we commit no sin with it, so we are not more ashamed to show it than you are when you show your hand or face or any other member which you do not employ in sinful lechery. It is because you employ this member in sin and lechery that you cover it and are ashamed of it.

Source: Polo, Marco. *The Travels.* London: Penguin, 1958, pp. 279–280.

16. A Story of Pre-Muslim Delhi: Justice for a Crow, c. 1320

Amir Khusrau (1253–1325) was a Turkish soldier who gained a high reputation as a scholar and poet. Able to read Sanskrit, he also wrote in two languages, Persian and Hindi. The following selection from his writings tells a mythical tale of an eighth-century Hindu ruler of Delhi.

I have heard a story that, in Delhi, about five or six hundred years ago, there was a great *rai*, called Anangpal. At the entrance of his palace he had placed two lions, sculptured in stone. He fixed a bell by the side of the two lions, that those who sought justice might strike it, upon which the *rai* would order them to be summoned, would listen to their complaints, and render justice. One day, a crow came and sat on the bell and struck it, when the *rai* asked who the complainant was. It is a fact, not unknown, that bold crows will pick meat from between the teeth o lions. As stone lions cannot hunt for prey, where could the crow obtain it usual sustenance? As the *rai* was satisfied that the crow justly complained of hunger, having come to sit by his tone lions, he gave orders that some goats and sheep be killed, on which the crow might feed himself for some days.

Source: Khusrau. "Nuh Siphir." In H. M. Elliot and John Dowson, eds., *The History of India as Told by Its Own Historians: The Muhammadan Period.* Vol. 3. London: Trübner and Company, 1869, p. 565.

17. Ibn Battuta: The Pepper Tree of South India, c. 1325

Ibn Battuta (1304–c. 1368/1377) was a fourteenth-century Moroccan Berber scholar and jurist who is best known as a traveler and explorer. Ibn Battuta's travels covered more than 30 years and over 70,000 miles, extending across the entire Islamic world, from North and West Africa to southern Europe, the Middle East, Central Asia, China, Southeast Asia, and India. At the direction of the sultan of Morocco, Ibn Battuta dictated a detailed account of his travels, which, for sheer distance traveled, far outstripped those of his near contemporary, Marco Polo (*see* Documents 13, 14, and 15). The following except is a description of pepper trees in South India. For another selection from the writings of Ibn Battuta, *see* Document 18.

The pepper trees resemble grapevines; they are planted alongside coco-palms and climb up them in the same way that vines climb, except that they have no shoots, that is to say tendrils, like those of vines. The leaves of the tree resemble those of stocks, and some of them resemble the leaves of briar. It produces its fruit in small clusters. In the autumn they gather the grains and spread them on mats in the sun, just as is done with grapes to obtain raisins; they keep on turning them until they are thoroughly dried and become black, and then sell them to the merchants. Most people in our country suppose that they roast them with fire and that it is because of that they become crinkled, but it is not so since this results only from the action of the sun upon them. I have seen pepper grains in the city of Qaliqut being poured out for measuring by the bushel, like millet in our country.

The First town in the land of Mulaibar that we entered was the town of Abu Sarur [Barcelore], a small place on a large inlet and abounding in coco-palms. Two days' journey from there brought us to Fakanur [Bacanor], a large town on an inlet; here there is a large quantity of fine-flavoured sugarcanes, which are unexcelled in the rest of the country. Three days after leaving Fakanur we reached Manjarur [Mangalore], a large town on the largest inlet in the land of Mulaibar. This is the town at which most of the merchants from Fars and al-Yaman disembark, and pepper and ginger are exceedingly abundant there. The sultan of Manjarus is one of the principal rulers in that land, and his name is Rama Daw. There is a colony of about four thousand Muslims there, living in a suburb alongside the town. Warfare frequently breaks out between them and the townspeople, but the sultan makes peace between them on account of his need of the merchants.

After staying with them for three days, we set sail for the town of Hili, which we reached two days later. It is large and well built, situated on a big bay which is navigable for large vessels. This is the farthest town reached by the ships from China; they enter only this port, the port of Kawlam, and Qaliqut. The town of Hili is venerated both by Muslims and infidels on account of its cathedral mosque, for it is of great blessedness, and resplendent with radiant light. Seafarers make many votive offerings to it, and it has a rich treasury. I met in this mosque a pious jurist . . . called Sa'id, of fine figure and character. He used to fast continually, and I was told that he had studied at Mecca for fourteen years and for the same length of time at al-Madinah, and that he traveled in India and China.

Source: Mackintosh-Smith, Tim, ed. *The Travels of Ibn Battutah.* London: Macmillan, 2002, pp, 221–222.

18. Ibn Battuta: A Pious Holy Man of Delhi, c. 1325

The selection from the writings of the fourteenth-century Muslin scholar and traveler Ibn Battuta (1304–c. 1368/1377) describes a Muslim holy man that the writer met in Delhi in about 1325. For another excerpt from the writings of Ibn Battuta, *see* Document 17.

Another of the pious men of Delhi is the learned and saintly Shaikh Sadr al-Din Kuhrani. He used to fast continually and stand all nights (in prayer). He renounced the world entirely and rejected all its goods, and wore nothing but a wollen cloak. The Sultan [Muhammad Adil Shah] and the officers of state used to visit him but he often refused to see them, and when the Sultan asked permission to give him a grant of some villages with the revenues of which he could supply food to poor brethren and visitors, he would have nothing to do with it. . . . It was said that he broke his fast only after three nights and that when someone remonstrated with him about this he replied: "I do not break fast until I am under such compulsion that carrion becomes lawful to me. . . . "

I had a slave boy who ran away from me, and who I found in the possession of a certain Turk. I had in mind to reclaim the slave from him, but the sheikh said to me "This boy is no good to you. don't take him." The Turk wished to come to an arrangement, so I settled with him that he paid me a hundred dinars and I left him the boy. Six months later the boy killed his master and was taken before the Sultan, who ordered him to be handed over to his master's sons, and they put him to death. When I experienced this miracle on the part of the sheikh I attached myself entirely to him, withdrawing from the world and giving all that I possessed to the poor and needy. I stayed with him for some time, and I used to see him fast for ten and twenty days on end and remain standing (in prayer) most of the night. I continued with him until the Sultan sent for me and I became entangled in the world once again—may God give me a good ending!

Source: Ibn Battuta. *The Travels of Ibn Battuta, A.D. 1325–1325.* Translated by A. R. Gibb. Vol. 3. Cambridge, UK: Cambridge University Press, 1971, pp. 626–627.

19. The Values of Concubines and Slave Girls in Delhi, c. 1348

This excerpt from the writings of the fourteenth-century Syrian geographer Shihab al-Din Al-Umari (d. 1349), describes the value of a good concubine in Delhi. That value increases dramatically if the slave can read, write, play games such as chess, and recite by heart verses of the Qur'an.

All of my informers related that the price of a slave girl for service in Delhi does not exceed eight *tankas.* The slave girls who are fit for both service and cohabitation cost fifteen *tankas.* But in other cities . . . they are still cheaper. Abul Safa Umar al-Shibli told me: I purchased a competent slave of adolescent age for four *dirhams.* One can guess the cheapness of slaves on account of this. . . . Al-Shibli states: Inspite of this cheapness of the slaves, there are in India such concubines also who coast twenty thousand *tankas* or even more. Ibn-Ul-Taj also testified to this fact. I enquired how a slave girl could cost so much inspite of so much cheapness? All the informers told me without any contradiction that the reason was the grace of her deportment and the refinement of her manners. Many of the slave girls of this type know the Quran by heart, can write, recite verses, relate stories and play on the sitar. They also make display of their ability in the games of *Chausar* and Chess. They take pride in these things. One of them says: "I shall capture the heart of my master within three days"; another says: "I shall be the queen of his heart within a day." The third says: "I shall captivate his heart in an hour"; while the fourth says: "What is to say about day and hour, I shall capture him in the twinkling of an eye."

Source: Al-Umari, Shihab al-Din. *Masalik al Absar fi-Mamalik al-Amsar: A Fourteenth Century Arab Account of India under Sultan Muhammad Bin Tughluq.* Translated by Iqtidar Husain Siddiqi and Qazi Mohammad Ahmad. Aligarh, India: Siddiqi Publishing House, 1971, p. 51.

20. An Uprising in Delhi during the Reign of Sultan Muhammad bin Tughluq, c. 1350

The following excerpt from the writings of the fourteenth-century Muslim historian Ziau-d Din Barni describes a serious rebellion that erupted in Delhi during the last years of the reign of Sultan Muhammad bin Tughluq (1325–1351).

While the Sultan was prosecuting the siege of Rantambhor, a revolt of some importance broke out in Delhi. . . . Haji, a maulaa or slave of the late *Kotwal,* Amiru-l umara Fakhru-d din . . . was a man of violent, fearless, and malignant character and he was charged with the guard of the exchequer. A man called Turmuzi was kotwal of the city and greatly oppressed the people. . . . Haji Maula, seeing the city empty, and the inhabitants distressed by the violence and tyranny of Turmuzi . . . knowing also that not a man could be spared from the army . . . thought the people would support him. He secured the support of the old *kotwali* officers, and excited a somewhat formidable revolt. It was the month of Ramazan, and the sun was in Gemini. The weather was very hot, and at midday people kept indoors taking their siesta, so there were few in the streets. At this time Haji Maula, with several armed followers, went to the house of *kotwal,* carrying with them as a blind a letter which he pretended to have received from the Sultan. The *kotwal* was taking his nap, and had none of his men with him. When he was called he roused himself, put on his slippers, and came to the door. Haji Maula instantly gave the signal, and his followers cut off the unsuspecting victim's head. He then brought out the pretended royal *farman,* and showing it to the crowd, he said that he had killed the *kotwal* in obedience to orders received from the Sultan. The people were silent. The keepers of the gates were creatures of Haji Maula, so they closed them. . . . Haji Maula then proceeded with the riotous followers to the Red Palace, seated himself upon a balcony, and set free all the prisoners, some of whom joined his followers. Bags of gold *tankas* were brought out of the treasury and scattered among the people. Arms were brought from the armoury, and horses from the royal stables, and distributed among the rioters. Everyone that joined them had gold *tankas* thrown into his lap. There was an Alawi (descendent of Ali) in Delhi who was called the grandson of Shah Najaf, who, by his mother's side, was grandson of Sultan Shamsu-d din. The Maula set off from the Red Palace with a party of horse, and went to the house of the poor Alawi. They carried him off by force and seated him on the throne in the Red Palace. The principal men of the city were brought by force and made to kiss his hand. . . . These riotous proceedings were on for seven or eight days, and intelligence was several times conveyed to the Sultan, but he kept it secret, and it did not become known to the army.

On the third or fourth day of the riot, Malik Hamidu-d din, Amir of Koh, whith his sons and relations, all valiant men, opened the Ghazni gate and went into the city. They proceeded towards the gate of Bhandar-kal, and arrows began to fly between them and the rioters, who became desperate and obtained gold from Haji Maula. After Hamidu-d din, the Amir of Koh, had been in the city two days, he and his loyal followers prevailed over the rebels. . . . He then entered the gate of Bhandar-kal, and a struggle ensued between him and the shoe-makers, and between him and Haji Maula. The Amir of Koh alighted from his horse, dashed Haji Maula to the ground, and sat upon his breast. Swords and clubs were aimed at him all round and he was wounded, but he neverquitted his fallen foe till he had dispatched him. After this the victors proceeded to the Red Palace. They decapitated the miserable Alawi and carried his head about the city on a spear.

Source: Barni, Ziau-d Din. "Tarikh-I-Firoz Shahi." In H. M. Elliot and John Dowson, eds. *The History of India as Told by Its Own Historians: The Muhammadan Period.* Vol. 3. London: Trübner and Company, 1869, pp. 175–177.

21. The Plunder of Delhi by Timur's Army, 1398

In 1398, the city of Delhi was sacked by the armies of the Turco-Mongol invader Timur (1336–1405), who is often known as Timur the Lame or Tamerlane. Timur eventually ruled much of Central Asia, and his descendents, the Mughals, ruled much of India from Delhi from the sixteenth to the nineteenth centuries. In this excerpt from his memoirs, Timur vividly describes why and how his soldiers slaughtered the Hindu inhabitants of Delhi, whose frenzied resistance is explained by the fact that prior to the capture of the city Timur executed thousands of Indian captives, mostly Hindus.

On the 16th of the month [December 1398] some incidents occurred which led to the sack of the city of Delhi, and to the slaughter of many of the infidel inhabitants. One was this. A party of fierce Turk soldiers had assembled at one of the gates of the city to look about them and enjoy themselves, and some of them laid violent hands upon the goods of the inhabitants. When I heard of this violence, I sent some amirs, who were present in the city, to restrain the Turks. A part of soldiers accompanied these amirs into the city. Another reason was that some of the ladies of my harem expressed a wish to go into the city and see the palace of Hazar-sutun (thousand columns). . . . I granted this request, and I sent a party of soldiers to escort the litters of the ladies. Another reason was that Jalal Islam and other *diwans* had gone into the city with a party of soldiers to collect the contribution laid upon the city. Another reason was that some thousand troopers with orders for grain, oil, sugar, and flour, had gone into the city to collect these supplies. Another reason was that it had come to my knowledge that great numbers of Hindus and *gabrs*, with their wives and children, and goods, and valuable, had come into the city from all the country round, and consequently I had sent some amirs with their regiments . . . into the city and directed them to pay no attention to the remonstrances of the inhabitants, but to seize and bring out these fugitives. For these several reasons a great number of fierce Turki soldiers were in the city. When the soldiers proceed to apprehend the Hindus and *gabrs* who had fled to the city, many of them drew their swords and offered resistance. The flames of strife were thus lighted and spread through the whole city . . . burning up all it reached. The savage Turks fell to killing and plundering. The Hindus set fire to their houses with their own hands, burned their wives and children in them, and rushed into the fight and were killed. The Hindus and *gabrs* of the city showed much alacrity and boldness in fighting. The amirs who were in charge of the gates prevented any more soldiers from going into the place, but the flames of war had risen too high for this precaution to be of any avail in extinguishing them. On that day, Thursday, and all the night of Friday, nearly 15,000 Turks were engaged in slaying, plundering, and destroying. When morning broke on the Friday, all my army, no longer under control, went off to the city and thought of nothing but killing, plundering, and making prisoners. All that day the sack was general. The following day, Saturday, the 17th, all passed in the same way, and the spoil was so great that each man secured from fifty to a hundred prisoners, men, women, and children. There was no man who took less than twenty. The other booty was immense in rubies, diamonds, garnets, pearls, and other gems; jewels of gold and silver; . . . vessels of gold and silver; and brocades and silks of great value. Gold and silver ornaments of Hindu women were obtained in such quantities as to exceed all account. Excepting the quarter of the *saiyids*, the *ulama*, and the other Musulmans, the whole city was sacked. The pen of fate had written down this destiny for the people of this city. Although I was desirous of sparing them I could not succeed, for it was the will of God that this calamity should fall upon the city.

On the following day, Sunday, it was brought to my knowledge that a great number of infidel Hindus had assembled in the Masjid-i-jami of Old Delhi, carrying with them arms and provisions, and were preparing to defend themselves. Some of my people who had gone that way on business were wounded by them. I immediately ordered Amir Shah Malik and Ali Sultan Tawachi to take a party of men and proceed to clear the house of God from infidels and idolaters. They accordingly attacked these infidels and put them to death. Old Delhi then was plundered.

Source: Timur. "Malfuzat-i-Timuri." In H. M. Elliot and John Dowson, eds., *The History of India as Told by Its Own Historians: The Muhammadan Period.* Vol. 3. London: Trübner and Company, 1869, pp. 445–447.

22. The Mughal Conqueror Babur Describes India, c. 1526

In the excerpt from his memoirs, the Babur-nama, Babur, the founder of the Mughal dynasty in India, describes India and the Hindu Indians as he perceives them. To get an idea of the conqueror's mindset, note carefully what he things are the "charms" of India and what he thinks are not.

Most of the inhabitants of India are infidels, called Hindus, believing mainly in the transmigration of souls; all artisans, wage-earners and officials are Hindus. . . . Every artisan follows the trade handed down to him from his forefathers.

India is a country of few charms. The people lack good looks and good manners. They have no social life or exchange of visits. They have no genius or intelligence, no polite learning, no generosity of magnanimity, no harmony or proportion in their arts and crafts, no lead-wire or carpenter's square. They lack good horses and good dogs; grapes, melons, and any good fruit; ice and cold water; good food or good bread in the markets. They have no baths and no advanced educational institutions. . . . There are no running streams in their gardens or residences, no waters at all except the large rivers and the swamps in the ravines and hollows. Their residences have no pleasant and sa-lubrious breezes, and in their construction no form of symmetry. . . .

Among the charms that India does possess is that it is a large country, with large quantities of gold and silver. Its air in the rainy season is very fine. Some-times it rains ten or fifteen or even twenty times a day, and in such torrents that rivers flow where no water was previously. While it rains, and throughout the rainy season, the air is remarkably fine, not to be surpassed for mildness and pleasantness. Its only fault is its great humidity, which spoils bows. . . .

For all these reasons, most of the best warriors were unwilling to stay in India; in fact, they determined to leave. . . .

When I discovered this unsteadiness among my people, I summoned all the leaders and took counsel. I said, "Without means and resources there is no em-pire and conquest, and without lands and followers there is no sovereignty and rule. By the effort of long years, through much tribulation and the crossing of distant lands, by flinging ourselves into battle and danger, we have through God's favor overcome so many enemies and conquered such vast lands. And now, what force compels us, what necessity has arisen, that we should without cause, abandon a country taken at such risk of life? And if we returned to Kabul, we would again be left in poverty and weakness. Henceforth, let no well-wisher of mine speak of such things! But let not those turn back from going who cannot bear the hardship and have determined to leave." With such words I reasoned with them and made them, willy-nilly, quit their fears.

Source: Babur. *The Babur-nama in English (Memoirs of Babur).* Translated by Annette Susannah Beveridge. London: Luzac, 1922. (translation slightly modernized.)

Appendix: Dynasties of Medieval India

Gupta Dynasty
Chandra Gupta I (c. 320–c. 335)
Samudra Gupta (c. 335– c. 375)
Rama Gupta (c. 375?)
Chandra Gupta II Vikramaditya
   (c. 375–c. 415)
Kumara Gupta (c. 415–455)
Skanda Gupta (455–467)
Narasimha Gupta (467–477)
Buddha Gupta (477–c. 495)
Vishnu Gupta (c. 540–c. 550)*

*The line of Gupta rulers is uncertain after about 495, when the Hun invasions overwhelmed the Gupta Empire and North India eventually splintered into various states and kingdoms. Vishnu Gupta, who reign ended about 550, is believed to be the last ruler of the Gupta line.

Sultans of Delhi
Mamluk Dynasty
Qutb al-din Aybak (1206–1210)
Aram Shah (1210–1211)
Shams al-Din Iltutmish (1211–1236)
Rukn al-din Firuz (1236)
Raziya Sultan (1236–1240)
Muiz al-din Bahram (1240–1242)
Ala al-din Masud (1242–1246)
Nasir al-din Mahmud (1246–1266)
Ghiyas al-din Balban (1266–1286)
Muiz al-din Qaiqabad (1286–1290)
Kayumars (1290)

Khilji Dynasty
Jalal al-din Firuz Khilji (1290–1294)
Allauddin Khilji (1294–1316)
Qutb al-din Mubarak Shah Khilji
   (1316–1320)

Tughluq Dynasty
Ghiyas al-din Tughluq Shah I (1320–1325)
Muhammad Shah II (1325–1351)

Mahmud Ibn Muhammad (1351)
Firuz Shah Tughluq (1351–1388)
Ghiyas al-din Tughluq II (1388–1389)
Abu Bakr Shah (1389–1390)
Nasir al-din Muhammad Shah III
   (1390–1393)
Sikander Shah I (1393)
Mahmud Nasir al-din (Sultan Mahmud II)
   at Delhi (1393–1394)
Nusrat Shah at Firuzabad (1394–1398)

Timur sacks Delhi in 1398, leading to a period of political turmoil.

Sayyid Dynasty
Khidr Khan (1414–1421)
Mubarrak Shah II (1421–1435)
Muhammad Shah IV (1435–1445)
Aladdin Alam Shah (1445–1451)

Lodhi Dynasty
Bahlul Khan Lodi (1451–1489)
Sikandar Lodi (1489–1517)
Ibrahim II (1517–1526)

Babur, the first Mughal ruler, conquers Delhi in 1526.

Vijayanagar Empire
Sangama Dynasty
Harihara Raya I (1336–1356)
Bukka Raya I (1356–1377)
Harihara Raya II (1377–1404)
Virupaksha Raya (1404–1405)
Bukka Raya II (1405–1406)
Deva Raya I (1406–1422)
Ramachandra Raya (1422)
Vira Vijaya Bukka Raya (1422–1424)
Deva Raya II (1424–1446)
Mallikarjuna Raya (1446–1465)
Virupaksha Raya II (1465–1485)
Praudha Raya (1485)

Saluva Dynasty
  Saluva Narasimha Deva Raya (1485–1491)
  Thimma Bhupala (1491)
  Narasimha Raya II (1491–1505)

Tuluva Dynasty
  Tuluva Narasa Nayaka (1491–1503)
  Viranarasimha Raya (1503–1509)
  Krishna Deva Raya (1509–1529)
  Achyuta Deva Raya (1529–1542)
  Sadashiva Raya (1542–1570)

Aravidu Dynasty
  Aliya Rama Raya (1542–1565)**
  Tirumala Deva Raya (1565–1572)***

Sriranga I (1572–1586)
Venkata I (1586–1614)
Sriranga II (1614–1617)
Ramadeva (1617–1632)
Venkata II (1632–1642)
Sriranga III (1642–1646)
Venkata III (1646–1652)

**Aliya Rama Raya, who was slain at the Battle of Talicota, was regent for the last Tuluva ruler.
***Tirumala Deva Raya, who succeeded his brother as regent, took the throne in 1570.

EAST ASIA

William B. Ashbaugh

Chronology

206 B.C.E–220 C.E.	Han dynasty rules China
c. 200 C.E.	Porcelain developed in China
c. 200–300	Creation of the Yamato state in Japan
c. 220–589	Buddhism reaches China and begins to spread
221–280	Three Kingdoms Era in China
c. 300–500	China suffers a series of barbarian invasions
c. 405	Adoption of Chinese writing in Japan
c. 500	Magnetic compass and manufacture of glass developed in China
c. 550	Buddhism begins to spread in Japan
581–618	Sui dynasty unifies China after nearly four centuries of political division
618–907	Tang dynasty rules China
645	Emperor of Japan promulgates Taika reforms to promote centralization and enhance the power of the imperial court
710	City of Nara established as capital of Japan
712–755	Reign of Emperor Illustrious August (Xuanzong) marks the golden age of China's Tang dynasty
751	Battle of Talas River between Chinese and Muslim forces halts the Chinese advance to the west and the Muslim advance into Central Asia
794–1185	Heian Period in Japanese history sees Confucianism and other Chinese influences at their height; the period is also considered the peak of the Japanese imperial court and is noted for a flowering of art, especially poetry and literature
c. 900	Woodblock printing of books develops in China, Japan, and Korea
907–960	Fall of China's Tang dynasty initiates the Era of the Five Dynasties, a period of decentralization with warlords dominating various regions of China
938	Vietnamese repel the Chinese at the Battle of Bach Dang
960–1279	Song dynasty rules in China
c. 1000–1200	Development of Neo-Confucianism in China
1021–1086	Life of Wang An-shih, Chinese writer and political reformer
1024	First paper money is introduced into China

1141–1279	Height of landscape painting in China
c. 1150	Explosive powder begins to be used in weapons in China
1192	Establishment of shogunate in Japan
c. 1200	Zen Buddhism reaches Japan; inoculation for smallpox is undertaken in China
1206–1227	Reign of Chinggis (Genghis) Khan, who unites nomadic Asiatic tribes and establishes the vast Mongol Empire
1219–1221	Mongols conquer Persia
c. 1235	Development of Chinese drama
1237–1241	Mongols conquer Russia
1254–1324	Venetian traders Marco Polo and his family visit the Mongol court in China to trade
1258	Mongols sack Baghdad
1264–1294	Reign of Kublai (Khubilai) Khan, grandson of Chinggis Khan, who centers Mongol rule in China
1274	Mongols launch an unsuccessful invasion of Japan
1279	Mongol conquest of Song dynasty of China
1279–1368	Yuan (Mongol) dynasty rules in China
1281	Mongols launch a second unsuccessful invasion of Japan
c. 1300–1550	Rise of the daimyo, the powerful feudal lords of Japan
1330s	Plague erupts in China and begins to spread westward
1368	Rebel Chinese forces capture Yuan capital of Khanbaliq; remaining Mongol forces retreat to the central Asian steppes, ending the Mongol dynasty in China
1368–1644	Ming dynasty rules China
1405	Zheng He/Cheng Ho (a former Muslim slave) sails west with a fleet of three-hundred ships, invading Sumatra and Ceylon and eventually reaching the coast of Africa
1421	Construction of the Forbidden City begins in Beijing

Three Kingdoms, 264

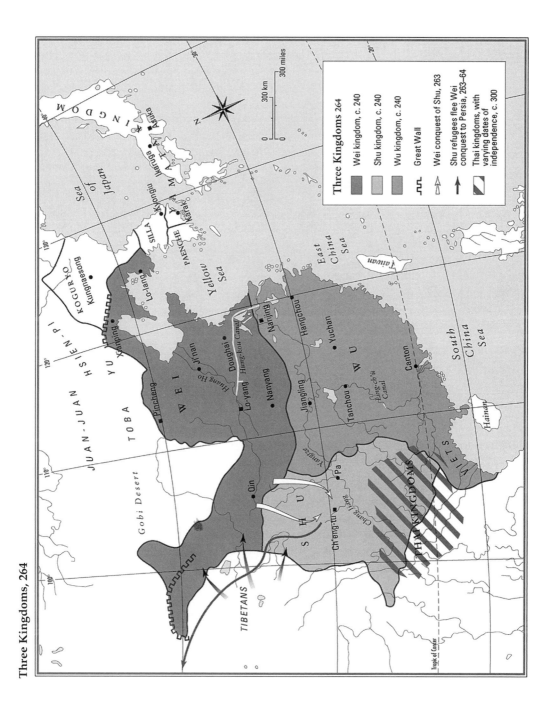

T'ang Empire, c. 645–700

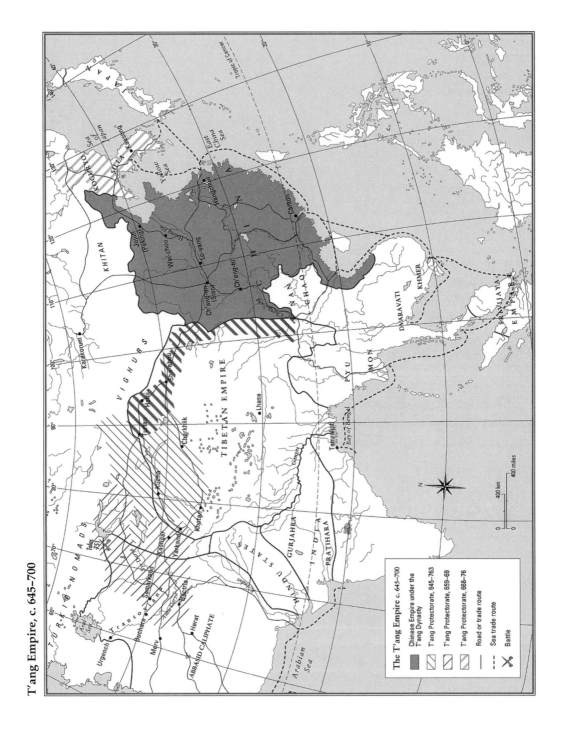

The T'ang Empire c. 645–700

- Chinese Empire under the T'ang Dynasty
- T'ang Protectorate, 645–763
- T'ang Protectorate, 659–69
- T'ang Protectorate, 668–76
- Road or trade route
- Sea trade route
- Battle

Mongol Conquests, 1209–59

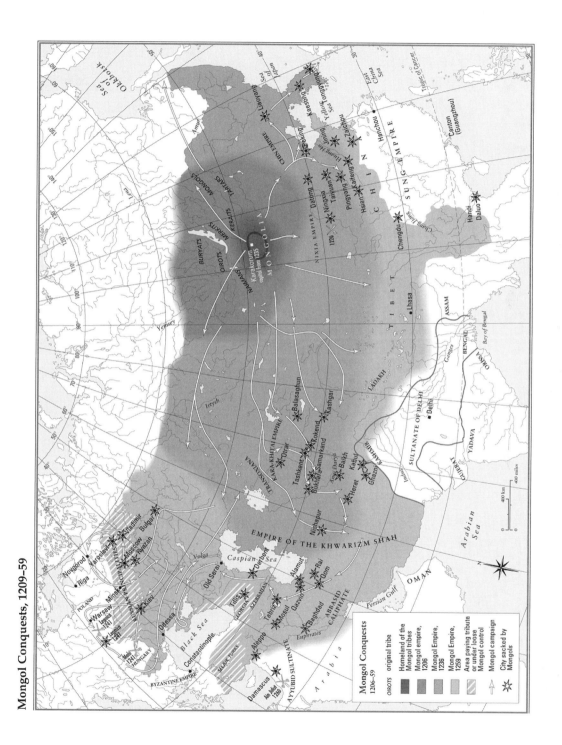

Route of Marco Polo, 1271

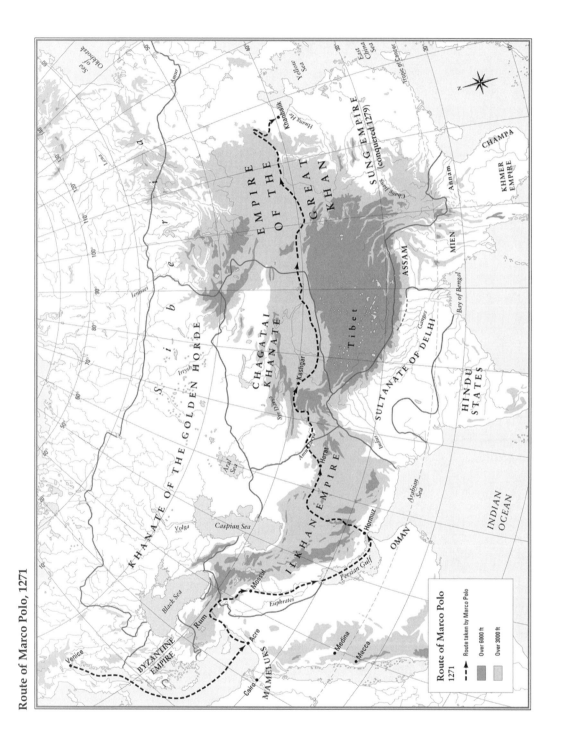

Mongol China, The Yuan Dynasty, 1272–1370

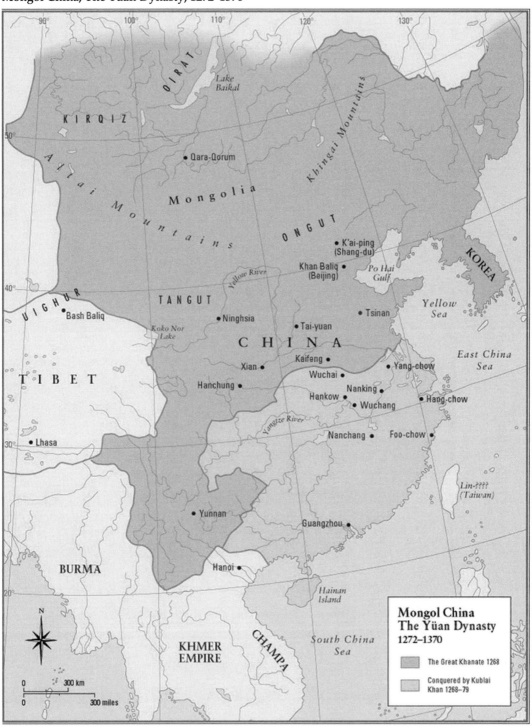

Overview and Topical Essays

1. HISTORICAL OVERVIEW

China

To paraphrase Mark Twain, history does not repeat itself, but it sure rhymes a lot. Such is the case with Chinese history and the almost cyclical nature of the rise and fall of dynasties. First, a new dynasty rose up on the ashes of the old. Peasant life improved, with lower taxes and a much higher percentage of land ownership by the common people. As the years progressed, large land-holders began to reemerge (or expanded their dominating hold over more lands, depending on the dynasty in question). These gentry raised the rents on their lands and demanded more and more taxes from the fewer and fewer peasant freeholders—all due to the fact that the gentry served as the tax officials, police, and judges at their local level and were thus immune to taxation. One popular ploy used by local gentry was to offer to buy land and rent it back to the same peasant family at a lower sum than that previously collected in taxes. Another was simply to steal a part of the tax receipts, as the bottom of the civil service was often chosen solely by status and not by passing various levels of the **examination system**. Within 100 years of the dynasty's founding, these ploys, coupled with many peasant families' inability to afford the higher tax rates, periodic crop failures, and general overpopulation, all led to the creation of a powerful landlord class controlling huge swaths of land. Under them struggled the millions of now-landless peasants, forced to become either lowly tenant farmers working hard to survive oppressive rents and usurious loans, or part of the unemployed masses with only begging or petty banditry left as options to feed themselves. Soon thereafter angry peasant rebellions began, often led by Daoist or Buddhist secret societies, aiming at the now-disreputable dynasty, rich landlords, or both. Many times nomadic forces would take advantage of the strife or outright civil war within China to take lands on the perimeter of the dynasty, and sometimes much more. At this point the government, lacking skilled leaders, often began begging for help from the landlords. These obvious weaknesses show a clear loss of the **mandate of heaven** and result in one of the following: conquest of half or more of China by outside nomads; a rich landlord crowning himself emperor of a new dynasty after leading a powerful army that defeated the peasant armies and the imperial forces; or, in the rarest outcome, a peasant leader starting a new dynasty after victories against nomads, rich landlords, the state, or all three.

These dynastic patterns help us to make sense of otherwise complicated events. But to understand Chinese history from 400 to 1400, much more detail is necessary. China in 400 was a divided country since the fall of the Han dynasty in 220; this era is often called the **Period of Disunity** (220–589). Geographically, China was isolated by jungle in the south, ocean in the west, and mountains in the east; it was the north where China traditionally interacted with nomadic or seminomadic groups. In the case of the Period of Disunity, a series of pastoral nomadic groups conquered north China for differing periods of time, causing many Chinese to flee southward. In the south strong landlords led many short-lived so-called dynasties, as battles for control led to constant change in the rulership of the south. The south's population explosion led to some conflict: rich landlords fleeing from the north demanded a share of governance and poor peasants competed with newcomers and the rich for ever-dwindling southern lands. These internal problems kept the more populous south from mounting successful wars to retake the north.

The history of the northern half of China during these times was no less chaotic. The region had seen a series of nomadic conquests, with each different nomadic group borrowing Chinese culture to rule and collect agricultural taxes, something quite unknown to these hunter/herding cultures prior to their successful conquest. The year 400 found the Tuoba nomads winning control northern China after military victories over the previous herding culture, the Tibetans. The victorious Tuoba proclaimed their lands and dynasty the **Northern Wei** (386–534), deciding to use leading Chinese landowning families to help administer laws and collect the taxes they hoped would make them rich.

The system agreed upon by the Confucian-educated gentry of north China and their Tuoba overseers was "land equalization," also known as the **equal field system**. The idea behind this system was to maximize the number of landholding peasant families to create an enduring tax base by adding or subtracting land from a peasant family based on its size. The system worked remarkably well in China for 300 years, guaranteeing the state stable taxation. Yet in addition to predictable taxes, the state also added to the **corvee** (unpaid labor—usually irrigation or flood-control projects) of the peasants the new task of forming a militia to serve as infantry along side the Tuoba cavalry in battles with their neighbors.

As the Tuoba ruled, they borrowed more ways to govern and more customs from their Chinese advisors and neighbors. Soon the Tuoba required the use of Chinese language as the official language, Chinese family surnames for Tuoba aristocrats, and Chinese social customs at the elite level. They at first encouraged and then supposedly demanded marriage between their leaders and Chinese gentry-class women! The Tuoba moved too far from their military exploits toward civilization, and the Northern Wei was swept away by new nomads; northern China was divided into two new states.

At first, **Religious Daoism** played the role of most popular religion in north and south China, due to its reputed healing and life-extending properties. The Period of Disunity also saw the introduction and adoption of Buddhism, which began slowly to erode Daoist appeal in both sections of China. Just as Confucianism and Daoism had become important philosophies/religions during the Warring States Period (480–221 B.C.E.), so did many Chinese accept Buddhism in the divided, disordered country. Yet Buddhism early on faced some opposition among more traditional followers of Confucianism and Daoism, as it demanded of its ardent followers actions considered "un-Chinese," including shaving one's head and practicing celibacy. Twice purges in the north halted the growth of Buddhism, yet only temporarily. None of these religions demanded the exclusive nature of Western religions, allowing a Chinese the ability to follow one, two, or all three teachings—Confucianism, Daoism, and Buddhism—simultaneously or at different phases of one's life. But the uncertain, confused times in the south and north, and the coming of a newer, more simple sect called **Pure Land Buddhism**—which appealed to commoners as well as monks and nuns—allowed Buddhism to spread across China. The Period of Disunity saw Buddhism become China's third great religious/philosophical tradition.

In 581, a prominent general of mixed Chinese-nomadic origin overthrew the king of the Northern Wei's successor state, killed the royal family, and assumed the throne. He declared himself the first emperor of the **Sui dynasty**, Emperor Wen. Quickly he conquered the rest of north China, then headed south across the Yangzi River to unify all of China under his control, an effort accomplished easily by 589.

Wen (ruled all China as emperor 589–604) first sought to create a strong central government. He reorganized the administration and bureaucracy, at first placing mixed Chinese-nomad families from the north in key positions. Quickly southern families married into the newcomer families from the north. The emperor established a limited examination system and a series of rules to prevent corruption by officials: local officials could not appoint subordinates; officials could not serve in their native place; and officials could spend no more than one tour of duty in the same location.

Wen secondly worked to restore the economy by instituting the successful equal field system throughout China. By creating new peasant landowners, he built up the tax base as had been done in the Northern Wei. Wen used **corvee** labor to build granaries around the capital of Changan, located along a major tributary of the Yellow River. Peasant labor also started a **Grand Canal** to link the Yangzi and Yellow rivers so grain and taxes could flow to the capital easily for more than half the year. The reforms strengthened the economy for a time. Then Emperor Wen of the Sui dynasty set out on some further wars of conquest. He fought wars to protect and then extend the empire west, north, south, and east. Wen was then murdered, likely by his son, who took the throne in 604 and ended up exceeding the megalomania of his father.

Emperor Yang (r. 604–617) decided to spend his time and China's money first on elaborate building projects. He decided to build a new capital, Loyang, around 200 miles down the Yellow River from Changan. He employed two million peasants on the project, and thousands died hauling rare timber to the treeless plain. He needed 1.2 million peasants starting in 607 to work on the **Great Wall**, where at least half perished. And supposedly five and one-half million peasants worked on the various canal projects; most important was finishing and extending the Grand Canal north and south. These forced laborers faced death if they fled and the whip if they worked too slowly. Once the Grand Canal reached the capital, Emperor Yang took his four-story, 270-foot long dragon boat south to the Yangzi River, towed by peasant power. His entourage reached eighty-thousand men and stretched out as many as 60 miles. He had forty palaces built so he could avoid sleeping on the barge.

Emperor Yang coupled his mistreatment of the peasantry and waste of taxes with renewed wars of conquest that turned out to be failures in Korea, even with perhaps the largest army in world history before the twentieth century. China faced bankruptcy and two large peasant rebel armies when Turkish nomads captured Yang and held him for ransom in 615. In the end, the emperor's own entourage assassinated Yang in 617, and chaos in China deepened. Key Sui dynasty officials joined the scramble for power. The winner was a Chinese-nomad military governor of the north. He claimed power in 618 and spent the better part of 8 years consolidating his hold on China using the same Turks as mercenaries. Thus began the short reign of Tang Gaozu, the first emperor of the Tang dynasty (*see* **Early Tang Dynasty; Late Tang Dynasty**). After his second son killed his other sons, Gaozu abdicated in 626 to Emperor Taizong.

The Tang dynasty made China the largest, richest, most powerful, and most civilized country in the world. Chinese historians consider Taizong one of the greatest of all emperors. He helped create for China a governing, bureaucratic system utilized from this period forward to the twentieth century (*see* **Tang Governance**) by Chinese emperors to control their vast empires, including a system of laws and divisions of the state down to the county level. Besides these reforming efforts, Taizong also got to the root of government problems: peasant distress. He began the equal field system anew, this time on a larger scale than ever before. In addition, the tax system allowed flexibility. If people wanted to avoid spending time doing **corvee**, they would simply pay extra taxes. If others wanted to avoid taxes, they could spend more time with corvee. And corvee included militia duty, which guaranteed a large army cheaper than mercenaries.

Agricultural production grew rapidly in the first century of the Tang, and government revenues increased with only moderate tax rates. Large landlords when the equal field system was implemented and Buddhist holdings were hardly affected by the changes. In fact, both were exempt from taxation. Large landholders (usually officials at the district level or local level—below the county level) and government officials in charge at the circuit level (like modern provinces), prefectural level, and county level practiced a lavish lifestyle that soon promoted the growth of the economy, including the import trade: Chinese silk for foreign luxuries.

China's capital reverted to Changan, along a **Yellow River** tributary. It was a planned city—the largest planned city built to that point and perhaps the largest ever. It stretched over 30 square miles, not including the extensive palace grounds, which, like the city itself, faced south. One million people lived within city walls, while perhaps another million lived just outside the perimeter. The city became the most prosperous, civilized, and cosmopolitan city in the world for its time. Many foreigners, especially Arab traders, arrived through the impressive 500-foot city gate to conduct business,and were afforded religious toleration during their stay as a result.

Although the Tang emperors created stability within China's borders as long as the census and redistribution of land under the equal field system continued, wars with their neighbors began quickly. Although some of the Turk allies who made Gaozu and Taizong emperors remained loyal, other groups attacked their erstwhile ally, invading from the north all the way to the capital across the great north China plain. A successful counterattack, coupled with disorder among their enemies' leaders, allowed China to recapture the **Silk Road**—lost during the Han dynasty—and the oases the caravans depended on, by 648. The subject peoples conquered in the far west, although officially part of the Tang Empire, had relative autonomy on local matters and would shake off Chinese rule when the Tang dynasty grew weak.

The Tang dynasty also fought with its eastern neighbors, the three kingdoms of Korea. The war proved difficult at first. But once the Chinese went back to their classic ploy—use barbarians against barbarians—the Tang, with an alliance with one Korean state, **Silla**, defeated the rest. The result was a unified Korean state with local autonomy, but a tributary state of China nonetheless.

Then an abnormality occurred in Chinese history. The concubine of a just-deceased emperor started running China from behind the scenes in starting in 660, before she dropped the facade in 690 and proclaiming herself **Empress Wu**. She ruled as China's only female emperor until forced out in a coup in 705 when she was 82 years old after years of her killing potential rivals in the imperial clan. She did do some good in her years in control of the Tang dynasty, from expanding the examination system, to pushing China's borders to their furthest extent in all directions. She also encouraged the worship of all three of China's great traditions as equals. In fact, Buddhism reached its highest point of political and economic power during her years in charge—in this case Pure Land Buddhism.

Chinese historians consider the early years of the 700s as the high point of the Tang dynasty and China in general, politically, economically, and culturally. New Emperor Xuanzong had reformed the coinage, repaired and extended the Grand Canal, and briefly renewed land registration for the equal field system. Yet soon he would withdraw from politics and let his chief minister rule as a virtual dictator. First came the abandonment of a militia army for an expensive, paid mercenary force. Frontier generals led nomadic troops in great numbers to protect China's new gains, sometimes with little thought of loyalty. Couple that with a defeat with Arab forces in 751 and a deepening social crisis as fewer peasants paid increasing taxes—all due to Buddhism taking away land from the tax rolls and putting aside yet again the equal field system, this time forever.

The biggest damage to the dynasty started in 755 with the illiterate slave of nomad origin An Lushan. Grotesquely obese yet charismatic and cunning, he had gotten into the confidences of Emperor Xuanzong's favorite consort and thus the emperor by playing the buffoon. He used this trust to send one hundred fifty thousand troops from north China to Loyang without meeting resistance. He then closed the short gap and attacked the capital Changan, proclaiming himself the new emperor. The real emperor fled south in remorse; his escorts forced him to kill his betrayed consort. Then Xuanzong's heir apparent fought An's forces until victory in 763.

The victory proved hollow, as loss of the capital showed the dynasty's weakness. Quickly between 25 percent and 30 percent of China fell into the hands of the autonomous military governors, and parts of the empire to the far west obtained their independence. Throughout the final half of the dynasty, emperors periodically had to fight these generals to keep from independence. In addition, **eunuchs** rose up at the end of the eighth century. Although originally hired to protect the emperor's wives, consorts, and concubines, by this late date they took charge of the secret police and became virtual masters of the country. Eunuchs chose eight out of the nine emperors to mount the throne after 800. Only conflict between eunuch factions held them back from total control.

Hoping to stop the dynasty's decline and to increase tax receipts otherwise stolen along their way to the capital by the empire's own collectors, the Emperor Wuzong—a fervent Daoist—persecuted Buddhists to bring their lands back onto the tax rolls. From 841 to 846, the new emperor through edict destroyed 4,600 temples and monasteries, 40,000 smaller shrines, and secularized 260,000 monks and nuns. Pure Land Buddhism in China would never recover, nor would Buddhism ever again have as much influence, even as successor emperors repealed Wuzong's efforts. Instead, **Chan Buddhism (Zen Buddhism** in Japan) would become the most popular form, even taking over some of the church-like behaviors of the Pure Land sect. Besides, the monetary windfall expected from the elimination of Buddhism turned out to be too little to help save the dynasty. Discontent among the peasantry, coupled with famine in parts of the country and enormous floods along the path of the Grand Canal, led to rebellions. The largest of these became one of the largest in Chinese history—the Huang Chao Rebellion—and its merchant-family leader even declared himself emperor over part of China for 2 years, until the few surviving members of the Tang dynasty, allied with Turkish fighters, defeated him. But at what cost? The Tang dynasty disintegrated in 907 into another disunited period, this time only 53 years in duration.

In 960, General Zhao Kuangyin became **Emperor Taizu** and worked hard to limit the power of other generals, founding the Song dynasty (normally called the **Northern Song dynasty**). His mercenary force, subject to periodic rotation of its commanders, would remain loyal to the emperor and prove valuable in the reconquest of China. Like unifiers before him, Taizu applied moderate force to those opposing him and welcomed those to join him when defeated. He and his successor brother fought to the north and used the Great Wall as the dividing line between China and a seminomadic conqueror, the Liao, for three generations.

The wars that ended the Tang and the period after its fall with little government control left a strange situation among the rich and poor, educated and uneducated, as the Song dynasty began. Some long-time gentry families had lost everything, and new families had become wealthy. The Song dynasty instituted an examination system used up until the twentieth century (with the exception of most of the **Yuan dynasty**) that ended hereditary officials (save the emperor). The central government chose its officials based on Confucian exams, with three levels to pass. At the start, over one hundred thousand scholars competed for five hundred government positions. The printing press in full use made Confucian books for study widely available. Of course the usual degree-earner came from a wealthy, educated family; it took time to learn classical written Chinese, let alone understand the Confucian canon. But once in a while, a smart village boy received backing from a village to allow him to study, take the exams, and make the village famous.

Throughout the Song dynasty, Confucianism became the most important of the three teachings, but it had evolved over time into **Neo-Confucianism**. Borrowing ideas from Chan Buddhism and Daoism, Neo-Confucianism, starting slowly in the ninth century, made Confucian ideas more meaningful in the starkly different world of the Late Tang and Song dynasties. This form of

Confucianism tried to answer certain Buddhist questions about heaven and hell, the nature of humans, and other fundamental matters. Some scholars then used their interpretations of Neo-Confucianism to try and remake the Northern Song dynasty, like the unsuccessful modernizer Wang Anshi. More important for the long term were the interpretations of Southern Song thinker **Zhu Xi** (1130–1200), whose ideas in two generations would be the respected interpretation of Confucianism. He sought to show that people were inherently good, but needed training and self-cultivation through meditation to show this goodness to the world. The downside to choosing one interpretation in the examination system is that it led to stagnation among China's intellectuals, who needed to memorize the style and even substance of this one particular version of Neo-Confucianism rather than rely on their own interpretations. Along with the memorization, Neo-Confucianism brought new restrictions on elite women to seclude themselves and practice the painful art of **footbinding**.

The Northern Song dynasty ended up making a terrible mistake based on the traditional Chinese custom of playing barbarian against barbarian. The nomadic Jurchen had recently thrown off the yoke of the Khitans, also called the Liao, so the Chinese decided to ally with the Jurchen against the Khitans and gain lands to the north of the Great Wall. But where the Jurchen succeeded, the Song failed in fighting the Khitans, and so the Jurchen decided after their victory to attack China itself. Like other nomadic invasions to this point, the Jurchen conquered just northern China after a 14-year war, with the Huai River (halfway between the Yellow River and the **Yangzi River**) serving as the dividing line between the Jurchen state and the **Southern Song dynasty**, established in 1127.

Although the Song dynasty had suffered a major blow, the loss of the north had the strange effect of improving China's economy. For one, more and more peasants fled Jurchen rule to join up with the Southern Song. These newcomers worked and lived on the new strains of rice (taken from southern Vietnam) that allowed for two crops of rice a year from the Yangzi River southward. Tea growing also expanded, as did cotton growing. And with these excess commodities, foreign and regional trade expanded so much that there was not enough copper currency to conduct business. China first used weighed amounts of gold and silver before turning to paper money, yet the government's urge to print paper money led to damaging inflation (*see* **Money/Coinage**).

The Song then made another costly error, again playing barbarian against barbarian. The Chinese stupidly allied with the **Mongols** against the Jurchen, hoping to get back north China in the process. The Mongols, disparate tribes living a nomadic existence in the plains that bear their name, became a unified and highly successful fighting force under Genghis Khan (one of many transliterations of his name) starting in 1206. He died in 1227, after many victories in Central Asia and into Russia, having only just begun to attack northern China. The alliance between his heir, Ogodei, and China resulted in the loss in 7 years of the Jurchen buffer state. The Mongols then slowly conquered the Southern Song dynasty over the next 45 years, as most Chinese landlords decided to ally with the Mongols in return for leaving their property intact.

Khubilai Khan (r. 1260–1294), the grandson of Genghis, moved the Mongol capital to Beijing and became the first ruler of the Yuan dynasty (1279–1368). Soon China became a realm within an empire, as China was easily the wealthiest possession of the Mongols. Khubilai had the population of China divided into four groups to help him rule: Mongols at the top of the bureaucracy, Central Asian peoples in less important bureaucratic positions, recent north China defeated-peoples in the least important positions, and southern Chinese completely out of government. The Chinese were also not allowed arms and forbidden from meetings. This would be the first time in history that Chinese landlords felt deprived of their official positions. The one benefit they received was to keep their estates intact.

Mongol control over Central Asia stimulated trade between China, the rest of the empire, and Europe, but the profits to this trade left Chinese hands. These losses increased rapidly due to a mistaken printing of too much paper currency; Mongol corruption and unsuccessful invasions of Southeast Asia and Japan (both twice), crippling China's economy in the long run. In addition, Mongols confiscated land in north China for pasturing horses, Mongol aristocrats, and Buddhist temples. As this land left tax rolls, peasants made up the difference. Taxes increased rapidly due to these economic problems, and because the Mongols built and extended the Grand Canal to move receipts and grain to this new capital. Although the Mongols expanded the Grand Canal, they did nothing about shoring up the Yellow River dykes or irrigation systems, which failed, leading to massive famine in some parts of China. In addition, peasants faced one hundred percent interest on loans as landlords attempted to recoup the funds they used to take from the government as local or regional bureaucrats.

Peasant unrest led to rebellion against the foreign Mongols. It started under the leadership of a leader claiming Song heritage, a Buddhist secret society called the White Lotus, and their Red Turban soldiers. Recruiting in the north was easy for this group, especially as one hundred fifty thousand peasant conscripts were working on repairing the Yellow River there in the 1340s. Open rebellion broke out in 1352, and for 3 years major parts of south and central China were lost to the Mongols and the Chinese landlords. The Mongols finally ended this rebellion by using Chinese troops led by the gentry against the peasant rebellion.

This victory for the Mongols and their allies would be short lived. Peasants continued to fight against the dynasty. A former peasant and one-time Buddhist monk rose in rank to become the leader of the southern Red Turban armies. Zhu revised the plan of attack, deciding to ally with Chinese landlords to attack the Mongols, rather than having both as enemies. Even though not all Chinese gentry broke from the Mongols, enough did to allow Zhu to push the nomads out of China in 1368 and form a new dynasty with its capital on the Yangzi at Nanjing: the **Ming dynasty** (1368–1644).

Zhu changed his reign name to Hongwu but is better known to history as his posthumous title Taizu, founder of the Ming or Brilliant dynasty. As a former peasant who led a peasant uprising, he understood the importance of agriculture and keeping the peasants complacent. He worked to promote agriculture by giving title to abandoned land cultivated by peasants, even exempting them from 3 years' taxation and corvee. Taizu also fixed the irrigation systems and tried to settle garrison troops on reclaimed land for the military to farm their own grain. Even artisans were better off under the Ming, as they could buy their way out of the corvee by paying higher taxes.

Although shrewd in managing peasants, Taizu was a harsh and autocratic ruler, executing those who spoke out or even made a pun on his name or position. He forced his advisers and ministers to kneel in front of him rather than the previous Chinese practice of standing at attention or even sitting. He restored the imperial university and examination system in 1382, but he only trusted his own family members and gave out huge land grants to his many sons and grandsons. He also divided the Ming empire into fifteen provinces, all corresponding with minor differences to present-day ones. Although he restored China to **Tang governance** with the six ministries, he controlled important parts of the government himself rather than having help by high Confucian bureaucrats in the secretariat or chancellor's office. These decisions would prove a mistake in the long run, as emperors and imperial family members later in the Ming dynasty would rely on the help of **eunuchs** for running the government and maneuvering for succession, disregarding Taizu's warnings on the matter—eunuchs became more and more powerful and helped cause the dynasty to weaken and fall in the seventeenth century.

Taizu also went to war with the Mongols, first capturing Beijing before pushing them back over the Great Wall in 1382. He followed up these successes with difficult and expensive expeditions into Mongolia to keep the pressure on the Mongols. In the midst of these inconclusive battles, Japanese pirates began to prey on Ming shipping, a problem not solved in two centuries. But these negatives did not outweigh Taizu's agricultural growth, especially when taking into account the renewed spread of south Vietnamese strains of rice that allowed three crops a year in the south and two crops a year in the Yangzi delta. China's population rebounded to 110 million.

Taizu chose his grandson, known later as Huizong (r. 1399–1402), to succeed him, but a civil war broke out over his choice. The winner was Yongle, Taizu's son, known to later historians as Chengzu (r. 1403–1425). It was he who rebuilt Beijing as the capital of the Ming and continued work on the Great Wall—to keep the Mongols at bay, as well as sending out a huge trading fleet seven times. All these actions are beyond the scope of this encyclopedia. However, it was after his reign that Confucian leaders began a crackdown on the merchant class, destroying the plans to build ships over 400 feet in length as well as many of the merchant maps of the Southeast Asian and Indian Ocean trading regions. Mongol rule had led to renewed distrust of merchants and foreigner and made most Confucianists believe—perhaps rightly—that Chinese civilization was the greatest in the world and did not need foreign influence. These factors are important to explain why Europe "discovered" the world instead of China.

Korea

Head east from Manchuria and cross the Yalu River one then enters the Korean peninsula. It is approximately the size of Britain or Minnesota, roughly 600 miles long by 135 miles wide. Korea's mountainous terrain only allows 20 percent of the land to be farmed. Yet those valleys early became large-yield rice-growing regions with organized irrigation systems, as Korea benefitted moisture wise from its position between the Yellow Sea and Sea of Japan. Although the Koreans, like the Japanese, borrowed important parts of China's culture, it is a mistake to assume Korea became a "little China" from 400 to 1400. This is true even considering that the peninsula served as a metaphoric bridge for Chinese ideas and Buddhism to cross first from the Shandong peninsula, across the Yellow Sea to southern Korea, and then move from there across the Tsushima Straights to Kyushu, Japan. Even with the borrowing of Confucianism and Buddhism, Koreans kept the shamanistic aspects of their folk religion and never in these years gave up their aristocratic, hereditary governing system unlike China did in the Song dynasty, using the more egalitarian-in-theory **examination system** to populate Chinese government posts.

Korea in 400 was divided into kingdoms of Koguryo in the north, Silla in the middle and south, and Paekche to the southwest. Koguryo especially copied the Chinese model of the defunct Han dynasty, using a Chinese-style bureaucracy paid for out of Chinese-style agricultural taxes and the **corvee**. It sought to increase its population and thus power by conquests of its Korean neighbors. Wealth gained by taxes or victories, however, trickled up only, allowing for enormous tombs for kings and nobles.

Koguryo's neighbors worked together, but the pinprick attacks from Silla and Paekche were not enough to hurt militarized Koguryo. Its forces pushed back the military might of China's **Sui dynasty** in 598, 612, and 614, helping to fell the brief dynasty. The **Tang dynasty** exacted revenge with the famous Chinese tactic of "barbarian against barbarian," uniting by sea with Silla in 660 to attack and defeat Paekche before turning successfully on Koguryo. Tang leadership thought with this last victorious battle China would rule Korea. Silla had other ideas. War returned, and, with the addition of indigenous uprisings, by 676 the Chinese had to retreat from the peninsula.

Silla Korea served as a little Tang. The country borrowed the Confucian structure of the government, including the bureaucracy and regional divisions of Tang China. Government posts, however, remained in the hands of the hereditary aristocrats in their hierarchical "bone ranks" instead of opening to anyone capable of passing the Confucian examination system. Yet Buddhism had more direct effect on Silla Korea. As the state religion, the government sponsored an elite corps of aristocratic youths called "**flower squires**," who attended an exclusive military academy devoted to protect Buddhism and the nation. It also promised more to the individual than the Korean folk traditions. But just like Japan, Korea adopted Buddhism without rejecting its previous shamanistic faith. Buddhist art and architecture spread throughout Korea, paid for by the taxes collected by the state and by the rich. The government also controlled the Buddhist orders and temples. It used art, dance, music, and literature to try to bring **Pure Land Buddhism** to the masses.

Religion did not fell Silla Korea, however. Instead, internal squabbling over royal succession after the king was assassinated in 780 became a common occurrence, as did regionalism and even a rebellion by an obscure group calling themselves the Red Trousers. Korea fell apart and back into three kingdoms toward the end of the ninth century.

It took a former merchant, Wang Kon, to reunify in 935 Koryo, from which we get Korea. Because so many of the aristocrats had died in the wars for control of Korea, Wang and his successors were able to create a government much closer to the Chinese model, including a civil service examination system in place after 958 based on Confucian ethics and Chinese history. Government schools soon taught these subjects, allowing some of society's lower-ranking members into important positions, if they could learn to read Chinese!

Koryo's civilian government was overthrown in 1170 by the military. A century of military rule followed, but not peacefully. Military men fought each other for control, and widespread social turbulence—peasant and slave rebellions. Only one military strongman was able to bring a semblance of order to Korea: General Choe Chung-hon. He eliminated rivals and put down rebellions, and he and his descendants kept the Mongols out of Korea until he was assassinated. Only then did Koryo stop fighting the Mongols to become their tributary state in the 1250s. For the next one hundred years or so, Korean kings were forced to marry Mongolian princesses; self-rule ended.

Mongolian control over Korea mostly meant catastrophe for the common people, starting with two-hundred thousand sent into slavery in 1254. Later came the destruction of Korean forests and more forced labor of Korean workers to build and man the ships needed to invade Japan, first in 1274 and then 1281. These failed invasions meant Japan would be unconquered, but Korea felt Mongol control until the 1340s. What was left of the Korean government proved confused when the Mongols were pushed out of China by the new **Ming dynasty**. General Yi Song-gye was sent to attack Ming forces in northwestern Korea in 1388. Seeing Ming strength firsthand, he marched his troops back and conquered the rest of Korea for himself with his capital at Seoul. Yi became a tributary state under the Ming and pushed Neo-Confucianism on Koreans, common and elite. Although Buddhism and Korea's old folk traditions would remain, especially among the illiterate majority, Korea became more Confucian than China! Confucian education spread wildly. The matrilineal power of women was pushed aside in favor of filial piety to fathers, seclusion of women, and a ban on widow remarriage. This idealized Neo-Confucian state, called the Yi dynasty or Chosen Period, would last in Korea until the Japanese takeover in 1910.

Japan

The people known today as Japanese were not the original inhabitants of the islands of Japan. The Japanese came over in different waves from Korea, starting first around 300 B.C.E. in southern Kyushu. Slowly these newcomers displaced the aboriginal inhabitants north and eastward, the Ainu (today these proto-Caucasian Ainu inhabit mostly Hokkaido, the northern of Japan's four main islands, and make up around 2 percent of Japan's total population). Around 250 C.E., another burst of people came over from Korea, this time on horseback in military clans and likely subjugating the earlier group and building enormous grave sites for their leaders–hence Japan's Tomb Period (ca. 250–ca. 400). These clans, called *uji* in Japanese, admired Japan for its beauty as well as for its mild climate; hence the Japanese **Shinto** religion's nature focus. The clans took different *kami*, or gods, as their different ancestors. But because of these mountains, volcanoes, and rugged forested hillsides, Japan's three southern islands only have approximately 10 percent arable land. As the clans' population grew, so did the need to expand. By around 400, these military clans had settled Kyushu and Shikoku and had pushed as far as the Yamato Plain in southern/western Honshu, driving the Ainu before them.

Historians date the beginning of this **Yamato Period** differently, but it makes sense to start it when the uji arrived on Honshu. The clans who chose the sun goddess to worship as ancestor used the fact that the sun is so important and gives light to all Japan to convince the other clans to follow its leadership. This is how the imperial family took the steps toward leadership in Japan. Even today there are those that claim that the imperial line flows unblemished from this early emperor.

By the sixth century, ideas from China via Korea streamed into Japan, and the battle for control of the imperial family became a fierce contest between three clans, with Soga—chief sponsor of Buddhism and by affiliation things Chinese—the temporary victor. The emperor, under Soga leadership, was to sponsor the adoption of Chinese ideas and influence in the law, arts, religion, society, and eventually even the idea of a capital city. Leaders of Soga decided to intermarry with the imperial line and have a regent control the niece of the family, Empress Suiko (r. 592–628). This regent was **Prince Shotoku**.

Prince Shotoku became famous for sponsoring Buddhism and Buddhist temples, as well as creating the **Seventeen Point Constitution** in 604. This constitution was more of a list of advice for rulers and the ruled and was written in Chinese, the only written language for the Japanese for centuries. Its articles heavily advocated **Confucianism** and Buddhism, with a sprinkling of **Daoism** and Shinto's consensus building thrown in for good measure. But the constitution was really a way to show forcefully that the emperor or regent for the emperor would serve as a powerful central government, including collecting taxes. Prince Shotoku also opened up relations with China and sent four missions to the short-lived **Sui dynasty**.

After the death of Prince Shotuku in 622, a new round of fighting for control of the empire broke out. The winner, the renamed Fujiwara family, would control or influence the empire for centuries to come. This leading Shinto family decided to keep Buddhism and the centralizing of the state. It even copied the Chinese **equal field system** and taxation policies of the Tang dynasty. And with the building of a permanent capital, the Yamato Period ended, and the short **Nara Period** began in 710.

Heijo, known today as Nara, was laid out as a miniature Changan, China's Tang dynasty capital. The main differences between the capitals was Japan built mostly with wood due to its availability and fear of earthquakes (while using wood increases fear of fire), and the city lacked a protective wall as Japan did not fear invasion. Even though Japan continued to borrow Chinese ideas, there were some differences. For example, emperors ruled not with the mandate of heaven but because they were related to heaven. This meant anyone trying to take control of the government would rule through the emperor, keeping his lineage intact. In addition, the equal field system was weakened from its creation by aristocrats keeping control of their land. The final blows to the system were the periodic smallpox epidemics that led the government in 743 to allow any new rice fields created to be owned forever.

The Nara Period saw six missions sent to Tang China, each of up to six hundred men. Japanese learned architecture from their Chinese hosts. In fact, the Buddhist temples in Heijo and later Heian (Kyoto) are the best examples of Tang dynasty buildings left in the world.

Buddhism grew very quickly during the Nara Period. The emperor's 741 edict required a Buddhist temple and pagoda to be built in every province. The emperor also worked to link Shinto gods to the Buddhist canon to keep both coexisting in peace and helping to spread to the common people. In 752 the huge Todaiji temple in Nara was finished, including the 50-foot great Buddha made out of a million pounds of metal. Emperor Kammu, either as part of the rivalry between families over control of the emperor or due to fears that Buddhist priests had become too powerful, decided to move the capital, successfully achieved in 794 with the move to today's Kyoto with the start of the **Heian Period** (794–1185).

As the Tang dynasty grew weak, Japan created more and more of its own high culture. Using literary sources, historians have a good idea how the aristocrats in the capital—again made out of wood—lived. The most important work is *Tale of Genji*, not only the world's first novel, but the first surviving work in Japanese and a work written by a woman, Lady Murasaki, probably from 1008 to 1021. The story takes place over 75 years, following three generations of the imperial family and five hundred characters in fifty-four chapters originally written in haphazard order most likely to amuse ladies of the court and not for publication. The story became famous first because the beautiful poetry—for a long time considered the only important Japanese language literature—written within the sprawling tale.

In brief, *Tale of Genji* is a story about looking for love where it is forbidden or unlikely to be found. The protaganist's popularity among Japanese then (and now) lies in his capacity to be deeply moved and emotional through poetry, painting, music, and affairs of the heart. Most important, the novel helps to explain the aesthetics of Heian Japan, at least for the 5 percent of Japanese living in the capital. But what the Heian Period aristocrats considered beautiful was not necessarily the obvious. Instead of the tune, the smell, or the sight, Heian Japanese elites, in contrast to Chinese, admired the transient nature of life heard in the last few notes of a song fading away, fragrance wafting on the breeze, or shadows present at dusk or dawn.

After centuries controlling the imperial family, the Fujiwara needed to keep the size of the imperial family—its relatives—limited in size. To do so it cut off branch families after a certain number of imperial generations. The collateral families had new **names** and wealth from provincial posts, but many elites would rather live in Heian with its many urban delights made famous by Lady Murasaki and so appointed others to do their jobs and run their estates. Other branch families, most famously Taira and Minamoto, became great warrior families with money for horses and expensive weapons and armor. Fighting soon broke out in the provinces between different groups in the eleventh century. This showed the weakness of the Heian system and lack of centralized military forces. Even rule by the emperors changed. Retired or "cloistered emperors" ran the government while the emperor just reigned and performed the Shinto rites. The system finally broke down when in 1156 military force from the provinces was used to control the government starting a cycle of violence across Japan. The eventual victors were the Minamoto family in 1185. Again, the emperor kept his position, as the victorious family forced the emperor to establish in 1192 a new position for control of the secular (and military) government, the **shogun**–barbarian quelling generalissimo.

This new era, the **Kamakura Period** began with the shogun controlling Japan from the Kanto Plain, near where Tokyo is today. The emperor granted the shogun the secular power needed to appoint bureaucrats to staff provincial posts. This made it easier to rule the country. Unfortunately for the Minamoto family, the shogun Minamoto Yoritomo distrusted his own family and had many members killed. Upon his death his widow and her father started to control from behind the scenes. Instead of taking the shogunate directly, these Hojo family members decided to rule through the shogun as regents. Within three generations the shogun was from the Fujiwara family, with the Hojo family actually running the country through its role as regent.

The late Heian Period and Kamakura Period saw the rise of the military class, the bushi or warrior. Not quite the samurai of film and comic book fame, the bushi owned lands like a European knight that enabled him to be able to own the horse, armor, and sword needed for combat. These warriors were rewarded for their victories in the long wars that ended the Heian Period. Warriors began to work on an informal code, although not quite the samurai bushido code of the seventeenth century. Kill or be killed was part of the code. *Seppuku* (ritual disembowelment often called "harakiri") was for those dishonored on the battlefield. In 1274 war was renewed, this time when Khubilai Khan sent an invasion fleet made up of Korean ships, Korean warriors, and Mongol horsemen—a total of thirty-thousand men—to invade Kyushu. Fierce fighting broke out, but an unexpected storm destroyed much of the fleet and led the invading force to retreat. In 1281, Khubilai Khan sent envoys to urge Japan to surrender. Instead, the Japanese executed the envoys. Luckily for Japan, when the Mongols invaded they again chose Kyushu; this time the Japanese had built a wall to make breaching defenses more difficult, even in the face of one-hundred forty thousand enemies. Again a typhoon halted the attack, and the Mongols again retreated, this time for good.

Although a military victory, no additional lands or wealth were won in the struggle and divided up among the warriors. As a result, the bushi became less enamored of their leaders. So when Emperor Go-Daigo launched his Kemmu Restoration in 1333, seeking to return the power to rule to the emperor, many disgruntled bushi joined his cause, so ending the Kamakura Period.

The Kemmu Restoration only briefly put the emperor back into power. His foe, then ally, then foe again—Ashikaga Takauji—pushed the emperor south and out of power. He then founded the **Ashikaga shogunate** in 1336, using Kyoto as his capital.

Although Takauji was a fighter, Yoshimitsu, the third shogun, was mainly interested in cultural pursuits. These were made easier with the choice to keep the capital in Kyoto near the emperor. With the rise of the **Ming dynasty**, trade between China and Japan reopened. Japan traded its famed **samurai swords**, illustrated folding fans, and painted silk screens—all Japanese inventions—for porcelain, great paintings, and sculptures of the Ming. The influx of art and ideas from China, combined with the huge following of **Zen Buddhism**, all had a huge impact on religion, aesthetics, and culture in the Ashikaga shogunate. Zen's inward-looking nature, Japanese ideals of beauty, and Ming Chinese sensibilities all worked together to create iconic Japanese arts: **noh theater**, the rock garden, flower arranging, and the tea ceremony.

The Ashikaga shogunate was far weaker than the Hojo regency. It tried to control the countryside through regional capitals staffed by branch families. These appointed rulers—if they stayed in their posts and did not move to the capital for the high culture practiced there—had to deal with regional warrior powers that were not integrated into the state after the Hojo fell from power. These independent warlords fought one another and the appointed officials to extend personal control. The officials took half of all taxes paid, as per the shogun's authorization, and levied troops. These troops were supposed to be in case of invasion, not to fight for control over Japan. This situation would explode out of control starting in 1467.

Japanese history in this encyclopedia begins and ends with Chinese influence on the rise. But in the middle years it was mostly responsible for its own take on beauty. It is true that Japan borrowed what it liked best about foreign ideas. It is also true that it modified these ideas or discarded them entirely when they did not fit Japan, such as the case with the **examination system** or walls around a city.

Further Reading

Asdshead, S.A.M. *China in World History.* 2nd ed. New York: St. Martin's Press, 1995.

Fairbank, John King, and Merle Goldman. *China: A New History.* 2nd enlarged ed. Cambridge, MA: Belknap Press of Harvard University Press, 2006.

Hane, Mikiso. *Premodern Japan: A Historical Survey.* Boulder, CO: Westview Press, 1991.

Kim, Chun-gil. *The History of Korea.* Westport, CT: Greenwood Press, 2005.

Weatherford, Jack. *Genghis Khan and the Making of the Modern World.* New York: Crown Publishers, 2004.

2. RELIGION

When first encountering East Asian religions, many challenges occur to the Western-educated reader, in part due to differences from Europe. Instead of believing in only one religion, East Asians often follow the teachings and rituals of two or even three religions. For example, in Japan a person might have a **Shinto** wedding and a Buddhist funeral. In China, a high official in the **Song dynasty** would follow **Confucianism** in his work but upon retirement would often retreat into the countryside and practice **Daoism** (written "Taoism" in earlier transliterations). In addition, the word *religion* is somewhat problematic itself. Many of the so-called religions that started in or migrated to China, Korea, and Japan began more as philosophies and expanded into a more religious form as they became popularized for the peasants. These philosophies/religions greatly influenced East Asian cultures, even if the people of the region did not necessarily confine themselves to one exclusive belief system. For ease of use and consistency, we continue to use the word *religion.*

In addition to the four religious traditions of China, Korea, and Japan, East Asia developed older ideas that some in the West consider "**ancestor worship.**" Most scholars reject this label, while others call it semireligious. At a funeral, during certain holidays each year, and perhaps on the deceased's annual death day, families provide real or symbolic food, items, or money for use in the afterlife and to honor the past. "Ancestor commemoration" might be a better term for what was practiced more extensively and further back along the family tree by large, wealthy families, **lineages**, or **clans** in China. Although part of ancestor worship worked itself into Confucianism, filial piety, and family rites, much of the folk tradition that grew up with ancestor worship split off and became subsumed into Daoism in China and Korea, Buddhism sometimes in China and Japan, or kept its separation as did Shinto in Japan.

In China, three religions came out of the period of great societal and political upheaval during the Eastern Zhou Period (771–256 B.C.E.), which overlaps in part the Warring States Period (453–221 B.C.E.). The tumultuous Eastern Zhou began with the slow downfall of the one controlling state and the creation of many different states, all fighting one another for survival or supremacy. The end of the Warring States Period led to the end of feuding Chinese kingdoms and instead a single Chinese Empire, the Qin (although it only lasted a handful of years). At the societal level, the slave-like farmers of the Western Zhou Period (1122–771 B.C.E.) became landowning peasants during the Eastern Zhou, and in a few, rare cases, fabulously wealthy. In addition to war and societal changes, urbanization began as more and more land fell under the till. The three religions, Confucianism, Daoism, and **Legalism**, competed with other new ideas in what Chinese call the "Hundred Schools"—not literally one hundred, but *hundred* meaning "many." At almost the same time in India, state creation, incessant warfare, and urbanization led to changes in religion leading eventually to Hinduism, as well as belief systems opposed to Hinduism on different levels such as Buddhism and Jainism. New philosophical ideas also began in contemporary Greece. When periods of division or uncertainty hit Korea and Japan, so too did new ideas from China lead to religious conversions, primarily Confucianism and Chinese-style Buddhism.

Legalism

Ideas fought one another figuratively during the Hundred Schools, just as a hundred states fought each other literally until only one controlled all of China. The Qin state began its conquests with Legalism as its state ideology. Through ruthless war, the Qin achieved victory. The Qin dynasty inaugurated imperial China in 221 B.C.E. with the first emperor. Under Legalism, the leader of the state was always right and ordered repressive laws for the people to follow. An individual only existed to serve the state in wartime and harvest time. People need laws to regulate their behavior because according to Legalism people are evil, or at their best lazy. Laws had stiff penalties, including death. A whole family might pay the punishment, under the theory that collective responsibility made rebellion less likely and families would not shield a law-breaker. Leaders raised taxes to obscene levels in peacetime to help pay for wars already waged; in some ways the populace looked forward to war as a period of less repression! Luckily for the Chinese people, the Qin dynasty only lasted until 207 B.C.E., as peasant unrest over repression and taxes helped to eliminate those who sought to continue the Qin. Unfortunately, Legalist ideas would continue in future dynasties such as the Han and the **Sui**, and even in more recent times with the Cultural Revolution under Communist Mao Zedong (1966–1969) or the Tiananmen Square massacre in June 1989 under Deng Xiaoping.

Daoism

Leaders imposed **Legalism** to create a repressive future; Daoism harkened back to an idealized past just after the discovery of cultivation. It cared more about the individual. It too came out of the Hundred Schools era but unlike Legalism played a much more positive role in Chinese history. The term *Dao* comes out of the first text of Daoists, the *Dao De Jing*, usually translated as "The Way and Its Power." Supposedly written before the works of Confucius by the mysterious Laozi (although some doubt Laozi ever existed), *Dao De Jing* preaches following the "Way"; yet the Way cannot be defined: "The Way that can be named is not the eternal Way." Not only is the Way nameless, so are its ideas behind how the world or society functions. Much of the *Dao De Jing* continues in this vague and cryptic way, leading some to speculate that the text, written in verse, is also a guide to meditation. In the midst of vague philosophizing, the book also offered some advice for attempting to solve the troubles of the Eastern Zhou Period: "Do not prize possessions and the people will not steal." Perhaps even more difficult to enact by leaders of the time was this pithy sentence: "The best ruler is one whose presence is barely known by his subjects."

A key term of Daoism is *wu wei*, an idea also difficult to describe. It means "nonaction." Daoist texts describe a butcher who cuts meat for years without ever sharpening a knife by simply following the meat where a microscopic gap already existed. Modern equivalents include firing the perfect tennis shot made without applying much swing to a racket or scoring a lay-up in a basketball game without any conscious thought of dribbling the ball or shooting. In these examples the mind is absent from the action; one's body simply flows to what is right after lots of practice. Water is another example of wu wei in action: water yields, flows down, and fills pools, but over the years its channel cuts through rock.

The second Daoist classic was named after its author, *Zhuangzi* (Master Zhuang). Again, some do not believe Master Zhuang Zhou lived, using as evidence the fact that the work in question was written over a couple centuries. Zhuang extolls the beauty of nature and meditation in everyday life and avoids advice to rulers. The book in many ways seems a direct attack on **Confucianism**. Confucius himself appears at times, only to be outargued or made the fool by Zhuang Zhou. As we see, Confucianism holds to the importance of ritual and honoring parents and loved ones. When Zhuang's wife died, instead of mourning her ritually and avoiding public displays of cheer as a Confucianist would demand, Zhuang sang and played drums. When he was chastised by a friend for quitting his mourning, Zhuang replied that his wife long ago had no spirit and no body, then had a spirit, then was born with a body. With death came another change. If he had continued to mourn her it would show he did not understand the Way.

Zhuang challenged Confucian and other philosophies' emphasis on morality. Good and bad, right and wrong, true and false, all these distinctions become problematic if one was to understand the Way in its totality. Avoid drawing distinctions, wrote Zhuang. Hence it makes sense that ideas of the yin and yang (the dualities that worked together—evil and good, female and male, weak and strong) found their way quite early into Daoism and helped to move it from its philosophical form into a more religious one.

The *Zhuangzi* also engages in some interesting metaphysics, not in the sense of discussing gods or the hereafter, but rather being and existence. Zhuang described a dream he had where he was a butterfly and did not know he was Zhuang Zhou. When he awoke, he was not sure he was Zhuang who had dreamt he was a butterfly or a butterfly now dreaming he was Zhuang. Maybe all life was but a dream. That would fit into Zhuang's discussion of death as just another part of life. In fact, Zhuang theorized that the dead might be wondering why they clung to life!

Soon the *Dao De Jing* and *Zhuangzi* would be interpreted for new times, partially due to repression by Legalists and partially due to the nature of the written word. The Qin dynasty ordered many books burned, and in other cases these "prepaper" books fell apart when the leather strap holding the bamboo slats rotted away and when put back together often became rearranged. But as only the most educated could read classical Chinese with its thousands of ideograms (and the fact that pre- and post-Qin ideograms were often different), Daoism came to the common folk through a more religious outlook. Toward the end of the Han dynasty (202 B.C.E.–220 C.E.), a Daoist religious movement known as the Celestial Masters won acceptance with the peasantry in the spiritual and civic realms, actually conquering and governing parts of China. The Celestial Masters helped move Daoism away from its roots to a religion focused on nature, the yin and yang, healing, and even trying to cheat death! With the fall of the Han (220 C.E.) and the **Period of Disunity** (316–588), Daoism became further entrenched in the north, as the Celestial Masters continued their teaching and healing services (even providing free food to travelers). Soon they added meditation and breathing exercises. Some wealthy patrons began searching for everlasting life from religious Daoists, who emulated later European alchemists in handling exotic ingredients to concoct supposed life-sustaining elixirs. Ironically, mercury often turned up in these potions, leading to horrible suffering and death instead of everlasting life.

Daoism also faced competition from a new direction, the coming of Buddhism into China. During the **Northern Wei** dynasty, north China's Emperor Taiwu persecuted Buddhists from 446 C.E. until his death in 452, gaining him ceremonial trappings of Daoism, as well as the support of Confucianists. A second Buddhist purge of north China occurred from 574 to 578; just like the first it was an attack on the wealth and political power of Buddhists by destroying monasteries, not forcing individual religious change. In this case Daoism became the official state religion, but the advent of the Sui dynasty and reunification 10 short years later brought Daoism away from imperial sanction and back into steady competition with Buddhism and Confucianism. The Celestial Masters faded with a revived strong, central state, and Daoism splintered into different religious groups founded on beautiful mountains away from cities. Many former Confucianist government officials would retire to mountain areas to spend their days reflecting on the Way and drawing or painting the landscapes. Daoism for the common people, on the other hand, tied itself to folk traditions and local gods.

The emperors of the **Sui**, **Tang**, and **Song** dynasties drew equally on what became known as China's "Three Teachings": Confucianism, Daoism, and Buddhism. Each time emperors pushed for more universal recognition of Daoism, like having the *Dao De Jing* required reading along Confucian classics as part of the **examination system** (**Empress Wu**) or statues of Laozi placed throughout China (Emperor Xuanzong), emperors would also proclaim the importance of Buddhist teachings or sponsor Buddhist festivals. Only when the Mongols overran China and established the **Yuan dynasty** (1279–1368), did the emperor favor a religion, in this case Tibetan Buddhism; but as the **Mongols** also practiced religious freedom and only occupied all of China for 90 years, Daoism maintained its importance.

As for other East Asian states, Daoism influenced the culture of Korea and Japan, but never to the extent as in China. Daoism first came to Korea from Chinese emigrants and conquerors during the Han dynasty, around 109 B.C.E. By the time the Chinese empire collapsed and the last Chinese either left or merged into the Korean population, Daoism, Confucianism, and even some

Buddhism had made their way to the Three Kingdoms of Korea. Daoism, with its love of nature, ended up merging well with the local folk traditions and gods, whereas Confucianism and Buddhism ended up the most powerful influences. As for Japan, Daoist ideas on nature and meditation struck a nerve. The Chinese worldview came to Japan through Korea between the fourth and sixth centuries, and Japanese leaders officially adopted Confucianism and Buddhism after the start of the Sui dynasty (around 604 with **Prince Shotoku** and his **Seventeen Point Constitution**). The Japanese kept **Shinto**, their nature-worshiping and animistic religion. Hence Daoism lost out in formal allegiance, yet it influenced Japanese culture, especially through **Zen Buddhism**.

Confucianism

Confucianism also began during the Hundred Schools Period, around 500 B.C.E. It looked to an idealized past of the Shang dynasty (1766–1122 B.C.E.) or the Western Zhou Period (1122–771 B.C.E.), times where people understood their place in society and family. Master Kong Qiu, Latinized Confucius, thought order was the answer to the chaos of his times, when a lower ranking peasant could climb to the top of the hierarchy and almost constant war

Tsong-Kha-Pa, 1357–1419 founder of Tibetan Buddhist sect Dge-lugs-pa, literally Model of Virtue but called Yellow Hat. Gilded bronze, 14th–15th century Tibetan. The Art Archive/Musée Guimet Paris/Gianni Dagli Orti.

plagued the land. Perhaps jealously fueled Confucius: his family was of poverty-stricken nobility. Confucius turned to books and histories of the past and perhaps wrote or collated parts of them—the historical record is vague. These "Five Classics"—*Book of Odes, Book of History, Book of Changes, Book of Rites*, and the *Spring and Autumn Annals* (this last book a history of the recent Eastern Zhou past)—became the foundation of Confucianism. The Confucian canon would also eventually include works or proverbs by Confucius or his key followers, the "Four Books": *Analects* (sayings of Confucius), *Book of Mencius, Great Learning*, and *Doctrine of the Mean*. Confucius idealized the early years of the Western Zhou and believed that society could be saved if it replicated the past through understanding old books, renewing old rituals, and reinstituting systems of order. A natural order existed before; replicate it again and conflict and chaos will evaporate.

Confucius himself wanted to be a sage, a scholar who could advise the rulers of his time. Instead he became a great teacher, imparting his ideology to willing disciples chosen for their ability and not their birth. Confucius philosophized about the here and now, not the hereafter. He placed emphasis on good government, morality, and ethics. Rigid hierarchy also played a large role in his philosophy; he combined the idea of knowing one's place in society with patriarchy and filial piety (respect for one's parents). These ideas became explicit in his

Five Relationships: ruler to subject, father to son, husband to wife, elder brother to younger brother, and friend to friend. Notice that all the relationships but the final one showed hierarchy, women only fit into the system in a subordinate role (as wife), and one only existed in relation to others. Each of these relationships was reciprocal, however, with the subordinate owing the superior respect and obedience, while the superior owed the subordinate benevolence. A benevolent ruler might forgive taxes a drought-stricken region.

Benevolence (*ren* in Chinese) and ritual (*li*) played key roles in Confucianism. In fact, benevolence under Confucianism is very similar to the golden rule of Western thought, only in a negative form: "Do not do unto others what you would not wish yourself." Those below needed to treat you with loyalty and obedience, performing the proper rituals. These included 3 years of mourning when a parent died. The ruler needed to observe the correct rituals to please the gods and allow his rule to continue. But ritual should not be observed blindly; real, sincere feeling had to occur during the rites or they were useless. The ruler, like the father, also served as a model of behavior, teaching morality through his actions. Confucius did not believe laws prevented immorality; laws just created criminals. If those at the top of the social hierarchy acted morally and with benevolence, the lower ranks of society would behave well, too. At the top, just below the ruler, stood the scholar-official (*junzi* in Chinese), to explain Confucian ideology to the leader.

Confucianism preached the importance of hierarchy, but with a small rebellious streak. A leader was only a leader if he behaved as one, with benevolence to those below and propriety in rituals. If a leader did not provide those below with benevolence or shirked his ritual duties, the leader could be replaced. But ordinarily Confucianism would be used historically by the elite to keep order; rebellions were started by Daoist secret societies at first, then Buddhist secret societies once Buddhism became popular in China.

Mencius is the Latinized name of the second key extoller of Confucianism, one Meng Ke, who lived and wrote around 300 B.C.E. He brought into Confucianism two ideas many associated with Confucius: All people are good and can become sages, and the leader rules because of the **mandate of heaven**. Mencius argued that all people are good. As evidence, Mencius pointed out that all people would be shocked to see a child fall into a well; this, he said, was humaneness that he saw as the glimmerings of benevolence. Because benevolence is within everyone, so is the possibility of sagehood, if only one studied and applied Confucianism. And because sages could best predict how to respond to the current conditions in China, it was right and proper for a king to cede his rule to a sage. Not surprisingly, this never happened.

Mencius also argued a king only ruled with the mandate of heaven. The Xia, Shang, and Eastern Zhou dynasties lost out not because of the actions of rebels who should be shunned, but due to losing the mandate of heaven. The mandate provided good weather and compliant subjects. In return the king engaged in proper rituals and treated his subjects with benevolence. Natural disasters or rebellious peasants might mean the king was losing the mandate, hence his overthrow or even regicide was divinely inspired and not immoral under the Five Relationships. Worthy men established the new dynasties under the new mandate.

Not long after the days of Mencius, Qin dynasty took over China; Confucianism had to go underground or face elimination. The few Confucian scholars who tried to stand up to the new emperor met hideous deaths, and the Qin emperor burned books to keep Confucianism or any other philosophies out of the hands of his subjects. Copies of books that survived often were just piles of old bamboo straps with writing of an older form of Chinese than introduced (and kept) by the Qin. The Han dynasty realized it was the heir to the Qin, so continued many Legalist practices. But a clever scholar-official figured out a way to put Legalism and renewed Confucianism together. Confucianists claimed that laws were unnecessary and a ruler should lead by example to get the people to do good. Although perhaps true in the time of the Shang, Zhou, or even the Warring States Period, he argued, the world of the Han was much different. It needed the laws of the Legalists in conjunction with the moral example of Confucianists, just like the world needed the dark of the yin with the light of the yang. Confucianism became part of the ruling ideology of China, at the expense of a little corruption from **Legalism** and mysticism/religious ideas from the yin/yang (just as **Daoism** had been mildly altered by the introduction of symbol and its principles).

Also during the Han, the emperor sponsored an imperial university to teach Confucianism. It began with fifty students; in one hundred years three thousand students attended. With the **Sui** and **Tang** dynasties, the university continued to grow in size, as more and more government positions required the passing of exams based on Confucianism (and for a brief time on Daoism as well). By the **Song dynasty** and then during the **Ming,** almost all central government positions required passing the Confucian exams. These exams were open to all in theory, allowing the best and the brightest to pass the exams and work in government. Yet the difficulty of learning the thousands of characters of classical Chinese, as well as the Confucian canon and commentaries, meant normal members of the gentry ran the government bureaucracies. Only rarely an intelligent peasant boy, backed by his village, earned a spot in government.

By the time of the Sui dynasty, Confucian temples and shrines could be found in all provinces. Religiously Confucianism remained important for rites the emperor engaged in or sponsored for the good of China, and at the family level for the poorly named "ancestor worship." But Buddhism, starting slowly at the end of the Han dynasty, briefly overshadowed Confucianism. From 800 to 1200, important scholar-officials studied Buddhism, before some rejected its philosophy. Using ideas gleaned from Buddhism or even Daoism, these scholars created **Neo-Confucianism**.

The Neo-Confucian movement brought new ideas to Confucianism. Yet the Confucian exams remained unaffected by these changes until a generation after the death of Neo-Confucianism's most important thinker, **Zhu Xi** (1130–1200). Zhu used the two terms qi and li in much the same way as earlier scholars had attached the yin and yang to Confucianism or Daoism. In this case, li (a different Chinese character than "ritual") meant "principle," and qi, like in Daoism, meant "energy," as in Tai Qi (sometimes still written in the old transliteration as "T'ai Chi"). Just like a house needed a plan (li) before beginning building with materials (qi), people were on the path of goodness (li), but needed to be taught to obtain the qi, its outward expression. This was an elegant solution needed to prove Mencius correct in the face of contradictory evidence: if all people are good, why do so many do bad? The answer: not enough training. One must study the Confucian canon but also look within oneself through meditation and reflection, just like **Chan Buddhism**. With these Neo-Confucian teachings and rulers leading by example, all people could eventually be good.

Zhu's Neo-Confucianism became the accepted interpretation of Confucianism for passing the exams and getting the appointment to government positions during the Later Song dynasty and until the twentieth century. This would be one of several problems with Neo-Confucianism (or its predecessor). No longer would an examinee dare to interpret the Confucian canon himself; this led to students and teachers valuing memorization not intellectualism, and leading to a weakened Chinese intelligencia when the Europeans arrived by sea. In addition, Neo-Confucianism was also behind a backlash against women. **Footbinding** became popular for the gentry's daughters during the Song dynasty. This incredibly painful procedure, which kept the girl/woman's feet the size of a 5-year old's, pushed women out of society, where they had a place before, and into their homes' shadows. Finally, although Confucianists made intelligent government officials, the Confucian importance of family and thus making sure one's children were well taken care of made some scholar-officials less than honest when it came to remitting tax receipts. This embezzlement by men the government depended on eventually led to financial problems and thus the beginning of the end for many dynasties.

As for Korea and Japan, both societies were profoundly influenced by Confucianism. After 1391 and the establishment of the Yi dynasty, Korea became perhaps more Neo-Confucian than even China! In Japan's case, the **Seventeen Point Constitution** reflects equal parts Confucianism and Buddhism. But neither Korean kings or Japanese emperors (let alone Japanese regents or Japanese "**shogun**") ended or even modified their respective hereditary systems like China did for all but the emperor. The **examination system** in non-China East Asia, when offered, was superfluous.

Buddhism

Buddhism arose in the Nepal region of South Asia around 500 B.C.E. Prince Siddhartha Gautama worried about what life meant once he realized at age 29 that he would become sick, age, and die. Giving up his father's palace, his wife, and his son, Siddhartha became an ascetic, living with no possessions and starving — popular philosophical strategies for the region at the time. After 6 years of mistreating his body like this and almost starving to death, and apparently no closer to the answers to suffering he sought, he took food and drink. Then, while meditating, the answer came to him, a middle way between treating himself with luxury and maltreating his body through pain and hunger. He described his Four Noble Truths: humans suffer, desire causes suffering, there is a way to stop suffering and achieve liberation, and that way to liberation is the Eightfold Noble Path (ways of treating oneself and others, including meditation until one loses thought of a "self"). Humans suffer because they seek pleasure, worry about losing pleasure, or wish they had pleasure again, and stubbornly believe in their individual soul. Humans had forgotten to live in the moment and recognize the community of living creatures. Siddhartha, called by his new followers Buddha ("enlightened one"), developed an order of monks for those to practice his teachings and spread his ideas.

Clearly the Buddha had created a philosophical way of dealing with the sorrows of life: Live simply, live for the moment, treat all living things with respect, and be ethical. True enlightenment, "nirvana," only came after long hours of meditation, something only open to celibate and poor monks willing to beg for food before meditating each day. The mysticism associated in South Asian culture with meditation and the word of the Buddha and his teachings soon transformed philosophic thought into a new religion, with the Buddha as a god. Buddhism then took three paths: the traditional teachings of the god Buddha (now in Sri Lanka and South-East Asia); Mahayana ("Greater Vehicle") Buddhism in East Asia, where even laypeople could obtain enlightenment, through worshiping the original Buddha or one of the many to come; and Tibetan Buddhism, a more complicated form of Buddhism with a hierarchical system not seen in other religions practiced in East Asia.

According to legend, Mahayana Buddhism first arrived during the Han dynasty. But Buddhism did not become a popular choice among the Chinese until the **Period of Disunity**. Then, like during the Warring States, China was undergoing upheaval and so welcomed what at first glance seemed very unChinese. The first sects of Mahayana Buddhism that arrived still favored the monks and had a complicated cosmology that said the world was an illusion or was empty. Monks had strict vows of celibacy and shaved their heads to show dedication to their order. Both of these actions insulted their parents and ancestors by not providing a new generation to follow Confucian or ancestor rituals and harming the body "given" to you by parents. But Buddhism, by discussing what happened when you died (transmigration of the soul, similar to reincarnation) and sorrow itself, provided to the Chinese ideas not available under **Legalism**, **Daoism**, or **Confucianism**.

Buddhism's popularity exploded in the **Tang dynasty**. **Empress Wu**, although backing both Daoism because of supposed family ties to Laozi and Confucianism as part of the **examination system**, claimed to be the current incarnation (called a **Bodhisattva**) of the future Buddha (Maitreya) to come at the end of the world. The two most popular sects of Chinese Buddhism were **Pure Land** and **Chan Buddhism**. Pure Land believed the world was in terrible shape, but luckily Buddha had foreseen this, and explained secretly to a few followers that one specific Bodhisattva (being of wisdom) could help ordinary people achieve enlightenment. By believing in his saving grace and reciting his name ("Amituofo" Buddha—Amida in Japanese) in true devotion, a follower could be reborn in the land of paradise. Many Chinese did not understand this stay was temporary, assuming the Pure Land was heaven. Theoretically they would come back to earth and help others obtain enlightenment before permanently seeking it themselves as Bodhisattvas under Mahayana Buddhism were supposed to do. Just at the high point of Buddhism in China, Emperor Wuzong, a devote Daoist, attacked Buddhism. During his brief reign (840–846), due to his Daoist beliefs, xenophobia toward foreigners (with Buddhism obviously foreign), and acting on his chance to take back lands into taxation, Wuzong defrocked over two-hundred fifty thousand Buddhist monks and nuns (leaving only forty-nine monasteries and eight hundred monks), sold off their lands, destroyed 4,600 temples, and wrecked forty-thousand shrines. His death in 846 saved Buddhism in China, but not Pure Land; instead Chan Buddhism gained adherents to be the most popular form of Buddhism in China.

Chan Buddhism (called **Zen** in Japan) favored monks in their quest for enlightenment, believing meditation the key. But Chan Buddhism also provided churches for regular peasants to take part in, making up for the loss of Pure Land, and those churches survived the coming of the **Mongols** and their adherence to Tibetan Buddhism. Other forms of popular Buddhism also remained, albeit underground: Buddhist secret societies. Different versions helped to weaken or even destroy many of the Chinese dynasties since the Sui.

Korea accepted Buddhism early from China and was the key cultural transmitters to Japan. Although the folk religion in Korea already absorbed Daoism, Buddhism found almost universal acceptance. Japan, too, welcomed Buddhism. Japan also had many different sects vying for power. Some of the earliest actually took to the streets to fight government officials and each other over temple appointments. By the time the warrior classes in Japan made their first push at dominance to move the capital away from the Kyoto in 1185, the most popular forms of Buddhism in Japan were Pure Land (this time, the lay members repeated Amida's name many times to insure entrance into the Pure Land) and Zen (Chan Buddhism for Japanese), which added thinking about illogical puzzles called "koan" to meditation to achieve enlightenment.

Shinto

Japan's original animistic, folk religion survived the coming of new religious ideas. The Japanese coined "Shinto," meaning "way of the gods," after Buddhism arrived and absorbed a few local gods. But what were gods, called "kami," under Shinto? Gods were anything awe inspiring in a beautiful, powerful, or even scary way. Nature often played this role, probably because people in Japan came from Korea; Japan has far more beautiful mountain forests than the Koreans did by this point in history. A giant tree could be a kami, as could a mountain or even an interesting boulder. Even a man could be a kami if he had incredible abilities; upon death he might obtain even more fame as stories about his exploits got more and more exaggerated and people's knowledge of his kami-hood spread.

Shinto also provides multiple explanations on how the world, and more important, Japan, was created. One family claimed the sun goddess was a direct ancestor and used those stories to gain control of the state and become Japan's emperor. Shinto, however, does not handle death or a woman's menstruation well. Anyone who touched a dead body or animal was considered unclean; eventually an outcaste class developed from those who performed such jobs, called "**burakumin**." If a woman happened to touch a wrestling ring, Shinto priests would have to help rebuild it before refereeing **Sumo wrestling** again. Japan therefore differs from Korea and China, and for that matter almost all the world, in that its original religion survives into the twenty-first century!

Further Reading

Bresnan, Patrick S. *Awakening: An Introduction to the History of Eastern Thought.* 2nd ed. Upper Saddle River, NJ: Prentice Hall, 2002.

De Bary, William T., Wing-tsit Chan, and Burton Watson. *Sources of Chinese Tradition.* Vol. 1. New York: Columbia University Press, 1960.

Lee, Ki-baik. *A New History of Korea.* Translated by Edward W. Wagner. Cambridge, MA: Harvard University Press, 1984.

Osborne, Richard, and Borin Van Loon. *Introducing Ancient Eastern Philosophy.* New York: Totem, 1996.

Tsunoda, Ryusaku, William T. De Bary, and Donald Keene. *Sources of Japanese Tradition.* Vol. 1. New York: Columbia University Press, 1958.

Wright, Arthur F. *Buddhism in Chinese History.* New York: Atheneum, 1965.

3. ECONOMY

China

Chinese wealth comes first from the surplus grain generated by overworked and overtaxed peasants. During the **Period of Disunity**, north China tried to help the peasantry and maintain a strong tax base by implementing the **equal field system**. Yet due to climate, north China grew wheat, barley, and millet. It was south China that could grow rice. Growing rice requires close work with neighbors to drain or flood fields at the proper times. The more people who worked in a rice field, the greater the yield, although obviously there was an upper limit to the output of the crop. In fact, owning animals to help farm was a luxury restricted to the rich peasant during these dynasties. When China was reunified under the **Sui dynasty**, the government squandered its newly found southern resources on wars and extravagance, with the exception of the **Grand Canal,** which allowed goods to head north to the capital from the **Yangzi River** region for half the year.

The next rulers of China, the **Tang dynasty**, made China the richest country on earth, first by lowering taxes on the peasants. It then built up transportation and irrigation using **corvee** labor; sometimes they were part of the same system. Canals in the south linked the many small rivers and lakes. Travel by land had been made easier centuries earlier with rules requiring carts to have the same axle lengths, but trade by land was not as lucrative as trade by sea, even in this age of lost ships. China's isolated position led to trade in two directions: east across the sea (from there north to Korea and Japan, or south to southeast Asia and the Indian Ocean) or northwest along the **Silk Road**. It was said at the time that trade with China's northern capital Changan was so great the sky was obscured with dust from the caravans coming in all directions, as China sold silk, tea, and some ceramics to traders from as far away as North Africa. But the Tang was a more Buddhist society than Confucian, so merchants did not face the discrimination of future dynasties like the Ming.

Silk was highly cherished by the elite throughout the known world. Although silk is a natural by-product, the West did not find out the secret of its creation for centuries. Silk traveled from China into the West through the Silk Road. The Silk Road started in China and traveled through Central Asia and into Constantinople. This Silk Road helped create the major trading centers of Central Asia. Silk grew expensive as each new trader along the route took his own share of the profit before selling it to the next merchant. However, the fall of Rome in 476 hurt the silk trade for a couple of centuries. Yet the market for it rebounded, even as Arab traders figured out how to get to China by sea. Trade always continued along the Silk Road, but the weakening of the Tang led to a couple centuries of turmoil in China.

The Chinese were also able to build many trading ships, called "junks" during the Tang and Song Periods—these ships grew massive by the start of the Ming. These junks were primarily based out of southeastern China, helped along by the Yangzi River and the extensive canal systems of the region. Seaports proved readily available in the south, whereas the Yellow River moved too rapidly and chaotically to allow for much carrying trade. Many trade routes were opened that would have been the envy of the West. Routes went to the East Indies, Africa, India, and even the Middle East, although Chinese sailors had to compete for trade, especially with Arab merchants.

During the early Song, the increases in trade and resource development led to a period of relative prosperity. With the sea lanes protected by a Chinese navy, China's wealth increased. These Chinese warships even made use of rockets to fight off attackers (usually pirates). The technology of the Chinese ships were impressive and the best in the world. Ships could carry hundreds of passengers or tons of exotic goods. Intricate sail systems helped the ships travel easier and faster. The junk's compartments were watertight, which helped preserve ships that struck reefs and would otherwise be lost at sea. Differences such as these facilitated the Chinese Empire's rise as an important trading partner.

Trade by sea brought in many exotic goods. From India and Africa came prized ivory. Coral, pearls, crystal, cloves, and incense were also bought from foreign markets. On the other hand, China was a major exporter. People throughout Asia, Africa, and Europe demanded Chinese goods, which were seen as the pinnacle of craftsmanship or simply out of the ordinary. Many Europeans and Middle Easterners bought goods such as silks, porcelain, other ceramics, and tea at high prices. However, many of the rich Chinese during the Song dynasty were enamored of foreign goods and became ravenous purchasers. To pay for these goods, gold and silver (especially silver) were traded out. This large amount of specie, or hard currency, leaving China led to a large foreign debt. This trade deficit hindered the Chinese imperial budget and placed disproportionate power in foreign hands.

The Song dynasty showed weakness in fighting its wars against different nomadic groups, but it did have a strong economy. Paradoxically, its economy grew again when the Jurchen conquered north China, sending a flood of refugees southward. These newcomers arrived just in time; Vietnamese rice strains coming into the **Southern Song dynasty** allowed two crops of rice a year in areas south of the Yangzi. More peasants meant a greater yield. The Southern Song economy exploded, leading to commercialization of agriculture and the monetization of the economy. Peasants now paid their taxes in coin rather than in kind.

Although most of China dealt with dirt roads that turned to mud in the rainy season, the Southern Song capital of Hangzhou had paved roads to facilitate travel and trade. Hangzhou, located along a canal a short distance from the Yangzi, was a tremendous center of trade. This was the largest city in the world at this time. There were ready supplies of the major foodstuffs: rice and pork. Secondary foods such as salted fish could also be found easily. It was said that in the city things could be found that were not found in all of the rest of the empire.

There were different markets in Hangzhou for just about everything. There were shops for flowers, olives, oranges, pearls, medicinal plants, and books. Within the city, due to its commercial and imperial status, were service buildings such as inns, restaurants, taverns, and tea houses. In the lake near Hangzhou were hundreds of boats serving similar purposes. The city was known for being one of the premier makers of jewelry in all of China.

Goods in demand in the West such as salt and different spices were easily available in Hangzhou. The markets sold other rare goods such as perfumes, pets, and mosquito repellant. Workers also performed intricate tasks such as repairing ovens and making instruments out of bamboo. Rivers and canals connected to other nearby cities, making the transferring of goods easy.

China was also one of the first nations to create porcelain. The practice was not learned in the West until the eighteenth century, thus providing China a valuable monopoly. Porcelain is so difficult to make because it involves heating pure clay to very high temperatures. This form of ceramics was highly esteemed and delicate, making Chinese traders rich. Chinese trade in porcelain was so well known and prevalent that the word *china* means the same as the ceramic. Products of porcelain were anything from teacups to plates to figurines. Chinese porcelain at the time of the Song was almost the finest in the world, second only to neighboring Korea. And its abilities to make these items only increased with the coming of the **Ming dynasty**.

China's coinage was developed centuries before with the famous cash coin, and new coins were still made 1,000 years after its first appearance (*see* **Money/ Coinage**). This copper coin with a square hole in the center, had the value of one-thousandth of a Chinese ounce of silver (37.301 grams). These coins were often strung together with string in "hundreds." Despite the name, the strings were likely not exactly one hundred cash coins, depending on the inflation/ deflation of the period. The main trouble with cash coins their weight and bulk. The state banned the export of these coins. Song officials believed export would take away from the Imperial stockpile of precious metals and cause economic hardships if the coins were unavailable for the peasants to pay taxes. China used weighed amounts of gold and silver — never minted — for exchange.

In the eleventh century, the Song dynasty introduced paper money. This paper made trade easier. A merchant carrying many strings of cash would have been severely impeded by their sheer weight. This new paper money was backed by the state and further backed by promises of gold or silver. Just as in early Western paper monies, there was an admonition on the bill that stated that counterfeiters would be summarily killed. The introduction of paper money was a major first in the world of commerce and state power. Yet the Song printed too much money, leading to economic woes. When the **Mongols** conquered China they too tried their hand at paper money, this time backed with silk. The **Yuan dynasty** too overprinted the currency, and the system collapsed.

Under the Song, the Chinese economy changed rapidly and dramatically. Many forms of resource extraction became easier and cheaper. Paper making became quicker, and salt processing less laborious. The coal and iron industries grew markedly, becoming the most advanced the world. Coal usage and trade also increased as more coal was burned as forests were being depleted. When Marco Polo traveled to China during the Yuan dynasty, one of the most impressive things to him was the use of coal. The Chinese were also the first people in the world to use natural gas and crude oil for energy. These could be burned for heat or for light. Oil was not used in the West until the nineteenth century.

During this period, the city of Quanzhou, in Fujian province, overtook Guangzhou (Canton) as the main trading port of the Chinese Empire. Quanzho was not only a major center of Chinese culture, but also brought in other cultures to create a melded society. There was a large mosque in the city for its large Muslim population. In addition, two pagodas were built in the Indian style. In this manner, trade not only brought in physical goods, but also traditions and religions.

During and largely due to the Mongol invasions, the Chinese population fell dramatically. In 1220, it is estimated that 108 million people lived in China.

By 1229 this number fell to 75 million. Although China's population was still the largest in the world, this sharp decline badly damaged trade. To make matters worse, floods, droughts, and harsh winters made growing food more difficult, and the subsequent fall in food production led to starvation and malnutrition. Diseases such as the Black Death also assisted in the striking fall in the Chinese population. Yet all was not desolation. An awestruck Marco Polo visited Hangzhou during the Yuan (Mongol) dynasty. He called Hangzhou "the most noble city and the best that is in the world." And he had already travelled to the capitals of the Mongol empire for comparison. But China would come out of the Mongol with economic troubles.

Even with the Mongol domination and the other terrible circumstances, the silk and porcelain trade remained strong. In the south, cotton became a major cash crop. Although the Chinese had known about cotton since the third century, cotton growing expanded dramatically during the Southern Song Period and continued under the Mongols. The cotton trade made it easier to clothe the many peasants of China.

The conquest of the Mongols helped tie China indirectly to the West. With the Mongol Empire traversing from China and Korea all the way to central Europe, the one empire helped spread Chinese ideas to the West. But by putting the profits of trade in the hands of the middle man, the Yuan dynasty damaged the Chinese economy and hurt the reputation of foreigners and merchants. The Chinese emperors of the Ming dynasty would take actions to prevent merchants from gaining much power in the future.

One of China's most prevalent trading partners from the Tang to the Ming was the Arabs. With the expansion of the Arab empires, trade with China increased dramatically. The Arabs desired Chinese goods such as tea and silk. It is through the Chinese that peoples such as the Turks and the Arabs learned the secret of gunpowder. With their strategic location, the Arabs and later Turks were an excellent intermediary between China and Europe.

The Chinese government also needed trade to supplement its military. China needed to trade with central Asia for horses to build its cavalry. Usually the nomadic groups gelded the horses to prevent Chinese breeding programs. This lack of horses is ironic because the Mongols that invaded China were masters of cavalry. Lacking horses put the Chinese military and government at a large disadvantage and help explain the loss of the **Northern Song dynasty** and the victory of the Mongols.

Tea was a major trade item of China. Tea was a favorite drink of the elite and the poor. This drink also caught on in the West eventually. But it was nomads north of China that used tea as more of a food source than a drink and so purchased many tons of it across the **Great Wall**. Much of the tea was grown and transported from central China and Szechwan province. Tea leaves needed to be cured before they could be mixed with water. The tea was not only a major portion of the commercial society of China, but also served to improve public health. Because tea water needed to be boiled, many microorganisms that could have led to epidemics died. Tea is still popular in China today and is still exported.

The printing press was a Chinese invention not adopted in the West for many years. Although the press was a tremendous feat of science and literature, it was not a dominating force in China. Because calligraphy was highly prized and the fact that there were so many different Chinese characters, the usage of the printing press was seen as almost unnecessary. Calligraphers could be cheaply hired, and their work contained a more personal touch. The printing press became an important tool, however, for the printing of paper money and edicts.

Some scholars trained in economics wonder why China's society advanced to a money economy during the Song dynasty but did not make the jump to an industrial, capitalist one. Instead, the nation remained between medieval ways and modern ones. This is an ethnocentric way of looking at China. Capitalist development is not the only path to modernization. It turns out that in China there have always been so many people that it was cheaper to hire them than to build a machine to do the work of one hundred men. In addition, rents and loans to peasants paid landlords and moneylenders well—between 20 percent and 100 percent a year—that it made little sense to invest money in capitalist ventures that paid only 10 percent (and usually worse). Better to buy more land. Europe, with its dearth of people after the Black Death, turned to machines to keep society advancing. That was not the Chinese experience.

Although China did not trade overland as much as its geographical borders might suggest, it did trade with the nations south of the kingdom. Vietnam was an important trading partner, a key source of tin. Other lands of Southeast Asia brought to China tropical and other exotic woods. Chinese traders became familiar with these regions. To the northeast the Chinese traded with Korea and Japan, both by sea.

Chinese resource industries were helped by the fact that China contained many different geographical landforms of the world. With deserts, forests, an ocean, jungles, and mountains, all sorts of resources were available within one empire. Trade surpluses were maintained for centuries, even though they would later become large deficits, especially during the Yuan dynasty. With a uniform writing system, trade became easier. China's large population made the gathering of resources cheaper and more efficient.

Korea

Korea in many ways served as the direct conduit between its two larger neighbors: China and Japan. In many ways, Korea has been forced to play second fiddle to them in history, but in trade Korea has its own traditions. Chinese culture and goods traveled across the Yellow Sea to the Korean peninsula on its way to Japan. Because Korea is Japan's closest neighbor, often trade relations with China were done through Korea, whether divided into three kingdoms or unified into one.

Korea is best known for its ceramics trade. Korean ceramics are not only of great aesthetic quality but are unmatched for sheer quality. After adapting the technique of making porcelain from the Chinese, the Koreans made great strides in its production. The Koreans created inlaid porcelain, which enables better looking sculptures of higher quality. Although Chinese porcelain is much better known and traded in the Western world, Korean porcelain was of much higher quality. Quality is so much higher that historians today still revel in the level of skill of the medieval Koreans. The quality of thirteenth-century Korean porcelain would not be replicated in the West for almost 600 years.

Korean ceramics makers became a staple of the society. Many pieces of Korean earthenware still exist today. Their intricacy of designs and illustrations are such that even Chinese wares are nowhere near the quality. Ceramics were the most highest prized of Korean traded goods. Many different types of ceramic ware were made. These included tea cups (tea was imported from China), bowls, and figurines. Yet Chinese influence could be seen on many of Korea's ceramics. Korean earthenware, however, created its own identity as time progressed. It is this distinctiveness that helped Korea put its own name on ceramics and their trade. Often these pieces would be painted with slices of life or other parts of Korean culture. The most valuable were the celadon in different colors of green, or the light green glaze uniformly crackled that was developed after numerous mistakes.

In many ways, the ceramics industry was how Korea was best known. Stuck behind China geographically made it difficult for it to stand out. Trading of these ceramics helped buoy the Korean economy. Today, these porcelains are studied as classics.

Korea is home to native gold mines, making its trading capabilities far larger than its geographic size. Being home to gold and silver mines helped Korean precious metals be traded across the world even if its point of origin was not known. In addition, Korean jewelers made jewelry of the highest quality. There was much demand among the rich in Korean society for jewelry. Most of the people in medieval Korea were farmers.

During China's **Song dynasty** (960–1279) Korean trade boomed. In the harbor of Yesong, near the capital, major buying and selling occurred. Ships came in from as far as the Arab world. The Koreans were able to trade the Arabs fur, leathers, and porcelain. Trade with close neighbor Japan that started even earlier, in the mid-500s was brisk as the two neighbors built a lucrative business relationship, especially for religious art. Korea was able to carry on trade that went geographically far beyond East Asia. This is fortunate for the Koreans as it only bordered one state, China, and could have been dominated economically had the Chinese wanted to do so.

The Koreans' largest trading partner was its giant neighbor China. The Chinese considered the Koreans as a legitimate civilization, as it offered tribute to the current Chinese emperor. The Chinese traded Koreans silk, their own porcelains, and printed books. This is particularly important because Korea used the Chinese for writing official documents, so both could read what the other wrote. Korea did not develop its own alphabet that would last until the fifteenth century. To China, Korea sent gold, silver, and ginseng. The gold and silver trade was especially important due to the large number of gold and silver coins the empire minted. After the Chinese aristocrats began to buy foreign goods excessively, Chinese gold and silver disappeared. Thus Korean precious metal became even more valuable than before.

Korean boat makers were particularly skilled. When the **Mongols** invaded Korea and China they forced the Koreans build them two massive fleets to conquer the recalcitrant Japanese. With a nation surrounded by water on three sides, one can easily see why ship making became so important and widespread. Fishermen also used these well-crafted Korean boats and brought fish and shellfish onto the Korean markets. Once the Mongols were on the run, Korea went through a period of **Neo-Confucianism** that briefly treated merchants poorly.

Japan

Japan is even more geographically isolated than China. The islands of Japan are inhabited by people of Japanese ancestry who arrived from Korea. The Japanese trade relied exclusively on sea routes for trade, especially with the Koreans. The largest problem for Japan was its lack of a market system for so many centuries. It took convincing the other clans to allow the imperial family to rule, then copying the Chinese governing system before Japan would urbanize with one city—the capital Heijo (Nara), built out of wood to avoid earthquake problems in a scaled-down replica of China's Changan.

Early in Japanese history, much of the land was controlled by familial clans. During the Taika reforms of the seventh century, much of the land in the nation was nationalized through the **equal field system** borrowed from China. By doing this, much of the power of the clans was reduced. In addition, the state's power became greater as the only one able to tax. The first person to give his land to the state was Prince Naka No-Oe, the initiator of the Taika reforms. Under the Taika reforms, the land was to be redistributed to the peasants through a census. Each male over the age of 6 was to receive 2 tan of land, while females would receive one and one-third tan. Even after this redistribution, the administration of the land would be done by the local authorities. Nobles were entitled to more land under the redistribution than the poor. This land equalization, which kept the tax base intact, was supposed to take place every 6 years afterwards to avoid corruption. Yet the system would not survive 100 years.

The property tax was approximately 2 percent to 3 percent of its value per year, paid in kind. Religious institutions like Buddhist monasteries or temples were exempt. Peasants were also expected to perform **corvee** duties each year. Corvee is unpaid labor for the state. In this case, corvee was owed to the national government as well as the local one. Usually corvee was 10 days per year. However, it could be extended to up to 60 days, and if there were special projects peasants could be forced to work extra time.

In Japan, cities were not a natural occurrence. Although in other societies, cities were built and maintained as centers of trade, this did not occur in Japan during this time. With a lack of domestic or foreign surplus, trade was seen as unnecessary or ignored. However, the Japanese did develop its capital cities by copying their neighbors, the Chinese. The Japanese again copied the Chinese capital when building Heian (Kyoto).

The Taika reforms and equal field system soon fell into disuse. Many of the edicts surrounding it were simply not followed. Land redistribution started to fail as other groups of Japanese began to consolidate large tracts of land. Buddhists, aristocrats, and government officials were able to consolidate great amounts of tax-free land. With the lack of tax revenue and the dissolution of nationalized land, the central government became substantially weaker. This was a problem, as trade in luxuries had finally begun in Heian, especially in high-quality silks.

With the declining of the government came the rise of the warrior class, the bushi (origins of the samurai). War broke out, and the winner, the Minamoto family, started the **Kamakura Period**, ruling from near where modern Tokyo is today.

Under the 1232 Joei Code and Confucianism, Japanese society was broken down into four classes. These were the bushi, peasants, artisans, and merchants.

Under this system the upper classes were not given preferential treatment as compared to peasants. Land began to accumulate in the hands of the warriors as their power increased.

With the **Mongol** invasion came the weakening of the military class. They had not been rewarded for their meritorious service twice in defeating the Mongols. This gave rise to moneylenders. In 1297 an edict was made attempting to forgive all outstanding debt. Instead of solving the problem, this simply led to more disputes. Due to all of these circumstances, land became concentrated in the upper echelons of the military, rather than in the hands of any soldier.

During the fourteenth century, the standing of independent farmers increased. The state had less control over lands. Local constables began taking half of the land of owners. With corruption on the rise, the economic well-being of the average citizen diminished.

As with China and the rest of the world from 400 to 1400, the most common profession was farming. As in China, rice was the most common staple. However, under strict **Zen Buddhism** animal meat was forbidden to be consumed. However, the Japanese did eat fish, and some called birds "mountain fish" to consume them.

Unlike Korea and China, the Japanese imported porcelain during this period. Japan had little trade with the outside world during this time period. The Chinese did not favor trade for trade's sake, even though Japan desperately wanted Chinese goods and culture. To China, Japan did not have very many desirable goods. In addition, China saw the Japanese as simple barbarians. With China open to trading partners such as the Arabs, Europe, the Turks, and Vietnam, Japan's products seemed almost insignificant. Japan, did, however trade **samurai swords**, fans, and painted folding screens to China in exchange for Ming art and religious items. In the second half of the fourteenth century, Japan sent a series of trading ships to China. The Chinese saw this ship as bringing tribute instead of trading goods. However, this was still beneficial to the Japanese as the Chinese sent gifts back of greater value than those sent to China. Japan also had trade with its closest partner, Korea, especially in the sixth century.

One way that Japanese citizens made money was through the practice of piracy. These Japanese pirates would harass Chinese trading and fishing vessels. By using these tactics, Japanese pirates became a scourge on Chinese maritime activities, then the most advanced in the world. Piracy did not stimulate trade with China, and it would be two centuries before the Japanese closed their borders to foreign ships under the Tokugawa regime.

Further Reading

Benn, Charles. *Daily Life in Traditional China: The Tang Dynasty*. Westport, CT: Greenwood Press, 2002.

Gernet, Jacques. *Daily Life in China on the Eve of the Mongol Invasion, 1250–1276*. Stanford, CA: Stanford University Press, 1962.

Kim, Chewon, and Won-Yong Kim. *Treasures of Korean Art: 2000 Years of Ceramics, Sculpture, and Jeweled Arts*. New York: Harry N. Abrams, Inc., 1966.

Lvov, Norman Basil. *Japanese Daily Life from the Stone Age to the Present*. New York: Carlton Press, Inc., 1977.

Temple, Robert K. G. *China: Land of Discovery*. Wellingborough, UK: Patrick Stephens, Ltd., 1986.

4. THE ARTS

Describing the arts for three cultures as different as China, Korea, and Japan over a thousand-year period posses many problems. It is probably best to see "The Arts" as high art tied to the elite class, public art tied to politics or religion, and low art of the commoners. All three of these countries, but especially China, hold history in high regard, making the retelling of the past and historical fiction fertile grounds for storytellers in different media. In fact, some historical dramas are really meant to criticize current leadership, meaning playwrights can act as journalists or even politicians.

China

Three forms of art were considered necessary for the Chinese elite to learn: calligraphy, poetry, and painting. All three were completed with the same tools, unlike in the West: brushes and ink on either paper or silk. Sometimes ink of many colors would be used as a watercolor-style painting. Many times part of the painting would have poetry either describing the scene in the painting or elaborating on the feeling the painting was meant to evoke. But paper and silk deteriorate over time or can be victims of wars and other property destruction. Some Chinese works from pre-Yuan times survive only in Japan or in written descriptions.

The painter Gu Kaizhi (344–c. 406) attempted to frame the subject's essential character in his works. It is said that by adding three hairs to a man's chin Gu could depict the subject's inner wisdom. Perhaps Gu's most famous work is painted on silk, named "Admonitions of the Instructress to the Court Ladies." This artwork shows the tendency to practice all three arts together, because the panels of art alternate with text.

With the advent and rise of **Chan Buddhism** in the **Late Tang** and Song dynasties, monochrome art again took center stage. Simple black ink drawings of items like bamboo, or splashed ink onto silk to see its creation in a flash (with uninspiring versions thrown away). Eventually Chinese tired of or rejected the Chan Buddhist–inspired works (especially with the coming of **Neo-Confucianism**), although the Japanese continued to admire these paintings.

Evoking feelings did not mean all Chinese painters did not try to be "realistic" by trying to show a three-dimensional world or painting wondrous landscapes and nature in abundance. This was especially true of painters interested in **Daoism**. Oftentimes these landscapes would have small images of people, like a house, boat, or an old man, just barely visible. The paintings would also not lead the eye to any one place; all parts of the painting were to be perused. Fan Kuan (d. c. 1023) is perhaps best known for this style in his painting "Traveling among Streams and Mountains." In Fan's work, humans are placed in a smaller scope than of other artists. Fan painted the work in dark tones and used the painting to portray an unusually large setting, dramatizing the land.

Painting was so important to elites that "freshness" in Chinese art—meaning to try to be original in subject and style, especially important considering the number of sheer counterfeit paintings sold to collectors at the time—was reinforced at one point by an edict by the emperor. This edict stated that artists were not simply supposed to copy the style of those who preceded them, but instead artists should attempt to paint their subjects in the way in which they actually appear.

Calligraphy is one of the most frequent expressions of elite Chinese art, surviving more often than paintings. The Chinese written language is made up of over ten thousand unique characters; the old style of Chinese writing was a tapestry of inking. Only the richest segments of society were able to learn to read and fewer were able to create the magnificent calligraphy of the true gentleman.

Calligraphy flourished in China after the fall of the Han dynasty. Chinese calligraphy was one of the major outlets for the Chinese upper classes, taking simple writing and transforming it into a unique art form. According to one Tang scholar, one written character of Chinese was enough to show the onlooker the character of the writer. In these calligraphic traditions, flow and rhythm were more important to the writer than even legibility.

In Chinese society, it was considered imperative to a gentleman to be able to be able to write passable poetry. Although calligraphy required only a few words or a short phrase, poetry would be longer, and written in a more official style of characters to be easily legible to the literate. Poetry became an important vehicle of expression; even Korean and Japanese men would create poetry in Chinese. Poetry appeared on paintings, and for many paintings, only the poetry, reprinted in wood-block or type-set books (both Chinese inventions), survives to the present day. In fact, this poetic ability was required to pass China's **examination system**, during the Tang dynasty. As a result, there are over forty-eight thousand different poems preserved from the Tang dynasty by 2,200 different authors.

One of the seminal poets of the Tang was Du Fu (712–770). Du wrote in an altogether new style of poetry, a regulated verse called *lushi*: eight lines of five or seven characters per line, with rules about tone, rhyme, and parallelism. Du wrote about all sorts of subjects but was most famous for his compassionate stories of commoners. One of his most poignant poems tells of an army recruiter preparing to take a man for military service. Only two males remain in the village: an old man (in the process of fleeing) and an infant. A grandmother offers to go the army instead, insisting that she is useful because she can at least cook.

During the time of the Neo-Confucian revival, China experienced a new era in its history. During the **Song dynasty** (pronounced "soong"), a torrent of new poetry was created. In fact, at least 3,812 poems still exist. Much of this Song dynasty-era poetry focused on the difficulties encountered by ordinary Chinese. Some of these were set to song, which increased their familiarity — but it must be remembered that spoken Chinese differed from location to location, whereas written Chinese stayed the same, and that the tunes have not often survived to the present day. Other subjects that came up in Song poetry included remarks about government policy or other issues of the day.

Although some paintings, calligraphy, or poetry might become famous and pass into society as a whole, public art exists for the enrichment and education of the masses. In western portions of the Chinese Empire, Buddhism played an integral role along the **Silk Road** in caves made for adherents as well as proselytizing. Statutes of Buddha spread rapidly starting during the **Period of Disunity**, and even more so in the Tang dynasty, as emperors often commissioned the works. Chinese art was briefly influenced by India. Yet this "skinny

Buddha" would be replaced in future dynasties by the common "fat, happy Buddha"—Chinese could not explain through their culture how one so thin could be successful or content.

At the city of Keifing during the Festival of the Lanterns, statues of Buddhist gods were constructed for all to see. These popular deities were shown in thanks of another successful year. Dragons were paraded showing their green cloth exteriors. These dragons were made with wicker interiors and made to show jubilation. From a distance, these dragons looked not just almost realistic, but also as though they were actually flying. To a peasant, however, this was quite the sight. From his pavilion, the emperor shared in the good times.

Although many of the large-scale sculptures and buildings of the Tang Buddhists have not survived to the present day—or were sealed off to protect them, as happened along the Silk Road—historians are able to see smaller artworks that still exist. Many of these sculptures set in bronze are of the Buddha. The Buddha in these pieces of art are skinnier and in a more agile form than those prevalent later. This cultural transformation shows how Chinese culture accepted Buddhism into its foundation. As years progressed, the Buddha fattened up, as his aspects became uniquely Chinese, especially for those in **Pure Land Buddhism**.

Architecture, in the form of pagodas, was also descended from Indian architecture, copied by monks who made pilgrimages to India. The top of the *stupas*, or buildings containing Buddha's ashes, had many umbrella-like objects arranged on the roof, one on top of the other. So Tang dynasty pagodas featured floor with roofs made of colored tile alternating six, seven, or eight stories high; unfortunately, only copies of these structures still exist today in Japan. A few Song dynasty pagodas still remain, but most are from the **Ming dynasty** or later.

The Sui-Tang capital of Changan was planned before construction, intended to show the great power of China. At 30 square miles, it is the largest planned city in world history, allowing at least a million citizens. The layout of the city was intended to resemble the average Tang large house. There was a service area in the front where official business could be conducted and in the rear was a classic garden. Gardens on the properties of those rich enough to afford them included a pond. These gardens were meant to give the owner a sense of meditation, and the one built in the capital was meant to do this for the emperor. Architecture became a major part of the new capital. Places of worship were built for the Buddhism, Daoism, Zoroastrian, and even Christian faiths. However, the city lacked massive stone buildings, either to reflect feelings of the ephemeral popular in Buddhism or to prevent loss of life in the event of a major earthquake.

For the annual Chinese Festival of Lanterns, the common and noble people rejoiced for three days. There were troupes of dancers, as well as acrobats and singers. Often these performers danced or sang at the houses of rich citizens. However, even the urban poor could take part in the festivities. People often drank and sang during the nights as the city was lit up with charcoal, fireworks, and other fires. Celebrations seemed to unify Chinese society. Fancy costumes were crafted so that people could look their finest for the special days. Women wore special hats and went to see the celebrations. These special forms of wearable art were shown as sources of pride.

The victory of the Mongols over China coincided with the Golden Age of Chinese drama. At least 171 different Yuan plays survived to the present. One play from the thirteenth century was known as *The Romance of the Western Chamber*. This play by the writer Wang Shifu tells the tale of a romance between characters known as Ying-Ying, the girl, and Zhang, the boy. However, Ying-Ying's mother refuses to allow the two to marry. In an earlier Tang version, the play ends tragically. However, in this version, the play concludes happily for all characters, including the conniving mother of Ying-Ying. Apparently the Mongols wanted happy endings!

During this golden age of drama a recurring theme was of justice. One included that of a judge based on Bao Zheng (999–1062). This character stopped even the most well crafted schemes of the corrupt. Other times, however, heroes are outlaws, defying laws to fight for what they believe is right. One of the innovations and important portions of theatre during this time is the use of music. Characters are tasked with singing, including Autumn in the Palace of Han, where the emperor sings. Even in *The Romance of the Western Chamber* the characters sing accompanied by instruments.

On the streets of Chinese cities, performers such as comedians, storytellers, and shadow puppeteers could be seen, helping to explain dramatic or comical episodes in Chinese history to the illiterate masses. Others like jugglers, acrobats, rope-walkers, and performers of animal acts could be encountered. Many times these performers could be seen near marketplaces or the entrance of bridges. There, people of all different economic classes would come to see the acts. These performers were frequently hired by the wealthy for the benefit of all during official celebrations, like holidays. These performers were able to spread Chinese culture even to the peasants with elaborate plays or music. Fortunetellers and mediums were common in China, for everyone from widows to the emperor himself.

Put together street theater, acrobats, singing, and drama, and Chinese opera comes to mind. Slightly different in presentation in the different provinces throughout China, opera played an important roll in bringing ideas about **Confucianism**, Daoism, and Buddhism to the masses, as well as Chinese literature and history (oftentimes the same thing). These exciting stories combined music, song, dance, acrobatics, comedy, and drama to entertain and educate. Music was in five tones and used silk to act as strings in traditional Chinese instruments. To this day Chinese opera holds an important place for the jumping off point of Chinese film, especially the martial arts spectatulars.

Art is enjoyed by elites and commoners alike, but it also can be made to sell. The Chinese knew the secrets of silk making (sericulture) centuries before any one else; the same was true of paper and porcelain. As craftsmen are wont to do, Chinese working in silk and porcelain spent many hours perfecting their craft, and adding color and patterns to their work. Three-color Tang ceramics became very popular for elites, in China as well as abroad; the years that followed brought even more fame (and sales) to Chinese pottery makers and sellers. The reason was the innovation of high-temperature kilns with the clays and glazes to take advantage of these newer techniques. They heralded what came to be called "china" in the rest of the world, or officially "porcelain." During the Song dynasty, well-crafted porcelain became prevalent, both for tea-ware rich with iron glazing each piece turned out individually, patterns being difficult to imitate, to statuary of Buddhist **Bodhisattvas**, or Confucian and Daoist leaders. Innovation would continue after the brief Mongol Period of the **Yuan dynasty** in the Ming dynasty, with its whiter white and later famous blue and white glazing. These ceramics were sought after then and are especially sought-after now, with "Ming vases" almost a television cliché.

Korea

Art in Korea followed the China pattern, when it was not just copying the Chinese style. Art was for the wealthy, but that art tended to reflect Chinese tastes. Public art, especially for Buddhist purposes, became the most important art form for the common people to enjoy. In fact, Korea became so well known for its Buddhist art that Buddhist monks began coming to Korea from all over Asia, as far away as India, to partake in the Buddhist temples, statuary, and paintings.

In 400 C.E., Korea was divided into three different kingdoms. The largest, **Silla**, was known for being a land rich in gold. This advantage played well for the Korean economy, as well as its art. Korean aristocracy wore elaborate jewelry, particularly using this indigenous gold. And because Chinese influence came more often by sea to Silla, this jewelry showed a surprising amount of artistic talent.

Buddhism came to Korea from China in the fourth century, and its acceptance accelerated in the next century. And as Korea periodically became a tributary state, Koreans went to China where they brought back more Buddhist ideas, statues, and texts (in Chinese). Temples and statues began to spring up across the peninsula. This trend accelerated once Korea was unified under Silla, with temples made out of ever-present granite. In 806, however, King Aejang banned new temple construction. That energy to proselytize moved in a new direction: Buddhist monks spread Buddhist carvings across Korea, fashioned bronze bells, and made many more statues of the Buddha and **Bodhisattvas** (the latter often tied to Korean shamanist "gods"). This period became known as the golden age of Korean art, even if few if any statues appeared out of gold (or even bronze) compared to granite.

The last version of public art was in theory for the elite that could read, but of course writing made these ideas spread eventually to the masses through public readings, storytelling, and dramas. Like Japan, early Korea had not developed writing. Instead, the Korean language, which is not related to Chinese in any way, eventually used Chinese characters based on sounds to write "Korean," a system called *idu* (not used after the midfifteenth century). Educated Koreans thus could then write in Chinese and this form of Korean. Using woodblocks, the **Koryo** rendered a Korean version of the Buddhist cannon, first in 1087, and then, this version was destroyed by the Mongols (or lost, depending on the scholarly interpretation), a second was completed in 1251 and can still be viewed today. Koreans also created their first history, "History of the Three Kingdoms," in 1145. Finally, Koreans argue they invented moveable metal type in 1234, before the Chinese and two centuries before the Germans.

However, the artwork that medieval Korea is best known for is its ceramics, of course influenced early on by neighboring China. These ceramics were considered of high quality and would sell to traders for transport abroad. Much of the pottery made in Korea was fired in "tunnel kilns" carved into a hill or mountainside.

Silla pottery was very elaborate, and the most exquisite examples come from the Three Kingdoms Period (for our purposes, 400–668). These ceramics include figurines of people and animals. Despite their small size, some of the statuettes still exist today, taken by archeologists from burial mounds. One of the most frequent forms of Silla ceramics found in burial sites was ceremonial urns, which became more prevalent after the introduction of Buddhism.

Ceramic roof tiles were used all across Korea, just as they were in ancient Rome. These tiles were used not only for religious sites or palaces, but also at places in the countryside. Some of these tiles were elaborately decorated and created as a form of art. One of the most popular decorations on the tiles was the lotus. Another was a face of a demon, meant to distract evil spirits.

During the time of the Silla Korea (668–918), Korean pottery began to use glazes, an idea borrowed from China. But the more elaborate tombs now favored by rich Koreans made grave robbing easy, so there are much fewer examples extant, even though some experts believe this period is the most truly "Korean" for the making of pottery and ceramics. It would be the next era, Koryo, when ceramics from Korea get their rightful fame. Even though the porcelain in the tenth and eleventh centuries reflect a great deal of borrowing from Song China, the Chinese highly prize these wares, considering them immensely well crafted. Ceramic experts claim they are among the most beautiful porcelains ever made!

Koreans exported many examples of celadon porcelain during the Koryo Period. It made an important contribution to the world of ceramics. By using this forgotten method, Korean pottery was able to become the prettiest, most complex in the world, especially that made in the eleventh century. Despite the heavy influence of Song China porcelain, celadon adopted a more Korean character over the next several centuries. In fact, celadon was the most widely made ceramic of Korea during this time. Three basic types remain the most popular forms of celadon. First is the differing green colors obtained from an iron oxide glaze difficult to duplicate. The more popular objects tend to be a celadon with soft green color, compared to the skies of the Korean peninsula during the fall, or, more commonly, to jade. The second form still uses this beautiful light green color, but through a controlled "mistake," potters create a cracked pattern throughout the glaze over the piece. This form is called crackle glaze. Finally, the most distinctive celadon were decorated by overlaying glaze on contrasting clay bodies. Artists inlaid designs made up of small pieces of different colored clay adhered to the base clay of the piece. The layers were then carved away to reveal varying colors. Still, regardless of the popularity of celadon, other types of porcelains, including painted pieces, were also created.

However, Korean pottery suffered a severe setback with the Mongol invasions of the thirteenth century. With the coming of the **Mongols** came the diminishing of Korean sovereignty and culture. Degradations of quality can be seen not only in Korean celadon, but also in their porcelains and other ceramics as well. Koreans were well aware that ideas from abroad and conquerors from abroad can mean the difference between art spreading outward or skills being diminished.

Japan

Japan was separated from other civilizations by the ocean. However, Japan was also indelibly changed by cultural diffusion. From the start to the end of the period in question, Japan borrowed ideas from China and Korea, except in those times when the sea connection was breached—when China or Korea faced internal disorder or when the **Mongols** controlled them. Buddhism and **Confucianism** took Japanese elites by storm. In terms of the arts, Japan was influenced greatly by Chinese painting, sculpture, and architecture, for example. In early Heian architecture one can see foreign designs clearly showing the Chinese **Tang dynasty** influence. In fact, Tang-era buildings are better represented in Japan than China, due to losses to the tall Tang pagodas through war and earthquake. In Japanese sculptures, wood replaced the more traditional Chinese mediums of clay, bronze, and stone. Sometimes these sculptures were painted. However, the onlooker was to see the original wood grain.

Japan's first system of writing came over the Sea of Japan from China, most likely by way of Korea. Japanese elites had to learn Chinese to have writing. This system of symbols represented words instead of sounds. From these characters arose an original Japanese form of calligraphy. Just as in China, the writer's character and intellectual setting could be gleaned from the way that they drew characters. Japanese women, however, likely did not learn Chinese. They, or perhaps the famous monk Kukai, leader of Shingon Buddhism exposed to syllabaric languages in India, simplified a small number of Chinese characters to create a sort of alphabet so Japanese could be written. Unlike in other cultures, East and West, women wrote most of the Japanese literature from around 1000 onward.

The world's first novel was Japan's *Tale of Genji* by Lady Murasaki (her given name is unknown), written probably from 1008 to 1021. This novel has been translated into modern Japanese (and many other languages) and is still read to this day. It is a source of Japanese cultural pride, although attacked at first due to the sexual conduct in the book. The story takes place over 75 years, following three generations of the imperial family and five hundred characters in fifty-four chapters originally written in haphazard order, most likely to amuse ladies of the court and not for publication. The story became famous because the beautiful poetry—for a long time considered the only important Japanese language literature—written within the sprawling tale. Only later it became an icon as the first book in Japanese.

In brief, *Tale of Genji* is a story about looking for love where it is forbidden or unlikely to be found. The hero is not one by standard Western definition. His heroism lies in his capacity to be deeply moved and emotional through poetry, painting, music, and affairs of the heart. Most important, the novel helps to explain the aesthetics of Heian Japan, at least for the 5 percent of elite Japanese living in the capital. Elite women have their eyebrows shaved and drawn on higher than before and their teeth blackened. They wear many layered robes of fine colored silk but can be almost mortally embarrassed if one layer does not quite match the rest. Instead of the tune, the smell, or the sight, Heian Japanese elites, in contrast to Chinese, admired the transient nature of life heard in the last few notes of a song fading away, fragrance wafting on the breeze, or shadows present at dusk or dawn.

For Buddhist monks practicing esoteric Shingon Buddhism under Kukai, one form of art borrowed from abroad but manipulated for the monastic Japanese audience was the mandala. These mandalas were painted, trying to represent the universe as an art form including the Buddhas and Bodhisattvas. In the center of the "Womb Mandala," a lotus is situated in the center, to represent the heart of the universe. In the "Diamond Mandala," a full 1,314 different deities are represented. Kukai believed that words could not explain Shingon Buddhism, a special sect of Buddhism that would not survive long after his passing. Instead pictures would make the intellectual and emotional understanding of Shingon more easily.

The **Heian Period** came to a violent end with the rise of a warrior culture. These fighting men, slowly given the name samurai, began to engage with **Zen Buddhism**. Zen is all about making right actions, staying in the moment, and not worrying about death, all things a warrior needs to do. With the spread of Zen Buddhism came Zen gardens. These creative uses of rock and sand were meant to be true representations of patience and the awe of creation.

Like in China, drama flourished in medieval Japan but became a different aesthetic experience during the Ashikaga Period. The **noh** form of drama became popular in the fourteenth century, growing out of folk dances that paid homage to **Shinto** gods to provide an abundant harvest. In noh plays, again an upper-class phenomenon, Zen Buddhist simplicity reigned. The stage sits open on three sides, with the only background scenery an old pine tree painted on a wall. An all-male cast, with the lead either wearing a mask or holding his face frozen as if he has a mask, expresses feeling by symbolic gestures and movements while wearing a brilliant costume. The actors are accompanied by a chorus that chants narration in sing-song voices to help explain what is going on. The noh experience included five or six plays, which lasted for 6 hours, usually divided between stories about a god, a warrior, a woman, an insane person, and a demon.

As for samurai going to war, the samurai's entire outfit was a work of art. Helmets and decorative armor showed different creativity across the main three southern islands of Japan. Above all, the sword of the samurai was immensely prized. Many samurai believed the sword a living object, imbued with supernatural powers. Japanese sword makers were revered as an honored class in society. These crafters went through elaborate ceremonies while creating these masterworks, the highest quality swords ever made. To make the blade, these sword makers followed an elaborate method of alternating layers of soft and hard steel to provide a sword with flexibility and superior sharpness. These special warrior swords were highly prized family heirlooms, passed down from generation to generation. They also fetched high prices when sold to China or Korea.

Japanese folding fans were invented in the seventh century. The Japanese creator modeled the fan after the physiology of a bat. At the imperial court, emperors would give folding fans away. Many times these fans were adorned with a favorite poem, a family crest, or a certain painting, all only visible when opened. Folding fans were too expensive for the common people of Japan, as were samurai swords, but both proved valuable for Japan to trade China or Korea for Buddhism texts, statuary, and porcelain. Japan's arts were thus mostly for elites, no matter their origin.

Further Reading

Benn, Charles. *Daily Life in Traditional China: The Tang Dynasty*. Westport, CT: Greenwood Press, 2002.

Frederic, Louis. *Japan, Art and Civilization*. New York: Harry N. Abrams, Inc., 1971.

Gernet, Jacques. *Daily Life in China on the Eve of the Mongol Invasion, 1250–1276*. Stanford, CA: Stanford University Press, 1962.

Kim, Chewon, and Won-Yong Kim. *Treasures of Korean Art: 2000 Years of Ceramics, Sculpture, and Jeweled Arts.* New York: Harry N. Abrams, Inc., 1966.

Sickman, Laurence, and Alexander Soper. *The Art and Architecture of China.* Baltimore: Penguin Books, 1956.

5. SOCIETY

To explore East Asian society, it is necessary to do two things: describe **Confucianism** and its role in ordering society and specify individually each of society's layered components, starting from the lowest (household), and conclude with how those lower layers interact on the state level. This method will not yield a perfect description of society. First, the thousand years of this study means many changes in society occurred: we will have to look at what was true for a longer time than not. This essay's length also does not allow for regional or ethnic variation. In China, besides the majority Han people, are people living in China for centuries, many who look the same to the foreign eye, but whose cultures were (and are) significantly different. The Hakka and Uighurs are two quick examples, the former an ethnic group of north China pushed into southern China and becoming a boating culture, and the latter a nomadic group from the far west along the **Silk Road**. Even Japan has the Ainu, the original inhabitants of the four great islands, pushed north and east to Hokkaido by 1400. And the society's description will be based on times where government was reasonably stable, not always true in China for over a third of the years in question.

Confucianism, one of the three great philosophical/religious traditions of East Asia, had by 400 indoctrinated the Chinese at all levels of society and even government, by 500 heavily influenced the different Korean states and their inhabitants, and by 600 had started converting the Japanese, helping create their nascent state. Confucianism in its simplest conception attempted to provide the alleged order of the past to the present so people understood their place in family and society, thus mitigating the possible chaos of the times. Thus it proposed a hierarchical system, the idea of knowing one's place in society with patriarchy and filial piety (respect for one's parents). These ideas became explicit in Confucianism's Five Relationships: ruler to subject, father to son, husband to wife, elder brother to younger brother, and friend to friend. Notice that all the relationships but the final one showed hierarchy. Women only fit into the system in a subordinate role (as wife). Each of these relationships was reciprocal, however, with the subordinate owing the superior respect and obedience, while the superior owed the subordinate benevolence. A benevolent ruler might forgive taxes from a drought-stricken region, for example.

Benevolence and ritual played key roles in Confucianism. In fact, benevolence under Confucianism is similar to the golden rule of Western thought, only in the negative form: "Do not do unto others what you would not wish yourself." Those below needed to treat you with loyalty and obedience, performing the proper rituals. These included 3 years of mourning when a parent died as part of filial piety. The ruler needed to observe the correct rituals for the state to please the gods and allow his rule to continue. But ritual should not be observed blindly; real, sincere feeling had to occur during the rites or they were useless.

Confucianism placed emphasis on good government, morality, and ethics. The ruler, like the father, also served as a model of behavior, teaching morality through his actions. Confucius did not believe laws prevented immorality; laws just created criminals. If those at the top of the social hierarchy acted morally and with benevolence, the lower ranks of society would behave well and not cheat or steal. Chinese government ignored this aspect of Confucianism, believing it too optimistic, as it ignored Confucius's hope that a scholar-official would be allowed to rule.

The household serves as the lowest level of society. As a moralistic society, albeit with a specific law code for most of its history, China often kept track of its subjects through household registration (listing members of the household older than the age of 5 with their respective occupations), whether to implement positive projects like the **equal field system**, taxation systems like the **corvee**, or collective responsibility programs like the *li-jia* system, where any criminals not apprehended would result in punishment of many families for the crime. At the very bottom of the Confucian hierarchy within the household were girls and women (*see* **Women, role of**).

Throughout East Asian traditional society, the birth of a girl was not as happy a day as the birth of a boy. Male children were needed to continue the family name and take care of the ancestors, including the parents in old age and then death. In difficult times for the poorest peasant family, a daughter might be the victim of infanticide or be sold into service or prostitution (or concubinage in China if an elite could be found that wanted more permanent sexual partners). The girl would then have to work until adulthood (and perhaps beyond) as a poorly treated maid, or become one of the extra wives or concubines of a rich, old man, the difference being a concubine could be bought and sold.

The first 7 years for a daughter—assuming no infanticide or the regular deaths children faced in the years before modern medicine—were probably the most joyful. East Asian families let children of both sexes—although perhaps allowing even more freedom for boys—play, with a little work thrown in the more poverty a family faced. Seven years did not mean seven Western years, however, children's ages were measured one for the birth, one at the first lunar New Year, and another year every lunar New Year, so a child 7 years of age might be only 5 years old in the Western reckoning.

The years of childhood after age 7 meant hard work, within the home with domestic tasks if the family had some money and in the fields and in the home if part of a poor-to-average peasant family. The family might make clothes to wear or sell out of local materials, be they hemp, cotton, or silk. And if a girl was not sold to a wealthy family or worse a brothel, she would expect to marry. A middle-income peasant family (or wealthier) would employ a matchmaker to find a suitable wife for their son from a neighboring village. If wealthy, the tie with another wealthy family would insure the continued prosperity of both. If normal peasants, an agreeable match would be all that was necessary. If poor peasants, the family might just seek someone from a nearby village. When the potential groom's family of average peasant status or higher was satisfied with the match, it would send to the bride's family a set of traditional, symbolic gifts like lacquer and glue to show the joining of the two in marriage, as well as a small dowery for the loss of a worker in the bride's home.

The newlywed was usually just a teen-aged girl who had no choice over her marriage partner, and this part of life was the most difficult, especially if married to the eldest son or a family wealthy enough to own a house and land for all the brothers to benefit from. Not only would she be expected to start a family and have children (hopefully sons) almost immediately—with all the dangers childbirth entailed—she was also run ragged by her new mother-in-law who had her working almost as hard as a slave. Because three generations—the father and mother, the newlyweds, and their new children—all lived under the same roof in an average peasant and higher family, the mother-in-law had the power as the elder and often abused that power. She would complain that the new wife was useless and did not do her chores properly. There were cases of suicide or fleeing back to her parents' home due to this cruelty, which ironically the mother-in-law no doubt herself endured when she was a newlywed. Conditions would likely improve upon the birth of a son, and of course the mother was owed respect by her children (and her nephews and nieces, if not adults yet). The birth of a series of daughters might lead her in-laws to send her back to her parents, divorced for not producing an heir or for lousy cooking (see **Food**)! But a new wife of a second son of average peasant background or lower would avoid the outward sadistic treatment—or just passive aggressive behavior—living in a home without a mother-in-law.

The woman's middle years were still times of difficulty and sadness: surviving multiple births and experiencing the likely death of some of her children. If a peasant, she kept the home as well as worked the fields. If an elite, she might get some education to pass on to her sons and daughters, and before the **Song dynasty** and **Neo-Confucianism**—which often confined her in her own home because of **footbinding**—she might play a role running the family or extended family.

Becoming a mother-in-law as her eldest son married and brought his new wife to live in the home was the high point of many East Asian women's lives. But it also meant, as she and her husband kept aging, her husband might die first. The life of an East Asian widow could go in two directions. If she had a son, her son and daughter-in-law would be expected to care for her until death. If she did not have a son, and lacked money after her husband's death, life would turn out full of difficulties. Widows were forbidden to marry, so could not hope to have a second family if their husbands died first.

The eldest son within the household held the highest status for his generation or lower—as seen in the Five Relationships—and he could expect to lead the house when his eldest son was old and wise enough to take control of the family. But there were expectations placed on the eldest son, as in most cultures, particularly taking care of aged parents and generations that preceded his: the so-called **ancestor worship**. If in a rich peasant or higher household, he was also responsible for taking care of his younger siblings, although he did have a large measure of control over them in matters such as marriage. A rich family would also invest in education, learning to read and write, as well as how to understand the Confucian classics. Government positions, starting in the early **Tang dynasty** with around one-third of such positions, soon required passing through the **examination system**. By the late Song, all jobs needed degree holders, and the study of Neo-Confucianism.

China's household system comes to the fore in legal matters. If a member of a household commits a crime of violence or property, the perpetrator usually confesses. If not, the leader of the household might pressure him to confess. If that did not work, the state would torture a confession out of him. Punishment would shame the criminal, and most important his family, as this local level justice had its greatest effect on the family's reputation.

A group of households made up a village. The imperial government could not reach down far enough to appoint officials at this, or even district level, in an era of slow transportation and nonexistent modern communication technology. The richest and most established family's head would lead the village as a gentry, whose jobs (usually unpaid by the state) included tax collector, police, and judge, all in one. It made sense therefore that not all the local tax revenue made it to imperial coffers. The villagers, especially those living in south China, also needed to work together to get the crops planted and harvested. This was even more true in the south, because farming rice takes much coordination throughout the growing season—when to plant, flood fields, dry fields, and harvest worked better when villagers worked as a team. And of course the corvee needed to be dealt with in a fair manner at the village level to avoid one family losing more than one worker at a given time.

The next step up, a group of villages, would have a centralized market within a few hours, sometimes a small town and other times just another village. There peasants could exchange news, gossip, and goods, not to mention finding eligible marriage partners for their children. If a town, it had a wall around it, so landowners could live in relative safety from unhappy tenant farmers (or nomadic invasions, if in north China). In the early years of Chinese unification, one market town (or just "market village") and its assorted villages likely made up a district, the highest level of government still controlled by local gentry. In the middle of a successful dynasty, with the resulting population explosion, it might be four or more market towns/series of villages in the district, all run by a local gentry. At this level in China, the Confucian class hierarchy came into use. The four classes, from top to bottom, were the scholars (essentially gentry—those who owned land but rented it out rather than cultivate it themselves), peasants, artisans, and merchants. This hierarchy had nothing to do with wealth, but on importance Confucians placed on the profession for helping the state. Peasants, except for a brief period in the Song dynasty, provided the majority of the taxes for China (or any East Asian premodern country) through **agriculture**, not even counting the food grown by the hard-working class. Artisans were tolerated, but Confucianists never trusted merchants, considering any profit they made to be theft or at the very least unfair dealings—after all, merchants created wealth by buying low and selling high. Not on this descending scale because Chinese considered them so unimportant or unsavory were soldiers, bandits, prostitutes, and other undesirables. But this is a class system, not a caste system. It was possible to move within this hierarchy within one's lifetime, or more important, move one's family within a generation or two. All it took was hard work and luck to become a rich peasant and perhaps leading gentry of a village, or intelligence with education to pass the exams and become a scholar-official at the central government level.

In Korea and Japan, the Confucian hierarchy was different—and much more permanent—in part because these two countries never eliminated hereditary offices like China did by the time of the Song dynasty (except for the emperor). Korea's hierarchy placed at the top the civil officials and the military officers, together called the *yangban* (the two orders). Next came a small group, the *chungin* (middle people), lower ranking government officials. Below these hereditary aristocrat ranks came the commoners and peasants called the *yangmin* (good people), whose taxes and corvee labor supported the government and aristocracy. Their poverty was obvious: trade was conducted usually in barter. At the very bottom, making up at least thirty percent of the population, were the *chonmin*. The "lowborn" were made up of slaves descended matrilineally, government workers in mines and porcelain factories, and workers made outcast because of Buddhism, like the **burakumin** in Japan: butchers, tanners, leatherworkers, and entertainers. Japan's four steps of the class system resembled China's, but the top of the class structure changed from the early years (starting c. 700) with the effete aristocracy on top and to the warrior class for Japan's militarized period after 1185. The rest of the hierarchy followed China's, and outside the list were the entertainers and finally the burakumin, so outcast that contemporary maps did not reveal their villages.

In China, all classes mixed in the many urban centers, cities walled off from the countryside that allowed for traded goods to move and be sold throughout the huge empire. The small size of Korea and Japan relative to China meant that trade had not progressed to the imperial level. In fact, most trade in Korea and Japan was by barter. Most spectacularly were the capitals of China's various dynasties, all facing south. These cities could hold a million-plus subjects and were defended by miles of city walls and towers. Japan decided that capitals are what countries needed, so they created capitals on the model of China, but on a reduced scale without walls. Koreans also copied Chinese capital cities.

The top ranks of the hierarchy ran their respective countries through inherited position in the case of Korea and Japan, and by the examination system in China for much of the period in question (save the emperor, of course). Passing a series of examinations, usually on Confucianism, allowed the degree-holder the right to be placed in the numerous positions the central government staffed. The early Tang dynasty divided China into first ten (later fifteen) large circuits that resemble modern day provinces in their borders; over 350 prefectures; and more than fifteen hundred counties managed by magistrates and other officials, the lowest part of the central bureaucracy chosen by exam. There were rules about how to choose these officials: they could not be from the same area as the job; they had to change positions periodically; and they could not work with assistants from their same region.

For the top degree-holders with experience, or mandarins, central government positions in the capital would be the ultimate promotion. Under the emperor were three departments: Department of State, Imperial Secretariat, and the Imperial Chancellery. The last, under the chancellor, was next in command after the emperor and served as a chief advisor. The Secretariat helped create policy and write imperial decrees. The main, daily, essential tasks of government were entrusted to the Department of State, which included six ministries: Officials, Finance, Rites, Army, Justice, and Public Works. The Ministry of Officials appointed, promoted, and demoted the officials that helped run the government through the use of the examination system. The Ministry of Finance gathered both census data and the taxes that allowed the state to function. The Ministry of Rites attended to Confucian, Buddhist, and Daoist matters, including state ceremonies and rituals. These state rituals became increasingly important over the years as emperors moved away from the public worship of their own imperial ancestors, and these public ceremonies became the way to show the emperor was the father of the nation in a very Confucian manner, and thus held the **mandate of heaven**. The Ministries of Army, Justice, and Public Works all functioned as might be expected by their names, with the exception that the Ministry of Army dealt with the organizing the military just in times of peace.

In a few dynasties, the Confucian scholars at the top of the government faced an implacable foe: the **eunuchs**. Originally created to guard the emperor's wives and concubines, there numbers sometimes grew and were used as secret police to help certain heirs realize their dreams of becoming emperor, only to find out too late that the eunuchs would continue to control them, even on the throne itself. If the dynasty's emperors were smart enough to avoid using eunuchs, palace intrigue might continue, but this time between consorts, wives, and concubines and their respective children. That is not to say that Confucian scholars/government officials were blameless when it came to law breaking, especially corruption. One could argue that a Confucianist's first duty is to provide for his family, so stealing a small percentage of tax receipts would be in keeping character rather than an immoral, illegal act frowned upon by his colleagues.

Just because the focus to this point has been on Confucian order does not mean **Daoism** and Buddhism not are practiced by the Chinese, or that Buddhism does not have an especially important influence on elite Koreans and Japanese. None of the religions mentioned, even Shinto in Japan or Korean shamanism, require repudiation of other faiths. One could be married in Japan through a Shinto wedding and be laid to rest in a Buddhist funeral. The focus is on Confucianism more because of the three traditions, it is the least religious and plays a larger role in the secular world than the other two or indigenous religions. Besides, for the lower classes that make up the majority of the populations, Buddhism and Daoism are too intellectual for much of the 400 to 1400 years. However, for those Confucianists so entrenched in the government—and for those who could not get government positions due to the lack of them or through failure at some point in the examination system—retirement meant moving to a more secluded part of the empire and starting the practice of Daoism. It might not be **Religious Daoism**, with its fixation on finding the magical elixir to live forever, although it might. It might just be the fondness for nature, painting, and obscure poetry inspired so much by Daoist thought.

The intellectualism of Buddhism slowly waned with the introduction and growing property in East Asia of **Pure Land Buddhism**. It believed the world was in terrible shape. Luckily Buddha had foreseen this and explained secretly to a few followers that one specific **Bodhisattva** (being of wisdom) could help ordinary people achieve enlightenment instead of the "hard" way by becoming a monk or nun. By believing in his saving grace and reciting his name (*Amituofo Buddha* in Chinese, *Amita* in Korean, and *Amida* in Japanese) in true devotion, a follower could be reborn in the land of paradise, the Pure Land of the West. Many Asians did not understand this stay was temporary, assuming the Pure Land was heaven. Theoretically they would come back to earth as Bodhisattvas and help others obtain enlightenment before permanently seeking it themselves. Just at the high point of Pure Land Buddhism in China, Emperor Wuzong defrocked over 250,000 Buddhist monks and nuns (leaving only forty-nine monasteries and eight hundred monks), sold off their lands, destroyed 4,600 temples, and wrecked forty-thousand shrines. His death in 846 saved Buddhism in China, but not Pure Land; instead Chan Buddhism (called

Seon or Son Buddhism in Korea and Zen Buddhism in Japan) gained adherents to be the most popular form of Buddhism in China. Even though this form of Buddhism was really for monks willing to put hours and hours of meditation to work, churches of Chan sprung up in China. It must be remembered that however peaceful Buddhism proclaims itself, in Chinese history secret Buddhist societies have helped organized disgruntled (or starving!) peasants to fight against the state, and in the long run have become successful.

That revolutionary impulse of Buddhism is not really found in Korea or Japan. Korea first accepted Buddhism early from China and were the key cultural transmitters of it to Japan. Silla Korea, as the imitation Tang dynasty, government also controlled the Buddhist orders and temples. It used art, dance, music, and literature to try to bring Pure Land Buddhism to the masses. Only in the fourteenth century did Chan overtake Pure Land in popularity in Korea. Pure Land Buddhism came to Japan much later, during the wars to conclude the **Heian Period**. It pushed its adherents to chant "Namu Amida Butsu," or nembutsu when said quickly. It required ten pure moments to achieve the help from Amida, along with one's good works. Only a few years later, during the start of the **Kamakura Period**, a splinter group called True Pure Land Buddhism also pushed chanting the nembutsu. Its difference lay in priests being able to marry (priests inherited control of the church) and in how only through the hard work of Amida could one achieve rebirth in the Pure Land. A criminal, because of his evil, was closer to being sent to the Pure Land if he only believed because nothing he did in his life would warrant such a reward. Nothing but the nembutsu and the gift granted by Amida would allow entrance into the Pure Land. These two forms together quickly became the most popular sect of Buddhism in Japan.

The change in sects of Buddhism practiced in Japan also helps explain the change in the treatment of the people. When heavily esoteric forms of Buddhism dominated the capital, the aristocrats treated the peasants as animals and ignored them whenever possible. What these Heian Period aristocrats considered beautiful was not necessarily the obvious. Instead of the tune, the smell, or the sight, Heian Japanese elites, in contrast to Chinese, admired the transient nature of life heard in the last few notes of a song fading away, fragrance wafting on the breeze, or shadows present at dusk or dawn. Because marriages were arranged as part of political expedience, men and women in Heian Japan apparently had many secret affairs, tales of courtly love. But a man would fall in love with a women not based on her beauty—women often hid behind screens when courting—but on her writing style or poetry recited. Genji excelled at dance, poetry, and calligraphy, and could cry in front of people should his love be out of reach. Genji is not a hero by standard Western definition that always puts his feelings out of reach to fight the bad guy.

Buddhism and these forms of aesthetics did not push into the lower classes for many centuries to come. Once the military took control of Japan from the twelfth century onward, the introduction of Pure Land Buddhism became very popular among the peasantry. But the warrior, and some artists, pursued **Zen Buddhism** instead. Although meditation had long been a practice of Japanese Buddhists, it was not until the twelfth century that Zen first arrived in Japan from China. It pushed the ideas of meditation and *koans* (literally "public cases," but really logic puzzles meant to snap the mind out of its harmful logic), the keys needed for enlightenment. Warriors became the chief nonmonk practitioners of Zen, needing the clarity of meditation, the elimination of fear of death, and the ability to make repetitive moves until one could attack without thinking. Zen also had a large impact on Japanese arts and culture of common folk, including **noh theater**.

As can be seen, East Asian societies share far more than they differ, at least in the period 400 to 1400. The Confucian-based system of control—in the family, village, and country—does not stop the practice of other religious traditions in China, Korea, or Japan. But there are major differences. The warrior on top of the Korea and late Japan hierarchy contrasts with the Chinese soldier far below even fourth place. Chinese soldiers behaved little better than bandits. It is bandits that Chinese peasants often became when high taxes and a brutal economy left them landless and without hope, living where two provinces come together to avoid patrols from either area. It made sense that Confucianists, so enamored with order, would look down on those who could challenge such order. Usually the dynastic cycle, as explained in the "Historical Overview" section, meant the dynasty had little time left once the bandits became prevalent, and a new dynasty with renewed effort to help the poor peasants for a generation would occur.

Further Reading

Benn, Charles D. *Daily Life in Traditional China: The Tang Dynasty*. Westport, CT: Greenwood Press, 2002.

Dien, Albert E. *State and Society in Early Medieval China*. Stanford, CA: Stanford University Press, 1990.

Ko, Dorothy, JaHyun Kim Haboush, and Joan R. Piggott. *Women and Confucian Cultures in Premodern China, Korea, and Japan*. Berkeley: University of California Press, 2003.

Lvov, Norman Basil. *Japanese Daily Life from the Stone Age to the Present*. New York: Carlton Press, 1977.

6. SCIENCE AND TECHNOLOGY

China

China led the world in science and technology for centuries. Some historians have wondered why it was not China in the fifteenth century to discover the rest of the world (instead of the Europeans), or why capitalism did not develop until China was turned into a semicolony at the end of the nineteenth century. Both questions make the mistake of assuming that the path taken by European countries to trade and conquer the world or move from feudalism to capitalism was the "normal" path. It turns out that two of China's greatest strengths for the longest time—**Confucianism** and its population—would serve to prevent either from occurring. It proved cheaper to hire a man to do heavy lifting than to build a machine. More money could be made owning and renting out land than traditional corporations pay to investors. Confucian distrust of merchants prevented continuing exploration or even the ships necessary for long-distance trade. An empire has more to react to than a small nation-state; tremendous Chinese borders needed defending for thousands of miles, more than an individual Western European nation could imagine. Finally, although these inventions were first created and used in China, that fact does not preclude independent creation 1,000 years later by Europeans for many of the items. Obviously, silk, paper, gunpowder, porcelain, and the compass all came across the **Silk Road** to Europe long before they spurred on Europeans to try and make these items themselves.

Several technological innovations predating the fifth century in China are worth mentioning before describing the advances between 400 and 1400. Silk and sericulture developed approximately 2700 B.C.E. remained a secret of the Chinese culture for millennia. Paper made out of cotton and plant fiber for writing was probably invented in 105; earlier versions were used for protecting bronze mirrors or making paper clothing (including shoes), blankets, and even armor. The Chinese also used it for sanitary purposes like toilet paper. Cast iron allowed China to make iron tools in large numbers by the fourth century B.C.E. The waterpower made smelting easier by 31 C.E. The waterwheel was in widespread use by the third century to mill minerals and grain. Related to the waterpower and invented in the fourth century B.C.E. were pneumatic and hydraulic pistons. Three hundred years later came the belt drive (first century B.C.E.). Pistons and the belt drive were not seen in Europe for at least another 1,500 years. Chinese used the chain pump—an application of the waterwheel to move water, rather than power other machinery—to irrigate land. The Chinese developed a system of agriculture for intensive hoeing and row cultivation—not endorsed in Europe until the eighteenth century—in the sixth century B.C.E. In addition to the iron hoe, made possible through cast iron, the efficient harnessing of horses for the plow or transport of crops improved the efficiency, although farm animals proved much less common historically in China than Europe. The now-familiar collar harness may have been in use as early as the first century B.C.E., as was steel made from cast iron and the drilling for and use of natural gas.

Mathematics was already highly advanced by the fifth century. Decimals, places, zero, pi, extraction of higher roots, negative numbers, algebra of geometry, were all long in use far before Europe or even the Arab world.

The compass had been in use since the fourth century B.C.E., with the great advancement of having the magnetized needle floating in water to allow more accurate readings developed by the eighth century. It should come as no surprise that Chinese science had discovered and studied the declination of the earth's magnetic field in the ninth century, even though the Chinese used their compass to determine south. By the eleventh century, Chinese scientists understood that heating or cooling iron influences its magnetic field. That same century, experiments with magnetic fields succeeded in making compasses without lodestones.

China, with lots of rivers and gorges, needed bridges, something science and mathematics excelled at making possible. In the sixth century came the invention of the suspension bridge. But other bridges were also possible. In 610, Li Chun designed a segmented stone arch bridge that still stands today, 500 years before anything similar in Europe could be built. It is important for its use of a segmental arch rather than the semicircular arch familiar in Roman architecture as well as four semicircular arches at either end. The semicircular arch allowed for a stronger structure using less material while the four smaller arches further reduced material and weight as well as to reduce the likelihood of flood damage by allowing the water to flow more freely. This Great Stone Bridge spans almost 125 feet, greater than the largest Roman whole arch bridge still standing. The so-called Marco Polo Bridge, a bridge near Beijing described by the Genoan traveler built in 1189, includes eleven segmental arches and spans 700 feet. More amazing still, both of these bridges are still in use today!

Some bridges did not quite survive as long. A pontoon bridge—built by attaching boats together, secured on shore with huge iron anchors in the shape of oxen—survived 350 years of use over the turbulent **Yellow River**. It was washed away in the eleventh century during a tremendous flood, dragging its iron oxen anchors along with it! These anchors ended up deep in the river, but though they could be located recovering them would require some innovation. Using principles later put into use in the 1950s to recover the ship *Andrea Doria*, the Chinese filled two large boats with earth. Divers connected lines to the sunken anchors and then the earth was slowly removed. The increased buoyancy caused the oxen to rise enough that they could be dragged to shore by simply steering the boats that way. Once close enough they could be dragged out from the shallows.

Often considered iconic of American ingenuity, the paddle wheel boat has been invented by the Chinese in the fifth century. The designs used varied tremendously in size and complexity. The first of these boats were used militarily in the early part of the century. Later designs used more and more men to power them. Where as the Mississippi riverboat centuries latter had one or two wheels, many of these boats had more—one had eleven!

The lock, or pound-lock, familiar to anyone who has traveled by or near canals, was developed in the tenth century, hardly surprising given the civilization's reliance on river travel. The locks work somewhat like an elevator or escalator made of water. The vessel enters one side, while the other side is closed. Then the entrance is closed, and the water level altered to match the other side. When these levels matched the second gate would be opened and the vessel could continue its journey.

Centuries before the Siemens-Martin process for steel manufacturing (regenerative furnace), a similar system was in use in China. Wrought iron and cast iron were mixed to create high-carbon steel. This was made possible in the fifth century by the double-acting piston bellows, already in wide use, to provide a constant stream of air. Keeping constant temperature makes the Siemens-Martin process possible. From this model, it is easy to see how the Chinese understood the basics behind a steam engine.

Some scientific or technological advances of the Chinese were more mundane. In the sixth century the modern match was developed. There is evidence to suggest that phosphorescent paints were in use in the tenth century. Almost taken for granted these days but a really important precursor to modern textiles is the spinning wheel. It is hard to date exactly, but a conservative estimate would be the eleventh century. It likely was an adaptation of the technology that had already been being used in sericulture to wind silk for centuries. Belt drive technology had been available since the first century B.C.E. and allowed these spinning machines to operate at extraordinary speed.

Some innovations remained unique to East Asia. The "permanent" lamp was an effort to conserve the fuel oil used for light. The process of burning the oil for light produced so much heat that half the oil was lost to evaporation. The solution to this was simple. The oil reservoir was surrounded with a second reservoir of water. This innovation has never been adopted in the West! Today, this water-cooled equipment is echoed in all manner of machinery, from the familiar automobile radiator to the liquid-cooled super computer.

The mechanical clock was developed in the eighth century. Although it could be used for telling time it was designed primarily as an astronomical and astrological instrument. Chinese astrology places more significance on the time of conception rather than birth so it was important to track the likeliest moments the emperor, his wives, and his concubines started life. Astrology meant the Chinese watched the heavens closely and were the first to record observations of comets, solar eclipses, and supernova. Over the centuries several of these clocks, at first powered by water, faced troubles with the freezing of water with the changing seasons. Later versions of these clocks would use mercury as the powering liquid. These were not wall clocks, but three-story towers. It would be over 500 years before the technology made its way to Europe for tracking the hours in monasteries.

One of these clocks featured an innovation now common on roadways all over the world: the chain drive. In 976, one scientist needed a more efficient way to transfer power to his clock, and he stumbled upon the by-now-familiar system that transfers power from the pedals to the wheel of bicycles everywhere began.

Just as astrology tries to describe the person by observing the universe, Chinese scientists looked to using items in the world to extend life and possibly cheat death. Scientists, especially Daoists seeking the secret elixir of life, began categorizing plants, herbs, animals, and even parts of animals, to determine if they contained any useful properties. Thus was born Chinese medicine. Some of its practice causes troubles today, when rare or endangered animals are killed for small body parts supposedly giving the cure for impotence or cancer, but for centuries this medicine was important to Chinese culture.

Chinese science and medicine depend on what Western Europeans today might consider superstitions, but Chinese have been using techniques based on these simple observations about people and the world in general for thousands of years. The Chinese believed that energy or qi moves throughout the body at different times, and that qi can affect different organs or body parts. Through belief in the yin (negative energy) and yang (positive energy), as well as the five elements that make up all matter (metal, wood, water, fire, and earth), Chinese doctors use acupuncture (stabbing with little needles) and moxibustion (burning small cones of the mugwort herb) on the right places to affect matter and energy.

Chinese medicine understood much about the human body even before the medieval period. It understood the circulatory system (sixth century B.C.E.), circadian rhythms (humans function on a 24-hour physiological and psychological cycle that is highly dependent on the cycle of light and dark or day and night), and endocrinology (science of hormones, glands, and organs) by 400. By the seventh century Chinese physicians could correctly diagnose diabetes and would recommend dietary changes similar to those still recommended today. Diagnosis was made by the sweet taste of the urine; the physician would recommend the patient forgo starchy and sweet foods as well as alcoholic beverages. Possibly earlier, but certainly by the seventh century, physicians were using animal thyroids to treat goiters. Even more striking, in the 900s Chinese doctors began vaccinating against smallpox. The method was simple. Because they could distinguish between the major and minor strains of the virus, scabs from those already exposed to the minor strain would be wrapped in cotton and placed in the nose of the patient to be inoculated against the disease. As today, every possible precaution was taken to prevent outright infection. In fact, the ideal "donor" of the scabs would have been one who had been inoculated himself.

Daoists also discovered gunpowder in their alchemist attempts to find the elixir of immortality around the ninth century. It is made up of potassium nitrate, charcoal, and sulfur. The Chinese made fireworks out of gunpowder, but there was an important military application as well. China always faced trouble from the north and the nomadic horsemen. Any way to disrupt their attacks, especially by hurting and scaring the cavalry, was useful. In the eleventh century Chinese made incendiary bombs to throw at siege engines and smoke bombs. By the end of the twelfth century, Chinese had cast iron grenades to throw at adversaries that could kill or maim many. In the thirteenth century, when parts of China tried to withstand the Mongol invasion, soldiers used rockets to attack horses from a distance; more experienced military men used the first guns in combat and cannonballs filled with explosives.

Movable type—so often attributed to Johannes Gutenberg—was first invented in China. Block printing on silk and paper had existed since the 700s. In fact, remarkable techniques were developed to produce near-photographic reproductions of three-dimensional objects as well as prints with three or four colors. When block printing proved impractical ink, rubbings of stone-engraved originals were popular quick solutions. In 1045, Pi Sheng invented movable type. These original type sets were made from baked clay, but later ones would be made from everything from bronze to various light woods. With the proliferation of movable type in China some truly staggering print runs occurred, even by modern standards. Printings of hundreds of thousands were not uncommon and possible millions. Over four-hundred thousand copies of a Buddhist text from the late tenth century still exist today.

The Chinese first invented checks, so a merchant did not have to travel with his trading wealth threatened by bandits or robbers. Money could be deposited in the capital, replaced with "flying money" (so named because the light paper was easy to lose to the wind) with him to more remote locations in the empire. The money would be safe, and once the transaction was complete safer ways of transferring money could be used, from other checks to lines of credit. This ninth-century invention paved the way for paper money as a government-backed method of exchange evolved from these merchant drafts. Copper cash coins weighed too much to use in large amounts over any distance, and for reasons that must be only cultural, China's government did not mint coins in gold or silver until the twentieth century—Chinese did use weighed silver or gold in transactions, however. As the inventors of multicolored printing the Chinese were also the first to use the technique as a method of discouraging counterfeiters. But it was not counterfeiting that doomed the paper money experiment of the **Song dynasty**, but greedy government officials that could not help themselves but to print more money.

Finally, the Chinese had a monopoly on high-class ceramics. By the time of the Song dynasty the use of high-temperature kilns with new clays and glazes to take advantage of these fiery techniques, Chinese invented what came to be called "china" in the rest of the world, also known as "porcelain." Well-crafted porcelain became prevalent, for tea-ware using iron glazings where each piece created during the Song dynasty remained a singular work of art and pattern perfectly imitated. Innovation would continue after the brief Mongol Period of the **Yuan dynasty** when potters in the **Ming dynasty** created porcelain with its bright white appearance and later famous blue and white glazing. Ceramics from the Song and Ming dynasties were especially sought after in the medieval world by wealthy in other countries, and that search continues to this day.

Finally, when the Ming dynasty began, southern Chinese ship builders began to build ocean-going craft of a kind never before seen. Ships were larger than ever before, with the biggest coming in well over 400 feet long. To put that in perspective, Christopher Columbus's flagship was 90 feet long. These tremendous ships also had the advantage of older technology from the first and second centuries—rudders and watertight compartments to prevent quick sinking, respectively. Yet after only a few decades, the emperor and his Confucian advisers burned the plans for these massive vessels as well as the ships themselves. The Confucian advisers pushed through laws limiting the size of ships constructed, in their push to prevent more merchant activity abroad and to put China's focus on the north and the remnants of the Mongol threat.

Korea

Korea from 400 to 1400 was heavily influenced by Chinese science and technology. The small country only excelled in a couple of areas. Koreans always made superior ceramics and pottery throughout these years in question. They excelled at roof tiles, for example, as well as pots and serving items for the home. But in the **Koryo** Period, their fame grew in making celadon porcelain. Although Korean potters borrowed ideas from Song China, the Chinese highly prized celadon items, considering them immensely well crafted. Ceramic experts claim they are among the most beautiful porcelains ever made.

By using a forgotten method, Korean pottery was able to become the prettiest, most complex in the world. Celadon became more Korean over the tenth and eleventh centuries. Three basic types remain the most popular forms of celadon. First is the differing green colors obtained from an iron oxide glaze difficult to duplicate. The more popular objects tend to be a celadon with soft green color, compared to the skies of the Korean peninsula during the fall, or, more commonly, to jade. The second form still uses this beautiful light green color, but through a controlled "mistake," potters create a cracked pattern throughout the glaze over the piece. Finally, the most colorful celadon were constructed by overlaying glaze on contrasting clay bodies. Artists inlaid designs made up of small pieces of different colored clay adhered to the base clay of the piece. The layers were then carved away to reveal varying colors.

However, the Korean celadon industry, so important for foreign sales, suffered a severe setback with the Mongol invasions of the thirteenth century. With the coming of the **Mongols** came the diminishing of Korean sovereignty and culture. Degradations of quality can be seen not only in Korean celadon, but in their porcelains and other ceramics as well. Koreans were well aware that ideas from abroad and conquerors from abroad can mean the difference between art spreading outward or skills being diminished.

The second invention claimed by Korean historians is moveable metal type in 1234, two centuries before the Germans. This is a difficult claim to prove, because Chinese had been printing for centuries by this time and had used moveable type made of clay and wood. But because historians have no specific date for when Chinese printers decided to try metallic, moveable type, the Koreans get the credit for this invention.

Japan

Japan, too, depended on Chinese ideas for much of the period 400 to 1400. Like the Koreans, the Japanese artisans created in valuable trade goods. And like the Koreans, the Japanese came up with two key innovations. The first item, Japanese folding fans, were invented in the seventh century. The Japanese creator modeled the fan after the physiology of a bat. At the imperial court, emperors would give folding fans away. Many times these fans were adorned with a favorite poem, a family crest, or a certain painting, all only visible when opened. Even though quite small, maybe two hand lengths at the largest, folding fans were too expensive for the common people of Japan due to the art placed on one or both sides of the fan.

Japanese Weights and Measures, c 1100–1400

Distance

1 Rin   10 →   1 Bu   10 →   1 Sun   10 →   1 Shaku 6 →   1 Ken →
.303mm.   3.03mm   3.03cm.   30.303cm   1.908m

Cloth

1 Shaku 25–30 → 1Tan 1.25 1 Kujira-Shaku 2 tan →   1 Hiki

Land

1 Ken 50–60 →   1 Cho 36 →   1 Ri

Square Measures

1 Ken squared 1 Tsubo 30 →   1 Se   10 →   1 Tan 10 →   1 Cho   10 → 1 Sq. Ri
                  ~3.35 sq m.   ~100 sq. m.   ~1,000 sq. m. 10k sq. m. 16 sq km.

Volume

1 Shaku 10 → 1 Go 10 → 1 Sho 10 → 1 To 10 → 1 Koku   4 → 1 Hyo →
1.8 cl.   1.8 dl.   1.8 l.   18 l. 180 l.   720 l.

Weight

1 Momme 100–180, varies → 1 Kin 1000 Momme → 1 Kan
3.75 g.   3.75 kg.

Currency

Wado-Kaiho: (708–958) Mainly copper currency struck in Japan
Mon: (958-late 1500s) Imported Chinese *Sen* coins
Kan: 1,000 Mon

Source: Adapted from Louis Frederic, *Daily Life in Japan at the Time of the Samurai 1185–1603.* New York: Praeger Publishers, 1972, pp. 251–252.

Japan's second great innovation, like Korean celadon, owed much to China, in this case Chinese steel makers. Many samurai—members of Japan's warrior caste—believed the sword a living object, imbued with supernatural powers. Japanese sword makers were revered as an honored class in society. Rather than a single artisan, a smith made the rough shape, the apprentice folded and beat the metal, a polisher made the sword beautiful to view, and other craftsmen made the various, noncutting parts of the blade, like the hilt and sheath. These crafters went through elaborate ceremonies and methods while creating these masterworks, the highest quality swords ever made. Sword makers followed an elaborate method of alternating layers of soft and hard steel to provide a sword with flexibility to avoid breakage and superior sharpness. These special warrior swords were highly prized family heirlooms, passed down from generation to generation. They also fetched high prices when sold to China or Korea.

China dominated science, technology, and innovation in East Asia over the period 400 to 1400, which was not surprising considering its size and population compared to Korea and Japan. But its domination in these categories is far more substantial than other ones tackled in this encyclopedia. The fact that China remained ahead of Europe (and the rest of the world) shows the difference between Chinese innovators and Chinese so absorbed with memorizing **Neo-Confucian** texts to gain entrance to government through passing the **examination system** that the inventive spirit was pushed aside.

Further Reading

Benn, Charles. *Daily Life in Traditional China: The Tang Dynasty*. Westport, CT: Greenwood Press, 2002.

Clark, Donald N. *Culture and Customs of Korea*. Westport, CT: Greenwood Press, 2000.

Frederic, Louis. *Daily Life in Japan at the Time of the Samurai, 1185–1603*. Translated by Eileen M. Lowe. New York: Praeger, 1972.

Gernet, Jacques. *Daily Life in China on the Eve of the Mongol Invasion, 1250–1276*. Stanford, CA: Stanford University Press, 1962.

Needham, Joseph. *The Grand Titration: Science and Society in East and West*. Toronto, Canada: University of Toronto Press, 1969.

Temple, Robert K. G. *China: Land of Discovery*. Wellingborough, UK: Patrick Stephens, Ltd., 1986.

7. GLOBAL TIES

China

The Chinese Empire was one of the few nation-states of the ancient and medieval world that could be called a legitimate superpower. Chinese rule spread over an area that is larger than the continental United States. During the years 400 to 1400, China's power and influence expanded and exceeded its previous size in the middle of this period.

China's impact on the wider world cannot be easily overstated. Its impact helped Europe with important inventions that the Europeans would perfect in the realms of war and discovery. Its inventions were exported more than any other country's technology during this period. Other inventions were lost in time, to be reinvented by Europeans centuries later. China was at the height of its culture, wealth, influence, and technology while Europe was still overrun by barbarian hordes.

Yet China rarely had direct relations with many countries. Chinese believed that their civilization was the greatest on earth and ignored other cultural ideas. China's mistreatment under the **Mongols**—a period where China was hooked into the world community in its simplest form, the Mongol empire—made Chinese even more xenophobic than before. And just in the heyday of Chinese technological advantages in shipping and interest in trade and exploration, its Confucian leaders pulled the plug and permanently ended Chinese naval supremacy.

In many ways, China started as accepting of foreigners and their ideas, even if Chinese did not want to change their ideas further than practicing the newest sect of Buddhism to make its way around China. China contained speakers from the Indo-European, Altaic, Sino-Tibetan, and Polynesian language families. However, most Chinese spoke one or more of the eight largest Chinese languages of the Sino-Tibetan language family. These languages could be as different as French and German. But China had a uniform system of writing that helped facilitate government function and trade. Many of the world's most important religions could be found in China, even if Chinese did not necessarily practice them. These included Islam, Christianity, Judaism, Zoroastrianism, Buddhism, and **Confucianism**. Chinese freedom of religion for foreigners living in Tang China occurred even as many other nations and empires worked to crush opposing religious views.

China, even with its long borders, is relatively isolated from other countries. It is separated from north Asia by the steppe and desert. Mountain chains keep it from directly touching Central Asia. In the southwest, it is kept separate from the Indian subcontinent by the largest mountains in the world, the Himalayas. Dense jungles and rivers separate China from Southeast Asia. It has a large coastline, which facilitates sea trade and fishing. Many times it is easier to go by sea than to trek through the deserts, jungles, or mountains on China's borders. To understand China's global ties, it is necessary to cover briefly China's influence on its East Asian neighbors.

China was the predominant cultural and trading force on the Korean peninsula. Through China came Korean adoption of Buddhism and the implementation of the Chinese writing style. China was Korea's number one trading partner, even though Korea did trade with Japan and through Arab sailors as far away as the Muslim world.

Korea, well known for its pottery and other ceramics, learned much about creating porcelain from the Chinese. And the Chinese adored Korean celadon with its beautiful green coloring. Even after the Koreans learned the secret of porcelain and improved on it, they still imported the Chinese version.

Korea readily converted quickly to Chinese sects of Buddhism, as already explained in the essay on religion. However, the peninsula also took up Confucianism, including **Neo-Confucianism** under the Yi dynasty. Anything Chinese was of high cultural and commercial value. The histories of China and Korea are indelibly and inexorably tied together.

Some of the same things could be said of the Chinese–Japanese connection. Japan was for most of its history an isolated nation. Not only was it geographically isolated 200 miles off the mainland, but it had little relation to any other nations save China and Korea. Like Korea, Japan adopted Buddhism. This Buddhism came through Korea from China.

Also similar to Korea, Japan used the Chinese to develop a writing system. Just like Korean, Japanese is not even in the same language family as Chinese. Even though Japan eventually used another writing style—this time a simplified version of some characters to mimic the sounds of Japanese and thus be able to read and write Japanese. However, throughout the period all important or official communication was in Chinese.

Japan also traded with the Chinese, even though the trading contacts were not fully developed because of the danger of the extra distance to north China by sea. In many ways, Japan simply tried to copy China. Japan traded some of its innovations, such as illustrated folding fans, painted silk screens, and samurai swords to China in exchange for porcelain, art, and Buddhist relics. Japan also adopted the Chinese invention of the parasol. This umbrella was originally a valuable symbol of the imperial courts of the two countries. However, they trickled to the aristocracy and then to more common people. In addition, societal structures were borrowed from China. In many ways, the Chinese were like a parent in its cultural relations with Japan and Korea.

China was heavily influenced by India. From India came the Buddhist religion, which China adopted after some cultural modifications. Although China and India are of different language families, the two nations had substantial contacts. However, the two are separated by the Hindu Kush and Himalayan mountains, hurting the facilitation of more relations. Trade was frequent with India, especially through sea routes. Chinese ships traded indirectly with India for such goods as ivory. India desired Chinese precious metals.

India and China were the two largest populations in the world and shared a border along the mountains. Indian influence is particularly heavy on the Chinese province of Tibet. There Buddhism and Indian culture morphed Tibet into a capital for the religion. Even as Buddhism was repressed in India, it flourished in China.

When the Chinese traveler Fa Xian, a Buddhist monk, went to India, he returned to China easily. This was not done through the mountains, but rather he simply found a ship going from Ceylon to the island of Java back to Guangzhou. This shows the tremendous level of trade done by Chinese merchants. That same trip would be duplicated by Xuanzang, another monk, only this time entirely by land along the **Silk Road** two centuries later.

Chinese traders had visited east Africa at least 100 and maybe 300 years before Portuguese sailors did. The Chinese traded for valuables on the continent such as ivory and rhinoceros horn. Chinese even took a giraffe back to China, thinking it was a Chinese unicorn called *kirin*.

Part of the trade network heading west from China, Persia had long been a world power. The Chinese enjoyed relations with the Persians, including strong trading ones. The Silk Road, which started in China, traversed Persia on its way to Europe. Part of China even speaks the Persian language, in the far west of the country. Chinese paper money has even been recovered in archeology sites in modern Iran. Chinese high society adopted polo from the Persians.

The Chinese traded with the Muslims, Arabs after their rise in the seventh century and Turks. For a period, the Chinese and the Arabs were the two strongest empires on the planet. In many ways, the Arab civilization acted as a firm intermediary between Asia and Europe for trade, ideas, and weaponry. The religion of the Arab Empire, Islam, spread to China. Some people in the southern port city of Quanzhou were converts to the religion, although the majority of its adherents were Arabs being given freedom of religion. Heavy trading ties existed between the Arabs, and Chinese Empire made the idea of a prominent mosque in the city an obvious need.

Much trade occurred between the two, and Chinese technology, inventions, and science found themselves being transferred to the Arabs. In trade relations, the Arabs knew the Chinese merchants were honest, which increased Chinese prestige among the Arab world.

In the northwest, Islam spread amongst the Turks living along the Silk Road in Chinese Xinjiang province; it is still a Muslim stronghold to this day. This landmass takes up almost one-fourth of all of China's geographic area, even though it is relatively underpopulated because of desert. Mosques are frequent structures in that part of China.

The Turks learned to use gunpowder. They developed cannons that would slowly but effectively cancel out the use of many medieval castles and other strongholds. This can be most clearly demonstrated by the Turks' destruction of city walls in the powerful albeit weakening Byzantine Empire.

Chinese influence cut through Central Asia along the Silk Road. These important arteries helped create and keep wealthy important Central Asian cities, such as Bokhara and Samarkand.

China was also a major influence for the countries of Southeast Asia, especially Vietnam. Chinese writing style spread into Vietnam, which, as another member of the Sino-Tibetan language group, could use the system as written. They traded especially for goods like tin. The Chinese also led military intrusions into this area. Chinese and Vietnamese history is so intertwined that the Vietnamese do not like China even to this day. Chinese traded with other Southeast Asian countries, but they tended to be influenced more by India and Indian-style Buddhism or even Islam as filtered through India. Going back to China were things such as tropical wood and spices.

The Mongols under Genghis Khan built the world's largest empire in history. The Chinese and Mongols were geographic neighbors and had relations for centuries before the invasion. The two were normally separated, however, by steppe and desert. When another nomadic called the Jurchen conquered north China ending the **Northern Song dynasty**, China had a buffer state until it stupidly allied with the Mongols against the Jurchen after the Mongols had already conquered central Asia and most of Russia. The Mongols took four decades to take all of China—south China was not the best place for armies specializing in cavalry. But when victory was finally achieved, the Silk Road would be safer than any time in history, and Chinese goods, technology, and ideas were spread across the Mongol realm all the way to central Europe.

The Mongols left their mark on China, as central Asian middlemen grabbed all the profits and made the Chinese more xenophobic than ever before. From the Mongol supremacy, other cultures were brought to China. The Chinese rejected borrowing them because of this distrust of foreigners and feeling—probably quite right at the time—that Chinese culture was the most advanced in the world at the time and did not need foreign ideas anymore.

Although the Mongols practiced general religious tolerance, many converted to Islam and Christianity. This helped bring Islam to the nomadic edges of China.

Before the years covered in this encyclopedia, the Chinese Empire made a tremendous amount of money from selling silk to the Roman Empire. But increased activity by nomadic groups temporarily made trade difficult in the fifth century, and Rome had other problems besides how much silk to purchase. Yet the fifth century also brought Christian monks to China and Mongolia. These monks, part of the heresy known as the Nestorians, introduced the faith to the Chinese but were much better at gaining converts with the Mongols. There were even Nestorian churches in the different Chinese capitals. This cultural transfusion was unique because Christianity did not again directly come to China for over a full millennium, besides the Mongolian Christians that practiced slightly corrupted versions of it.

After Rome fell, the Chinese carried on substantial trade with the Byzantine Empire, the successor state to Rome. These ties, however, were heavily strained by the Persian and Arab invasions of the latter. When the Byzantines and the Chinese first traded, the two were the most powerful nations on earth. Many Chinese goods made it to Constantinople, the Byzantine capital.

The most famous example of direct travel between the European world and China is that of the Italian Marco Polo. He was not the only European to come to Asia, nor even the only one in his family to come to Asia. But by writing a book and describing the wealth of the Mongol **Yuan dynasty**, Polo created a sensation. Comparatively speaking, at this time, Europe was relatively backwards. Polo saw how China was the premier power of the world in trade, culture, and technology. When Polo returned to Europe, he told disbelieving audiences of little black rocks that the marvelous Chinese burned for heat. He was, of course, speaking of coal.

The Europeans were indebted to the Chinese for many inventions. The Chinese innovation of gunpowder revolutionized the world of warfare. This invention came to the Europeans from the Chinese via the Turks. The Chinese invention of gunpowder also lent itself to a popular use in China and Western nations: fireworks. These celebratory rockets were perfected in China and used during state and religious celebrations. The crossbow had been invented in the West, but for some reason its knowledge had been lost. However, it was reintroduced to Europe by the Chinese, thanks to the Arabs.

The Chinese used the printing press and moveable type centuries before Johann Guttenberg "invented" it, which shows another theme about inventions—sometimes the idea did not come from China but was independently created by others. To be fair, a few historians see some circumstantial evidence that traces the idea for moveable type back to Asia, but nothing definitive. China also pioneered paper money. Even paper itself came to Europe from China, albeit long before 400. The Chinese invented the compass, which is perhaps the most important navigational tool ever created. Interestingly, Chinese used it to find south instead of north, important for their geomancy called **feng shui**.

Europe and China's views of each other were filtered through the prism of in-between civilizations. China was revered in the West as a major power during these years. Even though even the most educated did not know much about China, there was a clear understanding that China was a major force in many ways. Tales of the Chinese exploits came through sources such as Marco Polo and the Mongols. China played a major role in early European maps of Asia.

European demand for Chinese products was immense. Chinese silks and porcelain (known in Europe as china) went to Europe by land and partially by sea. Chinese silk layered the sheets of the kings and regents of the states of Europe. The finest foods were served on genuine porcelain, which was not invented in the West until the eighteenth century. European fascination of things Chinese became so great—especially in the post–Marco Polo world—that it helped get investors and nation-states interested in finding a direct connection, using this Chinese idea of a compass, and cutting out the Arab and Venetian middlemen starting in the fifteenth century. The Chinese were less enamored of things European, as they normally regarded the Europeans as barbarians, especially after the hard times of Mongol rule.

Korea

Stuck in history between China and Japan, Korea is often overlooked. In many ways, Korea is not just geographically in between China and Japan, but is also a study of being almost a balance between the two. Although Japan had few foreign contacts outside of East Asia and China visited far and wide in Southeast Asia and the Indian Ocean basis, Korea started off with relations with first their neighbors, then long-distance Arab traders, before closing off its foreign relations under China as a tributary state to take on the title of the Hermit kingdom by the sixteenth or early seventeenth century.

Korea is indelibly influenced by its massive neighbor, China. Korea adopted many practices first brought about by their neighbors. Korea also adopted Chinese for writing. Anything important or official would be written in Chinese for this period. This meant the only the rich or otherwise elite would be able to read or write, a common factor in world cultures in this period. After trying a system of simplified Chinese characters to be used as Korean sounds, Koreans left this complicated system for a logical phonetic system developed in the fifteenth century.

Chinese literature came into Korea, and demand increased. Chinese plays and poetry were considered the pinnacle of civilized writing. This prevented native Korean writers from flourishing, except in the Chinese language. Most important, Korea borrowed Chinese religions. **Confucianism** and Chinese-style Buddhism were enthusiastically embraced by Korea, even as shamanism and folk religion continued. Buddhist temples, monasteries, and statues were constructed across the peninsula. The nobility of Korea tried to model themselves after their Chinese counterparts. In many ways, especially early in its history, Korea tried to be a little China.

Just as with China, when Korea was building a new capital, it was planned out. This new city was copied from the amazing Chinese capital. Chinese architecture seeped into Korean styles. Such a connection showed that many of the similarities between the two nations was not simply on the surface but instead had affected all levels of Korean society and government. China was a tremendous geographical neighbor as well as a dominating cultural and economic one. Most trade done by the Koreans was done with their western neighbor, usually by sea to Shandong peninsula from far-south Korea.

The Korean kingdom of **Silla** did not hesitate to ally itself with Tang China to defeat one of the other two Korean kingdoms in the seventh century. This was done even though victory (or even defeat) could have undermined Korean sovereignty. In fact, the Tang tried to dominate the Koreans, but Korea fought back. Still, the newly unified Korea became a tributary state to the Chinese Empire. In this role, Korea was still autonomous in its self-rule but relied on China for foreign relations. The Chinese saw the Koreans as a civilized nation, which was a fairly high complement. With Korea's new status, trade continued unimpeded, and both sides generated incomes. This trade became especially important as China ran a trade deficit. Korean silver and gold help replace Chinese coins traded to foreign markets, even though the Chinese only used precious metals other than copper as weighed materials and not minted.

After the Chinese introduced porcelain to the Koreans, Korea became widely praised for its excellent quality pottery and other ceramics, especially the different greens of celadon porcelain. Korean artisans improved porcelain, making the highly prized inlaid porcelain and crackled glaze celadon. Korea traded these cups, plates, and figurines. Although Chinese earthenware is much better known, Korean ceramics of the period from the tenth to the start of the thirteenth century are considered of much higher quality and craftsmanship by those who collect Asian art. However, Korean society was so connected to China that Korea continued to import Chinese porcelain. In exchange, Korea sent precious metals. This gold and silver were important for the large amount of Chinese imperial coinage. Jewelry was another important and unique product of medieval Korea.

Korea also had a trading relationship with its other neighbor, Japan. Even though the Sea of Japan was treacherous, Koreans came to Japan with knowledge of Buddhism and even staffed the early monasteries and temples. Japan purchased many religious objects from Korea and sent Buddhist pilgrims back to Korea and sometimes from Korea to China to study. Later, Koreans traded porcelain and precious metals to Japan. This came to an end with the coming of the **Mongols**. The attempted invasion of Japan in the thirteenth century was launched from Korea by Mongols and Koreans in ships made in Korea. Koreans also had to contend with aggressive Japanese pirates after 1350.

Korea, like China, had trading partners with the outside world, only many fewer than the Middle kingdom (China) due to its small size. One Korean deepwater harbor traded with these foreign nations. Some of the clientele came from as far away as the Arab world. These traders purchased Korean furs and leathers. But for the most part Korea had very little effect on the world outside of East Asia.

Japan

The same could be said of Japan. Unlike China and Korea, Japan is geographically isolated from the rest of the world by ocean and sea. In times when other countries in East Asia are fraught with internal disturbance or foreign invasion, Japan creates its own culture and retreats from the outside world. But when China or Korea have civilizations that have much to offer, the Japanese borrow and use what works best for their culture. In a few cases, Japan collected ideas and items from a much wider world, yet Japan had little presence on the global stage apart from providing some ideas to its East Asian neighbors.

The Japanese borrowed many ideas from the Chinese, including written language, architecture, music, law, and religion. At first anything important or official Japanese men wrote in Chinese, even though the Japanese language has nothing in common with Chinese, as it is an Altaic language. Later, someone—either Kukai, a Buddhist leader, or a group of women—simplified a set of Chinese characters to make the forty-eight separate syllables. Later a second "alphabet" of characters joined the first, both called *kana*. And even later, Chinese characters were used with the kana to provide a sophisticated Japanese language. At first the use of kana was relegated to Japanese poetry and writing by educated women.

Anything Chinese brought over in the sixth and seventh centuries was considered almost intellectually sacred by the Japanese. Chinese-style Buddhism spread in many flavors and sects throughout Japan. The dominant sects of this religion included **Pure Land Buddhism** and **Zen Buddhism**, both developed in China and undergoing only a few changes in Japan. Buddhist temples, first staffed by Korean monks, sprang up across Japan with statues of the Buddha. Japanese culture was not only formed by these outside influences, but many times native styles and traditions were combined with these foreign pressures to create something uniquely Japanese. Zen gardens are examples of how foreign stimulus was combined with native artistic and religious ways.

Japan adopted Chinese codes of conduct and laws early on, especially **Confucianism**. Japanese architecture in the seventh through ninth centuries is based on Chinese **Tang dynasty** buildings—in fact, the best examples of Tang architecture today is Japan. Even the most famous alcoholic beverage of Japan—sake, or rice wine—was invented in China.

Japan had a healthy trading relationship with its closest neighbor, Korea. Korea in many ways served as the conduit of communication, trade, and culture between its larger neighbors, especially in the beginning of Japan's cultural borrowing from China in the sixth to eighth centuries. Later, Japan also traded for fine Korean porcelain, as the Japanese did not have the knowledge of how to create the ceramic in such beautiful forms yet. Korean gold and silver were also valued commodities. **Mongols** launched their two failed assaults on Japan from Korea.

On the other hand, the Japanese desperately wanted to trade with China. Being the richest nation in the world, China was a potential gateway to the rest of the world for Japan. China, however, saw the Japanese as barbarians who would not follow the proper traditions, with its leaders daring to put themselves up as equals to the Chinese emperor. Usually Japan was able to smooth over these disturbances and reopen trade. Japan traded its painted folding fans, **samurai swords**, and painted folding screens to China for Buddhist religious articles, Chinese art, and porcelain.

Japan had limited contacts with other peoples due to the movements of the monk Kukai, leading to some more Indian influence on Japan. However, in many cases Japan had no real relations with nations other than China and Korea. There was some indirect influence on Japan from India thanks to China. These influences included building styles and religion. Unlike the other two, there was no substantial trading with faraway kingdoms for the import of exotic goods; Japan was too far away and did not offer the profits trade with China or even Korea allowed.

The West had little knowledge of Japan. Although trade with China had occurred on and off since ancient times, Europe did not have this same relationship with Japan. Western maps showed Japan as a loose group of islands off the coast of China or India. Western travelers did not visit Japan like Marco Polo in Asia.

Japan did have another set of relations with China, Korea, and Southeast Asia after the defeat of the Mongols. Japanese pirates began to prey first on shipping and then on coastal towns and villages. Even though China had the finest and most technologically advanced navy in the world, the Japanese pirates still succeeded in harassing Chinese trade ships and fishermen so much the Chinese rebuilt the **Grand Canal** to allow year-round transit. But after 1425, Japan did not have to worry about the might of the Chinese navy, as Confucianists against the power of **eunuchs** and merchants in China destroyed not only the ships but the plans to make them. Japanese pirates also harassed Korea and Southeast Asian islands. One group eventually settled in the Philippines.

Japan had little effect on the world outside of East Asia, but it did have a clever traveler relay his experiences and Japanese leaders did collect objects from other countries. That traveler was a Buddhist monk named Kukai. He visited China and learned the ways of a complicated form of Buddhism called Esoteric Buddhism. He also supposedly visited India, where he learned more of Buddha's life and was introduced to Sanskrit. He learned to read this new language that used symbols to represent syllables. Some Japanese believe the basic ideas behind the kana and Japanese writing came from Kukai's adventure in India. As for the collection of foreign goods, in Nara, the Japanese built a clever storehouse built of logs attached to their large Buddhist temple the *todaiji*. When humid, the logs expand and keep out the moisture. When dry, the logs contract, letting in a breeze. Inside the storehouse were (and are) over ten thousand objects of art from not only Japan, China, and Korea, but from India, Persia, Greece, and Rome, all collected in the eighth century. So though Japanese usually visited only China and Korea, and rarely did visitors from anywhere other than China and Korea grace their shores—with the exception of a few monks from India—Japan did try to be part of the global scene through its collection of books, weapons, mirrors, and jewelry from around the world.

Further Reading

Asdshead, S.A.M. *China in World History*. 2nd ed. New York: St. Martin's Press, 1995.

Kim, Chewon, and Won-Yong Kim. *Treasures of Korean Art: 2000 Years of Ceramics, Sculpture, and Jeweled Arts*. New York: Harry N. Abrams, Inc., 1966.

Schirokauer, Conrad, et al. *A Brief History of Chinese and Japanese Civilizations*. 3rd ed. Belmont, CA: Thomson Wadsworth, 2006.

Temple, Robert K. G. *China: Land of Discovery and Invention*. Wellingborough, UK: Patrick Stephens, Ltd., 1986.

Weatherford, Jack. *Genghis Khan and the Making of the Modern World*. New York: Crown Publishers, 2004.

Wood, Frances. *The Silk Road: Two Thousand Years in the Heart of Asia*. Berkeley: University of California Press, 2002.

Short Entries: People, Ideas, Events, and Terms

Agriculture

Agriculture began in East Asia along the **Yellow River**. Its unpredictable flooding and swift currents had the benefit of bringing loess soil to a large part of the flat north China plain. In fact, it is from the loess that the Yellow River and the Yellow Sea get their names—the dirt appears a yellowish brown color in the water. This soil was (and is) rich in nutrients and only required wooden tools to farm. The Chinese grew first millet (in the West today millet is used as birdseed), then barley and *kaoliang* (sorghum), before the coming of wheat around 1500 B.C.E. Even before the first imperial dynasty, the Chinese had started to use metal agricultural tools and beasts of burden to help prepare the soil outside the Yellow River's influence. Yet animals were expensive to feed, and most peasants plowed using only their own human power, leaving the oxen or water buffalo for the rich peasants to use.

As Chinese civilization moved southward, it came in contact with farmers growing rice. The Chinese soon adopted growing rice, which came mainly from the **Yangzi River** southward. Wet rice farming requires neighbors to work together to make sure water is added or drained from the different fields at the correct times. And the more people working on a plot of rice land (to weed and make sure the rice is growing properly), the higher the yield. There is of course an upper limit to this increase yield where it would be wasteful to add workers, but historically south China needed more workers, and this increased yield of rice could feed them. In any event, rice fields produced the largest number of calories per acre than any other foodstuff of the time. Whatever body of fresh water was nearby, the state worked to build irrigation systems through the use of **corvee** labor to increase the fields in cultivation; many Tang and Song dynasty irrigation systems survive and still work to this day.

So though wheat was for the more affluent in north China—turned into flour for noodles and dumplings—and millet for the poor, rice was the dish of choice in the south (and for the rich in the north after the creation of the **Grand Canal**). Peasants also grew bamboo (for the shoots), taro, melons, chestnuts, and citrus trees. To protect mandarin oranges, southern Chinese hung thin bags filled with reddish-yellow ants to kill pests, perhaps the first time humans used insects to control insects. Silkworms were another insect used by East Asian peasants who had access to the mulberry tree. The peasants killed the larva of the silk moth by tossing in boiling water to produce silk. Then it was just a question of winding the silk and preparing it for sale. Better-off peasants also raised pigs, chickens, ducks, and geese. Most important, Chinese grew soybeans. Soybeans served as protein—either eaten alone, turned into *doufu* (bean curd or tofu in Japan), or made into a soy flour for baking or other uses—for those who could not afford to eat meat or those whose religion forbade meat. Soy oil could be extracted for use in cooking or lighting lamps, with the residual soy mash fed to livestock. Soy beans also made excellent plants to use in crop rotation. Bacteria associated with the plant served as a nitrogen fixer for the soil, allowing a greater yield for the next crops grown on the associated land. Soybeans grew best in river valley soil in north China and later Manchuria (and in Korea and Japan).

Soybean cake would be used as fertilizer after the seventeenth century, but before—and even during its use, as there was never enough soybean cake to be used by all Chinese farmers—the traditional fertilizers were animal and human feces. "Nightsoil" was its euphemism. Its use meant peasants would do their best to use their own outhouse, collectors would scour cities for the commodity to sell in the countryside, and water and many raw vegetables could not be consumed. This was due to all the bacteria and viruses from the nightsoil that first contaminated raw vegetables and then with a rain ran off farmland and into rivers and streams. That is one reason for stir-frying—getting food hot enough to kill the dangers present in the water—and for drinking so-called white tea. Although Chinese would prefer to drink real black, fermented tea, one too poor to buy it often would drink "white tea," which was just water boiled long enough to be safe for drinking.

Taxes on agriculture were the most valuable for the Chinese state, with the exception of a brief period in the **Southern Song dynasty** when taxes on merchants temporarily rose to great heights. That is one reason peasants were placed in the second spot of the Confucian class system. But as the dynasty continued, free, tax-paying peasants began to dwindle. Peasants who lost their lands became tenant farmers or, in hard times, escaped to the countryside along the border between two or more provinces and pillaged as bandits. Elites rarely paid taxes on their lands, meaning it was in the state's best interest to keep land in the hands of the peasants. Hence the starting of the **equal field system**, which lasted into the **Tang dynasty** before indifference set in (with similar effects in Korea and Japan). The equal field system was an attempt to maximize land in the hands of independent peasants to keep the tax base from crumbling.

Korean agriculture started out with rice and soybean farming in its many river valleys. Growing rice also required the cooperation of the local peasantry. In Japan, rice too was cultivated before 400, although probably later, as rice was likely introduced by Korea. To please the **Shinto** gods or kami, scare off the demons, and record a large harvest, the biggest toughs in two nearby villages would battle in **sumo wrestling**. In addition, villagers put on folk dances and plays to pray for a large harvest or to give thanks for the harvest. These folk traditions later evolved into **noh theater**. In Korea and Japan, fishing was even more important than raising livestock for the people's diet (and health). The Chinese on the coast or rivers could become fishermen, but to provide maximum protein benefits per acre of land in south China, farmers with excess or depressed land would construct fish ponds.

Further Reading

Kolb, Albert. *East Asia: China, Japan, Korea, Vietnam; Geography of a Cultural Region*. London: Methuen, 1971.

Ancestor Worship

Ancestor worship is too strong of a phrase for what is an ancient practice still performed throughout East Asia. At best it involves semireligious ceremonies performed by families at funerals, during certain holidays each year, and perhaps on the deceased's annual death day. The oldest surviving son had the responsibility to provide for his dead parents (and sometimes all the ancestors) real or symbolic food, useful items, or money for use in the afterlife and to honor the past. The family was home for living and spirit worlds. These ceremonies stressed the importance of family and generational continuity. *Ancestor commemoration* might be a better term for what was practiced more extensively and further back along the family tree by large, wealthy families, **lineages**, or **clans** in China, and only for a few generations in Japan and Korea. Although part of ancestor commemoration worked itself into Confucianism, filial piety, and family rites, much of the folk tradition that grew up with ancestor worship split off and became subsumed into **Daoism** in China and Korea, Buddhism sometimes in China and Japan, or kept its separation as did Shinto in Japan and folk religion in Korea. For example, in Japan the Buddhist Obon Festival is when people return to their ancestral family places to clean their ancestors' graves and honor their ancestors' spirits. Koreans do it on the anniversary of their ancestors' deaths and for famous Confucian scholars and kings. In China, joss sticks (incense) are placed in the offered items or with messages.

Further Reading

Hansen, Valerie. *Negotiating Daily Life in Traditional China: How Ordinary People Used Contracts, 600–1400.* New Haven, CT: Yale University Press, 1995.

Scott, Janet Lee. *For Gods, Ghosts and Ancestors: The Chinese Tradition of Paper Offerings.* Seattle: University of Washington Press, 2007.

Ashikaga Shogunate (1336–1477)

Some historians date this period of Japanese history all the way through the Warring States Period (1477–1603) to the Tokugawa victory at Shimonoseki (1600), but doing so makes it seem that Japan has a legitimate government from the end of the Onin War (1467–1477), when a contest for **shogun** broke out, to 1603, when Tokugawa Ieyasu became the new shogun. Other historians date the start of the shogunate with Emperor Go-Daigo's Kemmu Restoration in 1333, where he sought to return the power to rule to the emperor. It makes more sense to use the date Go-Daigo retreated southward after Ashikaga Takauji decided to turn on his former ally.

The Kemmu Restoration only briefly put the emperor back into power. His foe, then ally, then foe again — Ashikaga Takauji — attacked Go-Daigo when he realized the emperor planned to make his son shogun and could not reward his allies enough. Ashikaga's second changes of sides pushed the emperor south and out of power, although he could not muster the troops necessary to finish off Go-Daigo. Ashikaga instead founded the Ashikaga shogunate in 1336, using Kyoto as his capital and thus unifying those who reigned (a branch of the imperial family that disagreed with Go-Daigo) with those who ruled as shogun. It would not be until the third shogun, Ashikaga Yoshimitsu (r. 1367–1395), tricked the Kemmu supporters into coming back to Kyoto to resume their traditional and restricted role in government that the country was again unified. Once they arrived, they were denied positions, leading some historians today to note that the imperial line of the twenty-first century may not be the correct line.

Yoshimitsu's main interests were cultural pursuits. These were made easier with the choice to keep the capital in Kyoto near the emperor. With the rise of the **Ming dynasty**, trade between China and Japan reopened. Japan traded its famed **samurai swords**, illustrated folding fans, and painted silk screens—all Japanese inventions—for porcelain, great paintings, and sculptures of the Ming. The influx of art and ideas from China, combined with the huge following of **Zen Buddhism** that the trade with China further encouraged, all had a huge impact on religion, aesthetics, and culture in the Ashikaga shogunate. Followers of Zen brought new styles of architecture through imitating Chan temples. Zen's inward-looking nature, Japanese ideals of beauty, and Ming Chinese sensibilities all worked together to create iconic Japanese arts: **noh theater**, the rock garden, flower arranging, and the tea ceremony. Zen Buddhism also influenced the economy and later politics through loaning money at between two and 10 percent a month.

However powerful the regime seemed in Kyoto, it was actually weaker than the Hojo regency. It tried to control the countryside through regional capitals staffed by branch families. More distant relatives were in charge of province-sized areas on the frontiers of Japan. These appointed rulers—if they stayed in their posts and did not move to the capital for the high culture practiced there—had to deal with regional warrior powers that were not integrated into the state after the Hojo fell from power. These independent warlords fought one another and appointed officials to extend personal control. The officials took half of all taxes paid, as per the shogun's authorization, and could levy troops. These troops were supposed to be in case of invasion, not to fight for control over Japan. Like Ashikaga Takauji himself, the bushi were hard to trust. They could change sides at any time. Sometimes they even placed sons on both sides of the battlefield to "win" no matter the outcome. Untrustworthy warriors help explain why Japanese chess, *shogi*, has pieces of only one color. When one captures an opponent's piece, the next turn you may place that piece behind his lines as a traitorous unit. Chess, after all, is a simple simulation of war.

The fixation of the shogun on cultural pursuits and the fighting in the countryside showed weaknesses in the structure of government in Japan that those in the fifteenth century would exploit, ending the Ashikaga shogunate in 1467.

Further Reading

Hall, John Whitney, and Takeshi Toyoda. *Japan in the Muromachi Age*. Berkeley: University of California Press, 1977.

Keene, Donald. *Yoshimasa and the Silver Pavilion: The Creation of the Soul of Japan*. New York: Columbia University Press, 2003.

Louis-Frederic. *Daily Life in Japan at the Time of the Samurai, 1185–1603*. New York: Praeger, 1972.

Bodhisattva

Boshisattva literally means "a being of wisdom." In the branch of Buddhism called Mahayana Buddhism, people believe that an enlightened person chose to keep their spirit available on earth to help others achieve enlightenment. The main difference from the old doctrine to Mahayana Buddhism was the belief that everyone had a Buddha nature in them and could be saved, and not just by becoming a monk. Bodhisattvas, who already understood enlightenment, could help one achieve personal nirvana, but one was supposed to come back to life as a baby and help others, for then you were a Bodhisattva too. Most Chinese, Japanese, and Korean believers did not understand becoming a Bodhisattva to help others but did understand that under **Pure Land Buddhism** a future Buddha was promised as Bodhisattva to help anyone obtain the Pure Land upon death if they would call out and ask for help. Occasionally there were those who claimed to be the current Bodhisattva incarnation of the future Buddha called Maitreya. This female Buddha would come at the end of the world to save those last humans who believed.

Bodhisattva Kuan-Yin. Polychrome wood Chin, 1115–1234, to early Yuan, 1260–1367. Tan Kian Khoon/Shutterstock.

Further Reading

De Bary, William Theodore. *The Buddhist Tradition in India, China and Japan.* New York: Modern Library, 1969.

Burakumin

The Japanese class system, modeled after **Confucianism**, had four classes, but the burakumin existed outside the class system entirely. This group is made up of people who were considered outcasts from birth or due to the jobs they performed that were considered ritually unclean under either Buddhism, Shintoism, or both. These jobs included butchers, tanners, shoemakers, or people who handled dead human bodies like gravediggers. One could become a permanent member if one's family continued to perform these tasks, or perhaps burakumin status came about due to minor ethnic differences or having had long ago descended from slaves.

In censuses, the outcasts were not counted. Their villages were not even marked on official maps. Some of the outcasts were considered inherently unclean and as such people avoided them. This caused widespread bigotry and cruelty toward them. They were not able to marry outside of their birth caste. They were also not allowed to speak with members of other castes or enter into their houses. They had to live in their segregated villages. They could not wear wooden clogs, nor any clothes not made of cotton. Strangely enough this discrimination still exists to this day.

Further Reading
Weiner, Michael. *Japan's Minorities: The Illusion of Homogeneity*. New York: Routledge, 2008.

Chan Buddhism

Chan Buddhism is part of the Mahayana ("Greater Vehicle") Buddhism in East Asia, although some of its ideas about meditation and becoming a monk harken back to early Indian Buddhism and **Daoism**. Everyone has the Buddha in them, it just takes individual effort underneath a master to find the path and follow it.

Chan was one of the two most popular sects of Chinese Buddhism, the other (and most popular during most of the **Tang dynasty**) was **Pure Land Buddhism**. At the high point of Buddhism in China near the end of the **Late Tang dynasty**, Emperor Wuzong, a devote Daoist, attacked Buddhism. Wuzong defrocked over two-hundred fifty thousand Buddhist monks and nuns (leaving only forty-nine monasteries and eight hundred monks), sold off their lands, destroyed 4,600 temples, and wrecked forty-thousand shrines. His death in 846 saved Buddhism in China, but not Pure Land; instead Chan Buddhism gained adherents to be the most popular form of Buddhism in China.

Chan Buddhism (called **Zen Buddhism** in Japan) favored monks in their quest for enlightenment, believing meditation the key, but also practiced *kungan*, logic puzzles designed to shake up one's view of the world and allow enlightenment to come. Chan was divided into two schools in China, one that believed in slow progress to enlightenment through working with a master and the other that believed enlightenment came in a sudden stroke. But Chan Buddhism also provided churches for regular peasants to take part in, making up for the loss of Pure Land houses of worship, and those churches survived the coming of the Mongols.

Korea accepted Buddhism early from China and was the key cultural transmitters to Japan. In late **Silla Korea** Chan Buddhism slowly filtered into Korea. Called Seon Buddhism, it received kungan puzzles and meditation training on a large scale during the Mongol occupation. In 1354, Seon groups tried to work together under the Jogye Order, becoming the largest sect of Buddhism in Korea and stressing meditation, monasticism, and asceticism. Japan, too, welcomed Buddhism. Probably the second most popular form of Buddhism in Japan starting in the **Kamakura Period** was Chan, called Zen Buddhism in Japanese. The warrior class particularly used the philosophy behind Zen to empty their minds in combat.

Further Reading
De Bary, William Theodore. *The Buddhist Tradition in India, China and Japan*. New York: Modern Library, 1969.
Keel, Hee-Sung. *Chinul, the Founder of the Korean Son Tradition*. Seoul, Korea: Pojinjae, 1984.
McRae, John R. *The Northern School and the Formation of Early Ch'an Buddhism*. Honolulu: University of Hawai'i Press, 1986.

Clan

In early Japan, especially before the foundation of the Chinese copycat state during the **Nara Period** the clan or *uji* controlled western/southern Japan as military groups on horseback. The uji was also how elites traced their descent to a common ancestor, usually a kami or **Shinto** god. An example of a kami as a common ancestor was the imperial family with the sun goddess. The system also made the leader of the clan the chief priest under Shintoism and secular ruler. Members of the clan or uji all worshiped the same kami. Eventually some of these uji weakened and became subordinate to the more powerful ones. After the shake-up, what was to become the imperial clan found itself the most powerful clan, a first-among-equals status, due to its military might but more importantly its diplomacy through marriage alliances. Plus it made some sense that the leader of Japan should be related to the sun goddess, the most important kami, thought leaders of many uji. Because of Japan's mountains and rugged geography, the imperial clan let the other clan leaders manage the internal affairs of their regions and peasants living there as unelected and unchosen governors. In fact, the word to describe this government was the same in early Japanese as the word for religion. Once the imperial house strengthened with the coming of the Nara Period, the uji at the top became a cultural and political aristocracy, having the power to tax their original areas of control as well as being paid enormous stipends from the central government's tax receipts. By the late **Heian Period**, the term *uji* was more about the trained clan warriors who could raise armies through their control of the countryside. Some of the most powerful were related to some of the families that intermarried with the imperial house, but these uji — and others away from the capital — all prided themselves on skill of battle as bushi or warriors. Their battles for control of first the countryside and then the state led to the end of effete civilian rule and to the bakufu or tent (military) government of the **Kamakura Period**. (To avoid confusion with the term *clan* and the militarist uji, the term *lineage* will be used here to describe the extended kinship systems used in China and Korea.)

Further Reading
Barnes, Gina Lee. *State Formation in Japan: Emergence of a 4th-Century Ruling Elite*. London: Routledge, 2007
Kidder, J. Edward. *Japan before Buddhism*. New York: F.A. Praeger, 1966.

Confucianism

Confucianism, one of the three great philosophical/religious traditions of East Asia, started in China in the fifth century B.C.E. Confucianism looked back to an idealized past of the Shang dynasty (1766–1122 B.C.E.) or the Western Zhou Period (1122–771 B.C.E.), times where people understood their place in society and family. Master Kong Qiu, Latinized as Confucius, thought this past order was the answer to the chaos of his times, when a lower-ranking peasant could climb to the top of the hierarchy and almost constant war plagued the land. Perhaps jealously fueled Confucius — his family was of poverty-stricken nobility. Confucius turned to books and histories of the past and perhaps wrote or collated parts of them–the historical record is vague. These "Five Classics" — *Book of Odes, Book of History, Book of Changes, Book of Rites*, and the *Spring and Autumn Annals* (this last book a history of the recent Eastern Zhou past) — became the foundation of Confucianism. The Confucian canon would also eventually include works or proverbs by Confucius or his key followers, the "Four Books": *Analects* (sayings of Confucius), *Book of Mencius, Great Learning*, and *Doctrine of the Mean*. Confucius believed that society could be

The Confucius Temple (Fuzimiao). Confucius statue, detail. tamir niv/Shutterstock.

saved if it replicated the past through understanding old books, renewing old rituals, and reinstituting systems of order. A natural order existed before; replicate it again and conflict and chaos would evaporate.

Confucius himself wanted to be a sage, a scholar who could advise the rulers of his time. Instead he became a great teacher, imparting his ideology to willing disciples chosen for their ability and not their birth. Confucius philosophized about the here and now, not the hereafter. He placed emphasis on good government, morality, and ethics. Rigid hierarchy also played a large role in his philosophy; he combined the idea of knowing one's place in society with patriarchy and filial piety (respect for one's parents). These ideas became explicit in his Five Relationships: ruler to subject, father to son, husband to wife, elder brother to younger brother, and friend to friend. Notice that all the relationships but the final one showed hierarchy. Women only fit into the system in a subordinate role (as wife). Each of these relationships was reciprocal, however, with the subordinate owing the superior respect and obedience, while the superior owed the subordinate benevolence. A benevolent ruler might forgive taxes a drought-stricken region, for example.

Benevolence (*ren* in Chinese) and ritual (*li*) played key roles in Confucianism. In fact, benevolence under Confucianism is very similar to the golden rule of Western thought, only in the negative form: "Do not do unto others what you would not wish yourself." Those below needed to treat you with loyalty and obedience, performing the proper rituals. These included 3 years of mourning when a parent died as part of filial piety. The ruler needed to observe the correct rituals for the state to please the gods and allow his rule to continue. But ritual should not be observed blindly; real, sincere feeling had to occur during the rites or they were useless. The ruler, like the father, also served as a model of behavior, teaching morality through his actions. Confucius did not believe laws prevented immorality; laws just created criminals. If those at the top of the social hierarchy acted morally and with benevolence, the lower ranks of society would behave well, too. At the top, just below the ruler, stood the scholar-official (*junzi* in Chinese), to explain Confucian ideology to the leader.

Confucianism preached the importance of hierarchy, but with a small rebellious streak. A leader was only a leader if he behaved as one, with benevolence to those below and propriety in rituals. If a leader did not provide those below with benevolence or shirked his ritual duties, the leader could be replaced. But ordinarily Confucianism would be used historically by the elite to keep order; rebellions were started by secret societies in China's other two great teachings.

Mencius is the Latinized name of the second key extoller of Confucianism, one Meng Ke, who lived and wrote around 300 B.C.E. He brought into Confucianism two ideas many associate with Confucius: all people are good and can become sages and the leader rules because of the **mandate of heaven**. Mencius argued that all people are good. As evidence, Mencius pointed out that all people would be shocked to see a child fall into a well; this, he said, was humaneness that he saw as the glimmerings of benevolence. Because benevolence is within everyone, so is the possibility of sagehood, if only one studied and applied Confucianism. And because sages could best predict how to respond to the current conditions in China, it was right and proper for a king to cede his rule to a sage. Not surprisingly, this never happened.

Mencius also argued a king only ruled with the mandate of heaven. The Xia, Shang, and Eastern Zhou dynasties lost out not in the end because they lost mandate of heaven. The mandate provided good weather and compliant subjects. In return the king engaged in proper rituals and treated his subjects with benevolence. Natural disasters or rebellious peasants might mean the king was losing the mandate, hence his overthrow or even regicide was divinely inspired and not immoral under the Five Relationships. Worthy men would then establish new dynasties under the new mandate.

Not long after the days of Mencius, Qin dynasty took over China; Confucianism had to go underground or face elimination. The few Confucian scholars who tried to stand up to the new emperor met hideous deaths, and the Qin emperor burned books to keep Confucianism out of the hands of his subjects. Copies of books that survived often were just piles of old bamboo straps with writing of an older form of Chinese than introduced by the Qin and used ever since. The Han dynasty realized it was the heir to the Qin, so continued many of these Legalist practices. But a clever scholar-official figured out a way to put **Legalism** and renewed Confucianism together. Confucianists had claimed that laws were unnecessary and a ruler should lead by example to get the people to do good. Although perhaps true in the time of the Shang, Zhou, or even the Warring States Period, he argued, the world of the Han was much different. It needed the laws of the Legalists in conjunction with the moral example of Confucianists, just like the world needed the dark of the yin with the light of the yang. Confucianism became part of the ruling ideology of China, at the expense of a little corruption from Legalism and mysticism/religious ideas from the yin/yang.

Also during the Han, the emperor sponsored an imperial university to teach Confucianism. It began with fifty students; in 100 years three thousand students attended. With the Sui and Tang dynasties, the university continued to grow in size, as more and more government positions required the passing of exams based on Confucianism (and for a brief time on Daoism as well). By the Song dynasty and then during the Ming, almost all central government positions required passing the Confucian exams (really Neo-Confucian exams by the **Southern Song dynasty**). These exams were open to all in theory, allowing the best and the brightest to pass the exams and work in government. Yet the difficulty of learning the thousands of characters of classical Chinese, as well as the Confucian canon and commentaries, meant normally members of the gentry ran the government bureaucracies. Only rarely an intelligent peasant boy, backed by his village, earned a spot in government.

By the time of the Sui dynasty, Confucian temples and shrines could be found in all provinces. Religiously Confucianism remained important for rites the emperor engaged in or sponsored for the good of China, and at the family level for the poorly named "**ancestor worship**." But Buddhism, starting slowly at the end of the Han dynasty, briefly overshadowed Confucianism. From 800 to 1200, important scholar-officials studied Buddhism, before some rejected its philosophy. Using ideas gleaned from Buddhism or even Daoism, these scholars created **Neo-Confucianism**. Confucianism in this new guise roared back into the limelight as the most important of the three teachings.

As for Korea and Japan, both societies were profoundly influenced by Confucianism. After 1391 and the establishment of the Yi dynasty, Korea became perhaps more Neo-Confucian than even China! In Japan's case, the **Seventeen Point Constitution** reflects demands adherence to Confucianism, as well as Buddhism. But neither Korean kings or Japanese emperors (let alone Japanese regents or Japanese "**shogun**") ended or even modified their respective hereditary systems like China did for all but the emperor. The examination system in non-China East Asia, when offered, was superfluous.

Further Reading

Berthrong, John H., and E. Nagai-Berthrong. *Confucianism: A Short Introduction*. Oxford, UK: Oneworld, 2000.

Kang, Jae-eun, and Suzanne Lee. *The Land of Scholars: Two Thousand Years of Korean Confucianism*. Paramus, NJ: Homa & Sekey Books, 2006.

Waley, Arthur. *Three Ways of Thought in Ancient China*. Garden City, NY: Doubleday, 1956.

Corvee

Corvee is free labor performed by East Asian peasants as part of taxes or tribute. Peasants would work a certain number of days a year, or in hard times, a few days a month. This work was done for local warriors who owned their land in feudal Japan, or to local officials in China's empire. In China the work usually consisted of building or repairing irrigation systems, flood-control devices, canals—30,000 miles of canals connecting rivers, lakes, and each other by 1400—and fortifications. Conscription for military purposes was usually considered over and above the corvee and therefore in a different category. By the time of the **Southern Song dynasty**, artisans and merchants could pay extra taxes to avoid serving the corvee, and poor peasants having trouble paying the new, monetized taxes, could work extra days of corvee to meet their tax responsibilities. Increased corvee was high on the list of peasant complaints toward the end of many Chinese dynasties.

Further Reading

Benn, Charles D. *Daily Life in Traditional China: The Tang Dynasty*. Westport, CT: Greenwood Press, 2002.

Lvov, Norman Basil. *Japanese Daily Life from the Stone Age to the Present*. New York: Carlton Press, 1977.

Daoism

Daoism is the second of the three great teachings of China. Daoism harkened back to an idealized past further back than the Shang to just after the discovery of cultivation. It cared more about the individual than the state. The term *Dao* comes out of the first text of Daoists, *Dao De Jing*, usually translated as "The Way and Its Power." Supposedly written before the works of Confucius by the mysterious Laozi (although some doubt Laozi ever existed), *Dao De Jing* preaches following the "Way"; yet the Way cannot be defined: "The Way that can be named is not the eternal Way." Not only is the Way nameless, so are its ideas behind how the world or society functions. Much of the *Dao De Jing* continues in this vague and cryptic way, leading some to speculate that the text, written in verse, is also a guide to meditation. In the midst of vague philosophizing, the book also offered some advice for attempting to solve the troubles of the Eastern Zhou Period: "Do not prize possessions and the people will not steal." Perhaps even more difficult to enact by leaders of the time was this pithy sentence: "The best ruler is one whose presence is barely known by his subjects."

A key term of Daoism is *wu wei*, an idea also difficult to describe. It means "nonaction." Daoist texts describe a butcher who cuts meat for years without ever sharpening a knife by sim-

Lao Tzu. Courtesy of photos.com.

ply following the meat where a microscopic gap already existed. Modern equivalents include firing the perfect tennis shot made without applying much swing to a racket or scoring a lay-up in a basketball game without any conscious thought of dribbling the ball or shooting. In these examples the mind is absent from the action; one's body simply flows to what is right after lots of practice. Water is another example of wu wei in action: water yields, flows down, and fills pools, but over the years its channel cuts through rock.

The second Daoist classic was named after its author, *Zhuangzi* (Master Zhuang). Again, some do not believe Master Zhuang Zhou lived, using as evidence the fact that the work in question was written over a couple of centuries. Zhuang extolls the beauty of nature and meditation in everyday life and avoids advice to rulers. The book in many ways seems a direct attack on Confucianism. Confucius himself appears at times, only to be outargued or made the fool by Zhuang Zhou. Confucianism holds to the importance of ritual and honoring parents and loved ones. When Zhuang's wife died, instead of mourning her ritually and avoiding public displays of cheer as a Confucianist would demand, Zhuang sang and played drums. When he was chastised by a friend for quitting his mourning, Zhuang replied that his wife long ago had no spirit and no body, then had a spirit, then was born with a body. With death came another change. If he had continued to mourn her it would show he did not understand the Way.

Zhuang challenged Confucian and other philosophies' emphasis on morality. Good and bad, right and wrong, true and false, all these distinctions become problematic if one was to understand the Way in its totality. Avoid drawing distinctions, wrote Zhuang. Hence it makes sense that ideas of the yin and yang (the dualities that worked together—evil and good, female and male, weak and strong) found their way quite early into Daoism and helped to move it from its philosophical form into a more religious one, or, for lack of a better term, **Religious Daoism**.

The *Zhuangzi* also engages in some interesting metaphysics, not in the sense of discussing gods or the hereafter, but rather being and existence. Zhuang described a dream he had where he was a butterfly and did not know he was Zhuang Zhou. When he awoke, he was not sure he was Zhuang who had dreamt he was a butterfly or a butterfly now dreaming he was Zhuang. Maybe all life was but a dream. That would fit into Zhuang's discussion of death as just another part of life. In fact, Zhuang theorized that the dead might be wondering why they clung to life!

Soon the *Dao De Jing* and *Zhuangzi* would be interpreted for new times, partially due to repression by Legalists and partially due to the nature of the written word. The Qin dynasty ordered many books burned, and in other cases these "prepaper" books fell apart when the leather strap holding the bamboo slats rotted away and when put back together often became rearranged. Only the most educated could read classical Chinese with its thousands of ideograms (and pre- and post-Qin ideograms were often different), so Daoism changed. Although it started out as more of a philosophy for the educated to question, Daoism came to the common folk through a more religious outlook.

As for other East Asian states, Daoism influenced the culture of Korea and Japan, but never to the extent as in China. Daoism first came to Korea from Chinese emigrants and conquerors during the Han dynasty, around 109 B.C.E. By the time the Chinese empire collapsed and the last Chinese either left or merged into the Korean population, Daoism, Confucianism, and even some Buddhism had made their way to the Three Kingdoms of Korea. Daoism, with its love of nature, ended up merging well with the local folk traditions and gods—which also survived—whereas Confucianism and Buddhism ended up the most powerful influences. As for Japan, Daoist ideas on nature and meditation struck a nerve. The Chinese worldview came to Japan through Korea between the fourth and sixth centuries, and Japanese leaders officially adopted Confucianism and Buddhism after the start of the Sui dynasty (around 604 with **Prince Shotoku** and his **Seventeen Point Constitution**, which had a small taste of Daoism in it). Ironically, Daoism's biggest influence in Japan turned out to be **Zen Buddhism**.

Further Reading

Kirkland, Russell. *Taoism: The Enduring Tradition*. New York: Routledge, 2004.

Renard, John. *101 Questions and Answers on Confucianism, Daoism, and Shinto*. New York: Paulist Press, 2002.

Waley, Arthur. *Three Ways of Thought in Ancient China*. Garden City, NY: Doubleday, 1956.

Early Tang Dynasty (618–751)

Most Chinese historians herald the first half of the Tang dynasty as the peak of Chinese culture and China's preeminent place in world culture. The fall of the **Sui dynast**y led to a mad scramble for power. The winner over these pretenders and the peasant armies was another Chinese-nomad military governor of the north who proclaimed power in 618 and spent the better part of eight years consolidating his hold on China using the same Turks as mercenaries — Tang Gaozu, the first emperor of the Tang dynasty. After his second son killed his other sons, Gaozu abdicated in 626 to Emperor Taizong and served behind the scenes as retired emperor until his death in 635.

The Tang dynasty made China the largest, richest, most powerful, and most civilized country in the world, the shining example Japan would follow. Chinese historians consider Taizong one of the greatest of all emperors. He helped create a governing, bureaucratic system utilized from this period forward to the twentieth century (*see* **Tang Governance**) by Chinese emperors to control their vast empires, including a system of laws and divisions of the state down to the county level. Besides these reforming efforts, Taizong also got to the root of government problems: peasant distress. He and his father understood that the **Sui dynasty**'s collapse was mostly due to peasant discontent. So the **equal field system** began anew, this time on a larger scale than ever before. In addition, the tax system allowed flexibility. If people wanted to avoid spending time doing **corvee**, they would simply pay extra taxes. If others wanted to avoid taxes, they could spend more time with corvee. And corvee included militia duty, which guaranteed a large army cheaper than mercenaries.

Agricultural production grew rapidly in the first century of the Tang, and government revenues increased with only moderate tax rates. Large landlords when the equal field system was implemented and Buddhist holdings were hardly affected by the changes. In fact, both were exempt from taxation. Large landholders (usually officials at the district level or local level — below the county level) and government officials in charge at the circuit level (like modern provinces), prefectural level, and county level practiced a lavish lifestyle that soon promoted the growth of the economy, including the import trade: Chinese silk for foreign luxuries. Chinese historians and storytellers alike described the billowing dust created by constant flow of luxury goods to the capital from almost every direction.

China's capital reverted to Changan, along a **Yellow River** tributary. It was a planned city — the largest planned city built to that point and perhaps the largest ever. It stretched over 30 square miles, not including the extensive palace grounds, which, like the city itself, faced south. One million people lived within city walls, while perhaps another million lived just outside the perimeter. The city became the most prosperous, civilized, and cosmopolitan city in the world for its time. Many foreigners, especially Arab traders, arrived through the impressive 500-foot city gate to conduct business and were afforded religious toleration during their stay as a result. China and the Byzantine Empire periodically connected in these years.

Although the Tang emperors created stability within China's borders as long as the census and redistribution of land under the equal field system continued, wars with their neighbors began quickly. Although some of the Turk allies who made Gaozu and Taizong emperors remained loyal, other groups attacked their erstwhile ally, invading from the north all the way to the capital across the great north China plain. A successful counterattack, coupled with disorder among their enemies' leaders, allowed China to recapture the **Silk Road** — lost during the Han dynasty — and the oases the caravans depended on, by 648. The subject peoples conquered in the far west, although officially part of the Tang Empire, had relative autonomy on local matters and would shake off Chinese rule when the Tang dynasty grew weak.

The Tang dynasty also fought with its eastern neighbors, the three kingdoms of Korea. The war proved difficult at first. But once the Chinese went back to their classic ploy—use barbarians against barbarians—the Tang, with an alliance with one Korean state, **Silla**, defeated the rest. The result was a unified Korean state with local autonomy, but a tributary state of China nonetheless.

Then an abnormality occurred in Chinese history. The concubine of an ill emperor started running China from behind the scenes in 660. When he finally died, she deposed her eldest son and ruled though another son, before deposing him. Finally, in 698, she dropped the facade and proclaimed herself **Empress Wu**, ruling until forced out in a coup in 705 when she was 82 years old. She expanded the **examination system**, pushed China's borders to their furthest extent in all directions, and encouraged the worship of all three of China's great traditions as equals: Confucianism, Daoism, and Buddhism. In fact, Buddhism reached its highest point of political and economic power during her years in charge—in this case **Pure Land Buddhism**.

Chinese historians consider the early years of the 700s as the high point of the Tang dynasty and China in general, politically, economically, and culturally. New Emperor Xuanzong had reformed the coinage, repaired and extended the Grand Canal, and briefly renewed land registration for the equal field system. Yet soon he would withdraw from politics and let his chief minister rule as a virtual dictator. First came the abandonment of a militia army for an expensive, paid mercenary force. Frontier generals led nomadic troops in great numbers to protect China's new gains, sometimes with little thought of loyalty. More problems plagued China as Arab forces beat Chinese armies in 751; a deepening social crisis arose as fewer peasants paid increasing taxes. Finally, Buddhist monks took away land from the tax rolls, ignoring yet again the equal field system. Unfortunately for peasants not yet born, no dynasty would ever again succeed in implementing land equalization. *See also* **Late Tang Dynasty.**

Further Reading

Benn, Charles D. *Daily Life in Traditional China: The Tang Dynasty*. Westport, CT: Greenwood Press, 2002.

Wright, Arthur F., and Denis Crispin Twitchett. *Perspectives on the T'ang*. New Haven, CT: Yale University Press, 1973.

Education

Education in China was divided between religious (Buddhist and Daoist especially through their churches and monasteries/nunneries, where they taught religious views, healing, and rarely martial arts) and secular, which included **Confucianism**. As the **Tang dynasty** made the **examination system** increasingly important in getting government position—and by the Song almost all government positions were obtained by passing the different exam levels to become the so-called mandarins—it made sense that the government reestablished the imperial university to teach Confucianism. By imperial decree, at the high point of the Tang dynasty, schools spread down to the county level, with government-sponsored education supposedly teaching over one-hundred thirty thousand students out of around fifty million people. This was not a large number per se, but it was leaps and bounds larger than any other society at the time and does not include private schooling or tutoring, or religious training for the future monks and nuns of Buddhism and Daoism. After learning the ten thousand-plus characters necessary for reading, secular education included the Confucian classics, etiquette, divination, medicine, mathematics, music, poetry, calligraphy, plays, fiction, and history.

These activities of the educated help to explain why the Chinese think historically, constantly remarking on the present with examples from the past. It also showed that as the examination system became the sole route to higher bureaucratic positions with the Song and Ming dynasties, there were no restrictions based on class on who could attend the schools and take the exams. If a smart peasant child–often through the efforts of a village to hire a tutor collectively or through a **lineage**—read well and understood the Confucian classics, he could attend schools or perhaps even the imperial university to prepare for the exams. Of course the elites had the advantage of money for lessons and the time away from the fields to learn to read and write to become by far the majority of the test takers, but by at least allowing a form of meritocracy over aristocracy, China became a model for the West during the Enlightenment in the eighteenth century. This model, however, had a huge weakness discovered centuries later—memorization over independent thought.

The disadvantage of the Chinese educational system were its reliance on memorization and, with the coming of the **Zhu Xi** form of **Neo-Confucianism**, the move away from one's own interpretation of Confucius to instead a slavish copying of Zhu Xi's ideas and even the format of his essays. By focusing on memorization, Chinese bureaucrats lost the ability to think for themselves on the fly and thus leading to troubles for China in the nineteenth century vis-a-vis the Europeans.

Koryo Korea adopted in 958 a Chinese-style civil service examination system, emphasizing mastery of Confucian ethics. Korea's educational institutions quickly followed suit, yet the educated became Sinophillic (ones who love China). The government schools were really just for the elites of Korean society. A number of petty restrictions based on class prejudice kept the potential pool of the poor scholars quite low and helped exclude all but the elite from many government schools.

In Japan from 400 to 1400, education was restricted to those wanting to become Buddhist monks or nuns and the elite of the capital city. Toward the end of the period, a burst of learning by the bushi class began, but the coming of well-educated samurai who could cut down and kill peasants for not knowing their place before crafting an exquisite haiku poem would have to wait until the seventeenth century.

Further Reading

De Bary, William Theodore, John W. Chaffee, and Bettine Birge. *Neo-Confucian Education: The Formative Stage*. Berkeley: University of California Press, 1989.

Lee, Thomas H. C. *Government Education and Examinations in Sung China*. New York: St. Martin's Press, 1985.

Emperor Taizu (d. 976)

With the collaspe of the **Tang dynasty**, China fell into multiple states. The lack of control over the majority of China did not stop elites from bestowing the title of emperor over and over to a series of short-lived dynasties. One night, in 960, the head of the imperial guard awoke to find the yellow robes of the emperor being thrown over his body. General Zhao Kuangyin realized he could be killed and replaced at any time, just like his predecessors, so he sought a solution as Emperor Taizu (r. 960–976). First, he worked hard to limit the power of other generals. He invited the most powerful generals to a banquet. There he succeeded in persuading them to relinquish their military posts in return for generous rewards. By detaching the generals from their military units, Taizu found a way to attach the military units to the state. The central government quickly exerted strict control on the military, even though it was primarily a mercenary force. Periodic and mandatory rotation of its commanders and eliminating the post of military governor helped for the conquest of the rest of China and the founding the Song dynasty—pronounced "soong"—had begun (normally this period is called the **Northern Song dynasty**). Like unifiers before him, Taizu applied moderate force to those opposing him and welcomed those to join him when defeated. However, a seminomadic group made Manchuria and parts of north China its home. With the help of his brother and successor, the **Great Wall** would serve as the dividing line between China and a seminomadic conqueror, the Liao, for three generations.

Further Reading

Brandauer, Frederick Paul, and Junjie Huang. *Imperial Rulership and Cultural Change in Traditional China.* Seattle: University of Washington Press, 1994.

Hon, Tze-Ki. *The Yijing and Chinese Politics: Classical Commentary and Literati Activism in the Northern Song Period, 960–1127.* Albany: State University of New York Press, 2005.

Empress Wu Zetian, imperial concubine until marriage to Emperor Gaozong. Tang dynasty, from album of portraits of 86 Chinese emperors, with Chinese historical notes, 18th century. The Art Archive/British Library.

Empress Wu (d. 705)

During the **Tang dynasty**, an abnormality occurred in Chinese history: a woman became emperor for the only time in Chinese history. At first, she was just the concubine of an ill emperor. She started running China from behind the scenes in 660. When her husband finally died, she deposed her eldest son, Zhongzong, and then ruled through her other son, Ruizong. Finally, in 690, she dropped the facade, deposed Ruizong, and proclaimed herself Empress Wu, ruling until forced out in a coup in 705 when she was 82 years old. Chinese historians find her one of the most ruthless, unscrupulous, and tyrannical rulers in Chinese history, but this might be an exaggeration based on historical Chinese sexism. She killed many of the imperial clan, using terror against her opponents. But her paranoia created more opponents than reality would dictate: she ended up murdering many more than just her outright enemies.

Empress Wu did do some good in her years in control of the Tang dynasty, from expanding the **examination system**, to pushing China's borders to their furthest extent in all directions with military victories. She also encouraged the worship of all three of China's great traditions as equals: Confucianism because of and through her rule and as its literature played the strongest role in most of the examinations; **Daoism** because she believed her family was descended from its founder; and Buddhism from her belief that she was the Bodhisattva of the final Buddha to come as the world ended—Maitreya. In fact, Buddhism reached its highest point of political and economic power during her years in charge—in this case **Pure Land Buddhism**.

Further Reading

Clements, Jonathan. *Wu: The Chinese Empress Who Schemed, Seduced and Murdered Her Way to Become a Living God*. Stroud, UK: Sutton, 2007.

Dien, Dora Shu-fang. *Empress Wu Zetian in Fiction and in History: Female Defiance in Confucian China*. New York: Nova Science Publishers, 2003.

Fitzgerald, C. P. *The Empress Wu*. London: Cresset Publishers, 1968.

Equal Field System

This was first utilized by the Tuobans in the **Northern Wei** dynasty during the **Period of Disunity**. The nomadic conquerors, unfamiliar with how to tax agriculture, decided to use the ideas of leading Confucian-educated Chinese landowning families to help increase and stabilize taxes over the long term, called either "land equalization" or the **equal field system**. The idea behind this system was to maximize the number of landholding peasant families to create an enduring tax base. Theoretically all regular farm was now owned by the monarch or state, but allocated for use based on family size by a peasant for his lifetime. When the peasant or members of his family died or moved away, some or all of the land went back to the state for renewed distribution. If the family grew, it would receive more land for every person older than the age of 5. Orchards, however, would belong forever to the peasant's family for starting the long process of growing the trees without immediate reward. In reality, the system as used during the Northern Wei, **Sui dynasty**, and part of the **Tang dynasty** did little to harm the large, landowning Chinese families, or more importantly take away their land. But other than allowing this concentration of land to continue, the system worked remarkably well for 300 years, guaranteeing the king or emperor with a stable tax base and more quiescent peasants—it even led to increased agricultural yields as new and marginal lands were brought under cultivation.

Within a few short decades after a brief reintroduction, land registration was again discarded. The equal field system ceased to function, leading to a social crisis where landed peasants paid more and more taxes as the elite avoided them and created more tenant farmers.

Japan tried to copy China's equal field system during the late **Yamato Period** and early **Nara Period**. It lasted only a century before its collapse due to exempting aristocrats, changing the rules on bringing new land into cultivation, and tendency to allow hereditary land ownership as the years progressed.

Further Reading

Fairbank, John K., and Denis Crispin Twitchett. *The Cambridge History of China*. Vol. 3, *Sui and T'ang China, 589–906*. Part 1. Cambridge, UK: Cambridge University Press, 1979.

Mole, Gabriella. *The T'u-Yu-Hun from the Northern Wei to the Time of the Five Dynasties*. Roma, Italy: Istituto italiano per il Medio ed Estremo Oriente, 1970

Eunuchs

Eunuchs were castrated males who played a large role at certain times in Chinese history at the government and economic levels. In Chinese histories, eunuchs are often blamed for the decline and fall of a dynasty due to their corrupt ways, placed into opposition with honest Confucian officials by Chinese historians. But Confucianists most often have written the histories of China and neglect the corruption of Confucian officials in their taking of bribes or tax receipts—taking care of their families was more important than the state to these Confucianists. And conversely some eunuchs worked hard to help China.

Eunuchs in China had all their genitalia cut off before their 12th birthday. This was very dangerous in the world before the twentieth-century's antibiotics. Supposedly almost half the castrated died from the procedure. Those that survived kept their genitalia in a small box that would be buried with their body, thus satisfying at least part of their filial piety obligation to leave their bodies in (almost) the condition of their birth. They obviously failed the obligation to produce offspring.

Eunuchs provided China (and Korea, who used eunuchs to a lesser extent) with the same services as elsewhere: guarding the wives and concubines of the emperor to prevent illegal pregnancy. The educated eunuchs could teach members of the imperial family. From there it was only a short distance to power. Because they did not have families, and often served in intimate settings, eunuchs found that Chinese emperors and the imperial family trusted them with more and more governing tasks. Some eunuchs served as chief advisers, generals, an admiral, and chief of the secret police. But Chinese eunuchs, by choosing among the newcomers, created artificial "families" that took later formed factions that fought for power, prestige, and profits, the latter from the tax receipts from the empire.

Although a form of punishment in the **Sui dynasty**, castration created a new class of Chinese who could live close to the imperial family. These eunuchs rose up in power the eighth century, just after the high point of the **Tang dynasty**. One, as general in the invasion of Vietnam, was guilty of horrible atrocities. By the ninth century, eunuchs took charge of the secret police and became virtual masters of the country. Eunuch factions chose eight out of the nine emperors to mount the throne after 800 and fought with the Confucian officials, although eunuchs won more than they lost. Only conflict between eunuch factions kept them as a class away from total control over the last years of the dynasty.

The **Song dynasty** used eunuchs, but not to the same extent as the Tang, believing the eunuchs helped lead to the downfall of the previous dynasty. There were some wealthy eunuchs in the Southern Song, however. The Mongol **Yuan dynasty** did not face troubles from the eunuchs, but the next dynasty would. Imperial family members in the **Ming dynasty** starting in the midfifteenth century would rely on the help of eunuchs for running the government and maneuvering for succession, disregarding the first Ming emperor's warning not to trust eunuchs. In 1400, just after his death, there were only a few hundred eunuchs in the capital, but that number would swell to tens of thousands. Confucianists did have the last word on maritime expeditions, cancelling them not only because they aided merchants, but because Admiral Zheng He was a Muslim eunuch. But afterwards eunuchs became more and more powerful and helped cause the dynasty to weaken and fall in the seventeenth century, and historians cite many examples of corrupt eunuchs stealing millions of ounces of silver in tax receipts starting in the late fifteenth century.

Further Reading

Anderson, Mary M. *Hidden Power: The Palace Eunuchs of Imperial China*. Buffalo, NY: Prometheus Books, 1990.

Mitamura Taisuke. *Chinese Eunuchs: The Structure of Intimate Politics*. Rutland, VT: Charles E. Tuttle, 1992.

Examination System

The examination system was an idea to allow top government officials—those positions chosen by the imperial government and not local ones that the gentry filled—to be placed based on passing a series of exams that would push the smartest to the top. To help the exam takers, the idea of the imperial university of the Han dynasty was reborn and expanded to teach Confucian ideas starting with the **Sui dynasty**. The percentage of government positions given to the degreed candidates, the so-called mandarins, varied based on dynasty, with the tendency to give more jobs to these educated elites as the years went by. The exception was the **Yuan dynasty**, which allowed exams for 20 years before abolishing them briefly for 7 years until resumption in 1342. But even with the examination system, the Mongols only appointed a small number of mandarins, instead using a simplified test that guaranteed **Mongols** the majority of positions. Some historians argue that the great beauty and large numbers of paintings, poetry, and drama of the Yuan Period occurred because the educated classes had so much time on their hands due to their lack of employment by the dynasty.

The examination system was open to all in theory, allowing the best and the brightest to pass the exams and work in government and make China a meritocracy. Yet the difficulty of learning the thousands of characters of classical Chinese, as well as the Confucian canon and commentaries, meant normally members of the gentry ran the government bureaucracies. Only rarely an intelligent peasant boy, backed by his village, earned a spot in government.

The examiners had to worry about cheating and favoritism. The exam takers would write their answers while locked in cells to prohibit cheating. At least one creative student wrote his answers on an undershirt and simply took it off and copied it for the test. To prevent those who graded the exams from recognizing the handwriting of a test-taker or being influenced by his name, other scholars would copy the answers and put a number on the answers instead of a name to keep the examination system fair.

The Sui dynasty's first emperor, Wen (r. 589–604), first sought to create a strong central government in his reunification of China. To give access to government positions to those he just brought back into imperial China, he established a limited examination system to choose officials and a series of rules (adopted by other dynasties as well) to prevent corruption by officials: local officials could not appoint subordinates; officials could not serve in their native place; and officials could serve no more than one tour of duty in the same location. Although Emperor Taizong, the second emperor of the celebrated **Tang dynasty**, was most famous for his bureaucratic system of rule and his legal system—utilized from this period forward to the twentieth century by

Chinese emperors to control their vast empires—he also increased the positions granted to those passing the examination system. Instead of the haphazard system of the Sui, the exams were used for filling positions that were newly created or when a position would become vacant due to the official in question lacking an heir. This meant about one-third of all positions during the early Tang. His Ministry of Officials appointed, promoted, and demoted the officials that helped run the government, down to the local magistrate, leaving local affairs to the local gentry. It was under Tang's **Empress Wu**, the only female to rule in her own name, that the examination system became even more important, although again not universal. Because she believed her family was descended from Laozi, creator of Daoism, the test in her and husband's day also had questions about Daoism to answer. After her expulsion from the throne in 705 at the age of 82, Confucianists resumed their monopoly over the questions.

The wars that ended the Tang and started the Song left a strange situation among the rich and poor, educated and uneducated. Some longstanding gentry families had lost everything, and new families had become wealthy. Only holding a degree allowed the elites to separate themselves from just those who owned land. The Song dynasty instituted an examination system more fair than ever before, used up until the twentieth century (with the exception of the Yuan dynasty) and ending hereditary officialdom (save the emperor and during the Yuan dynasty). All central government officials would be chosen based on Confucian exams; for five hundred spots over one hundred thousand competed—that second figure would grow throughout the centuries, making it difficult for those who completed the exams to obtain an appointment. The printing press—not just a block printing but with moveable type—in full use made Confucian books for study widely available. Of course the usual degree earner came from a wealthy, educated family; it took time to learn classical written Chinese, let alone the Confucian canon. But once in a while, a smart village boy received backing from his neighbors (or his **lineage**) to allow him to study, take the exams, and make the village (or lineage) famous.

Also during the Song dynasty **Neo-Confucianism** replaced older **Confucianism**. Its most famous scholar, **Zhu Xi**, looked at Confucianism through the lens of his own time. For example, people were born good but needed training and self-cultivation through meditation to show this goodness to the world. Zhu's ideas became the orthodox interpretation of Neo-Confucian thought. So important were his ideas that in the late Southern Song, his was the sole interpretation used to pass through the examination system; students even needed to copy the format of his writing for the tests, the so-called eight-legged essay. The downside to Zhu's work is that it led to stagnation among China's intellectuals, who needed to memorize the style and substance of one particular version of Neo-Confucianism from the thirteenth through the nineteenth century. No longer would a degree seeker dare to interpret the Confucian canon himself to show off his brilliance. Students (and those who graded the different levels of the examination system) instead valued memorization not intellectualism, leading eventually to a weakened Chinese intelligencia.

The Yuan dynasty either ignored or marginalized the examination system, so it was up to the first emperor of the **Ming dynasty** (Taizu), to bring it back in all its glory. Taizu was a harsh and autocratic ruler, executing those who spoke out or even made a pun on his name or position. He restored the imperial university and examination system to full prominence in 1382, holding the tests more often than ever before.

As for other countries, Korea, as the country most apt to copy China, also used the examination system, although never to the extent China did. **Koryo Korea** adopted in 958 a Chinese-style civil service examination system, emphasizing mastery of Confucian ethics. Although implementing this system helped broaden the possibility of upward social mobility for talented Koreans of low social background in theory, it, like other memorization tests, tended to stifle intellectual creativity and kept educated Korean Sinophillic (ones who love China). Besides, the system really had the effect of continuing aristocratic rule. The difficulty of mastering written Chinese, the lack of time to learn the Chinese classics, the exclusion from many government schools, and the number of petty restrictions based on class prejudice kept the potential pool of the poor quite low, unable to take any real advantage of the theoretical opportunity Chinese ideas allowed commoners. Status was essentially determined at birth. High government posts went to those at the top of the "bone ranks," a hereditary and not merit-based system.

The Yi dynasty took hold in Korea with the expulsion of the Mongols in the late fourteenth century. The new dynasty was profoundly influenced by Neo-Confucianism. Some scholars have argued that Korea became perhaps more Neo-Confucian than even China, with the exception of allowing anyone to take part in the examination system to obtain government positions—the system still only catered to the elite.

Japan experimented with the examination system with the Taiho Code established in 702. Not only did the code divide the country into three levels of administration and used the **equal field system**, but it also set up the examination system for Japan. However, it really only worked for minor positions in the aristocracy: Japan would remain controlled by hereditary rule, unlike China, and would soon let the tests fall by the wayside.

Further Reading

Herbert, P. A. *Examine the Honest, Appraise the Able: Contemporary Assessments of Civil Service Selection in Early Tang China.* Canberra: Faculty of Asian Studies, Australian National University, 1988.

Lee, Thomas H. C. *Government Education and Examinations in Sung China.* New York: St. Martin's Press, 1985.

Lo, Winston Wan. *An Introduction to the Civil Service of Sung China: With Emphasis on Its Personnel Administration.* Honolulu: University of Hawai'i Press, 1987.

Feng Shui

Feng shui is Chinese geomancy that is practiced also in Korea and Japan; *feng shui* literally means "wind-water," with water the yin of the yin–yang duality. Water is also one of the Five Elements so important to geomancy (fire and wood are yang, water and metal are yin, with the earth in balance between yin and yang). It was a part of **Religious Daoism**. Feng shui was used at the time to decide where to put cities, graves, and houses. The Chinese invented the magnetic compass to insure buildings and cities faced south (like the needle did in China). Geomancy sought to increase the positive energy flowing to the people while pushing away the vapors or negative energy. It also

meant trying to live in peace with nature. A geomancer might warn a landowner not to dig in certain parts of his land. The feng shui specialist might also
tell a government official to build a pagoda to block the vapors coming out of a
stagnant lake near the capital; nonmoving water was even more charged with
yin than flowing water.

Koreans followed a similar system of geomancy. Theirs, however, mixed the
original Chinese ideas with Buddhist thought, a combination that greatly influenced traditional Korean thought. A government bureau in **Silla Korea**, headed
by an official of either the first or second bone rank, built more Korean Buddhist
monasteries on top of high mountains at certain points to have a beneficial influence on the surrounding terrain. These locations were chosen by geomancy.

In Japan, geomancy was mainly used for choosing grave sites, building sites,
and city sites. It used topography and yin–yang ideas to come up with the best
settings for these places. It was more popular in the **Heian Period** and helped
choose the placement of the capital of Heian/Kyoto, the only real city until the
sixteenth century.

Further Reading

Bruun, Ole. *Fengshui in China: Geomantic Divination between State Orthodoxy and Popular Religion*. Honolulu: University of Hawai'i Press, 2003.
Yoon, Hong-key. *The Culture of Fengshui in Korea: An Exploration of East Asian Geomancy*. Lanham, MD: Lexington Books, 2006.

Flower Squires

Flower squires is an organization set up in Silla in the sixth century before
unification of the Korean peninsula. In Silla, one of Korea's three kingdoms,
Buddhism was welcomed and made the state religion. Its king, who, like his
successors, took on Buddhist names, hoped it could help the unification process. These were the days, after all, when three kingdoms divided the peninsula in state building, religion, and philosophy. Only a few years after the king
converted his kingdom to Buddhism in 527, the king created the flower squires,
in Korean the *hwarang*. The flower squires were an elite corps of aristocratic
youth who attended an exclusive military academy dedicated to the protection of Silla and Buddhism. The deity worshiped by the flower squires was the
last Buddha Maitreya, in Korean Miruk; most Koreans in this period followed
suit. Only later did the majority of Koreans change to **Pure Land Buddhism**.

Chinese culture greatly influenced the flower squires. At the flower squires'
military academy, the initiates were taught the six traditional arts of China: etiquette, music, archery, riding, writing, and arithmetic. They even learned swords-
manship, stone throwing, javelin throwing, ladder climbing, and polo. They
wore incredible, awe-inspiring clothing and makeup. They followed a new code
of behavior called the Five Commandments, which was mostly Confucian with
some Buddhism mixed in: loyalty to the King, filial piety toward parents, sincerity in friendship, courage in battle, and discrimination in killing.

There were several hundred bands of flower squires by the seventh century,
and they worked successful to create a unified Korea under Silla after the coming of the Tang Chinese. From their ranks the king was able to choose good
generals, brave soldiers, and able ministers, all depending on the aristocratic
ranks of the individual.

Further Reading

McBride, Richard D. *Domesticating the Dharma: Buddhist Cults and the Hwaom Synthesis in Silla Korea*. Honolulu: University of Hawai'i Press, 2008.

Food

Most Americans understand that ethnic cuisines change greatly when adapted to U.S. taste buds. So it should not come as a surprise that the foods eaten in East Asia from 400 to 1400 were very much different from American versions of Chinese, Korean, and Japanese food. But differences go further than this. Before the Columbian exchange starting around 1500, many common foodstuffs were simply unavailable to the Asian Old World until introduced from Native American cultivators. Foods such as corn, hot peppers, and peanuts—all part of a dish called "Hunan chicken" in the United States today—were unheard of in China before 1500. In fact, it is hard to narrow down a historic cuisine like China's in any event, as the huge size of the empire—even just counting the acres of arable land—dwarfed that of Western Europe. So where you would have French, German, or Italian cuisines in Europe, Chinese people had far different foods depending on which part of the country they lived. There were, however, similarities between Chinese, Korean, and Japanese foods for those who lived by the ocean or sea. All three civilizations ate kelp and fish. Especially useful in soups, kelp provides a fullness of flavor also called savory, the fifth of the different kinds of tastes the human's taste buds distinguish. This savory sense, called *umami* today by researchers from the Japanese (*xianwei* in Chinese), was first discovered by Asians long before Western scientists finally concurred. Finally, fish and seafood delicacies did not count as meat for the Buddhists in these countries, just as in contemporary Christian Europe—and if Chinese lived too far from the sea, the extensive river and lake systems of inland China at the time teemed with fish and river varieties of prawns.

When one thinks of food and China, rice races to the top of the list. But traditional China was north China, where the first Chinese grew millet (in the West today millet is used as birdseed), then barley and kaoliang (sorghum), before the coming of wheat in around 1500 B.C.E. Wheat was for more affluent in north China—turned into flour for noodles, dumplings, and steamed bread—and millet for the very poor. Rice was the dish of choice for those living south of the **Yangzi River** (and for the rich in the north after the creation of the **Grand Canal**). Peasants also grew bamboo (for eating the shoots), taro, melons, chestnuts, bananas, lychee, and palm and citrus trees. The better off also ate long-domesticated pigs, sheep, chickens, ducks, geese, and much more rarely oxen, cattle, or camel. They ate as much of these animals as possible, making delicacies out of sweetbreads and deep-fried intestines, for example. The oxen and cows ate too much grain compared to the calories the meat or milk would provide (plus most Chinese lacked an enzyme in their stomachs to digest cow's milk properly). This led peasants to use these large beasts as work animals only or not keep them on the farm at all. For most of the period 400 to 1400, if one lived well away from cities and towns, Chinese could expect to hunt game or even vermin for food. They consumed bear, deer, marmots, otters, pheasant, elephants, monkeys, rabbits, snakes, rats, cockroaches, and turtles. In fact, under the Mongols much of north China and Manchuria served as private hunting grounds for the elite. And from abroad, elite Chinese dined on peaches from Samarkand; pistachios, figs, and dates from Persia; mangoes from Southeast Asia; and pine nuts and ginseng roots from Korea. But most important, Chinese grew soybeans. Soybeans served as protein—either eaten alone, turned into tofu, or made into a soy flour for baking or other uses—for those who could not afford to eat meat or those who decided to follow meticulously Buddhist religious restrictions on meat.

Because China's traditional fertilizers were animal and human feces, water and many raw vegetables could not be consumed directly if one lived in a place with lots of farmland or many towns and cities. All the bacteria and viruses in the "nightsoil"—the euphemism for human feces used as fertilizer—contaminated the vegetables and when rain came it washed into rivers and streams. That is why Chinese cooking called for quickly increasing the temperature through boiling, steaming, broiling, roasting, and frying—getting food hot enough to kill the dangers present in the raw food. Baking was rarer, with no "oven" in a regular Chinese household—even rich ones—made for the job. By placing food in a pot or wrapping it in clay and throwing on embers one could get an approximation of baking. Chinese cut up food into small pieces before cooking to allow a diner to eat using just chopsticks, and if soup, a spoon.

In terms of beverages, starting in the sixth century in the south and the eighth century in the north tea became a popular drink, especially among monks and nuns wanting to stay alert during meditation. Tea came from the hilly regions in China's southwest and remained a secret for many centuries. Nomads often traded or raided for tea, using it with mare's milk or sheep's milk as a soup instead of just a drink. Although Chinese would prefer to drink tea, one too poor to buy it often would drink "white tea," which was just water boiled long enough to be safe for drinking. Wine was available to the elite, but rice wine was drunk all over China. Rice wine is perhaps a misnomer, as the beverage was manufactured through brewing like beer. In the north millet was used, in the south rice. In addition, nonalcoholic fruit juices—including the invention of an instant fruit drink—slaked the thirst of middle-income peasants and richer Chinese.

Korea's cuisine was influenced constantly by China and once due to Mongol invasion. Because of peninsula-moderated the weather, rice could be grown in most river valleys, while peasants in the northern plains struggled with wheat and uncertain rainfall. Korean peasants thus ate similarly to the Chinese peasant: vegetables and a tiny bit of meat or fish mixed with noodles, dumplings, and rice. The **Mongols** left behind the habit of eating grilled meat (still popular in Korean restaurants to this day), as well as a taste for black pepper that needed to be imported. Among the food innovations by the Koreans were fermented kimchi (in theory any fermented vegetable with seasonings, but usually meaning spicy Chinese cabbage) and fermented soybean paste called *miso*.

The Japanese copied outright from the Koreans miso as the starter for soup, whereas the elites of the **Heian Period** ate wheat noodles like the Chinese did—it would be seven centuries before common Japanese ate wheat noodles. The elites also ate polished white rice and suffered stomach disorders as a result—rice needs its husk or an infusion of vitamins for a consumer to get the full dietary benefits of rice. During Heian times Japanese elites cared more for how food looked and was presented over its preparation and taste. This ideal continues to this day to some extent: Japanese gauge if they are eating properly if they have eaten food of every color. Also during Heian times Buddhism was so popular in the capital that the eating of meat virtually stopped there. There was even a brief attempt to end the eating of fish, but it did not hold up over the years. Those living in the mountains, even Buddhists, decided that because fish were difficult to catch in the quick-moving streams, birds were an acceptable alternative as "fish of the air." And to appease elites in the capital who longed for boar's meat, Japanese Buddhists collectively looked the other way as a boar was also declared a bird!

Peasants ate rice as gruel but did not polish the rice, which left the nutrients intact. They also lived on other grains and vegetables with a little fish. With the rise of the bushi or warrior class in the **Kamakura Period**, hunting resumed for the new elites, and cuisine moved a step closer to modern Japanese food. The warriors also demanded rice; it became a custom that warriors had to be paid one and a quarter pounds of rice daily. Eventually modern delicacies like *sashimi* (sliced raw fish) or *sushi* (fish with vinegar rice) became popular for those who could afford them. Apparently tofu (soybean curd) came about very late in the Ashikaga Period to help the peasants eat a useful animal-free protein. And by this late date the Japanese had adopted the chopstick (early on they used a two-pronged wooden device to eat) but discarded the spoon, preferring to bring the soup bowl up to their lips to drink. Zen Buddhist monks brought over tea, and the Japanese began drinking leaves picked earlier and not fermented like Chinese black tea. The elites even turned the whole tea-drinking experience (the tea ceremony) into a highly ritualized form that helped Zen Buddhism teach some of its ideas.

Further Reading

Anderson, Eugene N. *The Food of China*. New Haven, CT: Yale University Press, 1988.

Clark, Donald N. *Culture and Customs of Korea: Culture and Customs of Asia*. Westport, CT: Greenwood Press, 2000.

Lvov, Norman Basil. *Japanese Daily Life from the Stone Age to the Present*. New York: Carlton Press, 1977.

Footbinding

Footbinding was a vivid and crippling reminder that Chinese elite society had changed after the fall of the **Tang dynasty** and help stand for the Neo-Confucianist backlash against women. Footbinding became popular for the gentry's daughters during the **Song dynasty**. This incredibly painful procedure — wrapping a 5-year-old's feet so they would not grow — kept the elite women's feet smaller than their fist. It made it difficult to walk and thus showed that the family was wealthy enough to do without the work of the woman in question. It also pushed these women out of society, where they had a place before, and into their homes' shadows. Unless planning to sell a daughter to be a concubine, poor girls and women did not experience this torture; husband, wife, and daughters all needed to work the fields together to survive.

Footbinding also had a sexual component. As the foot tried to grow, the bones snapped and left the foot looking a little like a lotus flower, and was considered erotic. A woman with her feet bound up as a youth would use a really small shoe as an adult. Due to acupuncture beliefs, the Chinese looked at the body as having two different body parts "attached" to each other for certain hours of the day, in this case the feet and genitals. In addition, some men believed that the hobbled walking-style footbound women used made the muscles of her genitalia stronger. Many Chinese men believed that the body would supposedly pass that tight feeling of her feet and her awkward walking to her vagina, increasing the male's pleasure during sexual intercourse. The foot fetish may give pause to the Western reader, but remember in the United States today women inflate their breasts with bags full of potentially poisonous materials or otherwise alter their appearance through dangerous plastic surgery. Body image in the United States leads teen-aged girls (and others) to risk their health by not eating or purging after a large meal.

Further Reading
Wang, Ping. *Aching for Beauty: Footbinding in China*. Minneapolis: University of Minnesota Press, 2000.

Grand Canal

The Grand Canal is a system of man-made canals and rivers that connect the area just south of the **Yangzi River** delta to north China and the **Yellow River**. The two emperors of the **Sui dynasty** decided to link a few canals together and extend them to allow grain the state received in taxes to come up from the rice-rich south from Hangzhou (south of the mouth of the Yangzi) to the new capital of Loyang in north China for the 6 months the water levels allowed transit. Another segment of the canal went northeast to an area south of Manchuria that served as a staging area for the invasion of Korea. Built with **corvee** labor of supposedly five and one half million peasants, these forced laborers faced death if they fled and the whip if they worked too slowly. Along the canal were an imperial road, post offices, a courier service, and trees planted for shade. Once the Grand Canal was completed, the second emperor, Emperor Yang took his four-story, 270-foot long dragon boat south to the Yangzi River, towed by peasant power. His entourage reached eighty-thousand men and stretched out as many as 60 miles. He had forced labor build forty palaces so he could avoid sleeping on the barge (water was associated by Chinese with yin, negative energy).

During the **Tang dynasty**, China reached its high point politically, economically, and culturally. Emperor Xuanzong repaired and extended the Grand Canal further west to the new capital Changan. The Tang dynasty was also when new boats were designed for the different parts of the canal for safety and increased usage. This allowed over 150,000 tons of grain and other goods to move north to the capital. Late in the Tang dynasty, discontent among the peasantry, coupled with famine in parts of the country and enormous floods along the path of the **Grand Canal**, led to rebellions that helped to end the dynasty in 907.

After a 53-year period of lack of central control, the Song dynasty rebounded, and with a new invention—a more efficient lock for the canal—built a parallel addition to avoid the Tang-era problems with flooding along the older route of the Grand Canal. The loss of the north led to the Southern Song dynasty, and the northern part of the canal suffered great decay under the Jurchen while the southern, shorter parts functioned beautifully. Once the Mongols took over north China from the Jurchen, all the way to the fall of the Song and start of the **Yuan dynasty**, Mongols—uncharacteristically for nomadic peoples—rebuilt the northern-most segment of the canal and extended it to their capital Beijing. The Grand Canal was its longest, over 1,100 miles. The later days of the **Mongols** again led to trouble with the canal. The third emperor of the Ming, after deciding to move his capital from Nanjing in the south to Beijing in the north, would be left with the problem of repairing the canal's northern-most section, only with newer technology that allowed the canal to function year-round. With a few exceptions, the Grand Canal has continued along this path from this period onward, with much of it widened and used to this day, although no longer human powered through the muscles of canal workers that would haul the ships up or down the system before communism took hold of the government.

Further Reading

Lu, You, and Philip Watson. *Grand Canal, Great River: The Travel Diary of a Twelfth-Century Chinese Poet.* London: Frances Lincoln, 2007.

Great Wall

The Great Wall of China is in many ways a misnomer. The Great Wall is really a series of walls created throughout history by many different dynasties and even smaller states. And sometimes the wall is not even a wall at all; it might be a ditch, a mountain, or a deep valley. The traditional wall would continue on the other side of the obstruction. And the wall varied in materials based on the year and place of manufacture. In the east, large stones and bricks made up the foundation and top of the wall. In regions to the west, the wall was made of stamped loess soil, and in the desert far to the west, Chinese used sand mixed with reeds and branches.

The wall was started during the Warring States Period for protection from neighbors and northern mounted nomads. The first series of connected Great Walls occurred during the first dynasty. Supposedly the emperor of the Qin dynasty sent three million peasants to connect and extend the wall. It served to keep out the less-determined nomads of the north and mark the boundary between the agricultural region of China and the plains and deserts beyond. It could serve as a defensive barrier when sufficiently manned (although a determined attack would always succeed), a watchful eye on nomads when just a few in towers could light signal fires or explode fireworks, and a base of operations when trying to bring the fight to the nomad homelands. Successive dynasties repaired or built new walls for almost 2,000 years, oftentimes using prison labor. The Han and the Ming dynasties were the biggest builders. If all wall systems in the north were to be measured and added together, they would probably exceed 30,000 miles in length. What we consider the Great Wall today was built or rebuilt during the Ming dynasty, and is called by Chinese "The Ten Thousand Li Long Wall," where a li is approximately a little less than one third of a mile. Today's wall (the Ming Great Wall) stretches over 3,000 miles, from Shanhaiquan on the sea near Beijing westward to Jiayuguan in Gansu province, although sometimes the wall doubles back on itself or heads directly south to a dead-end. The wall also varied in size from 10 feet to 35 feet high and from 6 feet to 10 feet wide. It included square walled enclosures with a watchtower and gate-tower on top, with a fortified complex series of inner gates to allow traffic from one side of the wall to the other. Beacon towers dotted the wall at visual intervals to pass messages by sight, sound, or horsed/running courier.

Two of the great myths surrounding the Great Wall: one, that it is all one wall built at one time, and two, that it is the only human-made object visible from the moon or orbit. Even the Chinese "astronaut" Yang Liwei announced in 2003 upon his return to earth that it was impossible to see the Great Wall from space.

Further Reading

Waldron, Arthur. *The Great Wall of China: From History to Myth*. Cambridge, UK: Cambridge University Press, 1990.

Heian Period (794–1185)

This period of Japanese history started when Japanese Emperor Kammu moved the capital from Nara to Heian (today's Kyoto). As the Tang dynasty grew weak, Japan created more and more of its own culture. Historians, however, know little about the lives of the peasants up through the Heian Period. The aristocracy took little notice of the commoners. When they did write about the peasants, 90 percent of society, authors would describe them like animals. But because the period was a vibrant one for literature, historians have a good idea how the aristocrats in the capital—again made out of wood—lived. The most important work is *Tale of Genji*, not only the world's first novel, but the first surviving work in Japanese and a work written by a woman, Lady Murasaki, probably from 1008 to 1021. The story takes place over 75 years, following three generations of the imperial family and five hundred characters in fifty-four chapters originally written in haphazard order most likely to amuse ladies of the court and not for publication. The story became famous first because the beautiful poetry—for a long time considered the only important Japanese language literature—written within the sprawling tale.

In brief, *Tale of Genji* is a story about looking for love where it is forbidden or unlikely to be found. The hero of the tale is popular among Japanese then (and now) because of his capacity to be deeply moved and emotional through poetry, painting, music, and affairs of the heart. Most important, the novel helps to explain the aesthetics of Heian Japan, at least for the 5 percent of elite Japanese living in the capital. But what the Heian Period aristocrats considered beautiful was not necessarily the obvious. Instead of the tune, the smell, or the sight, Heian Japanese elites, in contrast to Chinese, admired the transient nature of life heard in the last few notes of a song fading away, fragrance wafting on the breeze, or shadows present at dusk or dawn. Because marriages were arranged as part of political expedience, men and women in the *Tale of Genji*—and we assume in Heian Japan—had many secret affairs, tales of courtly love. But a man would fall in love with a women not based on her beauty, because women often hid behind screens when courting, but on her writing style or poetry recited. Genji excelled at dance, poetry, and calligraphy, and could cry in front of people should his love be out of reach. Genji is not a hero by standard Western definition that always puts his feelings out of reach to fight the bad guy.

Buddhism rebounded from the move with new sects—although neither was at first allowed to initiate monks—including the rivals Saicho with his Lotus School and Kukai with his Esoteric (or Shingon) Buddhism. The latter sect used pictures to explain Buddhist mysteries and was only open to monks studying with him, a position that led to bitterness between the two leaders. Kukai had visited China and India, and some scholars claim his knowledge of Sanskrit led him to simplify certain Chinese ideograms to represent Japanese sounds, thus making it possible to Lady Murasaki to write in Japanese two centuries later. Saicho built his monastery overlooking the city on Mt. Hiei. Within a few centuries the temple grounds grew to include three thousand buildings. Unfortunately, the Mt. Hiei monks, led by lesser men than Saicho, often times fought in the streets of the capital, demanding titles and land rights. With little military after the end to the conscription system, Heian leaders had to give in many times.

After centuries controlling the imperial family, the Fujiwara needed to keep the size of the imperial family—its relatives—limited in size. To do so it cut off branch families after a certain number of imperial generations. The collateral families had new names and wealth from provincial posts, but many elites would rather live in Heian with its many urban delights made famous by Lady Murasaki and so appointed others to do their jobs and run their estates. Other branch families, most famously Taira and Minamoto, became great warrior families with money for horses and expensive weapons and armor. Fighting soon broke out in the provinces between different groups in the eleventh century. This showed the weakness of the Heian system. Even rule by the emperors changed. Retired or "cloistered emperors" ran the government while the emperor just reigned and performed the Shinto rites. The system finally broke down when in 1156 military force from the provinces was used to control the government starting a cycle of violence across Japan. The eventual victor was the Minamoto family in 1185.

Further Reading

Lvov, Norman Basil. *Japanese Daily Life from the Stone Age to the Present*. New York: Carlton Press, 1977.

Morris, Ivan I. *The World of the Shining Prince: Court Life in Ancient Japan*. New York: Knopf, 1964.

Murasaki Shikibu. *Genji and Heike: Selections from The Tale of Genji and The Tale of the Heike*. Translated by Helen Craig McCullough. Stanford, CA: Stanford University Press, 1994.

Kamakura Period (1185–1333)

This period of Japanese history started with the victory of the Minamoto family after a series of civil wars. Seven years into their de facto control over Japan, Minamoto left his position and forced the emperor to establish in 1192 a new position for control of the secular (and military) government, the **shogun**–barbarian quelling generalissimo.

This new era, the Kamakura Period or *bakufu* (tent government—government by the military) began with the shogun controlling Japan from the Kanto Plain, near where Tokyo is today. The emperor granted the shogun the secular power needed to appoint bureaucrats to staff provincial posts. This made it easier to rule the country. Unfortunately for the Minamoto family, the shogun, Minamoto Yoritomo distrusted his own family and had many members killed. Upon his death his widow and her father started to control from behind the scenes. Instead of taking the shogunate directly, these Hojo family members decided to rule through the shogun as regents. Within three generations the shogun was from the Fujiwara family, with the Hojo family actually running the country through its role as regent.

The late **Heian Period** and Kamakura Period (both eras where China was weak, leaving the Japanese to create their own culture) saw the rise of the military class, the bushi or warrior. Not quite the samurai of film and comic book fame, the bushi owned lands like a European knight that enabled him to be able to own the horse, armor, and sword needed for combat. These warriors were rewarded for their victories in the long wars at the end of the Heian Period. They also were subject to the Joei Code in 1232. This code provided rules for the bushi in matters that might well have been solved by violence, such as land tenure, succession, and property rights of widows and divorced women. The shogunate, under the Hojo, would work to solve such disputes in the fairest ways possible. Warriors began to work on an informal code of their own, although not quite the samurai bushido code of the seventeenth century. Kill or be killed was part of the code, and *seppuku* (ritual disembowelment often called "harakiri") was for those dishonored on the battlefield. These men were aided by new sects of Buddhism, especially **Zen Buddhism** for its single mindedness and lack of fear of death. Nichiren Buddhism, with its strong appeal to patriots and simple ways to nirvana, and **Pure Land Buddhism** (and its splinter group True Pure Land Buddhism) with its nembutsu chanting and optimism about being reborn in a heaven-like Pure Land, also helped bushi, commoners, and elites alike.

There were some brief outbreaks of violence, but the bakufu retained control over Japan quite easily until the coming of the Mongols. In 1274, Khubilai Khan sent an invasion fleet made up of Korean ships, Korean warriors, and Mongol horsemen—a total of thirty-thousand men—to invade Kyushu. Fierce fighting broke out, but an unexpected storm destroyed much of the fleet and led those on the ground to retreat. In 1281, now leading the **Yuan dynasty** in China, Khubilai Khan sent envoys to urge Japan to surrender. Instead, the Japanese executed the envoys. Luckily for Japan, the Mongols again invaded Kyushu; this time the Japanese had built a wall to make breaching defenses more difficult, even in the face of one-hundred forty thousand enemies. Again a typhoon halted the attack and the Mongols again retreated, this time for good.

Although a military victory, no additional lands or wealth were won in the struggle and divided up among the bushi. As a result, the bushi became less enamored of their leaders. So when Emperor Go-Daigo launched his Kemmu Restoration in 1333, seeking to return the power to rule to the emperor, many disgruntled bushi joined his cause, so ending the Kamakura Period.

Further Reading

Louis-Frederic. *Daily Life in Japan at the Time of the Samurai, 1185–1603*. New York: Praeger, 1972.

Oyler, Elizabeth. *Swords, Oaths, and Prophetic Visions: Authoring Warrior Rule in Medieval Japan*. Honolulu: University of Hawai'i Press, 2006.

Koryo (Korea) 935–1254

A former merchant, Wang Kon, reunified his country in 935 as Koryo, from which we get Korea. Because so many of the aristocrats had died in the wars for control of Korea, Wang and his successors were able to create a government much closer to the Chinese model, including a civil service **examination system** in place after 958 based on Confucian ethics and Chinese history. Government schools soon taught these subjects, allowing some of society's lower-ranking members into important positions, if they could learn to read Chinese!

Koryo soon faced trouble from without, as a formerly nomadic people, the Khitans, settled down in Manchuria and defeated the Koreans, forcing Koryo to become a weak tributary state in 1010. Only 8 years later, Koryo decisively defeated the Khitans, allowing the Koreans to build a wall to prevent a future invasion. Later that century, the Khitans were defeated and replaced by the Jurchen–Koreans put down the Jurchen quickly thereafter.

Although the bone ranks ceased to exist, Korea's hereditary aristocracy slowly rebuilt itself and divided society into different sectors. At the top were the civil officials and the military officers, together called the *yangban* (the two orders). Next came a small group, the *chungin* (middle people), lower-ranking government officials. Below these hereditary aristocrat ranks came the commoners and peasants called the *yangmin* (good people), whose taxes and **corvee** labor supported the government and aristocracy, as those on top passed on the tax burden to those below through their growing, tax-free estates. Their poverty was obvious—trade was conducted usually in barter. At the very bottom, making up at least 30 percent of the population, were the *chonmin*. The "lowborn" were made up of slaves descended matrilineally, government workers in mines and porcelain factories, and workers made outcast because of Buddhism, like the **burakumin** in Japan: butchers, tanners, leatherworkers, and entertainers.

Koryo's civilian government was overthrown in 1170 by a military coup. A century of military rule followed, but not peacefully. Military men fought each other for control, and—peasant and slave rebellions brought widespread social turbulence. Only one military strongman was able to bring a semblance of order to Korea: General Choe Chung-hon. He eliminated rivals, put down rebellions, and he and his descendants kept the **Mongols** out of Korea until assassinated so Koryo could stop the fight with the Mongols to become their tributary state. For the next 100 years or so, Korean kings were forced to marry Mongolian princesses, and self-rule ended.

Further Reading

Kim, Kumja Paik. *Goryeo Dynasty: Korea's Age of Enlightenment, 918–1392*. San Francisco: Asian Art Museum—Chong-Moon Lee Center for Asian Art and Culture, 2003.

Lancaster, Lewis R., Kikun Suh, and Chai-Shin Yu. *Buddhism in Koryo: A Royal Religion*. Berkeley: Institute of East Asian Studies, University of California, 1996.

Vermeersch, Sem. *The Power of the Buddhas: The Politics of Buddhism during the Koryo Dynasty (918–1392)*. Cambridge, MA: Harvard University Asia Center, 2008.

Late Tang Dynasty (751–907)

Emperor Xuanzong spent the first half of his reign (712–765) as an active emperor. Yet he tired of the position. He withdrew from politics and let his chief minister rule as a virtual dictator. Then came a series of minor catastrophes. First came the abandonment of a militia army for an expensive, paid mercenary force. Frontier generals led nomadic troops in great numbers to protect China's new gains, sometimes with little thought of loyalty. Couple that with a defeat with Arab forces in 751 and a deepening social crisis as fewer peasants paid increasing taxes—all due to Buddhism taking away land from the tax rolls and ignoring yet again the **equal field system**. And unfortunately for peasants not yet born, no dynasty would ever again succeed in implementing land equalization.

The biggest damage to the dynasty started in 755 with the illiterate slave of nomad origin An Lushan. Grotesquely obese but charismatic and cunning, he had gotten into the confidences of Emperor Xuanzong's favorite consort and thus the emperor by playing the buffoon. He used this trust to send one-hundred fifty thousand troops from north China to Loyang without meeting resistance. He then closed the short gap and attacked the capital Changan, proclaiming himself the new emperor. The real emperor fled south in remorse; his escorts forced him to kill his betrayed consort. Then Xuanzong's heir apparent fought An's forces until victory in 763.

The victory proved hollow, as loss of the capital showed the dynasty's weakness. Quickly between 25 percent and 30 percent of China fell into the hands of autonomous military governors, and parts of the empire to the far west obtained their independence. Throughout the final half of the dynasty, emperors periodically had to fight these generals to keep from independence. In addition, **eunuchs** rose up at the end of the eighth century. Although originally hired to protect the emperor's wives, consorts, and concubines, by this late date they took charge of the secret police and became virtual masters of the country. Eunuchs chose eight out of the nine emperors to mount the throne after 800. Conflict between eunuch factions held them back from total control.

Hoping to stop the dynasty's decline and to increase tax receipts otherwise stolen along their way to the capital by the empire's own collectors, the Emperor Wuzong—a fervent Daoist—persecuted Buddhists to bring their lands back onto the tax rolls. From 841 to 846, the new emperor through edict destroyed 4,600 temples and monasteries, forty-thousand smaller shrines, and secularized 260,000 monks and nuns. **Pure Land Buddhism** in China would never recover, nor would Buddhism ever again have as much influence, even as successor emperors repealed Wuzong's efforts. Instead, **Chan Buddhism** (**Zen Buddhism** in Japan) would become the most popular form, even taking over some of the church-like behaviors of the Pure Land sect. Besides, the monetary windfall expected from the elimination of Buddhism turned out to be too little to help save the dynasty. Discontent among the peasantry, coupled with famine in parts of the country and enormous floods along the path of the **Grand Canal**, led to rebellions. The largest of these became one of the largest in Chinese history—the Huang Chao Rebellion—and its merchant-family leader even declared himself emperor over part of China for 2 years, until the few surviving members of the **Tang dynasty**, allied with Turkish fighters, defeated him. But at what cost? The Tang dynasty disintegrated in 907 into another disunited period, this time only 53 years in duration.

Further Reading

Benn, Charles D. *Daily Life in Traditional China: The Tang Dynasty*. Westport, CT: Greenwood Press, 2002.

Wright, Arthur F., and Denis Crispin Twitchett. *Perspectives on the T'ang*. New Haven, CT: Yale University Press, 1973.

Law

The idea that China needed laws was anathema to Confucianists. But starting with the Han dynasty, emperors decided that although it would be wonderful if Confucian ideals about morality worked in the Han dynasty, the **Period of Disunity**, or **Tang dynasty**, the emperors believed that the Qin dynasty's **Legalism**, the idea that people are evil or at least lazy and the government needs laws to control them, needed to work with **Confucianism**—leading by moral example—to keep China ordered and peaceful. Yet moralism is writ large all over how China enforces its laws. China's legal system goes back to the celebrated Tang dynasty and Emperor Taizong, its second emperor. He first divided China into first ten (later fifteen) large circuits that resemble modern-day provinces in their boundaries. He then subdivided them into over three-hundred-fifty prefectures and more than fifteen-hundred counties managed by magistrates and other officials, the lowest part of the central bureaucracy that could be appointed by the emperor. The final division, sixteen-thousand districts, were under control of the local elites, as the central government could not control what happened at the local level with the size of the empire and the technology of the time. Most important, Taizong also created laws of two types—primary (meant for all time) and secondary (regulations that would be adjusted over time).

The worst crimes were the Ten Abominations, which covered four different categories of criminal behavior. Most were about the emperor and included plots to eliminate the current emperor, as well as what to feed him and how to treat him if diseased. Laws even covered criticism of the emperor or destruction of his property. The second category of abominations were crimes against the state (helping a foreign ruler or killing a top official), although as the emperor was a stand-in for the state, oftentimes a crime was a first and second abominations. The third category of abominations was crimes against one's own family—beating or murdering any elders in the family or one's husband. Of course violence, on the other hand, as long as not fatal, was not a crime. For example, a father could beat his son with impunity. Even making accusations against one's elders was a crime, as was selling them into slavery. Finally, the final category of abominations were depraved crimes: dismembering or burning a body, implementing poisons to kill, using sorcery, or killing three members of the same household.

The rest of the primary crimes were the ordinary crimes seen in society then and now: murder, robbery, rape, and so on. These crimes would be tried a the local level by local gentry, while at least the top two levels of abominations would be tried by imperial courts by mandarins. It was hard to get a fair trial locally, because at the lowest levels of government a gentry member might be the tax collector, police chief, and judge all in one! In larger districts, all these positions might be held by members of the same household. Guilt was determined by the judge examining the evidence and interrogating the suspect. The judge was supposed to see if the suspect's statement made logical sense; find if the suspect was blushing or breathing strangely while telling his or her story and thus lying; check to see if the suspect could hear the questions asked; and look into his or her eyes to see if they were clear (to see if not insane or otherwise unfit to stand trial). Key to determining guilt, like Europe at the time, was the confession. As a moral society, the elites expected the criminal to admit guilt.

If the criminal refused, but facts bore out the suspect's guilt, the judge could demand the suspect be tortured until the court received a guilty confession. But
whether at the local level or some higher level with judges appointed by the
emperor (or later, in the Song dynasty, appointed through the **examination system**), judges had little leeway in sentencing the criminal, as the punishments
were often printed on the walls of the judge's office. Five different punishments
awaited Chinese criminals: thrashing with the rod up to fifty blows; hitting with
a thick stick up to one hundred blows; enslaving by the state for up to 3 years
(jails were only to hold suspects temporarily); exiling up to 1,000 miles; and executing by either strangulation (preferred) or decapitation (worse because of the
belief that one's ancestor's provided one with a body and it was a disgrace to
not leave the world as one came into it). The emperor had to review all death
sentences and often commuted the sentence to a lesser one. Notice that except
for death, all forms of punishment relied on embarrassment; even with laws
Chinese Confucianism influenced society in a moralistic fashion.

Another was of controlling subjects at the local level—reinstituted by **Emperor Taizu**, first emperor of the **Ming dynasty**—used the *li-jia* system for
local control and allocating corvee service. Every ten families in an area were a
jia and ten jia formed a *li*. All were responsible for each other following the
laws and making sure corvee work was done. If anyone broke the law, all in
that jia and perhaps in the li (depending on the seriousness of the crime) would
face the same sentence as the one who did the crime, unless someone turned
in the suspect immediately.

Korea and Japan from 700 to 1400 followed closely Chinese law. Although
the exact crimes and penalties would not necessarily be enforced, the Korean
and Japanese codes of law worked in similar ways to Tang China's law codes.

Further Reading

Hansen, Valerie. *Negotiating Daily Life in Traditional China: How Ordinary People Used
Contracts, 600–1400.* New Haven, CT: Yale University Press, 1995.

Johnson, Wallace. *The T'ang Code.* Vol. 1, *General Principles.* Harvard Studies in East
Asian Law. Princeton, NJ: Princeton University Press, 1979.

McKnight, Brian E. *Law and Order in Sung China.* Cambridge, UK: Cambridge University Press, 1992.

Legalism

Legalism is the idea that all a ruler does is right, and that repressive, restrictive, and punishing laws need to be placed on the rest of society. The Qin
state, which unified China for the first time, began its conquests with Legalism
as its state ideology and kept the philosophy through its short history as a dynastic empire. Through ruthless war, the Qin achieved victory. The Qin dynasty inaugurated imperial China in 221 B.C.E. with the first emperor.

Under Legalism, an individual only existed to serve the state in wartime
and harvest time. People needed laws to regulate their behavior because according to Legalism people were evil, or at their best, lazy. Laws needed stiff
penalties, including death. A whole family might pay the punishment, under
the theory that collective responsibility made rebellion less likely and families
should not shield a law breaker. Leaders raised taxes to obscene levels in
peacetime to help pay for wars already waged; in some ways the populace

looked forward to war as a period of less repression! Luckily for the Chinese people, the Qin dynasty only lasted until 207 B.C.E., as peasant unrest over repression and taxes helped to eliminate those who sought to continue the Qin. Unfortunately for peaceful Chinese, Legalist ideas would continue in future dynasties like the Han and the **Sui**, and even in more recent times with the Cultural Revolution under Communist Mao Zedong (1966–1969) or the Tiananmen Square massacre in June 1989 under Deng Xiaoping. Leaders imposed Legalism to create a repressive future.

During the Han dynasty, a Confucian scholar figured out the reason for continuing the Legalist tradition with harsh laws. He realized the Han dynasty was the heir to the Qin, so it needed to continue many of these Legalist practices. Confucianists had claimed that laws were unnecessary and a ruler should lead by example to get the people to do good. Although perhaps true in the time of the Shang, Zhou, or even the Warring States Period, he argued, the world of the Han was much different. It needed the laws of the Legalists in conjunction with the moral example of Confucianists, just like the world needed the dark of the yin with the light of the yang. Legalism stayed as part of the ruling system in China, but never as a popular philosophy. It was also tempered by Confucian benevolence in government.

Further Reading

Waley, Arthur. *Three Ways of Thought in Ancient China.* Garden City, NY: Doubleday, 1956.

Lineages

In China and Korea, families kept track of their ancestors for what in the West has been mistakenly called "**ancestor worship**." Lineages were families that could trace their ancestors back to the same source, always a male and usually the male who settled the area where the lineage held its ancestral hall. The lineages that could trace back their ancestors the furthest—meaning the lineage would likely be the largest—came from southern China. Nomadic incursions in the north no doubt made this the case, although some lineages cheated by claiming relations far into China's prehistory. Not all Chinese were in contact with lineages, moving because of war, revolution, or to begin lives with a fresh start. Chinese lineages were often well organized, with the wealthiest members of the lineage in charge of the lineage's ancestral hall, graves, and ritual land. At the spacious ancestral hall, the lineage's members would meet usually twice a year to commemorate the ancestors—hence the Western idea that these meetings were ancestor worship—whose names were written on a wooden tablet along with his title and birth and death dates. The lineage hoped that the ancestors would help them, or at the very least not harm them as ghosts. Once a year in the spring, the leaders of the lineage would use their maps of ancestral graves to locate them so that they could be cleaned and maintained before they offered sacrifices of wine and food to the departed. They would use **feng shui** or geomancy to determine the best plots for future graves. The lineage leaders also made sure the ritual land brought funds to the lineage to help pay for the hall, graves, and sacrifices, and perhaps even a fund to educate the best and brightest students of the whole lineage, as well as provide help to downtrodden members of the lineage like widows and other poor members. Use of this land was often controversial. Members of the lineage who farmed the land thought they should get preferential rents, whereas the clan leaders argued they needed to maximize income for the good of all. There was also the fear by the poor relations that the lineage leaders siphoned off rents for their private use to the detriment of the entire lineage. If it happened with elites and taxes, it would make sense for rents and the lineage leaders.

The Korean lineages provide a much more confusing mix compared to the Chinese lineage system. Much of it is due to historic Korea's matrilineal system. By the time of Chinese influence on Korea, Koreans believed that a child's bones came from the father and the flesh from the mother. Both showed kinship and thus prevented marriage among the kin. But because flesh was soft, the kinship of the female line faded after eight degrees of kinship (a first cousin is four degrees of separation). Marriage between any relations on the father's direct side, however distant, was prohibited—much like the Chinese taboo on marrying someone with the same family name.

Lineages played a huge role in Korean "ancestor worship" as well. By the time of Yi Korea those of the elite *yangbang* status often set aside fields to support annual ancestor worship on the father's side (the **Neo-Confucianism** of the Yi dynasty had pulled elites away from the old days and commemorated matrilineal ancestors) more distant than the great-great-grandfather. The tenant of this land, the gravekeeper, had to use income from the land to prepare elaborate ancestral sacrifices during the tenth lunar month. Ancestral tombs in Korea were usually scattered all over the hills and mountains surrounding the farmland of the villages. The Korean aristocrats and the correct gravekeeper were thus forced to spend a month or more traveling over mountains and streams from tomb to tomb. They had to carry the sacrificial materials to hold ancestor commemoration ceremonies ("ancestor worship") starting with the earliest ancestor to arrive in the village and working to the great-great grandfather.

Further Reading

Bossler, Beverly Jo. *Powerful Relations: Kinship, Status, and the State in Sung China (960–1279)*. Cambridge, MA: Council on East Asian Studies, Harvard University, 1998.

Freedman, Maurice. *Lineage Organization in Southeastern China*. London: University of London: Athlone Press, 1965.

Kang, Hildi. *Family Lineage Records As a Resource for Korean History: A Case Study of Thirty-Nine Generations of the Sinch'on Kang Family (720 A.D.–1955)*. Lewiston, NY: Edwin Mellen Press, 2007.

Mandate of Heaven

Mandate of heaven is the Chinese idea that the emperor rules China due to a proper relationship with the gods and the nation's ancestors. Historically minded Chinese like Confucius faced a conundrum. If an imperial family has the right to rule because of the gods, how does one explain the fact that dynasties in ancient times, like the Xia and the Shang, collapsed. The Xia and Shang dynasties lost out in the end because they lost mandate of heaven. The mandate provided good weather and compliant subjects. In return the king engaged in proper rituals and treated his subjects with benevolence. Natural disasters, poor growing weather, or rebellious peasants might mean the leader was losing the mandate, hence his overthrow or even regicide was divinely inspired and not immoral under **Confucianism**'s Five Relationships. The fall of dynasties actually followed a pattern before worthy men could then establish new dynasties under the new mandate.

First came the natural disasters, trouble with crops, and gross overtaxation of the peasantry. Soon thereafter angry peasant rebellions began, often led by Daoist or Buddhist secret societies, aiming at the now-disreputable dynasty, rich landlords, or both. Many times nomadic forces would take advantage of the strife or outright civil war within China to take lands on the periphery of the dynasty, and sometimes much more. At this point the government, lacking skilled leaders, often began begging for help from the landlords. These obvious weaknesses showed a clear loss of the mandate of heaven and resulted in one of the following: conquest of half or more of China by outside nomads; a rich landlord crowning himself emperor of a new dynasty after leading a powerful army that defeated the peasant armies and the imperial forces; or, in the rarest outcome, a peasant leader starting a new dynasty after victories against nomads, rich landlords, the state, or all three.

Even though Japan borrowed many Chinese ideas, including Confucianism, there were some differences in how they were interpreted. For example, emperors ruled not with the mandate of heaven, but because they were related to heaven through the imperial **clan** and the sun goddess. This meant that in Japan people did not take over and become emperor. Instead, anyone trying to take control of the government would rule through the emperor, keeping his lineage intact. Regents and **shogun** were two ways around the emperor for secular and military power, leaving to the imperial house the religious aspects of reigning rather than ruling.

Further Reading

Marshall, S. J. *The Mandate of Heaven: Hidden History in the I Ching*. New York: Columbia University Press, 2001.

Renard, John. *101 Questions and Answers on Confucianism, Daoism, and Shinto*. New York: Paulist Press, 2002.

Ming Dynasty (1368–1644)

Zhu Yuanzhang, a former peasant and one-time monk who led the Red Turbans of the secret Buddhist sect White Lotus, defeated the **Mongols** and its **Yuan dynasty** by allying with the Chinese landlords. This proved a winning change of strategy, even though the peasants were oppressed by the gentry class and had started their uprising almost two decades earlier by challenging Mongol and rich Chinese alike. Once Zhu became emperor he changed his reign name to Hongwu but is better known to history as his posthumous title Taizu, founder of the **Ming** or Brilliant dynasty. As a former peasant who led a peasant uprising, he understood the importance of **agriculture** and keeping the peasants complacent. He warned his officials that peasants were like young trees that should not be shaken. Taizu worked to promote agriculture by giving title to abandoned land cultivated by peasants, even exempting them from 3 years' taxation and **corvee**. He also ordered the irrigation systems be fixed and tried to settle garrison troops on reclaimed land for the military to obtain their own grain by farming. Even artisans were better off under the Ming, as they could buy their way out of the corvee by paying higher taxes.

Although shrewd in managing peasants, Taizu was a harsh and autocratic ruler, executing those who spoke out or even made a pun on his name or position. He even denied being a part of the White Lotus and declared the group an illegal organization. He forced his advisers and ministers to kneel in front of him rather than the previous Chinese practice of standing at attention or even sitting. He restored the imperial university and **examination system** in 1382, but he only trusted his own family members and gave out huge land grants to his many sons and grandsons. He also divided the Ming empire into fifteen provinces, all corresponding with minor differences to present-day ones. Yet he was also a hard worker, supposedly reading over sixteen hundred memorials in only 10 days. Although he restored China to **Tang governance** with the six ministries, he controlled important parts of the government himself rather than having help by high Confucian bureaucrats in the secretariat or chancellor's office; in fact, he eliminated the latter. These decisions would prove a mistake in the long run, as emperors and imperial family members later in the Ming dynasty would rely on the help of **eunuchs** for running the government and maneuvering for succession, disregarding Taizu's warnings on the matter. By 1400, there would only be a few hundred eunuchs in the capital, but that number would swell to tens of thousands—eunuchs became more and more powerful and helped cause the dynasty to weaken and fall in the seventeenth century. Finally, at the local level, Taizu used the li–jia system for local control and allocating corvee service. Every ten families in an area were a *jia* and ten jia formed a *li*. All were responsible for each other following the laws and making sure corvee work was done.

Taizu also went to war with the Mongols, first capturing Beijing before pushing them back over the **Great Wall** in 1382. He followed up these successes with difficult and expensive expeditions into Mongolia to keep the pressure on the Mongols. In the midst of these inconclusive battles, Japanese pirates began to prey on Ming shipping, a problem not solved in two centuries. But these negatives did not outweigh China's agricultural growth during Taizu's reign, especially when taking into account the renewed spread of south Vietnamese strains of rice that allowed three crops a year in the south and two crops a year in the Yangzi delta. China's population rebounded to 110 million.

Taizu chose his grandson, known later as Huizong (r. 1399–1402), to succeed him, but a civil war broke out over his choice. The winner was Yongle, Taizu's son, known to later historians as Chengzu (r. 1403–1425). It was he who rebuilt Beijing as the capital of the Ming and continued work on the Great Wall—to keep the Mongols at bay—as well as sending out a huge trading fleet seven times. The Forbidden City, the part of Beijing where the emperor lived and ruled, remains the best example of Ming architecture and aesthetics. After Chengzu's reign, however, Confucian leaders began a full-scale crackdown on the merchant class, destroying the huge ships over 400 feet in length used in the fleet, including the plans on how to make them. They also destroyed many of the merchant maps of the Southeast Asian and Indian Ocean trading regions. The smaller Chinese ship size meant only short voyages could be contemplated, and Japanese pirates prevented much trade or exploration in these small ships. Mongol rule had led to renewed distrust of merchants and foreigners and made most Confucianists believe—perhaps rightly—that Chinese civilization was the greatest in the world and did not need foreign influence. These factors are important to explain why Europe "discovered" the world instead of China less than a century later.

Further Reading

Chan, Hok-lam. *China and the Mongols: History and Legend under the Yuan and Ming*. Aldershot, UK: Ashgate, 1999.

Farmer, Edward L. *Zhu Yuanzhang and Early Ming Legislation: The Reordering of Chinese Society Following the Era of Mongol Rule*. Leiden, the Netherlands: E.J. Brill, 1995.

Money/Coinage

Early in its history the Chinese minted the famous copper cash coins. These little coins with square holes in the center became widespread. These copper coins became very useful. However, the small value of a single cash led to these coins being put on strings to facilitate trade. These strings were supposed to be one-hundred cash coins but were rarely if ever an actual hundred. These coin strings were traded for more expensive items, including the purchasing of markets. Peasants had no need for this currency because they could pay their debts in kind. Due to this fact, the supply of these coins was readily available.

However, during the **Southern Song**, this changed. More coins were minted to meet increased demand. When this was not enough, the Chinese Empire resorted to trading goods for weighed gold and weighed silver. China did not, in fact, mint their own silver or gold coins during this time period. "Flying money"—essentially a check or promissory note—were developed in the ninth century to compensate for this problem. In 1024 flying money gave way to the invention of paper currency, as the Song dynasty became monetized and peasants had to pay taxes in coin instead of in kind. The Chinese government even created a central bank system and dated the money to be good for only 3 years. At first, this helped facilitate trade as less of the bulky cash coins or ingots of gold or silver were needed. However, the government printed too much paper money, leading to large-scale inflation; its trading value sharply diminished.

Counterfeiting also became a problem in China. Paper money was much easier to counterfeit than metal coins, allowing greater latitude for potential crooks. Like in the West, counterfeiting was punished by death. When the **Mongols** conquered China, they issued their own paper money, backed by silk, and tried to stop trade in other kinds of currency. These "silk notes" have been found far outside of China and replaced the older paper currency. But they too printed too many and were hurt when inflation hit.

Because Korea and Japan's economies were so far behind China's, barter proved the easiest way to trade goods. Eventually, Chinese coins were used in Korea and Japan. These coins were used as local currency, even in the string form. Japan later would mint its own copper coins and used weighed silver and gold once it realized that its minting process led to more gold in the early coins and less gold in the later coins. Once Korea's economy boomed with the introduction of celadon (fine porcelain), it issued iron and copper coins, with silver shaped like a miniature vase. But even after this introduction in 996, Koreans still often traded in amounts of grain and linen, and Japan used *koku*, or how much rice an average person ate in a year, to conduct business.

Further Reading

Hansen, Valerie. *Negotiating Daily Life in Traditional China: How Ordinary People Used Contracts, 600–1400*. New Haven, CT: Yale University Press, 1995.

Von Glahn, Richard. *Fountain of Fortune: Money and Monetary Policy in China, 1000–1700.* Berkeley: University of California Press, 1996.

Wang, Yu-ch'uan. *Early Chinese Coinage.* New York: S.J. Durst, 1980.

Mongols

The Mongols were a nomadic people living on the steppes to the north of the Chinese Empire. Like other nomadic or herding societies, these various tribes were considered to be barbarians to the peoples of China and Korea. And like other nomadic groups, the Mongols had launched brief raids into China, stealing goods or demanding tribute to stop the attacks. For this reason, the **Great Wall** was constructed and constantly rebuilt throughout history to put up a border between the civilized, farming world and the nomadic lands of groups like the Mongols. It was hoped the wall could thwart or at least slow down a nomadic raid.

The Mongols did have connections with other societies through trade and conquest along the **Silk Road**. They learned and followed different faiths, depending on their tribe. By the time Genghis Khan unified the tribes into an unstoppable fighting force there were Christian, Muslim, Buddhist, and even Manicheanist Mongols, all allowed religious freedom.

The Mongols were expert horse riders; their skills honed by centuries of herding animals. The Mongol horses were of the highest quality, making it much easier for the Mongols to carry out their conquests. This mobile lifestyle, as well as a great proficiency in archery with a powerful composite bow and in-battle formation, helped the Mongols become a force to be reckoned with. The Mongols also had a system of fast couriers that could transmit messages up to 200 miles per day! But until they settled down in China, Mongols did not read or write. To keep oral messages from being garbled, the Mongols put the orders into music and rhyme. This allowed the most important ability in war to occur—clear communication which allowed commanders to split an army and have it come back together as one once the battle was joined.

Mongol victories came about due to some important tactics and strategy. When in combat for the first time against a foe, the Mongols would attack directly with only part of their force and retreat like they had been defeated. They might even retreat for days, just a step ahead of the overconfident pursuit teams of their enemy. At the appropriate time—usually when another force got behind their adversaries—the fighting would continue. Using their powerful bows and maneuverable horses, Mongols would usually win. If an enemy decided to hide in fortified cities, the Mongols would warn that they would kill everyone inside if they did not surrender, then called for engineers from conquered peoples to build siege equipment. The Mongols, this time with support of previously captured soldiers, assaulted and then killed the civilian populace. When the Mongols arrived at the next city or state, the threat of terror led many to surrender without a fight.

Genghis Khan united the various Mongol tribes in 1206. This young man, whose birth name was Temujin, created an empire so vast that he earned the name that he is known by today: Genghis Khan means "supreme ruler: in Mongolian. He died in 1227, after many victories in Central Asia and even European Russia, having only just begun to attack the Jurchen, a seminomadic group in control at the time of north China.

His descendants did away with the Jurchens, with only a little help from the Chinese, in 7 years. But the battle for the **Southern Song dynasty** for complete control took another 45 years; battles on horseback were difficult in the watery, rugged south. While that conquest slowly rolled on, Mongols continued their attacks to the west, including riding into central Europe. In this manner, the Mongol Empire not only became the largest land empire of its time, but also of all history. The Mongols were also able to conquer China's neighbor Korea, while still fighting for control of the rest of China. Ghengis Khan's grandson Khubilai Khan then tried his unsuccessful invasions of Japan, using Korean ships and men, in 1274 (and again in 1281), while Chinese landlords finally agreed to stop fighting back in return for leaving them alive and in control of their estates.

Mongol control over Imperial China was known as the **Yuan Dynasty** (1279–1368). In the meantime, the Mongol empire was cut into four parts, with China the richest quarter by far. The Mongols and their conquests helped the spread of culture and trading. With this massive empire connected by imperial routes, the Mongols were able to stretch from Kiev to Beijing. This helped facilitate trips to Asia and renewed interest from Europe about to enter the Renaissance. Marco Polo himself was in the Mongol court during his famous travels.

After the Mongols lost control of China, squabbles within their ranks prevented a renewed alliance of the tribes. But Mongols remained a raiding threat to the new **Ming dynasty** who sent several armies into the steppes to contain the Mongols. The Chinese even built their capital in the north and again worked on the Great Wall, all so future generations would remember to have enough military force in the north to prevent any nomadic threat out of Mongolia. Ironically, in the seventeenth century the nomadic threat came from Manchuria, to the northeast of Beijing.

Further Reading

Grousset, Rene, and Naomi Walford. *The Empire of the Steppes: A History of Central Asia.* New York: Barnes and Noble Books, 1996.

Lane, George. *Daily Life in the Mongol Empire.* Westport, CT: Greenwood Press, 2006.

Weatherford, J. McIver. *Genghis Khan and the Making of the Modern World.* New York: Crown, 2004.

Names

East Asian names follow the family name, given name convention. Most Chinese family names were (and are) one character in length, although a few have two characters. Chinese had a taboo against marrying any one with the same family name. The family names also helped keep track of ancestors for **lineages** and what has been called **ancestor worship**. If a family kept track of its lineage—usually meaning if the family was wealthy or had local, middle-class or wealthy relatives nearby—the given names of a generation (all the cousins) often would have the same first character, with the second character different for everyone. These characters would be planned out by the lineage for generations. So usually a Chinese name would be made up of three characters, the family name always first.

Korean names also followed the usual Chinese example, although a much smaller number of family names: one-character family name; two-character given name, with the first character of the given name generational and the second personal. Only during the Mongol occupation of Korea did this change; many Koreans remade their names in Mongol style.

In Japan, names varied between one and three characters for the family name, and between one and three characters for the given name. But because written Japanese had so many different pronunciations per character, one would have to explain which pronunciation to use for the given name, if the name was to be known—it often was off limits to all but family, close friends, and, perhaps, bosses. But only elites in Japan had family names until the end of the feudal period in 1868, which explains why lineages are not as important until the modern era in Japan for the majority of Japanese.

Further Reading

Des Forges, Roger V., and John S. Major. *The Asian World, 600–1500.* New York: Oxford University Press, 2005.

Nara Period (710–794)

In this brief period, Japan decided to copy China and create a capital city, unusual in Japan because of the lack of urbanization at the time. The new capital, Heijo, known today as Nara, was laid out as a miniature Changan, China's **Tang dynasty** capital. The main differences between the capitals was Japan built mostly with wood due to its availability and fear of earthquakes (though using wood increases fear of fire), and the city lacked a protective wall as Japan did not fear invasion. By this time, emperors reigned (and sometimes ruled) from this city not with the **mandate of heaven**, but because they were related to heaven. This meant anyone trying to take control of the government would rule through the emperor, keeping his **lineage** intact. In addition, Japanese bureaucracy had continued to borrow from China, with the Taiho Code established in 702 but having a greater effect on the Nara Period. It divided the country into three levels of administration: provinces, districts, and villages. Peasants were organized at the village level to monitor each others' behavior. And the **equal field system** was tried again, this time using square rice fields divided into standard sizes and redistributed based on the number of people older than the age of 5. Taxes, as in all East Asia until the **Song dynasty**, were paid in kind: grain, textiles, the **corvee**, and military service. Finally, the Taiho Code set up the **examination system** for Japan. However, it really only worked for minor positions in the aristocracy—Japan would remain controlled by hereditary rule, unlike China, and would soon let the tests fall by the wayside.

The equal field system was weakened from its creation by aristocrats keeping control of their land. The final blows were the periodic smallpox epidemics that led the government in 743 to allow any new rice fields created to be owned forever.

The Nara Period also saw six missions sent to Tang China, each of up to six hundred men. This was in addition to Koreans visiting Japan armed with Chinese ideas. The journeys to China encouraged the Japanese to write their own history, which became Japan's oldest works, albeit in Chinese for the most part. In these books, Japanese exaggerated how long the imperial family had controlled three of the four main islands of Japan. Supposedly an emperor

Jimmu founded the state in 660 B.C.E., almost a thousand years before the true event in the **Yamato Period**. Japanese learned architecture from their Chinese hosts as well. In fact, the Buddhist temples of Heijo and later Heian (Kyoto) are the best examples of Tang dynasty buildings left in the world.

Buddhism grew very quickly during the Nara Period. The rich donated huge sums of money to the temples. The emperor's 741 edict required a Buddhist temple and pagoda to be built in every province. Within them would be twenty monks and ten nuns chanting for the good of Japan. The emperor also worked to link **Shinto** gods to the Buddhist canon to keep both coexisting in peace and helping to spread to the common people. In 752 the huge Todaiji temple in Nara was finished, including the 50-great Buddha made out of a million pounds of metal. After its eyes were painted, the emperor presented a feast to ten thousand monks. Finally, one problem with Buddhists did crop up in this period. Empress Shotoku grew close to a Buddhist priest called Dokyo. She even tried to give him the throne but was thwarted. When the empress finally died, Dokyo was banished from the capital in 770. Emperor Kammu, either as part of the rivalry between families over control of the emperor or due to fears that the Buddhist priests had become too powerful, decided to move the capital, successfully achieved in 794 with the move to Heian (today's Kyoto), and hence the **Heian Period**.

Further Reading

Barnes, Gina Lee. *Protohistoric Yamato: Archaeology of the First Japanese State*. Ann Arbor: University of Michigan, Center for Japanese Studies and the Museum of Anthropology, 1988.

Kidder, J. Edward. *The Lucky Seventh: Early Horyu-Ji and Its Time*. Tokyo, Japan: International Christian University, Hachiro Yuasa Memorial Museum, 1999.

Van Goethem, Ellen. *Nagaoka: Japan's Forgotten Capital*. Leiden, The Netherlands: Brill, 2008.

Neo-Confucianism

Neo-Confucianism is a new interpretation of **Confucianism** that was founded after about 300 years of Buddhist ascendance in China. From 800 to 1200, important scholar-officials had studied Buddhism, before many rejected its philosophy. Using ideas gleaned from Buddhism or even **Daoism**, these scholars created Neo-Confucianism.

The Neo-Confucian movement brought new ideas to Confucianism. Yet the Confucian exams remained unaffected by these changes until a generation after the death of Neo-Confucianism's most important thinker, **Zhu Xi** (1130–1200). Zhu used the two terms *qi* and *li* in much the same way as earlier scholars had attached the yin and yang to Confucianism or Daoism. In this case, *li* (a different Chinese character than "ritual") meant "principle," and *qi*, like in Daoism, meant "energy," as in Tai Qi (sometimes still written in the old transliteration as "T'ai Chi"). Just like a house needed a plan (li) before beginning building with materials (qi), people were on the path of goodness (li), but needed to be taught to obtain the qi, its outward expression. This was an elegant solution needed to prove Mencius correct in the face of contradictory evidence: if all people are good, why do so many do bad? The answer: not enough training. One must study the Confucian canon but also look within oneself through meditation and reflection, just like **Chan Buddhism**. With these Neo-Confucian teachings and rulers leading by example, all people could eventually be good.

Zhu's Neo-Confucianism became the accepted interpretation of Confucianism for passing the exams and getting the appointment to government positions during the Later Song dynasty and until the twentieth century. This would be one of several problems with Neo-Confucianism. No longer would a degree seeker dare to interpret the Confucian canon himself to show off his brilliance. Students (and those who graded the different levels of the **examination system**) instead valued memorization not intellectualism, leading eventually to a weakened Chinese intelligencia. In addition, Neo-Confucianism was also behind a backlash against women. **Footbinding** became popular for the gentry's daughters during the Song dynasty. This incredibly painful procedure, which kept the girl/woman's feet the size of a 5-year-old's, pushed women out of society, where they had a place before, and into their homes' shadows. Finally, although Confucianists made intelligent government officials, the Confucian importance of family and thus making sure one's children were well taken care of made some scholar-officials less than honest when it came to remitting tax receipts. This embezzlement by men the government depended on eventually led to financial problems and thus the beginning of the end for many dynasties.

Although Japan did not pay much attention to Neo-Confucianism until the Tokugawa Era (1600–1868), led as it was after 1185 by the warrior elite, Korea, on the other hand, was profoundly influenced by Neo-Confucianism after 1391 and the establishment of the Yi dynasty. In fact some scholars have argued that Korea became perhaps more Neo-Confucian than even China, with the exception of allowing anyone to take part in the examination system to obtain government positions.

Further Reading

Chan, Wing-tsit. *Chu Hsi and Neo-Confucianism*. Honolulu: University of Hawai'i Press, 1986.

De Bary, William Theodore. *The Unfolding of Neo-Confucianism*. New York: Columbia University Press, 1975.

De Bary, William Theodore, and JaHyun Kim Haboush. *The Rise of Neo-Confucianism in Korea*. New York: Columbia University Press, 1985.

Noh Theater

Like **sumo wrestling**, noh plays grew out of Japanese **Shinto** festivals that prayed for an abundant harvest and to give thanks for the harvest. Villagers put on folk dances and plays during these festivals, which became entertainment for the common people. By the time of the **Ashikaga shogunate**, the dances and plays had been refined and emerged as a serious dramatic form. Noh theater became an upper-class aesthetic entertainment heavily influenced by **Zen Buddhism** in its simplicity.

A noh performance was an all-day affair. A theatrical troop would put on five or six plays on a simple stage open on three sides, without a curtain or background scenery except for a painting of an old pine tree on the rear wall. The plays themselves relied on symbolic and abstract properties. Usually the principal actor wore a mask, or at least kept his face frozen as if it were a mask. The actors would not speak. The movements and gestures performed by he and the rest of the all-male cast were highly stylized and carefully measured. Mime played an important part of the drama. Weeping, for example, was signified by raising the hand to the eyes. The lead actor manipulated his fan to symbolize a variety of other events, such as falling leaves, rippling waves, or a moon. In fact, all actors had folding fans to help tell their stories through mime and were on stage dressed in brilliant, fancy costumes. A chorus that chanted the story in a sing-song voice accompanied the performers on stage, along with four musicians, each playing a different instrument.

The series of plays performed often followed a pattern, although this too could have been tinkered with by the playwright. The first short play might be about a famous Japanese, and the next the story of a particular Shinto kami (spirit or god). Sometimes these two plays were part one and part two, as the human became a kami due to his heroic efforts during his lifetime. The next would demonstrate the life of a famous warrior, then the story of his death as told by his ghost. Finally, the series would end on an energetic note, usually about monsters and demons, all told in a fast-paced, colorful style.

The noh plays were perfected by the father and son dramatists, Kan'ami Kiyotsugu and Seami Moptokiyo, during the reign of the third Ashikaga shogun. The son, Seami, was profoundly influenced by Zen in his writing, even though he and his father practiced **Pure Land Buddhism**, which also helps show that Zen did not have a monopoly on religion in this era even if Zen played a large role in affecting the culture. This Zen influence can be seen in his plays that had a sense of mystery, those that emphasized the idea of what lies beneath and the subtle as opposed to the obvious.

Further Reading
Nakamura, Yasuo. *Noh: The Classical Theater*. New York: Walker/Weatherhill, 1971.

Northern Song Dynasty (960–1126)

In 960, General Zhao Kuangyin became **Emperor Taizu** and worked hard to limit the power of other generals, founding the Song dynasty (normally called the Northern Song dynasty to differentiate from when nomads took over northern China in 1127). His mercenary force, subject to periodic rotation of its commanders, remained loyal to the emperor and proved valuable in the reconquest of China. Like unifiers before him, Taizu applied moderate force to those opposing him and welcomed those to join him when defeated. The **Great Wall** would serve as the dividing line between China and a seminomadic conqueror, the Liao, for three generations.

The wars that ended the Tang and started the Song left a strange situation among the rich and poor, educated and uneducated. Some longstanding gentry families had lost everything, and new families had become wealthy. Only degree holding allowed the elites to separate from just those who owned land. The Song dynasty instituted an **examination system** more fair than ever before, used up until the twentieth century (with the exception of the Mongols) and ending hereditary officials (save the emperor). All central government officials would be chosen based on Confucian exams; for five hundred spots over one hundred thousand would compete. The printing press in full use made Confucian books for study widely available. Of course the usual degree earner came from a wealthy, educated family; it took time to learn classical written Chinese, let alone the Confucian canon. But once in a while, a smart village boy received backing from a village to allow him to study, take the exams, and make the village famous.

The Northern Song dynasty ended up making a terrible mistake based on the traditional Chinese custom of playing barbarian against barbarian. The nomadic Jurchen had recently thrown off the yoke of the Khitans, also called the Liao, so the Chinese decided to ally with the Jurchen against the Khitans and gain lands to the north of the Great Wall. But where the Jurchen succeeded, the Song failed. China was forced to pay the Jurchen the same tribute it had paid the Khitans. The Jurchen decided that was not enough and attacked the Chinese capital and demanded increased tribute: fifty million ounces of silver, five million ounces of gold, and one million rolls of silk. They took half immediately and headed back north. But only a few months later, the Jurchen attacked the Song again, this time taking the capital, the Song emperor, and the treasury. One son of the Song managed to escape to the south to continue the war against the nomadic invasion. Because of its flat geography, the mounted Jurchen conquered northern China after a 14-year war but could not push south of the Huai River (halfway between the **Yellow River** and the **Yangzi River**) where terrain starts to become difficult for cavalry. The Huai River would serve as the boundary between the Jurchen state and the **Southern Song dynasty**, established in 1127, with tribute set at 250,000 ounces of silver/rolls of silk.

Further Reading

Ebrey, Patricia Buckley, and Maggie Bickford. *Emperor Huizong and Late Northern Song China: The Politics of Culture and the Culture of Politics.* Cambridge, MA: Harvard University, Asia Center, 2006.

Egan, Ronald. *The Problem of Beauty: Aesthetic Thought and Pursuits in Northern Song Dynasty China.* Cambridge, MA: Harvard University, Asia Center, 2006.

Williamson, Henry Raymond. *Wang An Shih: A Chinese Statesman and Educationalist of the Sung Dynasty.* Westport, CT: Hyperion Press, 1973.

Northern Wei (386–534)

The Tuoba (sometimes called "Toba") were a Turkish nomadic group that settled in northern China during the **Period of Disunity**. The year 400 found the Tuoba nomads winning control of northern China after military victories over the previous herding culture, the Tibetans. The victorious Tuoba proclaimed their lands and dynasty over the Northern Wei. Like the string of nomadic conquerors before it, the Tuobans had an important decision to make. Should they too copy the ways of the Chinese left in north China to govern and collect taxes, or should they drive away or exterminate the ethnic Chinese to turn the north into huge pasture lands? The Tuobans decided to do the former, using leading Chinese landowning families to help administer laws and collect taxes.

The system agreed upon by the Confucian-educated gentry of north China and their Tuoba overseers was "land equalization," also known as the **equal field system**. The idea behind this system was to maximize the number of landholding peasant families to create an enduring tax base by adding or subtracting land from a peasant family based on its size. The system worked remarkably well in China for 300 years, guaranteeing the state stable taxation. Yet in addition to predictable taxes, the state also added to the **corvee** (unpaid labor—usually irrigation or flood-control projects) of the peasants the new task of forming a militia to serve as infantry along side the Tuoba cavalry in battles with their neighbors.

The Tuoba encouraged Buddhism, as it was not Chinese in origin. That positive feeling toward Buddhism diminished rapidly, if only temporarily, in the middle of their reign. In 444 and 445 the Tuoban leader decided to purge Buddhists—killing monks and destroying monasteries—all in an attempt to increase taxable land and trumpet his alliance with Daoists and Confucianists. Buddhism rebounded after his death.

As the Tuoba ruled, they borrowed more and more customs from the Chinese who had stayed in northern China. The governing structure was heavily influenced by the leading Chinese landlord families in the north. Soon the Tuoba required the use of Chinese language as the official language, Chinese family surnames for Tuoba aristocrats, and Chinese social customs at the elite level. They at first encouraged and then supposedly demanded marriage between their leaders and Chinese gentry-class women!

The Longmen cave-temple complex, which extends for about 1,000m along the Yi River. There are 1,352 grottoes, over 750 niches and about 40 pagodas of various sizes. They contain more than 100,000 Buddhist images. Work on the caves began in about 494 C.E. and continued into the Tang period. Werner Forman/Art Resource, NY.

The Tuoba ended up weak militarily as they moved toward civilization, and the Northern Wei was swept away by new nomads; northern China was divided into two new successor states, out of which would arise the **Sui dynasty** in two generations.

Further Reading

Frodsham, J. D., and Hsi Ch'eng. *An Anthology of Chinese Verse: Han Wei Chin and the Northern and Southern Dynasties.* London: Oxford University, 1967.

Mole, Gabriella. *The T'u-Yu-Hun from the Northern Wei to the Time of the Five Dynasties.* Roma, Italy: Istituto italiano per il Medio ed Estremo Oriente, 1970.

Yu, Taishan. *A History of the Relationships between the Western and Eastern Han, Wei, Jin Northern and Southern Dynasties and the Western Regions.* Philadelphia: University of Pennsylvania, Dept. of East Asian Languages and Civilizations, 2004.

Period of Disunity (220–589)

The Period of Disunity was the period after the fall of the Han dynasty and until the start of the **Sui dynasty**. During this time China was divided into one large southern kingdom and one or two northern kingdoms that often claimed to be heirs to imperial China, even though started by different nomadic groups. After the failure of the Three Kingdoms Period (soon after the Han) to bring back imperial China, the country faced northern invasion and constant struggle for control over the Chinese south. A series of pastoral nomadic groups conquered north China for differing periods of time. In the south strong landlords led many short-lived so-called dynasties. More and more ethnic Chinese from the northern half of the country fled south to avoid nomadic rule. The movement of population the south led the economy there to grow as agricultural production increased; soon the **Yangzi River** delta region became the center of China's economy, replacing the **Yellow River**. Besides the normal battles for control and the temporary establishment of these petty southern dynasties, new pressures compounded the problems of the ruling class of the south, mostly due to the population explosion: rich landlords fleeing from the north demanded a share of governance and poor peasants competed with newcomers and the rich for ever-dwindling southern lands. The result was a destructive but failed rebellion known as the Five Bushels. These internal problems continued, keeping the populous south from mounting successful wars to defeat the north and restore ethnic Chinese borders to those of the Han dynasty; the great landholding families had too much power compared to the state.

In the north, a barbarian group called the Tuoba decided to use Chinese elites in the north to help them rule and tax their so-called **Northern Wei** dynasty. Effective use of the **equal field system** allowed the Tuoba to rule for almost 150 years, until borrowing too much civilized Chinese ideas weakened the former nomads and allowed their defeat northern China was divided into two new states.

At first, **Religious Daoism** played the role of most popular religion in north and south China, due to its reputed healing and life-extending properties. Although Buddhism may have made its first appearance in China during the Han dynasty, coming as it did by way of the **Silk Road**, it was in the Period of Disunity that Buddhism began slowly to erode Daoist appeal in both sections of China. Just as **Confucianism** and **Daoism** had become important philosophies/religions during the Warring States Period (480–221 B.C.E.), so did many Chinese accept Buddhism in the divided country, as both regions faced almost constant disorder. Yet Buddhism early on faced some opposition among more traditional followers of Confucianism and Daoism, as it demanded of its ardent followers actions considered "un-Chinese," including shaving one's head and practicing celibacy. Yet none of these religions demanded the exclusive nature of Western religions, allowing a Chinese the ability to follow all three teachings—Confucianism, Daoism, and Buddhism—simultaneously or at different phases of one's life. The Tuoba and their Northern Wei state encouraged Buddhism, as it was not Chinese in origin. Twice in the north that positive feeling toward Buddhism diminished rapidly, if only temporarily. In 444 and 445 the Tuoban leader decided to purge Buddhists—killing monks and destroying monasteries—all in an attempt to increase taxable land and trumpet his alliance with Daoists and Confucianists. Buddhism rebounded after his reign. Yet even the Northern Wei's successor state in the north—the one that would eventually reunify all China under the Sui dynasty—practiced a Buddhist purge almost 100 years later. But the uncertain, confused times in the south

and north, and the coming of a newer, simpler sect called **Pure Land Buddhism** —
which appealed to commoners as well as monks and nuns — allowed Buddhism, even in its differing doctrines, to spread across China and survive the
purges and slanders against it. The Period of Disunity saw Buddhism become
China's third great religious/philosophical tradition.

In 581, a prominent general of mixed Chinese-nomadic origin overthrew the
king of the Northern Wei's successor state, killed the royal family, and assumed the throne. He declared himself the first emperor of the Sui dynasty,
Emperor Wen. Quickly he conquered the rest of north China, then headed
south across the Yangzi River to unify all of China under his control, an effort
accomplished easily by 589.

Further Reading

Dien, Albert E. *State and Society in Early Medieval China*. Stanford, CA: Stanford University Press, 1991.

Mole, Gabriella. *The T'u-Yu-Hun from the Northern Wei to the Time of the Five Dynasties*.
Roma, Italy: Istituto italiano per il Medio ed Estremo Oriente, 1970.

Yu, Taishan. *A History of the Relationships between the Western and Eastern Han, Wei, Jin
Northern and Southern Dynasties and the Western Regions*. Philadelphia: University of
Pennsylvania, Dept. of East Asian Languages and Civilizations, 2004.

Prince Shotoku (d. 621)

Prince Shotoku was Japanese regent to Empress Suiko and member of the
Soga family; he was temporarily victorious in controlling the imperial family
through marriage and the regency. The prince became famous for sponsoring
Buddhism and Buddhist temples, especially the famous
Horyuji temple (today the oldest wooden buildings in the
world). However, not enough Japanese understood the
complexities of these early Chinese forms of Buddhism — as
well as the Chinese in the books about Buddhism — so he
brought in Korean monks to run the different temples.

Prince Shotoku also opened up relations with China and
sent four missions to the short-lived **Sui dynasty**. He made
a terrible faux pas in sending a note to the emperor of
China from "the emperor of the sunrise country," when
the Chinese believed the Japanese were vassals to China,
not equals!

Prince Shotoku is most famous for writing the **Seventeen
Point Constitution** in 604. This constitution was heavily influence by Chinese ideas. It is really a list of advice for rulers
and the ruled written in Chinese, the only written language
for the Japanese for centuries. Its articles heavily advocated
Confucianism and Buddhism, with a sprinkling of **Daoism**
and Shinto's consensus building thrown in for good measure. But the constitution was really a way to show forcefully that the emperor/regent for the emperor would serve
as the head of a more powerful central government, including collecting taxes. No longer would local elites have that
opportunity or that resource.

Prince Shotoku Taishi and his
sons Yamashiro Oe and Ekuri,
(Shotoku Taishi gazo). Color on
paper, late 7th century. The Art
Archive/Imperial Household
Collection Kyoto/Laurie Platt
Winfrey.

Further Reading

Anesaki Masaharu. *Prince Shotoku: The Sage Statesman*. Tokyo, Japan: Boonjudo, 1948.

Como, Michael. *Shotoku: Ethnicity, Ritual, and Violence in the Japanese Buddhist Tradition*. Oxford, UK: Oxford University Press, 2008.

Pure Land Buddhism

Pure Land Buddhism is another of the most popular Mahayana ("Greater Vehicle") Buddhist sects in East Asia, where even laypeople could obtain enlightenment through worshiping the Amiotabha Buddha.

Pure Land Buddhism came to China during the **Northern Wei**. It believed the world was in terrible shape at the time of the **Tang dynasty** (ironic considering most people of the day and historians looking back see the Tang as the high point not only in Chinese civilization, but also in world civilization at the time). Luckily Buddha had foreseen this and explained secretly to a few followers that one specific **Bodhisattva** (being of wisdom) could help ordinary people achieve enlightenment. By believing in his saving grace and reciting

Avalokiteshvara as Guide of Souls, early 10th C.E. He is identified by the figure of the Buddha Amitabha in the headdress of this figure. He is leading the soul of a female devotee to the halls of paradise, depicted by the three top nabds each with tiny buildings. He has a censer in his left hand and a long staff with a banner. Erich Lessing/Art Resource, NY.

his name (*Amituofo Buddha* in Chinese, *Amita* in Korean, and *Amida* in Japanese) in true devotion, a follower could be reborn in the land of paradise, the Pure Land of the West. Many Chinese did not understand this stay was temporary, assuming the Pure Land was heaven. Theoretically they would come back to earth as Bodhisattvas and help others obtain enlightenment before permanently seeking it themselves. Just at the high point of Pure Land Buddhism in China, Emperor Wuzong defrocked over two-hundred fifty thousand Buddhist monks and nuns (leaving only forty-nine monasteries and eight hundred monks), sold off their lands, destroyed 4,600 temples, and wrecked forty-thousand shrines. His death in 846 saved Buddhism in China, but not Pure Land; instead **Chan Buddhism** gained adherents to be the most popular form of Buddhism in China.

Korea accepted Buddhism early from China and were the key cultural transmitters to Japan. **Silla Korea**, as the imitation Tang dynasty, government also controlled the Buddhist orders and temples. It used art, dance, music, and literature to try to bring Pure Land Buddhism to the masses. Only in the fourteenth century did Chan (*Seon* in Korean) overtake Pure Land in popularity in Korea. Pure Land Buddhism came to Japan much later, during the wars to conclude the **Heian Period**. It pushed its adherents to chant "Namu Amida Butsu," or *nembutsu* when said quickly. It required ten pure moments to achieve the help from Amida, along with one's good works. Only a few years later, during the start of the **Kamakura Period**, a splinter group called True Pure Land Buddhism also pushed chanting the nembutsu. Its difference lay in priests being able to marry (priests inherited control of the church) and in how only through the hard work of Amida could one achieve rebirth in the Pure Land. A criminal, because of his evil, was closer to being sent to the Pure Land if he only believed because nothing he did in his life would warrant such a reward. Nothing but the nembutsu and the gift granted by Amida would allow entrance into the Pure Land. These two forms together quickly became the most popular sect of Buddhism in Japan.

Further Reading

De Bary, William Theodore. *The Buddhist Tradition in India, China and Japan.* New York: Modern Library, 1969.

Foard, James Harlan, Michael Solomon, and Richard Karl Payne. *The Pure Land Tradition: History and Development.* Berkeley: Regents of the University of California Press, 1996.

Religious Daoism

Although **Daoism** started out as more of a philosophy for the educated to question, Daoism came to the common folk through a more religious outlook.

Toward the end of the Han dynasty (which existed 202 B.C.E. to 220 C.E.), a Daoist religious movement known as the Celestial Masters won acceptance with the peasantry in the spiritual and civic realms, actually conquering and governing parts of China. The Celestial Masters helped move Daoism away from its roots to a religion focused on nature, the yin and yang, and healing. It now also tried to cheat death! With the fall of the Han (220 C.E.) and the coming of the **Period of Disunity** (316–588), Daoism became further entrenched in the north, as the Celestial Masters continued their teaching and healing services (even providing free food to travelers). Soon they added meditation and breathing exercises. Some wealthy patrons began searching for everlasting life from religious Daoists, who emulated later European alchemists in handling exotic ingredients to concoct supposed life-sustaining elixirs. Ironically, mercury and later gunpowder often turned up in these potions, leading to horrible suffering and death instead of everlasting life.

Daoism also faced competition from a new direction, the coming of Buddhism into China. During the **Northern Wei** dynasty, north China's Emperor Taiwu persecuted Buddhists from 446 until his death in 452, gaining him ceremonial trappings of Daoism, as well as the support of Confucianists. A second Buddhist purge of north China occurred from 574 to 578; just like the first it was an attack on the wealth and political power of Buddhists by destroying monasteries, not forcing individual religious change. In this case Daoism became the official state religion, but the advent of the **Sui dynasty** and reunification 10 short years later brought Daoism away from imperial sanction and back into steady competition with Buddhism and Confucianism for adherents. The Celestial Masters faded with a revived strong, central state, and Daoism splintered into different religious groups with retreats founded on beautiful mountains away from cities. Many former Confucianist government officials would retire to mountain areas to spend their days reflecting on the Way and drawing or painting these landscapes. Daoism for the common people, on the other hand, tied itself to folk traditions and local gods.

Further Reading

Renard, John. *101 Questions and Answers on Confucianism, Daoism, and Shinto.* New York: Paulist Press, 2002.

Robinet, Isabelle, and Phyllis Brooks. *Taoism: Growth of a Religion.* Stanford, CA: Stanford University Press, 1997.

Samurai Swords

Japanese samurai swords were highly prized, in Japan, the wider sphere of Asia, and today all around the world as they are the best-made swords in world history. Japanese sword makers perfected the art of sword toward the end of the thirteenth century. These swords were made for the warrior class by the most esteemed of sword-making masters. These swords were not only considered as superior weapons, but also as living creatures, which were revered. With these swords have come the Japanese traditions of warfare and honor. They are still revered today as important parts of Japanese past and of the present.

Perhaps it is a mistake to call them samurai swords, as the true samurai of film and comic book fame is really a seventeenth-century creation with the laws of bushido. The warriors of the **Kamakura Period** and **Ashikaga shogunate** (1185–1467) were really just bushi or warriors just starting to refine themselves with learning to read and write poetry. The closest thing to bushido, or the warrior's code of seventeenth century (and beyond) samurai, was the bushi's vow to kill or be killed. If unsuccessful in combat and not killed outright, the bushi would either ask his enemy to behead him or stab himself in the entrails to die (*seppuku* or more vulgarly "harakiri"—ritual suicide). In addition, the sword of this period is not the *katana* of the samurai, but the *tachi*, a slightly longer weapon, made with similar (or even better) precision.

The samurai sword as perfected in the thirteenth century solves two age-old problems that plagued the profession of sword making. One was that a sword could be sharp but brittle or strong but dull. Bushi who got too close to their Korean or Mongol enemies during the attempted Mongol invasions of 1274 and 1281 often complained that their swords were not tough enough to cut through enemy leather armor. To solve these problems, Japanese sword makers pounded two different parts of iron collected from sandy river bottoms together. Then they would reheat the mixture and keep folding over the layers of the two. By the end of the process, over a million layers created a sword with a sharp outer blade to cut and a softer inner core to take abuse but not break from other swords or armor. Not only was the tachi extremely sharp, but it was also rugged and reliable, with a curve that allowed the user to swing his sword without worrying that it might get stuck in the opponent's body. Stories passed down claim that master sword makers would take their just-completed sword to a local stream. One sword may cut a floating leaf cleanly in half while another would have the leaf float by it. It would be the latter sword that would be greater valued because it was considered to have spiritual powers (and possible additional sharpness). These powers were believed to help protect a warrior.

These swords became valuable family heirlooms. These swords were passed from generation to generation as symbols of a family's strength. After 1400 sword makers would cut these tachi down to make them more like the popular katana. These swords were also in demand in China as the best made in the world, ironic because China used to export iron swords to Japan 1,000 years before. These swords became known around Asia (and later the world) as a testament to Japanese sword-making skills.

Further Reading
Yumoto, John M. *The Samurai Sword: A Handbook*. Rutland, VT: C.E. Tuttle Co, 1958.

Seventeen Point Constitution

The Seventeen Point Constitution was created in Japan in 604, supposedly by **Prince Shotoku**, regent to Empress Suiko and member of the victorious Soga family. Some historians argue the language used in this document is too sophisticated for the time and thus is a later creation. In any event, this constitution was a list of advice for rulers and the ruled and was written in Chinese, the only written language for the Japanese for centuries. It contains many ideas from China and Korea, as Japan was greatly influenced by China's **Sui dynasty** as interpreted by Korea (ideas traveled from China by sea to southern Korea then by sea to Japan).

The constitution begins by advocating Confucian ideas, including provisions for keeping harmony, following orders, leading by example, maintaining honesty, punishing the bad, encouraging the good, understanding one's place, working hard, avoiding anger or envy, and treating peasants fairly. The second article specifically honors Buddhism, within the rest there is a sprinkling of Daoist thought. Finally, Shinto's consensus building closes out the last article. Although these words of advice are important, what the constitution really does is make the state more powerful and puts the power of taxation solely in the hands of the emperor (or the emperor's regent). No longer would local elites have that opportunity. These last points about increased imperial power is important, for even after Prince Shotoku's death and the loss of control over the imperial house by the Soga's, the power of the state would continue with the victors in the brief power struggle, the Fujiwara family. The Fujiwara would also leave alone the Buddhist ideas and sects that had come to Japan, even though the family had championed Shintoism in the past.

Further Reading
Como, Michael. *Shotoku: Ethnicity, Ritual, and Violence in the Japanese Buddhist Tradition*. Oxford, UK: Oxford University Press, 2008.
Kuroita Katsumi. *Prince Shotoku and His Seventeen-Article Constitution*. Tokyo, Japan: Nippon Bunka Chuo Renmei, 1940.

Shinto

Shinto is Japan's original animistic, folk religion, which, like Korea's shamanistic faith, survived the coming of new religious ideas. The Japanese coined *Shinto*, meaning "way of the gods," after Buddhism arrived and absorbed a few local gods. But what were gods, called *kami*, under Shinto? Gods were anything awe inspiring in a beautiful, powerful, or even scary way. Nature often played this role, probably because people in Japan came from Korea; Japan has far more beautiful mountain forests than the Koreans did by this point in history. A giant tree could be a kami, as could a mountain or even an

Fertility offering of boiled rice made to Shinto gods, Rice Cultivation Scroll (Ta-warakasane kosaku emaki). Color on paper, late 16th century. The Art Archive/Tokyo University/Laurie Platt Winfrey.

interesting boulder. Even a man could be a kami if he had incredible abilities; upon death he might obtain even more fame as stories about his exploits got more and more exaggerated and people's knowledge of his kamihood spread.

Shinto also provides multiple explanations on how the world, and more importantly, Japan, was created. One family claimed the sun goddess was a direct ancestor and used those stories to gain control of the state and become Japan's emperor. Shinto, however, does not handle death or a woman's menstruation well. Anyone who touched a dead body or animal was considered unclean; eventually an outcaste class developed from those who performed such jobs, called "**burakumin**." If a woman happened to touch a wrestling ring, Shinto priests would have to help rebuild it before refereeing **Sumo wrestling** again. Sumo also began as a Shinto sport, albeit with little rules at first. It was a way to appease the kami and work for an abundant harvest. Later rules made the wrestlers unarmed and restricted certain painful attacks. A Shinto priest served as referee, and the goal became to push the opponent out of the ring or make any part of his body touch the ground other than the soles of his bare feet.

Further Reading

Breen, John, and Mark Teeuwen. *Shinto in History: Ways of the Kami*. Honolulu: University of Hawai'i Press, 2000.

Grapard, Allan G. *The Protocol of the Gods: A Study of the Kasuga Cult in Japanese History*. Berkeley: University of California Press, 1992.

Renard, John. *101 Questions and Answers on Confucianism, Daoism, and Shinto*. New York: Paulist Press, 2002.

Shogun

In Japan, the term *shogun* is a shortening of *sei-i-tai shogun*, meaning "barbarian-quelling generalissimo." Originally *shogun* was a title given to those commanding troops against the non-Japanese inhabitants of Honshu and Hokkaido, usually the Ainu. After victories and the "barbarian" retreat to Hokkaido, the term fell into disuse. It was resurrected by the Minamoto family, a branch family of the Fujiwara, who won a series of wars for control of Japan at the beginning of the **Kamakura Period**. Instead of eliminating the emperor or intermarrying with him to help control Japan, Minamoto Yoritomo took the title shogun and expanded its meaning beyond simple military control to include all facets of secular control from the Kanto Plain (near modern-day Tokyo). The emperor would handle state religious ceremonies and continue to reign and not rule. Yet Minamoto Yoritomo's paranoia meant he killed many of his relatives, leaving his widow to put in place her family (Hojo) as the true rulers behind the shogun as regents and soon a Fujiwara (an important family that had become distant cousins to the Minamoto family) as the puppet shogun.

Minamoto Yorimoto, Japanese warrior, military dictator and founder of the Shogunate, wearing ceremonial sokutai robe rather than general's uniform. Color on silk, 12th century, attributed to Fujiwara Takanobu. The Art Archive/Laurie Platt Winfrey.

The shogun would again take control of Japan's secular world (civilian and military government), this time from the same city as the emperor, Kyoto, in the **Ashikaga shogunate**. The Ashikaga family had taken power and the position as shogun in part because many warriors were disappointed over boons not awarded after the "defeat" of the **Mongols** (their fighting plus the two lucky typhoons that forced the Mongols back to Korea). Yet the Ashikaga shogun had trouble rewarding those loyal as well and ruled Japan from a position of weakness compared to the Hojo or Minamoto families. In fact, the end of the importance of the title *shogun* for 125 years would occur as a result of the Onin War (1467–1477) due to a civil war over who should inherit the position.

Further Reading
Hall, John Whitney, and Takeshi Toyoda. *Japan in the Muromachi Age*. Berkeley: University of California Press, 1977.

Silk Road

The Silk Road is well known as one of the principal arteries of trade connecting China to central and western Asia, the Near East, and eastern Europe. From these two main routes (northern and southern), some of the most valuable goods that traversed Asia were brought over the course of weeks or months, changing hands many times along the way.

As a route through Central Asia, the Silk Road served not only as a means of trade, but also as a way for cultural diffusion to occur. Along the road traveled the noted Buddhist Pilgrim Xuanzang, who traveled from China through East Turkestan to India. Silk was perhaps the most demanded of all of China's exotic goods. Along the Silk Road sprang up trading centers along desert oases.

Although the secret of spinning silk was known in China, it took centuries for the West to produce its own fabric. Due to this fact, the Chinese silk was in tremendous demand due to its low availability. Along the Silk Road during the **early Tang dynasty** lay tributary states to the Chinese emperor, expanding

Chinese influence. Later the **Mongols** and **Yuan dynasty** would control those oasis states. The road allowed not only silk to be brought across the vast steppes of Asia but also some porcelain and lots of tea to be traded; central Asian nomads used tea as a foodstuff. These valuable resources helped build China's reputation in the wider world as a legitimate superpower. Porcelain from China was so well known and in demand it was and still is known as china throughout the Western world.

Although there were sea routes available to transport Chinese goods, the Silk Road became the most well known in Europe. The Chinese merchants would only bring their goods to the eastern edge of what is today Chinese Xinjiang before passing it to the next number of merchants. However, Chinese power and influence spread during the Tang dynasty further west. From this route, along with others, the Chinese Empire was able to amass a large trade surplus with empires and states further west. In addition, the expansion of the Chinese control afforded the empire more defensible borders and a wider amount of latitude over how to treat tributary and vassal states. However, this control was only temporary, despite the fact that China controls these territories today.

One contemporary source wrote that so many caravans were entering the eastern terminus of the Silk Road — the Chinese capital of Changan — during the Tang dynasty that dust rose from all four directions to obscure the sun. West from there, in an oasis called Dunhuang in today's Gansu province of China, Buddhists traveling on the Silk Route founded the famous Caves of the Thousand Buddhas. These caves are actually 420 temples started in 366, with continued building for around 1,000 years. There sculpture and cave painting explain Buddhism, particularly the type of Buddhism practiced in China, Korea, and Japan, Mahayana Buddhism. It turned out one of the reasons for the caves was that this arid region was perfect for preserving wooden and paper items about Buddhism, many hidden behind a false wall for centuries. Along the route were various Buddhist caves. Along this route traveled Buddhist monks with their teachings, allowing the religion to flourish in Asia starting with the **Northern Wei** dynasty during the **Period of Disunity**.

Persian middlemen and Turkish people living in the oases of the Silk Road controlled most of its traffic until the Mongols conquered the entire lengths of the roads. But instead of making money on these now-safer roads, Mongols let the middlemen continue to profit. But in the fourteenth century, the retreat and then internecine war of the Mongols and the Black Death (or simply fear of the Black Death) led to the disuse of the Silk Road in favor of travel by sea across the South China Sea and Indian Ocean. By 1400, the Silk Road was more of a legend than a viable commercial highway.

Further Reading

Grousset, Rene, and Naomi Walford. *The Empire of the Steppes: A History of Central Asia.* New York: Barnes and Noble Books, 1996.

Weng, Weiquan. *Xinjiang, the Silk Road: Islam's Overland Route to China.* Hong Kong: Oxford University Press, 1986.

Silla Korea (674–892)

Silla Korea served as a tributary state to Tang China, at the elite level borrowing Chinese culture and institutions, while the Silla ruling family received yearly presents at least as valuable, if not more so, than the tribute they provided China. Silla Korea, like Japan at that time, was remade into a little Tang. The country borrowed the Confucian structure of the government, including all the bureaucracy of Tang China, as well as dividing Korea into prefectures, subprefectures, and smaller units. Most government posts, however, remained in the hands of the hereditary aristocrats in their hierarchical "bone ranks" instead of to anyone capable of passing the Confucian examination system. The government remained more part of the personal household of the royal family.

Buddhism had more direct effect on Silla Korea. Large numbers of Korean Buddhist monks and lay students left by sea for study in China. The optimistic Buddhism coming out of China appealed to the Koreans. It appeared to offer protection to the state. As the state religion, the government sponsored an elite corps of aristocratic youths called "**flower squires**," who attended an exclusive military academy devoted to protect Buddhism and the nation. It also promised more rewards to the individual than the Korean folk traditions. But just like Japan, Korea adopted Buddhism without rejecting its previous shamanistic faith. Buddhist art and architecture spread throughout Korea, paid for by the taxes collected by the state and by the rich. The government also controlled the Buddhist orders and temples. It used art, dance, music, and literature to try to bring the deep ideas of **Pure Land Buddhism** to the masses. In fact, the man who created the first system of writing Korean using Chinese characters, *idu*, was the son of the man charged briefly with bringing Buddhism to the masses. Yet success brought temporary problems—at one point, Buddhist orders owned so much land and wealth that the government had to place restrictions on their holdings.

Religion did not fell Silla Korea, however. Instead, internal squabbling over royal succession after the king was assassinated in 780 became a common occurrence, as did regionalism and even a rebellion by an obscure group calling themselves the Red Trousers. Korea fell apart into its previous three kingdoms toward the end of the ninth century.

Further Reading

Adams, Edward Ben. *Korea's Golden Age: Cultural Spirit of Silla in Korea*. Seoul, Korea: Seoul International Publishing House, 1991.

Lancaster, Lewis R., and Chai-Shin Yu. *Assimilation of Buddhism in Korea: Religious Maturity and Innovation in the Silla Dynasty*. Berkeley, CA: Asian Humanities Press, 1991.

Pratt, Keith L. *Everlasting Flower: A History of Korea*. London: Reaktion, 2006.

Vainker, S. J. *Chinese Silk: A Cultural History*. London: British Museum Press, 2004.

Song Dynasty. *See* **Northern Song Dynasty**; **Southern Song Dynasty**

Southern Song Dynasty (1127–1279)

The Southern Song dynasty began when the Jurchen took advantage of Chinese military weakness and conquered northern China up to the Huai River (halfway between the **Yellow River** and the **Yangzi River**).

Although the Song dynasty had suffered a major blow, the loss of the north had the strange effect of improving China's economy. For one, more and more peasants fled Jurchen rule to join up with the Southern Song. These newcomers worked and lived on the new strains of rice (taken from southern Vietnam) that allowed for two crops of rice a year from the Yangzi River southward.

The Yangzi delta became the most important region for economic development. Tea growing also expanded, as did cotton growing. Commercialization of agriculture meant that peasants would pay taxes in money and not in kind. The landlord class began to take up residence in luxury, which led to the development of quality artisan goods like silk and porcelain. Even better was to live in the new capital of Hangzhou. The city was a short canal journey from the eastern reaches of the **Yangzi River**. There all manner of luxury goods could be purchased, from jewelry to books. The elite did not work and showed off this idleness through growing long fingernails. And elite women faced the torture known as **footbinding**. Footbinding came about because elite women did not need to work and the growing popularity of **Neo-Confucianism** took elite women out of public life. The poor did not experience either; husband and wife needed to work the fields together to survive.

With these excess commodities, foreign and regional trade expanded so much that there was not enough copper currency to conduct business. China first used weighed amounts of gold and silver before turning to paper money, yet the government's urge to print paper money led to damaging inflation.

The Song then made another costly error, again playing barbarian against barbarian. The Chinese stupidly allied with the **Mongols** against the Jurchen in 1227, hoping to get back north China in the process. The alliance resulted in the loss in 7 years of the Jurchen buffer state. The Mongols then slowly conquered the **Southern Song dynasty** over the next 45 years, as most Chinese landlords decided to ally with the Mongols in return for leaving their property intact.

Further Reading

Bossler, Beverly Jo. *Powerful Relations: Kinship, Status, and the State in Sung China (960–1279)*. Cambridge, MA: Council on East Asian Studies, Harvard University, 1998.

Gernet, Jacques. *Daily Life in China, on the Eve of the Mongol Invasion, 1250–1276*. Stanford, CA: Stanford University Press, 1962.

McKnight, Brian E. *Village and Bureaucracy in Southern Sung China*. Chicago: University of Chicago Press, 1972.

Sui Dynasty (589–617)

In 581, a prominent general of mixed Chinese-nomadic origin overthrew the king of one of two of north China's states near the end of the **Period of Disunity**, killed the royal family, and assumed the throne. He declared himself the first emperor of the Sui dynasty, Emperor Wen. Quickly he conquered the rest of north China, then headed south across the **Yangzi River** to unify all of China under his control, an effort accomplished easily in 589.

Wen (r. 589–604) first sought to create a strong central government, so lacking throughout China during the split. He reorganized the administration and bureaucracy, at first placing mixed Chinese-nomad families from the north in key positions. Quickly southern families married into the newcomer families from the north. The emperor established a limited **examination system** and a series of rules to prevent corruption by officials: local officials could not appoint subordinates; officials could not serve in their native place; and officials could serve no more than one tour of duty in the same location. To unite symbolically China, the emperor enshrined thirty supposed Buddha relics in buildings called *stupas* in the thirty regional capitals in 601.

Emperor Yang Ti, 560–618 C.E., Sui dynasty, on his boat on the Grand Canal China. Painting on silk, 17th century, Chinese. The Art Archive/Bibliothèque Nationale Paris.

Wen secondly worked to restore the economy by instituting the successful **equal field system** throughout China. By creating new peasant landowners, he built up the tax base as had been done in the Northern Wei. Wen used **corvee** labor to build granaries around the capital of Changan, located along a major tributary of the **Yellow River**. Peasant labor also started a **Grand Canal** to link the Yangzi and Yellow rivers so grain and taxes could flow to the capital easily for more than half the year. The reforms strengthened the economy for a time. Then Emperor Wen of the Sui dynasty set out on some further wars of conquest. He fought wars to protect and then extend the empire west, north, south, and east. Wen was then murdered, likely by his son, who took the throne in 604, and ended up exceeding the megalomania of his father.

Emperor Yang (r. 604–617) decided to spend his time and China's money first on elaborate building projects. He decided to build a new capital, Loyang, around 200 miles down the Yellow River from Changan. He employed two million peasants on the project, and thousands died hauling rare timber to the treeless plain. He needed 1.2 million peasants starting in 607 to work on the **Great Wall**, where at least half perished. And supposedly 5.5 million peasants worked on the various canal projects; most important was finishing and extending the Grand Canal north and south. These forced laborers faced death if they fled and the whip if they worked too slowly. Once the Grand Canal reached the capital, Emperor Yang took his four-story, 270-foot long dragon boat south to the Yangzi River, towed by peasant power. His entourage reached eighty-thousand men and stretched out as many as 60 miles. He had forty palaces built so he could avoid sleeping on the barge.

Such building projects proved expensive. Emperor Yang coupled this mistreatment of the peasantry and waste of taxes with renewed wars of conquest that turned out to be failures, even with perhaps the largest army in world history before the twentieth century used to fight one of the Korean states. China faced bankruptcy and two large peasant rebel armies when Turkish nomads captured Yang and held him for ransom in 615. In the end, the emperor's own entourage assassinated Yang in 617, and chaos in China deepened. Key Sui dynasty officials joined the scramble for power. The winner over these pretenders and the peasant armies was another Chinese-nomad military governor of the north who proclaimed power in 618 and spent the better part of 8 years consolidating his hold on China using the same Turks as mercenaries: Tang Gaozu, the first emperor of the Tang dynasty. *See also* **Early Tang Dynasty** and **Late Tang Dynasty**.

Further Reading

Bingham, Woodbridge. *The Founding of the T'ang Dynasty: The Fall of Sui and Rise of T'ang, a Preliminary Survey*. New York: Octagon Books, 1970.

Dien, Albert E. *State and Society in Early Medieval China*. Stanford, CA: Stanford University Press, 1990.

Fairbank, John K., and Denis Crispin Twitchett. *The Cambridge History of China*. Vol. 3: *Sui and T'ang China, 589-906*. Part 1. Cambridge, UK: Cambridge University Press, 1979.

Sumo Wrestling

Sumo likely predates the Japanese arrival on the Yamato Plain at the start of the fifth century. Sumo's governing body today says the sport is at least 1,500 years old. It started as a harvest ritual for Shintoism. The fight between two neighboring peasants would include prayers for a bountiful harvest. There were no real rules at first, so punching and strangling attacks were allowed for centuries before the sport organized under the Tokugawa regime (after 1600). In fact, sometimes the wrestlers would use weapons to kill their opponent.

During the **Nara Period** sumo was introduced to the imperial court and no doubt took on further characteristics of Shintoism that are still seen today, like having a **Shinto** priest as referee, tossing salt to purify the arena, and stomping to scare away the evil spirits. The emperor began to hold a yearly wrestling festival the seventh day of the seventh lunar month, including music and dancing for the wrestlers. Slowly rules were added so the fight was no longer about maiming or killing them an adversary. Instead, later rules made the wrestlers unarmed and restricted certain painful attacks. A Shinto priest served as referee, and the goal became to push the opponent out of the ring or make any part of his body touch the ground other than the soles of his bare feet.

In the Kamakura and then Ashikaga Periods, sumo wrestling became something to teach the nascent samurai warrior who might lose his weapon or have his sword broken. Out of sumo came jujitsu, a useful martial art for the bushi.

Further Reading

Adams, Andy, and Ryo Hatano. *Sumo History and Yokozuna Profiles*. Tokyo, Japan: Bat Publications, 1979.

Tale of Genji

The world's first novel was Japan's *Tale of Genji* by Lady Murasaki (her given name is unknown), written probably from 1008 to 1021. This novel has been translated into modern Japanese (and many other languages) and is still read to this day. It is a source of Japanese cultural pride, although attacked at first due to the sexual conduct in the book. The story takes place over 75 years, following three generations of the imperial family and five hundred characters in fifty-four chapters originally written in haphazard order, most likely to amuse ladies of the court and not for publication. The story became famous because the beautiful poetry—for a long time considered the only important Japanese language literature—written within the sprawling tale. Only later it became an icon as the first book in Japanese.

In brief, *Tale of Genji* is a story about looking for love where it is forbidden or unlikely to be found. The hero is not one by standard Western definition. His heroism lies in his capacity to be deeply moved and emotional through poetry, painting, music, and affairs of the heart. Most important, the novel helps to explain the aesthetics of Heian Japan, at least for the 5 percent of elite Japanese living in the capital. Elite women have their eyebrows shaved and drawn on higher than before and their teeth blackened. These aristocratic men and women wore white powder on their faces. They wear many layered robes of fine colored silk but can be almost mortally embarrassed if one layer out of twelve does not quite match the subtle colors of the rest. It was more important for food to look beautiful than to taste delicious. The elite liked to dance, recite poetry, and concoct perfumes. But what the **Heian Period** aristocrats considered beautiful was not necessarily the obvious. Instead of the tune, the smell, or the sight, Heian Japanese elites, in contrast to Chinese, admired the transient nature of life heard in the last few notes of a song fading away, fragrance wafting on the breeze, or shadows present at dusk or dawn. Cherry blossoms were (and are) an excellent example of this aesthetic. The flowers in the cherry tree only last for a few days and thus were (and are) seen as reflecting how briefly humans live on earth or the fickleness of the human heart, both themes of Murasaki's work.

Because marriages were arranged as part of political expedience, men and women in the *Tale of Genji*—and we assume in Heian Japan—had many secret affairs. But a man would fall in love with a women not based on her beauty, because women often hid behind screens when courting, but on her writing style or poetry recited. Most important were the "morning after" letters sent by lovers after their night of love; the way it was folded, the perfume put on it, the calligraphy of the note, and the words within all foretold how the other viewed the relationship. Genji excelled at dance, poetry, and these letters and could cry in front of people should his love be out of reach. This sensitivity made him a hero for Heian Japan very different from a Western hero that always put his feelings out of reach to fight the bad guy.

Further Reading

Morris, Ivan I. *The World of the Shining Prince: Court Life in Ancient Japan.* New York: Knopf, 1964.

Murasaki Shikibu. *The Tale of Genji.* Translated by Edward Seidensticker. New York: Knopf, 1989.

Tang Dynasty. *See* **Early Tang Dynasty; Late Tang Dynasty**

Tang Governance

Emperor Taizong, the second emperor of the celebrated Tang dynasty, helped create a governing, bureaucratic system utilized from this period forward to the twentieth century by Chinese emperors to control their vast empires. It was a pyramid structure, with the emperor at the top. Three departments came at the next level: Department of State, Imperial Secretariat, and the Imperial Chancellery, the last, under the chancellor, was next in command after the emperor and served as a chief advisor. The secretariat helped create policy and write the imperial decrees. The main, essential tasks of government were entrusted to the Department of State, which included six ministries: Officials, Finance, Rites, Army, Justice, and Public Works. The Ministry of Officials appointed, promoted, and demoted the officials that helped run the government, down to the local magistrate level, and thus helped with the **examination system**. The Ministry of Finance gathered census data and the taxes that allowed the state to function. The Ministry of Rites attended to Confucian, Buddhist, and Daoist matters, including state ceremonies and rituals. These state rituals became increasingly important over the years as emperors moved away from the public worship of their own imperial ancestors and these public ceremonies became the way to show the emperor was the father of the nation in a very Confucian manner, and thus held the **mandate of heaven**. The Ministries of Army, Justice, and Public Works all functioned as might be expected by their names, with the exception that the Ministry of Army dealt with the organizing the military in times of peace.

Besides this bureaucratic system, Taizong also divided China into first ten (later fifteen) large circuits that resemble modern day provinces in their borders. He subdivided them into over 350 prefectures and more than fifteen hundred counties managed by magistrates and other officials, the lowest part of the central bureaucracy. The final division, sixteen thousand districts, were under control of the local elites, as the central government could not control what happened at the local level with the technology of the time. Taizong also created laws of two types — primary (meant for all time) and secondary (regulations that would be adjusted over time).

The Tang governance system also began to use the examination system to a greater and greater degree as the years progressed, although at the beginning it was an important, but not major method of recruitment. First it was used for filling positions that were newly created or when a position would become vacant due to the official in question lacking an heir. This meant only about one third of all positions. The Tang dynasty restored the Imperial University to teach Confucianism to its hoped-for officials.

It was under Tang's **Empress Wu**, the only female to rule in her own name, that the exam system became even more important, but still not all positions in government were subject to it. Because she believed her family was descended from Laozi, creator of Daoism, the test in her "husband's" day also had questions about Daoism to answer. She continued the tradition. After her expulsion from the throne in 705 at the age of 82, Confucianists resumed their monopoly over the questions. As the years progressed, the exams became conservative and subject to rote memorization, serving to hamper intellectual growth by emphasis on Confucian orthodoxy. *See also* **Early Tang Dynasty** and **Late Tang Dynasty**.

Further Reading

Bingham, Woodbridge. *The Founding of the T'ang Dynasty: The Fall of Sui and Rise of T'ang, a Preliminary Survey*. New York: Octagon Books, 1970.

Dien, Albert E. *State and Society in Early Medieval China*. Stanford, CA: Stanford University Press, 1990.

Johnson, Wallace. *The T'ang Code*. Vol. 1, *General Principles*. Harvard Studies in East Asian Law. Princeton, NJ: Princeton University Press, 1979.

Warfare

The Chinese military, once trousers and stirrups came on the scene, used cavalry to harass the enemy and usually militia-quality infantry armed with easy-to-use crossbow as the shock troops. The strategy Chinese used came from the Warring States Period, before the unification of China, in the book *Art of War* by Sun Zi. Sun advocated using diplomacy to win a country's desires. If that failed, disrupt enemy alliances, harass the enemy supply line to win without fighting, avoid combat except when and where you wanted it and had the advantage, and do not attack an enemy-fortified city. Sometimes the Chinese generals neglected these and other suggestions by the military genius Sun, almost always to China's disappointment.

Soldiers never obtained much status in China, usually falling even below mercenaries. During the **Late Tang dynasty** and into the Song, China changed its system by hiring seminomadic horsemen as mercenaries to fight for the empire. Like late Roman reliance on others to guard the frontiers, the Chinese mercenaries often turned on their employer and as a result helped end the dynasty.

By the time the **Song dynasty** decided to go back to a militia system, poor Chinese troop quality may have led to former allies attacking Chinese forces (first the Jurchen and then the **Mongols**), but their heavy infantry at least had the best equipment for the times. The Song soldiers also used crossbows (and regular bows) with thick, heavy metal armor (over 60 pounds) to protect themselves. They used a mish-mash of rockets, grenades, firearms, and cannon in attempts to scare their enemy's horses, as well as to harm them. The **Ming dynasty** also used militia and different gunpowder-driven weapons in their fights against the Mongols.

The **Yuan dynasty** used some of the classic Mongol combat tricks, at least through the first half of the dynasty. In the second half, it often used landlord armies to help it put down near-constant peasant rebellions. Mongol troops had already been organized by Chingess (Genghis) Khan: every warrior, with his family and possessions, was permanently assigned to a particular unit; those units were placed together in tens, and tens of tens, and so on, for a simple organizing system. There cavalry had great proficiency in archery with a powerful, long-range composite bow. The Mongols also had a system of fast couriers that could transmit messages up to 200 miles per day! This ability for rapid communication allowed the most important ability in war to occur—being able to split an army and have it come back together as one once the battle was joined. Another important tactics was used when in combat for the first time against a new foe. The Mongols would attack directly with only part of their force and retreat like they had been defeated. They might even retreat for days, just a step ahead of the overconfident pursuit teams of their enemy. At the appropriate time—usually when another force got behind their adversaries—the fighting would resume. Using their powerful bows and maneuverable horses, Mongols would usually win, until sedentary life ruling China diminished the skills of one fourth of the total Mongol empire.

As neighbors to China during the Sui, Tang, and **Northern Song dynasty**, Korean military forces fought on the battlefield in ways similar to the Chinese, with large numbers of quality militia soldiers armed with crossbows behind large shields with a small number of cavalry to harass the flanks. The main difference was that soldiers had more status in Korea than China. In terms of strategy and tactics, no Korean matched the war hero Ulchi Mundok of Koguryo in 612. He fought off a **Sui dynasty** invasion, rumored to be two million strong (likely an exaggeration of the times—it would be difficult to field an army larger than one-hundred thousand in the seventh century) of one of the three Korean states, Koguryo. It was the largest of the three, but still small by Chinese standards. He fought a brilliant campaign of retreat, scorched-earth policy (destroying food and shelter while retreating to deny the enemy comfort), and periodic probing attacks, all designed to keep the Sui army on the attack but unbalanced. Ulchi managed to lure the Sui forces deep within Korean territory; that was fine by the Chinese, for they planned to besiege the Koguryo capital of Pyongyang. Just before that siege could take place, Ulchi surprised the larger army at the Battle of Salsu—one of the most brilliant military victories in Korean history—forcing it to retreat. Throughout the retreat, Korean forces harassed the Chinese. Supposedly fewer than three thousand marched back to China, the rest lost to lack of supplies, disease, or combat.

Japanese warfare went through four phases during the years 400 to 1400. Archeologists call the 400s the century of armor. Japanese foot soldiers were protected by iron cuirass (a breastplate and backplate armor) and a helmet similar to that used simultaneously in southern Korea. Soldiers also had either handheld shields or planted into the ground 5 foot high and 2 feet wide wood and leather tower shields to hide from arrows.

By the sixth century, Japan converted to cavalry and used lighter, more flexible lamellar armor made up of eight hundred small iron slats to use while riding their short horses. They armed themselves with the bow, which took much dedication to fire accurately on the run and to be able to ride while not holding the reins. This style of armor and mounted warfare would be reflective of Japanese armor all the way through the time of the samurai. It was also how the Japanese uji or **clans** fought with one another for control of the coalescing state.

After leading Japanese learned of Chinese advancements in the Sui and Tang dynasties, they copied the Chinese army and left the cavalry for flanking maneuvers using their swords and to finish off the opponent. The Japanese brought back infantry armed with bows or crossbows behind the giant planted shields. Generals coordinated their different forces through the use of gongs, bells, drums, and banners. Even **Shinto** priests involved themselves in the military, perhaps explaining the continued Shinto operation of the controversial Yasukuni Shrine for Japan's Asia-Pacific War dead and the executed war criminals. Japan's **Yamato Period**, **Nara Period**, and beginning of the **Heian Period** mostly used this military to push their non-Japanese "barbarian" neighbors like the Ainu northeast to northern Honshu and hopefully Hokkaido.

The final phase reverted back to the expensive cavalry, the roots of the samurai, during the late Heian Period. These mounted soldiers soon came to dominate Japan's class system. Called at this time bushi (warriors), they borrowed the idea of a curved sword from the defeated "barbarians" and continued their skills with bow and arrow. Japanese battles now devolved into one-on-one fights, with the loser apt to lose his head from the squire-like infantry who moved to mop up after the swordfight had ended. This was because the non-Japanese had been forced away to the northeast and except for the two brief and abortive Mongol invasions of Kyushu, Japanese fought Japanese. Out of these fights and a few centuries would eventually emerge ritual suicide (*seppuku*, or more vulgarly "harakiri") and bushido, the way of the samurai warrior.

Further Reading

Graff, David Andrew. *Medieval Chinese Warfare, 300–900*. London: Routledge, 2002.

King, Winston L. *Zen and the Way of the Sword: Arming the Samurai Psyche*. New York: Oxford University Press, 1993.

Lorge, Peter Allan. *War, Politics and Society in Early Modern China, 900–1795*. New York: Routledge, 2005.

Sun Zi. *The Art of War*. Translated by J. H. Huang. New York: HarperPerenial, 2008.

Women, Role of

Women in traditional East Asia faced many hardships, although during the **Heian Period** in Japan and for much of Korea's history elite women had more power and prestige until the twentieth century. Average peasant women faced the normal hardships of being on the edge of poverty, but not as much discrimination as elites due to the poor family needing the equal work by all to survive the difficult farming life.

Throughout East Asian traditional society, the birth of a girl was not as happy a day as the birth of a boy. Male children were needed to continue the family name and take care of the ancestors, including the parents in old age and then death (at least in China and Korea). In difficult times, a daughter might be the victim of infanticide, or be sold into service or concubinage if an elite family could be found to make the sale. The girl would then have to work until adulthood (and perhaps beyond) as a poorly treated maid, or become one of the extra wives or concubines of a rich, old man, the difference being a concubine could be bought and sold.

The first 7 years for a daughter—assuming no infanticide or the regular deaths children faced in the years before modern medicine—were probably the most joyful. East Asian families let children of both sexes—although perhaps allowing even more freedom for boys—play, with a little work thrown in the more poverty a family faced. Seven years did not mean 7 Western years, however; children's ages were measured one for the birth, one at the first lunar New Year, and another year every lunar New Year, so a child 7 years of age might be only 5 years old in the Western reckoning.

The years of childhood after age 7 meant hard work, in the house if the family had some money, and in the fields and in the home if part of a normal peasant family. And if not sold to a wealthy family or worse a brothel, the girl might expect to marry. A middle-income peasant family (or wealthier) from a neighboring village would employ a matchmaker to find a suitable wife for their son. If wealthy, the tie with another wealthy family would insure the continued prosperity of both. If normal peasants, an agreeable match would be all that was necessary. If poor peasants, the matchmaker would likely be out of the picture. When the potential groom's family was satisfied with the match, it would send to the bride's family a set of traditional, symbolic gifts like lacquer and glue to show the joining of the two in marriage, as well as a small dowery for the loss of a worker in the bride's home.

The newlywed was usually just a teenaged girl who had no choice over her marriage partner, and this part of life was the most difficult—if she did not commit suicide on the way to her new home. Not only would she be expected to start a family and have sons almost immediately—with all the dangers childbirth entailed—she was also run ragged by her new mother-in-law who had her working almost as hard as a slave. Because three generations—the father and mother, the newlyweds, and their new children—all lived under the same roof, the mother-in-law had the power as the elder and often abused that power. She would complain that the new wife was useless and did not do her chores properly. There were cases of suicide or fleeing back to her parents' home due to this cruelty, which ironically the mother-in-law no doubt herself endured when she was a newlywed. Conditions would likely improve upon the birth of a son. The birth of a series of daughters might lead her in-laws to send her back to her parents, divorced for not producing an heir!

The woman's middle years were full of surviving multiple births and experiencing the likely death of some of her children. If a peasant, she kept the home as well as worked the fields. If an elite, she might get some education to pass on to her sons and daughters, and before the **Song dynasty** might play a role in the family or extended family.

Becoming a mother-in-law as your eldest son married and brought his new wife to live in your home was the high point of many East Asian women's lives, especially peasant lives. But elite women in China by the time of the Song dynasty faced a new horror, albeit for their girl children, the **Neo-Confucian** attack on women known as **footbinding**. This incredibly painful procedure—wrapping a 5-year-old's feet so they would not grow—kept the elite woman's feet smaller than their fist. It made it difficult to walk and thus showed that the family was wealthy enough to do without the work of the woman in question. It also pushed these women out of society, where they had a place before, and into their homes' shadows. Unless there was a plan to sell a daughter to be a concubine, poor girls and women did not experience this torture; husband, wife, and daughters all needed to work the fields together to survive. Footbinding also had a sexual component. As the foot tried to grow, the bones snapped and left the foot looking a little like a lotus flower, which was considered erotic, and was thought to increase sexual pleasure for the woman's husband.

The life of an East Asian widow could go in two directions. If she had a son, her son and daughter-in-law would be expected to care for her until death. If she did not have a son, and lacked money after her husband's death, life would turn out full of difficulties. Widows were forbidden to marry, so could not hope to have a second family if their husbands died young.

Chinese society rarely allowed a woman to rule, with **Empress Wu** the big exception. Korea was a matrilineal society, which remained important in Korean **lineages**, so a female leader was not out of the question—at least three ruled between 400 and 800—before **Confucianism** and especially Neo-Confucianism began to rule the ideas of Koreans. During a similar period, Japan had two empresses. During the Heian Period, elite women had many rights and were educated, if only in Japanese and not the Chinese needed for secular rule at the time. They had relationships with men on their own accord, even if neither party to the relationship saw the entire body of the other, what with the twelve layers of silk robes and paper screens. But when the warrior class took over Japanese society, elite women went back into the shadows, and the poor peasant woman continued to work hard in the fields and in the home.

Further Reading

Ko, Dorothy, JaHyun Kim Haboush, and Joan R. Piggott. *Women and Confucian Cultures in Premodern China, Korea, and Japan*. Berkeley: University of California Press, 2003.

Ruch, Barbara. *Engendering Faith: Women and Buddhism in Premodern Japan*. Ann Arbor: University of Michigan, Center for Japanese Studies, 2002.

Wang, Robin. *Images of Women in Chinese Thought and Culture: Writings from the Pre-Qin Period through the Song dynasty*. Indianapolis, IN: Hackett Publishing Co., 2003.

Yamato Period (c. 400–710)

This period of Japanese history begins with the Japanese pushing into the Yamato Plain on Honshu. Some scholars date its start from when Korean Buddhism hit the island in 552, but it makes more sense to start in the fifth century. It was around this time that the clan who chose the sun goddess to worship as ancestor used the fact that the sun is so important and gives light to all Japan to convince the other clans to follow its leadership and become subsidiary elites. It would take a bit of time to work out leadership, but by the next century this imperial house, drawing its lineage from Amaterasu the sun goddess, held loose control over the other clans, a first-among-equals arrangement. Even today there are those that claim that the imperial line flows unblemished from this early emperor.

In 552, the Korean kingdom of Paekche asked for help in its struggle against its two Korean neighbors, so it sent a bronze image of the Buddha and some Buddhist scriptures to the Soga family, triggering renewed interest in Buddhism. Although too weak to offer military help, the Soga family used the ideas coming from China via Korea as weapons in the battle for control of the imperial family. Two families besides Soga were the main contestants, which became a fierce contest: Nakatomi (virtually in charge of Shintoism), Mononobe (who controlled the military), and Soga (championing Buddhism even though intermarried with the imperial clan). Endorsing Buddhism had the dual function of endorsing Chinese/Korean ways; Japan was to copy laws, arts, religion, society, and eventually even the idea of a capital city from first Sui and later Tang China before too much time passed. Even though its enemies declared Buddhism caused an epidemic by irritating **Shinto** gods (kami), Soga defeated the Mononobe in a war and convinced Nakatomi to back out of the struggle, at least temporarily. Soga had the opportunity to eliminate the emperor and place a full-blooded Soga onto the throne, yet the leaders of Soga decided simply to intermarry and have a regent control the niece of the family, Empress Suiko (r. 592–628). This regent was **Prince Shotoku.**

Prince Shotoku became famous for sponsoring Buddhism and Buddhist temples, as well as creating the **Seventeen Point Constitution** in 604. This

constitution was more of a list of advice for rulers and the ruled and was written in Chinese, the only written language for the Japanese for centuries. Its articles heavily advocated **Confucianism** and Buddhism, with a sprinkling of
Daoism and Shinto's consensus building thrown in for good measure. But the
constitution was really a way to show forcefully that the emperor/regent for
the emperor would serve as a more powerful central government, including
collecting taxes. Prince Shotoku also opened up relations with China and sent
four missions to the short-lived **Sui dynasty**.

After the death of Prince Shotuku in 622, a new round of fighting for control
of the emperor broke out. The winner was the Nakatomi family, who changed
its name to Fujiwara. The Fujiwara family would control or influence the emperor for centuries to come, first by intermarrying with the emperor and later
by becoming regent. This leading Shinto family decided against discarding
Buddhism. The Fujiwara instead pushed for more centralization and adopted
more Chinese ideas. It continued centralizing of the state, even though the
family continued to practice Shintoism. For example, the imperial residence
changed with the death of each emperor until 645 — Shintoism abhors pollution and believes the dead defiled the previous palace. The Fujiwara then instituted new changes, called the Taika (Great Change) Reforms in 646, and
decided to leave the imperial residence as it was too much work to move it so
often. These reforms created a new system of provincial administration and a
series of roads to link the kingdom together. Private land ownership was
ended so Japan could copy the Chinese **equal field system** and taxation policies of the **Tang dynasty**. The rice fields would revert to state ownership each
generation for redistribution based on the census, but the census was not taken
until 670, and the equal field system was always incomplete. After three emperors, the Fujiwara decided to build a city, a permanent capital for Japan on
the Tang model in Heijo, also called Nara. Thus ended the Yamato Period and
the short **Nara Period** began in 710.

Further Reading
Hong, Wontack. *Relationship between Korea and Japan in Early Period: Paekche and Yamato
Wa*. Seoul, Korea: ILSIMSA, 1988.
Kidder, J. Edward. *Japan before Buddhism*. New York: F.A. Praeger, 1966.

Yangzi River

The Yangzi River is the third longest river in the world at just under 4,000
miles; it is wide and deep enough to allow navigation of ocean-going modern
vessels 1,000 miles from the sea to its famous gorges. With many men and ropes,
even the gorges were defeated by shallow draft vessels and skilled, determined
navigators. The river thus serves as a major transportation corridor into China's
interior, as well as the water to grow rice this far north in traditional China. Chinese traditionally founded their southern capitals on the river (Nanjing for the
Ming dynasty) or a short distance away on a tributary (Hangzhou during the
Southern Song dynasty). The river winds its way from a glacier on the eastern
border of Tibet southeast before turning around a third of its way to the sea
back in a general northeastern direction. The river gets wide with over seven
hundred tributaries and four of China's five great freshwater lakes feeding the
river. Although floods periodically do occur, putting the countryside for miles

and miles completely under water, the Yangzi does not compare to the **Yellow River** in its historic destructiveness and unpredictability.

The river and its tributaries were home to exotic Chinese animals now on the endangered species list, from the Yangzi River dolphin (called "goddess of the Yangzi"), to the finless porpoise (known as a "river pig"), and even alligators (the only place they exist outside of North America). Although the river does not flow muddy yellowish colors like its neighbor to the north, the Yellow River, as the years of agriculture on its banks increased the water became dangerous to drink–the nightsoil runoff described under **agriculture** was the main culprit.

The Yangzi River served as the dividing line between north and south China, and the boundary for rice growing for the 400 to 1400 period. Its width in the east and mountainous terrain in the west meant it was difficult to cross. Only a few strong, long, and wide bridges crossed the river, save in major urban centers. By the ninth century, the Yangzi delta and its rice farms had become the most densely populated area in China (and thus the world), and perhaps continues to hold this mark to this day. The center of China's growing economy was no longer the Yellow River, but instead the Yangzi. Under the Southern Song dynasty, Hangzhou, in the southern delta, was the largest city in the world with over 1.5 million inhabitants. It was also where the **Grand Canal** started its trek northward to the Yellow River and beyond.

Further Reading

Van Slyke, Lyman P. *Yangtze: Nature, History, and the River*. Reading, MA: Addison-Wesley Publishing Co., 1988.

Yellow River

The Yellow River is a long and powerful river in north China; it is where Chinese civilization first developed because of the fine, loess soil the river carved out of the earth in the west and deposited through floods throughout the north China plain. In fact, it is the loess that gives the Yellow River its name: the soil when in the water appears as a yellowish brown color. This soil was rich in nutrients and only required wooden tools to farm. The Chinese grew first millet (in the West today millet is used as birdseed) along its banks and tributaries, then barley and kaoliang (sorghum), before the coming of wheat around 1500 B.C.E. The itself river flows well over 3,000 miles across the mostly-flat north China plain, making it the sixth-longest river in the world, although not a good one for ships and boats because of its quick current and unpredictable nature. As the river deposited silt along its banks, the river itself rose from the plain. It needed constant peasant labor to maintain its banks and earthen dykes to prevent water from spilling down onto the flat farmlands below. When the major floods would finally occur, the river would jump its banks and flow down onto thousands of square miles of farms, leading to devastation of the flood itself and famine due to the destruction of that year's growing season. This unpredictable nature of the river is why it bears the nickname "China's Sorrow." Yet the river also supplies water for irrigation projects and loess soil for farming with even primitive tools.

Peasants near the river historically spent much of their corvee working to keep the Yellow River dykes in order. Unfortunately, many of the nomadic or seminomadic conquerors of north China did not spend sufficient resources to maintain the river, leading to disastrous floods, which the local peasants took to mean the rulers had lost the **mandate of heaven**. In 1194, when north China was under the control of the Jurchen, one of the worst of these floods spilled out over the southern portion of the north China plain, ruining the lives of thousands of peasants. The river and flood were so powerful that it changed the river's course. For the next few centuries, the Yellow River co-opted the Huai River basin, reaching the Yellow Sea over 600 miles south of its original exit to the sea. Under the Mongols—another nomadic group with difficulty understanding the importance of controlling the river—during the **Yuan dynasty** in the 1340s the river once again jumped its banks and flooded peasant lands. In this case the muddy waters fouled the **Grand Canal**. It took the efforts of one-hundred fifty thousand peasants to put the river back into its 1194 channel. Revolutionaries in the secret White Lotus Buddhist sect used the opportunity of thousands of disgruntled **corvee** workers to proselytize and thus set the stage for peasant rebellions in north China that would eventually fell the dynasty.

Further Reading

Sinclair, Kevin. *The Yellow River: A 5000 Year Journey through China*. Los Angeles: Knapp Press, 1987.

Yuan Dynasty (1279–1368)

The **Southern Song dynasty** made a costly error, just as the **Northern Song dynasty** did with the Jurchen. It again tried to play barbarian against barbarian. The Chinese stupidly allied with the **Mongols** against the Jurchen, hoping to get back north China in the process. The Mongols, disparate tribes living a nomadic existence in the plains that bear their name, became a unified and highly successful fighting force under Genghis Khan (one of many transliterations of his name) starting in 1206. He died in 1227, after many victories in Central Asia and into Russia, having only just begun to attack the Jurchen in northern China. The alliance between his heir, Ogodei, and China resulted in the loss in 7 years of the Jurchen buffer state. Because the Chinese armies again did poorly against nomadic troops, the Mongols decided to push their luck and continue the war, this time against the Chinese. The Mongols slowly conquered the Southern Song dynasty over the next 45 years—fighting proved difficult not due to the quality of Chinese troops, but because south China is not very suitable to cavalry attacks. The Mongols improvised, and had the advantage of most Chinese landlords deciding to ally with the Mongols in return for leaving their property intact.

Kublai Khan, 1216–1294, grandson of Genghis Khan, Emperor Shih-tsu of Yuan Dynasty China, 1279–1294. The Art Archive.

Khubilai Khan (r. 1260–1294), the grandson of Genghis, moved the Mongol capital to Beijing and became the first ruler of the Yuan dynasty (1279–1368). Soon China became a realm within an empire, as China was easily the wealthiest possession of the entire Mongol empire stretching to

Eastern Europe. Khubilai divided the population of China into four groups to help him rule: Mongols at the top of the bureaucracy, Central Asian peoples in less important bureaucratic positions, recent north China defeated peoples in the least important positions, and southern Chinese completely out of government. The Chinese were also not allowed arms and forbidden from meetings. This would be the first time in history that Chinese landlords felt deprived of their official positions. The Mongols would temporarily relent on this point and brought back ever so briefly the **examination system**. However, the Mongols made the test easier for non-Chinese, so the system did not endear itself to the Chinese gentry exam takers. The one benefit they received as a class was to keep their estates, the original reason they surrendered and then turned to help the Mongols.

Mongol control over Central Asia stimulated trade between China, the rest of the empire, and Europe, but the profits to this trade left Chinese hands for the middlemen involved along the **Silk Road**. These losses increased rapidly due to a mistaken printing of too much paper currency, Mongol corruption, and unsuccessful invasions of Southeast Asia and Japan (both twice), crippling China's economy in the long run. In addition, Mongols confiscated land in north China for pasturing horses, Mongol aristocrats, and Buddhist temples. As this land left tax rolls, peasants were forced to make up the difference. Taxes increased rapidly due to these economic problems, and because the Mongols built and extended the **Grand Canal** to move receipts and grain to this new capital. Although the Mongols expanded the Grand Canal, they did nothing about shoring up the **Yellow River** dykes or irrigation systems of north China, which both failed, leading to massive famine in some parts of China. In addition, peasants faced 100 percent interest on loans as landlords attempted to recoup the funds they used to take from the government as local or regional bureaucrats.

Peasant unrest led to rebellion against the foreign Mongols and the Chinese oppressive landlords. It started under the leadership of a leader claiming Song heritage, a Buddhist secret society called the White Lotus, and its Red Turban soldiers. Recruiting in the north was easy for this group, especially as one-hundred fifty thousand peasant conscripts were working on repairing the Yellow River there in the 1340s. Open rebellion broke out in 1352, and for 3 years major parts of south and central China were lost to both the Mongols and the Chinese landlords. The Mongols finally ended this rebellion by using Chinese troops led by the gentry against the peasant rebellion.

This victory for the Mongols and their allies would be short-lived. Peasants continued to fight against the dynasty. A former peasant and one-time Buddhist monk named Zhu Yuanzhang rose in rank to become the leader of the southern Red Turban armies. Zhu revised the plan of attack, deciding to ally with Chinese landlords to attack the Mongols, rather than having both as enemies. Even though not all Chinese gentry broke from the Mongols, enough did to allow Zhu to push the nomads out of China in 1368 and forming a new dynasty with its capital on the **Yangzi River** at Nanjing: the **Ming dynasty** (1368–1644).

Further Reading
Chan, Hok-lam. *China and the Mongols: History and Legend under the Yuan and Ming*. Aldershot, UK: Ashgate, 1999.

Franke, Herbert. *China under Mongol Rule*. Brookfield, VT: Variorum, 1994.
Weatherford, J. McIver. *Genghis Khan and the Making of the Modern World*. New York: Crown, 2004.

Zen Buddhism

Zen Buddhism is another type of Mahayana ("Greater Vehicle") Buddhism popular in Japan, especially among warriors and the literati. Everyone has the Buddha nature in them and can be saved, but in Zen your teacher only explains the path, it takes the monk-student to follow the path successfully to achieve enlightenment.

Zen was a translation of **Chan Buddhism** and shares many qualities with it. Although meditation had long been a practice of Japanese Buddhists, it was not until the twelfth century that Rinzai Zen arrived in Japan from China. It believes meditation and koans (literally "public cases," but really logic puzzles meant to snap the mind out of its harmful logic) the keys needed for enlightenment. A bit later, in the thirteenth century Soto Zen arrived from China. It focuses on sitting. Warriors became the chief nonmonk practitioners of both types of Zen, needing the clarity of meditation, the elimination of fear of death, and repetitive moves until one can attack without thinking. Zen also had a large impact on Japanese arts and culture, including **noh theater**.

Bodhidharma (Daruma). Momoyama period, Japan, late 16th century. Bodhidharma, known as Daruma in Japanese, was the Indian founder of Zen Buddhism which he brought to China. Erich Lessing/Art Resource, NY.

Further Reading

De Bary, William Theodore. *The Buddhist Tradition in India, China and Japan*. New York: Modern Library, 1969.

King, Winston L. *Zen and the Way of the Sword: Arming the Samurai Psyche*. New York: Oxford University Press, 1993.

Suzuki, Daisetz Teitaro. *Zen and Japanese Culture*. New York: Pantheon Books, 1959.

Zhu Xi (1130–1200)

Zhu Xi was a **Southern Song dynasty** Neo-Confucian thinker whose ideas in two generations would become the respected interpretation of Confucianism. He mixed ideas of Buddhism and **Daoism** to find a new interpretation of **Confucianism**. Zhu thought long and hard about how to cultivate the self. He believed through meditation one could suddenly become aware and achieve full Neo-Confucian enlightenment. These ideas sound suspiciously like **Chan Buddhism**.

Zhu looked at Confucianism through the lens of his own time. There was an immaterial and immutable principle in all things that gives them their form and essence. Once he grasped this basic idea, it was simple to show that people were inherently good, but needed training and self-cultivation through meditation to show this goodness to the world. This is much the same as a house plan: it only becomes a house once materials are used to build it. One's qi, the parts of the house, needs li, a plan, to make everything work properly. Zhu's ideas became the orthodox interpretation of Neo-Confucian thought. So important were his ideas that in the late Southern Song, his was the interpretation needed to pass through the examination system. The downside to Zhu's work is that it led to stagnation among China's intellectuals, who needed to memorize the style and even substance of one particular version of **Neo-Confucianism** from the thirteenth through the nineteenth century rather than coming up with their own ideas and interpretations for a changing world.

Further Reading

Brandauer, Frederick Paul, and Junjie Huang. *Imperial Rulership and Cultural Change in Traditional China*. Seattle: University of Washington Press, 1994.
Chan, Wing-tsit. *Chu Hsi and Neo-Confucianism*. Honolulu: University of Hawai'i Press, 1986.

Primary Documents

1. Selections from the *Analects* by Confucius (c. sixth century B.C.E.)

The following document comes from nine centuries before 400 but details some simple ideas of Confucius in what most historians agree are his words. Through these statements and answers to questions, Confucius explains such things as the Golden Rule and filial piety (honoring one's parents). Benevolence to those below and loyalty to those above, the four- or five-part hierarchical class system, and the five relationships are left out, but can be found in the entry on Confucianism or in the essay on "Religion."

40. Zi Gong asked: "Is there any one word that can serve as a principle for the conduct of life?" Confucius said: "Perhaps the word 'reciprocity': Do not do to others what you would not want others to do to you."

. . .

56. Zi You asked about filial piety. Confucius said: "Nowadays a filial son is just a man who keeps his parents in food. But even dogs or horses are given food. If there is no feeling of reverence, wherein lies the difference?"
57. Zi Xia asked about filial piety. Confucius said: "The manner is the really difficult thing. When anything has to be done the young people undertake it; when there is wine and food the elders are served—is this all there is to filial piety?"

. . .

95. Confucius said: "If a ruler himself is upright, all will go well without orders. But if he is not upright, even though he gives orders, they will not be obeyed."

Source: Bary, Wm. Theodore de, Wing-tsit Chan, and Burton Watson, comps. *Sources of Chinese Tradition.* New York: Columbia University Press, 1960, pp. 27, 29, 34.

2. Selections from the *Dao De Jing* (c. sixth century B.C.E.)

These selections from the *Dao De* Jing, supposedly written millennia before, are probably contemporary with the works of Confucius. Daoism became the chief challenger to Confucianism and like it survived the Warring States Period with practitioners to this day. Daoists often put their ideas in opposition to Confucianism, especially claiming Daoism allows one to be closer to nature, as Confucianism is too tied up in government and ritual, yet their views rejecting writing laws are actually quite similar. One of Daoism's key ideas is *wu wei*, which means completing a task through nonaction. A famous story shows *wu wei* in action: a butcher never needed to sharpen his carving knife because instead of cutting the meat and dulling the blade, his experience with the meat had him put the knife where there was no resistance.

1

The Dao [Way] that can be told of
Is not the eternal Dao;
The name that can be named
Is not the eternal name.
Nameless, it is the origin of Heaven and earth;
Namable, it is the mother of all things.

. . .

3

Refrain from exalting the worthy,
So that the people will not scheme and contend;
Refrain from prizing rare possessions,
So that the people will not steal;
Refrain from displaying objects of desire,
So that the people's hearts will not be disturbed.

Therefore a sage rules his people thus:
He empties their minds,
And fills their bellies;
He weakens their ambitions,
And strengthens their bones.

He strives always to keep the people innocent of knowledge and desires and to keep the knowing ones from meddling. By doing nothing that interferes with anything (*wu-wei*), nothing is left unregulated.

Source: Bary, Wm. Theodore de, Wing-tsit Chan, and Burton Watson, comps. *Sources of Chinese Tradition.* New York: Columbia University Press, 1960, pp. 53, 54.

3. Alchemy in Religious Daoism (c. fifth century)

Daoism changed with the coming of Buddhism, which borrowed some of Daoism's ideas and used them in new ways. Daoism therefore became more church-like, which historians dub Religious Daoism. Although the original Daoists professed to want to get close to nature and do what is natural, Religious Daoists were more concerned with avoiding death altogether. Daoists became alchemists, trying to find the secret ingredients in Chinese medicine to live forever, as this document from the Period of Disunity shows. Unfortunately, often the items they mixed, like mercury and gunpowder, proved to have opposite of the desired effect.

The immortals nourish their bodies with drugs and prolong their lives with the application of occult science, so that internal illness shall not arise and external ailment shall not enter. Although they enjoy everlasting existence and do not die, their old bodies do not change. If one knows the way to immortality, it is not to be considered so difficult.

Among the creatures of nature, man is the most intelligent. Therefore those who understand [creation] slightly employ the myriad things and those who get to its depth can enjoy [what is called in the *Lao Tzu* "long life and everlasting existence"]. As we know that the best medicine can prolong life, let us take it to obtain immortality, and as we know that the tortoise and the crane have longevity, let us imitate their activities to increase our span of life. . . . Those who have obtained Dao are able to lift themselves into the clouds and the heavens above and to dive and swim in the rivers and seas below.

Source: Bary, Wm. Theodore de, Wing-tsit Chan, and Burton Watson, comps. *Sources of Chinese Tradition.* New York: Columbia University Press, 1960, pp. 300–301.

4. Changing Wives in China (sixth century)

The following poem below by Yuan-di (508–554) illustrates the tenuous position of women in sixth-century Chinese society. The poem expresses the loss and sorrow felt by a wife as she returns to her home to discover that she has been replaced by a new wife.

Entering the hall, she meets the new wife:
Leaving the gate, she runs into her former husband.
Words stick: she does not manage to say anything:
She presses her hands together and hesitates.
Agitates moon-like fan—sheds pearl-like tears—
Realizes she loves him just as much as ever:
That her present pain will never come to an end.

Source: Waley, Arthur, trans. *A Hundred and Seventy Chinese Poems.* London: Constable, 1918, pp. 15, 90.

5. The Shinto Creation Story (eighth century)

Written down from oral tradition in the early eighth century, the *Kojiki*, is the oldest text written in Japanese and a core sacred document of Shinto, the indigenous religion of Japan. Comprising mainly folk beliefs and traditional rituals, Shinto is loosely organized and lacking any recognized governing body. This passage from the start of the *Kojiki* describes the creation of the world. Notice the sexual imagery in the creation of the island of Onogoro (Japan) and the courtship story.

The Beginning of Heaven and Earth

The names of the Deities that were born in the Plain of High Heaven when the Heaven and Earth began were the Deity Master-of-the-August-Centre-of-Heaven, next the High-August-Producing-Wondrous Deity, next the Divine-Producing-Wondrous-Deity. These three Deities were all Deities born alone, and hid their persons. The names of the Deities that were born next from a thing that sprouted up like unto a reed-shoot when the earth, young and like unto floating oil, drifted about medusa-like, were the Pleasant-Reed-Shoot-Prince-Elder Deity, next the Heavenly-Eternally-Standing-Deity. These two Deities were likewise born alone, and hid their persons.

The five Deities in the above list are separate Heavenly Deities.

The Seven Divine Generations

The names of the Deities that were born next were the Earthly-Eternally-Standing-Deity, next the Luxuriant-Integrating-Master-Deity. These two Deities were likewise Deities born alone, and hid their persons. The names of the Deities that were born next were the Deity Mud-Earth-Lord next his younger sister the Deity Mud-Earth-Lady; next the Germ-Integrating-Deity, next his younger sister the Life-Integrating-Deity; next the Deity Elder-of-the-Great-Place, next his younger sister the Deity Elder-Lady-of-the-Great-Place; next the Deity Perfect-Exterior, next his younger sister the Deity Oh-Awful-Lady; next the Deity the Male-Who-Invites, next his younger sister the Deity the Female-Who-Invites. From the Earthly-Eternally-Standing Deity down to the Deity the Female-Who-Invites in the previous list are what are termed the Seven Divine Generations.

The Island of Onogoro

Hereupon all the Heavenly Deities commanded the two Deities His August-ness the Male-Who-Invites and Her Augustness the Female-Who-Invites, or-dering them to "make, consolidate, and give birth to this drifting land." Granting to them a heavenly jeweled spear, they [thus] deigned to charge them. So the two Deities, standing upon the Floating Bridge of Heaven, pushed down the jewelled spear and stirred with it, whereupon, when they had stiffed the brine till it went curdle-curdle, and drew [the spear] up, the brine that dripped down from the end of the spear was piled up and became an island. This is the Is-land of Onogoro.

Courtship of the Deities the Male-Who-Invites and the Female-Who-Invites

Having descended from Heaven onto this island, they saw to the erection of a heavenly august pillar, they saw to the erection of a hall of eight fathoms. Then the August Male-Who-Invites asked his younger sister the August Fe-male-Who-Invites, "Who is your body made?" She responded, "My body grew by growing, but there is one part that did not grow fully." Then the August Male-Who-Invites said, "My body grew by growing, but there is one part that grew too much. Therefore, would it be good for me to insert this part that grew too much into your part that did not grew fully, so that I will generate regions?" "It would be good." Then the August Male-Who-Invites said, "Since this is so, let us place together our august parts, running around this celestial column." Having made this agreement, the August Male-Who-Invites said, "Run around from the right, and I'll run from the left." When they had run around, the August Female-Who-Invites said, "O pleasant and lovable youth!" and the August Male-Who-Invites said, "O pleasant and lovely maiden!" When they finished, the August Male-Who-Invites said to his sister, "A woman should not speak first." Nevertheless, they began the work of creation in bed, and they produced a son named Hirudo. This child they placed in a boat of reeds, and let it float away. Next they gave birth to the Island of Aha. This likewise is not reckoned among their children.

Source: Chamberlain, Basil Hall. *Translation of "Ko-ji-ki": or "Records of Ancient Matters."* n.p., 1919, pp. 15–18.

6. A Confucian Denunciation of Buddhism (ninth century)

In the following selection from the Tang dynasty period, the Confucianist writer Han Wengong (768–824), in an attempt to gain imperial favor, urges the emperor to reject Buddhism and favor instead traditional Confucianism.

The Buddhist religion was in fact introduced during the reign of Ming Ti of the Han dynasty; and that Emperor sat on the throne but eighteen years. After him came rebellion upon rebellion with short-lived monarchs.

During the [Period of Disunity] . . . , the Buddhist religion gradually spread. The duration of those [disunity] dynasties was comparatively short, only the Emperor Wu Ti of the Liang dynasty reigning for so long as forty-eight years. Thrice he devoted himself to the service of Buddha; at the sacrifices in his ancestral shrines no living victims were used; he daily took but one single meal, and that composed of fruits and vegetables; yet he was harassed by the rebel Ho Ching and died of hunger at T'ai-ch'eng, soon after which his dynasty came to an end. He sought happiness in the worship but found misfortune instead; from which it must be clear to all that Buddha himself is after all but an incompetent god.

When Kao Tsu obtained the Empire he contemplated the extermination of this religion; but the officials of that day were men of limited capabilities; they did not understand the way of our rulers of old; they did not understand the exigencies of the past and present; they did not understand how to avail themselves of His Majesty's wisdom, and root out this evil. Therefore, the execution of this design was delayed, to your servant's infinite sorrow.

Now your present Majesty, endowed with wisdom and courage such as are without parallel in the annals of the past thousand years, prohibited on your accession to the throne the practice of receiving candidates, whether male or female, for priestly orders, prohibiting likewise the erection of temples and monasteries; which caused your servant to believe that the mantle of Kao Tsu had descended on Your Majesty's shoulders. And even should prohibition be impossible, patronage would still be out of the question. Yet your servant has now heard that instructions have been issued to the priestly community to proceed to Feng-hsiang and receive a bone of Buddha, and that from a high tower in the palace Your Majesty will view its introduction into the Imperial Palace; also that orders have been sent to the various temples, commanding that the relic be received with the proper ceremonies. Now, foolish though your servant may be, he is well aware that your Majesty does not do this in the vain hope of deriving advantages therefrom; but that in the fullness of our present plenty, and in the joy which reigns in the hearts of all, there is a desire to fall in with the wishes of the people in the celebration at the capital of this delusive mummery. For how could the wisdom of Your Majesty stoop in participation in such ridiculous beliefs? Still the people are slow of perception and easily beguiled; and should they behold Your Majesty thus earnestly worshipping at the feet of Buddha they would cry out, "See! the Son of Heaven, the All-Wise, is a fervent believer; who are we, his people, that we should spare our bodies?" Then would ensue a scorching of heads and burning of fingers; crowds would collect together, and tearing off their clothes and scattering their money, would spend their time from morn to eve in imitation of Your Majesty's example. The result would be that by and by young and old, seized with the same enthusiasm, would totally neglect the business of their lives; and should Your Majesty not prohibit it, they would be found flocking to the temples, ready to cut off an arm or slice their bodies as an offering to the God. Thus would our traditions and customs be seriously injured, and ourselves become a laughing-stock on the face of the earth; truly, no small matter! For Buddha was a barbarian. His language was not the language of China; his clothes were of an alien cut. He did not utter the maxims of our ancient rulers, nor conform to the customs which they have handed down. He did not appreciate the bond between prince and minister, the tie between father and son. Supposing, indeed, this Buddha had come to our capital in the flesh, under an appointment from his own State, then your Majesty might have received him with a few words of admonition, bestowing on him a banquet and a suit of clothes, previous to sending him out of the country with an escort of soldiers, and thereby have avoided any dangerous influence on the minds of the people. But what are the facts? The bone of a man long since dead and decomposed, is to be admitted, forsooth, within the precincts of the Imperial Palace! Confucius said, "Pay all respect to spiritual beings, but keep them at a distance." And so, when the princes of old paid visits of condolence to one another, it was customary for them to send on a magician in advance, with a peach wand in his hand, whereby to expel all noxious influences previous to the arrival of his master. Yet now Your Majesty is about to causelessly introduce a disgusting object, personally taking part in the proceedings without the intervention either of the magician or of his peach wand. Of the officials, not one has raised his voice against such an act. Therefore our servant, overwhelmed with shame, implores Your Majesty that this bone may be handed over for destruction by fire or water, whereby the root of this great evil may be exterminated for all time, and the people know how much the wisdom of Your Majesty surpasses that of ordinary men. The glory of such a deed will be beyond all praise. And should the Lord Buddha have power to avenge this insult by the infliction of some misfortune, then let the vials of his wrath be poured out upon the person of your servant who now calls Heaven to witness that he will not repent him of his oath.

In all gratitude and sincerity your Majesty's servant now humbly resents, with fear and trebling, this Memorial for your Majesty's benign consideration.

Source: Giles, Herbert A. *Gems of Chinese Literature: Prose.* 2nd ed. London: Bernard Quaritch, 1923, pp. 124–128.

7. Criticism of Chinese Merchants (eleventh century)

Xia Song, a high official during the Northern Song dynasty (960–1127), considered himself a reformer in the Confucian mold. The following excerpt from his writings is a traditional Confucian critique: the growing power of the merchant class. First, he describes the outrageous wealth of the merchants, no doubt exaggerating, especially about slaves wearing silk. Then he uses the classic Confucian critique of the merchant class: merchants make money by cheating others out of their assets. Ironically, merchants in the Southern Song dynasty had even more wealth and power than during Xia's time, showing the difficulty the dynasty had in controlling the merchant class. After the Mongol interval ended in the fourteenth century, the Ming dynasty, after a burst of brief official trading by sea, never allowed such commerce to happen again.

Since the unification of the empire [after the fall of the Late Tang dynasty], control over merchants has not yet been well established. They enjoy a luxurious way of life, living on dainty foods, owning handsome houses and many carts, adorning their wives and children with pearls and jades, and dressing their slaves in white silk. In the morning they think about how to make a fortune, and in the evening they devise means of fleecing the poor. Sometimes they ride through the countryside behaving haughtily, and sometimes they inveigle rich profits from the poor. In the assignment of corvee duties they are treated much better by the government than average rural households, and in the taxation of commercial duties they are less rigidly controlled than commoners. Since this relaxed control over merchants is regarded by the people as a common rule, they despise agricultural pursuits and place high value on an idle living by trade.

Source: Haeger, J. W., ed. *Crisis and Prosperity in Sung China.* Tucson: University of Arizona Press, 1975, p. 43.

8. Tang Poetry on Old Age (ninth century)

Bo Juyi (772–846), a prominent poet during the rule of the Chinese Tang dynasty, wrote the following poems describing his feeling on old age and getting old.

On Being Sixty
Between thirty and forty, one is distracted by the Five Lusts;
Between seventy and eighty, one is a prey to a hundred diseases.
But from fifty to sixty one is free from all ills;
Calm and still—the heart enjoys rest.
I have put behind me Love and Greed; I have done with Profit and Fame;
I am still short of illness and decay and far from decrepit age.
Strength of limb I still possess to seek the rivers and hills;
Still my heart has spirit enough to listen to flutes and strings.
At leisure I open new wine and taste several cups;
Drunken I recall old poems and sing a whole volume.
Meng-te has asked for a poem and herewith I exhort him
Not to complain of three-score, "the time of obedient ears."

Last Poem
They have put my bed beside the unpainted screen;
They have shifted my stove in front of the blue curtain.
I listen to my grandchildren, reading me a book;

I watch the servants, heating up my soup.
With rapid pencil I answer the poems of friends;
I feel in my pockets and pull out medicine-money.
When this superintendence of trifling affairs is done,
I lie back on my pillows and sleep with my face to the South.

Source: Waley, Arthur, trans. *A Hundred and Seventy Chinese Poems.* London: Constable, 1918, pp. 161, 168.

9. Japanese Poetry (ninth century)

Reproduced here are two poems of the mid-ninth century poet Ono no Komachi.

A thing which fades
With no outward sign—
Is the flower
Of the heart of man
In this world!

The flowers withered,
Their color faded away,
While meaninglessly
I spent my days in the world
And the long rains were falling.

Source: Cortazzi, Hugh. *The Japanese Achievement.* New York: St. Martin's Press, 1990, p. 59.

10. Japan's *Tale of Genji*: The World's First Novel (eleventh century)

The *Tale of Genji* is a sprawling tale of three generations in and around the imperial household in Japan's Heian Period, as the characters try to find love in difficult circumstances. Besides being the first novel ever written, the book is also one of the first written in Japanese instead of Chinese, and by a woman. This book, besides being a primer on early Japanese poetry, also gives some idea of the aesthetics of Heian Japan and Japanese today.

The lady, when no answer came from Genji, thought that he changed his mind, and though she would have been very angry if he had persisted in his suit, she was not quite prepared to lose him with so little ado. But this was a good opportunity once and for all to lock up her heart against him. She thought that she had done so successfully, but found to her surprise that he still occupied an uncommonly large share of her thoughts.

Source: Lady Murasaki. *The Tale of Genji.* Translated by Arthur Waley. New York: Doubleday, 1955, p. 58.

11. The *Tale of Genji:* The Trials of Genji's Mother (eleventh century)

This second excerpt from the *Tale of Genji*, the eleventh-century novel of Japanese court life by Lady Murasaki, tells of the many hardships suffered at court by Genji's mother, a favorite of the emperor. The passage is an engaging description of the Japanese court at the height of the Heian Period in the early eleventh century.

In the reign of a certain Emperor, whose name is unknown to us, there was, among the Niogo and Kôyi [titled ladies] of the Imperial Court, one who, though she was not of high birth, enjoyed the full tide of Royal favor. Hence her superiors, each one of whom had always been thinking—"I shall be the one," gazed upon her disdainfully with malignant eyes, and her equals and inferiors were more indignant still.

Such being the state of affairs, the anxiety which she had to endure was great and constant, and this was probably the reason why her health was at last so much affected, that she was often compelled to absent herself from Court, and to retire to the residence of her mother.

Her father, who was a Dainagon [court official], was dead; but her mother, being a woman of good sense, gave her every possible guidance in the due performance of Court ceremony, so that in this respect she seemed but little different from those whose fathers and mothers were still alive to bring them before public notice, yet, nevertheless, her friendliness made her oftentimes feel very diffident from the want of any patron of influence.

These circumstances, however, only tended to make the favor shown to her by the Emperor wax warmer and warmer, and it was even shown to such an extent as to become a warning to after-generations. There had been instances in China in which favoritism such as this had caused national disturbance and disaster; and thus the matter became a subject of public animadversion, and it seemed not improbable that people would begin to allude even to the example of Yó-ki-hi [a Chinese woman whose favor with the emperor led to rebellion].

In due course, and in consequence, we may suppose, of the Divine blessing on the sincerity of their affection, a jewel of a little prince was born to her. The first prince who had been born to the Emperor was the child of Koki-den-Niogo, the daughter of the Udaijin (a great officer of State). Not only was he first in point of age, but his influence on his mother's side was so great that public opinion had almost unanimously fixed upon him as heir-apparent. Of this the Emperor was fully conscious, and he only regarded the new-born child with that affection which one lavishes on a domestic favorite. Nevertheless, the mother of the first prince had, not unnaturally, a foreboding that unless matters were managed adroitly her child might be superseded by the younger one. She, we may observe, had been established at Court before any other lady, and had more children than one. The Emperor, therefore, was obliged to treat her with due respect, and reproaches from her always affected him more keenly than those of any others.

To return to her rival. Her constitution was extremely delicate, as we have seen already, and she was surrounded by those who would fain lay bare, so to say, her hidden scars. Her apartments in the palace were Kiri-Tsubo (the chamber of Kiri); so called from the trees that were planted around. In visiting her there the Emperor had to pass before several other chambers, whose occupants universally chafed when they saw it. And again, when it was her turn to attend upon the Emperor, it often happened that they played off mischievous pranks upon her, at different points in the corridor, which leads to the Imperial quarters. Sometimes they would soil the skirts of her attendants, sometimes they would shut against her the door of the covered portico, where no other passage existed; and thus, in every possible way, they one and all combined to annoy her.

The Emperor at length became aware of this, and gave her, for her special chamber, another apartment, which was in the Kôrô-Den, and which was quite close to those in which he himself resided. It had been originally occupied by another lady who was now removed, and thus fresh resentment was aroused.

When the young Prince was three years old the Hakamagi took place. It was celebrated with pomp scarcely inferior to that which adorned the investiture of the first Prince. In fact, all available treasures were exhausted on the occasion. And again the public manifested its disapprobation. In the summer of the same year the Kiri-Tsubo-Kôyi became ill, and wished to retire from the palace. The Emperor, however, who was accustomed to see her indisposed, strove to induce her to remain. But her illness increased day by day; and she had drooped and pined away until she was now but a shadow of her former self. She made scarcely any response to the affectionate words and expressions of tenderness which her Royal lover caressingly bestowed upon her. Her eyes were half-closed: she lay like a fading flower in the last stage of exhaustion, and she became so much enfeebled that her mother appeared before the Emperor and entreated with tears that she might be allowed to leave. Distracted by his vain endeavors to devise means to aid her, the Emperor at length ordered a Te-gruma to be in readiness to convey her to her own home, but even then he went to her apartment and cried despairingly: "Did not we vow that we would neither of us be either before or after the other even in traveling the last long journey of life? And can you find it in your heart to leave me now?" Sadly and tenderly looking up, she thus replied, with almost failing breath:

> "Since my departure for this dark journey,
> Make you so sad and lonely,
> Fain would I stay though weak and weary,
> And live for your sake only!"
> "Had I but known this before—"

She appeared to have much more to say, but was too weak to continue. Overpowered with grief, the Emperor at one moment would fain accompany her himself, and at another moment would have her remain to the end where she then was.

At the last, her departure was hurried, because the exorcism for the sick had been appointed to take place that evening at her home, and she went. The child Prince, however, had been left in the Palace, as his mother wished, even at that time, to make her withdrawal as privately as possible, so as to avoid any invidious observations on the part of her rivals. To the Emperor the night now became black with gloom. He sent messenger after messenger to make inquiries, and could not await their return with patience. Midnight came, and with it the sound of lamentation. The messenger, who could do nothing else, hurried back with the sad tidings of the truth. From that moment the mind of the Emperor was darkened, and he confined himself to his private apartments.

Source: Murasaki Shikibu. *Genji Monogatari.* In *Japanese Literature.* rev. ed. Translated by Suyematz Kenchio. The World's Great Classics Series. New York: Colonial, 1900, pp. 11–14.

12. A Chinese Official's View of the Korean People (twelfth century)

Xu Jing, a Chinese official, traveled through Korea in 1123 (during the Song dynasty) as an observer. He explained the composition of the four classes of Koreans before complaining about them in relation to Confucian behavior. He calls Koreans greedy and complains about Korean women divorcing their husbands for petty reasons. This document therefore shows both the Neo-Confucian antiwoman stand of the Chinese and the Korean tradition of giving women more power than the other two East Asian countries.

Although the Koryo territory is not expansive, there are many people living there. Among the four classes of people, Confucian scholars are considered the highest. In that country it is considered shameful not to be able to read. There are many mountains and forests, but because there is not much flat land, their skill at farming has not developed as much as their craftsmanship. As the products of the countryside are all committed to the state, merchants do not travel widely. Only in the daytime do they go to city markets and exchange what they have for what they do not have. Although the people are prosperous, the favors they extend, however, are few. As they are lascivious, they love freely and value wealth. Men and women take marriage lightly and divorce easily. They do not follow proper ritual, which is deplorable.

Source: Lee, Peter H., et al., eds. *Sourcebook of Korean Civilization.* Volume I: *From Early Times to the Sixteenth Century.* New York: Columbia University Press, 1993, p. 325.

13. Corvee Labor in Korea (twelfth century)

Peasants occupied the second place in the Confucian hierarchy throughout East Asia. Yet peasants also faced the corvee, unpaid labor owed in addition to taxes. Corvee laborers built irrigation, flood control, urban centers, and buildings for those related to the royal family. This short document shows the plight of the poor peasant in the twelfth century, forced to work for no pay by the state. This peasant distress spread and led to peasant rebellions even after the military coup of 1170.

Earlier, when building pavilions, each corvée worker brought his own food. One worker was too poor even to do that, so the other workers shared with him a spoonful of their own food. One day his wife came with food and said, "Please ask your friends to come and share it with you." The worker said, "Our family is poor. How did you prepare food? Did you have intimate relations with another man to get it, or did you steal it?" His wife replied, "My face is too ugly to be intimate with anyone, and I am too stupid to know how to steal. I simply cut my hair and sold it." Then she showed her head. The worker sobbed and could not eat. Those who heard this story were all deeply moved.

Source: Lee, Peter H., et al., eds. *Sourcebook of Korean Civilization.* Volume I: *From Early Times to the Sixteenth Century.* New York: Columbia University Press, 1993, pp. 326–327.

14. The "Jottings" of the Japanese Writer Kamo no Chomei (thirteenth century)

The following excerpt from the *Hojoki*, a classic work of the Kamakura Period, describes the life of solitude lived by the Buddhist priest Kamo no Chomei at his mountain hermitage. The work is a Japanese *zuihitsu*, meaning "jottings," which describe the author's musings on nature and human life.

The flow of the river is ceaseless and its water is never the same. The bubbles that float in the pools, now vanishing, now forming, are not of long duration: so in the world are man and his dwellings. . . .

In the spring I see waves of wisteria like purple clouds, bright in the west. In the summer I hear the cuckoo call, promising to guide me on the road to death. In the autumn the voice of the evening insects fills my ears with a sound of lamentation for this cracked husk of a world. In winter I look with deep emotion on the snow, piling up and melting away like sins and hindrances to salvation.

Source: Cortazzi, Hugh. *The Japanese Achievement.* New York: St. Martin's Press, 1990, p. 93.

15. Slavery in Korea (1300)

Korea had an even more rigid hierarchical system than did China or Japan, with slaves at the bottom. Even if slaves bought their freedom, it would be generations before the descendants of that slave could compete for government positions—basically impossible. This memorial was written in 1300 to convince the Mongols not to change how slavery worked in Korea.

In the past, our founding ancestor, setting down instructions to posterity on the question of inheritance, stated: "In general, the offspring of the lowest class . . . are of different stock. Be sure not to allow the people of the lowest class to become emancipated. If they are permitted to become free, later they will certainly get government positions and gradually work into important offices, where they will plot rebellions against the state. If this admonition is ignored, the dynasty will be endangered."

Accordingly, the law of our country provides that only if there is no evidence of lowborn status for eight generations in one's official household registration may one receive a position in the government. As a rule, in the lowborn class, if either the father or mother is low, then the offspring is low. Even if the original owner of a lowborn person frees him, allowing him to achieve commoner status, the descendants of that freed individual must return to low status. If the owner has no heirs, the descendants of his freed lowborn belong to his clan. This is because they do not allow lowborns to achieve permanent commoner status.

Source: Lee, Peter H., et al., eds. *Sourcebook of Korean Civilization.* Volume I: *From Early Times to the Sixteenth Century.* New York: Columbia University Press, 1993, p. 327.

Appendix: Dynasties of Medieval China, Rulers of Medieval Japan, and Chinese Inventions

The following listing of Chinese dynasties is useful for quickly referencing which dynasties were most powerful during which periods, but it makes medieval Chinese history seem somewhat neater than it actually was. Rarely did one dynasty follow immediately upon the fall of its predecessor. Often a new dynasty was established some time before the final collapse of the old, and existing regimes often continued, at least in some parts of the country, for a number of years after a new dynasty came to power. For long periods, China was divided, with different regions being ruled by different families, and no one family ruling a unified China. Since the rise of the Qin dynasty is usually taken as the beginning of a unified, imperial China, the list starts there, even though the Qin era is somewhat before the medieval period as defined by this volume.

Qin Dynasty (221 B.C.E.–206 B.C.E.)
Han Dynasty (206 B.C.E.–220 C.E.)
Three Kingdoms Period (220–280)
Jin Dynasty (265–420)
Northern and Southern Dynasties (420–589)
Sui Dynasty (581–618)
Tang Dynasty (618–907)
Five Dynasties and Ten Kingdoms (907–960)
Song Dynasty (1960–1279)
Yuan (Mongol) Dynasty (1271–1368)
Ming Dynasty (1368–1644)

Sui Dynasty Emperors
Wen (589–604)
Yang (605–617)

Tang Emperors
Gaozu (618–626)
Taizong (626–649)
Gaozong (649–683)
Zhongzong (684)
Ruizong (684–690)
Empress Wu (690–705)
Zhongzong (705–710)
Shaodi (710)
Ruizong (710–712)
Xuanzong (712–756)
Suzong (756–762)
Daizong (762–779)
Dezong (779–805)
Shunzong (805)
Xianzong (805–820)
Muzong (820–824)
Jingzong (824–827)
Wenzong (827–840)
Wuzong (840–846)
Xuanzong (846–859)
Yizong (859–873)
Xizong (873–888)
Zhaozong (888–904)
Aidi (904–907)

Source: Charles Benn, *Daily Life in Traditional China: The Tang Dynasty* Westport, CT: Greenwood Press, 2002, xxi–xxii.

Song Emperors

Northern Song
Taizu (960–976)
Taizong (976–997)
Zhenzong (997–1022)
Renzong (1022–1063)
Yingzong (1063–1067)
Shenzong (1067–1085)
Zhezong (1085–1100)
Huizong (1100–1125)
Qingzong (1126–1127)

Southern Song
Gaozong (1127–1162)
Xiaozong (1162–1189)
Guangzong (1189–1194)
Ningzong (1194–1224)
Lizong (1224–1264)
Duzong (1264–1274)
Gongzong (1275)
Duan Zong (1276–1278)
Xiangzing (1278–1279)

Yuan Dynasty Emperors

Kublai Khan (1260–1294)
Temur Oljeytu Khan (1294–1307)
Qayshan Guluk (1308–1311)
Ayurparibhadra (1311–1320)
Suddhipala Gege'en (1321–1323)
Yesun-Temur (1323–1328)
Arigaba (1328)
Jijaghatu Toq-Temur (1328–1329 and
    1329–1332)
Qoshila Qutuqtu (1329)
Irinchibal (1332)
Toghan–Temur (1333–1370)

Ming Emperors (until 1425)

Temple Name	Era Name	Era Dates
Taizu	Hongwu	1368–1399
Huizong	Jianwen	1399–1402
Chengzhu	Yongle	1403–1425

"The Ming founder initiated the practice followed by all subsequent emperors of retaining a single era name . . . throughout his reign. . . . Ming emperors are often known by their era names rather than by their posthumous temple names."

Source: Conrad Shirokauer, et al. *A Brief History of Chinese and Japanese Civilizations,* 3d ed. Belmont, CA: Thomson Wadsworth, 2006, p. 264.

Japanese Secular Leaders from 1185–1400

Shogun of the Minamoto Clan
Yorimoto (1192)
Yoriye (1202)

Hojo Regents
Tokimasa (1203)
Yasutoki (1225)
Tsunetoki (1242)
Tokiyori (1246)
Nagatoki (1256)
Masamura (1264)
Toimune (1268)
Sadatoki (1284)
Morotoki (1300)
Takatoki (1315)

Shogun of the Ashikaga Clan
Takauji (1336)
Yoshiakira (1358)
Yoshimitsu (1367)
Yoshimachi (1395)

Source: Adapted from Louis Frederic, *Daily Life in Japan at the Time of the Samurai 1185–1603* (New York: Praeger Publishers, 1972), 249.

Periods of East Asian Medieval History

China	Japan	Korea
Northern Wei	*Tomb Period*	*Three Kingdoms*
386–534	250–592	c. 300s–674
Sui	*Yamato*	*Silla Period*
587–617	592–710	674–982
Early Tang 618–751	*Nara Period* 710–794	
Late Tang	*Heian Period*	*Koryo Period*
751–907	794–1185	934–1254
Northern Song 960–1126		
Southern Song 1127–1279	*Kamakura Period* 1185–1333	
Yuan	*Ashikaga Period*	*Yi Dynasty*
1279–1368	1336–1477	1392–1910
Ming 1368–1644		

Inventions in China: A Comparison with the West

Invention/Finding	Discovered in China	Discovered in West
Matches	577	1500s
Urinalysis for diabetes	600s	1600s
Printing press	700s	1400s
Mechanical clock	725	1310
Gunpowder	800s	1100s
Paper money	800s	1700s
Mercator projection	900s	1500s
Phosphorescent paint	900s	1600s
Chain drive (like bicycle)	976	1700s
Flamethrower	900s	1900s
Canal pound-lock	984	1300s
Grenades	1000	1400s
Rockets	1000s	1300s
Land mines	1277	1403
Guns and cannon	1280	1330

Source: Adapted from Robert Temple, *The Genius of China*: 3000 *Years of Science, Discovery and Invention.* New York: Simon and Schuster Books, 1986, frontpapers and backpapers.

OCEANIA

Nancy Sullivan, with the assistance of Robert D. Craig

Chronology

2000 B.C.E.–700 C.E.	Autronesian migrations to Pacific islands
c. 300 C.E.	Beginning of early eastern Polynesian culture
c. 500s	Polynesians, originally from Southeast Asia, settle in Hawaiian Islands and Easter Island; Polynesians continue to navigate eastward
c. 600–1200	Introduction of breadfruit into the islands of Micronesia and eastern Polynesia
c. 700	Easter Islanders begin to build stone platforms that form part of ceremonial enclosures; first Polynesians settle in the Cook Islands
c. 900	First settlers from the Cook Islands, ancestors of the Maoris, reach the South Island of New Zealand; establishment of the Tu'i Tonga dynasty
c. 900–1100	Construction of great megalithic features at Nan Madol
c. 1000	Māori people settle in New Zealand; Polynesians begin to build stone temples
c. 1100s	First statues erected on previously constructed platforms in Easter Island; beginnings of organized societies in Hawaiian Islands; earliest settlements by Polynesians in Pitcairn Island
c. 1150	Maoris begin to settle in the river mouth areas in the north of the South Island of New Zealand, notably at Wairau Bar
c. 1200	Tui Tonga monarchy builds coral platform for ceremonial worship on island of Tonga in South Pacific
c. 1250	Beginnings of intensive valley irrigation schemes in Hawaiian Islands
c. 1300	Hawaiian peoples start to develop class structure as a result of economic growth through agriculture; stone temple complexes, or marae, erected on Rarotonga, Cook Islands, and on Moorea Island in the Society Islands; huge stone statues erected on Easter Island; height of the Saudeleur dynasty
c. 1350	Maoris flourish in the North Island of New Zealand; first terrace-type fortifications, called pa, built in New Zealand
c. 1400	Tonga people build major ceremonial centre at Mu'a, on the largest island in the Tongatapu Group; widespread cultivation of wet taro in Hawaiian islands
c. 1500	A village of oval stone houses is built on Easter Island
c. 1511	Portuguese navigators begin to explore the Pacific Ocean

1519–1522	Ferdinand Magellan attempts voyage around the world: he navigates the Pacific but later dies; his crew completes the voyage
1525	Diego Ribeiro, official mapmaker for Spain, makes first scientific charts covering the Pacific Ocean; Portuguese probably visit Caroline Islands, northeast of New Guinea, and nearby Palau Islands
1526	Portuguese land on Papua New Guinea
c. 1550s	Maoris on the North and South Islands of New Zealand build fortified enclosures called pa
1567	Alvaro de Menda, a, Spanish sailor, sets sail from Callao in Peru westward across the Pacific; he reaches the Ellice Islands and Solomon Islands, east of New Guinea and returns to Callao in 1569
1595	Alvaro de Menda a visits the Marquesas Islands and then Nderic (Santa Cruz)
c. 1600s	Beginning of building of tupa, stone towers with inner chambers, on Easter Island
c. 1600	In Tonga, dominant political leadership passes from Tu'i Tonga dynasty to Tu'i Konokupolu dynasty

Societies of Oceania

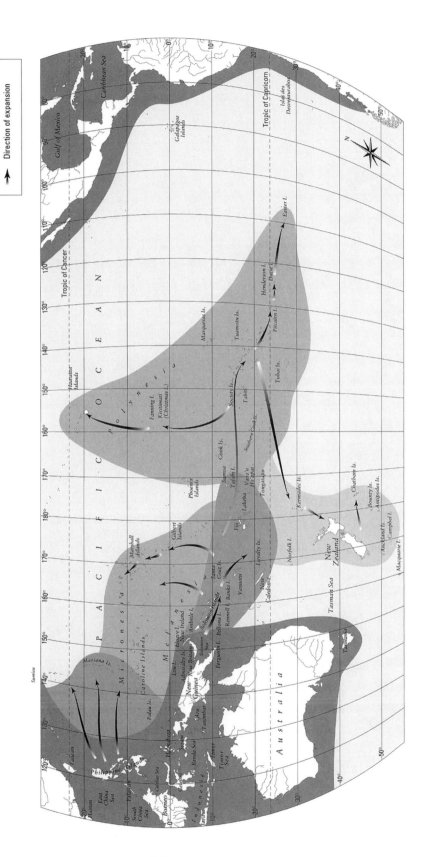

Overview and Topical Essays

1. HISTORICAL OVERVIEW

Great Sea Migrations and Explorations

Oceania, which includes the three large **island groups** of **Melanesia**, **Micronesia**, and **Polynesia**, was settled from the west, in three big waves. The first crossing of 50,000 years ago was made by the proto-Melanesians, across the Indonesian Archipelago (as it was at that time) to the Sahul, the landmass then combining New Guinea and Australia. Not until 5,000 years ago did the second migration begin, as people now called "**lapita**" started to move from points in Southeast Asia (probably Taiwan), through the Philippines, Micronesia, and on to the Bismarck Archipelago, the Solomon Islands, and Vanuatu. About 1200 B.C.E., this wave pushed off from Vanuatu to the Lau islands of Fiji and then on to Tonga, Samoa, Futuna, Uvea, and Niuatoputapu. These two purposeful migration waves are among human history's greatest accomplishments, and archaeology's greatest challenges, because we have so little physical evidence of the lapita people, and even less of the early Melanesians.

Thousands of years later, during the European Middle Ages, the third great Pacific wave of migration gained momentum. The first millennium C.E. is sometimes known as Polynesia's "dark age" because it represents the end of a long pause the lapita peoples seem to have taken in their migration across the Pacific once they had settled Fiji, Tonga, and Samoa, the islands now considered "ancestral" Polynesia. During this period, the lapita pottery style is abandoned, and it is several centuries yet before the monumental Polynesian architecture will be erected. But this period corresponding to the early Middle Ages in Europe is also a time of cultural elaboration in these islands of West Polynesia, and the beginning of a new age of ocean-going exploration. (*See* **Pulemelei Mound** for the location where the people of Western Polynesia made their final migration east.) Indeed, by the close of the Middle Ages in the fourteenth and fifteenth centuries, the entire eastern portion of Oceania will have finally been colonized. Some time around 600 C.E., explorers set off from the easternmost edge of Samoa, where it was more than 200 long, empty miles to the next island, Santa Cruz. By the end of the first millennium C.E., these mariners were moving through the Marquesas, the Society Islands (Tahiti), Hawaii to the north, and, finally, Aotearoa (New Zealand). The earliest evidence of settlement, for example, in southeastern Polynesia (the Cooks, Australs, Mangareva, Pitcairn Island, and Easter Island) dates to 900 to 1000, just after Hawaii, which was settled sometime before 800 (although some evidence suggests possibly 500 years earlier), and Aotearoa, where the earliest evidence of settlers also dates to 800 (*see* **Voyaging/Ancient Navigation**).

Polynesia as a geographic area comprises the island groups of Samoa, Tonga, Cook, Marquesas, Society, Austral, Aotearoa, and Hawaii, as well as the islands of Tuamotu, Tuvalu, and Tokelau. Many archaeologists argue that the dispersal from ancestral Polynesia (Tonga-Fiji-Samoa) to the east was actually a series of movements, all interacting with each other, and beginning as early as 1000 B.C.E. The wave that moved from Samoa in 600 to 800 C.E. to Tuvalu and Tokelau, then westward, looping back to Micronesia and northern Melanesia, became the inhabitants of what we call Polynesian "outlier" islands: Kapingamarangi and Nukuoro, and Sikaiana. Another dispersal moved eastward to the northern Cooks atolls, then the Society Islands and the western Tuamotus.

A third dispersal moved from Samoa down to the southern Cook Islands of Rarotonga and Mangaia, then to the Austral chain and finally to Mangareva. From here, they reached Pitcairn, the Marquesas, the eastern Tuamotus and ultimately sailed up to Hawaii. It is hard to convey how quickly and widely these colonizations occurred, and what kind of navigational feats they were for the time. It is clear, at least, that these were not shipwrecks or drifting fishing expeditions, but voyages of settlement. People arrived with families, animals, seeds, and foodstuffs, ready to find a homeland beyond the vast watery horizon.

Also in the first century C.E., the early Melanesians to the west were making contact at the coast with voyagers from Micronesia and central Polynesia, as the lapita migrations to coastal Melanesia were replaced by more concerted trade and intermarriage networks. People throughout the Massim region of New Guinea and the Bismarck Archipelago of New Guinea were already engaged in trading valuables made from tridacna, conus, pearl, spondyllus, bailer, cowrie, and nassa shells, as well as dog and flying fox (bat) teeth, all of which are still in circulation today. (*See* **New Guinea, Fauna of** and **New Guinea, Flora of** for a description of the rich biodiversity of this island.) In the Massim, the complex system of *kula* was already in existence, and similarly, in New Caledonia, the "jade cycle" would have begun to link the Loyalty Islands to the Grande Terre and the Isle of Pines (one Loyalty island ceremonial jade axe dates to 890–1200). Thus the first millennium C.E. really represents a time when cultural differentiation, and economic specialization, would have begun to knit people together over long distances and across overt cultural differences. It is when the Melanesians really begin to define themselves by their differences, and in so doing create the unity in diversity that still characterizes the area today.

By the second millennium C.E., Melanesia, which includes New Guinea, the Bismarck Archipelago, the Solomon Islands, Vanuatu, and New Caledonia, was also trading with Polynesia, as Polynesians moved westward into New Caledonia and Vanuatu. The burial site of **Roymata** in Vanuatu is evidence of these migrations, as well as a sign of increasingly hierarchical chiefly systems.

Meanwhile, in the interior highlands of New Guinea horticulture was intensifying, but it would be several hundred years before the sweet potato arrived. Irrigated fields of **taro** were grown in the valley floors, which gave lowlanders an advantage over their hillside neighbors. Some even postulate that this may have driven a two-tiered social structure, so that commoners might have labored for elites in the valleys, for example. If this was so, then the introduction of the sweet potato in the seventeenth century allowed everyone to grow food and gain access to surplus wealth, introducing democracy where there had been inherited hierarchy.

In the islands north of Melanesia some of the most sophisticated chiefdoms were also evolving. Micronesia, the area that covers the Marianas, Carolines, Marshalls, Kiribati, Nauru, Palau, Yap, Truk, Ponape, and Kosrae island groups, was settled during the lapita era from different points. The Marianas and Palau were probably reached first by people from the Philippines; the Caroline, Marshall, and Kiribati archipelagoes were settled by people probably from the Solomons or Vanuatu; and Yap, to the western end of Micronesia, may have been settled from the Bismarck Archipelago, although legend suggests the Admiralty Islands.

Island Empires: The Yap Empire and the Saudeleur Dynasty

Two great seats of power emerged in the Middle Ages. One in the eastern Caroline Islands of Pohnpei and Kosrae, was the Saudeleur dynasty, and the other, in the western Carolines, became what is called the "**Yap empire.**" Not coincidentally, this was the period when Carolinean navigational systems were perfected, absorbing such comprehensive databases on everything from astronomy to bird movements to wave patterns. It is said that a true Carolinean navigator would require 30 years of training to be considered an expert.

Yap was settled in the second millennium C.E., and its high island status secured its advantage over neighboring atolls. This height was critical to its rank because islands with mountains, even the smallest of mountains, can boast real security against typhoons, a fairly diverse ecosystem, and, not the least, more water sources than low-lying **atolls**. Yap also cultivated a reputation for sorcery, which allowed it to become the center of a wide system of "tributes" (or *sawei*), with surrounding atolls, from Palau to Chuuk, all ranked in accordance to their distance from Yap. Tributes would move from island to island until they reached Ulithi, which acted as intermediary to Yap. More accurately, the center of control rested in one village, Gatchepar, in Yap's eastern region of Gagil. Gatchepar chiefs used these tributes to hold all the islands from Ulithi to Namonuito in their thrall. But it can also be said that these islands gained at least as much as they gave in terms of insurance, especially when rising tides and bad weather can determine the survival of these precarious atolls.

> The name *Yap* comes from one of the first European ships to arrive in the sixteenth century. When the captain pointed to the island asking its name, the villagers responded by telling him the name of the pointer he was using, the canoe paddle itself: "yap." This story is reminiscent of the story of Vanuatu's island Ambrym, named not for the people or place, but for the yam villagers extended to Captain James Cook on his arrival there in the eighteenth century.

This insurance becomes all the more important when we realize that the Middle Ages underwent a Little Climatic Optimum, otherwise known as the Medieval Warm Period, from around 800 to 1300. Not only did this climatic event involve rising sea levels, but in Oceania it also meant floods, typhoons, and other weather disturbances associated with the **El Niño/La Niña** phenomenon, making the significance of high islands, not to mention the importance of having magical powers over the weather, all the more dramatic. From roughly 1300, this warming shifted to cooling, and the globe then experienced a Little Ice Age for about 500 years. Coming at the end of the Middle Ages, this cooling punctuated the era and led the way to more social and environmental changes.

The Yapese traded their high island resources for the navigational skills of *etak*, enabling them to travel to Palau and quarry their great limestone money. Some say that Yapese commoners themselves, and not Palauans, did most of the arduous carving and transporting of **stone money**, in a system of indentured labor for the Gatchepar chiefs. This stone money, called *rai*, came from islands as distant as the Bismarck Archipelago to the south and the Marianas to the north, but most of it is attributed to Palau. Ranging from several inches to several meters in size, the limestone disks were pierced in their centers to be rolled by logs. But the real chore would be towing the multiton "coins" by canoe back to Yap; we might assume that more money was lost en route than ever arrived on shore. The value of these stones was based on exactly these hazards of acquisition. Once on Yap, they lined the walkways to meeting houses as signs of a chief's political prowess, not to mention monuments to the lives and effort spent producing them.

At the peak of the Yap Empire the central island of Wa'ab probably had a population of fifty thousand or more. Its villages were divided by rank, and at the top of the order were seven elite villages led by the three even more elite, or paramount, villages. The Yapese also had a system of matriclans, which were divided into two groups, one called *Banpilung*, meaning "side of the chiefs," and the other *Banpagel*, or "side of the young men." Like many other places in Micronesia, Melanesia, and Polynesia, this dualism between older/younger brother, chief/commoner, paramount/lesser groups provided an element of rivalry between ruling bloodlines. That is to say, a system of older and younger sibling chiefs always makes succession more interesting; when a paramount chief dies, either his eldest son or his younger brother (and sometimes daughters and sisters) can lay claim to the title. One of the most compelling explanations for the rapid and successive migrations through Polynesia is this system of primogeniture, that is, inheritance through the elder sibling. If a title goes to one sibling, so too do all the trappings, leaving the other sibling little alternative but to push off to establish a new kingdom on the next island.

Genealogy in Oceania was also often dualistic, which adds another dimension to historical legend. Samoa and Tonga, for example, make distinctions between people who came from Pulotu in the west and those from Papatea in the east. In Hawaii, there are people said to come originally from Hawaiki and those from Kahiki, not to mention other groups. In the Marquesas, people from Vevau are distinguished from those from Hawaiki, marking two "tribes" who travelled from the same place by different routes and at different times. In the Society Islands, the people of Ra from Vavau are distinguished from the people of Ta'aroa from Rotuma. In the Cook Islands, there are the people of

Tangiia from Tahiti and the people of Karika from Manuka. And in New Zealand, Ngapuhi traditions tell us the ancestral pa-builders came from the north, while the fleet-people came from the east.

To the east of Yap, Pohnpei was the seat of the Saudeleur dynasty, and its great stone palace complex was called **Nan Madol**. This offshore community may have been inhabited by the first or second century C.E., and we know it was under construction by the ninth century. Not until the twelfth century, however, were the distinctive megalithic features erected, including mega-ton blocks of basalt that had to be moved from the far side of the island. It is said locally that a magician was needed to "fly" these massive stones from their quarry. Pohnpeian tradition claims that the builders of the contemporaneous Lelu complex on Kosrae (likewise composed of huge stone buildings) migrated to Pohnpei, where they used their skills and experience to build the even more impressive Nan Madol complex.

The complex includes residences, temples, and mortuary sites, and may have housed as many as one thousand people, both chiefs and commoners. Madol Powe, the mortuary sector, contains fifty-eight islets in the northeastern area. Elsewhere, separate islets were dedicated to activities like food preparation, coconut oil pressing, and canoe construction. The outer islets are accessible by waterways, which made the complex something of a Carolinean island Venice, and it is assumed that the Saudeleurs would sail to regional islands to collect tributes as a form of imperial taxation.

By the second millennium C.E., the Pohnpei and Kosrae dynasties were comparable to the chiefdoms of Polynesia. The Saudeleurs emerged around 1 C.E., constructed Nan Madol from 900 to 1100, and then flourished, peaked, and diminished just prior to European contact in the eighteenth century. By about 1300, the dynasty had a four-tiered hierarchy that rivaled the complexity of the Hawaiian chiefdoms. Kosrae's Lelu complex was similarly sophisticated, with artificial islets under construction by 1250. Population growth started to rise on Kosrae from 500 until roughly 1200 to 1300, when the megalith construction emerged. By 1600, Lelu had become a thriving community. The question remains whether Nan Madol's inhabitants moved to Lelu, or vice versa—and why?

Social Change

Beginning in 600 and running to about 1200 in the Marquesas, when populations expanded and warfare became more prevalent, breadfruit appears to have played a role in these political and social changes. Archaeologists tell us that the fruit revolutionized the Micronesian and Eastern Polynesian islands when introduced during the Middle Ages. The years between 1000 and 1500 in particular were filled with radical social transformations in these islands for which breadfruit was a clear catalyst. There are two distinct types of breadfruit in Oceania: one grows wild in Micronesia, in places like Palau and the Marianas; the other is found in Eastern Polynesia and points west to New Guinea. Botanists tell us these two types were brought together somewhere in the Eastern Carolines, and that they produced numerous hybrid forms, some of which were saltwater resistant enough for cultivation on atolls. The typical seedless breadfruit, *Artocarpus altilis*, was carried northward by early settlers into eastern Micronesia, where, at some point in the first millennium C.E., it hybridized with the wild, seeded Marianas *A. mariannensis*, and spawned the varieties that now thrive throughout Micronesia. Only this hybridized breadfruit grows on Polynesian islands, and even then, only on Tuvalu and Tokelau. But it thrives on Micronesian atolls, largely because of the salt tolerance, and because its roots help retain the island lens of freshwater. But drought, especially on coral atolls, will kill the tree. Otherwise it requires little labor and produces a variety of foodstuffs all year round. The efflorescence of breadfruit in Micronesia coincides with monumental stone architecture, which is significant: greater reliance on fruit appeared to free people up and enable the social complexity and expansion that characterizes the second millennium C.E. in Micronesia and Polynesia.

By the first century C.E., the islands of Fiji, Samoa, and Tonga had also established chiefdoms with some degree of complexity. The burials of **chiefs** became important, as did the burial mounds themselves. Settlements on Tutuila, Samoa, were established during the transitional period between the Little Climatic Optimum and the Little Ice Age, approximately 660 to 700 years ago, when coastal populations began to make extensive agricultural use of lowland valleys. Gradually, as rainfall increased and temperatures dropped, the sea levels also lowered and the violent environmental upheavals of the imminent Ice Age required people to find alternative land-use strategies. People began to move inland, to cultivate higher ground. Monuments were erected in mountain settlements, possibly as ownership markers for coastal villagers who would then have access to all the best resources. Many nonresidential sites in the mountains and ridge tops of Samoa seem to have functioned as forts or refuges for times of **warfare**.

During the first millennium C.E., the coastal settlements had been fairly dispersed, but in the second millennium, chiefly burials, small house mounds, and large chief mounds, or *malae*, begin to emerge. For example, the Samoan complex of Tataga Matau, established sometime after 1400, includes residential areas, basalt quarries, fortifications, and a ceremonial star mound. Samoan mounds were rectangular or star shaped, and some were used as foundations for chiefs' houses, shrines for ancestral worship, or lookout posts to watch for invading fleets. The most enticing explanation, however, is that star mounds were used in the ancient and important sport of pigeon snaring, which occurred in the company of feasting and hunting games, usually for religious occasions. Only high chiefs were allowed to walk on the platforms, some of which were half the size of a rugby field. Hunters would sit in blinds on the mound and manipulate decoy pigeons in what must have been a bizarre bit of theater. It says a lot about the lack of biodiversity in these Polynesian islands (as compared to the Melanesian islands to the west) that elite individuals would dedicate so much time and effort to snaring what elsewhere would be considered a common, and not too palatable, bird.

The Tu'i Tonga Empire and Other Dynasties

The Middle Ages were also the height of the **Tongan Empire**, which included Fiji, Samoa, and Tonga, and by extension Futuma, Rotuma, Tuvalu, and Tokelau. Fiji had its own lesser Tu'i Pulotu dynasty, just as Samoa had its

Tu'i Manu'a. But around 900, the Tu'i Tonga dynasty was formed from the legendary union of a sun god and a mortal Tongan woman, whose offspring, 'Aho'eitu, was its first chief.

Under the 10th Tu'i Tonga, Momo, and his son Tu'itātui (11th Tu'i Tonga) the empire was expanded to include parts of Fiji, including the distant Lau Islands, and all of Samoa, except for Manu`a island (which the Tongans considered sacred). Due to the success of the imperial navy, the empire continued to expand to include all of western and central Polynesia, and even parts of Melanesia and Micronesia. The largest of the long-haul canoes with square sails used by the imperial navy would be sailed by as many as one hundred men. Tribute networks to Fiji, Samoa, and surrounding island brought wealth back to the royal treasury where the Tu'i Tonga reigned supreme. Mats came from Samoa, while red feathers, mosquito curtains, ndrua canoes, and pottery came from Fiji. In turn, Tonga distributed mulberry bark cloth, weapons, and protection in war.

The glue between these chiefdoms was blood, or more accurately, the exchange of spouses between dynasties. Tongan elites took wives from Samoa, whereas Fiji exported male spouses to high-ranking Tongan women. The Tu'i Tonga's sister actually held a higher rank than her brother, so her children could outrank her brother's children were she to marry locally. The solution was to have her marry a Fijian chief and shift the succession issues to the other islands. The elites of Tongatapu also exchanged spouses (and multiple wives) with tributary islands. At its height, the empire covered over 3 million square kilometers of ocean, and those islands not under direct control were still forced to pay tribute. Under the 12th Tu'i Tonga, the capital moved to Mu'a, where it prospered further.

In the reign of the 13th or 14th Tu'i Tonga, the *falefa* were established as political advisors to the empire. These individuals could help negotiate political pressures but could not, in the end, prevent the assassinations of Havea I, Havea II, and Takalaua, the 19th, 22nd, and 23rd Tu'i Tongas. Takalaua's son and successor Kau'ulufonua I pursued his father's murderers to 'Uvea, where he established a second dynasty, the Tu'i Ha'atakalaua. The Tu'i Tongas were thereafter forced to live as exiles in Samoa for more than a century. When the 28th Tu'i Tonga, Tapu'osi, was allowed to return, his role was nevertheless limited to that of a priest, who only performed religious duties. In this way, the dynasties functioned as co-rulers—until 1610, when, ironically, Ngata, the younger son of Mo'unga-'o-Tonga (6th Tu'i Ha'atakalaua), broke away to start his own, a third, dynasty, the Tu'i Kanokupolu.

The high volcanic islands of French Polynesia were the base for the development of Polynesian social structure, art, and customs. Tahiti, in the Society Islands, is considered the typically complex Polynesian chiefdom because it developed three social classes: chiefs, *ari'i* (ariki or aliki); lesser chiefs, or *ra'atira* (ringatira), who held titled estates; and *manabune* (manahune), or commoners, most of whom were landless. Traditions and religious ceremonies in this area show that political aristocracy first arose in the western island of Raiatea, which was formerly called *Havaii*. Stone structures emerge in the second millennium C.E. in Tahiti, including religious temples or *marae*. This was also the period for the migrations from Tahiti to the Marquesas, 900 miles northeast, in the tenth century, and those to New Zealand in the thirteenth century. It is speculated that those who pushed off were of the ringatira class, chafing under their submission to the ariki; they were "second sons" in a metaphoric sense.

Although the inhabitants of Polynesia were physically akin to one another and shared a common culture, considerable differences arose in their manner of life in response to the widely different island environments. The high islands of Tahiti and Rarotonga had deep, sheltered, fertile valleys and alluvial plains; water was abundant, and there was a variety of **food** plants and material resources. On the low islands, the biodiversity and access to water was much more limited. Nevertheless, Eastern Polynesian cultures share a pantheon of anthropomorphic gods, including Tane, Tu, Rongo, and Tangaloa, and the temple or *marae* is common throughout, a variation on the western Polynesian *malae*, which is more of an open-air assembly hall (*see* **Gods and Goddesses**).

Hawaii, Rapa Nui, and New Zealand

The final points of eastern Polynesian colonization were Hawaii to the north, Rapa Nui (Easter Island) to the east, and Aotearoa (New Zealand) to the south. The valiant Polynesians who settled these distant islands, and all those in between, arrived with food plants like taro, bananas, coconut, **breadfruit**, and **yams**, as well as fiber plants like the paper mulberry, to make **tapa** cloth. They also brought the **pig**, the dog, the chicken, and the Pacific rat, in different combinations to different islands. People traveled 4,000 kilometers from Tahiti and the Marquesas to reach Hawaii, for example, so they certainly set out with provisions. Once ashore, they became an established chiefdom with already domesticated crops. These voyages between 400 and 1200 ended in windward arrivals, from whence people moved to the leeward sides of the island (*see* **Leeward and Windward**). In Hawaii, during this period, there were community chiefs and paramount chiefs. Between 1200 and 1650, the Hawaiian Islands each sustained three major chiefdoms and two to three minor chiefdoms, the total population peaking in 1500 at possibly one million people.

Hawaii is considered the most stratified of Polynesian chiefdoms, such that by the time of European contact in late eighteenth century a society once based on lineages of kinship had become a highly structured and hierarchical kingship. Hawaii was colonized between 300 and 600 C.E. (perhaps later) probably from the Marquesas. A voyaging period followed when Hawaiians traveled frequently between the Marquesas and the Society Islands. This long haul voyaging ceased by 1300, when the Hawaiian Islands became cut off, rather suddenly isolated from the rest of Polynesia. Agricultural development probably started as early as 800, leading to settled communities mainly on the coast. But between 1000 and 1650, the population expanded and people moved inland to different ecological zones. The population really exploded up until at least 1600, doubling in less than a century. With this population growth came agricultural intensification, fishponds, and systems of irrigation. Hawaiian religion emphasized Kane, god of flowing waters, and in the big islands of Maui and Hawai'i, chiefs were dedicated to the cult of Ku, a god demanding human sacrifice who would alternate with Lono, god of rain and thunder, for whom, it is said, Captain James Cook was mistaken, and ultimately killed (*see* **Agriculture**).

Rapa Nui is the most isolated spot on earth. It is the southeastern-most is-land in the Polynesian triangle and closer to South America than the ancestral Polynesia islands of Tonga, Samoa, and Fiji. Famous for its monumental stat-ues, called *moai*, the island and its people committed a kind of social and en-vironmental suicide to erect them. Where there once were forests of palms, there are now very few trees at all, and it is generally thought that the Rapa Nui people cut them down to transport their great stone statues from one side of the island to the other. Oral tradition (much like that of Pohnpei) says a form of spiritual power, or *mana*, actually "walked" the statues from their quarry. Archaeologists also suggest that the Little Ice Age (about 1650 to 1850) at the end of the Middle Ages would have contributed to the deforestation. Whether cause or effect, the decline of Rapa Nui's environment coincided with the decline of its sociocultural prosperity, and by the eighteenth century its people were starving, many native plants were extinct, and people may have been forced into cannibalism for survival.

Nevertheless the great *moai* megaliths are a tribute to the Rapa Nui Middle Ages. A total of 887 volcanic tuff statues appear to have been constructed, one fourth of which were successfully erected on the *ahu* platforms, others left in the Rano Raraku quarry and still others now buried in the sand after the archi-tectural project was abandoned. The dates of their construction range from 1000 to 1500 and 1500 to 1700. The *ahu* vary in size and may have been sculpted during or after the *huri mo'ai* or statue-toppling era. Many became ossuaries; others were destroyed by storms.

Eastern Polynesians reached New Zealand in a series of migrations sometime between around 800 and 1300. Legend says the Māori came from Hawaiki, the mythical Polynesian homeland, to settle the North and South Islands, and sev-eral smaller islands, including Rakiura (Stewart Island) and the Chatham Islands. Over the next few centuries, these settlers developed a distinctive Māori culture with two competitive *hapū* or subtribes. At some point a group of Māori mi-grated to the Chatham Islands where they developed a variant Moriori culture.

The Māori chiefs came from multiple lineages, and these hereditary posi-tions were distinct from the competitive and achieved status of elite warriors. New Zealand had its own monumental age from 1000 to 1500 on the northern end of the South Island, where the settlers shifted from horticulture to hunting and gathering.

The sweet potato was especially well suited to the warmer North Island of New Zealand and became the Māori staple food quite quickly because it could be planted on slopes and flat land and stored in cool pits or stilted *pataka*, or storehouses, within the ceremonial *marae*. Patakas symbolized the fecundity of the chief and were a symbol of his great *mana* or prestige. As such they were *tapu*, and almost as important as war canoes in terms of status symbols.

The Māori lived in settlements called *kainga,* which, with the rise of warfare eventually metamorphosed into *pa*, or fortified settlements. *Kainga* were estab-lished in sheltered coastal locations, near harbors or estuaries, such as those found at Palliser Bay, in the North Island, dating from the twelfth, fifteenth, and sixteenth centuries. The most famous *kainga* is at Wairau Bar, in the north of the South Island, and was constructed sometime between the eleventh and thirteenth centuries. Eventually, however, and just at the close of the Middle Ages, roughly 1500, these *kainga* transformed into complex defensive settle-ments, with ditches and palisades and multiple cooking areas. At the end of the Middle Ages in Oceania, life was much more fraught and defensive. *See also* Documents 1 and 2.

Further Reading
Chowning, A. *An Introduction to the Peoples and Cultures of Melanesia*. Menlo Park, CA: Cummings Publishing, 1979.
Crocombe, R. *The South Pacific*. Suva, Fiji: University of the South Pacific, 2001.
Feil, D. K. *The Evolution of Highland Papua New Guinea Societies*. Cambridge, UK: Cambridge University Press, 1987.
Finney, B. R. *Voyage of Discovery: A Cultural Odyssey through Polynesia*. Berkeley: University of California Press, 1994.
Kirch, Patrick Vinton. *On the Road of the Winds*. Berkeley and Los Angeles: University of California Press, 2000.
Malinowski, B. *Argonauts of the Western Pacific*. London: Routledge, 1922.

Nancy Sullivan

2. RELIGION

The religious life of Oceanic peoples has always been integrated with all other aspects of life: with politics, the arts, agriculture, fishing, trade and sea voyaging, not to mention everyday routines. The local religions varied by culture and **language** group, as these were nonliterate people without the equivalent of a Torah, Qur'an, or Bible. These beliefs were not just demographically localized, they were about localized subjects—like where our people come from, how we arrived here, who made us (and not them), with relatively little reflection on the origin of humanity. Religion is one of the few subjects about which we have no empirical evidence in the archaeological record, too, so whatever is said here would be speculation based on ethnographic reports very near "first contact" with Europeans. There were myths about the cosmos, as the sun, moon, and stars were vitally important to farmers and seafarers. And there were stories of fabulous creatures that lived with or preceded humans on earth, sometimes half-animal half-human or shape-shifting beings that are said to have created natural phenomena like mountains or lakes or coral reefs.

Island people are likely to have legends about the origin of the sea, and some creator god who would have made it. People in southern Vanuatu have a myth in which a woman became angry with her son because he disobeyed her. In her fury she knocked down a wall that surrounded the water of the sea. The water broke free, scattering people and coconuts to other islands. In Dobu Island, New Guinea, it is said that when the sea was first released it swept all the beautiful women to the neighboring Trobriand Islands.

On the Banks Islands of Vanuatu, the first being in the world was Qat, a creator god made all the islands and their flora and fauna, and carved humans from wood and then danced with them, as dolls, to give them life. In the Chambri Lakes of the Sepik River of New Guinea a mythical woman named Kolimanggi was the first clay pot maker, and she fashioned human features on the pots for they could come alive and act as her assistants. But when a handsome man from the neighboring Karawari River caused her to break taboo and sleep with him, these pots hardened and forever after stopped assisting her.

The myths of **Melanesia** are filled with animal characters. Snakes appear as symbols of fertility and power, sometimes wandering from place to place and distributing magical powers, sometimes actually birthing humans from their being. Virtually everywhere in New Guinea there are beliefs about composite animal creatures, called *masalai* in Tok Pisin, that live in the water and the bush, guarding their territory. The Arapesh believe that *masalai* live in rocks and pools and sometimes take the form of snakes or lizards. The Kiwai of Papua New Guinea say that they are descended from Nuga, a half-human, half-crocodile creature created long ago from a piece of wood.

Along the Sepik River, there are distinct historical time frames for *masalai* and culture heroes. People generally believe that *masalai* are from an earlier creation period, a deep historical era, which evolved into a time of the first humans, sometimes through a period of half-human creatures. Eventually the origin stories meld with ancestral hero stories and bring the chronologies to the present day.

Culture hero legends are always picaresque. Stories about twin brothers and older–younger sibling sets are common throughout Melanesia. Generally there is a wise brother and a foolish one, as for example, in New Britain, and Vanuatu, where a creator god made twin brothers by sprinkling his own blood on the ground: one became a hero of the people, the other, an evil-doer. Two brothers from the north coast people of New Guinea, Kilibob and Manut, are responsible for local landmasses, rivers, volcanoes, and sacred sites across the eastern top end of the island, in a series of sometimes hilarious, sometimes tragic episodes of their travels.

Then there are the trickster characters. According to the Kiwai people of New Guinea, the trickster Sido could change his skin like a snake. He was killed by a powerful magician and then wandered the world seducing women and children. He had a human wife, but lost her, and then transformed himself into a giant **pig**, splitting open so that his backbone and sides formed the house of death — the place where all Kiwai go when they die.

In other places, the first beings came from the sea or emerged from underground. Among the Trobriand Islanders, the ancestors of each clan emerged from a particular spot in a grove of trees, or from a piece of coral or a rock. The Keraki of Papua New Guinea believe that the first humans emerged from a tree, while others say that they came from clay or sand, blood, or pieces of wood. According to a myth from Vanuatu, a terrible ogre killed everyone except one woman hiding under a tree. She later gave birth to twin sons who destroyed the ogre and cut it into pieces, which freed the people formerly been eaten by the ogre, and they came to life again. There are unexpected twists and turns to these stories, very much the way stories from the Sanskrit *Mahabharata* epic mixes the spiritual and profane world events together.

Often these culture heroes introduce magical powers to the world of humans. According to a myth from the Trobriand Islands, a hero named Tudava taught the people various forms of garden magic, for which they have since become renowned. People use magical formulas to manipulate spirits across Melanesia. Learning the ritual incantations, performing the ablutions or abiding by the taboos, all take skills that are coveted by the entire community. Those with the power to control weather are always highly influential people.

A general Melanesian belief in life after death provides a second order of beliefs that coexisted with all these cosmological and ontological theories.

The spirits of ancestors and culture heroes remain present to be appeased and blamed by the living, sometimes eternally, and sometimes before they make their way to a final resting place or offshore "home" of ancestral beings. In some places, a successful journey for the dead will depend upon completing the funeral rites. By contrast, Fijians believe that the path taken by the deceased is dangerous and only the greatest warriors can complete it.

In Melanesia, ancestral spirits are not always good. They are just as likely to punish and trick their living relatives as they are to smooth their way in the world. In Melanesia it is impossible to distinguish between magic and religion, because spirits are not transcendental. They linger and behave in very human ways, sometimes petulantly or arbitrarily. The require ceremonies and obeisance, and in Manus Island, for example, they can punish lack of respect with illness or death. But the after death holds no punishment or reward, it has no ethical implications for the living. There are certainly ethical aspects to indigenous belief systems across Melanesia, in both highlands and lowlands areas, but the general rule is that afterlife is not related to how one led their life, for good or for bad.

But it is sorcery throughout Melanesia that is responsible for social control and punishment. Most illness and death is attributed to these human agents of supernatural power. Melanesians are less concerned with cosmogony than are Polynesians. They have no specialized priesthood (although there are sorcerer positions and hereditary powers). Sorcery is a very important aspect of social control, because it is public and community behavior that sorcerers are monitoring, and not the degree to which one respects ancestral spirits or not. You grow ill or die from something you have done, or a relative has done, in the material world, and the fear of sorcery is as powerful as its effects. People accord with community obligations and taboos to avoid sorcery.

The intentions and desires of ancestral spirits are usually revealed in dreams. People who have dreams, or are said to have summoned ancestor spirits, can sometimes have powerful sway in community matters. Not only do they invest themselves with the supernatural powers of the deceased, but they often claim to be able to influence the supernatural world through rituals and magic. Music is usually part of these rituals, and in the mainland of New Guinea, the flute is an especially meaningful instrument during ritual. A mythic storyline shared by a great deal of northeastern New Guinea people involves the primordial power of women: how the community was once ruled by its women who played magical flutes in a spirit house of their own. At some point, the myth tells us, the women either fell asleep or were duped by men who stole these flutes back and have forever after been the masters of magic and governance in society.

In Hawaii, families still conduct ceremonies to transform the deceased into the body of the family's totemic animal. Thus these totems or animals become embodied with ancestral powers, and a fisherman, for example, may be guarded by a shark, or lizard descendants may see lizards as particularly good omens. Along the north coast of New Guinea, people had ritual acts and dietary restrictions regarding their totems. The chicken family could not eat chicken, and the descendants of certain fish species could not disembowel these fish to use as bait for bigger fish. In this way, totems and deceased relatives remain living members of the community, governing behavior and providing benign assistance. In Vanuatu people say that humans have two souls—one goes to an afterlife while the other takes the form of an animal, plant, or object.

Micronesian religion is characterized by a vertical worldview; that is to say, a belief in sky gods responsible for creating the world and the forces of nature. This is related to the Polynesian pantheons of creators, and differs somewhat from Melanesian religions. By contrast, the Australian Aboriginal worldview might be called horizontal. It rests on the concept of the Dreaming, a sacred time before living memory when ancestors (human and animal) wandered the earth, creating everything from their own essence and adventures. Once the site had been made, the ancestor would merge with it as a manifestation of his or her self. Human life or soul derives from these ancestors, as incarnations of and at death, returns to them (a belief also common in island New Guinea).

The concepts of *mana* and *tapu*, which are central to Polynesian cultures, are also less significant in Melanesia. *Mana* is a sacred and generative potency, a power of the gods made manifest in the human realm. As a characteristic of persons and objects as well as of spirits, *mana* can be either helpful or harmful. It is a force of growth and vitality, as well as of harm and death, and must be harnessed at all costs. Anything uncommon or out of the ordinary—such as a weapon that has killed many animals or a great hero who defeats many foes— can be said to possess *mana*. The worldly acts of consumption and of sex are especially vulnerable to *mana*, and so, by way of controlling the force, taboos are placed on activities surrounding both. Transformations of life-giving to death-dealing *mana* are the central concern of ritual life, and the object is to balance or rectify the opposing forces into either the ritual state of *tapu*, or the ritual state of *noa*. *Tapu* is the state of contact between human and divine, but *noa* is a state of complete detachment.

Beneath the many variations between Melanesian and Micronesian and Polynesian belief systems lie very important distinctions in social organization. Most salient is the system of chiefly rule in **Polynesia** and **Micronesia**, or a ruling class set against a common or majority class. Chiefdoms also exist throughout island Melanesia, but the continuum of social organizations that ranges from councils of elders or meritocratic societies to inherited government runs from western Melanesia to eastern Polynesia, as from interior New Guinea to its easternmost island communities. Chiefdoms are pervasive in the Admiralty Islands of northwestern Melanesia and are highly developed in the Marshall Islands and Pohnpei, in eastern Micronesia, as they are in Polynesia. Chiefdoms are also found in the Papuan coast of New Guinea, in Manam Island, off its north coast; in the Trobriands Islands, off the eastern coast; in Vanuatu; in New Caledonia; and in the southeast Solomon Islands. In all these chiefdoms, however, the rules of succession are more pliant than European nobility (*see* **Chiefs**). One of the ways commoners could move up the system, for example, in Polynesia, was by mastering religious and esoteric supernatural and historical information. In the Murik Lakes of New Guinea, for example, oldest brothers and sisters could compete with each other for the designated title of *Sana*, or chief. In addition, a "loophole" that allowed noble lines to have first "unofficial" marriages before they married for life also allowed children from these earlier unions to compete with "legitimate" heirs when it came time to bequeath the chiefly title.

In this way, even the most tyrannical chiefdoms have always allowed for an element of competition, and competence, to enter the succession of leaders.

The eldest son deemed unfit or disagreeable could be passed over for a favorite. Even in Polynesia, where genealogies were fought over like the Holy Grail, there was also room for maneuvering, and rival claims could be made between different levels of entitlement. The principle of succession has always been primogeniture, or first son/daughter succession, but second and third siblings can also position themselves before their elder sibling's offspring, and the various cousins and second son lineages are complexly debated. In many of these societies, primogeniture marks a distinction between senior and junior lines of descent. The conical clan system gives all descent lines unique ranks. The ranks derive from elder siblings from younger siblings—elder brothers from younger brothers in patrilineal Polynesia and elder sisters from younger sisters in matrilineal Micronesia—and all of their descendants.

Ancestral Polynesia had hereditary ranks for priests. The paramount chiefs were also the embodiment of deities. In New Caledonia, by comparison, Kanaky chiefs had magical relationships with the ancestors and were embodiments of the lunar calendar, so they initiated the different planting and harvesting seasons. The Pleiades in the sky were important not just for navigation but for determining seasonal time.

Oceanic peoples were (and many still are) entirely dependent upon the weather for their garden food, fishing, housing security and ocean-going trade. Because the Pacific Islands are strung along the Ring of Fire, seismic activity throws up earthquakes, tsunamis, and volcanic eruptions that have always made life in these islands precarious, if not absolutely dangerous. At the eastern end, the Nazca and Cocos Plates are being subducted beneath the South American Plate, and to the west, the Pacific and Juan de Fuca Plates are being subducted beneath the North American Plate (to the west). Pacific island societies have always relied on beliefs that would control the weather by appeasing spirits or gods that might reside in volcanoes, hot springs, and the sea. The fact that high chiefs, priests, and sorcerers across this region have all made hereditary or supernatural claims to controlling the weather comes as no surprise. There are **yam** planting seasons and tapu seasons for Polynesian gardens, and in the Trobriand Island the pre-European garden magic alone fills two volumes of one of anthropology's classic tomes, *Coral Gardens and Their Magic*, by Bronislaw Malinowski (1935).

It stands to reason, then, that weather pattern changes during the Middle Ages would have deeply influenced their beliefs about themselves and their world. The entire Pacific Basin underwent radical changes during the Middle Ages because of the transition between the Little Climactic Optimum (c. 950–1310) and the Little Ice Age (c. 1425–1850). The transition peaked between 1310 and 1425, and was characterized by rapid temperature drops and an increase in rainfall. Agricultural impacts would have been severe. This transition era coincides with the end of long distance voyaging in Polynesia (*see* **Voyaging/Ancient Navigation**). It marks a period of increased social complexity in Samoa, for example. Islanders pulled back from the expansive interisland connections they enjoyed and stopped the pattern of exploration and colonization. Coastal populations grew during the Little Climactic Optimum, archaeologists tell us, and then when things cooled off and violent weather arrived, they started to expand to the interiors and mountain centers of the Polynesian islands. The rise in rainfall, cooler temperatures, lower sea levels, and increasingly violent weather patterns that gradually augured in the Little Ice Age also made alternative land-use strategies very important. Agricultural intensification began. Forests were cleared for gardens. No doubt **food** was a growing problem with violent weather, and the surpluses upon which so many chiefly tribute systems relied—from Micronesia through Polynesia—were drying up (*see* **Agriculture**).

In Micronesia, many changes can be attributed to the **breadfruit** revolution. Early settlers on Kosrae and Pohnpei depended on breadfruit with other things and grew to depend more on breadfruit alone. It probably came from the Solomon Islands and Vanuatu originally, and it became the staple of Micronesia, particularly in the western Carolinean high islands. Myths in the Marshall Islands tell of its introduction sometime between 1200 and 1300. In Chuuk, its introduction also marks a major sociopolitical shift, as the islanders became more dependent on the interisland tribute systems from Pohnpei and Kosrae. Across Micronesia, it is breadfruit—an easy staple to grow—that signals a cultural and social efflorescence during the Middle Ages.

Megaliths, stone money, stone forts, ceremonial platforms, monuments, plinths, burial platforms, and stone gods are all features of Oceania's Middle Ages and can be found from Micronesia across to Polynesia. Stone faces in Palau, ridge-top forts in the Solomon Islands, **stone money** disks in Yap, latte stones in the Marianas, limestone backrests in Tonga, burial mounds in Samoa, and *marae* altars in Tahiti—all date from the era just prior to European contact. They are reflections of the kind of interisland networks created during the early Middle Ages, and the social intensification characteristic of the later Middle Ages. What we call "shrines" or "altars" in Polynesia, however, were as much political as religious sites, where rituals were conducted, **kava** was drunk and debates, singing, chanting, and occasionally human sacrifice took place. *See also* **Gods and Goddesses.**

Further Reading

Ashby, G., ed. *Micronesian Customs and Beliefs*. Eugene, OR: Rainy Day Press, 1975.

Bellwood, P. *Prehistory of the Indo-Malaysian Archipelago*. 2nd ed. Honolulu: University of Hawai'i Press, 1997.

Chowning, A. *An Introduction to the Peoples and Cultures of Melanesia*. 2nd ed. Menlo Park, CA: Cummings Publishing, 1977.

Firth, R. *Tikopia Ritual and Belief*. Boston: Beacon Press, 1967.

Kirch, P. V. *On the Road of the Winds*. Berkeley: University of California Press, 2000.

Kirch, P. V., and R. C. Green. *Hawaiki, Ancestral Polynesia*. Cambridge, UK: Cambridge University Press, 2001.

Lawrence, P., and M. J. Meggitt. *Gods Ghosts and Men in Melanesia*. Melbourne, Australia: Oxford University Press, 1965.

Malinowski, B. *Coral Gardens and Their Magic*. 2 vols. London: George Allen and Unwin, 1935.

Moyle, R. *Fâgogo: Fables from Samoa in Samoan and English*. Auckland, New Zealand: Auckland University Press, 1981.

Orbell, M. *The Illustrated Encyclopedia of Mâori Myth and Legend*. Canterbury, UK: Canterbury University Press, 1995.

Shore, B. "*Mana*" and "*Tapu*." In A. Howard and R. Borofsky, eds., *Developments in Polynesian Ethnology*. Honolulu: University of Hawai'i Press, 1989, pp. 137–173.

Slone, T. H., ed. *One Thousand One Papua New Guinea Nights: Folktales from Wantok Newspapers*. 2 vols. Oakland CA: Masalai Press, 2001.

Swain, T., and G. Trompf. *The Religions of Oceania*. London: Routledge, 1995.

Thompson, R. C. *Religion in Australia: A History*. Melbourne, Australia: Oxford University Press, 1994.

Trompf, G. *Melanesian Religion.* Cambridge, UK: Cambridge University Press, 1991.
Williamson, R. W. *Religion and Social Organization in Central Polynesia.* Cambridge, UK:
    Cambridge University Press, 1937.

Nancy Sullivan

3. ECONOMY

The economic life of Oceanic peoples during the Middle Ages was largely
about subsistence **agriculture** and fisheries, as well as hunting and gathering.
But these societies were also deeply involved in trade, in a full range of systems, from gifts to high **chiefs**, and reciprocal exchanges of goods (like fish for
yams), to extensive cross-cultural trade in shell valuables, like the *kula* ring
in **Melanesia**'s Massim region. Before European contact, when there was no
monetary currency, traditional currencies consisted of consumables such as
pigs, tubers, meat, fish, and objects such as stone axes, red feathers, jade, shells,
ceramic pots, and so forth. These were important elements of all subsistence
economies, and their circulation created extensive interdependencies between
different peoples; but their role was by far more important in the construction
and maintenance of social relationships. Things are transacted between people, of course, and the transaction itself can speak volumes about the giver
and the receiver.

Before the advent of a market economy, driven by supply and demand,
there were two general types of transactions in the Pacific Islands. The first,
and more prevalent, was a redistributive economy, whereby the public tithed
or proferred resources to the leader (or chief or **bigman**), who then managed
its redistribution. This would characterize most of the trade networks throughout **Polynesia** and **Micronesia**, and a great many island trade systems in Melanesia during this period.

Reciprocal trade, on the other hand, is what most people think of as quid
pro quo or apples-for-oranges exchange. The Western world used to see the
vast majority of nonwestern or "primitive" trade as being just this, a functional
exchange of what one has for what one needs. In this way, "primitive man"
was easily understood as having very basic needs to fulfill, whether material
or social, and engaging in trade as a form of self-preservation. At the same
time, scholars were confounded by the prevalence of "gifts" in Polynesia
(especially) and found it hard to rectify functional motives with gift giving.
These reciprocal exchanges were not always functional; they made little sense
in terms of a notion of "primitive economics." Some gifts were returned in
kind, others seemed to create social indenture rather than material obligations.
In his classic work *The Gift* (first published in France in 1950), Marcel Mauss
argued that gifts are never "free"—he says his subject matter is "the gift, and
especially the obligation to return it." Acknowledging that human history is
filled with cases of reciprocal exchange, Mauss wanted to find out what it was
about an object that prompts a recipient to return the gesture. Mauss explains
that the gift is a "total prestation," imbued with "spiritual mechanisms," engaging the honor of giver and receiver (Mauss, 3). The giver is giving a part of
himself, Mauss says, so that "the objects are never completely separated from
the men who exchange them" (31).

This very simple redefinition of gift giving allowed scholars to finally see the social dimension of exchange in non-Western societies, and particularly in the many forms of reciprocal exchange throughout Oceania. Through this lens, anthropologists and historians could begin to make sense of the long-distance and multicultural interisland trade in shells valuables, as well as the great ritual exchanges of pigs, garden produce, and even women in the hinterland of New Guinea. It had to do with honor, status, mana (in Polynesia), and corporate identity.

In part, Mauss was responding to the provocative findings of Bronislaw Malinowski (1920, 1922) who studied the Trobriand Islanders during the period of the First World War. He wrote about the Kula Ring, a voyaging exchange network that is dominated by Trobriand Islanders but runs in a circle through two language groups and several islands in the Massim of Melanesia. The ring spans eighteen island communities, including the Trobriand Islands, and compels participants to travel hundreds of miles across dangerous waters to exchange two types of valuables: the mother-of-pearl and spondyllus disc necklaces (*veigun* or *soulava*) that move in a clockwise direction around the ring, and the *conus* shell armbands (*mwali*) that circle anticlockwise. Every armshell is exchanged for a necklace, and vice versa.

In this trade system (which would have been operating during the Middle Ages), no one grows wealthy, nor do they gain food or other natural resources in the process. Chiefs, commoners, and perfect strangers all participate (if they wish). Malinowski himself was confounded by the system (1920, 1922), which appeared to strengthen friendship and kinship ties in the most ritualistic ways. There was a more practical barter exchange (*gimwali*) running parallel to the *kula*, by which useful items like food, oils, building materials, and other items were exchanged in the process. But though the *kula* reciprocal trade and the *gimwali* barter trade were linked, they operated under different logics, and with very different objectives. Kula objects are never owned, never alienated from the ring itself, and do little more for the temporary "recipient" than give him (more rarely her) the right to tell the stories embedded in these shells.

The shells proffer temporary status only, although the entire system builds a hierarchy of players whose reputations survive over time and acts in counterpoint to the matrilineal descent and inheritance that governs these societies. Carefully prescribed customs, magic, and historical legends surround the exchanges, and these knit together men from various islands in lifelong exchange partnerships (called *karayta'u*, "partners"). The act of giving, as Mauss wrote, is a display of the greatness of the giver, and demands modesty from the recipient. There are proscribed roles for each player that involve acts of hospitality and security, and good players are held in very high esteem.

The *Kula* ring is a classical example of Mauss' distinction between a gift and a commodity exchange. *Kula* players are clear to distinguish between the gift exchange (*Kula*) and the barter or market exchange (*gimwali*). The *kula* involves public and ritualized display and underscores honor and integrity as cultural values. The barter is something else: it rides alongside the kula but involves purely economic values (Malinowski, 1990, 22–23). *Kula* valuables are *inalienable* in the sense that they can never be taken from the ring, they can never be individually owned. They pass through the hands of caretakers but are heirlooms on an unstoppable journey through time. Recipients can hold them, and even pass them on as gifts, but they can never become commodities for sale or barter. *Kula* valuables are never private property.

In a gift economy, the objects that are given are inalienable from the givers; they are always on loan, never sold. The identity of the giver is also necessarily bound up with the object given, and invests the valuable with the power to compel a recipient to reciprocate. In this way, kula objects have what Polynesians call **mana**, that is a power to impel or realize something. The act of giving creates a debt that must be repaid. Gift exchange creates an ongoing interdependence between giver and receiver. According to Mauss, the "free" gift is therefore no more than a myth.

The sociality of exchange in Pacific Island societies has opened up a great field of scholarship, so that more recently it is possible to see virtually all aspects of human interaction in these cultures in terms of reciprocity or gifting. For the Trobriand Islands, the anthropologist Annette Weiner played an important role in opening the public's eyes to **women** and their more immutable roles in a gift economy. She looked at the Trobriand system of social organization — through which subclans (*dala*) are reproduced, and pointed out that women reclaimed *dala* valuables that men had loaned their sons and daughters (who are in fact not part of the father's matrilineage). The children never own their father's valuables, but they enjoy a form of usufruct rights over them during their lifetime. In this way the presence of a father's *kula* valuables could become part of the success and status of a woman's line, in other words, a factor in the reproduction of the matrilineal *dala*. But more than this, Weiner called these gifts to the dala "free" gifts, offered of love from father to child, and not expected to be reciprocated. Nevertheless, they play an important role in enhancing a child's status, to the ultimate benefit of the child's matrilineage, not the father's. Such generosity had been overlooked by other scholars, and its acknowledgement helped restore some of the "gifting" quality to a gift economy. But Weiner was really arguing that to call gifts either unreciprocal (free) or reciprocal (commodities) is to overlook another important role they play: building social hierarchy in these island chieftainships.

A very different example of Oceanic reciprocity in exchange comes from the highlands of New Guinea, in Melanesia, where the *moka* is a form of ceremonial wealth exchange that primarily involves pigs. During the Middle Ages, pigs were well established throughout Melanesia, although the sweet potato (which has become currency for purchasing them) was just being introduced. It is hard to say that *moka*, or neighboring Engan *tee*, ceremonies were as elaborate at that time as they were just prior to European contact in the twentieth century, but it is fair to say that the principles upon which these ceremonies rest were already well entrenched.

Moka is from the Western Highlands of New Guinea, and, like *kula*, is a system of building status. Men are the players, although women have been known to perform *moka*, too. But it is really a vehicle by which a self-made or ambitious man can catapult himself to leadership by producing a ceremony in his (and his clan or tribe's) name. Successful moka players are ipso facto big men, and their influence grows with the number of moka partners they accumulate. He can also conduct small- or large-scale moka exchanges, which become like an entrepreneurial gambling system, each debt taken out to cover a previous obligation. The difference between moka and virtually all other island or coastal exchange system, is that it is profit bearing. The system rests on a principle of incremental returns. Thus, a gift of two pigs is returned with interest, as a gift of three pigs, and so forth. The complexity of one's obligations, as they are paid off in part and in total (much like a highly leveraged market venture), means that the truly big *moka* players are constantly calculating their risks and investments, trying to find the next windfall of pigs to stage a bigger yet *moka* and create even more staggering obligations from others.

These are bigmen societies, where no one inherits status or power, and where men must work to convince others that they represent everyone's best interests. Bigmen, in this system, are much like candidates in a democratic race, individuals whose sheer will to lead can charm or terrorize clansmen (in equal measure) into getting behind their ambitions. As a supporter, you throw your pigs into his *moka* exchange, knowing that his success will guarantee your success, and having his goodwill can also guarantee your future security. At any given time in the process, the *moka* partners are in unequal relations with each other—as debtors or creditors.

The extraordinary things about these moka (and similar tee) exchanges is that they escalate obligations, as well as rewards. Ambitious players can become extremely powerful, and their supporters (clansmen) benefit economically (with efficiently returned pigs, and a profit). Most important, successful moka networks can guarantee peace across otherwise hostile frontiers, and so the advantage of wealth accumulation and distribution can have very dramatic political consequences. Naturally, just as anthropologists have seized upon the kula as an example of complex economics (that defy previous notions of "primitive economic man"), so too have they seized the *moka* exchanges as signs of highlanders being "preadapted" to capitalism. *See also* Document 7.

Further Reading

Chowning, A. *An Introduction to the Peoples and Cultures of Melanesia.* Menlo Park, CA: Cummings Publishing, 1979.

Crocombe, R. *The South Pacific.* Suva, Fiji: University of the South Pacific, 2001.

Feil, D. K. *The Evolution of Highland Papua New Guinea Societies.* Cambridge, UK: Cambridge University Press, 1987.

Finney, B. R. *Voyage of Discovery: A Cultural Odyssey through Polynesia.* Berkeley: University of California Press, 1994.

Kirch, P. V. *On the Road of the Winds: An Archaeological History of the Pacific Islands before European Contact.* Berkeley: University of California Press, 2000.

Lutkehaus, N., ed. *Sepik Heritage: Tradition and Change in Papua New Guinea.* Durham, NC: Carolina Academic Press, 1990.

Malinowski, B. *Argonauts of the Western Pacific: An Account of Native Enterprise and Adventure in the Archipelagoes of Melanesian New Guinea.* London: George Routledge & Sons, Ltd., 1922.

Malinowski, B. "Kula; the Circulating Exchange of Valuables in the Archipelagoes of Eastern New Guinea." *Man* 20 (1920): 97–105.

Mauss, M. *The Gift: Forms and Functions of Exchange in Archaic Societies.* London: Routledge, 1990.

Neich, R., and F. Pereira. *Pacific Jewelry and Adornment.* Honolulu: University of Hawai'i Press, 2004.

Strathern, A. J. *One Father, One Blood: Descent and Group Structure Among the Melpa People.* London: Tavistock, 1972.

Strathern, A. J. *Rope of Moka: Big-Men and Ceremonial Exchange in Mount Hagen, New Guinea.* Cambridge, UK: Cambridge University Press, 1971.

Weiner, A. *Women of Value, Men of Renown: New Perspectives in Trobriand Exchange.* Austin: University if Texas Press, 1976.

Yed, D. E., and J. M. J. Mummery, eds. *Pacific Production Systems: Approaches to Economic Prehistory.* Canberra: The Australian National University, 1990.

Nancy Sullivan

4. THE ARTS

The arts of Oceania are wide and varied, and nowhere can they be separated from the sociocultural life of their creators (*see also* **Entertainment**). One essay cannot do the subject justice. What we can say, however, is that the arts of Oceania are best viewed in terms of their role in the lives of their peoples, rather than the prism of Western aesthetics. In context, they have always been a link between mankind and the spiritual realm. In some cases the act of carving or creating a material object was and still is itself a form of propitiation to the ancestors. Where the plastic arts (sculpture or painting) are part of one's tribal heritage, they may form a mnemonic device for stories that give a person entitlement to hunting, fishing, or gardening grounds. Or they may be symbols of genealogical information, or maps of where an ancestor roamed. In this way the very concept of authorship for Pacific art should be seen as fundamentally different. Oceanic artists are not auteurs realizing personal impulses, they are islanders performing, voicing, painting, or carving part of a community imperative. What is personal is the unique relationship between the artist and the ancestor, totem, or clan represented in the work, and not the form of its expression. Only since European contact have Pacific Islanders considered art as a form of personal expression, and part of a global (albeit largely Western) discourse on aesthetics.

The different regions of Oceania—**Melanesia, Micronesia**, and **Polynesia**— can be distinguished by their different art forms. In general, however, the material art objects include a range of functional objects such as altars, houses, stools, and instruments of war, for examples, along with decorated human skulls, carved stone and wooden figurines, bark paintings, sand paintings, woven mats and bags, decorated **tapa** cloth, and shell ornaments. Many of these items are also items of trade, acting as currency or valuables in networks of exchange that run from island to island and criss-cross the interior of the major islands (*see* **Shell Valuables**).

Melanesian Art

Melanesian art is well known for its elaborate stylizations, especially of the human form, where exaggerated facial and bodily parts come to represent sexuality, fertility, strength, cannibalism, and sometimes comic foibles. In the outer islands of Manus, New Britain, New Ireland, and the Massim these carvings and masks are especially finely wrought and bear the imprint of **lapita** migrations traveling through from Taiwan and the Philippines roughly 5,000 years ago. The carved canoe prows of stylized warriors in the Solomon Islands were called *NguzuNguzu* and were powerful reminders of the importance of warfare. The mortuary masks and carvings from New Ireland, part of a tradition called *malangan*, are especially dramatic and colorful, some might say hoary, and can be seen in Oceanic museum collections across Europe. But each region of the Bismark Archipelago is known for its striking ancestor masks and life-sized figures, some of which are made from less permanent materials, like leaves and bark, and discarded after ritual use.

Because many Melanesian carvings and masks have always been made for a ritual or occasional purpose, only the wooden articles have endured for collecting. Few objects that have been fashioned as "permanent" objects for trade, such as the shell valuables, actually remain from the period of 400 to 1400 C.E. One extensive trade network in the eastern islands, or Massim, area off New Guinea, called the *kula*, conveys old shell armbands and necklaces in a system of exchange and prestige building precisely because the shells contain so much history. But in general, older is not better for Melanesian art, and ancestral masks and carvings were made to be discarded, so that the next generation could learn their stories from the making and remaking of clan and tribal designs.

In the Sepik, to continue the example, it is the men's house or *haus tambaran* that is the focus of male ceremonial life. Even today, this is where the initiated men spend their days, where clan *sacralae* is stored, and where young boys are secluded and instructed by clan elders in preparation for **initiation**. The design for these houses may be as simple as a structure resembling a house, with an open ground floor, thatch roofing, and split palm floorboards for a second story. For the Iatmul and Blackwater peoples of the Middle Sepik, spirit houses are awe-inspiring structures as much as 164 feet long with soaring gables and saddleback rooflines that slope in the center, all raised above the floodlines on stilts up to 16 feet high. We have no evidence to confirm that his was how they looked 600 years ago, but there are carvings from such structures that have been carbon dated as far back as 650 to 780.

Inside the *haus tambaran* are the powerful *mwai* masks and basketwork *tumbuan* worn during initiation **dances**, along with cult hooks, food hooks, ancestor masks and figures, war shields, war canoe shields, sacred flutes, water drums, and slit-gong drums. Upstairs there are painted palm bark or carved wooden skull racks for displaying decorated enemy heads taken in war raids. The most striking features of the Middle Sepik *haus tambaran* are the ornately carved posts and roof beams, each representing clan totems and ancestral figures. But most of all, and most important, there is the *tambaran* — the spirits of the ancestors.

There is never anything unplanned about a *haus tambaran*. Most are divided in two by major clans, then subdivided by subclans which have their own seating platforms, carved posts, and entrances at each quarter of the ground floor. The older initiated men sit towards the center post, the younger men toward either end. Thus, when you enter a *haus tambaran* you would go to the center to speak to the most important men.

In the carvings of the Sepik River, major tribes and languages groups are distinguished by the images they carve and paint. Many of the Lower Sepik Yuat and Keram River peoples carve flying fox clan totems and surround their masks and figures with basketwork frames and a ruff of cassowary feathers. Some of the ancestor figures can be identified by place according to the way their hair is tied on top of their head, others by the shape of their nose or eyes. Each community has its own stylization of ancestral figures, embedded with human hair; feathers; crocodile, dog, or rats' teeth; tridachna, nassa and conus shells; and seeds.

North of the river itself, and inland, the Sawos and Abelam people have long made basketwork masks rather than wooden ones, and these are traded down to the Iatmul people at the riverside. In Maprik and the Waskuk areas inland, yam masks were woven to decorate large ceremonial **yams** during yam harvest celebrations so that they resembled humans. We can trace the emergence of these stylizations along the lines of migration n this region, as this floodplains region was just being settled during the late Middle Ages. The founding Iatmul tribe villages, for example were Japandai and Suapmeri, after which came Palembei and Kanganaman, and the styles of their carvings can be seen as variations on an original format. In Korogo, another early Iatmul village, the signature look for their masks is eyes that protrude from the face.

Up the tributaries that feed the Sepik River, such as the Karawari River, there is far less carving and more painting on sago bark. Each painting tells a clan specific story within a fixed iconography. They also carve tall cult hooks called *Kamanggabi* that embody protective spirits and are used for divination. Interestingly, these hooks would be abandoned when the Karawari people moved on to a new site, leaving the object while the spirit moved on.

Different villages have distinctive carving styles, but because trade is so prevalent in the region, there has always been great circulation of form and technique. Ancestral masks, skull racks, ritual paraphernalia, canoe prows, sacred flutes, and lime holders were variously traded across language groups and tribes. Sometimes great sickness, flood, or war casualties would drive a group to trade for a powerful ritual complex of another, with its song cycles, chants, and ritual objects. But the traveling generally vitiated much of the object's power. The importers would have the right to carve such images, but they might not know all the secrets embedded in them.

Virtually all Sepik masks are ancestor masks, mainly protective. Standing figures and finial or post carvings may depict ancestors or *masalai*—bush spirits. An ancestor figure may have a possum on its head or a crocodile wrapped around its legs, or a bird on its back. But *masalai* figures have part human-part animal features, like a crocodile's mouth and pig's nose or bird's beak, with human body and a snake's tail. These are variously evil or benevolent creatures who can change form according to their travels but are generally associated with the river, a patch of jungle, or a hill somewhere. Certain *masalai* figures are very powerful, comparable to a *haus tambaran*'s "orator chair," and so can only be carved by master carvers. As noted above, often a new figure will come to the carver in a dream.

Archaeologists and government officers in the same area of the Sepik, ranging eastward to the Ramu River area of Madang Province, have also found stone figures large and small that look like Polynesian stone carvings, in some cases, and war amulets in others. They even bear resemblance to the standing *tamtams* in Vanuatu with their stylized human features. This marks the overlap of what some might call the two forms of Pacific art: western and eastern. In Melanesia, must of the artistic expression is focused on secular purposes, or on ancestor worship, whereas in Polynesia and Micronesia there is more "idolatry" or god figures worshipped on altars and in public spaces. In eastern Melanesia, which can be called the "cradle" of Polynesian culture as people moved eastward right up through the Middle Ages, we see that combination of gods and ancestor figures, and more altars or places of public worship.

Micronesian and Polynesian Art

Micronesian art is similarly functional and is known for its fine hardwood finish. It often looks manufactured in comparison to Melanesian carving, so elegant and polished is its finish. But the Micronesian islands also place difference emphases on their material objects, and this is the only region that has traditionally woven textiles. In the Caroline Islands traditional navigational skills are reproduced through various string, shell, stone, and sand images that illustrate the wave patterns, stars, fish, bird, underwater iridescence, and other formula taught by specialists to novices over many years.

Polynesian art is known for its wide range of materials, including feathers in Hawaii, bark cloth (**tapa**) for exchange and ornamentation, finely woven mats, stone sculptures, jade amulets, and carved woodwork, including canoes. Again, it is usually more finely wrought and finished than Melanesian art, with the circular patterns such as you see in the Māori **tattoos** and public houses. These objects were meant to endure and to contain *mana* or supernatural powers by their particular stylizations of ancestral gods.

Turning to Polynesia, the most salient form of material art is the *marae*, or altar, which also functioned as a meetinghouse and the chief's throne in different locations. It is said that the most plausible origin of *marae* is in eastern Polynesia, specifically Rapa Nui, or Easter Island. The reddish volcanic rock, tufa, was carved to create enormous ancestral figures weighing as much as 20 tons. The relatively few early radiocarbon ages associated with these ceremonial stone architecture, or *marae*, of Rapa Nui are associated with earlier dates than those found in Tahiti, the Society Islands. *Ahu*, in Rapa Nui refers to the entire ceremonial stone structure, including the altar, the courtyard (where present), and the statue, or *moai*. In the Society Islands, *ahu* refers only to the altar of the *marae*. McCall (29–32) described the social structure of pre-Contact Rapa Nui culture as being divided into two confederations, and each of these contained several lineage groups called *mata*. The *moai* may, however, personify dead chiefs or some other aspect of religion, or they may represent segments of ancient society, rather than god figures.

The tradition of stone architecture is considered to have moved from east to west across Polynesia, starting from Rapa Nui's impressive *moai*. Martinsson-Wallin, for one, developed a comparative study looking at material culture traits of ancient Peru, Rapa Nui, and Polynesia and concluded that there must have been pre-Contact interaction between the people of Rapa Nui and South America.

These large stone monoliths are found in the Marquesas Islands as well, as are smaller objects of shell and stone. But what the Marquesas Islanders perfected was the art of body tattooing, in extraordinary patterns that would cover the entire body. This more mutable and living form of art eventually moved through the Hawaiian Islands and New Zealand during the migrations of the Middle Ages.

Further Reading
Chowning, A. *An Introduction to the Peoples and Cultures of Melanesia*. Menlo Park, CA: Cummings Publishing, 1979.
Craig, B. *Art and Decoration of Central New Guinea*. Aylesbury, UK: Shire Publications, 1988.
Eddowes, M. D. "Ethnohistorical Perspectives on the *Marae* of the Society Islands: The Sociology of Use." Unpublished M.A. Thesis, Department of Anthropology, University of Auckland (New Zealand), 1991.

Finney, B. R. *Voyage of Discovery: A Cultural Odyssey through Polynesia*. Berkeley: University of California Press, 1994.

Firth, R. *We, the Tikopia*. Stanford, CA: Stanford University Press, 1983 [1936].

Gathercole, P. et al. *The Art of the Pacific Islands*. Washington, DC: National Gallery of Art, 1979.

Kirch, P. V. *On the Road of the Winds: An Archaeological History of the Pacific Islands before European Contact*. Berkeley: University of California Press, 2000.

Lutkehaus, N., ed. *Sepik Heritage: Tradition and Change in Papua New Guinea*. Durham, NC: Carolina Academic Press, 1990.

Martinsson-Wallin, H. *Ahu – The Ceremonial Stone Structures of Easter Island. Analyses of Variation and Interpretation of Meanings*. Aun 19. Uppsala, Sweden: Societas Archaeologica Upsaliensis, 1994.

McCall, G. "Reaction to Disaster: Continuity and Change in Rapanui Social Organization." Ph.D. diss. Australia National University, 1976, 29–32.

Neich, R., and F. Pereira. *Pacific Jewelry and Adornment*. Honolulu: University of Hawai'i Press, 2004.

Nancy Sullivan

5. SOCIETY

Oceania's social organization during the Middle Ages varied considerably across the subregions of **Micronesia, Melanesia**, and **Polynesia**, and everywhere society's values were transmitted through informal, yet strong **education**. Although no written evidence exists for this era prior to European contact, the archaeological record is vivid enough. We can also project back from earliest contact reports by Europeans to what might have been the case in the preceding centuries.

Micronesian society would have been the most interesting by far during this period. This is because the region was its glorious height during the period between 400 and 1400 C.E. The Saudeleur dynasty flourished in Pohnpei at the center of the region during the beginning of this period and toward the end the **Yap Empire** was fully defined at its western end. Archeological evidence is inconclusive about Palau (Belau) during this period, but the remnants of basalt monoliths there suggest that there were meeting houses large enough to contain more than 1,000 people, and terraced hillsides as well.

Micronesian descent was matrilineal, except for Yap, which was patrilineal (although it also had matriclans). Here the small but high island of Yap in the west came to govern an empire of outer atolls stretching eastward that, by their lack of resources and vulnerability to weather and famine, were dependant upon the high island for security. In addition, the Yapese controlled weather magic, which impelled the lower islands to present tributes of fiber, ropes, timber, shells, and other valuables, like tumeric, to Wa'ab islands (Yap). The islands of Wa'ab may have had a population of more than fifty thousand during the Middle Ages. They had great vstone meeting houses (like Belau) and amphitheaters. Family houses were raised on stone platforms with thatched roofs, and connected by networks of stone paths. There were even ceremonial Women's Houses where young **women** came of age.

Villages were highly stratified by rank, gender, age and occupation, and ruled by a triumvirate of chiefs. They competed for wealth and status, although seven elite villages were led by three even higher ranking ones. In addition, Yap's clans were divided into two groupings, or moieties, which gave even more fluidity to the social organization. Villages staged elaborate and competitive celebrations for other villages, and young men in the Men's House would make raids to other villages to capture women as concubines. Yapese boats sailed to Palau to quarry the outsized and highly valued stone money.

To the east, the island of Pohnpei was home to the Saudeleur dynasty ruled from around 500 to 1450. The Saudeleurs were the inhabitants of **Nan Madol**, the great palace complex of islands offshore to the southeast that has come to be known as one of the region's great wonders, and undoubtedly the most spectacular structure of the Oceanic Middle Ages. Nan Madol consisted of a small medieval town with temples and markets and even burial grounds constructed sometime 900 to 1200. There are more than ninety platforms of coral rubble with basalt retaining walls (some 25 feet high) that were quarried on the opposite end of the island. Permanent settlements appear to date from the first two centuries C.E., but the entire complex, and especially the large basalt megaliths, would have been constructed after the arrival of the San Deleur family (or Saudeleurs) in the twelfth century. Perhaps as many as 1,000 people lived in the complex at its busiest.

The island of Pohnpei was itself divided into various (first three, then later five) principalities, where the chiefly class allowed the noble class to lease land to the commoners, for gardens and residences. The Saudeleur oversaw all of this as a form of paramount landlord who was paid in tributes of **food** and fish. He was considered sacred, as well, and dealt with the common people through the intermediary of the noble class.

Nearby, Kosrae's commoners lived on the main island of Ualang, while the chiefly lineages lived in the walled palace of Lelu, ad the nearby islands of Pisin, Tenyen, and Yenasr. Lelu was smaller, but no less sophisticated than Nan Madol, and included coral roads and a canal system for boats. Legend says Kosrae warriors sailed to Pohnpei and overthrew the tyrannical Saudeleur dynasty sometime in the fourteenth century.

Melanesian social organization in the Middle Ages would have been very different from its Micronesian neighbors, especially for the higher islands. Much smaller political and residential units, ranging from less than one hundred to only a few thousand people, would have been scattered across the islands and further divided by linguistic and cultural barriers. For the vast majority of mainland New Guineans, these language groups were described as tribes, or descent units, and further divided into clan and subclan lines. The most common organizing principle for these polities was a sibling set, usually two brothers, from whence the different clans of a single tribe descended. In this way, there is normally a dominant clan for a tribe or, where tribe is not used, a dominant subclan, representing the elder brother's line.

As with all of Oceania, primogeniture is the dominant form of succession. Land tenure and inheritance were always reckoned first through the older brother, and by extension, the elder brother clan, although the rules are flexible enough to allow variations. In addition, though the majority of Melanesian societies recognize patrilineal over matrilineal entitlements, cognatic descent is always recognized, so that a child can reckon entitlements through both or either parent. This means that if a woman lost her husband, and his family was hostile toward her, she could usually return to her father's land and make a garden. The rules would bend according to circumstance, and over time, so that if a descent line is killed in war or dies from malaria, the system can recalibrate itself much more quickly than a rigid hierarchical Polynesian chieftainship.

There are chieftainships in island Melanesia, and these are also not strictly systems of genealogical succession, either. In the Massim, along the north coast of New Guinea, and in the Admiralty Islands there are multiple ranks of descent, much like Polynesia. Certain families are commoners, others are nobility, and still others are chiefly lines, each with their special taboos and deference toward each other. Commonly there are several small chiefs responsible for different communities, and one paramount **chief** for the entire tribe, language, or cultural unit.

In the lowlands of New Guinea, the riverine cultures of the Sepik River and the Asmat, are classic gerontocracies, where councils of elders rule the community, and one gains more entitlements with age. This structure is often combined with male (and sometimes female) initiation rituals, which formally induct the young into the ruling elite. Whereas the highland societies, ruled by ambitious bigmen who come and go in one lifetime and never cede their power to their sons, can be visualized as horizontal polities, much like Western democracies—where individuals campaign for a wide following—the lowland societies are better visualized as vertical lines of descent. Highland societies value wealth, whereas lowland societies run on knowledge. Highlands bigmen become big from surplus production, but the more marginal subsistence bases of lowland societies means their focus is more on esoteric information, genealogical and historical knowledge, and, most important, control of secret information. In this way the men with the longest and best memories are always prominent, if not more powerful, in the lowlands, and young men spend much of their time currying the favors of their elders who may then impart their information before they lose their memories.

One interesting combination of chiefly and age-graded social organization can be found at the mouth of the Sepik River, in the Murik Lakes. These people have migrated in from the north coast and Bismark Archipelago, mixing with Sepik River peoples, perhaps as recently as 500 years ago. They retain a chieftainship, or a series of small chiefs, called *Sana*, but with unusually competitive features. Here, as elsewhere, primogeniture is important to succession, so that the eldest child has a prior claim to the father's title. But there's a twist: sons and daughters can compete for the title. This is not so unusual, as sisters sometimes step in to hold titles for their brothers in many Pacific societies (like, for example, Fiji). But the twist is more: in the Murik Lakes, children from an earlier premarital union may also be recognized and compete for a title. That is, the society recognizes a "starter marriage" that may have fallen apart before a young person really settled down. Then, for example, it is possible that the eldest daughter of the first union could win the favors of her father and thereby inherit the position of *Sana* before he dies.

In Polynesia, we know that the early Middle Ages was a period of early settlement for most of the region, especially for the Marquesas, Hawaii, and New Zealand. The comparative anthropology of Polynesia comprises a few core social institutions and cultural patterns that are consistent across the islands. This is based on a common assumption that Polynesian culture all comes from a single source, which anthropologist Marshall Sahlins explains with a biological metaphor by saying, "the Polynesian cultures derive from a common source; they are members of a single cultural genus that has filled in and adapted to a variety of local habitats" (ix).

These common patterns can be seen in the social organization of these widespread island states. Lineage is defined by the *kainanga* or *kainga*, as a descent group or clan, and patrilineal descent that governs land tenure, plus the concepts of **mana** and **tapu**, which are based on myths of origin. In addition, hereditary chiefs are present everywhere in Polynesia, in one form or another (commonly called *ariki*) (*see* Kirsch, 214).

The concept of primogeniture is also ubiquitous in the region. The concept of *mana*, for example, as a form of potency, is an inherited potential, transmitted genealogically through first-born children. The gods are incorporated into kinships systems in Polynesian societies, as the ultimate form of reckoning in a highly competitive environment. It is postulated hat after initial settlement of the islands, as the restricted amount and range of resources became more valuable, competition intensified along with agricultural production. Chiefly bloodlines became more important and grew deeper as rivals traced their origins back to the gods. In this way the supernatural power of *mana*, or efficacy, became a defining element of chieftainship as it passed through the oldest son. Of course *mana* is an ex post facto determination, and those individuals who succeeded in gaining power were necessarily those with *mana*. At the same time, there was no better way to demonstrate *mana* than to challenge and defeat a rival of equal or higher status. This created a constantly fluid and competitive dimension to these genealogically formal social structures (Howard and Kirkpatrick, 64). *See also* **Gods and Goddesses**; Documents 4, 5, and 12.

Further Reading

Brown, P. *Highland Peoples of New Guinea*. Cambridge, UK: Cambridge University Press, 1978.

Chowning, A. *An Introduction to the Peoples and Cultures of Melanesia*. Menlo Park, CA: Cummings Publishing, 1979.

Crocombe, R. *The South Pacific*. Suva, Fiji: University of the South Pacific, 2001.

Feil, D. K. *The Evolution of Highland Papua New Guinea Societies*. Cambridge, UK: Cambridge University Press, 1987.

Finney, B. R. *Voyage of Discovery: A Cultural Odyssey through Polynesia*. Berkeley: University of California Press, 1994.

Firth, R. *We, the Tikopia*. Stanford, CA: Stanford University Press, 1983 [1936].

Gewertz, D. *Sepik River Societies: A Historical Ethnography of the Chambri and Their Neighbors*. New Haven, CT: Yale University Press, 1983.

Howard, A., and R. Borofsky, eds. *Developments in Polynesian Ethnology*. Honolulu: University of Hawai'i Press, 1989.

Howard, A., and J. Kirkpatrick. "Social Organization." In A. Howard and R. Borofsky, eds., *Developments in Polynesian Ethnology*. Honolulu: University of Hawai'i Press, 1989, pp. 47–94.

Kirch, P. V. *On the Road of the Winds: An Archaeological History of the Pacific Islands before European Contact*. Berkeley: University of California Press, 2000.

Kirch, P. V., and R. C. Green. *Hawaiki, Ancestral Polynesia: An Essay in Historical Anthropology*. Cambridge, UK: Cambridge University Press, 2001.

Lebot, V., M. Merlin, and L. Lindstrom. *Kava: The Pacific Drug*. New Haven, CT: Yale University Press, 1992.

Lutkehaus, N., ed. *Sepik Heritage: Tradition and Change in Papua New Guinea*. Durham, NC: Carolina Academic Press, 1990.

Malinowski, B. *Argonauts of the Western Pacific*. London: Routledge, 1922.

Myers, F. R. *Pintupi Country, Pintupi Self: Sentiment, Place, and Politics among Western Desert Aborigines*. Washington, DC: Smithsonian Institution, 1986.

Sahlins, M. "Poor Man, Rich Man, Big Man, Chief: Political Types in Melanesia and Polynesia." *Comparative Studies in Society and History* 5 (1963): 285–303.

Sahlins, M. *Social Stratification in Polynesia*. Seattle, WA: American Ethnological Society, 1958.

Schieffelin, B. *The Give and Take of Everyday Life: Language Socialization of Kaluli Children*. Cambridge, UK: Cambridge University Press, 1979.

Shore, B. "*Mana*" and "*Tapu*." In A. Howard and R. Borofsky, eds. *Developments in Polynesian Ethnology*. Honolulu: University of Hawai'i Press, 1989, pp. 137–174.

Strathern, A. J. *Rope of Moka: Big-Men and Ceremonial Exchange in Mount Hagen, New Guinea*. Cambridge, UK: Cambridge University Press, 1971.

Strathern, Andrew. *One Father, One Blood: Descent and Group Structure among the Melpa People*. London: Tavistock, 1972.

Suggs, R. C. *The Island Civilizations of Polynesia*. New York: Mentor Books, 1960.

Weiner, A. *Women of Value, Men of Renown*. Austin: University of Texas Press, 1976.

Nancy Sullivan

6. SCIENCE AND TECHNOLOGY

The Oceanic peoples were developing technological advances in several areas during the Middle Ages. **Micronesia**, for example, was engaged in quarrying great limestone and basalt blocks and wheels for the megaliths in Pohnpei and Kosrae, and for stone in Yap. The stones were cut from limestone quarries on Palau (Belau), an island 220 miles to the southwest, and transported to Yap by way of small native canoes. The exact means by which these massive stones were rolled and sailed to their destinations at some distance from their quarries has always been a field of great interest to archaeologists and historians, and certainly constitute great technological achievements of the age.

At the same time, however, Eastern Oceania was enjoying a final burst of maritime exploration as populations continued to push eastward from central **Polynesia**, in the Society Islands and the Marquesas, to settle the region's final outposts in Easter Island, New Zealand, Mangareva, Kermadec, and the Sandwich Islands of Hawaii. There is no doubt that all of this could only be accomplished by the advanced navigational systems being developed during this period. Pacific navigation flourished as a science during the Middle Ages, and each region developed its own emphasis on stars, wave patterns, weather, and countless other components to this highly complex field on knowledge. With many types of ocean-going canoes, and their familiarity with the stars and other natural phenomena for navigation, Pacific Islanders were able to move through the sea with relative ease. They adapted to their watery setting with great precision, accumulating vast libraries of unwritten information regarding their surroundings, and even developing various iconographic systems by which to record and transmit this expertise over time. The wind, stars, swells, underwater phosphorescence, clouds, birds, rains, and every feature of these vast expanses between their homes on land became as familiar to them as signboards along a public highway. In the Caroline Islands of Micronesia, for example, it is still the case that expert navigators require decades of training before they have mastered the science completely (*see* **Voyaging/Ancient Navigation**).

In the age before compasses or sextants, Pacific Islanders conducted long-distance voyages by mastering the observation of these natural signs, the most important of which were the stars. The star compass was the basic instrument of traditional navigation. Each star is named by its location and trajectory, and in some places more than two hundred stars are memorized. Their movements anchor the entire system by creating measurable distances and timings for bird flights, wave patterns, cloud formations, and much more. In Micronesia the star compass, and the thirty-two points around the horizon that represent it, was taught by pebble diagrams. In this way, navigators memorized the star course for each possible destination from one starting point by starting with one point (usually rising of Altair) on compass and going round the compass. This creates twenty-eight possible courses from each point. The thirty-two-point compass was based on positions of only fifteen stars or constellations, with Polaris being the only star not used twice (as it marks magnetic North). Most stars are marked by their rising and setting points, although stars do not rise and set at the same time each day. Some are only visible near a rising or setting point at one time in the day, so other stars and their positions at the same time also must also be memorized, to complete the compass at any given moment. This is daunting memorization for anyone, and perhaps only possible for nonliterate peoples who continually exercise mnemonic strategies to remember details.

Gladwin says that on Puluwat Atoll (in the Caroline Islands of Micronesia) there are star courses known to twenty-six places from the island, and for most of the journeys between any pair of the twenty-six destinations. This means a total of 650 journeys and 325 unrelated courses would be memorized. Similarly, the nearby Wolai Islanders knew courses for eighteen island destinations, which, multiplied by twenty-eight compass points, created 504 possible courses. In the Caroline Islands, these systems of dead reckoning were, and still are, known by different names: *Hatag* on Woliei, and *Etak* on Puluwat (today the general Micronesian system is referred to as *Etak*).

The Southern Cross is also very important for all these navigational systems. For example, the two stars in the Southern Cross always point south, so that if you travel south by canoe, these stars appear to travel higher and higher in the sky each night. Should you travel down to the South Pole, they would lie exactly overhead. Conversely, if you were traveling to Hawai'i, the Southern Cross would move across the sky in a lower and lower arc each night, so that when you hit the latitude of Hawai'i, the distance from the top star to the bottom star would be the same distance from that bottom star to the horizon. These are the sort of details every traditional navigator would have on file.

But when the stars disappear in daylight, the wind, swells, shape of the waves, and the flight of birds are all the more important means for reckoning location. The mental charts to configure these locations also change, so that you can expand your target landfall positions. For example, if you know about the bird movements and wave swells for a given atoll, you can navigate toward that location with a much wider radius than the atoll itself. If you find yourself 20 kilometers (or just over 12 miles) off target but know the noddies travel that far at any given time of day, it is possible to reset the course. Island blocks are also much easier to find than single islands; and for longer voyages, two or more canoes would journey out at a given distance from each other, once again to expand the chance of finding landfall. It is thought that the Polynesian navigators may have measured the time it took to sail between islands in "canoe-days" or a similar type of expression.

Sometimes waves would be the only navigational touchstone for travel at night or in bad weather. Carolinean navigators mastered the art of mapping these waves according to wind directions and depth, especially in swell patterns as they move beyond certain points. Winds are seasonal, of course, so this kind of knowledge involved a certain expertise in calendar cycles and freak weather contingencies. But even within a single voyage winds could change and weather could throw a canoe off course. A canoe blown off course in the darkness of bad weather would nevertheless be able to tell an expert navigator something about its direction by how it moved within the swells, and in which manner it need move to correct a course.

Phosphorescence was another critical factor in reading the seas. Here the term has little to do with surface or subsurface phosphorescence, which sailors see all the time. What these navigators would search for was something called "underwater lightning," meaning long streaks or plaques of light beneath the surface, not unlike vein of ore in a mountainside. Sometimes these were no more than momentary flashes of brilliance, but they nevertheless could indicate directions to a landmass. Such phosphorescence usually radiates away from land, flickering or darting in straight lines. But calculations are complicated by reef systems, which also radiate phosphorescence, but at a slower rate, depending upon their depth. Reefs in general are indications of distance to land by their depth, as the sea changes color — it becomes more green — as you pass over them, even at 20 or more fathoms below. In good weather, short choppy waves will indicate the presence of reef if they are otherwise invisible. The movement of fish (feeding on the reef) will also be an indication.

In the Marshall Islands traditional navigators used stick charts to diagram swells and wave directions, including the breaks in the waves at certain distances off shore. In this way, one could chart a route between two islands by the indications of waves radiating from other islands, reefs, or atolls in between. Indeed, part of the long and arduous task of training to be a navigator in virtually all Pacific islands involved the use of shoreline materials for mapping or diagramming such course — pebbles, sticks, strings, and shells were most commonly used.

In bad weather at night, swells are hidden, and only the most experienced navigators could master a more sophisticated manner of reading the waves beneath their canoe. Sometimes they would lie down in the hull to sense their direction or source.

Color is another important observation. As a sailor moved toward land till below the horizon, he would judge the relative brightness over these "invisible" islands below the horizon. Such brightness can be viewed an average of 15 miles from land. Cumulus clouds provided other clues. Cumulus gathers in tower formations over islands, and heat refraction may even pull it down father to the surface, making an even greater punctuation on the horizon. Clouds also gather over land at different times of day, and different times of year, but whenever they do form, they are relatively impervious to wind or calms. Although normal trade winds are blowing, land clouds may pile up over atolls, as neighboring clouds move on. Slow-moving clouds may be being drawn over land, pulled down by it, so that navigators might be able to read the different speeds of a cloudy sky for the landmasses they respond to below the horizon.

Other methods for expanding landfall targets would involve reading the sun's rays. On a calm and clear day, when the sun is nearly overhead, you can look into the sea and observe that the sun's rays (in reflection) have different lengths. Some are short, some are longer. It is the shorter rays that point toward invisible land. Drift objects could also be read by experienced navigators. Freshly broken branches after a storm, coconuts, seaweed cut adrift from a reef, and old driftwood, are all directional markers in one way or another.

Scholars think that Polynesian voyaging followed the seasonal paths of various sea birds. Many islands have oral traditions about bird flight patterns, and some even include tables for marking flight ranges. There are references to shoreline marks that point to distant islands in triangulation with these flight paths, usually involving noddies, terns, boobies, and frigate birds. One theory is that Pacific navigators may have taken frigate birds with them. Because these birds cannot land on water (their feathers become water-logged and they cannot fly), they would be excellent landfall locaters as voyagers grew close to land. Indeed, they were boomerangs, because where they could not find land, they would return to the boat.

There is little doubt that the Middle Ages saw a great deal of Pacific exploration, especially throughout the eastern half of Oceania. But scholars posit different theories about how frequently and how far this voyaging occurred. For example, there is evidence in Tonga during this period that people travelled annually to Fiji, Samoa, and 'Uvea, but they may never have reached Futuna, and even as they did land in New Caledonia, Vanuatu, the Cook Islands, and Niue, they never established regular round-trip routes.

Furthermore, the fact that Polynesians valued **pigs** and chickens and dogs, but that many islands did not have one or another of them, indicates that voyaging was not that common in many places. But these theories revolve around another factor, and that is climate change, beginning in the 1300s. Before the Little Ice Age was in full swing (from 1400 onward), ocean travel was facilitated by warm temperatures and stable weather patterns. Winds and waves were very predictable from about 1,200 to 650 years ago. This was when most of Polynesia was settled. Westerly winds were frequent and helped nudge voyagers toward the sunset.

These vast open seas became increasingly familiar and less foreboding to Oceanic peoples. Their entire intellectual, technological, and scientific life centered on the skills required to traverse the ocean, to move from island to island in trade, migration, and communication. But with the colder weather and choppier seas, this freedom was suddenly curtailed, and long-distance voyaging very quickly became a thing of the past. Oceania demographics changed as people moved inland and away from the shore in most of the higher islands. Life changed dramatically and never really returned to the earlier period of oceanic exploration. It is possible that many island societies that once developed elaborate navigational systems actually lost them for lack of practice in the meantime. The few that have survived are important glimpses into an era of great intellectual and ecological sophistication.

Further Reading

Finney, B., ed. *Pacific Navigation and Voyaging*. Wellington, New Zealand: Polynesian Society, 1976.

Finney, B. R. *Voyage of Discovery: A Cultural Odyssey through Polynesia*. Berkeley: University of California Press, 1994.

Firth, R. *We, the Tikopia*. Stanford, CA: Stanford University Press, 1983 [1936].

Gladwin, T. *East Is a Big Bird: Navigation and Logic on Puluwat Atoll*. Cambridge, MA: Harvard University Press, 1970.

Howard, A., and R. Borofsky, eds. *Developments in Polynesian Ethnology*. Honolulu: University of Hawai'i Press, 1989.

Kirch, P. V. *On the Road of the Winds: An Archaeological History of the Pacific Islands before European Contact*. Berkeley: University of California Press, 2000.

Kirch, P. V., and R. C. Green. *Hawaiki, Ancestral Polynesia: An Essay in Historical Anthropology*. Cambridge, UK: Cambridge University Press, 2001.

Lewis, D. *We the Navigators, the Ancient Art of Landfinding in the Pacific*. Honolulu: University of Hawai'i Press, 1972.

Lutkehaus, N., ed. *Sepik Heritage: Tradition and Change in Papua New Guinea*. Durham, NC: Carolina Academic Press, 1990.

Makemson, M.W. *The Morning Star Rises: An Account of Polynesian Astronomy*. New Haven, CT: Yale University Press, 1941.

Malinowski, B. *Argonauts of the Western Pacific*. London: Routledge, 1922.

Yed, D. E., and J. M. J. Mummery, eds. *Pacific Production Systems: Approaches to Economic Prehistory*. Canberra: Australian National University, 1990.

Nancy Sullivan

7. GLOBAL TIES

The region called Oceania is a collection of three island groups—**Micronesia**, **Melanesia**, and **Polynesia**—ranging from Indonesia to the west and South America to the East. The global ties that integrated Oceania with the rest of the world during the Middle Ages were strongest to the West, where populations were higher and more settled.

Trade

Trade connections at the Melanesian western end of Oceania were established between the island of New Guinea and its East Indies (Indonesian) neighbors with bird of paradise pelts. This commerce boomed between 1 C.E. and roughly 300 C.E. The skins, and the uniquely long, colorful plumes they boast, were traded throughout Asia well before they ever made their way to Europe (where they arrived in the sixteenth century, but became the height of millinery fashion during the nineteenth century). Their movement through Asia led to the treasuries of sultans and kings, and most notably to the headdress of the King of Nepal, which, to this day, still bears multiple arched plumes of the Greater Bird of Paradise. The best account of this trade and its history through to the twentieth century comes from Pamela Swadling's 1996 *Plumes from Paradise*, which traces the exact trade routes and the commodities that traveled them from New Guinea to the rest of the world.

Swadling tells us that the first cycle of this plume trade between western Melanesia and Asia lasted from roughly 0 to 300 C.E. She maps the extent of this trade along the circulation of other luxury goods of the era, particularly bronze kettledrums that would have come from China, and which would have been exchanged for plumes. These have been found in eastern Indonesia and into New Guinea. Iron was not produced in New Guinea and could only have come from China and Vietnam, through Java and the Sunda chain. These trade networks are distinct from the much earlier **lapita** pottery distribution that accompanied Asian migrations throughout Melanesia from 5,000 to 3,000 years ago.

By the advent of the Middle Ages, however, Timor and the Spice Islands (the Moluccas) had been catapulted to the fore of regional trade dominance for their nutmeg, mace, and cloves. Nutmeg was a highly prized spice in medieval cuisine (and in the sixteenth-century times it was believed to ward off the plague). Trade was conducted by Indian Ocean Arabs, who moved it to the Middle East, where it was traded on to Europe. It became such a coveted commodity that the Portuguese were impelled to Oceania during the fifteenth-century European age of maritime exploration in the pursuit of it. They cornered the trade under the Treaty of Tordesillas with Spain and a separate treaty with the sultan of Ternate. But the authority Ternate held over the nutmeg-growing center of the Moluccan Banda Islands was limited, and so the Portuguese failed to gain a foothold in the islands themselves. This allowed the Dutch to eventually gain an edge in the trade by establishing military control over the Banda Islands (with a massacre and forced expulsion of island inhabitants in 1621). Archeologists found cloves within a ceramic vessel in Syria along with evidence dating the find to within a few years of 1721 B.C.E.

By 1500, Molucca had become the most important trade hub in Southeast Asia. Chinese, Indian, Malay, Javanese and other traders came to exchange goods there. Javanese traders supplied most of the cloves and nutmegs from the Spice Islands, and sandalwood from Timor, traveling through the Sunda Islands to the Moluccas. Chinese traders were active in the Talaud Islands, Sulawesi, and the Spice Islands during the thirteenth and fourteenth centuries, and by the fifteenth century they had reached the coast of New Guinea and were trading from the Bird's Head area at Onin and possibly with the Waropen people.

Spices

As the demand for spices grew, there must have been traders from Southeast Asia who surmised that the conditions for cloves and nutmeg in the Moluccas might also exist along the coastline of New Guinea. Pamela Swadling says some evidence to support this comes from the presence of pedestal pottery bowls compatible with those found in Philippine archaeological sites and dating from 500 C.E. found in the Collingwood Bay area of the eastern coast of New Guinea. Megaliths erected during this period in the Trobriand Islands off the eastern coast of New Guinea were also similar to Southeast Asian megaliths of the period, further suggesting that Asian traders had begun plying the coastlines—searching for spices? But by the end of the Middle Ages these ties had diminished considerably, and Melanesia, at the western end of Oceania, had become considerably more remote than before. Once part of an extensive trade network leading east, by the fifteenth century western Melanesia was cut off from the Asian markets. Instead, it generated elaborate internal trade networks.

In addition to archaeological records, the oral traditions of New Guinea contain evidence of Medieval Indonesian trade. Although oral histories cannot really be pegged to a linear timeline, there are plenty of stories in the Trans Fly area of New Guinea of Asian traders well before the Europeans arrived in the sixteenth century. Some are attached to sacred sites, or resources that would have been trade items, like the gum-producing damar tree (that locals burn to produce light). There are also stories of trade routes that inscribe the known boundaries of the Sultan of Tidore during this time. In the Morehead area east of the Fly River, however, the early foreigners were said to be Dutch (Wagner) — a very real possibility, considering the Dutch had usurped Portuguese trade with the Sultan of Tidore by the seventeenth century.

Borrowed words and cognates from Malay language are found throughout the Trans Fly area, and they tell their own stories, especially when they refer to natural resources items or of trade. But close readings of Papua myths lead to even more intriguing suggestions. Certain myth structures in the Trans Fly not only resemble Indonesian (East Indies) myths but point to origins as far away as Mesopotamia. These neither Christian nor Islamic storylines may have traveled up the Fly River to the interior of New Guinea, where the Mountain Ok people have a myth cycle that also bears resemblances.

One of the hubs in the long chain of a spice trade was in the southern Philippines. Cloves from the Moluccas traveled through the Philippines to South China, Indochina and south again along the coast to the Strait of Malacca. From there the cloves went to Indian spice markets and points further west. This Philippine–Moluccas route persisted into Muslim times and is chronicled in Arabic writings (allowing it to be recognized as part of world heritage by UNESCO).

The Philippines are the northern neighbors of Micronesia, an archipelago of islands stretching nearly 2,000 miles, whose original inhabitants are said to have come from the Philippines more than 3,000 years ago. In 1521, Magellan made landfall in the Marianas Islands, and in 1565, Spain laid claim to the Marianas group.

The Filipino sailing merchants who made first contact with Spaniards were said to be already engaged in long-range trade with Asia. Filipino island kingdoms ranged as far West as the Maldives on the southwest coast of India and as far north as Japan. But the evidence is inconclusive on whether or not they were trading with the Micronesian islands during the Middle Ages. Western Micronesia is one the only area in Oceania that had rice crops at European contact; the islanders also chewed **betel** nut and fermented coconut into wine, in the Filipino fashion.

Merchants and ambassadors from surrounding areas came to pay tribute to the Filipino King of Cebu before the Spanish arrived. Magellan's crew records that while they were paying tribute to the King, a representative from Siam was also there to see him (De Morga). The Spanish conquistador Legazpi wrote how merchants from Luzon and Mindoro had come to Cebu for trade, and that Chinese merchants regularly came to the north for the same purpose (López de Legazpi 1564–1572). Legazpi arrived in the Marianas in 1565 and conquered the Chamorro people before traveling on to Cebu. Thus, like Western Melanesia, Micronesia's islands bordered important and highly trafficked trade routes. It would be logical to imagine traders also traveled through Micronesia and Melanesia during this era. But because of a lack of spices, and a lull in the plume trade, these European contacts were impermanent for the time being. And as a result, there are no written records of the commerce that may have taken place.

Polynesian colonists spread quickly over the entirety of Polynesia in the period 1300 B.C.E. to 1100 C.E. They came from Fiji-Samoa-Tonga, at the western end of Polynesia, and farther east, the Marquesas; and they travelled in huge double-hulled canoes with all the requisite supplies for colonization: stone tools, animals (**pigs**, chickens, and dogs) and the seeds of their **food** crops. These plants included coconut, **yam, taro**, banana, **breadfruit**, and sweet potato. All the domesticated plants and animals were of Southeast Asian origin with one notable exception: the sweet potato, *Ipomoea batatas*. It is the sweet potato that provides an historical link with the regions eastern neighbors, South America, during the Middle Ages. It is said that the sweet potatoes first arrived in Polynesia from South America somewhere between 300 and 700 C.E.

Sweet potatoes originated in the Andes Mountains of Peru and Colombia. Peruvians call the sweet potato *kumar*, while Easter Islanders, for example, call it *kumara*. But it is said that the sweet potato arrived first in the Marquesas, not Easter Island, sometime after the Marquesas were settled around 300 C.E. It may have been possible for Polynesian traders to cross the 4,000 km (2,485 miles) distance to Peru against prevailing head winds, and return home safely. They would need to have carried trade goods to barter for the sweet potato, and to cart this commodity in one direction and sweet potatoes back to the Marquesas. Another possibility would be that Chinese traders moved between the Marquesas and South America during the fifteenth century, transporting sweet potato along with other goods.

Recently the archaeological record has provided an even earlier link between Polynesia and South America. Chicken bones have been excavated in a Chilean site that have been carbon dated to a century before European conquest, somewhere in the fourteenth century. In addition, a DNA test run on the bones revealed that they are not European chickens anyway but have come from a root stock in the Pacific Islands, no doubt traded to Chile through Easter Island.

Domestic chickens are said to derive from wild fowl somewhere on the Indian subcontinent. But it is also assumed that the people who migrated from Asia across the Bering Strait and into the Americas did not bring chickens with them. Yet in 1532 the Spanish conquistador Francisco Pizarro reported on his arrival in Peru that the local Inca were using chickens as part of their religious ceremonies. It had been thought that chickens arrived later, through European shipping routes. But the bones from the archaeological site at El Arenal in the Arauco region of Chile date from between 1321 and 1407, a good century before the Portuguese landed in Brazil. Without a European connection, it must be assumed the chicken came from Asia across the Pacific and finally to South America. Along with the sweet potato and the bottle gourd, the chicken bones now establish a Medieval connection between Polynesia and South America.

Further Reading

Kirch, Patrick Vinton. *On the Road of the Winds: An Archaeological History of the Pacific Islands before European Contact*. Berkeley: University of California Press, 2000.

Laba, Billai. "Oral Traditions About Early Trade by Indonesians in Southwest Papua New Guinea." In Pamela Swadling, ed., *Plumes from Paradise*. Port Moresby: Papua New Guinea National Museum and Robert Brown & Associates Pty Ltd., 1996, pp. 299–307.

Swadling, Pamela. *Plumes from Paradise*. Port Moresby: Papua New Guinea National Museum and Robert Brown & Associates Pty Ltd., 1996.

Wagner, Roy. "Mysteries of Origin: Early Traders and Heroes in the Trans Fly." In Pamela Swadling, ed., *Plumes from Paradise*. Port Moresby: Papua New Guinea National Museum and Robert Brown & Associates Pty Ltd., 1996, pp. 285–298.

Nancy Sullivan

Short Entries: People, Ideas, Events, and Terms

Agriculture

Most Oceanic peoples grew their own food, except the Indigenous Australians, who were primarily **food** gatherers and not cultivators. Archaeological evidence shows that thousands of years ago the islanders brought their food plants and their horticulture techniques with them as they settled across the Pacific Basin. Some food plants, of course, were native to the islands, but in most cases, they were introduced by human settlement. The various island environments and quality of their soils produced a wide variety of different farming techniques. The scarcity of soil on a small coral **atoll**, for example, created agriculture problems not usually encountered on the lush, green mountains of the large volcanic islands, and as a result, residents on atolls experienced much more difficulty in farming than their large-island neighbors. Traditionally, all islanders spent most of their days' activities in tending their gardens—even the highest of chiefs. Their basic food crops, of course, determined the way in which they farmed their lands. Basically, these food plants were certain trees (coconut and sago palms, **breadfruit**, pandanus, and bananas) and root crops (**taro**, **yams**, sweet potatoes, arrowroot, *pueraria*, and tumeric).

Tree cultivation generally took the least amount of time and energy. Coconut palms were self-propagating and were easily started by placing a fallen nut in a new location, where it would grow, and within 5 to 8 years, it would start producing mature nuts. Palms, of course, produced trunks for timber and wooden objects, and their leaves were used for various woven baskets, roofs, and protective clothing. The actual nuts provided "milk" (clear water inside), shells for bowls and cups, and "meat" for food—either by eating it raw or by squeezing the "cream" out and mixing it with other foods for baking. In some places in **Micronesia** and New Guinea, the islanders collected sap from coconut blossoms and then drank it fresh or fermented it into a "toddy." The trunk of the sago palm provided a starchy substance, which could be dried and cooked similar to a pancake, and it had the added advantage of being able to be stored for months. The ever-producing breadfruit (especially in Micronesia and **Polynesia**) yielded a starchy fruit that was cooked, peeled, and eaten like a potato, or pounded out like Hawaiian poi. The fruit of the pandanus (resembling a pineapple) was less used, but its fruit could be stored and eaten during times of famine. Bananas (the cooking variety) provided a sweet supplement to any meal. In all cases, once these food-producing trees had been established, they required little or no cultivation. A few coconut trees and a couple bread-fruit trees around one's property could provide food throughout the entire year, supplemented, of course, by protein from fish, **pigs**, or fowl.

On the other hand, root-crop production took most of the islanders' time. In some areas, land was cleared either by cutting (with stone adzes) or by fire, and then the soil was tilled to accept the new cuttings of the various root crops. There is no indication that islanders used any form of fertilizer, although some groups in the New Guinea Highlands used composting of grass cuttings in their gardens. Cuttings from the newly harvested root crops provided starts for the new plants. Holes were made in the ground with digging sticks, and the cuttings placed in them at various depths. Sometimes yam cuttings were planted in small mounds, which had been made to aid their drainage. Nor-mally, tall sticks were inserted close by so that the new plants had poles on which to vine. For the next several months, the islanders would tend their crops by weeding and sometimes performing magic spells, which they thought would bring them a fruitful harvest. Irrigation ditches were often constructed for proper water balance, and in Hawai'i, a massive stone aqueduct (24 feet high in some places) was constructed on Kaua'i to bring water from its wind-ward side to the drier side of the island.

Land tenure varied from one island group to another. But in most cases, an extended family lived on a plot of land, collectively owned by its particular social unit, and one that provided for its subsistence needs. Traditional cus-toms also influenced whether a certain crop was cultivated entirely by men (dry taro, for example) or by **women** (wet taro), whether the sexes ate together or separately, or what foods might be taboo to one or the other. Agricultural terms dominated the calendar, and certain names of the month indicated what particular agricultural task was to be performed that month. Mythologies ex-plained the origin of each food plant and how it was first "captured" from the gods by some remote and marvelous ancestor who brought it to earth for the benefit of humans. *See also* **Gods and Goddesses**.

Further Reading

Barrau, Jacques. *Subsistence Agriculture in Melanesia*. Honolulu, HI: Bernice P. Bishop Museum Press, 1958.

Barrau, Jacques. *Subsistence Agriculture in Polynesia and Micronesia*. Honolulu, HI: Ber-nice P. Bishop Museum Press, 1961.

Craig, Robert D. *Polynesian Mythology*. Santa Barbara, CA: ABC-CLIO Press, 2004, pp. 66–69, 88–90, 203–207.

Oliver, Douglas L. *Oceania: The Native Cultures of Australia and the Pacific Islands*. 2 vols. Honolulu: University of Hawai'i Press, 1989, pp. 185–217.

Robert D. Craig

Atolls

Thousands of various sized islands are scattered throughout the Pacific Ocean. Some are large enough to be called "continental islands" (New Zealand, New Caledonia, and New Guinea, for example), whereas others are smaller and tall and are called "volcanic islands" like Hawai'i and the Marquesas because they were anciently formed from volcanoes that pushed up from the ocean floor.

"Atolls," on the other hand, are coral remnants of large mountains or volcanoes that slowly sank beneath the surface of the ocean. As the land-mass disappeared, coral grew around its edge to form a circular, low-lying reef around a shallow lagoon where the mountain once stood. Although the term *atoll* has been used in the English language since the seventeenth century, it was Charles Darwin (1809–1882) who popularized the term in 1842 after his 5-year research trip aboard the HMS *Beagle*. The definition has been modified only slight since then.

Most of the world's atolls are found in the warm waters of the Pacific, primarily in the Polynesian island groups of the Tuamotu Islands, Tuvalu, Kiribati, and Tokelau (*see* **Polynesia**) and in the Micronesian island groups of the Caroline Islands, the Marshall Islands, and the Coral Sea Islands. The largest atoll in the Pacific, however, is Landsdowne Bank, located just west of New Caledonia (**Melanesia**) and stretches over 811 square miles.

For the ancient Pacific islanders, atoll living created challenges not faced by larger, mountainous island communities. Their landmass was much smaller, and its resources could not support a large population. Often water was

A string of atolls located in the Indian Ocean. © Hbbolten/Dreamstime.com.

unavailable and, for that reason, most of the Pacific atolls were uninhabited. Some may have provided enough water to sustain short visits by voyaging fishermen, who used the island on overnight fishing trips, or by a limited number of people who sustained themselves with a scant growth of vegetables and fruits, despite the fact that the lagoons often were teeming with rich marine life. In ages past, these small atoll societies were faced with overpopulation, and they had to wrestle with the decision to emigrate or to limit population (often through infanticide). They utilized every natural resource available and surprisingly from these created some of the most intricate and visual-stunning arts and crafts.

Limited resources on atolls sometimes pressed the islanders to specialize in the production of one commodity that could be traded throughout the area for others. In **Micronesia**, for example, this created a limited type of overseas trade and exchange in finely woven mats, shell ornaments, and certain types of dye and the use of a type of money (various sizes of stone discs) not found in other Pacific Island groups. (*See also* **Agriculture**.)

Further Reading

Dobbs, David. *Reef Madness: Charles Darwin, Alexander Agassiz, and the Meaning of Coral.* New York: Pantheon, 2005.

Kay. E. A. *Little Worlds of the Pacific: An Essay on Pacific Basin Biogeography.* Honolulu: University of Hawai'i Press, 1980.

Robert D. Craig

Betel

The custom of betel chewing in Oceania spread anciently from south Asia to western Oceania—the Melanesian islands, New Guinea, and the westernmost islands of **Micronesia**—Yap, Palau, and the Marianas. It was not found among the Polynesians or the Australian aboriginals. Betel chewing consists of mixing a husked betel nut from the *Areca catechu* palm with a pinch of lime, and then the concoction is wrapped in a betel leaf (*Piper betel* vine) and placed far back in the mouth, where it releases its chemicals to produce a sense of well-being, good humor, and relaxation, while at the same time appeasing hunger and lessening one's appetite.

The saliva produced by the betel mixture is a bright, brick red, and chewers normally discharge it frequently rather than swallowing it. If drooled on one's clothes, the spewed-out saliva produces a nasty stain. Excessive use causes the teeth to be stained permanently red and then to turn black. Betel chewing never attained the formal status that **kava** drinking did in parts of **Melanesia** and **Polynesia**. But it did play, and continues to play, an important social role private and public gatherings throughout Melanesia, where bringing a "hand" or bunch of betel nuts everything from goodwill, like a bottle of wine or a fruitcake to the party, to gravely serious exchange in compensation and reconciliation events. The custom continues in many of the islands.

Further Reading

Chowning, A. *An Introduction to the Peoples and Cultures of Melanesia*. Menlo Park, CA: Cummings Publishing, 1979.

Lum, J. K. "Central and Eastern Micronesia: Genetics, The Overnight Voyage, and Linguistic Divergence." *Man and Culture in Oceania* 14 (1998): 69–80.

Nancy Sullivan

Bigman (Melanesia)

"Bigman" in **Melanesia** is a position of leadership, not a physical description. The classic bigman is a central highlander of New Guinea, a man whose force of personality rather than his birthright has made him a "first among equals" for his clan and/or tribe. The highlanders of New Guinea may have had inherited systems of wealth in the past, but by the Middle Ages, their world had been transformed by the arrival of the sweet potato. Easier to plant than **taro**, the sweet potato suddenly made everyone wealthy and turned the have-nots into major players as surplus wealth created news systems of exchange.

To become a clan leader one now had to campaign to "produce" a major exchange event by which, at least in the Western Highlands, great public generosity could bring even greater returns. What wealth you gave out would obligate a return with profit. Thus, if you gave three **pigs** out, you could expect five pigs in return. Those individuals who could persuade clansmen to back them in these public wealth displays were entrepreneurs of sorts, and by their own powers of persuasion could transform themselves into wealthy and influential leaders, despite their circumstances at birth. Thus anthropologists have referred to them as "bigmen," and in some cases "great men," rather than **chiefs**.

Further Reading

Brown, P. *Highland Peoples of New Guinea.* Cambridge, UK: Cambridge University Press, 1978.

Chowning, A. *An Introduction to the Peoples and Cultures of Melanesia.* Menlo Park, CA: Cummings Publishing, 1979.

Feil, D. K. *The Evolution of Highland Papua New Guinea Societies.* Cambridge, UK: Cambridge University Press, 1987.

Marcus, G. "Chieftainship." In A. Howard and R. Borofsky, eds., *Developments in Polynesian Ethnology.* Honolulu: University of Hawai'i Press, 1989, pp. 175–210.

Sahlins, M. "Poor Man, Rich Man, Big Man, Chief: Political Types in Melanesia and Polynesia." *Comparative Studies in Society and History* 5 (1963): 285–303.

Strathern, A. J. *Rope of Moka: Big-Men and Ceremonial Exchange in Mount Hagen, New Guinea.* Cambridge, UK: Cambridge University Press, 1971.

Strathern, Andrew. *One Father, One Blood: Descent and Group Structure Among the Melpa People.* London: Tavistock, 1972.

Sullivan, N. *Papua New Guinea, with Trans Niugini Tours* [handbook]. Mt. Hagen, New Guinea: Trans New Guinea Tours, 1994.

Nancy Sullivan

Breadfruit

The tall breadfruit tree (*Artocarpus incisa* or *Artocarpus altilis*) provided the staff of life for Pacific islanders, especially those living in **Polynesia** and **Micronesia**. It was less known in **Melanesia** and Australia. Breadfruit spread eastward across the Pacific as the early peoples pushed out from Southeast Asia with their various tarts of plant foods to help them get established in their new homes. As a result of this eastward expansion, breadfruit spread throughout the region, but surprisingly not as far as Easter Island. It grew abundantly in the tropical islands and **atolls** (sparsely in New Zealand, however), and provided a year-round **food** source for the islanders. Breadfruit trees grow in a wide range of environments, they require very little care, and they begin to bear fruit in 3 to 5 years. They provided a substantial carbohydrate supplement (about 75 percent) to the often meager diets of Pacific islanders. They were also a good source of minerals and vitamins.

A mature tree often reaches 100 feet in height and produces round or cylindrical-sized fruit ranging in diameter from 4 to 12 inches. Islanders would grow several trees around their dwellings to provide not only food for their families but also shade from the tropical sun and wood for implements and clothing. For food, they merely had to cut the ripened fruit off the trees and cook it for their daily meal. In its natural state, it could be roasted over an open fire, peeled with a sharpened instrument like a cowry shell, and then eaten very much like a baked potato. A more popular

A breadfruit tree. © Begreen/Dreamstime.com.

method of preparation was roasting it in an underground oven with other plant, animal, or marine foods, after which it could then be eaten or mashed and mixed with other foods or ingredients.

Some islanders enjoyed fermented breadfruit. In this case, the breadfruit (cooked or uncooked) was left in underground pits for days, or even weeks, depending upon the desired taste. In Samoa, for example, there is evidence that *"masi"* was stored for several years! Other islanders peeled the raw breadfruit, wrapped it in various leaves, and then left it to ferment out in the open, while some placed it on coastal rocks where it could be covered by the salty waters of the ocean during high tide. Others processed the mashed "paste," rolled it out into thin sheets, dried it, and then wrapped it in pandanus leaves for long-term storage. All in all, it was a valuable source of food.

The fruit gained European fame in the late eighteenth century as a result of the famous story of the mutiny on the *Bounty*. The British government commissioned Lieutenant William Bligh to set sail for Tahiti to obtain starts of the breadfruit tree to be transported to the West Indies where they thought the local slaves would eat it as a staple of life, like it was in the Pacific. After spending months in the islands collecting the starts and then setting sail, Bligh's men mutinied and threw the starts overboard. Bligh made it back to England, however, where he again (1791) was sent out to gather additional starts. This trip was successful, and breadfruit was introduced to the West Indies. Ironically, however, the slaves there did not like the food and refused to eat it!

Further Reading

Alexander, Caroline. *The* Bounty: *The True Story of the Mutiny on the* Bounty. New York: Penguin Books, 2004.

Morton, Julia F. *Fruits of Warm Climates*. Miami, FL: Julia F. Morton, 1987, pp. 50–58.

Zerega, Nyree J.C. "The Breadfruit Trail: The Wild Ancestors of a Staple Food Illuminate Human Migrations in the Pacific islands." *Natural History* (December 2003): pp. 46–51. Available at http://www.findarticles.com/p/articles/mi_m1134/is_10_112/ai_111736244.

Robert D. Craig

Chiefs

Governance of any social group depends a great deal upon custom and culture. The same can be said of Oceanic peoples before the arrival of Westerners in modern times. When European explorers first visited Pacific peoples, they could only describe what they saw in terms of their own Western vocabularies. They often called leaders of significant power "kings" and those governing smaller areas "chiefs," and very often these designated terms continued into colonial times when Western powers molded Pacific islands into states and nations that fit their particular perceptions.

Prior to modern times, Polynesian rulers belonged to an aristocratic class called the *ali'i, aliki, ari'i, ariki,* or *'eiki.* They claimed the right to rule through genealogical descent from an important ancestor or from the gods. A similar allegation was made by Japanese emperors who, during this same period, claimed descent from the powerful sun goddess and were regarded divine by their subjects. Comparisons are also made to European rulers who, in the early modern period, claimed they ruled by "divine right." But the Japanese and European rulers had forces that restrained their absolute powers. Medieval Japanese emperors were figureheads whose governments were actually controlled by their shogun rulers and their feudal samurai. European rulers were restrained by their Christian beliefs, parliaments, and other feudal lords. Polynesian *ali'i*, however, were undeterred. They held absolute power. The highest ranking Hawaiian *ali'i* chiefs intermarried with their sisters to provide an even more sacred legacy. Their children had to be carried about on the shoulders of servants lest all the ground they touched reverted to them. Likewise, in Tahiti, *ali'i* names became so sacred, that similar words in the language had to be purged from use while the rulers were alive. In Tonga, lower ranking chiefs and commoners alike stripped down to their waists or prostrated themselves when the Tu'i Tonga (king of Tonga) approached. There was even a special form of speech that had to be spoken in his presence (*see* **Tongan Empire**).

The Head of a Chief of New Zealand, 1773. Plate XVI from *A Journal of a Voyage to the South Seas, in His Majesty's Ship, the Endeavour* by Sydney Parkinson (London, 1773). HIP/Art Resource, NY .

Although descent through the male line was the general rule, sometimes the first-born daughters claimed powers of their own. In New Zealand, for example, the *Tapiru* (first-born daughter of a high chief) assumed the duties of high priestess, a position not open to other **women**. No one could even eat in her presence. Sometimes women could rule, like Salsmasina, the 15th century Samoan Queen. A similar tradition continued in Tonga into modern times (eighteenth century), when Princess Sinaitakala outranked her younger brother, and she ruled jointly with him. Even her children by a Fijian chief were considered of higher rank than the Tu'i Tonga, but they did not rule.

Although genealogical descent was important among most of the Polynesian ruling classes, another power sometimes allowed a junior line to gain ascendancy. It was that "spiritual" power called *mana*—a powerful force normally inherited through descent, but one that could be obtained by accomplishing something outstanding during one's lifetime. In Hawai'i, for example, Chief Kamehameha (1758–1819) gained a formidable reputation through his military tactics. When the ruler of the island of Hawai'i died and his authority passed to his legitimate heir, Kamehameha declared war, usurped his authority, and became the ruling high chief. He continued his conquests for the next 20 years until the whole island chain recognized him as ruler and he was crowned Hawai'i's first "king." But, surprisingly, Kamehameha was outranked by his favorite wife Ka'ahumanu. It is said that when he entered her hut, he had to crawl on his hands and knees for she outranked even him.

Samoan chiefs, on the other hand, were generally more egalitarian because, in some cases, they had gained their titles (*matai*) through means other than inheritance—commoners could on, occasion, gain *matai* status or a title could be held by two different people at the same time. The village council (*fono*) also had its individual and self-perpetuating administration (electing their own membership) and they could oppose pressures from an outside, high-ranking ruler.

A different custom arose among some groups in **Melanesia**. These communities were dominated by what anthropologists have come to call a "**bigman.**" They rose in power and prestige not by hereditary or genealogical rights of succession but by a series of events that elevated them above all the lesser men in the community. In Bougainville, for example, village elders of the Siuai peoples usually decided most of their important matters. Sometimes, however, these communities were "ruled" by men known as *mumi* ("bigman"), whose influences (*potu*) often extended beyond their own villages. They gained this influence not by inheritance or by conquest but by giving lavish feasts one after another until they eventually outstripped the prestige of their rival *mumi*. A bigman would have started out gradually, spending liberally, impressing friends and family, and then spending more on the entire community. Through this process, he would become the most respected man in the village. A typical bigman would own his own male clubhouse, and after having renovated it (if inherited), would refurbish it with new drums, slit gongs, and protective gods (*see* **Gods and Goddesses**). All the while, of course, he offered lavish feasts to all those who worked on its restoration.

Once being recognized the dominant *mumi* in his village, a bigman could then extend his fame by competing with *mumi* from other communities. If he chose, he would lavish gifts of **pigs** and **shell valuables** to his rival, and the competition would begin. If his rival could not reciprocate with a greater feast, the rival was "defeated." If the reciprocal feast was of equal value, then a balance was acknowledged, and the two became equals. The whole competition, of course, depended upon the resources and ingenuity of the *mumi*. He often had to rely upon friends and family for "loans" until the competitive process had ended. The end result, of course, was the attainment of some political authority over those who respected and admired him. But once he had lost to a rival *mumi* or when he had grown too old, he lost his political influence and returned once more being an equal among his village kinsmen. No enduring political structure or ruling dynasty survived his rule.

Further Reading

Goldman, Irving. *Ancient Polynesian Society*. Chicago: University of Chicago Press, 1970.

Oliver, Douglas L. *Native Cultures of the Pacific Islands*. Honolulu: University of Hawai'i Press, 1989, pp. 81–83.

Sahlins, Marshall D. "Poor Man, Rich Man, Big-Man, Chief: Political Types in Melanesia and Polynesia." *Comparative Studies in Society and History*, 5, no. 3 (April 1963): 285–303.

Robert D. Craig

Dance

Dance in Oceania during the Middle Ages provided an important emotional and spiritual outlet for performers as they moved their bodies to various types of music during their religious and public celebrations. Most humans feel a need to move their bodies as they hear the beat and sound of musical voices or

musical instruments, and it was the same with the original inhabitants of Australia, **Melanesia, Micronesia**, and **Polynesia**. The exact nature of such dancing in Oceania, however, varied from the spectacular display of body art and costumes and less emphasis on precise dance steps as experienced in Melanesia to the exact, complex, and rehearsed drama found among the Polynesians and to a lesser extent the Micronesians.

Australian and Melanesian dances consisted primarily of impersonation — the imitation of animals or spiritual beings rather than relying on the words being chanted or sung by a group or director. The dancers often assumed a nonhuman status by lavishly decorating their bodies and donning elaborate costumes and masks that would impress the spectators (especially in Melanesia). Such heavy decoration made precise movements of the body difficult, and hands and upper body were primarily used to steady the costumes. As a result, dances were less exact, usually individual and personal, and very seldom rehearsed. The legs, feet, and swaying torsos, therefore, were the most important elements of the dance. Performers would move to the accompaniment of objects being beaten on the ground (sticks and bamboo, for example) or to a variety of drums, slit gongs, and flutes. Dance steps and movements had little to do with the musical accompaniment, except to keep in time with the rhythm. During important celebrations such as fertility, head-hunting, or funeral rites, the whole community would often join the dancers, but even then, the purpose was to present a vast moving body that would impress the gods and their human audiences, not to show how well they danced.

Polynesian dancing, on the other hand, was a visual extension of sung poetry (chanting), using complex hands, arms, hips, and leg movements either in a standing or sitting position and performed by men and women. Dances were usually performed by a group in unison and facing an audience. Despite the attempts of early Christian missionaries to eradicate traditional dancing, it did survive, but just barely, and during the last 30 years, there has been a remarkable resurgence in the performance of traditional dancing. This type of dancing was based upon poetry (stories being sung or chanted) and acted out by the dancers' use of their arms and hands during which their lower bodies kept time and the shoulders and back were unmoving, upright, and straight. All dances were choreographed in advance — there was little or no improvisation (although certain exceptions can be cited).

Costuming was important, but it was negligible and usually secondary to the movements of the dancers. Men usually wore only a loincloth while the **women** wore a variety of clothing, ranging from very little or nothing to yards of traditional **tapa** (bark cloth) wound about them. Almost all wore festive feathers, colorful flower leis, and wood ferns around their heads, arms, and legs.

Each island group — Hawai'i, Tahiti, New Zealand, Samoa, Tonga, for example — had particular characteristics that set one apart from another. Western Polynesian dancing (Samoa and Tonga) was characterized by the rhythmic pulsating of the legs and lower body and hand clapping, whereas Eastern Polynesia (Tahiti and Hawai'i) was characterized by the swaying of hips and the varied movements of the hands, wrists, and arms.

Searches on the Internet and especially at "Youtube.com" reveal a wide variety of videos of Pacific island dances. Some, of course, are modern interpretations done primarily for the benefit of the tourists who visit the islands. Keywords for traditional dances may include "*Hula Kahiko Kane*" (male dance, Hawai'i) and "*Kahiko kaahumanu*" (female dance, dedicated to Princess

Ka'ahumanu, Hawai'i), "Siva Sāmoa traditional" (Samoan dancing), "Tonga traditional dance" (Tongan dancing), "Otea Polynesia" (Tahitian dance, the *'ōtea*),
and "Traditional Māori dance" (New Zealand Māori dance). Searches could
also be done for Melanesian, Micronesian, or Australian (Aboriginal) dances.
See also **Gods and Goddesses**, **Tattoo**, and Document 9.

Further Reading

Kaeppler, Adrienne L. *Poetry in Motion: Studies of Tongan Dance.* Vava'u, Tonga: Vava'u
Press, 1993, pp. 1–18.
Kaeppler, Adrienne L. *Polynesian Dance: With a Selection for Contemporary Performances.*
Honolulu, HI: Alpha Delta Kappa, 1983.
Moulin, Jane Freeman. *The Dance of Tahiti.* Pape'ete:Tahiti Christian Gleizal/Les Edi-
tions du Pacifique, 1979.
Moyle, Alice Marshall, ed. *Music and Dance of Aboriginal Australia and the South Pacific:
The Effects of Documentation on the Living Tradition.* Sydney: University of Sydney,
1992.

Robert D. Craig

Dress

The warm and humid climate experienced by Oceanic peoples did not encourage their wearing of elaborate everyday clothing. In fact, many of them
went totally nude while the rest wore
as little as decorum would allow. When
Western explorers first visited the Pacific islanders and indigenous Australians, most of them recorded that the
people wore little or nothing at all. In
the hot climate of northern Australia,
for example, men and **women** worked
throughout the day without clothing,
but perhaps wearing only a few
stringed armlets or necklaces. Explorers who visited the other areas of Oceania — **Micronesia**, **Melanesia**, and
Polynesia — also recorded on various
occasions that men and women were
"totally nude." (What Europeans called
nude in the eighteenth century, however, may not be exactly the same
meaning as it is in our twenty-first century, but complete nudity in the area
was possibly more common than has
generally been assumed.)

Costumes of Oceania from A. Racinet, *Historical Costumes*, Vol. 2, Paris, 1888. The Art Archive/Musée des Arts
Décoratifs Paris/Alfredo Dagli Orti.

Not all Oceanic peoples went totally
nude, however. It appears that in many
island groups at least a simple loincloth
for men or perhaps a short skirt for
women was the normal practice for everyday use. This type of clothing is

mentioned frequently in the ancient tales and legends that have survived into historic times (nineteenth century). Traditional loincloths were made from **tapa**, which, had been made by beating the inner barks of certain tress (the mulberry, hibiscus, and the **breadfruit**) into lengthy strips. A loincloth, for example, was a rectangular piece of tapa measuring about 1 foot wide by 3 to 4 yards in length. It was wrapped around the waist, down the back, up the front covering the genitals, and then tied-off in front (depending on direction of wrap). Any excess material could be formed so that it hung down in front and back very much like an apron, and the sides were generally open. (The traditional Japanese *fundoshi* is very similar to the loincloths worn in the Pacific.)

Women usually wore some type of pliable, woven mat tied around the waist and extending to various lengths. In the Marshall Islands (Micronesia), for example, women wore square mats woven from strips of the pandanus or coconut tress and decorated with various borders associated with their social rank. In Samoa and Tonga, women wore ti leaf skirts "sewn" together or finely woven mats that extended from the waist down below the knee and tied around the waist with a string or type of girdle. Tongan men as well wore similar types of mats over their loincloths (the working garment) when showing respect or in the presence of members of the upper class. Remnants of this type continue today in the form of the lava-lava worn in many of the Polynesian islands or the *sulu* in Fiji.

In New Zealand and Hawai'i, where people experienced colder weather, warmer clothing had to be worn. Unlike the other Polynesians, the Māori made their common skirts from flax rather than tapa, and they were worn by both sexes. Hawaiians and Māori also fashioned elaborate cloaks that were worn in colder weather. Some of these were highly decorated and used only for ceremonial occasions. Simple cloaks were made of coarse fibers, tied around the neck, and rainproof. Longer ones were fastened at the shoulder with some sort of pin made of bone or wood. Ceremonial cloaks used by the high chiefs of Hawaiian were made from a woven base upon which intricate and colorful designs were created from various feathers, which had been plucked from native birds.

A unique form of "clothing" worn by several groups in western New Guinea was the male penis sheath (the *koteka* or *horim*). It was the ultimate in minimal clothing, because no other attire was worn. It consisted of a gourd that had been grown and shaped by various means into the form of a man's genitals. It was dried and hollowed-out and then cords attached to it so that it could cover one's private parts. It could be worn pointed straight up, out, or at various angles, depending upon the wearer's preference and customs. The size, color, and decoration (painted or adorned with shells and feathers) could also differ from one cultural group to another.

Although everyday clothing was minimal and plain, the reverse was true of the highly decorated dress worn on ceremonial or special occasions. During those times, everyone would put on their best attire and add whatever colorful ornaments they could. The Hawaiian high **chiefs** and chiefesses would sport their colorful colored cloaks and headdresses. Others would wrap yards and yards of decorative tapa cloth around them, and then add intricately woven gorgets around their necks and heads. Darker-skinned Melanesians and Australians would add colored paints to their bodies to dramatize the particular occasion. They would carry their colorful shields and carved masks, add enormous necklaces and arm bracelets, and don whatever else that might give enjoyment and dignity to the event. *See also* **Tattoo**.

Further Reading

Codrington, Robert Henry. *The Melanesians: Studies in Their Anthropology and Folk-Lore.* Oxford, UK: Clarendon Press 1891. Facsimile reprint ed. New York: Dover Publications, 1972.

Kennett, Frances. *Ethnic Dress.* New York: Facts on File, 1995.

Ucko, Peter J. "Penis Sheaths: A Comparative Study." In *Proceedings of the Royal Anthropological Institute of Great Britain and Ireland,* 1969, pp. 27–67.

Robert D. Craig

Education

In traditional societies in the South Pacific everyone in the community learned in formal and informal ways. Transmitting practical skills and their application was an ongoing part of a child's socialization, along with learning the one or more community languages. Throughout a lifetime, the stories of legend and origin would be learned, along with specialty information imparted by an older relative or expert. Young men and **women** learned their gender-related roles in subsistence, through gardening, hunting, and fishing with their family. Women who marry into a community must learn the practical skills of homemaking, from basketwork and pottery to **food** preparation and child care. All children are taught basic first aid, including the leaves, seeds, barks, and flowers that held reduce fever or heal wounds. More serious medicines and sorcery skills would be taught to an exclusive few.

Formal education also predates European schooling in many Pacific Island societies. It is possible to say that ceremony is a version of formal education, however intermittent it may be. Children of all ages can be found participating in the **dances** and chants of public ceremonies, and where appropriate, the more restricted rituals of a clan or tribe. Perhaps the most organized form of education in the Pacific was male **initiation**, where men were segregated from female company, oftentimes in a men's house, and systematically instructed on the genealogical, historical, and esoteric information required for being a full citizen of their community.

Further Reading

Bloch, M., ed. *Political Language and Oratory in Traditional Society.* New York: Academic Press, 1975.

Chowning, A. *An Introduction to the Peoples and Cultures of Melanesia.* Menlo Park, CA: Cummings Publishing, 1979.

Gewertz, D. *Sepik River Societies: A Historical Ethnography of the Chambri and Their Neighbors.* New Haven, CT: Yale University Press, 1983.

Herdt, G. H. *Guardians of the Flutes: Idioms of Masculinity.* New York: McGraw-Hill, 1981.

Schieffelin, B. *The Give and Take of Everyday Life: Language Socialization of Kaluli Children.* Cambridge, UK: Cambridge University Press, 1979.

Nancy Sullivan

El Niño/La Niña

El Niño refers to the El Niño Southern Oscillation (ENSO), an ocean-atmosphere phenomenon that causes temperature fluctuations in the surface temperature of the Pacific Ocean. Like its partner phenomenon, La Niña, which usually follows El Niño, this "little boy" (and "little girl") in Spanish is named after the Christ child because it is known to arrive around Christmastime. Unlike the Christ child, however, these youngsters wreak havoc on Pacific **agriculture**, fisheries, and general well-being every two to eight years or so, causing floods, droughts, coral bleaching, fish losses, and the ramifications from these to the island populations. ENSO was first described by Sir Gilbert Thomas Walker in 1923 and must be taken into account by historians looking back at the migrations and production economies of Oceanic peoples during the Middle Ages.

El Niño begins when the tropical trade winds weaken, air pressure rises over the Indian Ocean and Indonesia, and warm surface water begins to travel eastward across the Pacific. This set of conditions dissipates the cooler Humboldt Current and causes air pressure to fall over Tahiti and the central and eastern Pacific islands. Ultimately, warm air rises in the east, near Peru, releasing vital rains to Peru's deserts. As the warm water moves eastward across the Pacific, it takes the rain with it, leaving drought behind. Cooler water begins to upwell in the western Pacific, and because it fails to evaporate quickly, the rains do not come, causing drought and other weather disturbances throughout the western Pacific.

The La Niña phase of the phenomenon may have been dominant until recently, as winds blew westwards across the Pacific accumulating warm surface waters off the north of Australia, the Torres Straits, and New Guinea. The cold Humboldt or Peru Current then surfaces off the Pacific Coast of South America and feeds nutrients to the all-important local fisheries, called *achovetta*. La Niña often follows El Niño, especially when the El Niño effect has been particularly strong.

Further Reading

Flannery, T. *The Weather Makers: The History and Future Impact of Climate Change.* Melbourne, Australia: Text Publishing, 2005.

Kirch, P. V., and R. C. Green. *Hawaiki, Ancestral Polynesia: An Essay in Historical Anthropology.* Cambridge, UK: Cambridge University Press, 2001.

Yed, D. E., and J. M. J. Mummery, eds. *Pacific Production Systems: Approaches to Economic Prehistory.* Canberra: The Australian National University, 1990.

Nancy Sullivan

Entertainment and Recreation

Entertainment in ancient Oceania consisted of the simplest forms of amusement by children to the complex and intricate performances by their parents of music, **dance**, storytelling, and even skilled sporting events that often resembled Roman gladiator fights.

Most Pacific peoples treated their children with great affection, and they spent much of their preadolescent lives playing games that increased their particular skills. Boys practiced throwing spears, darts, or even boomerangs, while young girls imitated their mothers in beating **tapa** or digging out grubs and lizards in the wild with their small digging sticks. They would run, jump, swim, wrestle, roll in the sand, play in the trees, and otherwise pass their early days entertaining themselves.

One fascinating game they played was "string figures" or "cat's cradles," a form of entertainment commonly found elsewhere in the world. The game was played with a closed loop of string, made of plaited hair or coconut fibers, and with their fingers and sometimes their toes and teeth, the children created intricate geometric patterns that resembled something from their environment: stars, constellations, animals, birds, and so forth. Complex patterns required a certain amount of dexterity, especially when two players competed to finish a certain figure. Some figures required two players, while others proceeded from one to another in a long, continuous display of different forms.

In Tonga, young girls juggled small, round gourds or wooden balls in a competition to see which one could manage the greatest number and keep them aloft the longest. (The number often ran from six to ten.) Juggling was often accompanied by singing and dancing, which helped the girls keep time in passing the balls from one hand to another.

Because water played a paramount role in the lives of the islanders, it is not surprising that the ocean provided them with a constant source of pleasure. Body surfing was a sport that required no paraphernalia. Surfers would swim (or more often tread) out to the breaking waves, and when a suitable wave rolled in, they would push off with one hand in front and "ride" the wave as far as they could—often until their stomachs grazed the sandy bottom of the shore. When the waves were just right, a ride could last for many seconds, and when the waves were substantially brisk, a ride could be downright exhilarating. Another water sport was underwater "football." This took place in water from 4 to 10 feet deep. Two wooden posts were pounded into the sand under water from 140 to 300 feet apart. Midway between them was placed a heavy stone. Two teams were formed, consisting of both of men and **women**, and the object of the game was for one team to move the stone to their goal line and score a victory. The contestants could either "run" under water or swim with the stone, but of course, when they surfaced to breathe, one of their team members had to dive down and continue their push to the goal line. All the while, members of the opposing team were attempting to get the stone and thwart their rivals.

Surfing the waves with some sort of a wooden board, of course, was another popular water activity. Although practiced anciently in several places of the world, it probably reached its highest fervor in the Pacific islands and especially in Hawai'i. Although it appealed to all levels of society—including men, women, and children—only members of the chiefly class could surf the "long boards" and ride the best waves. The resurgence of interest in the sport in Hawai'i during the last 50 years of the twentieth century has lead to its becoming one of world's most popular sports.

Adult men practiced their spear throwing in several games. In one, a soft piece of wood (or an unhusked coconut) would be affixed to the top of a 6-foot, vertical pole. From a set distance, the teams would take turns throwing spears at the wood. The team that hit the target the most won the competition. Bareknuckle boxing and wrestling were enjoyed by men and women (competing separately) and were performed before a large audience that sat around in a large circle. The first player knocked to the ground ended the match. But the loser's place was often taken up by another opponent who rose up from the audience. Wrestling, boxing, and mock-fighting matches as well as foot races routinely took place between villages to the enjoyment of all. (Ancient Hawaiians also had a notorious passion for betting on these types of competitive games.)

Although considered a less vigorous sport, music, and dance, however, often provided more of a physical workout than one might assume. Some men's fast-paced dance steps, for example, were practiced to help them with their fighting dexterity. Women's stick dances provided training in protecting themselves, while other dances increased their graceful movements.

Storytelling at night around the fire provided entertainment for all. Because Pacific peoples had no written language, almost every village had a long tradition of storytelling. Usually, designated individuals within the community were trained in this tradition. They learned their stories, mythologies, and genealogies from their predecessor and would then present them at various times during the year. Many of these stories took the form of chants that extolled the virtues of their ancestors, told the stories of the creation of the heavens and earth, and in some cases, the migration of their forefathers from a mystical homeland (called Hawaiki). Some tales, we are told, were so long that it took several evenings to complete. Many of them have survived into the modern period and now provide contemporary scholars and authors with important data to help describe how these ancient peoples lived. *See also* **Musical Instruments.**

Further Reading

Ferdon, Edwin N. *Early Tonga as the Explorers Saw It, 1616–1810.* Tucson: University of Arizona Press, 1987, pp. 173–203.

Handy, E. S. Craighill, et al. *Ancient Hawaiian Civilization.* Honolulu, HI: The Kamehameha Schools, 1933 [reprinted Honolulu: Mutual Publishing, 1999], pp. 145–158.

Lal, Brij V., and Kate Fortune. *The Pacific Islands: An Encyclopedia.* Honolulu: University of Hawai'i Press, 2000, pp. 455–460.

Maude, H. C., and H. E. Maude. *String Figures from the Gilbert Islands.* Wellington, New Zealand: Polynesian Society, 1958. (Professor Maude has published numerous monographs on string figures from Oceania.)

Reed, A. W. *An Illustrated Encyclopedia of Maori Life.* Auckland, New Zealand: A. H. & A. W. Reed, 1963, pp. 37, 77, 83–84.

Robert D. Craig

Food

Until the arrival of Europeans in modern times, Oceanic peoples lived in highly sophisticated, Neolithic societies and depended upon subsistence food gathering, hunting, and gardening for their nourishment. Their environment determined to a great extent the types and amounts of food that could be obtained. The high volcanic islands of Oceania, for example, provided a much richer soil in which food plants could be cultivated and harvested compared to low-lying **atolls.** But even then, islanders on atolls turned to garden production to help provide for their daily sustenance. The Australian continent provided far greater possibilities for gardening, but surprisingly, the vast majority of the Indigenous Australians led a nomadic life of hunting and gathering for their food. Islands, of course, limited any type of nomadic existence—on some islands, for example, a person could walk around the entire parameter in a few hours' time. Geography, therefore, forced islanders to settle down and turn to garden production. Climatic differences also helped to determine what foods were available to both groups, and, therefore, there existed a wide variety of foods that were eaten by Oceanic peoples.

Like many other Pacific peoples, the Indigenous Australians spent most of their energy in seeking their daily food needs, and this work was generally divided between the sexes. Men excelled in hunting and fishing (along the coast), and they provided the meat (or fish) to augment the vegetable foods gathered by the **women** and children. The vast Australian continent provided such animals as kangaroos, emus, possums, large goannas (Australian monitor lizards), wombats, and snakes. Birds could be caught by throwing clubs (boomerangs, for example) at a flock or by nets. Fish were harpooned or caught in traps. Australian men were highly skilled in tracking and hunting animals, sometimes for long lengths of time before finally making the kill.

Women, on the other hand, stayed near their campsites and were food collectors, usually providing the larger portion of their daily rations. They usually scanned the surrounding areas looking for snakes, lizards, honey ants, small marsupials, witchetty grub larvae, and bird eggs. They dug up various roots and **yams** and collected grass seeds for making a type of bread. They, too, were the ones who prepared and cooked the food (as opposed to some other Pacific island cultures in which the men did the cooking). The main meal of the day was usually in the evening when the day's food had been gathered. A small depression in the earth was dug out and a fire built. Seeds were ground between stones, mixed with water, and then formed into a flat, oval cake and cooked over the hot ashes. Once the fire had died down, the various animals and vegetables would be placed in the hole and covered ("sealed") with leaves and parts of the hot ashes. Sometimes heated stones were added to the underground oven. After a length of time, the oven would be opened, food extracted and divided between family members. Fruit and berries that had been gathered during the day might supplement the evening meal, and any leftovers would provide food the next morning.

Like the Indigenous Australians, Pacific islanders spent most of their days gathering food for their primary meal, usually eaten late afternoon, but in addition to hunting and gathering wild animals and plant foods, islanders also raised domesticated animals and grew crops in and around their home sites. (Time spent in hunting and gathering as versus growing and raising of crops, of course, depended a great deal on the fertility of their lands.) Besides wild animals and plants, islanders' domesticated animals consisted of chickens, dogs, and **pigs** (not in Micronesia), and their cultivated food plants consisted of coconuts, bananas, **breadfruit**, **taro**, yams, arrowroot, pandanus, sago palm, and rice (found only in the Mariana Islands of Micronesia). Often complex social restrictions (*tapu*) dominated the cultivation and eating of these foods. In some places, for example, women could only grow wet taro while the men cultivated the dry. In some areas, women could not participate in fishing and hunting or even touch their husband's implements. Some Polynesian men ate food prepared only by themselves, and in the New Guinea highlands, the men and older boys ate in their separate male-only houses.

Although food pieces could be thrown onto an open fire for cooking, usually food was either broiled (in clay pots where available or in coconut shells into which hot stones were placed) or baked, usually in an underground oven. These "ovens" ranged in size from 1 to 2 feet deep and 5 to 6 feet wide, depending upon the quantity of food being cooked. Once dug, these ovens were used over and over again. Firewood and stones were arranged in the pit and the wood set on fire. The stones were turned frequently to get them evenly heated. Then leaves (often banana leaves) were placed over the stones and the various foods (wrapped or unwrapped) were placed at strategic spots on top of the leaves. More leaves and sand or soil were added to create a type of giant steam oven, which cooked the food and prevented its moisture from escaping. When finally uncovered, the food was then served on leaves from the banana or ti plants, accompanied with either fresh or seawater (for its salt content). Cooked taro and breadfruit could often be eaten as it was prepared in chunks, or it could further be mashed with a small amount of water into what was called in Hawai'i "poi" or in Tahiti "*po'e*." Coconut cream provided a rich sauce that could be mixed with pork or fish or cooked with leaves from the taro plant (like a creamed spinach). In some areas of the Pacific **kava** was drunk with meals. It was made from mashed roots of the *Piper methysticum* plant and mixed with water (as one would make tea). It had a type of stupor effect if drunk in excess. *See also* Document 8.

Further Reading

Alkire, William H. *An Introduction to the Peoples and Cultures of Micronesia*. Menlo Park, CA: Cummings Publishing, 1977.

Bellwood, Peter. *The Polynesians: Prehistory of an Island People*. London: Thames & Hudson, 1978, pp. 34–38.

Lal, Brij V., and Kate Fortune. *The Pacific Islands: An Encyclopedia*. Honolulu: University of Hawai'i Press, 2000, pp. 27–39, 343–345.

Oliver, Douglas L. *Oceania: The Native Cultures of Australia and the Pacific Islands*. 2 vols. Honolulu: University of Hawai'i Press, 1989, pp. 157–320.

Robert D. Craig

Gods and Goddesses

The animistic religions of ancient Oceania gave rise to the worship of a multitude of gods and goddesses. Isolated one from another for centuries, these island peoples developed a wide variety of different deities, very much like their individual, rich cultures. Legends of their gods and goddesses became a dominant part of their lives, and these stories developed into some of the most fascinating and elaborate mythologies in all of world history.

Indigenous Australians developed a widespread belief in a supernatural Rainbow Serpent who was creator and destroyer, associated with water in all forms, and often appeared in the form of a rainbow. It was worshipped under various names, such as Kanmare, Andrenjinyi, Julunggul, Ngalyod, and Yhi (some gods, other goddesses). Originally, they say, it emerged from the dark streaks of the Milky Way and slithered down to earth to roam through the mountains and valleys (which it created) as a benevolent protector and a malevolent punisher of those who broke the **law**. Another god was Altjira, or Sky-Father of the Alchera (Dreamtime), who created the earth but then returned to the upper limits of the sky where he no longer involves himself in the mundane affairs of humans. A similar god

Statue of Pele, the Hawaiian fire goddess. Hawaii, 17th–18th century. Wood and hair. Werner Forman/Art Resource, NY.

was Bunjil, a creator god among the Kulin and Wurunjerri peoples, who formed humans and taught them how to live, but then left them to live in the heavens, very much like Altjira. The formidable goddess Eingena, primordial mother and creator of the world, once became pregnant but had no way of allowing her new life to escape from her body. God Barraiya conceived a plan that would help her. He simply slit an opening in the lower part of her body through which her vast creation emerged. Eingena, they say, continues to live in Dreamtime, often awakening and continuing her creation. It is believed she holds a thread attached to all newly born humans, and when she lets go of the thread, they die.

Among the Pacific islanders, Micronesian mythology has been the least researched. These islands were the first to be visited by Western explorers in the early modern era, and their immediate conversion to Christianity (primarily Catholicism) destroyed much of their rich heritage. Their extant stories, however, tell of male and female creators, but the latter is more predominant. Ligoupup, for example, was the great creator goddess among the Caroline Islanders. She created the heavens and earth and then made her home at the bottom of the ocean. As she moved and turned, her movements caused earthquakes aboveground. Her son became the ruler of the underworld. Her daughter married sky-father and the two gave birth to Aluelp, the possessor of all knowledge. There existed, too, a male creator god, Anulap, who could do nothing for himself, not even open his eye lids or his mouth without assistance. Among the Marshallese, the great creator god was Loa (Lowa), and similar to Ligoupup, he lived under the sea. After creating the beautiful reefs and **atolls**, he created the first man (Walleb) and **woman** (Limdunanji).

Melanesian peoples were much more interested in rituals than they were with their gods. They believed that all unusual phenomenon resulted from the works of sorcery (magic) or the action of spirits rather then the gods. Certain gods, of course, were associated with specific activities and might have to be petitioned to undo certain spells, but they were generally felt to be too remote to affect human affairs. For that reason, Melanesian deities were less known and developed than elsewhere in the Pacific. One story among several Melanesian tribes tells of two brother gods whose adventures are noteworthy. One brother (To Kabinana) created all that was good and another (To Karvuvu) all that was wrong. In Vanuatu, the god Qat created everything important in the world, including humans, to the displeasure of his eleven brothers. Another widespread cultural hero was Sido (Sosom, Souw, Hido, Iko), whose sexual lust incensed his young female friend so much that in shame he fled to the mountains and in revenge showered everything evil upon the earth. Eventually, he turned himself into a monstrous pig whose body provided the inspiration for building the unique "great houses" in which Melanesian tribes lived. **Pigs** (called Marunogere) were widely worshiped as well as snakes (Randalo, Hatuibwari, and Agunua), sharks, dogs, and hawks.

The Polynesians, however, created the most elaborate and homogeneous pantheon of gods of any Oceanic peoples. Surviving chants are measured in thousands of lines, and some take several days to relate. Their creation stories tell of the great god Ta'aroa (Kanaloa, Tagaloa) who arose from his long sleep from a seashell and began the act of creation. From the top of his shell, he created the heavens and from the bottom the earth. He created fellow gods and goddesses who dwelt with him in the darkness until the shells were separated and the heavens were propped up on pillars. The first man (Ti'i or Kiki) was created followed by his female companion Hina (Sina). Other powerful Polynesian deities include Tū (Kū), a god of creation and of war; Kāne (Tāne), a god of creation and of light; and Rongo (Lono), one of Hawai'i's three major gods and also the name of an important son of the Māori sky father (Rangi) and earth mother (Papa). Although Hina (Sina, Ina) was the most popular Polynesian goddesses (she lived in the moon and was the goddess of **tapa** beating), it was the volcano goddess Pele that sparked the most veneration in the Hawaiian Islands. The demigods and heroes of ancient **Polynesia** were equally as popular. The exploits of Māui are legend and are found throughout Polynesia. Tinirau (Kinilau) became the romantic hero and god of the oceans. Tahaki (Kahai'i) was the perfect chief, and Rata (Laka) was the irreverent vagabond. Details of all of these Pacific deities can be found in the books listed below. *See also* **Melanesia** and **Micronesia**.

Further Reading

Allen, Tony et al. *Journeys Through Dreamtime: Oceanian Myth*. London: Time-Life Books, 1999.

Craig, Robert D. *Handbook of Polynesian Mythology*. Santa Barbara, CA: ABC-CLIO Press, 2004.

Graves, Robert, ed. *New Larousse Encyclopedia of Mythology*. New York: Prometheus Press, 1971, pp. 449–472.

Poignant, Roslyn. *Oceanic Mythology*. London: Paul Hamlyn, 1967.

Robert D. Craig

The God Rongo. Gambier Islands, Polynesia. Collected 1834–1836. Scala/Art Resource, NY.

Initiation (Melanesia)

Rarely do **women** in **Melanesia** undergo any formal initiation. But boys all across Melanesia become men through a period of separation from women and specialized instruction. The ideas behind initiation are simple. Women have the power to create people, but only men can create men. Whereas girls come to adulthood unproblematically, boys must become men through a combination of biological and psychological transformations. Some time in adolescence, boys are taken away from their mothers and sisters to sleep in the men's house and, eventually, to enter seclusion in the spirit house. They must avoid women's blood and bodily secretions, as well as their charms, because these nurturing elements can threaten their masculinity. Most initiation practices require the expelling of a mother's postpartum blood, by skin cutting, cutting the tip of one's penis, nose bleeding, vomiting blood, or shoving bamboo reeds down one's throat until it bleeds. Pain and fear are transformational. Usually it is the maternal **uncle** (in an otherwise tender relationship) who inflicts them. When the mother's blood is spilled it thus goes back to her line through this uncle.

Before European contact, up through the Middle Ages, a handful of New Guinea societies—along the rivers on the south coast, in the Papuan Plateau and Western Province of Papua New Guinea—would complement the initiatory spilling of mother's blood with the consumption of paternal semen. Boys would be invested with clan powers through the life-giving substance of semen during what are called "ritual homosexual" practices with clan elders. Rid of women's fluids, purified by special diets and filled with this masculine essence, the young men would then be ready to fight in battle and to face the more sustained dangers to their being: marriage and marital relations.

Fears of female pollution are even more widespread than ritual initiation practices. In the Southern Highlands of New Guinea, where Huli men marry across enemy lines, they so fear deliberate sabotage by their wives that they take the precaution of cooking their own food. It is thought that women's secretions will sap men's power. Moreover, in-married women are thought to gradually shift loyalties to their husband's clan by repeatedly taking in his semen. By the time she reaches menopause, a woman's biological danger has been neutralized, and her fidelity is rewarded by the cessation of menstrual blood. Like her son, she has become indebted to her husband's line for the gift of its semen and its socializing powers.

These ideas about pollution and the "wildness" of women by contrast to the "tameness" of initiated men are part of even more widespread beliefs regarding the origin of reproductive power. In places all over Melanesia (and Oceania generally) people say that it was men who originally gave birth to children and women who socialized them. In the Karawari region of the Sepik River, for example, they say that the women were so exhausted after a long series of rituals that they went home to sleep; that's when the men snuck into the spirit house and stole the sacred flutes and thereby reclaimed their power of "making" men.

Further Reading

Gewertz, D. *Sepik River Societies: A Historical Ethnography of the Chambri and Their Neighbors*. New Haven, CT: Yale University Press, 1983.

Herdt, G. H. *Guardians of the Flutes: Idioms of Masculinity*. New York: McGraw-Hill, 1981.

Herdt, G. H., ed. *Rituals of Manhood: Male Initiation in Papua New Guinea*. Berkeley: University of California Press, 1982.

Neich, R., and F. Pereira. *Pacific Jewelry and Adornment*. Honolulu: University of Hawai'i Press, 2004.

Sahlins, M. "Poor Man, Rich Man, Big Man, Chief: Political Types in Melanesia and Polynesia." *Comparative Studies in Society and History* 5 (1963): 285–303.

Schieffelin, E. L. *The Sorrow of the Lonely and the Burning of the Dancers*. New York: St. Martin's Press, 1976.

Sullivan, N. *Papua New Guinea, with Trans Niugini Tours* [handbook]. Mt. Hagen, New Guinea: Trans New Guinea Tours, 1994.

Nancy Sullivan

Island Groups

Although some thirty-thousand islands lie within the bounds of the Pacific Ocean, most of them were unknown to Europeans and Asians until well into modern times. Some archeologists theorize, however, that Chinese junks may have made their way across the Pacific during medieval times, but there is little evidence to substantiate their claims. Even the Europeans did not know the Pacific Ocean existed until its "discovery" by Balboa in 1513. After that, of course, competition between the Spaniards, Portuguese, Dutch, French, and British gave rise to the whole Pacific being "discovered" and mapped by 1790 (with special thanks to Captain James Cook in the 1770s). They were subsequently categorized into three main island groups that today often make little or no sense, but it is that grouping of **Melanesia, Micronesia**, and **Polynesia** that allows scholars a convenient system to study and describe these island peoples.

Melanesia

Melanesia consists of New Guinea (the second largest island in the world), the Admiralty Islands, and the Bismarck and Louisiade archipelagoes; the Solomon Islands and Santa Cruz Islands; New Caledonia and the Loyalty Islands; Vanuatu (formerly the New Hebrides); Fiji, and numerous other small islands lying to the north and northeast of Australia. The peoples that inhabit these islands created some of the most diverse and complex cultures in the whole world.

New Guinea

New Guinea, with its surrounding islands of Bougainville, the Louisiade Archipelago, and New Britain, was one of the first areas of Oceania to be settled. Papuan peoples first moved into the island over 40,000 years ago and by 10,000 years ago had created one of the first cultures in the world to establish sedentary communities, grow crops, and domesticate animals (especially pigs). Austronesian-speaking peoples arrived about 3,500 years ago, bringing with them additional skills, including pottery making and ocean navigation (*see* **Voyaging/Ancient Navigation**). This mixture of different peoples led to the great diversity in languages (over one thousand) and cultures that characterized later Papuan history. House styles varied from small lean-tos to the *grandhaus tambaran* (worship and meeting houses) of the Sepik peoples with their sweeping front gables and low backs. In some highland communities, village leadership was attained by a **bigman** who competed with rivals in lavish feast offerings and gift-giving for social advancement, while in other areas, chieftainship was inherited either through one's mother (matrilineal) or father (patrilineal). Complex trade and ceremonial cycles (*kula*) characterized the southeastern islands, but in most areas there was little support of anyone outside their own descent groups and villages. The remoteness of some New Guinean villages has allowed a few Melanesian cultures to survive into modern times, and there, in fact, still several uncontacted tribes living in central New Guinea.

New Caledonia

The long, thin island of New Caledonia lies directly east of Australia and south of the Solomon Islands. It was first inhabited over 3,000 years ago by Austronesia peoples, who divided their communities into families, clans, and tribes, all of whom claimed descent from a common ancestor. Tribal **chiefs** were considered representatives of their ancestors and, therefore, performed duties as chief priest. He lived in a unique conical house that also served as a place for tribal meetings and ceremonies.

Solomon Islands and Santa Cruz Islands

The Solomon Islands and Santa Cruz Islands consist of six large, mountainous islands of volcanic origin located directly east of Papua New Guinea. The first inhabitants arrived here about 10,000 years ago, and then about 4,000 years ago, Austronesian peoples arrived bringing their more advanced farming techniques, their food plants, and domesticated chickens, dogs, and **pigs**. They developed matrilineal and patrilineal descent groups. Villages averaged about one hundred to two hundred people, and their wood carvings, canoe making, and other crafts were highly developed. Large-scale **warfare** and head hunting took place frequently, and they believed in a world of spirits, ghosts, sorcery, and magic.

Vanuatu

Vanuatu, formerly called the New Hebrides, consists of about eighty-two islands lying in a "V" shape configuration northeast of New Caledonia and south of the Santa Cruz Islands. They were populated at least before 3000 B.C.E. by several different Pacific migrations. The various clans lived in small autonomous villages that remained hostile one to another. Chiefs emerged as bigmen, who had outstripped their rivals in competing village feasts. Wives were considered property and could be traded between villages. Cannibal raids by one village upon another prevented anyone from wandering too far from his home village. Their religion was aniministic, and magic was used to control the ever-present spirits.

Fiji Islands

During the medieval period, the inhabitants of the Fiji Islands developed one of the highest material cultures in the Pacific. Although there are over three hundred islands in the group, the two largest volcanic islands (Viti Levu and Vanua Levu) were more densely population and provided a wide variety of **agriculture** and village development. According to Fijian legend, the great chief Lutunasobasoba led his people across the seas to the new land of Fiji, where they mixed with their neighbors, the Polynesians (Tongans and Samoans), to produce a rich and vibrant medieval culture. Their large, ocean-going, double-hulled canoes were one of their legacies passed on to the migrating Polynesians, who passed through their group.

Micronesia

Micronesia comprises 2,106 islands, stretching across the northwestern Pacific Ocean, and includes the Caroline Islands (with its five districts of Kosrae, Ponape, Truk, Yap, and Palau), the Marshall Islands, the Mariana Islands (together with Guam), and Kiribati (formerly the Gilbert Islands). The western islands (Palau, Mariana Islands, and Yap) apparently were first settled about 1500 B.C.E. from people coming from Indonesia and the Philippines. The rest of the islands were settled by peoples sailing north from the Gilbert Islands, on to the Marshalls, and then westward across to Palau.

Marshall Islands

The Marshall Islands consist of five isolated islands and twenty-nine **atolls**, and although they are scattered over 230,000 square miles, the culture of the islanders was very much alike. Like other Micronesians, the Marshallese recognized matrilineal descent groups. Each lineage had its own headman (male or female), and land could be inherited by male and female children. In other areas of the Marshalls, a paramount chief could gain dominance over several atolls by warfare or its threat and exact tribute (mats, sennit, various forms of food, etc.) from their inhabitants. Frequent sailing between the islands led to the Marshallese to become expert canoe builders and seamen. They navigated the area by the use of stick and shell charts that approximated the relation of the islands one to another and showed sea swells that could influence their navigation.

Caroline Islands

The Caroline Islands consist of approximately five hundred coral atolls that stretch just east of the Philippines and north of New Guinea. Navigation was highly developed here as it was in the Marshall Islands, and their ocean-going canoes were built of irregular planks that were caulked and sewn together with coconut-made sennit (rope). Hereditary chiefs were recognized, but in general they were more egalitarian and worked for a living like everyone else. Their primary function was to preside over community meetings. Yap was perhaps an exception with its highly structured caste system that ranked chiefs as well as villages. Chiefs presided over what is often referred to as a **Yap Empire**, which stretched 700 miles east of the island and demanded tribute from their subordinate islands. Palauans were especially noted for the construction of their elaborate men's clubhouses, where they spent a good deal of their time.

Mariana Islands

The Mariana Islands (including Guam) stretch 1,565 miles southeast of Japan. The islands are actually the fertile tops of a submerged mountain chain rather than coral atolls found elsewhere in Micronesia. The native peoples are called *Chamorros*, and they most likely originated from the Philippines or Southeast Asia before 1527 B.C.E. The first settlers brought rice with them, and these islands were the only place in Oceania where it was produced before pre-European contact. Chamorros recognized matrilineal descent but recognized clans and lineages. They lived in nucleated villages, some of which included very impressive, large stone foundation columns (*latte*). The rapid destruction of their ancient culture by European explorers in early modern times limits our knowledge of their medieval past.

Gilbert Islands

The Gilbert Islands consist of a chain of sixteen atolls and coral islands stretching across the equator at 175 degrees east longitude and today make up part of the Republic of Kiribati (created in 1979). Culturally, the Gilbertese were basically Micronesian, but they were also highly influenced by their Polynesian neighbors to the south, possibly by immigrants from Samoa.

Polynesia

Polynesia comprises the modern states of Tonga, Samoa, French Polynesia (Marquesas Islands, Society Islands, Austral Islands, Tuamotu Archipelago, and Gambier Islands), Cook Islands, Hawai'i, New Zealand, Tokelau, Tuvalu, and Easter Island, plus nineteen small "outlier" islands located in the cultural areas of Micronesia and Melanesia.

Tonga

Tonga was the first group of the Polynesian Islands to be settled in ancient times, sometime around 1300 B.C.E., by settlers from eastern Melanesia to the west. Tonga's 172 low islands lie in the tropics between 15 and 23 degrees south latitude and are divided into three main groups: Tongatpu, Vava'u, and Ha'apai. Early Tongans developed a "classical" Polynesian culture based on chiefs and a paramount ruler called the Tu'i Tonga ("King" of Tonga). The 11th Tu'i Tonga, Tuitātui (c. 1200) supposedly built the great stone monument, the Ha'amonga-a-Māui, near the modern town of Nuku'olofa. Throughout the Middle Ages, Tonga had intermittent contacts with Samoa and Fiji (a Melanesian island group lying to the southwest).

Samoa

Culturally, Samoa consists of the two large islands of Savai'i and 'Upolu as well as the six islands that currently make up American Samoa, a U.S. territory: Tutuila, Ta'ū, Olosega, Ofu, 'Aunu'u, and Rose Island. The islands lie in the South Pacific at a latitude of 14 degrees south and longitude 168 to 171 degrees west. These high volcanic islands sustain a wide variety of tropical flora, including **taro**, coconut palm, and **breadfruit** along their coasts. The highest mountain peak is mount Matafao, at 2,303 feet. The islands were first settled by Austronesian-speaking peoples (Polynesians) who came from the area of Tonga about 1000 B.C.E., and in ancient times, the islands had occasional contact with Tonga and Fiji.

French Polynesia

French Polynesia is a modern political designation that includes the Marquesas Islands, the Society Islands, Austral Islands, Gambier Islands, and the Tuamotu Archipelago, all lying in the southeast Pacific Ocean. These 130 islands range in size from the high volcanic mountains of Tahiti (Mt. 'Orohena at 7,333 feet high) and the Marquesas to the small, low-lying atolls that make up the Tuamotu Archipelago. According to scholars, the Marquesas were first settled by Samoan explorers about 200 C.E., and from there, these "central Polynesian" peoples pushed out and settled the Society Islands (450 C.E.), Hawai'i (650 C.E.), Easter Island (700 C.E.), New Zealand (900 C.E.), and their surrounding islands and inhabitable atolls. Rā'iātea, an island in the Society Group, was anciently regarded as the most sacred in all of eastern Polynesia, and it is said that annual tribute was sent to its priests from islands as far away as New Zealand.

Cook Islands

The Cook Islands, consisting of thirteen inhabited and two uninhabited islands, are located between Samoa to the west and French Polynesia to the east. The islands range in height from the high mountains on Rarotonga to the flat surface of the Takutea atoll. Oral traditions maintain that the islands were settled from Samoa by the warrior Karika and from Tahiti by the warrior Tangi'ia, probably before 950 C.E. The islanders developed a traditional-styled Polynesian culture with each island being independent and separate from one another until modern times.

Hawai'i

Hawai'i, a collection of eight major islands and 124 minor islands in the North Pacific Ocean, was apparently settled twice in medieval times—once from the Marquesas Islands about 650 C.E. and then another from Tahiti or its surrounding islands about 1200. Both are over 2,000 miles to the south of Hawai'i. These early settlers set sail in their double-hulled, ocean-going canoes and brought with them their animals, plants, and eastern Polynesian culture, and during the next 600 years, they established a complex society based upon subsistence agriculture and fishing.

New Zealand

Traditional stories from New Zealand tell the epic history of the first migrations of the Polynesians to these islands from a distant homeland called Hawaiki (traditionally dated about 925 C.E.). The great chiefs Kupe and Ngāte and their fishing crews followed a great octopus from Hawaiki to a strange, new land they named Aotearoa (Long-White-Cloud). Returning to Hawaiki, they informed their friends and family, whereupon, Kupe's young brother-in-law, Turi, gathered his family and provisions and in his mighty canoe, the *Aotea*, set sail for the new land. Once there, they settled the islands, and their descendants became known as the Māori of New Zealand. The island group consists of two major islands—North Island and South Island—and numerous smaller islands. South Island's massive mountain chain has been nicknamed the "Alps of the Pacific," and its climate is temperate rather than tropical as the other Polynesian islands.

Easter Island

Easter Island, known also by its Polynesian name *Rapanui*, lies isolated in the southeastern Pacific and is considered the most remote island in the world. Traditions ascribe the first settlers to Hotu Matu'a and his followers, who arrived about 450 C.E., and to another group of immigrants, who arrived sometime after, both of whom became bitter rivals throughout their history. Despite the rivalry, however, the islanders created an advanced Neolithic culture over the years that produce two unique contributions—a type of written script called *kohau rongorongo* and the carving of thousands of stone structures (*ahu*) and monolithic statues (*moai*)—not equaled by any other Pacific peoples.

Tuvalu and Tokelau

Tuvalu and Tokelau are two groups of small islands and atolls that lie north of Fiji and Tonga. They were originally settled by Samoan immigrants, and Tuvalu also may have been settled by drifting canoes from Micronesia and Tonga.

Further Reading

Bellwood, Peter. *Man's Conquest of the Pacific*. New York: Oxford University Press, 1979.

Craig, Robert D., and Frank P. King. *Historical Dictionary of Oceania*. Westport, CT and London: Greenwood Press, 1981.

Motteler, Lee S. *Pacific Island Names: A Map and Name Guide to the New Pacific*. 2nd ed. Honolulu, HI: Bernice P. Bishop Museum Press, 2006.

Oliver, Douglas L. *Oceania: The Native Cultures of Australia and the Pacific Islands*. 2 vols. Honolulu: University of Hawai'i Press, 1989.

Robert D. Craig

Kava

Kava (*'awa* in Hawaiian) is a nonalcoholic drink consumed throughout most of **Polynesia** (except Easter Island and New Zealand), **Melanesia**, New Guinea, and parts of **Micronesia** (Ponape and Kosrae in the eastern Caroline Islands). Drinking of kava results in a type of euphoria or well-being feeling, and when drunk to excess, it results in immobilization or deep sleep. The drink is prepared by pulverizing (chewing or pounding) the roots of the *Piper methysticum* (pepper plant), mixing it with water, and then straining it through a sieve, usually made from the inner fibers of the coconut.

In the western Polynesian Islands of Samoa and Tonga and in Fiji (Melanesia), the drink is associated with important ceremonial occasions where chiefs attend and where it becomes an important ritual with its strict rules of preparation and proper serving protocols. In ancient Samoa, for example, preparing ceremonial kava was generally the responsibility of the chief's daughter, the *taupou*, and she was accompanied by several other young girls, the *'aumaga*, the official kava chewers. After all the important **chiefs** had been seated, a designated talking chief would begin the ceremony by calling forth kava roots from the community. Several young boys appeared with the best roots they could find, the largest and best, of course, being designated for the highest chief among the assembled body. The speaker then called forth the *taupou* and her assistants to prepare the ceremonial drink.

The cleaned kava pieces were brought forth, the girls washed their hands, and then masticated the roots by chewing and placing them in a large kava bowl. A young boy added water to the preparation while the *taupou* mixed, strained, and squeezed the juices out of the kava roots. The process continued until the kava was well prepared. The *taupou* would then clap her hands and announce that the kava was ready to be served, whereupon the chief called for its distribution. The kava was then served individually (usually in a coconut shell) to the seated chiefs in order of their rank, the presiding high chief, of course, being served first. Often, the orator announced the chief's name and rank as they were being served. After everyone had been served, then the kava ceremony ended and the official discussion of business began. In other areas of Polynesia, however, the drink carried no particular significance and could be drunk at any time of the day, and in parts of Melanesia, it was used to communicate with the supernatural world of one's ancestors. *See also* **Betel Chewing** and **Gods and Goddesses**.

Further Reading

Chowning, A. *An Introduction to the Peoples and Cultures of Melanesia*. Menlo Park, CA: Cummings Publishing, 1979.

Lebot, V., M. Merlin, and L. Lindstrom. *Kava: The Pacific Drug*. New Haven, CT: Yale University Press, 1992.

Lum, J. K. "Central and Eastern Micronesia: Genetics, The Overnight Voyage, and Linguistic Divergence." *Man and Culture in Oceania* 14 (1998): 69–80.

Marcus, G. "Chieftainship." In A. Howard and R. Borofsky, eds., *Developments in Polynesian Ethnology*. Honolulu: University of Hawai'i Press, 1989, pp 175–210.

Suggs, R. C. *The Island Civilizations of Polynesia*. New York: Mentor Books, 1960.

Robert D. Craig

Kula

During medieval times, Oceanic people essentially lived in Neolithic societies and had no money economy like what was found in Western Europe and Asia. What little trading was done was essentially bartering in kind, and this was confined largely to **Melanesia** and parts of **Micronesia** (*see* **Yap Empire**). One particularly unique gift exchange or barter that merits attention, however, was called the *Kula*, *Kula* Exchange, or *Kula* Ring. It existed among the various small islands off the southeast coast of Papua New Guinea (Melanesia), and the custom has continued down into modern times. Anthropologist Bronislaw Malinowski (1884–1942) first wrote extensively about it in the 1920s.

Essentially, it was a complex system of exchanging two types of *kula* articles — red shell and bead necklaces (*soulava*) and white shell arm bracelets (*muwali*) — not for commodities or goods, but for one another in a traditional trade route. The necklaces were traded only clockwise and the bracelets counterclockwise in a trade route that extended over hundreds of miles in circumference between the numerous islands found in this geographical area. Every act performed in the *kula* exchange was regulated by traditional rules, customs, and conventions, all of which were often performed with elaborate rituals and ceremonies. Only a limited number of men actually participated in the ceremony, but it tended to link tribes one to another in permanent and lifelong alliances.

Kula articles were "traded" only between established partners, some living on islands as far away as one hundred miles, while others were traded between partners on the same island. The trade was for nothing more than the intrinsic value placed upon the particular *kula* articles. Their value was determined by their size, age, craftsmanship, history, and prestige rather than by their actual consumable value. Extraordinary *kula* were highly prized, but ownership might only last a few minutes to a year before tradition maintained that they be "traded" again. Meeting one's *kula* exchange partner may take a canoe voyage of one hundred miles or more. In this case, the partner might be accompanied by dozens of other interrelated traders in ocean-going canoes who would transport consumable products to be exchanged among the tribal leaders at the other end. This way, ordinary bartering of commodities between island groups was facilitated, and a brisk trade and often friendly alliances between groups sometimes developed. But these exchanges were regarded as only secondary to the main purpose of the expedition, which was, of course, was the exchange of the *kula*.

Most men had several *kula* partners living in various directions, but at least one clockwise of him and the other counterclockwise, and *kula* articles were traded from one hand to another. Membership to the *kula* came only through inheritance through a matrilineal succession (from mother's brother to mother's son), although evidence shows that on rare occasions an affluent man might be able to "buy" his way in. The whole purpose, of course, was to give pleasure and prestige of ownership (albeit for a while) of a revered *kula* to a particular partner.

The origin of this unique and complex custom is unknown. It may have emerged, perhaps, in reciprocal gift exchanges and mutual alliances made after **warfare** and then developed over the years into this distinctive cultural phenomenon that provided peace, protection, and hospitality between partnered groups. *See also* **Markets/Trade**.

Further Reading
Malinowski, Bronislaw. *Argonauts of the Western Pacific: An Account of Native Enterprise and Adventure in the Archipelagoes of Melanesian New Guinea*. London: Routledge & K. Paul Ltd., 1922. [Reprinted Prospect Heights, IL: Waveland Press, 1984.] Available at http://www.archive.org/details/argonautsofweste00mali.

Robert D. Craig

Languages

Oceania, and specifically **Melanesia**, is home to roughly one-fifth of the world's languages. Fewer than five million people in Papua New Guinea alone speak nearly eight hundred distinct languages in this, the most linguistically diverse region of the world. It is the cultural doppelganger of Melanesia's vast biodiversity. Although there are large language groups of roughly thirty-thousand speakers, most languages are spoken by fewer than one thousand people, and one-third have fewer than five hundred speakers. Some languages are spoken by barely one hundred speakers, and even then there may be special dialects within it spoken by **women** or men. Today, when more and more people are leaving the village for town, these local vernaculars are rapidly being lost. When mothers start teaching their children English or Pidgin instead of local languages, it is the beginning of the end for a vernacular. And with it goes local ideas, customs, histories, even taxonomies of local flora and fauna, because all these may be locked in a local language where they simply do not exist in English or Pidgin.

But before Europeans, and before the (relatively recent) invention of Pidgins and Bislama as lingua franca, Melanesia was a hothouse of linguistic diversity. The extent of this actually stumped some of the earliest linguists to the region. It has been thought, for example, that people who traveled and traded with each other for hundreds and even thousands of years would eventually speak a common tongue, their languages bleeding and converging over time. Not so in Melanesia. In the most highly trafficked and traded area of Papua New Guinea, for example, along the Sepik River, there are more languages per capita than anywhere else. On the other hand, it was thought that isolated pockets of people would develop dialectical variations, one language eventually breaking down into several. Again, the opposite is true in Melanesia. In Enga Province (Papua New Guinea), where rugged mountains and warfare kept neighboring villages apart for generations, more people (thirty thousand) speak one language than anywhere else in Papua New Guinea. So it seems interaction does not always lead to language pooling, and isolation doesn't always lead to linguistic diversity.

People along the Sepik River have held onto their languages through conquest, migration, trade, and even depopulation. Wherever language is valued, wherever the unique information locked in a language is considered a valuable commodity, people will continue speaking it. In the Sepik region, knowledge is wealth, and ritual information, clan esoterica, genealogies, and technical knowledge are customarily traded along with fish, sago, shells, and pots. People have sustained distinct languages as a way of marking group identity, and hierarchy between and within groups. Some language groups are even subdivided by men's and women's dialects, or special oratorical registers for initiated men only.

In Enga Province, and throughout the New Guinea Highlands, it is material wealth that counts. The individual **bigman** (or woman) gains prominence through coercion and charm and by sponsoring traditional wealth exchanges. What matters is the political ability to convince as many others as possible that their interests are the same as yours. Bigmen pool tribal wealth for their own purposes, and their personal success often reflects upon the entire community. All this is made possible by the use of one common language, rather than the mutual intelligibility of many. *See also* **Markets/Trade.**

Further Reading

Bloch, M., ed. *Political Language and Oratory in Traditional Society.* New York: Academic Press, 1975.

Blust, R. "Austronesian Culture History: Some Linguistic Inferences and Their Relations to the Archaeological Record." *World Archaeology* 8 (1976): 19–43.

Foley, W. *The Papuan Languages of New Guinea.* Cambridge, UK: Cambridge University Press, 1986.

Goldman, L. *Talk Never Dies.* London: Tavistock Publications, 1983.

Green, R.C. "Linguistic Subgrouping within Polynesia: The Implications for Prehistoric Settlement." *Journal of the Polynesian Society* 75 (1966): 6–38.

Kulick, D. *Language Shift and Cultural Reproduction: Socialization, Self and Syncretism in a Papua New Guinean Village.* Cambridge, UK: Cambridge University Press, 1992.

Myers, F. R. *Pintupi Country, Pintupi Self: Sentiment, Place, and Politics among Western Desert Aborigines.* Washington, DC: Smithsonian Institution, 1986.

Schieffelin, B. *The Give and Take of Everyday Life: Language Socialization of Kaluli Children.* Cambridge, UK: Cambridge University Press, 1979.

Sullivan, N. *Papua New Guinea, with Trans Niugini Tours* [handbook]. Mt. Hagen, New Guinea: Trans New Guinea Tours, 1994.

Weiner, A. *Women of Value, Men of Renown.* Austin: University of Texas Press, 1976.

Wurm, S. *Papuan languages of Oceania.* Tubingen, Germany: Gunter Narr, 1982.

Nancy Sullivan

Lapita

The term *lapita* essentially refers to a distinctive form of ancient pottery found on beach sites in southwest Oceania—**Melanesia** and western **Polynesia**—and to the Austronesian culture that developed it. Ancient lapita potsherds were first found in New Britain (Melanesia) by Father Meyer, a Catholic missionary, in 1909 and by other researchers later in the twentieth century. Lapita pottery is distinguished by its unique decorative motifs, which were stamped or incised into the pot's soft clay with various types of wood or bamboo instruments. Its wide variety of motifs includes geometric patterns as well as human-type faces. Lapita pottery fragments have been found in the Melanesian islands of New Britain and New Guinea in the west to the Polynesian islands of Tonga and Samoa in the east. The importance of the discovery of these fragments has gained substance in the last half of the twentieth century for they have helped date and trace Pacific people's migrations eastward across Melanesia into Polynesia from about 1500 B.C.E. (see **Voyaging/Ancient Navigation**).

Recent archeological discoveries indicate that these lapita peoples originally emigrated from Southeast Asia into Melanesia, where they made settlements in islands that had already been populated for thousands of years. Lapita peoples built fairly large villages near the sea coast. They raised various domesticated animals — **pigs**, dogs, and chickens — and they appear to be the first Pacific island peoples to practice animal husbandry and have an agricultural economy. They had a wide range of working tools such as adzes, knives, and fishhooks made of stone or shell. Their main food sources came from fishing and hunting wild birds and animals and from raising a few root crops. In these Melanesian islands, lapita peoples eventually mixed with the population and became assimilated into that culture. Other lapita peoples, who may have already mixed with the Melanesian population, however, set sail eastward and were the first humans to settle the western fringes of Polynesia.

The oldest lapita site found in Polynesia comes from the island of Nukuleka in the Hapa'i group of Tonga. The ancient potsherds found there in 1999 reveal decorative motifs that are almost identical to the ones found in the Santa Cruz Islands of Melanesia to the west. Based on these new finds, it is now believed that the first lapita culture settlers (now called Polynesians) entered Tonga by 900 B.C.E. probably from the area of Santa Cruz rather than through Fiji as was once believed. From Tonga, lapita-pottery-making islanders made their way into Samoa, and, for unknown reasons, by 500 B.C.E., lapita pottery was no longer being made in Samoa and Tonga. Consequently, Polynesians who set out from Samoa to settle islands further to the east carried no knowledge of pottery-making with them, and, as a result, no pottery remains have been found in any of the other Polynesian islands.

Further Reading

Bedford, S., C. Sand, and S. P. Connaughton, eds. *Oceanic Explorations: Lapita and Western Pacific Settlement*. Canberra: Australian National University, 2007.

Lewis, D. *We, the Navigators: The Ancient Art of Landfinding in the Pacific*. Honolulu: University of Hawai'i Press, 1972.

Lum, J. K. "Central and Eastern Micronesia: Genetics, the Overnight Voyage, and Linguistic Divergence." *Man and Culture in Oceania* 14 (1998): 69–80.

Makemson, M. W. *The Morning Star Rises: An Account of Polynesian Astronomy*. New Haven, CT: Yale University Press, 1941.

Suggs, R. C. *The Island Civilizations of Polynesia*. New York: Mentor Books, 1960.

Summerhayes, G. *Lapita Interaction*. Canberra: Australian National University, 2000.

Yed, D. E., and J. M. J. Mummery, eds. *Pacific Production Systems: Approaches to Economic Prehistory*. Canberra: The Australian National University, 1990.

Nancy Sullivan

Law

Across Oceania, the social control has long been established by systems of taboos (*tapu*, *kapu*). These behavioral restrictions, dietary laws and privileges govern different classes or types of people. It is the fear of supernatural retribution from breaking these taboos that keeps law and order in most traditional Oceanic societies. By far more arbitrary than Western law, the concept of supernatural justice is oppressive, as the gods may target you in unexpected ways, or victimize relatives instead (*see* **Gods and Goddesses**). In many places, it is combined with an equally fearsome threat of human sorcery wielded for everything from jealousy to retribution.

A few key distinctions can be made between southwestern (or Melanesian) concepts of justice and those of the more eastern (Polynesian) and northern (Micronesian) island groups. Melanesian cultures are shaped by concepts of reciprocity, so that everything from supernatural to social relations are seen to be part of an ongoing dialectic between givers and receivers, those who are owed and those who owe. Any antisocial behavior can be viewed in terms of the given quid pro quo, as either a return for a former wrongdoing, or a misstep that requires compensation. The principle of restorative justice, or finding a social peace, is far more important than individual justice, and thus clansmen sometimes take the "punishment" for each other, and perceived injury may call for more compensation than real. In legal proceedings, cases were heard by the local **chief** (*alii*) or priest who might order a trial by ordeal for the wrongdoer. For everyday matters, however, Hawaiians use a form of family-based dispute resolution called *hooponopono* or "setting it right."

Further Reading

Horigan, Damien P. "Some Aspects of Law in Hawaii." *Journal of South Pacific Law* 5 (2001). Available at http://www.paclii.org/journals/fJSPL/vol05/1.shtml.

Stephen, M., ed. *Sorcerer and Witch in Melanesia*. New Brunswick, NJ: Rutgers University Press, 1987.

Trompf, G. W. *Payback: The Logic of Retribution in Melanesian Religions*. Cambridge, UK: Cambridge University Press, 1994.

Nancy Sullivan

Leeward and Windward

With its high temperatures and humidity, the climate of almost all of Island Oceania is considered tropical, except, of course, southern New Zealand and a few other remote islands. Variations in rainfall in some island groups extend from almost none at all to over 470 inches a year. Most of this variation has to do with the particular wind patterns that cross the Pacific.

Throughout most of the Pacific (especially the eastern two-thirds), the dominant wind system consists of the trade winds. They are affected, of course, by the earth's rotation so that they blow from the southeast in the southern hemisphere and from the northeast in the northern. These brisk and ever-continuous winds bring moderate showers occasioned sometimes by heavy downpours and then clear skies. The trades from both hemispheres conjoin along the equator in a low-pressure zone known as the Inter-Tropical Convergence Zone (ITCZ), or more popularly called "The Doldrums."

The trades are noted for their regularity and strength, especially in Hawai'i, where they blow continuously for months on end without stopping. As the trades blow across the open ocean, they pick up moisture, and when they hit the high mountain peaks of an island, they deposit rain on what is called the island's windward side. Rainfall is particular heavy, especially if the mountains lie close to the coast and at right angles to the rain-laden winds. A good example is the island of Kaua'i in the Hawaiian chain. Mount Wai'ale'ale averages 486 inches or more a year and is considered one of the rainiest spots in the world. Once across the mountains, the winds lose most of their moisture, and as a result, the leeward sides of the islands are much dryer. Kaua'i's leeward beaches, for example, receive a scant 5 inches a year! Frequently, the windward sides of the islands may experience a downpour, while the leeward sides bask in clear, blue skies. Other Pacific island groups experience this same phenomena, the most prominent being Fiji, Papua New Guinea, and Guadalcanal.

The seasonal movements of the ITCZ bring drastic climatic changes to the normal wind and rain patterns. Trades winds stop almost entirely and become variable, while moisture builds up more often, and then storm clouds drop their rain more widely over the islands, often days and weeks on end. This is generally referred to as the "wet season" of the year, and in the northern hemisphere, it occurs between December and March (winter months). During the same time in the western Pacific, monsoon winds from Asia bring rain to the Caroline Islands in **Micronesia** and to New Guinea and the Solomon Islands in **Melanesia**. *See also* **El Niño/La Niña**.

Further Reading

Craig, Robert D. *Historical Dictionary of Honolulu and Hawai'i.* Lanham, MD: Scarecrow Press, Inc., 1998, pp. 139–140.

Hinz, Earl R., and Jim Howard. *Landfalls of Paradise: Cruising Guide to the Pacific Islands.* 5th ed. Honolulu: University of Hawai'i Press, 2006.

Thomas, W. L. "The Pacific Basin: An Introduction." In A. P. Vayda, ed., *Peoples and Cultures of the Pacific.* Garden City, NY: Natural History Press, 1968, pp. 3–26.

Robert D. Craig

Mana

Mana is the power of the gods in human agency. Polynesian genealogies attribute divine origins to some of their greatest **chiefs**, and the line between human and divine is somewhat blurred in **Polynesia** cosmology. Thus *mana* is divine power that can be manifest and experienced in human form. But such power is never arbitrary, it must be inherited along very specific bloodlines, and as such, it legitimizes the succession of chiefs. *Mana* is not to be associated with some democratically available source of power. It is a form of life-giving fertility, of procreation and agricultural fecundity, and of political efficacy. Not least, it is a source of danger that must be channeled properly. These features are common throughout Polynesian cultures, although with regional variations. *Mana* is a force of nature that is irrational and destructive in its uncontrolled state, but beneficial when constrained by systems of *tapu* and *noa*. *Tapu* refers to the sacred and *noa* the profane—or the chiefly and the common, the pure and impure, and so forth.

Interestingly, in central and eastern Polynesia (Hawaii, Marquesas, New Zealand, Easter Island, Society Islands) the concept of *mana* tends to devalue the female, or feminine, whereas in western Polynesia (Samoa, Tonga, Tokelau, Tuvalu, Tikopia and Pukapuka) *mana* appears to exalt the feminine. In the east, **women** are considered common and polluting and dangerous; they must be rigidly controlled by systems of *tapu*. But it is apparent that the reproductive power of women is a prime source of *mana*, and not to be taken for granted. Where it is feared and deprecated as impure, it is also tacitly revered for its fecundity and force. So the east–west gender variation to *mana* is more of a continuum than an inversion of concepts. *See also* **Gods and Goddesses**.

Further Reading

Finney, B. R. *Voyage of Discovery: A Cultural Odyssey through Polynesia*. Berkeley: University of California Press, 1994.

Firth, R. *We, the Tikopia*. Stanford, CA: Stanford University Press, 1983 [1936].

Howard, A., and R. Borofsky, eds. *Developments in Polynesian Ethnology*. Honolulu: University of Hawai'i Press, 1989.

Kirch, P. V. *On the Road of the Winds: An Archaeological History of the Pacific Islands Before European Contact*. Berkeley: University of California Press, 2000.

Kirch, P. V., and R. C. Green. *Hawaiki, Ancestral Polynesia: An Essay in Historical Anthropology*. Cambridge, UK: Cambridge University Press, 2001.

Lewis, D. *We, the Navigators: The Ancient Art of Landfinding in the Pacific*. Honolulu: University of Hawai'i Press, 1972.

Makemson, M.W. *The Morning Star Rises: An Account of Polynesian Astronomy*. New Haven, CT: Yale University Press, 1941.

Marcus, G. "Chieftainship." In A. Howard and R. Borofsky, eds., *Developments in Polynesian Ethnology*. Honolulu: University of Hawai'i Press, 1989, pp. 175–210.

Sahlins, M. *Social Stratification in Polynesia*. Seattle, WA: American Ethnological Society, 1958.

Shore, B. *"Mana" and "Tapu."* In A. Howard and R. Borofsky, eds. *Developments in Polynesian Ethnology*. Honolulu: University of Hawai'i Press, 1989, pp. 137–174.

Suggs, R. C. *The Island Civilizations of Polynesia*. New York: Mentor Books, 1960.

Nancy Sullivan

Marae

In most Pacific cultures, community and/or religious ceremonies were conducted in open, public areas that could be associated with the modern terminology "the village green." In the western Polynesian islands of Samoa and Tonga it was called the *malae*, and in New Zealand (eastern Polynesian culture) it was called the *marae*. In other parts of eastern **Polynesia**, however, the term *marae* was used to identify certain megalithic, platformed structures that were used specifically for religious purposes, similar to "temples" or "churches" in other cultures. These monuments were dotted throughout eastern Polynesia—the Society Islands (Tahiti), the Marquesas, Cook Islands, the Tuamotu Islands, and Hawai'i (where they were called *heiau*).

Essentially, *marae* (*ma'ae* or *heiau*) were large raised stone platforms (*ahu*) upon which the islanders built structures for religious purposes. They often contained priests houses, altars, houses for the gods, and various stone slabs that were dedicated to one purpose or another, all of which were usually erected around a central, open platform area (the traditional "village green"). The largest of the stone *marae* are found in Taipivai Valley on the island of Nuku Hiva in the Marquesas. In the nineteenth century, Herman Melville described one "amazing" platform (*ma'ae* or *tohua*) that was subsequently measured at 550 feet long and 82 feet wide with a wall of enormous stones reaching a height of 10 feet. A massive *marae* at Mahaiatea on Tahiti consisted of a rectangular *ahu* upon which was built a type of step pyramid. It no longer survives in its original state, but fortunately, English missionary James Wilson made a drawing of it during his visit there in the 1760s. It measured 71 by 263

A cluster of tall wooden god figures at a Marae, temple site, near Hanaunau on the west coast of Hawaii. 1970. Werner Forman/Art Resource, NY.

feet upon which were eleven successive smaller steps were placed, raising it to a height of approximately 50 feet.

In Hawai'i, numerous *heiau* of various sizes were built throughout the islands. On the island of O'ahu, the largest was the *Pu'u-o-Mahuka* ("Hill of Escape") *heiau*, built on a cliff overlooking beautiful Waimea Bay on O'ahu's north shore. On the Big Island of Hawai'i, three heiau were enclosed in the City of Refuge at Hōnaunau (*Pu'uhonua-o-Hōnaunau*). The site is currently being restored and maintained by the U.S. Park Service. The complex at Hōnaunau contains a massive 13-foot-high wall enclosure that houses the three *heiau*, two of which have recently been reconstructed by using extant drawings made by Christian missionaries in the early nineteenth century.

Apparently, sizes of *marae* did not entirely indicate their relative importance. The relatively small *marae* of Taputapuatea, located on the southeast coast of the island of Rā'iatea (Society Islands), for example, is reputed to have been the most sacred of all *marae* in Polynesia. Sources tell us that the various Polynesian island chiefs (even as far away as New Zealand) would send yearly sacrifices to Taputapuatea. Its simple, stone-slabbed *ahu* is only 130 by 23 feet, and it is surrounded by numerous upright stone slabs, some measuring 13 feet, which anciently served for backrests for the officiating priests or high **chiefs**. (For more details regarding the various religious ceremonies conducted in Pacific cultures, refer to the "Religion" essay, above.) Folklore and legends tell us that Rā'iatea was the "homeland" of many of the Polynesians who set sail to establish new homes across the seas.

Although Tongans did not erect stone *marae* like the eastern Polynesians, they did construct sacred stone structures (*langi*) to mark important burial grounds, especially those surrounding the Tui Tonga ("King" of Tonga) ceremonial center located at Mu'a on the island of Tongatapu (*see* **Tongan Empire**). Likewise, the Ponapeans in **Micronesia** suggest that their monumental ruins at **Nan Madol** may have included a religious center. The Melanesians and Australians, unfortunately, produced nothing similar to what their neighbors to the east constructed. *See also* **Gods and Goddesses**.

Further Reading

Bellwood, Peter. *Man's Conquest of the Pacific.* New York: Oxford University Press, 1979, pp. 273, 289–295, 331–377.

Emory, Kenneth P. *The Natural and Cultural History of Hōnaunau, Kona, Hawaii.* Honolulu, HI: Bernice Pauahi Bishop Museum, 1986.

Handy, E.,S. Craighill. *The Native Culture in the Marquesas.* New York: Kraus Reprint Company, 1986 [1923].

Robert D. Craig

Melanesia

Melanesia is a group of Oceanic islands ranging from the big island of New Guinea, to the west, and Fiji to the east. The term was coined by Jules Dumont D'Urville in 1832 as a reference to the black-skinned inhabitants of these islands, which is perhaps the only thing that these diverse cultures hold in common. The term is useful politically to describe treaties that unite the states of Papua New Guinea, Vanuatu, Solomon Islands, Fiji and sometimes New Caledonia, although these neither exhaust the Melanesian states nor indicate any political cohesion.

As a geographic term, Melanesia is easier to map, and the most pronounced characteristic of the region is its extraordinary cultural and linguistic diversity. New Guinea, the Bismark Archipelago, the Admiralty Islands, the Solomon Islands, Vanuatu, Norfolk Island, Fiji Torres Straits Islands, New Caledonia, Manus, Aru Island and the offshore islands of West New Guinea, have all been included in the term. In addition, the peoples of Flores, Nauru, Sumba, Timor-Leste, and Rotuma are sometimes included for their mixed Melanesian heritage.

Interestingly, though the Indonesian islands of the Banda Sea are not included in the term Melanesia, reference is sometimes made to the Andaman Sea islands of Andaman and Nicobar, politically part of India, and geographically at the western edge of Indonesia and Malaysia. This is because the inhabitants of these islands are "Papuans," ethnologically the same as the Melanesians of the interior of New Guinea (who share the Papuan language phylum).

Melanesia is truly a jangle of terms. Where cultural definitions exclude certain islands, geographic ones may include them. Most of the region speaks languages from the Austronesian phylum, although Melanesian peoples are often lumped together as "Papuans." The south coast of Eastern New Guinea was once called "Papua" by its British colonizers, as distinguished from German "New Guinea," but currently the term *New Guinea* refers to the entire large island as a whole, while *Papua* is reserved for the Indonesian half of the island.

The enormous biological and cultural diversity of this region tends to thin out as the map moves eastward to Polynesia, northward to Micronesia, and southward through Australia. To talk about the region's flora and fauna we therefore do our best to focus on the largest island, New Guinea, whose flora is one of the richest in the world, particularly within rainforests. The larger islands of Melanesia are from 50 to 100 miles in length with their mountains ranging from 1,000 to 10,000 feet in height.

The island of New Guinea, which includes Papua New Guinea in the east and Indonesia's Irian Jaya Province (now West Papua) to the west, is the second largest island in the world, after Greenland. It is about 1,300 miles by 700 miles and is the world's highest island, with the ice-capped Cartensz Massif in West Papua rising to over 16,000 feet, and 60 percent of the land rising above 900 feet.

About 75 percent of New Guinea s covered by rainforest—some of the most extensive and unspoilt rainforests in the world. Rainforests have greater plant life than any other habitats, which in New Guinea include mangrove forests, swamps and lakes, flood plains, grasslands, savannahs, scrubland, woodlands, and cultivated areas.

In New Guinea there are actually five types of rainforest: lowland alluvial and lowland hill; and then lower, middle, or upper montane or highland rainforest. Lowland rainforests support the most plant species (up to twelve hundred) with gingers, palms, strangler figs, climbing palms, woody lianas and orchids, most notably.

In the rainforest plants and animals are adapted to three strata: the forest floor, the understory, and the canopy. The entire system depends on a lot of rainfall, and the humidity within it may reach saturation. Inside the canopy this moisture may be absorbed directly by tree bark or plant roots, or it may evaporate; the excess rains off and down into mountain gullies and creeks which eventually cascade over waterfalls and flow into lowland rivers to the sea.

It is impossible to give the exact number of species found in New Guinea, as many of them, particularly invertebrates, remain undescribed and/or undiscovered. There are about 190 species of mammals in New Guinea, representing all three types. Monotreme mammals lay eggs and, after they hatch, nurse the young on milk. The two species of New Guinea monotremes are spiny anteaters, or echidnas. The marsupial mammals include about seventy species: bandicoots, certain rats, wallabies, tree kangaroos, gliders, possums, and cuscuses, all have pouches for their newly born young to develop further. Placental mammals, such as ourselves, stay in the womb longer where they get nourishment through the placenta. These include bats (seventy species), such as flying foxes, blossom bats, and insect-eating bats; and rodents (about fifty-five species), such as tree mice, melomys, and rats.

All around the coasts and out on the beautiful coral reefs, New Guinea teems with marine life. Divers say there are more fish per cubic meter than any other place in the world. Yet there are relatively few native freshwater species, and most edible ones like carp and tilapia are introduced.

There are at least twenty-five thousand species of beetles, and six thousand moths and butterflies in New Guinea. There are also grasshoppers, earwings, termites, bees, wasps, ants dragonflies, damselflies, lacewings, mayflies, cicadas, aphids, flies, and (the ubiquitous) mosquitoes. Of the frogs alone there are about 160 species.

New Guinea has two species of crocodile. The estuarine or saltwater crocodile is widespread throughout the Indo-Pacific, including tropical Australia. It lives in marine habitats and coastal river systems. The New Guinea crocodile is found in freshwater rivers, lakes, marshes, and swamplands. The two actually exist together in rivers throughout New Guinea.

New Guinea has a rich lizard fauna with about 170 species, including geckoes, legless lizards, dragon lizards, monitor lizards or goanna; and one hundred species of skinks. Approximately 110 species of snakes can be found, including sea snakes, tree snakes, pythons, and (more rarely) poisonous front-fanged snakes such as death adders and taipans.

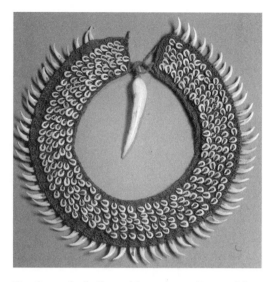

Tooth and shell necklace from Papua New Guinea. The Art Archive/Alfredo Dagli Orti.

During the Middle Ages the Melanesian islands were thoroughly settled and engaged in extensive networks of exchange and interaction, bellicose and peaceful. Toward the east of the region in the islands of New Caledonia, Vanuatu, and Fiji, social organization was chiefly, and trade networks involved tributes to the local chiefs that included **shell valuables**, implements, and others valuable objects. To the western side of the region, the interior of New Guinea was dotted with small communities living in defensive suspicion of their neighbors, raising sweet potato and **taro** gardens that became the basis of their more egalitarian, democratic systems of governance, otherwise known as "**bigman**" societies. *See also* **New Guinea, Fauna of** and **New Guinea, Flora of**.

Further Reading

Bedford, S., C. Sand, and S. P. Connaughton, eds. *Oceanic Explorations: Lapita and Western Pacific Settlement*. Canberra: Australian National University, 2007.

Brown, P. *Highland Peoples of New Guinea*. Cambridge, UK: Cambridge University Press, 1978.

Gewertz, D. *Sepik River Societies: A Historical Ethnography of the Chambri and Their Neighbors*. New Haven, CT: Yale University Press, 1983.

Herdt, G. H. *Guardians of the Flutes: Idioms of Masculinity*. New York: McGraw-Hill, 1981.

Herdt, G. H., ed. *Rituals of Manhood: Male Initiation in Papua New Guinea*. Berkeley: University of California Press, 1982.

Malinowski, B. *Argonauts of the Western Pacific*. London: Routledge, 1922.

Myers, F. R. *Pintupi Country, Pintupi Self: Sentiment, Place, and Politics among Western Desert Aborigines*. Washington, DC: Smithsonian Institution, 1986.

Neich, R., and F. Pereira. *Pacific Jewelry and Adornment*. Honolulu: University of Hawai'i Press, 2004.

Sahlins, M. "Poor Man, Rich Man, Big Man, Chief: Political Types in Melanesia and Polynesia." *Comparative Studies in Society and History* 5 (1963): 285–303.

Schieffelin, E.L. *The Sorrow of the Lonely and the Burning of the Dancers*. New York: St. Martin's Press, 1976.

Suggs, R. C. *The Island Civilizations of Polynesia*. New York: Mentor Books, 1960.

Strathern, A. J. *Rope of Moka: Big-Men and Ceremonial Exchange in Mount Hagen, New Guinea*. Cambridge, UK: Cambridge University Press, 1971.

Strathern, Andrew. *One Father, One Blood: Descent and Group Structure Among the Melpa People*. London: Tavistock, 1972.

Weiner, A. *Women of Value, Men of Renown*. Austin: University of Texas Press, 1976.

Nancy Sullivan

Micronesia

The term *Micronesia* comes from two Greek words—*mikros*, small and *nesos*, island—and is used to designate one of the three major geographical areas of the Pacific Basin. The term was first used by the French scholar Jules Dumont d'Urville in 1831 to distinguish these small Pacific islands north of the equator from those of **Polynesia** lying to their south and east. The third geographical area is **Melanesia**, a large group of Pacific islands lying directly south of Micronesia and the equator. Although scholars may disagree with d'Urville's classification (because of the great diversity in each group), the designation is still a convenient way to divide the area for general discussion.

Geographically, Micronesia consists of approximately 2,106 small islands and atolls in the north Pacific tropics lying between 13 and 20 degrees north latitude and stretching in a slight arc from 130 to 180 degrees east longitude. The main groups include Guam and the Marianas (with Palau and Yap), the Carolines, Marshalls, Kiribati (formerly the Gilbert Islands), and Nauru.

Archeological and linguistic evidence suggests that the high islands of western Micronesia were first settled from the Philippines possibly between 2000 and 1500 B.C.E. and then the eastern Micronesian islands were settled 2,000 years later by voyagers coming from eastern Melanesia (probably near Vanuatu). Although some eight cultural groups are recognized, ancient Micronesians were alike in many ways. They were subsistence farmers living in small villages or in single out-lying farmsteads, and they augmented their simple diet of plant **foods** primarily with fish caught in the lagoons or out in the deeper depths of the Pacific. Their main plant foods consisted of **breadfruit, taro**, coconuts, and pandanus kernels, but often these could not grow sufficiently on the low atolls to allow people to survive. The islanders in the Marianas also raised rice, a food unknown to the rest of Oceania.

Linguistically, the Micronesians spoke a multitude of languages, distinct and often unintelligible one from another, although they are recognized as being Austronesian in origin. Without a written language, the Micronesians depended upon oral tradition to pass down their knowledge from one generation to another. Oratory and storytelling were highly respected "professions" within their culture.

The lack of local resources often forced the Micronesians to turn to trade with their island neighbors. Using outrigger canoes and sailing by observing the stars and the wind and water currents, they became extremely competent navigators, often traveling vast distances within Micronesia (and perhaps beyond). Island "fleets" from Yap and Truk frequently sailed to Guam and other parts of Micronesia to trade food stuffs, shell ornaments, fine mats, special dyes, or even large stone discs that the Yapese used for money. These expert navigators even developed a type of navigational map—called "stick charts," made of wooden sticks and shells—to aid them in sailing between the islands.

Status in Micronesian society depended primarily upon birth, however, there were instances where one could gain ascendancy through some special ability, but this was not the norm. Unlike the Polynesians who developed highly structured patriarchal societies, the Micronesians (except for Yap and the Gilberts) developed unique matrilineal societies. (Matriliny should never be considered a system that somehow empowers women—and should not be confused with matriarchy.) Chiefly authority varied from one group to another. Chiefs on Palau, for example, exercise little authority while those in the Marshalls held absolute authority over lands and persons. Living in such close proximity to one another, the Micronesians developed techniques of adjustment and reconciliation that created societies that were less aggressive and more reconciliatory than often found in other parts of the Pacific.

Most Micronesians lived in some form of extended-family group. Members usually did not marry within the same lineage—some newlywed couples would live with the husband's family while others with the wife's. Monogamy was the general rule, but sometimes a more affluent Micronesian had more than one wife or concubine. In this case, the principal wife exercised strong authority over family affairs. Commoners generally lived in lean-to huts that have not survived the ages, however, some large stone house foundation columns (*latte*) still survive on Guam and on the Mariana Islands. Approximately ninety-two stone platforms on the island of Ponape suggest the remains of a small "royal" town, including a religious center. Large and often elaborate meeting houses or men's club houses were commonly found in villages that served for gathering places for communal affairs.

Back-strap loom weaving by **women** was practiced throughout the Caroline Islands (except Palau) and was found only again in the northern Melanesian islands. (Loom weaving was unknown in Polynesia.) Richly colored Micronesian threads of black, brown, and red were woven into colorful loincloths, sashes, skirts, and burial shrouds. Other art forms consisted of shell ornaments and artifacts, decorative mats, tattooing, and woodcarvings. *See also* **Voyaging/ Ancient Navigation**.

Further Reading

Akire, William H. *An Introduction to the Peoples and Cultures of Micronesia*. 2nd ed. Menlo Park, CA: Cummings Publishing, 1977.

Bellwood, Peter. "Prehistory of Oceania." *Current Anthropology*. 16, no. 1 (March 1975): pp. 9–28.

Mason, Leonard. "The Ethnology of Micronesia." In Andrew P. Vayda, ed., *Peoples and Cultures of the Pacific*. New York: Natural History Press, 1968, pp. 275–298.

Oliver, Douglas, 1951. *The Pacific Islanders*. Cambridge, MA: Harvard University Press, pp. 57–60.

Rainbird, Paul. *Archeology of Micronesia*. Cambridge, UK: Cambridge University Press, 2004.

Robert D. Craig

Moai (Easter Island)

One of the greatest artistic achievements ever fashioned by any civilization was the creation of the six-hundred megalithic statues that still stand on Easter Island. They were carved by a Polynesian, stone-age people, who immigrated to the small island around 500 C.E. and who spent the next 1,000 years forming these unique structures. Exactly why and how they formed the statues have intrigued modern scholars since the island was first "discovered" on Easter day, 1722, by the famed Dutch explorer Jacob Roggeveen. This enigma is often referred to as the "mystery of Easter Island."

Modern scholars in the nineteenth and twentieth centuries, such as Katherine Routledge, Alfred Métraux, Henri Lavachery, Thor Heyderdahl, and William Mulloy, have provided theses that illuminate much of Easter Island's distant past as well as the "mystery of Easter Island." Although Heyerdahl suggested that drifting rafts from South America may have brought the first inhabitants to the island, most other authorities, using archeology and linguistic sources, agree that they immigrated most likely from the Marquesas islands in eastern Polynesia. (Others have argued that they came from a lost continent called Mu or even from outer space!)

Easter Island history is divided into three major periods—Early (500–1000 C.E.), Middle (1000–1600), and Late (1600–). In the Late Period, continual civil war broke out between the island clans that brought an end to their *moai* carving and the decline in their population and culture. Many of the unfinished statues (about 150) were left in the quarry sites or partly moved to their final resting places, and an examination of these reveals the exact way in which they were formed. Using only their primitive stone mauls, carvers in the stone quarry cut trenches around the statue as the rest of it was being carved out of the limestone. The statue was kept intact during its construction by an uncut spine running down its back until completion. The workers would then string rope around the statue in strategic places, and when the spine was severed, the statue was then raised upright. After these huge statues were finished, they were then hauled several miles to their final resting places. Considering that some of the statues attained a height of 37 feet and weighed almost 100 tons, it is remarkable that this could be done without modern equipment.

Ahu Nau nau in Anakena beach. According to local tradition, the first Polynesian settlers arrived on this shore in the 6th century, led by their chief Hotu matua. All Anakena statues have red tuff topknots. 10th–12th c. © Ivonne Wierink/Dreamstime.com.

In the 1960s, archeologist William Mulloy suggested that the statues were transported by a system of leverages and a large forked sled attached to the front of the statue. He estimated that an average-sized statue would have taken thirty men one year to carve, then ninety men 2 months to move it from the quarry to its final resting place, and then another 3 months to get it erect.

Several mysteries still remain. To begin with, what was the inspiration behind creating these huge monuments? And second, were they meant to portray their ancestral chiefs or their powerful gods? These questions may never be answered. Easter Islands today use all forms of modern gas and electrical engines to help stand many of these statues upright so that they may be more appealing to the growing number of tourists who visit the island. But there is no suggested proposal that they try carving out new *moai* that rival their ancestors' work done 1,000 years ago. *See also* **Gods and Goddesses**.

Further Reading

Bellwood, Peter. *Man's Conquest of the Pacific*. New York: Oxford University Press, 1979, pp. 361–377.

McCall, Grant. *Rapanui: Tradition and Survival on Easter Island*. 2nd ed. Honolulu: University of Hawai'i Press, 1994.

Orliac, Catherine, and Michel Orliac. *Easter Island: Mystery of the Stone Giants*. New York: Abrams, 1995.

Robert D. Craig

Musical Instruments

Music played a major role in the cultural life of Oceanic peoples, although the number and types of their musical instruments were extremely limited. In one Micronesian Island group, for example, the only two "instruments" known were the conch shell, used primarily for signaling purposes, and the rolled-leaf oboe, used primarily as a toy. Despite these limitations, however, European explorers who first visited the islands of the Pacific were deeply impressed with the expertise with which the islanders performed, although their instruments seemed extremely primitive. Traditional musical instruments in Oceania consisted primarily of a variety of drums, slit gongs, flutes, and panpipes, although not all existed in every island group. Most music was performed not for entertainment but for religious and ritual ceremonies.

The most common instrument was the drum, cylindrical in shape with a sharkskin membrane stretched over the hollow end and secured with a type of rope made of coconut fibers through slotted holes in the drum's base. Sizes of the drum ranged from the small knee variety (uniquely found in Hawai'i) to the hourglass-shaped drums found in New Guinea and **Melanesia** and the tall, slender drums with elaborate carvings found in Tahiti and other Polynesian groups. These drums were beaten by one's fingers and the full hand in a variety of percussion rhythms, depending upon the desired sound.

Slit gongs were found in various cultures throughout the world, except for Australia. They were made of various sizes of bamboo or hollowed-out wooden logs with one or more slits cut into them. Many gongs had three slits cut into them in the shape of an "H." The ends of the logs were closed, and sound was produced by striking the log with a wooden mallet. The size and the thickness of the gong and mallet determined the pitch and volume of the sound. Large gongs pounded with heavy mallets could be heard for miles and were used for signaling as well as for accompanying singers and dancers. Smaller slit gongs were struck with a variety of sticks at various speeds and rhythms to accompany performers in their dances. Precision drumming in the islands continued into modern times, and drumming groups from Bora Bora, the Cook Islands, Tonga, and Tahiti are especially noted for their precision and skill.

Nose flutes were popular in **Polynesia** but found less often in the rest of the Pacific. They were usually made from a section of bamboo about 12 to 18 inches long and up to an inch in diameter. In New Zealand, however, where bamboo was scarce, the Māori made their nose flutes (*gnuru*) from hollowed out soapstone. Nose flutes had a hole on one side at one end and up to six holes on the other side. The performer placed the thumb of the right hand against the right nostril and held the flute with the right fingers up to the left nostril through which air was blown. Covering and uncovering the other holes produced a variety of notes. Its sound was described as soft and plaintive, but its range was extremely limited, consisting of three to four notes and unlike Western music could produce half and quarter notes on the scale. The flute was played to accompany singing and dancing.

A unique form of wind instrument was the panpipe, sometimes referred to as the pan flute. It was found throughout the ancient world—Europe, Asia, and South America—and in the Pacific. It became a highly sophisticated instrument among the 'Are'are people of Malaita (Solomon Islands in Melanesia). Panpipes usually consisted of three to nine closed tubes, doubled by open tubes, which produced a higher octave, and all were then secured together in irregular distribution of lengths. Sound was produced by blowing across the open end of a tube. Its length and width determined its particular pitch and sound, while at the same time, the main tube vibrated its neighboring tubes, which added a varied dimension to the main sound. During village performances, many members of the community would join in so that there could be fifty or more performers. Complex ensemble playing was the norm among the 'Are'are. Their music depicted sounds from nature, like bird and animal calls, the sounds of the ocean and rivers, as well as human sounds and actions. In modern times, contemporary musical groups have revived their unique panpipe-playing traditions and have performed to sold-out audiences around the world.

Although the Indigenous Australians had far fewer sound-producing instruments than the rest of Oceania, one that stands out as unique to them was the didjeridu (didgeridoo), found primarily in northern Australia among the Yolngu people. The didjeridu accompanied most singers and dancers in their religious ceremonies, or it could be used for signaling or communicating with one another for several miles. It was constructed from a wooden branch or log that had been hollowed-out by termites or ants. The bark was removed and the surface smoothed and sharpened. A rim of beeswax was placed around the rim of one of the ends to form a mouthpiece. It was then played with one's vibrating lips very much like a trumpet, trombone, or other similar instrument. What made the didjeridu unique was its special technique of circular breathing, a feat not easily accomplished without training. Air is breathed in through the nose while at the same time it is blown out of the mouth to produce a continuing droning type of sound. (Contemporary players have been known to sustain a single note for over 40 to 50 minutes!)

Internet searches (at YouTube.com, for example) can find actual video clips of performances of the various instruments described above, for example, "slit gong" or "slit drums," "Cook Island drummers," "Tahiti drummers," "Pacific nose flutes," "Solomon Islands/Malaita panpipes," and "Australian didjeridu." *See also* **Dance**.

Further Reading

Feld, Steven. "Bamboo Boogie-Woogie." In Simon Broughton and Mark Ellington, eds., *World Music*, Vol. 2: *Latin & North America, Caribbean, India, Asia and Pacific*. London: Rough Guides Ltd., 2000, pp. 183–188.

Malm, William P. *Music Cultures of the Pacific, the Near East, and Asia*. 3rd ed. Upper Saddle River, NJ: Prentice Hall, 1996.

Zemp, Hugo. "Melanesian Solo Polyphonic Panpipe Music." *Ethnomusicology* 25, no. 3 (1981): 383–415.

Robert D. Craig

Nan Madol

The house platform ruins on the island of Ponape (Pohnpei) in **Micronesia** rank as some of the most magnificent in all of Oceania, including the *moai* statues found on Easter Island. Nan Madol lies on the southeastern side of the island and consists of ruins of a small town including a religious center that perhaps date back to 900 to 1200. Approximately ninety-two platforms of coral rubble faced with basalt retaining walls (some 18 to 25 feet high) make up the site with the most impressive structure being the chiefly burial site called Nan Douwas. Most of the platforms were surrounded by water, and travel between the "islets" was by boat. For this reason, Nan Madol is often referred to as the "Venice of the Pacific."

The exact date of the settlement of the island is still unknown, but permanent settlements existed from the first two centuries C.E. Apparently, the building of the megalithic structures only began, however, with the conquering San Deleur (Lord of Deleur) family around the twelfth or thirteenth centuries. The entire island population may have reached twenty-five thousand with Nan Madol sustaining a population of about one thousand. Ponapean oral traditions maintain that the San Deleur dynasty was overthrown, perhaps in the early 1600s by a legendary hero named Isokelekel, and he divided the island into three separate, autonomous districts in order to prevent any future centralization of power on the island. Isokelekel's title was Nahnmwarki of Madolenihmw, and he ruled from the center of Nan Madol. By the early modern period (c. 1700), the Nahnmwarki family had abandoned Nan Madol, and, consequently, the site fell into ruins.

Nan Madol was first observed by Western outsiders to the island in 1828 and 1833. Other visitors to the island reported their finds throughout the century, but it was only in 1910 that the German archaeologist Paul Hambruch seriously made any precise site measurements and detailed observations of the site. Since then, numerous scientific research teams have visited the island (especially the Smithsonian Institute in 1963) and have contributed to the understanding of the site and its relationship to the other neighboring monuments in the islands.

Further Reading

Ballinger, Bill S. *Lost City of Stone: The Story of nan Madol, The "Atlanti" of the Pacific.* NY: Simon & Schuster, 1979.

Robert D. Craig

New Guinea, Fauna of

The fauna of New Guinea is one of the richest in the world, particularly within rainforests. It is impossible to give the exact number of species found in New Guinea, as many of them, particularly invertebrates, remain undescribed or undiscovered.

There are about 190 species of mammals here, representing all three types. Monotreme mammals lay eggs and, after they hatch, nurse the young on milk. The two species of New Guinea monotremes are spiny anteaters, or echidnas. The marsupial mammals include about seventy species: bandicoots, certain rats, wallabies, tree kangaroos, gliders, possums, and cuscuses all have pouches for their newly born young to develop further. Placental mammals, such as ourselves, stay in the womb longer where they get nourishment through the placenta. These include bats (about seventy species), such as flying foxes, blossom bats and insect-eating bats; and rodents (about fifty-five species), such as tree mice, melomys, and rats.

All around the coasts and out on the beautiful coral reefs, New Guinea teems with marine life. Experts say there are more fish per cubic meter than any other place in the world. Yet there are relatively few native freshwater species, and most edible ones like carp and tilapia were introduced by Europeans very recently.

There are at least twenty-five thousand species of beetles, and six-thousand moths and butterflies in New Guinea. There are also grasshoppers, earwings, termites, bees, wasps, ants, dragonflies, damselflies, lacewings, mayflies, cicadas, aphids, flies, and those ubiquitous mosquitoes. Of the frogs alone there are about 160 species.

New Guinea has two species of crocodile. The estuarine or saltwater crocodile is widespread throughout the Indo-Pacific, including tropical Australia. It lives in marine habitats and coastal river systems. The New Guinea crocodile is found in freshwater rivers, lakes, marshes, and swamplands. The two actually exist together in New Guinea rivers.

New Guinea has a rich lizard fauna with about 170 species, including geckoes, legless lizards, dragon lizards, monitor lizards or goanna; and one hundred species of skinks. Approximately 110 species of snakes can be found, including sea snakes, tree snakes, pythons, and (more rarely) poisonous front-fanged snakes such as death adders and taipans. *See also* **New Guinea, Flora of**.

Further Reading

Flannery, T. *Mammals of New Guinea*. rev. ed. Ithaca, NY: Cornell University Press, 1995.

Marshall, A., and B. M. Beehler, eds. *The Ecology of Papua, Parts One and Two: The Ecology of Indonesia Series, Volume VI.* Singapore: Periplus Editions, Conservation International, 2007.

Strathern, A. J. *Rope of Moka: Big-Men and Ceremonial Exchange in Mount Hagen, New Guinea.* Cambridge, UK: Cambridge University Press, 1971.

Strathern, Andrew. *One Father, One Blood: Descent and Group Structure Among the Melpa People*. London: Tavistock, 1972.

Sullivan, N. *Papua New Guinea, with Trans Niugini Tours* [handbook]. Mt. Hagen, New Guinea: Trans New Guinea Tours, 1994.

Yed, D. E., and J. M. J. Mummery, eds. *Pacific Production Systems: Approaches to Economic Prehistory*. Canberra: Australian National University, 1990.

Nancy Sullivan

New Guinea, Flora of

The island if New Guinea, which today comprises Papua New Guinea in the east and Indonesia's West Papua Province to the west, is the second largest island in the world, after Greenland.

About 75 percent of New Guinea is covered by rainforest—some of the most extensive and unspoilt rainforests in the world. Rainforests have greater plant than any other habitats, which in New Guinea include mangrove forests, swamps and lakes, flood plains, grasslands, savannahs, scrubland, woodland, and cultivated areas.

In New Guinea there are actually five types of rainforest: lowland alluvial and lowland hill; and then lower, middle, and upper montane or highland rainforest. Lowland rainforests support the most plant species (up to twelve hundred) with gingers, palms, strangler figs, climbing palms, woody lianas, and orchids the most notable.

In the rainforest plants and animals are adapted to three strata: the forest floor, the understory, and the canopy. The entire system depends on a lot of rainfall, and the humidity within it may reach saturation. Inside the canopy this moisture may be absorbed directly by tree bark or plant roots, or it may evaporate; the excess rains off and down into mountain gullies and creeks that eventually cascade over waterfalls and flow into lowland rivers to the sea. One need only look at the mighty Sepik River to comprehend how much water drains off the mountain rainforests of New Guinea.

The forest floor is covered with a maze of surface roots in shallow systems that extend horizontally from trunk bases and buttresses. Plant seeds germinate on the warm moist forest floor, developing into saplings that strive toward the lighter understory and canopy.

The forest understory is made up of hundreds of tree trunks, most of which produce flowers in their canopy. But some, such as cluster figs, produce flowers and fruits from their main trunks in the understory. Plants in the understory may be terrestrial, epiphytic, climbing, strangling, or parasitic; they include tree ferns, gingers, wild taros, cordylines, pandanus, some orchids, and many shrubs and trees.

Ginger plants have large leaves and red, orange, yellow, and even blue flowers or fruits; and cordyline are thin-stemmed plants with clusters of leaves in red. Highlands peoples use bundles of cordyline for "arse-gras" and plant it to symbolize peace. The variety of rainforest palm trees includes pandanus, or what some call screw palms, which produce bright orange, red, or yellow fruits with edible kernels and oily seeds much prized as food. Coconut palms are the most thoroughly exploited palm, as their trunk fiber provides a kind of netting, their leaves a range of woven materials, and their fruit all kinds of food. Tall, thin, small-crowned betel palms provide the center nut that people chew everywhere; they mix it with crushed coral or limestone to make a mildly stimulating pulp (*see* **Betel Chewing**).

The rainforest canopy is crowded with interlocking tree crowns and their beautiful flowers and succulent fruits, supporting an arboreal garden of tangled vines, mosses, lichens, orchids, and bird's nest ferns. Lowland rainforests are taller than mountain rainforests, and their canopies fuller, rounder, sometimes consisting of three crown layers. Giant emergent trees several hundred to more than 1,000 years old project well above the canopy. The red, pink, and purplish pigmentation on some young leaves in the rainforest protects them from strong radiation. *See also* **New Guinea, Fauna of**.

Further Reading

Malinowski, B. *Argonauts of the Western Pacific*. London: Routledge, 1922.

Marshall, A., and B. M. Beehler, eds. *The Ecology of Papua, Parts One and Two: The Ecology of Indonesia Series, Volume VI*. Singapore: Periplus Editions, Conservation International, 2007.

Strathern, A. J. *Rope of Moka: Big-Men and Ceremonial Exchange in Mount Hagen, New Guinea*. Cambridge, UK: Cambridge University Press, 1971.

Strathern, Andrew. *One Father, One Blood: Descent and Group Structure Among the Melpa People*. London: Tavistock, 1972.

Sullivan, N. *Papua New Guinea, with Trans Niugini Tours* [handbook]. Mt. Hagen, New Guinea: Trans New Guinea Tours, 1994.

Yed, D. E., and J. M. J. Mummery, eds. *Pacific Production Systems: Approaches to Economic Prehistory*. Canberra: Australian National University, 1990.

Nancy Sullivan

NguzuNguzu

In the Western District of the Solomon Islands the canoe prows are carved as stylized human warriors with their hands clasped together, sometimes holding a totemic bird or miniature skull. Inlaid with mother of pearl or nautilus shell eyes, tortoise shell ears, and bright red lips, these striking black heads with beard-like jaw lines have become national symbols for the Solomon Islands. They are called *Toto isu* (in New Georgia Island) or *NguzuNguzu*, and they originated in the fierce western islands of New Georgia, Choiseul, Santa Isabel, and Nggela.

These warrior figureheads were important protection during headhunting raids throughout the pre-Contact era. They watched out for enemies and evil water spirits as they also helped navigate around dangerous reefs and shorelines. Where the figures hold small birds, these are considered to be deity figures than help avoid submarine perils during the journey. Where they hold skulls, the latter are considered sources of *mana* or power transferred from the victims to the victors.

The anthropologist Edvard Hviding, in the following passage, describes these figures as dog-like:

> These small anthropomorphic images (often with dog-like features) were carved from light wood, stained black, and elaborately inlaid with nautilus shell. They are depicted as holding either a human head (for success in headhunting) or a

bird (for navigational aid) in the hands. A toto isu was lashed to the bow of every departing New Georgian war canoe to ensure safe passage and success in warfare; its wide open staring eyes were supposed to ward off any troublesome maritime spirits. (Hviding, 76–78)

Further Reading

Hviding, Edvard. *Guardians of the Marovo Lagoon: Practice, Place and Politics in Maritime Melanesia.* Pacific Islands Monograph Series 14. Honolulu: University of Hawai'i Press, 1996.

Nancy Sullivan

Pigs

Pig production is the most important smallholder livestock management in mainland New Guinea. In Papua New Guinea alone, more than one half the rural population raises pigs. How they arrived in New Guinea, and Oceania more generally, is still a subject of archaeological debate, however. The current consensus seems to be that the pig came to **Melanesia** within the last 3,500 years (possibly only 2,000 years ago), during the later **lapita** migrations from Southeast Asia.

Throughout Oceania pigs are important sources of wealth and are ceremonially killed at all major occasions, from funerals to births, to peace-making and compensation ceremonies. In Melanesia, where they play key roles in highlands exchange systems, the owner rarely consumes his or her pig and indeed looks at the transaction of a pig with some remorse, especially where it has been raised lovingly by hand. Highlands bigmen must cajole their wives into separating from their pigs for a public exchange, as in some cases, where a sow has a large litter, the wife may have nursed a pig at her own breast.

Robin Hide tells a story from the Madang Province of New Guinea that describes the relationship between domestic and feral pig husbandry in Melanesia. In 1979, he says, an interesting practice was observed by a visitor while hunting for wild pigs on Long Island. When the hunter caught a feral boar, they castrated him, and docked the tail and ears, before letting him loose to the wild. The hunters explained that this way the pig would grow fat and they could capture it again, guaranteeing a portion of the meet by the marks they just made (Hide, 13–14).

One of ecological anthropology's classic studies was conducted in the highlands of New Guinea by the anthropologist Roy Rappaport, who collected meticulous quantitative and qualitative data on food consumption and energy expenditure, as well as the world-views of the Maring people, demonstrating exactly how important pigs are to the material and ideological life of these people. *See also* **Bigman**.

Further Reading

Hide, R. *Pig Husbandry in New Guinea: A Literature Review and Bibliography.* Canberra: Australian Centre for International Agricultural Research, 2003.

Rappaport, Roy. *Pigs for the Ancestors: Ritual in the Ecology of a New Guinea People.* New Haven, CT: Yale University Press, 1968.

Nancy Sullivan

Polynesia

The term *Polynesia* comes from two Greek words—*polys*, many and *nesos*, islands—and is used to designate one of the major geographical areas of the Pacific Basin. The term was first used in the English language by Charles de Brosses in 1756 to mean all the islands of the Pacific, but the word was re-stricted to only one section of the Pacific by the French scholar Jules Dumont d'Urville in a lecture he gave in 1831. That geographical area is represented roughly by a vast triangle drawn from the islands of Hawai'i in the north, south-west to New Zealand, east to Easter Island, and then north back to Hawai'i.

Early European explorers to the Pacific (eighteenth century) noticed a simi-larity in the language, customs, and cultures of the island peoples living within that region as they did with the peoples living in what became known as **Mel-anesia** ("Black Islands") and **Micronesia** ("Small Islands"). Essentially, Poly-nesia today includes the modern states of American Samoa, Cook Islands, French Polynesia, Hawai'i, New Zealand, Samoa, Tonga, Tokelau, Tuvalu, and Wallis and Futuna and the isolated islands of Nauru, Niue, Pitcairn, and Eas-ter Island. There is a group of nineteen small Polynesian islands lying outside of this area in the cultural areas of Melanesia and Micronesia. They include Nukuoro and Kapingamaangi (Micronesia); Nukuria, Taku'u, Nukumanu, Ontong Java Atoll, Sikaiana, Rennell and Bellona, Tikopia, Anuta, Pileni, Tau-mako, Mae, Aniwa, Mele, Fila, West Futuna, and West 'Uvea (Melanesia). Al-though modern scholars find the terms—*Micronesia, Melanesia,* and *Polynesia*— less useful in their scholarly pursuits, the words still are convenient in less intel-lectual settings.

Early Mongoloid-type humans pushed out of Southeast Asia about 3000 B.C.E. As they sailed into the Melanesian islands to their southwest, they picked up certain genetic traits from the local population that set them apart—a tall, heavy build, for example—and then they sailed further eastward into the un-populated territories of the Tongan and Samoan islands. There they remained for several hundred years where they developed their unique culture before setting out again into unknown waters. The settlement of the vast Pacific by the Polynesians is considered one the greatest navigational exploits in all of human history. From Samoa, they pushed out across the ocean in their large, double-hulled, ocean-going canoes to the east where they reached the Mar-quesas Islands before the second century before Christ, and from the Marque-sas they reached Hawai'i, the Cook Islands, Tuvalu, Tokelau, Tahiti, and Easter Island by 1000. For the next 600 years, here in these isolated islands of the Pa-cific, the Polynesian developed complex political, social, religious, and cultural characteristics that formed a sophisticated and unique Neolithic society.

Having no written language, the Polynesians were proficient in the art of story and genealogical recitation. They passed these myths, legends, and fam-ily histories down from one generation to another, despite the fact that many are thousands of lines in length. It was only in the nineteenth century that con-cerned Westerners and then island scholars began to collect, transcribe, and translate these for posterity. Unfortunately, we do not know how many thou-sands of others that may have been lost. It is from these extant documents, that we draw much of our knowledge of ancient Polynesia.

Polynesian societies tended to be highly structured and complex, although essentially the classes were divided between the rulers (high **chiefs**, chiefs, priests) and commoners. The communities were organized in clans and tribes around a particular island in districts over which the tribal chieftains pretty much ruled as they saw fit. There existed no "king" as such over an island or even an island group, but certain island groups had begun to show this tendency by the time of European contact. Chiefs were semidivine whose rule was absolute, and fighting (warfare) between them was frequent. Commoners had little or no say in the "affairs of state." Their daily life consisted of subsistence farming and hunting and paying dues (in kind) required of them by their superiors. Women were subordinate to men (except those with high-ranking chiefly status) and their duties consisted of making **tapa** cloth, weaving mats, growing **food** crops befitting their status, and rearing the smaller children. Complex social restrictions (called *tapu*) kept classes and genders in harmony with their age-old traditions. Subsistence living took most of the islanders' daytime hours, but evenings were taken up with various entertainments, including storytelling, swimming, dancing, and playing various games. This way of life changed drastically once Europeans started visiting the islands, and by the mid-nineteenth century, this old order had pretty much disappeared. *See also* **Voyaging/Ancient Navigation.**

Further Reading

Bellwood, Peter. *The Polynesians: Prehistory of an Island People*. London: Thames & Hudson, 1978.

Craig, Robert D. *Historical Dictionary of Polynesia*. 2nd ed. Lanham, MD and London: Scarecrow Press, 2002, pp. 1–3.

Craig, Robert D., and Frank King, eds. *Historical Dictionary of Oceania*. Westport, CT and London: Greenwood Press, 1981, pp. 236–243.

Robert D. Craig

Pulemelei Mound

On Samoa's Savai'i Island, the great pyramid mound Pulemelei is the largest Oceanic fortification of the Middle Ages. Believed to be the point from which the people of Western **Polynesia** made their final migration eastward, this curious stone structure measures 197 feet by 164 feet at the base and 39 feet in height. Actually a complex of structures, the central mound is surrounded by smaller mounds discovered to be burial sites.

The main mound is considered to have been a shrine or temple of worship. But what makes Pulemelei special is a stone pathway that runs right through the center and is said to represent the gateway to *Pulotu*, the afterlife (an important part of the Samoan funeral ritual, called *auala*, or path). Carbon dating has revealed the site to date from around 900. Some believe it was originally constructed as a pigeon-snaring mound for chiefs—that is, a platform for the bizarre sport of pigeon snaring that was exclusive to the western Polynesian islands of Samoa and Tonga. But it is also believed to have played a part in the defense of Savai'i against Tongan warriors in roughly 950, as they passed through to conquer the island of "Upolu."

Further Reading

Kirch, P. V. *On the Road of the Winds: An Archaeological History of the Pacific Islands Before European Contact*. Berkeley: University of California Press, 2000.

Makemson, M. W. *The Morning Star Rises: An Account of Polynesian Astronomy*. New Haven, CT: Yale University Press, 1941.

Sahlins, M. *Social Stratification in Polynesia*. Seattle, WA: American Ethnological Society, 1958.

Suggs, R. C. *The Island Civilizations of Polynesia*. New York: Mentor Books, 1960.

Nancy Sullivan

Religion. *See* Gods and Goddesses

Roymata (Roy Mata) (fl. c. 1265)

Traditional legends from the islands of Vanuatu (once called the New Hebrides) maintain that in the thirteenth century (about 1265), a foreign **chief** arrived on the shores of the island of Efete, united the warring tribes under his command, and brought a great period of peace and stability to the island. It was said that he instituted a peace-making ceremony called the *natamwate*, which was held every 5 years and during which rival factions could talk out their differences. Sometime later, however, Roymata's jealous brother seems to have killed him by a slow death with a poisoned dart to the throat. The villagers carefully carried the great chief from one village to another to say his good-byes, and after his death, he was taken to the nearby islet of Retoka (Hat Island) where he was buried along with forty-seven men and women (as was the custom in those days). Afterwards, the island became taboo, and until the modern day, very few outsiders ever ventured near the island.

In 1967, a French anthropologist—José Granger—gained permission to do some archeological digs of the gravesite as long as everything was returned to its original state. Sure enough and according to traditional legends, Granger found the Roymata's tomb and the numerous skeletons mentioned in those legends. Most of the skeletons unearthed were adorned with beautiful bracelets, shells, and carved bones, and evidence indicates that some may have been buried alive, as also was the custom. Roymata's head was supported by a slab of limestone, and he, too, was adorned with similar ornaments.

Archeological evidence derived from Granger's excavations indicate that Vanuatu was settled by 1300 B.C.E. by distinctive **lapita** potter immigrants from the Melanesian islands to the west, and by the time of Roymata, the people had developed a highly stratified society. Recent archeological work in the 1990s, suggests, however, that the traditional dating of Roymata may have been distended. The redating of artifacts from his burial site and other archeological evidence now place Roymata's death in the 1660s and not in 1265. Traditional legends also suggest that Roymata emigrated from the islands to the south, possibly from **Polynesia**, but the scientific finds suggest that Roymata was indigenous to the island, possibly a chief who was able to bring an end to the Takarua War and peace to the island.

Further Reading

Bedford, Stuart, Matthew Spriggs, and Ralph Regenvanu. "Australian National University—Vanuatu Cultural Centre Archaeology Project, 1994-97: Aims and Results." *Oceania* 7, no. 1 (September 1999): Available at http://www.vanuatutourism.com/vanuatu/cms/en/history/roymata.html.

Nancy Sullivan

Salamāsina (fl. late fifteenth century)

Salamāsina is the most famous of Samoan queens. Born in the late fifteenth century, she was the first Samoan and the first queen to hold all four of Samoa's highest *pāpā* titles. Her genealogy united the kingdoms of Tonga, Fiji, and Samoa, as well as a lesser line from 'Uvea (Wallis Island), making her the perfect regent of ancestral **Polynesia**. In the main, Polynesian families tend to be patrilineal rather than matrilineal, but titles often pass to and through first-born or otherwise high-ranking women. But this also means that women are sometimes, as was the case in Tonga, Samoa and Fiji, of higher status than their brothers.

To preserve their rank, royal Tongan women married Fijian men, and their brothers, in turn, took Samoan brides. Rather like the royal houses of Europe, this sometimes meant that a sister-in-law would also be a cousin, and a cousin might also be a wartime enemy. It was inevitable that the royal houses of Tonga, Fiji, and Samoa would eventually combine in one person, Salamāsina. Her mother was the daughter of the Tuitoga of Tonga, and her father was a descendant of Tuitoga and Tuifiti lines, as well as the high chiefs of Samoa and Fiji. She was made Tupu O Samoa and Tafaifa (supreme monarch of Samoa) as a child and the 40-year period of her adult reign was peaceful. This is attributed, by legend, to her kindness, her sense of justice and her skills at diplomacy. *See also* **Tongan Empire** and **Women**.

Further Reading

Howard, A., and R. Borofsky, eds. *Developments in Polynesian Ethnology*. Honolulu: University of Hawai'i Press, 1989.

Marcus, G. "Chieftainship." In A. Howard and R. Borofsky, eds., *Developments in Polynesian Ethnology*. Honolulu: University of Hawai'i Press, 1989, pp. 175–210.

Sahlins, M. *Social Stratification in Polynesia*. Seattle, WA: American Ethnological Society, 1958.

Shore, B. *"Mana"* and *"Tapu."* In A. Howard and R. Borofsky, eds. *Developments in Polynesian Ethnology*. Honolulu: University of Hawai'i Press, 1989, pp. 137–174.

Suggs, R. C. *The Island Civilizations of Polynesia*. New York: Mentor Books, 1960.

Nancy Sullivan

Shell Valuables

One of the best ways to view the diversity of cultures across the Pacific is to study the variety and circulation of shell valuables. Considering the fairly limited palette of materials, the variety of their assemblage and purpose in all manner of currencies and bodily decorations is truly remarkable. Just as language is a means by which people create and sustain differences, so too are these shells and their combinations a way of distinguishing between people who live in the vast watery domain of the Pacific. As jewelry, functional instruments, monetary valuables and objects of aesthetic beauty, shells are still extremely important markers of gender, status, culture, and kinship, and the people of the highest mountains of interior New Guinea are just as obsessed with their clam shells as those in the Tuamotu Islands of Eastern **Polynesia** (Strathern).

Shells are combined with a wide variety of other ingredients as well, from bark and rattan to stones, seeds, beads, feathers, teeth, bones, and human hair.

Turtle shell, **pig** tusks, beetle carapaces, whale ivory, ebony wood, even flowers are included in the ceremonial dress or daily currency of Oceanic peoples. We know from **lapita** excavations that some of these shell networks have an antiquity of over 3,000 years, in particular the exchange of clam shell armbands found everywhere from the Micronesian islands through the Solomons and Vanuatu to Polynesia. Archaeologist Patrick V. Kirch, for example, published a photo from one example of a burial crypt in the Ndughore Valley of Kolombangara Island, in the Solomon Islands, that is full of shell valuables from roughly 2,000 years ago. He postulates that the shells have something to do with the forts and the sophisticated irrigation systems found in the same area, as reflecting a kind of intensification of production and inter-island raiding that might have led to taking slaves (Kirch, 133–134). What is fascinating is that these conus and clamshell armbands are ubiquitous across chiefly societies in Oceania, where they are used in mortuary, marriage, and other ceremonial exchanges, as well as to indicate a person's rank. This same shell is also a major player in the *Kula* Ring of the D'Entrecasteaux and Trobriand Islands off New Guinea, where it is circulated across language and culture groups around a widespread ring of islands in exchange for highly decorated necklaces of different seashells (Malinowski).

Further Reading

Kirch, P. V. *On the Road of the Winds: An Archaeological History of the Pacific Islands Before European Contact*. Berkeley: University of California Press, 2000.

Malinowski, B. *Argonauts of the Western Pacific*. London: Routledge, 1922.

Neich, R., and F. Pereira. *Pacific Jewelry and Adornment*. Honolulu: University of Hawai'i Press, 2004.

Strathern, A. J. *Rope of Moka: Big-Men and Ceremonial Exchange in Mount Hagen, New Guinea*. Cambridge, UK: Cambridge University Press, 1971.

Nancy Sullivan

Stone Money (Yap)

Before the modern period and the introduction of Western culture to the Pacific islanders, "money" as a means of economic exchange was generally unknown. On the Micronesian island of Yap, however, there existed the practice of executing certain exchanges and evaluating one's wealth by the use of stone "money" called *rai*. These *rai* stones ranged in size from a few inches in diameter to over 12 feet in diameter, some of the latter weighing thousands of pounds. Holes were carved in each for ease in carrying—the small ones with a sennit (coconut) rope often strung around the neck and the larger ones with wooden poles that were carried by several men.

The stones were unique and not indigenous to the island of Yap. They were actually cut from limestone quarries on Palau (Belau), another island, some 220 miles to the southwest. They were then carried back to Yap by way of small native canoes where the stone-cutting was completed. Chiefs on the island were primarily responsible for *rai* production, and it is estimated that approximately 10 percent of the adult male population was involved in the business. The value of the stones was determined by their size, the difficulty of cutting and transporting them back to Yap, and the amount of time to finish the stones. The larger and more valuable stones were given names of important chiefs of the island. These stones, of course, could hardly be transported from one place to another. When the "value" of such a large stone was actually transferred from one person to another, the ownership of the stone was "transferred" to its new owner, such as we do today with deeds to property.

Not money in the modern sense of the word, *rai* stones acted as reminders of gifts or goods that were given at one time to someone with the expectation that sometime in the future a comparable favor would be given in return. Anthropologists call this a "gift economy." The stones were not used in exchange between Yap and its trading partners. In these cases, the common means of exchange was finely woven mats, prized by most Pacific islanders. *Rai*, however, continued to be used into the twentieth century, and the most renown continue to retain their cherished value to this day. *See also* **Yap Empire**.

Further Reading
Gillilland, Cora L. C. *The Stone Money of Yap: A Numismatic Survey*. Washington, DC: Smithsonian Institution, 1975.

Nancy Sullivan

Tapa

Tapa is the name given to bark cloth that was produced in most of the Polynesian Islands as well as in the Melanesian islands of Fiji and Papua New Guinea. The English word *tapa* comes from the Tahitian language, while it is called *siapo* in Samoa, *kapa* in Hawai'i, *masi* in Fiji, and *ngatu* in Tonga. Anciently, it was created for decorations and more important for everyday clothing. Today, it is produced primarily in Fiji, Samoa, and Tonga as an art form, and the cloth is principally used only on important ceremonial occasions. Stereotyped designs, hand painted on the fabric, represent unique motifs that come from various cultural groups, and one can differentiate the different tapas that come from Samoa, Tonga, or Fiji.

Tapa production was a time-consuming task, most usually performed by **women** in the community. First, the inner bark of the mulberry, hibiscus, or breadfruit was stripped from the trees, dried in the open air, and then soaked in water for several days to make it pliable. (These strips usually measure approximately 6 inches in width and about 5 feet in length.) The strips were then placed over a smooth wooden anvil (often a large tree trunk) and then pounded with a grooved ironwood beater until the width of the strip stretched to almost 9 times its original width. The final beating was then done with the smooth, flat side of the beater. After several strips were made, they were "glued" together with starch made from the tapioca or similar tree to form a larger strip. It was then hung up to dry. Afterwards, another strip of similar size was glued cross-grain to add stability to the cloth.

The undecorated cloth was ready for everyday use, but in many cases, it usually underwent some form of painted decoration. Each island group had its own particular designs and means of decoration. Freehand painting could be done with brushes made from the seeds of the pandanus plant, while stencil blocks made from the ribs of the coconut fronds were placed under the fabric and then the brush (dabber) was rubbed over the surface to produce the desired design. The stencils were then moved to a new section of the tapa, and the design repeated again. Paints were made from the various roots, berries, leaves, bark, or flowers. Final touches and accents were given to the cloth once it was rolled out on the ground. Some traditional tapa measured 10 feet wide and 60 feet long, but these were usually done in a community effort for some very important occasion—such as a wedding, installation of a new chief, and the like.

Further Reading

Christensen, Barbara Gae. *Bark Cloth or Tapa: Its Past and Present-Day Uses in Selected Areas of the Pacific as related to Social Change.* Ann Arbor, MI: University Microfilms, 1971.

Kooijman, Simon. *Tapa in Polynesia.* Honolulu, HI: Bishop Museum Bulletin 234, 1972.

Robert D. Craig

Tapu

The English word *taboo* is derived from the Polynesian word *tapu*, which essentially means sacred, forbidden, or banned from general use. In ancient **Polynesia**, *tapu* was used to protect chiefly prerogatives, to regulate society, and to keep certain properties sacred or holy, although it varied in intensity from the very strict use in Hawai'i (where it is called *kapu*) to the less stringent approach in the Polynesian outliers like Tikopia (eastern Solomon Islands). *Tapu* was also closely associated with the Polynesian principal of *mana* – power, authority, prestige, honor—and one who possessed more *mana* was generally more *tapu*.

In many islands, *tapu* was proportionate to one's rank. Māori high chiefs and priests, who were infused with very potent *mana*, for example, were so *tapu* that they ate apart and commoners could not come near them. Their first-born sons were even more so. In Tahiti, they were carried about on a dais so that they could not touch the ground, otherwise that particular land would forever belong to them. Even the passing of their shadow upon a commoner might mean death, a excruciating death brought about by being burned alive, being strangled, or being stoned to death. It was this form of prohibition that regulated Polynesian aristocratic societies, and in the more populated islands such as Hawai'i, Tahiti, and New Zealand, for example, every male member of society had a certain amount of sanctity (or *tapu*) proportionate to his rank or status. Females were generally excluded, except the first-born daughters of the high chiefly class. **Women** normally ate separate from the men, could not eat food prepared by men, and could not touch occupational tools associated with manly work, such as fishing and hunting. Hundreds of other *tapu* restrictions regulated women's daily lives. Of course, sexual restrictions existed throughout the whole Pacific region other than just in Polynesia.

Chiefs often proclaimed *tapu* over certain fishing and hunting grounds to prevent commoners from entering them. Certain fish were *tapu*, and certain days were set aside for high chiefs to fish and other days for the commoners. Such prohibitions were often proclaimed to prevent the over use of fishing and hunting areas, but in other instances, it was merely a means for self-aggrandizement or for selfish reasons. In a preliterate society such as Polynesia, such *tapu* areas could be recognized by the several poles on the reef or shore on which were attached bunches of bamboo leaves or **tapa** cloth similar to the "No Trespassing" signs one might see today on fences or poles surrounding private property. But in ancient Polynesian, *tapu* "signs" were far more feared than the written "No Trespassing" signs in our modern society. To them, it might mean death.

Further Reading

Ferdon, Edwin N. *Early Tonga as the Explorers Saw It, 1616–1810.* Tucson: University of Arizona Press, 1987, pp. 219–223.

Goodman, Irving. *Ancient Polynesian Society.* Chicago: University of Chicago Press, 1970, pp. 10–13.

Oliver, Douglas. *Ancient Tahitian Society.* 3 vols. Honolulu: University of Hawai'i Press, 1974, pp. 66–67, 90, 226, 310, 314, 330.

Robert D. Craig

Taro

One of the chief root crops widely found throughout all three geographical regions of the Pacific islands—**Polynesia, Melanesia**, and **Micronesia**—was taro. It first originated in the tropic, wetlands of Malaysia thousands of years ago and then spread westward through India to the ancient civilizations of Greece and Rome. (The Roman recipe book, the *Apicius*, for example, gives several ways of cooking taro.) As the Pacific islanders moved out of Southeast Asia and settled the Pacific, they also brought with them their basic food starts, including various species of taro.

Of the three varieties known to these early Pacific islanders, "true" taro (*Colocasia esculenta*) had a much wider distribution and was much more popular than the other two (the *Cyrtosperma chamissonis* and the *Alocasia macrorrhiza*). In Palau, *Colocasia* was the traditional prestige staple of all their foods. *Cyrtosperma* (swamp taro), however, was more prominent in coastal Melanesia and in the **atolls** of Micronesia. *Colocasia* grew year round in shaded, wet soil up to an altitude of about 7,000 feet. In dry areas where water was not immediately available, irrigation brought water from near-by ponds, streams, or man-made dams. Ancient bamboo aqueducts or extensive canal systems have been found in New Caledonia, Fiji, and Hawai'i.

The corm (underground bulb or rhizome) of the taro was harvested (dug up and cut from its leaves), and the top portion was planted again to produce a new crop of taro. A new crop could be harvested within 7 to 12 months. *Colocasia* taro was much less hardy than *Cyrtosperma* and had to be harvested and eaten much quicker. Once harvested, taro corms were then eaten in a variety of ways. The universal method was broiling uncovered or leaf-wrapped over hot ashes or stones. The corms could also be boiled in clay

Taro farm, Waipio Valley, Island of Hawaii, Hawaii. © Gary Hartz/Dreamstime.com.

pots, coconut shells, marine shells, or wooden bowls. (Heated stones were placed in the water of the coconut shells and wooden bowls to heat it up.) Another popular alternative (especially in Polynesia and Micronesia) was to bake it in an underground oven, consisting of heated stones and ashes and covered with banana leaves and sand. Once cooked, taro could then be sliced or diced and eaten with other foods. In Hawai'i and other islands of Polynesia, it could be pounded (mashed) and served as poi.

Because ripe *Colocasia* needed to be harvested and eaten rather quickly, some island groups developed a unique method of preservation in case of possible famine. Poi was stored in underground pits where fermentation preserved it for months on end.

Taro leaves were often used as a vegetable (like spinach). The most common dish was a food packet made of taro leaves into which either fish, pork, or fowl pieces were placed along with some coconut cream. This was then tied up and placed with other items in the underground oven. (Uncooked taro leaves are toxic and can cause sickness, thus it was important that they be thoroughly cooked for several hours.)

Further Reading

DeYoung, John E., ed. *Taro Cultivation Practices and Beliefs* (Micronesia). 2 vols. Hagatna, Guam: Trust Territories of the Pacific Islands Anthropological Office, 1960.

Handy, E. S. Craighill, and E. G. Handy. "Taro." In *Native Planters in Old Hawaii: Their Life, Lore and Environment.* Honolulu, HI: Bernice Pauahi Bishop Museum Press, 1972, pp. 71–118.

Robert D. Craig

Tattoo

The word *tattoo* only entered the English language in the late eighteenth century. It came from the Polynesian languages in the Pacific (Samoan, Tahitian, Marquesan, Māori, etc.) where the word *tatau*, means "tapping." Apparently, the English sailors aboard the European ships of "discovery" first saw the elaborate tattoo designs practiced by the Pacific peoples and returned home with their own personal "souvenirs" of their trips to the Pacific. They popularized an ancient art form that has continued to the present day.

Actually, the art of tattooing (applying permanent colored designs to one's body) goes back to Neolithic times where it existed in various parts of the world. It had a resurgence of popularity in Western civilization, however, only after Europe's contact with the peoples of the Pacific, primarily **Polynesia** and **Micronesia**. Captain James Cook first recorded the word in his journal of 1769 when he made references to the Marquesan custom of "*tattaw*." Tattooing was common throughout ancient Polynesia and Micronesia, but to a far lesser extent in **Melanesia** and Australia because the darker skin of these peoples did not show off the dark inks as it did with the lighter brown color of the other Pacific islanders.

Māori performing the Haka dance (war dance). Jose Gil/ Shutterstock.

The variety of design, the number of tattoos on one's body, and the original social or religious purpose of tattooing varied from one island group to another. In the Marshall Islands (Micronesia), for example, only the chiefs and noble families were tattooed, and in other parts of the Pacific, it carried little or no social distinction. Tattoos were more commonly found on men, however, on Ponape (Micronesia), tattoo was far more extensive and decorative on **women** than men. In the Marquesas (Polynesia), both sexes were tattooed, but not far away on Mangareva, only the men were tattooed. In Polynesian, the tattoo artist was generally a male (often associated with a religious order), but on Palau (Micronesia), the women did the tattooing.

Anciently, the Pacific tattoo artist used a sharp serrated comb (usually made of bone) attached to a handle or rod about 12 to 18 inches in length. The sharp comb was first dipped into a type of ink made from various dyes from plants, ashes, or soil, mixed with oil, and then placed on the exact location of the body. The skin was stretched tightly, and then the comb hit sharply with a small mallet that caused the comb to pierce the skin and deposit the colored pigment beneath it. Any blood flow was wiped away with a piece of **tapa** cloth either by the artist or by one of his assistants. Finer lines could be drawn by the use of a type of sharp needle made of bone or other material. Depending upon the extent and size of the tattoo, the process could take hours, even days, and often the procedure was accompanied with chanting, singing, and periods of silence.

In some areas of the Pacific, tattooing was associated with the rite of passage to adulthood. In Samoa, for example, boys were tattooed from the age of 15 in groups of six to eight during a special feast called the *umusāga*. Samoan tattoos were unique in that they covered their bodies only from the lower part of the torso to the knee, while in the Marquesas, where tattooing reached its peak, men were tattooed from the head to their toes. Several European artists to the Pacific left drawings of what traditional Marquesan tattooing looked like.

Despite having been settled from the Marquesas Islands, the Hawaiians developed a relatively conservative approach to tattooing. Their designs were more restrained with simpler motifs than found in the Marquesas or in Samoa. It was also limited to a relatively small area of the body—on the right chest and shoulder, for example, balanced with another on the upper left leg—and consisted of checkered patterns and triangle motifs.

New Zealand Māoris also limited their elaborate tattoos (*ta moko*) primarily to the face, but simpler tattoos might be found elsewhere on the body. Male tattoos were highly decorative and covered the whole face, while female tattoos generally were limited to the lips and chin area. Māoris tattoos also differed from other island tattoos by being "incised" or carved deeply into the flesh rather than just the skin being punctured. Naturally, the incising caused considerable swelling and, consequently, a small area of tattoo could be undertaken at any one time. Throughout the islands, the complexity and extent of one's tattoo increased the *mana* (prestige, power, respect) of that particular individual.

Māori Carving. Māori culture in New Zealand. Sam Dcruz/Shutterstock.

Christian missionaries to the islands generally banned all forms of tattooing, and it was not until 20 to 30 years ago that there has been a resurgence of tattooing in many of the islands. It is a traditional art form that islanders wear with great respect and dignity. *See also* **Dress**.

Further Reading

Barbieri, Gian Paolo. *Tahiti Tattoos*. New York: Taschen, 1998.

Graham, Pita. *Māori Moko or Tattoo*. Auckland, New Zealand: Bush Press, 1994.

Handy, Willowdean C. *Tattooing in the Marquesas*. Honolulu, HI: Bernice P. Bishop Museum Press, 1922.

Robert D. Craig

Tongan Empire (c. 1250–1450)

Traditions tell us that from about the middle of the thirteenth to the middle of the fifteenth centuries, the Tu'i Tonga (the Ruler of Tonga) dominated many of the islands around him, including the three major Tongan island groups—Tongatapu, Ha'apai, and Vava'u—as well as parts of Samoa (lying further to the north) and parts of the Fijian islands (lying further to the west). This period in Tongan history is usually referred to as the "Tongan Empire." Some contemporary writers further claim that Tonga dominated the entire area, including *all* of Fiji and Samoa as well as parts of **Micronesia** in the North Pacific Ocean.

Actual historical records regarding the "empire," however, are scant. Tonga had no written language until the coming of the Europeans in the late eighteenth century, therefore, the only records we have are a few comments made to Captain James Cook and his fellow explorer William Anderson in 1777 while visiting Tonga. One islander told Cook that Tonga had once conquered "*Hamoa*" far to the north, but we should not assume that this meant all of the Samoan islands in the chain. By the tenth and eleventh centuries, only Tonga had indeed developed a unitary, centralized political system under a single ruler. Neither Fiji nor Samoa had similar developments, but both island groups had close connections to Tonga. The rulers of Tonga, for example, traced their lineage back to the sacred island of Manu'a in Samoa, and intermarriage between them and Samoan women was common. Fiji lay within such close proximity to Tonga that there was substantial trade and travel between the two island groups, and as a result cultural traits certainly passed from one people to another. War tribute may have initially been exacted from the defeated Samoan chiefs, but a continuous domination of one government with a centralized bureaucracy over another is hard to imagine during this period in Polynesian history. Neither is there any evidence of a sustained occupation of Samoa by the Tongans, in fact, each new Tu'i Tonga after Talakaifaiki had to reestablish his own right to tribute. Also, the Manu'a islands in Samoa appear to never have been touched by the Tongan conquest at all.

It is true that for several centuries, Tonga acted as a type of middleman between Samoa and Fiji most likely because Tonga's very few natural resources had forced its islanders to take to sea. Canoe building and navigation had, therefore, become far more advanced in Tonga than the other areas. Its large, double-hulled *lomipeau* canoes plied the ocean (perhaps as far away as Micronesia) trading for red feathers, timber for boat building, adze blades, **tapa**, and pandanus cloth. Rather than a marketplace type of trade as one might think of in Europe or Asia at the same time, exchange came primarily during traditional ceremonies, often coupled with treaties, marriage alliances, and the like.

Also associated with this expansion of Tongan trade and influence was the building of monumental stone works, as evidenced in the surviving triathlon monument the *Ha'amonga-a-Māui* (The Burden of Māui), located about 20 miles from the modern capital of Nuku'alofa. Tongan traditions say it was built by Tu'i Tuitatui, the conqueror of Samoa, as a reminder to his sons (represented by the two upright supports) not to quarrel and to remain always united (represented by the lintel). Today, the structure is nicknamed the "Stonehenge of the Pacific" and rivals the other stone structures found in the Marquesas or the *moai* statues on Easter Island.

The decline of the Tongan empire came to an end with the frequent assassinations of the 19th, 22nd, and 23rd Tu'i Tonga, all of which introduced a new period of violence and instability in the realm. A new political practice of dividing royal authority similar to the Samoan custom was eventually established, and the Tu'i Tonga was relegated to a lower, but complementary authority. By 1610, the central authority was divided again creating yet another new title, the Tu'i Kanokupolu, which, of course, led to the foundation of the current ruling dynasty in Tonga.

Further Reading

Craig, Robert D. *Historical Dictionary of Polynesia*. 2nd ed. London: Scarecrow Press, 2002, pp. 226–227, 236.

Denoon, Donald. *The Cambridge History of the Pacific Islanders*. Cambridge, UK: Cambridge University Press, 1997, p. 444.

Ferdon, Edwin N. *Early Tonga: As the Explorers Saw It, 1616–1810*. Tucson: University of Arizona Press, 1987, pp. 255–257.

Robert D. Craig

Uncles

Uncles in Oceania play very important roles throughout a person's life. These vary by region ad place, but the mother's brother, or *kandare*, for example, of the Sepik River of New Guinea, is a classic example. Because he has given his sister to the brother-in-law, those in-laws remain forever indebted to him. When his sister's son comes of age and enters confinement for **initiation**, the *kandare* plays a major part in symbolically finishing off the child and handing him over to his brother-in-law's clan.

In the Sepik River region, as in many parts of **Melanesia**, these coming of age ritual involve cutting skin and bloodletting. This is a figurative way of releasing the postpartum mother's blood so as to re-create the child as a full member of his father's clan. In so doing, the mother's brother also reclaims the substance of his line. For Sepik initiates of the Iatmul tribe, a mother's brother will cradle him on a log as a special cutter incises his back and chest with hundreds of small notches by a bamboo knife. These keloid cuts are irritated and become raised welts on the skin, in a pattern of scars that is designed to resemble the totemic crocodile. But it is crucial that the Uncle take his nephew through this process with the kind of loving and firm hand of a father figure. For his service, the young man is forever indebted to the *kandare*, even as he is symbolically handed over by the *kandare* to his father.

Further Reading

Chowning, A. *An Introduction to the Peoples and Cultures of Melanesia.* Menlo Park, CA: Cummings Publishing, 1979.

Gewertz, D. *Sepik River Societies: A Historical Ethnography of the Chambri and Their Neighbors.* New Haven, CT: Yale University Press, 1983.

Herdt, G. H. *Guardians of the Flutes: Idioms of Masculinity.* New York: McGraw-Hill, 1981.

Herdt, G. H., ed. *Rituals of Manhood: Male Initiation in Papua New Guinea.* Berkeley: University of California Press, 1982.

Lutkehaus, N., ed. *Sepik Heritage: Tradition and Change in Papua New Guinea.* Durham, NC: Carolina Academic Press, 1990.

Malinowski, B. *Argonauts of the Western Pacific.* London: Routledge, 1922.

Schieffelin, E. L. *The Sorrow of the Lonely and the Burning of the Dancers.* New York: St. Martin's Press, 1976.

Nancy Sullivan

Voyaging/Ancient Navigation

One of the greatest of achievements of any people anywhere was the human settlement of the thousands of islands scattered throughout the Pacific Ocean. Although living in a Stone-Age culture and without iron and the benefit of a literate society, these peoples set out thousands of years ago from Southeast Asia and the Philippines and pushed eastward from one island to another until the farthest points were reached—Hawai'i and Easter Island—by 1100. This could only have been accomplished by the remarkable development of boat-building and advanced navigational skills.

Most of the Melanesian islands lying to the east of Southeast Asia are within 50 miles of one another, so the movement through these islands was without difficulty and could be accomplished by the use of rafts or small dug-out canoes. As the islanders moved further, however, the distances increased substantially, and by the time Hawai'i and Easter Island were settled, the crossings increased to nearly 1,700 miles one way. These vast distances could only have been made by the development of larger sea-going vessels—the Polynesian double outrigger canoe with sails, for example—and the development of advanced sailing techniques gained from observing astronomical and marine phenomenon.

As the early migrants entered **Polynesia** (via Tonga and Samoa), they used canoes similar to the Fijian *drua*, a double-hulled canoe with lateen sails that could carry several hundred people in addition to cargo. The Fijians had developed this peculiarly unique sailing vessel by improving upon the fast-sailing outrigger canoes of the Micronesians in the north Pacific, and by 1000 B.C.E., this new design moved eastward from Fiji into Tonga and Samoa. Here the design was modified to include a full covered deck, a large raised platform (with crew housing), and booms connecting the hulls midship. By 200 C.E., this type of sailing vessel made its way into eastern Polynesia—into the Marquesas Islands—where it too underwent substantial design changes to become the model upon which the richly decorated canoes of New Zealand and Hawai'i were fashioned.

Polynesian canoe building was not only an arduous physical task, but it was highly religious in nature. All workmen were duly consecrated for the duration of the task, and every step of the process involved the recitation of traditional chants and prayers by them or by their priests. Construction usually occurred near the beach, and the site was *tapu* (forbidden) to foreigners and women. A ceremonial feast usually marked the end of its construction, and upon launch, human sacrifices might be offered. Navigation of the canoe was usually restricted to priests or highly skilled **chiefs** who had received the exact knowledge of canoe construction and navigation from their fathers. The Marquesan canoes were elaborately decorated with carved sternposts of stylized birds and human masks and figures. Large Māori canoes of New Zealand included beautifully carved canoe prows and sterns. These vessels were often carved with grotesque human figures in the front to frighten the enemy whereas the stern pieces were highly carved with scroll-like patterns.

These large double-hulled canoes plied the Pacific throughout the Middle Ages, accomplishing tasks that not even the expert Vikings or Chinese could fathom. They sailed long voyages (making trips back and forth) from Tahiti and the Marquesas to Hawai'i and to New Zealand. Traditional chants detail numerous crossings with the names of their intrepid navigators. The Māori tell of chief Kupe from Hawaiki who first discovered New Zealand and upon returning home gave such a glowing report of the new land to his relatives that they quickly packed up and left for good. The Hawaiians tell stories of their three major navigational heroes—Hawai'i-loa, Pa'ao, and Moikeha from the islands of Tahiti far to the south (over 2,000 miles)—and their back-and-forth voyages over several generations. The Easter Islanders tell of their Hotu-Matua who left Marae-Renga (possibly in the Marquesas) because of family squabbles and with his hundreds of followers settled Rapanui (Easter Island) over 1,500 years ago. Then there are the demigod heroes of Polynesian myth—Rata (Laka), Māui, Tahaki (Kaha'i), and Tinirau (Kinilau)—whose superhuman voyaging trips are well known throughout the islands.

Unfortunately, by the time of European contact (eighteenth century), long-distant, ocean-going voyaging had all but ceased in the Pacific, and very few islanders retained the knowledge and expertise to build and captain one of these vessels. When British explorer Captain James Cook visited Tahiti in 1777, however, he witnessed a gathering of 170 smaller double-hulled war canoes that he estimated carried 7,760 men. He was so impressed with the Tahitian war canoe that he personally drew an accurate blueprint for one with instructions for building.

In the last part of the twentieth century, Pacific scholars and island experts began to detail the exact science of how the Pacific peoples were able to navigate between the islands so well. It was a matter of heading the boat out in the known direction by lining up landmarks at one's homeland (island), keeping the proper direction while out to sea, and then finding the correct destination when close to land. The direction at sea (a voyage of 3 or 4 weeks, for example) was determined by the various wind, sea swells and currents, and meteorological observances (the sun during the day and especially the stars at night). The suggested readings below will provide technical details for those interested. All this navigational knowledge could only be gained over hundreds of

Captain James Cook eating with Tahitians. Engraving. The Art Archive/Musée des Arts Décoratifs Paris/Alfredo Dagli Orti.

years of experienced sailing, but unfortunately in the Pacific, it could only be transferred from one generation to another by word of mouth. *See also* Documents 6 and 10.

Further Reading
Haddon, A. C., and James Hornell. *Canoes of Oceania*. 3 vols. Honolulu, HI: Bernice Pauahi Bishop Museum Press, 1936–1938. Reprinted in one volume, 1975.
Lewis, David. *We, the Navigators: The Ancient Art of Landfinding in the Pacific*. 2nd ed. Honolulu: University of Hawai'i Press, 1994.

Robert D. Craig

Warfare

Warfare in Oceania during the Middle Ages was much unlike warfare in Europe or samurai Japan whose governmental structures were based on a constant feudal order of fighting. Certainly Oceanic peoples spent a good deal of their time in some form of fighting between communities and between islands, but the complexity and extent of their organized battles were far less than we might see elsewhere, except perhaps in Papua New Guinea and some parts of island **Melanesia** where their cultures were shaped by an aggressive war ethic.

The extent and scope of fighting that did occur depended, of course, upon the size of the communities and their available resources. Family units, subsisting on far-flung **atolls**, might fight against another family across the lagoon using primitive weapons fashioned from the available trees, stones, and coral.

War pirogue, New Zealand. Engraving from 1811, travels to Australian lands. The Art Archive/Bibliothèque des Arts Décoratifs Paris/Gianni Dagli Orti.

Complex populations, however, living on large islands such as Hawai'i or Papua New Guinea might launch major pitched battles on land using a wide variety of weapons while at the same time being accompanied by large naval contingent.

The reasons for conflicts among Pacific peoples were many, just as in modern times. Often it was for revenge, breaking a mutual treaty, jealousy between leaders or groups over land or food, competition for the love of a beautiful woman, rivalry over genealogical rights to rule, or even just for the pleasure of it! The list was extensive.

Organized group training of warriors was found only in a few societies. Most men learned to fight from childhood as they were taught by their fathers to use the spear and club in the daily hunt. Most adult men took their protective weapons with him whenever they left the bounds of their home community or district, not just for protection against their enemy, but for protection against wildlife they might confront along the way. Male children often participated in daily sports consisting of mock skirmishes and exercises to increase their fighting abilities. In Fiji, for example, young children were allowed to use captured prisoners as targets to improve their skill with the spear and club. Other groups often participated in war **dances** that gave the performers experience in quick footwork and in the use of clubs or other weapons. There were no standing armies as such, but some larger island societies had some skilled fighters attached to the **chief**'s court while the rest of the needed fighters consisted of adult males from the villages that could be mustered when needed.

War weapons consisted of handmade slings, javelins, spears, scythes, and clubs, all of various lengths and sizes (iron was unknown in those days). Bows and arrows were used only in Melanesia, and the unique boomerang-shaped club only in southeastern Australia. Long spears with sharp or barbed tips were more frequently used, but like their arrows, having no feathers (unfledged), they were less accurate in hitting the target. Some warriors painted colored designs upon their faces and bodies to make them look more frightening, and the Māori warriors attempted to frighten their enemies by extreme facial and tongue gestures, fierce shouting, and unusual body gestures, not to mention their elaborate facial **tattoo**s.

A few societies used protective shields made of bark that varied in size from the small parrying shields used in Australia to those colorful Melanesian shields big enough to shield a whole man. Many warriors threw off all clothing that was not essential, while others put on additional clothing to help protect them from their enemies' weapons—protective cane armor around the torso was used along the Digul River in New Guinea and elaborate headdresses and gorgets around the neck in Tahiti.

War preparations might include calling a general council to discuss the advisability of going to war; petitioning the high priests for divine guidance through the use of trances, dreams, or auguries; and perhaps offering a human sacrifice if the occasion was significant enough. Once all had been said and done, the chief made the final decision. If it was war, the council would be dismissed and the whole community would prepare for a battle. Men would ready their weapons, psyche themselves up, and collect at the designated gathering place.

On the day of the battle, the "armies" would face each other and sometimes each side would send in its favored champion to do hand-to-hand combat against the other. Eventually, one side would rush the other without any real preplanned strategy for attack, although at times warriors fought in ranks or groupings in various formations. Fighting would continue until the enemy was routed and fled the battlefield. The victors then buried their own dead, but let the enemys rot on the battlefield.

Various forms of peace treaties were negotiated—either between victor and vanquished or between sides acknowledging a draw—and religious prayers and thank offerings were made, often in the form of **food** or human sacrifices being offered up in the temples by the high priests. Oftentimes, the victors would return home to celebrate their victory with feasting, dancing, and **entertainment**. *See also* Documents 3 and 11.

Further Reading

Henry, Teuira. *Ancient Tahiti*. Honolulu, HI: Bernice P. Bishop Museum, pp. 1928, 297–322.

Oliver, Douglas. *Oceania: Native Cultures of Australia and the Pacific Islands*. 2 vols. Honolulu: University of Hawai'i Press, 1989, pp. 423–500.

Robert D. Craig

Windward. *See* Leeward and Windward

Women

In Australia during the Middle Ages, women were the main **food** collectors and providers for the family. While their husbands were out hunting, they spent long hours gathering plant foods (fruits, **yams**, and grass seeds) and small animals (lizards, snakes, witchetty grubs, and ants) from the desert as well as seafood from the rivers and lagoons. They were also responsible for fetching drinking water and firewood, caring for babies, helping build the family hut or lean-to, making household utensils (bags, baskets, nets, and mats), and preparing meals, which took place early evening. Virtually all of her life was focused upon her family unit and its successful operation. Although most women's lives were held secondary to men and final authority within the family units rested with the husband, wives were not necessarily servile and submissive. If a fight between husband and wife occurred, the battered wife, who often fought back, could easily pick up her children and goods and move to a camp of a near relative until her husband came to his senses. In general, Australian wives were not inhibited to voice their own opinions. This attitude may have been a result of the more egalitarian character of Australian family and clan units, which were less organized and had far less hierarchical social structures than elsewhere in Oceania.

Woman and child from Easter Island, from the 1796 Travel Encyclopaedia with engravings by Grasset de Saint Sauveur and Labrousse. The Art Archive/Bibliothèque des Arts Décoratifs Paris/Alfredo Dagli Orti.

On the other hand, almost all Polynesian societies adhered to a highly structured, patriarchal form of governance. The right to rule was inherited by male **chiefs** through their fathers' senior blood lines, but on occasion, it could come through their mother's line, if, for example, it outranked her husband's. High-ranking chiefesses were recognized throughout the islands, but their actual rule was negligible, although on occasions they did challenge the ruling authority for one reason or another. Common women, on the other hand, were regulated by custom and *tapu* (things being forbidden). They were forbidden to participate in public religious ceremonies, they could not eat with men, they had to cook their own food, they were forbidden to touch their husbands' fishing equipment, and they could not eat specific foods (certain fish, dog, pork, sea turtles, and whales, for example). Each month during their menstrual period, they had to live in an isolated hut set away from the main village complex because they were considered "unclean." Women reared the children at home, fished in lagoons and shallow waters for food, produced **tapa** in the construction of clothing and decorative coverings, plaited all of the baskets and mats for clothing and household furnishings, gathered firewood, and often helped in the family's garden. In all of this, however, Polynesian women were not considered chattel, for they had the freedom to choose their husbands as well as the liberty to leave them. A beautiful woman was highly prized and much sought after in a Polynesian marriage. Surprisingly, the social status of a Polynesian woman was much higher in medieval Oceania than it was after having adopting European "civilization" in the late eighteenth and early nineteenth centuries.

Hundreds of different social and cultural groups lived on the 2,100 Micronesian islands in the North Pacific Ocean. Their lives reveal a far more complex scenario than Australia or **Polynesia**, and, as a result, generalizations about these peoples are much more difficult to make. Unlike Polynesians, most male chiefs inherited their status through their matrilineal descent (through their mothers), although patrilineal and other descent groups did exist. Families lived on lands belonging to their particular matrilineal clan, and often husbands had little decision regarding descent affairs in the community in which they lived. Men usually worked the gardens, gathered and cut wood, made their boats, fishing tackle, rope, domestic utensils, and weapons, while the women attended to the domestic chores—planting and weeding yams, weaving mats and baskets, making the clothing, caring for the children, cooking the food, and even doing the tattooing. Similar to other areas of Oceania, Micronesian women separated themselves from the community each month during their menstrual cycles and for birthing of children, actions considered "unclean" by the male population. Polygamy was allowed, but it was not widely practiced. Divorce was easy and simple. The couple parted by mutual agreement, although the father usually retained the right to keep the children. For all indications, it appears that Micronesian women were well respected and held in high esteem. On Truk, for example, it was unmanly to hit a woman whatever the provocation might have been, and on Kosrae, women would never be asked to do a chore that rightly "was not hers." It was also expected, however, that women would show total respect for their older brothers by not speaking to them directly and by crouching in their presence.

The widest diversity in the status of women occurred in **Melanesia**. At one extreme, the men of Sambia (Highlands of New Guinea) considered their women irresponsible, licentious, dangerous to men, and ready to "siphon off their strength." As a result, they adopted numerous hygienic practices to prevent the absorption any of their wives' "infectious" body fluids or smells. They also ate and slept in their own male-clubhouses to avoid the closeness of women. The Nagovisi women of south Bougainville (Papua New Guinea), on the other hand, controlled all matters regarding their descent group affairs. Land was inherited by the eldest daughters, and their husbands had to ask permission to use it because they were considered "outsiders." Heads of the various clans were women, and they had the final say over clan affairs, including the marriage of all the young women. Women supervised the gardening and food production, while their husbands helped in the heavier tasks of clearing land and weeding. Although Nagovisi wives deferred to their husbands as heads of their particular household, the husband knew that if his wife left, she would take everything with her— including the children and all the wealth he had helped build up. *See also* **Trukese Love Stick.**

Further Reading

Alkire, William H. *An Introduction to the Peoples and Cultures of Micronesia.* 2nd ed. Menlo Park, CA: Cummings Publishing, 1977.

Craig, Robert D. "Polynesian Woman." In Joyce E. Salisbury, ed., *The Greenwood Encyclopedia of Daily Life.* Vol. 2. Westport, CT: Greenwood Press, 2004, pp. 67–69.

Fischer, John L. *The Eastern Carolines.* New Haven, CT: Human Relations Area Files Press, 1966.

Lessa, William A. "An Evaluation of Early Descriptions of Carolinian Culture." *Ethnohistory* 9, no. 4 (Autumn, 1962): pp. 313–403.

Nash, Jill. *Matriliny and Modernization: The Nagovisi of South Bougainville.* Canberra: Australia National University, 1974.

Robert D. Craig

Yams

Cultivation of yams (various varieties of the *Dioscorea* family) occurred throughout Africa, Latin America, Asia, and Island Oceania, but not in Australia, where the indigenous peoples were primarily food gatherers and not cultivators. Along with **taro** and sweet potatoes, yams provided islanders with a substantial starchy food stock that was high in various vitamins and minerals and one that, unlike the others, could be stored for months at a time. Some Pacific island societies valued yams to such a degree that their whole way of life revolved around yam cultivation. Scholars refer to these societies as "yam cultures."

Two particular species of yams were primarily cultivated in Oceania—*Dioscorea exculenta* and *Dioscorea alata* (great yam), the former being the tastier and the latter being the larger. They were propagated through cuttings from the last tubers harvested. These cuttings were planted deep in well-drained soil or earth mounds usually before the beginning of the wet season. The leafy vine that emerged above the soil had to be trained either on poles or trees, and because all of this process took time, energy, and patience, yams were more time-consuming than the cultivation of taro or sweet potatoes. Harvesting took place between 5 and 8 months after planting, and the mature tubers that had been well cared for could measure up to 12 feet in length and weigh up to 150 pounds.

Several island societies developed remarkable yam cultures that venerated its cultivation. In Tonga (western **Polynesia**), for example, yams were their most important food crop. The months of the year were named in reference to its cultivation, and the most important ceremony of all, the *'inasi*, would take place 10 days after the announcement of the first yam harvested (usually at the beginning of October). During the festival, all types of **food** and crafts would be on display, but it was the huge ceremonial yams (*kahokaho*) that gained most of the peoples' admiration.

The Abelam people in Papua New Guinea (**Melanesia**) represent the ultimate in yam-growing cultures. Their whole lives were influenced by its cultivation and harvest. The size of harvested yams determined the status of not only the individual farmer, but the whole village as well. At a yearly festival, ceremonial yams would be put on display, after which, a farmer would present his largest yam to a particular rival who in return had to grow even a larger sized yam the following year, otherwise he would risk "losing face." Similar exchanges took place between villages, whose prestige and political powers were dependent upon the size and quality of their ceremonial yams.

The growing cycle of the yams determined the social intercourse of the whole village. Only men grew yams, and they spent their entire time in the garden tending to their best plants. **Women** were forbidden to enter the gardens. Even sexual relations were deterred in fear that any outpouring of emotions might disrupt the tranquility needed for successful yam cultivation. (Disagreements, anger, hunting, the eating of red meat, and other emotional actions were also prohibited.) It was believed that yams contained spirits of one's ancestors, and for that reason, they were highly revered. The plants were lovingly cared for during each stage of cultivation, and every possible means was employed so that the final product was the largest and finest yam ever produced. That included reciting certain magical spells, applying special fertilizers, and arranging the vines in particular patterns.

Once the first tubers were harvested, all sexual relations commenced in earnest again and repressed hostilities reappeared, but everyone looked forward to the festival that was to come. On that day, all of the prominent yams were exhibited on long poles in the display area. Many of them were highly decorated with yam masks, which had been hand-woven or carved from wood and colorfully painted. The women of the villages prepared lavish feasts for everyone, after which the ceremonial exchanges began. These exchanges usually led to friendly alliances with men from other villages and certainly to the distribution of the best breeding stock throughout the area. Once all the ceremonies were finished, most of the men began to contemplate the next year's harvest and the best methods of producing the finest ceremonial yam.

Further Reading

Ferdon, Edwin N. *Early Tonga as the Explorers Saw It, 1616–1810*. Tucson: University of Arizona Press, 1987, pp. 82–95.

Scaglion, Richard. "Yam Cycles and Timeless Time in Melanesia." *Ethnology*, 38, no. 3 (Summer 1999): 211–225.

Robert D. Craig

Yap Empire

Fiefdoms, kingdoms, and empires were unknown in medieval Oceania. Instead, one hears of local, district, and tribal chieftains governing through a decentralized system of personal rule. Two exceptions, however, might be suggested that could be interpreted as "empires" in the broadest sense of the word. They are the **Tongan Empire** in **Polynesia** and the Yap Empire in **Micronesia**.

For several hundred years, "subject" peoples living on the **atolls** east of Yap would set sail in their ocean-going canoes (every 2 or 3 years) and deliver "tribute" goods to the tribal leaders on the island of Yap. No one knows the origin of this complex custom. Some assume that it was established by the inhabitants of the poorer and more vulnerable atolls to the east so that, in case of hurricanes or tidal waves, they could find protective shelter on the larger island of Yap. Tribute gifts to tribal leaders on Yap, they believed, would provide that needed hospitality. Yet the tribute and gift giving was not entirely reciprocal. The various tribal leaders on Yap claimed "ownership" of these eastern atolls and asserted that they could punish any community that failed to pay their tribute. (Not much unlike the Athenian empire in classical Greece, for example.) Atoll visitors were also treated like tenants or persons of lower-caste status when visiting Yap. These last two statements suggest that perhaps there had at one time been a military defeat of the small atolls by Yap, but this has never been suggested or confirmed from island traditions.

Once a planned expedition had been announced, ocean-going canoes would set sail from Namonuito, Pulap, and Pulusuk atolls, almost 700 miles away from Yap. They would make their way to the next group of islands, where their leaders would give up their responsibilities to the new canoe "captains" of those islands who now joined them. The larger group would then continue westward and meet up again with other canoes and relinquish their leadership to the new captains. It was the **chief** of Mogmog who then represented the whole fleet when it arrived at the main district of Gatchepar on Yap.

The canoes carried with them three kinds of gifts—religious tribute, canoe tribute, and tribute of the land. The first two, of course, were given to the tribal leader of Gatchepar, while the third was given to the various Yap chiefs who claimed ownership over the atolls or districts from which the canoes had come. Tribute consisted of woven fiber skirts and mats, loincloths, sennit twine (rope made from twisted coconut husks), coconut oil, and various shell articles.

After a length of time and when the seasonal winds changed in their favor, the atoll dwellers would pack their gifts (food, turmeric, flint stones, and hand-carved wooden objects) from their Yapese hosts and return home in the same manner in which they had arrived.

Further Reading
Alkire, William H. *An Introduction to the Peoples and Cultures of Micronesia*. Menlo Park, CA: Cummings Publishing, 1977, p. 51.

Robert D. Craig

Primary Documents

For written descriptions of life in Oceania, we are often forced to rely on docu-ments generated by the first European contacts with the peoples of Oceania in the seventeenth and eighteenth centuries, and thus the selections provided below date from that period. Note that Europeans came to the region as ex-plorers, traders, and missionaries; and, as the following documents indicate, their accounts of the peoples they met and the traditions and practices they encountered were influenced by their own political ambitions, economic goals, social backgrounds, and religious beliefs.

1. Captain James Cook's Account of an Encounter with the Māori of New Zealand, 1769

James Cook (1728–1779), a British explorer, navigator, and cartographer, is best known for his three voyages to the Pacific Ocean, during the course of which he explored the Hawaiian Islands and the eastern coast of Australia, and also achieved the first circumnavigation of New Zealand. The following excerpt from Cook's journal of his first voyage describes an encounter with the Māori, whom he describes as "Indians," that occurred on October 8, 1769 along the shores of a bay on the North Island that is today known as Poverty Bay. This encounter, and another the next day, ended with the death of a Māori warrior and greatly disappointed Cook, who had hoped to establish friendly relations with the people of New Zealand and learn from them about the geography of their islands. For a Māori perspective of a second encounter between Cook's party and the people of New Zealand, see Document 2, below.

[S]eeing some of the natives on the other side of the River of whom I was desirous of speaking with, and finding that we could not ford the River, I order'd the yawl in to carry us over, and the pinnace to lay at the Entrance. In the mean time the Indians made off. However we went as far as their Hutts which lay about 2 or 300 Yards from the water side, leaving 4 boys to take care of the Yawl, which we had no sooner left than 4 Men came out of the woods on the other side of the River, and would certainly have cut her off had not the People in the Pinnace discover'd them and called to her to drop down the Stream, which they did, being closely pursued by the Indians. The coxswain of the Pinnace, who had charge of the Boats, seeing this, fir'd 2 Musquets over their Heads; the first made them stop and Look round them, but the second they took no notice of; upon which a third was fir'd and kill'd one of them upon the Spot just as he was going to dart his spear at the Boat. At this the other 3 stood motionless for a Minute or two, seemingly quite surprised; wondering, no doubt, what it was that had thus kill'd their Comrade; but as soon as they recovered themselves they made off, dragging the Dead body a little way and then left it. Upon our hearing the report of the Musquets we immediately repair'd to the Boats, and after viewing the Dead body we return'd on board.

Source: Reed, A. H., and A. W. Reed, eds. *Captain Cook in New Zealand: Extracts from the Journals of Captain James Cook.* 2nd ed. Wellington: A. H. and A. W. Reed, 1969, pp. 34–35.

2. Hore-ta-te-Taniwha's Account of Captain James Cook's Visit to New Zealand, 1769

Although not written down by Europeans until about 1852, this account by an aged Māori chief remembering his youth relates to events that occurred in November 1769 near the mouth of the Whitianga River on New Zealand's North Island. After the disappointing encounter with the Māori at Poverty Bay (*see* Document 1, above) Captain James Cook sailed his ship *Endeavor* along the east coast of the island seeking a suitable site to observe the transit of Mercury, which occurred on November 9. As this account for a Māori perspective indicates, the Māori–European interaction at Whitianga was, at least initially, more friendly, though the Māori considered their visitors to be very strange and referred to them as "goblins." Nonetheless, Cook was able to view the transit of Mercury and to get information about the shape of the islands. A brisk trade also developed during Cook's 10-day stay between his crew and the Māori, though it was a dispute arising from this trade that led to another Māori death.

In days long past, when I was a very little boy, a vessel came to Whitianga. Our tribe was living there at that time. We did not live there as our permanent home, but were there according to our custom of living for some time on each of our blocks of land, to keep our claim to each, and that our fire might be kept alight on each block, so that it might not be taken from us by some other tribe.

We lived at Whitianga, and a vessel came there, and when our old men saw the ship they said it was a *tupua*, a god, and the people on board were strange beings. The ship came to anchor, and the boats pulled on shore. As our old men looked at the manner in which they came on shore, the rowers pulling with their backs to the bows of the boat, the old people said, "Yes, it is so: these people are goblins; their eyes are at the back of their heads; they pull on shore with their backs to the land to which they are going." When these goblins came on shore we (the children and women) took notice of them, but we ran away from them into the forest, and the warriors alone stayed in the presence of those goblins; but, as the goblins stayed some time, and did not do any evil to our braves, we came back one by one, and gazed at them, and we stroked their garments with our hands, and we were pleased with the whiteness of their skins and the blue eyes of some of them. . . . .

After the ship had been lying at anchor for some time, some of our warriors went on board, and saw many things there. When they came on shore, they gave our people an account of what they had seen. This made many of us desirous to go and see the home of the goblins. I went with the others; but I was a very little fellow in those days, so some of us boys went in the company of the warriors. Some of my playmates were afraid, and stayed on shore. When we got on board the ship we were welcomed by the goblins, whom our warriors answered in our language. We sat on the deck of the ship, where we were looked at by the goblins, who with their hands stroked our mats [clothing] and the hair of the heads of us children; at the same time they made much gabbling noise in talking, which we thought was questioning regarding our mats and the sharks' teeth we wore in our ears . . . but as we could not understand them we laughed, and they laughed also. They held some garments up and showed them to us, touching ours at the same time; so we gave our mats for their mats, to which some of our warriors said "*Ka pai*," which words were repeated by some of the goblins, at which we laughed, and were joined in the laugh by the goblins.

There was one supreme man in that ship. We knew that he was the lord of the whole by his perfect gentlemanly and noble demeanor. He seldom spoke, but some of the goblins spoke much. But this man did not utter many words: all that he did was to handle our mats and hold our *mere*, spears, and *wahaika* [all types of weapons], and touch the hair of our heads. He was a very good man, and came to us—the children—and patted our cheeks, and gently touched our heads. His language was a hissing sound, and the words he spoke were not understood by us in the least. We had not been long on board the ship before this lord of these goblins made a speech, and took some charcoal and made marks n the deck of the ship, and pointed to shore and looked at our warriors. One of our aged men said to our people, "He is asking for an outline of this land"; and that old man stood up, took the charcoal, and marked the outline of Te Ika-a-Maui. And the old chief spoke to that chief goblin, and explained the chart he had drawn. The other goblins and our people sat still and looked at the two who were engaged with the chart marked with charcoal on the deck. After some time the chief goblin took some white stuff, on which he made a copy of what the old chief had made on the deck, and then spoke to the old chief. . . .

One of our tribe was killed by the goblins. . . . We—that is, our people—went again and again to that ship to sell fish, or mats, or anything that we Māori had to sell; and one day one of our canoes, in which were nine persons, paddled off to the ship; but one of that nine was a noted thief, and this man took a dogskin mat to sell to the goblins. There were five of them at the stern of the canoe and four in the bow, and this thief was with those in the stern. When they got alongside the ship, the goblin who collected shells, flowers, tree-blossoms, and stones was looking over the side [probably the naturalist Joseph Banks]. He held up the end of a garment which he would give in exchange for the dogskin mat belonging to this noted thief; so the thief waved with his hand to the goblin to let some of it down into the canoe, which the goblin did; and, as the goblin let some of it down into the canoe the thief kept pulling it towards him. When the thief had got a long length of the goblin's garment before him, the goblin cut his garment, and beckoned with his hand to the man to give the dogskin mat up to him; but the their did not utter a word, and began to fold up the dogskin mat with the goblin's garment into one bundle, and told his companions to paddle to the shore. They paddled away. The goblin went down into the hold of the ship, but soon came up with a walking-stick in his hand, and pointed with it at the canoe which was paddling away. Thunder pealed and lightening flashed, but those in the canoe paddled on. When they landed eight rose to leave the canoe, but the thief sat still with his dogskin mat and the garment of the goblin under his feet. His companions called to him, but he did not answer. One of them went and shook him, and the thief fell back into the hold of the canoe, and blood was seen on his clothing and a hole in his back. He was carried to the settlement and a meeting of the people called to consult on the matter, at which companions told the tale of the theft of the goblin's garment; and the people said, "He was the cause of his own death, and it will not be right to avenge him."

Source: White, John. *Ancient History of the Māori, His Mythology and Traditions.* Vol. V. Wellington, New Zealand: George Didsbury, Government Printer, 1889, pp. 121–128.

3. Captain James Cook's Description of War Canoes in Tahiti, 1774

Taken from the journal kept by Captain James Cook during his second South Pacific voyage (1772–1775), the following selection is important because it is one of the few descriptions we have of how an Oceanian crew worked together to move a large boat through the water. The canoes described here were part of a Tahitian war fleet assembled in 1774 for an attack on the nearby island of Mo`orea. For a later account of Tahitian rowers, see Document 6, below.

[W]e saw a Number of War Canoes coming round the point of Oparre, being desirous to have a nearer view of them I hastened down to Oparre (accompanied by some of the officers etc.) which we reached before the Canoes were all landed and had an opportunity to see in what manner they approached the shore which was in divisions consisting of three or four or more [boats] lashed close a long side each other, such a division one would think must be very unwieldy, yet it was a pleasure to see how well they were conducted, they Paddled in for the Shore with all their might conducted in so judicious a manner that they closed the line a Shore to an inch. . . .

The rowers were encouraged to exert their strength by their leaders on the stages, and directed by a man who stood with a wand in his hand in the fore part of the middlemost Vessel, this man by words and actions directed the paddlers when all should paddle when either the one side or the other should cease etc. for the steering paddles alone were not sufficient to direct them: all these motions they observed with such quickness as clearly shewed that they were expert in their business.

Source: Beaglehole, J. C., ed. *The Journals of Captain James Cook on His Voyages of Discovery. Volume 2: The Voyage of the Resolution and the Adventure, 1772–1775.* Cambridge, UK: Cambridge University Press for the Hakluyt Society, 1961, p. 401.

4. Tahitian Sexual Practices: The *Mahu*, c. 1790 and 1797

The *mahu* were Tahitian boys who were kept in the households of local chiefs for sexual purposes. The *mahu*, though male, behaved like women in all social settings and engaged in sex only with other men. Just as they reacted to the berdaches found among many North American tribes, the first Europeans to encounter the *mahu* found them to be largely incomprehensible. The first selection below was written about 1790 by James Morrison, one of the *Bounty* mutineers, who spent almost a year on Tahiti. His account is mainly descriptive. However, the second selection, from almost a decade later, is much more judgmental, using words like *vile* and *depraved* to describe the *mahu* and refusing altogether to detail their sexual practices. This selection was written by James Wilson, captain of a missionary expedition sent into the South Pacific in the late 1790s by the London Missionary Society. The *mahu* were clearly an affront to the religious sensibilities of Captain Wilson.

These men are in some respects like the Eunuchs in India but are Not Castrated. They Never Cohabit with women but live as they do; they pick their Beards out & dress as women, dance and sing with them and are as effeminate in their Voice; they are generally excellent hands at Making and painting of Cloth, Making Matts and every other Womans employment. They are esteemed Valuable friends in that way and it is said, tho I never saw an instance of it, that they Converse with Men as familiar as women do.

Source: Morrison, James. *Journal.* London: Golden Cockerel Press, 1935, p. 238.

These mawhoos [*mahu*] chuse this vile way of life when young; putting on the dress of a woman, they follow the same employments, are under the same prohibitions with respect to food, etc. and seek the courtship of men the same as women do, nay, are more jealous of the men who cohabit with them, and always refuse to sleep with women. We are obliged here to draw a veil over other practices too horrible to mention. These mawhoos, being only six or eight in number, are kept by the principal chiefs. So depraved are these poor heathens, that even their women do not despise those fellows, but form friendships with them.

Source: Wilson, James. *A Missionary Voyage to the Southern Pacific Ocean Performed in the Years 1796, 1797, 1798.* London: T. Chapman, 1799, pp. 370–371.

5. Marriage in the Marquesas Islands, c. 1800

Edward Robarts deserted from the whaleship *New Euphrates* on Christmas Day 1798 and spent the next 7 years, until February 1806, in the Marquesas Islands. He married a Marquesan wife, Ena, by whom he had a daughter. Many years later, with his wife and child dead and he himself living in poverty in India, Robarts wrote a detailed account of what he saw and experienced in the Marquesas during the first years of the nineteenth century. The following excerpt from that account describes a Marquesan marriage ceremony. For a description of the sexual aspects of the marriage ceremony in the Gilbert Islands, see Document 12, below.

Their Marriages are some what singular. A Chief or other great man having a son, perhaps not more than two or three years of age, now another great man has a daughter, and most likely pregnant. Word is sent to the Ladys Parents a few days fefore hand to inform them of the intended union. If they give consent, it always puts every one in motion in the Neighborhood for several days, some preparing cloths, some food and others gathering flowers and sandal wood.

A[t] length the days come. The Young Gentleman sets out with several attendants. When they arrive near the house of the Lady, Her friends give the signal by the Beat of a Drum. They are ushered in with shouts of Joy. The Young Lover is then seated by the side of his bride on the cloth of his mother in Law. This is the greatest respect they can show, as the Cloth or turban is held, as it were, Sacred. The Moria Drum is then brought with several of the Prophets & their retinue, who being seated the drum beats, and the Prophets party begins to sing their ceremonies [in] a dialect peculiar to themselves, which continues for several hours. A good Hog is roasted, and fish is brought for the Guests with every thing suitable. Plenty of food is brought from the Ladys several relations. The Drums Beat up at the Play ground. The Inhabitants assemble. The merry dance leads off and continues until sun set. In the even[ing] the House is crowded, and they sing the whole night.

In a day or two the father of the Bride groom visits the young couple, followed by a number of attendants, every one bearing a present. This visit causes another feast which continues for several days. On the even[ing] before his departure he gives notice of His wish to remove his daughter in law to her husbands estate. This being complied with, they set out early the next day. Being just Arrived at her new habitation, every mark of esteem and respect is showed to her. The merry day begins, and great plenty of food is provided for the different ranks of Ladies that comes to welcome her to their part of the country. The day is past over with all mirth and festivity. The evening is come.

Source: Dening, Greg, ed. *The Marquesan Journal of Edward Robarts 1797–1824.* Honolulu: University Press of Hawaii, 1974, pp. 269–270.

6. English Missionary William Ellis: Another Description of Tahitian Canoes, c. 1814

This selection by English missionary William Ellis, like the excerpt from the journal of Captain James Cook in Document 3, above, is a rare description of how a crew of Oceanians coordinated the paddling of their larger canoes. Writing about 40 years after Cook, Ellis is also describing a Tahitian crew, although his description of the rowers' coordination is even more detailed.

The rowers appeared to labour hard. Their paddles, being made of the tough wood of the hibiscus, were not heavy; yet, having no pins in the sides of the canoe, against which the handles of the paddles could bear, but leaning the whole body over the canoe, first on one side, and then on the other, and working the paddle with one hand near the blade, and the other at the upper end of the handle, and shoveling as it were the water, appeared a great waste of strength. They often, however, paddle for a time with remarkable swiftness, keeping time with the greatest regularity. The steersman stands or sits in the stern, with a large paddle; the rowers sit in each canoe two or three feet apart, the leader sits next, the steersman gives the signal to start, but striking his paddle violently against the side of the canoe, each paddle is then put in and taken out of the water with every stroke at the same moment; and after they have thus continued on one side for five or six minutes, the leader strikes his paddle, and the rowers instantly and simultaneously turn to the other side, and thus alternately working on each side of the canoe, they go along at a considerable rate. There is generally a good deal of striking the paddle when a chief leaves or approaches the shore, and the effect pretty much resembles that of the smacking of the whip, or sounding of the horn, at the starting or arrival of a coach.

Source: Ellis, William. *Polynesian Researches.* Vol. 1. London: Fisher, Son, and Jackson, 1829, p. 166.

7. Trade and Barter on Fiji in the 1840s

The two following selections describe trade and barter as it was conducted in Fiji in the 1840s. The first selection is by the Wesleyan missionary Thomas Williams (1815–1891), who worked among the Fijians from 1840 to 1852. His 1858 publication, *Fiji and the Fijians: The Islands and Their Inhabitants*, made him a recognized expert on Fijian culture as it existed at the time of first contact with Europeans. Williams was also a gifted artist, and his many drawings of Fijian life, which were later transformed into engravings to illustrate his book, are valuable depictions of mid-nineteenth-century Fijians.

Charles Wilkes (1798–1877), the author of the second selection, was an American naval officer and explorer. He commanded the United States Exploring Expedition (commonly known as the Wilkes Expedition), a small flotilla of ships authorized by the U.S. Congress that carried–botanists, naturalists, taxidermists, mineralogists, and artists on a voyage of exploration into the Pacific between 1838 and 1842. The following selection is an excerpt from Wilkes' narrative of the voyage.

The commercial transactions of the Fijians, though dating far back, have been on a small scale, consisting of barter trade, which is chiefly in the hands of the Levuka, Mbutoni, and Malaki people, who regard the sea as their home, and are known as "the inhabitants of the water." Although wanderers, they have settlements on Lakemba, Somosomo, Great Fiji, and other places. They exchange pottery for *masi* [barkcloth], mats, and yams. On one island, the men fish, and the women make pots, for barter with the people on the main. Their mode of exchange is very irregular. The islanders send to inform those on the mainland that they will meet them, on such a day, at the trading-place,—a square near the coast paved for the purpose. The people of the continent bring yams, taro, bread, etc., to exchange for fish. The trade is often left to the women, among whom a few transactions take place quietly, when some misunderstanding arises, causing excited language, and ending in a scuffle. This is the signal for a general scramble, when all parties seize on all they can, and run off with their booty amidst shouts and execrations of the less successful.

Source: Williams, Thomas. *Fiji and the Fijians: The Islands and Their Inhabitants.* Vol. 1. London: Alexander Heylin, 1858, pp. 93–94.

I also had an opportunity of seeing their manner of trading among themselves. This is entirely conducted by barter. The market is held on a certain day in the square, where each one deposits in a large heap what goods and wares he may have. Anyone may then go and select from it what he wishes, and carry it to his own heap; the other then has the privilege of going to the heap of the former and selecting what he considers an equivalent. This is all conducted without noise or confusion. If any disagreement takes place, the chief is there to settle it; but this is said to rarely happen. The chief has a right to take what he pleases from each heap.

Source: Wilkes, Charles. *Narrative of the United States Exploring Expedition During the Years 1838, 1839, 1840, 1841, 1842.* Vol. 3. London and Philadelphia: Wiley and Putnam, 1845, pp. 300–301.

8. Andrew Cheyne's Account of Food and Feasting on Ponape in Micronesia, 1843

Andrew Cheyne (1917–1866) was a Scottish trader who in 1841 set up two trading stations in the Yap Islands, which at that time were virtually unknown to Europeans. Offering the first written description of various island societies, such as Ponape, and of previously unknown sites, such as the now famous ruins at Nan Madol, Cheyne's account of his trading voyages to Yap and elsewhere in the South Pacific is an important historical resource. The following excerpt from Cheyne's account describes food and modes of cooking on the Micronesian island of Ponape (now Pohnpei).

The following description may give some idea of their mode of cooking. A fire is made of wood and covered with small stones. When the wood is all consumed, they rake the ashes out, and place a layer of the heated stones on the ground, on which they place their food well wrapped up in banana and wild taro leaves to prevent it from burning; the remainder of the heated stones are then laid on the top of the leaves containing the food, when that is done the whole is then closely covered up with leaves, mats etc. so as to prevent the steam from escaping. In a couple of hours the food will be sufficiently done. Whole pigs, turtle, dogs, yams and breadfruit are cooked in this way, and persons unacquainted with this South Sea mode of cooking would be rather surprised to find the food so well done. I consider this to be a superior mode of cooking yams and breadfruit to any with which we are acquainted.

Breadfruit being the chief food of these natives, they have, from the little time occupied in cultivating their vegetable productions, a great deal of leisure. It is true that yams are cultivated to a considerable extent, but the process of planting requires but very little time. They have no regular plantations, but small spots of ground here and there are cleared, in which the yams are planted. They merely make a small hole in the ground sufficiently large to admit the seed, and do not even loosen the earth around it to allow the yam to grow to any size; the consequence is that they are of a very small size and many of them of an indifferent quality. They generally have them planted near trees and have strings fastened to the branches for the vines to entwine round. At other islands small reeds are generally stuck in the ground by each seed for the vine to run up; but these islanders with respect to their cultivation, are far behind others who are in a much greater state of savage ignorance; consequently, their time being much less occupied, amusements and feasting occupy a great part of it. Their feasts generally claim priority to everything else. The King makes an annual visit to every village in the tribe, at which time the greatest festivities take place, the chiefs then vying with each other who shall entertain him the best. Immense quantities of breadfruit and yams are cooked . . . and Kava drinking is also carried to excess. These feasts commence in the morning and continue until near sunset, at which time the greater part of the chiefs are quite insensible with Kava. . . . young people then commence dancing and continue until Midnight, at which time they all retire to rest. The festivities last for two days at each village during the King's annual visit; but feasting on a smaller scale is of a daily occurrence.

Source: Shineberg, Dorothy, ed. *The Trading Voyages of Andrew Cheyne 1841–1844*. Honolulu: University of Hawai'i Press, 1971, pp. 186–187.

9. An English Sea Captain's Account of Dancing on Bora Bora, 1846

The following description of dancing on the island of Bora Bora was written by Henry Byam Martin, a British naval officer and member of a prominent naval family. Between August 1846 and August 1847, Martin commanded H.M.S. *Grampus*, which was on station between Hawaii and Tahiti. Based on his experiences during this service, Martin's account, like Captain Wilson's in Document 4, above, betrays a certain cultural disapproval of island society and practices.

The news of our arrival had brought in the population from all parts of the island; I found them assembled in front of the chapel celebrating their orgies in *honour of me*!

Nothing can be more uncouth or barbarous than the "*Bora Bora* dance." The performance would have been void of interest, but that it has been handed down from their earliest & most savage days—and if I am not mistaken I have seen it described and drawn n Cook or one of the early voyagers.

Twenty-five men—naked all but the Maro [loincloth]—sat side by side in a line—with the left leg tucked under the rump and the right projected in front. They grunted and gesticulated in chorus to a sort of wild song, executed by one who sat in the middle. After the exhibition Tivivi, the Regent, invited me to visit another group, which was far more numerously attended.

This was the real native dance, & seemed more attractive, the performers being mostly of the fairer sex. A circle was formed for the dancers, within which 11 drums were hammered with might & main. As for the dance itself, it was a gross exaggeration of that of the Egyptian Almehis. A girl or young man stepped into the circle & for a couple of minutes exhibited the most indecent movements; with certain gymnastical motions of the legs & arms. The great trial of skill seemed to be how nimbly they could wag their sterns. None the less the half naked figures decked in garlands, flitting about in the torch light were highly picturesque and the scene altogether was one that Salvador Rosa might have made something of.

I believe this ball was got up for my amusement, and therefore I remained as long as patience permitted. Then each chief seized a torch and lighted me to the boat—the 11 drums followed, and the multitude shook hands so vehemently that I was glad to be clear of their rough though cordial greetings.

Source: Martin, Henry Byam. *The Polynesian Journal of Captain Henry Byam Martin, R.N.* Salem, MA: Peabody Museum of Salem, 1981, pp. 71–72.

10. Description of a New Guinea Canoe, c. 1846

Between 1846 and 1850, Captain Owen Stanley commanded the H.M.S. *Rattlesnake* on a voyage of survey and exploration around New Guinea and neighboring islands. The following excerpt is taken from the narrative of that voyage written by the expedition's naturalist, John MacGillivray. Unlike Documents 3 and 6, above, which focus on how a Tahitian crew handled a large canoe, this description of the boats used in parts of New Guinea focuses on the craft itself, not on the crew.

The canoe of this part of New Guinea is usually about twenty-five feet in length, and carries seven or eight people. It is made of the trunk of a tree, hollowed out like a long tough, roundly pointed at each end, a foot and a half in extreme width, with the sides bulging out below and falling in at top, leaving only eight inches between the gunwales which are strengthened by a pole running along from end to end. the ends—which are alike—are carved like those of the catamaran in imitation of the head of a turtle or snake, but more elaborately. The outrigger consists of a float as long as the canoe, attached by small sticks or pegs let into the wood to eight or nine supporting poles the inner ends of which rest in notches in both gunwales, and are secured there. A portion, or the whole of the framework, is carefully covered over with planks or long sticks, and occasionally a small stage is formed on the opposite side, over the centre of the canoe, projecting a little outwardly, with room upon it for two people to sit and paddle. The canoes of this description which we saw were not provided with any other sail than a small temporary one, made by interlacing the leaflets of the cocoa-palm, and stuck up on poles when going with the wind free. The paddles used here are similar in shape to those seen in the Louisiade Archipelago, with spear-shaped blades and slender handles, but are larger—measuring six feet in length—and of neater construction, the end of the handle being carved into some fanciful device.

Source: MacGillivray, John. *Narrative of the Voyage of H.M.S. Rattlesnake Commanded by the Late Captain Owen Stanley, R.N., F.R.S. etc. during the Years 1846–1850.* London: T.W. Boone, 1852, pp. 256–257.

11. Settling a Dispute among the People of Australia's Cape York Peninsula, c. 1848

Edmund B. C. Kennedy (1818–1848) was a British surveyor and explorer who was instrumental in the exploration of northeastern Australia, particularly the Cape York Peninsula. The following selection is from a narrative of Kennedy's last expedition, an unsuccessful attempt to traverse the Cape York Peninsula that ended with Kennedy's death at the hands of hostile aborigines in December 1848. This account describes the resolution of a dispute for an unknown cause involving two groups of aborigines.

One day I witnessed a native fight, which may be described here, as such occurrences, although frequent enough in Australia, have by Europeans been witnessed only in the settled districts. It was one of those smaller fights, or usual modes of settling a quarrel when more than two people are concerned, and assumed quite the character of a duel upon a large scale. At day-break, I landed in company of six or seven people who were going out on different shooting parties. The natives came down to the boat as usual, but all carried throwing-sticks—contrary to their usual practice of late; and at the place where they had slept, numbers of spears were stuck up on end in the sand. These preparations surprised me, but Paida would not explain the cause and seemed anxious to get me away. The shooters marched off—each with his own black— but I loitered behind, walking slowly along the beach.

About 200 yards from the first camping-place, two groups of strange natives, chiefly men, were assembled with throwing-sticks in their hands and bundles of spears. While passing them they moved along in twos and threes towards the Evans Bay party, the men of which advanced to meet them. The women and children began to make off, but a few remained as spectators on the sands, it being then low water. A great deal of violent gesticulation and shouting took place, the parties became more and more excited, and took up their position in two scattered lines facing each other, extending from the margin of the beach to a little way in the bush, and about twenty-five yeards apart. Paida, too, partook of the excitement and could refrain no longer from joining in the fight; he dropped my haversack and bounded away at full speed to his camping-place, where he received his spears from little Purom his son, and quickly made his appearance upon the scene of action.

The two parties were pretty equally matched—about fifteen men in each. The noise now became deafening; shouts of defiance, insulting expressions, and every kind of abusive epithet were bandied about, and the women and children in the bush kept up a wailing cry all the while rising and falling in cadence. The pantomimic movements were of various descriptions; besides the singular quivering motion given to the thighs placed wide apart (common to all the Australian dances), they frequently invited each other to throw at them, turning the body half round and exposing the breech, or dropping on one knee or hand as if to offer a fair mark. At length a spear was thrown and returned, followed by many others, and the fighting became general, with an occasional pause. The precision with which the spears were thrown was not less remarkable than the dexterity with which they were avoided. In nearly every case the person thrown at would, apparently, have been struck had he stood still, but, his keenness of sight enabled him to escape by springing aside as required, variously inclining the body, or sometimes merely lifting up a leg to allow the spear to pass by, and had two been thrown at one person at the same moment he could scarcely have escaped, but this I observed was never attempted, as it would have been a would have been in war,—here each individual appeared to have a particular opponent. I had a capital view of the whole proceedings, being seated about fifty yards behind and slightly on the flank of one of the two contending parties. One spear thrown higher than usual passed within five yards of me, but this I was satisfied was the result of accident, as I had seen it come from Paida's party. Soon afterwards I observed a man at the right extreme of the line next me, who had been dodging round a large scaevola bush for some time back, make a sudden dart at one of the opposite party and chop him down the shoulder with an iron tomahawk. The wounded man fell, and instantly a yell of triumph denoted that the whole matter was at an end.

Paida rejoined me five minutes afterwards, apparently much refreshed by this little excitement, and accompanied me on my walk, still he would not explain the cause of the fight. The wounded man had his arm tied up by one of our people who landed soon afterwards, and, although the cut was both large and deep, he soon recovered.

Source: MacGillivray, John. *Narrative of the Voyage of H.M.S. Rattlesnake Commanded by the Late Captain Owen Stanley, R.N., F.R.S. etc. during the Years 1846–1850.* London: T.W. Boone, 1852, pp. 313–316.

12. The Sexual Aspects of Marriage in the Gilbert Islands, c. 1920

A British civil servant, Sir Arthur G. Grimble (1888–1956) was a member of the Gilbert and Ellice Islands Colony Administrative Service from 1914 to 1932, serving as colony lands commissioner from 1922 to 1925. During this period, Grimble spent his spare time in ethnographic research, and when colony resident commissioner from 1926 to 1932 he wrote numerous papers on aspects of Gilbert Islands culture. The following excerpt from one of his papers describes the sexual consummation of a new marriage.

[T]he families of the bridal pair came together, as soon as the sun had passed zenith. When all were present and silent, the bride was brought into the house by her mother, mother's sister, mother's mother, or adoptive mother. The girl and the old woman immediately mounted into the loft, and there the younger was stripped of all her clothing and laid upon a new sleeping mat especially woven for the occasion. Thus she was left, awaiting the arrival of her groom.

As soon as the groom was known to be ready, the boy was brought by his mother or father's sister into the lower room. Aided by pushes and encouragement from all his nearest female relations he climbed into the loft; there he stripped off his waist mat and threw it down among the waiting people. As soon as it was seen to fall the whole audience broke out into clamorous exhortation to both the young people, beseeching them to cast off coyness and quickly to consummate the union. Nevertheless, the bride's kinfolk would have been much disappointed and ashamed had she surrendered herself without demur to the embraces of the bridegroom, for that would have denoted a lack of modesty unseemly in a well-born maiden. Without moving from her mat, it was therefore customary for her to resist the advances of her mate, and to intimate to those below that she was so doing by struggles of which the reverberation could not fail to reach them.

At the moment when her virginity left her she emitted a single piercing scream. Soon after, the bridegroom would call from above, and at that signal his mother would mount into the loft. There she would at once search for traces of blood on the girl's sleeping mat and, having found them, would cry in a loud voice, "*Te tei! Te tei!*" ("A virgin! A virgin!"). She then descended alone to exhibit the mat to all eyes, whereupon, taking up the cry of the old woman, the father and uncles of the bridegroom rubbed a little of the virgin's blood upon his cheeks, where it would remain for the rest of the day. The mat was afterwards carefully burned that no enemy of the family might obtain it and, by using evil magic upon the blood, curse the bride with barrenness.

Source: Grimble, A. G. "From Birth to Death in the Gilbert Islands." *Journal of the Royal Anthropological Institute* 51 (1921): 31.

Appendix: Major Island Groups of Oceania

Western Oceania

Micronesia

Yap (the Yapese Empire islands and atolls: Woleai, Yap, Ifalik, Fais, Satawal, Lamotrek, Elato, Satawal, Faraulep, Eauripik, Ulithi Sorol, Gaferut, Ngulu, West Fayu, Pikelot, and Olimarao)

Belau (Palau)

Marianas (Guam, Saipan, Tinian, Rota Islands)

Caroline Islands

Chuuk (Truk)

Pohpei

Kosrae

Marshall Islands (Majuro Atoll, Kwajalein Atoll and outer islands)

Nauru

Kiribati

Gilbert Islands

Phoenix Islands

Line Islands

Tuvalu

Melanesia

New Guinea

New Guinea's outer islands:

Biak Island

Numfor Island

Waigeo Island

Torres Strait Islands

Bismark Archipelago

Admiralty Islands

Trobriand Islands

D'Entrecasteaux Islands

Louisiade Archipelago

Solomon Islands

Bougainville

Malaiata

Santa Cruz Islands

Vanuatu

Banks Islands

New Caledonia

Loyalty Islands

Central Oceania

Polynesia

Fiji

Rotuma

Tikopia

Futuna

Wallis

Vanua Levu

Viti Levu

Lau Group

Tokelau

Samoa

Savaii

Upolu

Tutuila

Tonga

Niuatoputapu

Vava'u

Ha'apai

Tongatapu

Niue

Cook Islands

Eastern Oceania

Polynesia

Society Islands

Moorea

Tahiti

Austral Islands
Gambier Islands
Tuamotu Islands
Marquesas Islands

Pitcairn Island
Easter Island
Hawaiian Islands
New Zealand (Aotearoa)

Index

Note: page numbers in **bold** indicate topical essays and short entries.

Abbasid Caliphate (750-1258), 455, 528, 529–30, 545–46, **581**; Fatimids and, 602–3; history, 517; Mamluk troops, 564–65, 631–32; translation of classical texts into Arabic, 566, 567–68

Abd al-Malik (c. 646-705), 534, 542, 553, 567, **581–82**

Abdallah ibn Yasin (d. 1059), **435**, 442

Abelard, Peter, 68, 86, 105, 142–43, 167

Abi Bakr, 'Aisha bint (d. c. 678), 583, **585–86**, 592, 599, 635

Abi Talib, 'Ali ibn (d. 661), 529, 576, 583, **586–87**, 627

ablutions, 535, **582**

Abu Bakr (d. 634), 517, 528–29, **583**

Abu Bakr ibn 'Umar (d. 1087), **435–36**, 442

acephalous (stateless) societies, Africa, 413–15

achievements, African social standing and, 409, 414

Acre, 72, 101, 136

Acutuba, 195, 204, **259–60**, 327

Adi Shankara, 696

aesthetics: African, 398, 400–401, 405; European, 42; Heian Period Japan, 883, 909, 962, 995; mosque architecture, 404, 423, 431, 550–51, 647–48, 734–35

Afghanistan, 662, 663, 684, 824

Africa: the arts, **395–405**; East Africa coast description, 509–11; ecological zones, 370; economy, **386–95**, 454; global ties, **425–33**; historical overview, **367–77**; history, periodizing of, 369; history, sources of, 374–77; medieval period and European context, 367–69; physical geography, overview, 371–74;

political structures, 409–15; religion, **377–86**, 426, 436–37; science and technology, **415–24**; social organization, 406–9; society, **405–15**; Sub-Saharan/European interactions, 71, 73, 369; traditional religions, overview, 378–82

afterlife, see death and afterlife

age hierarchies, see gerontocracy

Age of Faith, 24, 61

agriculture, Africa: overview, 387–90, **437–39**; ecological zones and, 456–57; Ethiopian Highlands, 461; farming technology, 420–21, 438–39, 453; herding technology, 421–22, 453–54; Iron Age effects, 370, 389–90; Niger Delta, 411

agriculture, Americas: Aztec, 246; chinampas, 274–75; development of, 181; economy and, 204–5; Incan, 351; maize, 240; the Pleiades and, 310; Shabik'eschee, **315–16**; Snaketown, 316; terra preta, 250, 259, **326–27**

agriculture, East Asia, 919, **935–36**, 947, 1003

agriculture, Europe, **79–80**; challenges to, 33–34; dispersed pattern and clustered villages, 33–35; fourteenth century, 21; instruction manual, 168–69; labor shortages and peasant revolts, 41; manorialism, 52–53, 79; technology and advances in, 18, 34–35, 67, 80

agriculture, North Africa and the Middle East, **583–85**

agriculture, Oceania, **1067–68**, 1079, 1088

agriculture, South Asia: overview, **775–77**; agrarian base of Indian

states, 703; South Indian trade guilds and, 711–14; technology, 716

ahisma, 799

Ainu, 881

Ajanta, 722–24, 793

Ajita atheists, 692

Ajivakas, 691–92

Akan, 391, 411, 416, **439–40**, 464

Aksâ Mosque, 647–48

Aksum: Christianity and, 383, 459; global ties, 425, 433; stelae, 359, 396, 404, 423, 440; trade and, 412, **440–41**, 450, 498–99

Al Minhaj Bin Siraj, 848–49

Alberuni's India, 737

alchemy, 62, 1010

alcohol: Africa, 462; Indian culture and, 777; Khilij prohibition, 685; Qur'anic prohibition, 604

ale, 110

The Alexiad (Comnena), 99

Alfonso VI, 20

Alfred the Great (849-899), 17, **81–82**, 157–58

Alhambra (Red Fortress), 552

Alighieri, Dante, see Dante Alighieri

Allauddin Khilji, Sultan (d. 1316), 663, 685–86, 716, 735, **778–79**, 788

Almoravid and Almohad Movements, 360, 412, 426, 430–31, **441–42**, 446, 464, 484–85

alms (*zakat*), 537

Alp Arslan, Sultan (r. 1063-1073), 531

Amazonia and the Caribbean: the arts, 223–24; economy, 212–13; global ties, 257; historical overview, 195–96; religion, 203–4; science and technology, 250; society, 237–38

American Southwest and the Great Basin: the arts, 215–16; economy,

205–7; global ties, 252–53; historical overview, 191; religion, 197–99; science and technology, 240–42; society, 226–29

Americas: the arts, **213–24**; culture area chronologies, 189–90; economy, **204–13**; geographic culture areas, 189; global ties, **251–58**; historical overview, **189–96**; The Inca Empire (map), 188; The Maya (maps), 187; religion, **196–204**; The Rise of the Aztec Empire (map), 186; science and technology, **238–51**; society, **224–38**; South and Mesoamerica (map), 185

An Lushan, 875, 966

Analects (Confucius), 889, 941, 1009

Anasazi, 182, 191

ancestor veneration, Americas: Chimor, 274; curaca and, 280; Moche, 203; overview, **260–61**; Southern Cult, 197

ancestor veneration, East Asia, **937**; overview, 885

Ancestral Pueblo (750-1450): the arts, 215–16; economy, 206–7; global ties, 253; religion, 198; science and technology, 241–42; society, 227–29

ancestral spirits: African traditional religions and, 379, 436; Melanesia, 1041–42

Andes, *see* Lower Central America and the Andes

Anglo-Saxon Chronicle, 81

Anglo-Saxons, 16, 81–82

Angor Wat, 816–17

animal husbandry, *see* domesticated animals

Anjuvaranam guild, 707, 712

Anselm of Canterbury (1033-1109), 142, 143

anti-Semitism, 5, 37, 123–24

Aphorisms of Love (Vatsyanana), 661

apostolic life, 32, 115

Aquinas, Thomas (1225-1274), 45, 63, 143

Arabic language, classical science in the Islamic world, 567, 570, 581, 615

Arabic numerals, 568, 755, 793

Arafat, 539, 540

Arawak speakers, 195, 203–4, 212, 223–24, 237, 257, 336–37

archaeology: African history and, 375; African trade and, 428, 471; Ajanta murals, 724; gold objects, 465; Nubian, 480; Pavement

Period of Ife, 397–98, 494; Sijilmasa, 484

Archimedes Screw, 585

architecture, Africa, 401–3, 422–23, 440, 444–45, 461; Cairene, 447; mosques, 404, 423, 431, 478, 550–51; Swahili, 402–3, 411, 422–23, 474, 488

architecture, Americas: Chaco Canyon, 271–72, 292–93; Cuzco, 281; Mayan, 232, 243; Mitla, 300–301; Moche, 301; Pueblo, 228; Tarascan, 336; Tawantinsuyu, 322; Teotihuacán talud-tablero, 243, 321–22; Wari, 339. *see also* kivas; mound building

architecture, East Asia, 905, 930–31, 977

architecture, European, 46–49, **82–83**

architecture, Islamic world: mosques, 404, 423, 431, 478, 550–51, 647–48, 734–35; palaces, 551–52

architecture, Oceania: Nan Madol, 1027, 1035, **1109–10**; Pulemelei Mound, 1115; Rapa Nui, 1039, 1053; stone structures, 1027, 1036, 1045, 1053, 1115

architecture, South Asia, *see* cave monasteries; temples, South Asia

Arctic and Subarctic: the arts, 216–17; economy, 207; global ties, 253; historical overview, 192; religion, 199; science and technology, 242; society, 229–30

Arians, 17, 114

aristocrats, *see* nobility

armor: European knights, 144–46; Muslim soldiers, 629–30

Art of War (Sun Zi), 997

Artocarpus altilis (seedless breadfruit), 1035

Artocarpus mariannensis (seeded breadfruit), 1036

the arts: Africa, 376–77, **395–405**, 476, 495; Americas, **213–24**; East Asia, **903–11**; Europe, **42–51**; North Africa and the Middle East, **549–56**; Oceania, **1050–54**; South Asia, **719–36**. *see also* ecclesiastical art; sculptures

Aryabhata I (476-550), 757–58, 759–60

ase, Yoruba art and, 399

Ashikaga Shogunate (1336-1477), 884, **937–38**, 959, 978, 989

Ashoka pillars, 687, 824

Asia, European interactions with, 73

Askiya Muhammad (c. 1442-1538), **443**, 485

Asser, Bishop, 157–58

astrolabe, 68

astrology, Islamic palaces and, 551–52

astronomy, *see* celestial observations

Atalhuapa (1532-1533), 183, 323, 349–50

Atlantic-based trade, Africa with Europe, 368

atlatl, 219, **261–62**

atolls, 1033, 1067, **1068–69**, 1089

atomic theory, Indian, 760–62

Augustine (354-430), 27, 32, 149–50, 153

Australia: Cape York Peninsula, 1146–48; dance, 1075; didjeridu, 1108; food gathering, 1067, 1081–82; gods and goddesses, 1083–84

Autronesian migrations, Pacific islands, 1027

Avalokiteshvara as Guide of Souls, 984

Averroes (1126-1198), 143

Avicenna (980-1037), 134

Avignon popes, 30, 56, 97

Avonlea, **262**

Aybak, Qutb al-Din (d. 1210), 734, **778**, 788, 792

ayllu, **262–63**

ayurvedic medicine, 764–66, 777

Ayyavole guild, 707, 712, 713

Ayyubids (1169-1250), 455, 532

al-Azhar University, 412–13, 431

Aztecs: the arts, 220–21; Aztlan and, 263–64; calpollis, 269–70; economy, 210; education, 269; "flowery wars," **285–86**; global ties, 253–54, 255–56; historical overview, 193; religion, 201–2; rise of the Aztec Empire (map), 186; rulers, 355; science and technology, 246–47; society, 235; Tenochtitlán, 345–47; Triple Alliance, 288–89, 306, **332–34**; Tula, **334–35**

Aztlan, **263–64**

Babur (1483-1530), 663, **779–80**, 831, 832, 857–58

The Baburnama, 780

Babylonian captivity, 30, 56, 97

Bach Dang, Battle of, 863

Bacon, Roger, 64

Baghdad, 517, 530, 543–45, 581, 615, 645–46, 657, 864

Bahmani Kingdom, 663, **780–81**, 788, 813, 829

al-Bakri, 360, 394, 428, **441**, 500–502

Balban, Ghiyas al-Din (d. 1286), 663, **781–82**, 788

ballgame: Caribbean ball courts, 203; Hohokam, 227, 265; Mesoamérican, 195, 215, **264–65**; Snaketown ball courts, 206, 317

Balochistan, 662

Banabhatta (Bana) (fl . seventh century C.E.), 662, 677–78, **782–83**, 794, 845–46

banking, 37, 136, 137–38

Bantu Expansions, 359, 370, **443–44**

baqt, 500

Barrancoid, 259

Basava (1134-1196), 697

Batán Grande, 194, **265–66**

Baybars, Sultan (r. 1260-1277), 533, 614, 633

Becket, Thomas, 30, 122

Bede the Venerable (c. 672-735), 41–42, 81, **83–84**, 153–54

belt drive technology, 919, 920

Benedictine monasteries, 84

Benedictine *Rule*, 28

benevolence, Confucianism, 890, 911, 942

Bengal, 662, **783–84**

Benin, 360, 411, **444–46**

Beowulf, 43

Berbers: overview, **446–47**; camels and, 391, 422, 432; Christianity and, 359, 382–83, 448; Islam and, 360, 384, 441–42, 446, 469; Sanhaja, 435–36, 442

Bernard of Clairvaux (1090-1153), 26, 50, **85–86**, 143, 167–68

betel, 702, 776–77, 1064, **1070**, 1112

Bhagavad Gita, 661, 696, 739, 818, 834, 837–38

bhakti, 695–97

bhakti yoga, 834

Bharata, 661

Bhaskara II (1114-1185), 759

bigman (Melanesia): overview, **1070–71**, 1074; New Guinea *moka* exchange and, 1049, 1087

bilateral descent, Africa, 407

birds, navigation and, 1059, 1061

Black Death, *see* bubonic plague

black earth sites, 250, 259, **326–27**

Boccaccio, Giovanni (1313-1375), 44, **86–87**, 172–73

Bodhisattva, 676, 893, **938–39**, 984

body art: African, 403–4; Marquesas Islands, 1053; tattoos, 403–4, 1053, **1122–24**

Bonampak murals, 219–20

Bonaventure(ca. 1217-1274), 139

Boniface VIII, Pope, 30

Book of Divine Works (Hildegard of Bingen), 117

Book of Government or Rules for Kings (Nizam al-Mulk), 617, 651–53

The Book of Highways and Kingdoms, 441

Book of Kells, 42

Book of Margery Kempe, 175–76

The Book of the Abacus (Fibonacci), 62–63

The Book of the City of Ladies (Pizan), 148

The Book of the Islamic Market Inspector (al-Shayzari), 559, 561, 598, 653–54

Book of Travels (Ibn Jubayr), 555

Bora Bora, 1145–46

Borobudur, 824

bow and arrow, Great Plains and, 262

Brahmagupta (c. 598-c. 660), 757, **784–85**

Brahmin caste, 738–39, 785

Brahmin theory, 771–73

Brahminical Hinduism: Buddhism and, 676–77; Gupta Empire and, 675–77

Brahmins of Lar, Marco Polo's account of, 850–51

brass sculptures, African, 397–98

breadfruit: overview, 1027, **1071–72**; social change and, 1035–36, 1045

Bretigny, Treaty of, 4

bridges, 919–20

broadcast sowing, 34

bubonic plague (Black Death): in Africa, 374, 452; in Asia, 75; in China, 864, 898; deaths from, 21, 41; described, 86, **87–88**, 172–73; map of spread, 12; medieval medicine and, 135; outbreak of, 4

Buddha: copper icon, 763; as *Dipamkara*, 769; Siddhartha Gautama, 892–93

Buddhism: Brahminical Hinduism and, 676–77; China overview, 892–94; Indian decline of, 689–90; in Japan, 882, 977, 984–85; in Korea, 880, 907, 984; Mahayana, 893, 938–39, 940; Nalanda University and, 814–15; Northern Wei and, 981; South Asia overview, 688–90; spread in China, 863, 872–73; *stupas* and, 675, 679, **823–25**; texts, 678; Tibetan, 682, 815

Buddhist literature, Faxian and, 661

Buddhist monasteries, 678

burakumin, 894, 915, **939–40**, 965, 988

burgers, rent and property charters, 40

burial practices: Chimor, 274; cremation, 839–40; Hohokam, 191; Igbo, 468; Luba kingdom, 475; Muslim, **595–97**, 735; Nan Madol, 1027, 1035, **1109–10**; Oceania chiefs, 1036; Pacific Coast, 199; Rivas, **314–15**; tomb of K'inich Janaab' Pakal, 292; tombs of the imams, 609–10. *see also* mound building; Southern Cult (Southeastern Ceremonial Complex); Spiro

bushi, 884, 901–2, 999

business management, Italian merchants, 41–42

Buyids (945-1055), 518, 530, 576–77, 581, **587**

Byzantine Empire: Battle of Manzikert, 531; c. 1270 (map), 523; churches, 47–48, 82; Constantinople and, 21, 58–59; Crusades and, 71; Golden Age, 18; iconoclasm and, 119–20; Justinian rule of, 3; Manzikert battle, 3; Ottoman conquest of, 23; Roman law and, 18, 59–60

cacao, 208, 209, **266–67**

Cahokia, 182, 190, 197, 205, 214, 226, 240, 252, **267–68**

Cairo: overview, 360, **447**; economy overview, 545–48; eleventh century description, 650–51; Fatimid Caliphs, 658; Islamic dynasties, 454–55, 459; Islamic scholarship, 385, 412–13, 431, 443; poll tax on Jews and Christians, 561; social complexity and, 371

Calakmul, **268–69**, 291, 328–29

calendars and dating systems: Aztec, 247; Coptic, 450; Dionysian, 84; Gregorian, 539, 588–89; Islamic, 517, 527, 538–39, 570–71, **588–90**; Jewish, 588; Mayan solar, 181; Mesoamérican, 219, 232, 242, 243–44, 278, **297–99**

caliph, 528, **590–91**

caliphate fragmentation, 529–33

calligraphy: Arabic, 404–5, 552–53, 735; Chinese, 904

calmecac, **269**

calpolli, **269–70**

camels, 359, 391, 421–22, 432, 453, 574

canoes, Polynesian, 1037, 1058, 1060, 1065, 1126–27

canon law, 25, 56–57, **128–30**
Canon of Medicine, 134
The Canterbury Tales (Chaucer),
    94–95
Canticle of the Sun, 112
Canute, King, 3
Capet, Hugh, 20
Capetian dynasty, 20, 23
Caraka Samhita (Caraka), 764
caravans, 574–75, 708
Carib peoples, 195, 294–95
Caribbean, *see* Amazonia and the
    Caribbean
Carmelites (White Friars), 29
Carmina Burana, 46
Caroline Islands, 1058–59, 1060,
    1089, 1105
Carolingian dynasty, 17, 20, 25,
    53, 93
carpet weaving, 714–15
Casas Grandes, 206, **270–71**
cash crops, European, 80
caste system, 676, 698, 700, 717,
    737–44, **785–86**
castles: European, 48–49, **89–90**;
    in literature, 166–67; manors
    and, 53
castration, *see* eunuchs
Catalan Atlas, 361, 429
Catherine of Siena (1347-1380), 22,
    27, 30, 97, 108
Catholic Church: decrees, 25–26;
    formation, 3, 18; organizational
    structure, 24–25; popular
    religion and, 26–27; reform of,
    25; secular life and, 19
cattle: African domestication of,
    452–53; Indian agriculture and,
    777; sacred cows, 745; wealth
    and, 388, 421, 454
Causae et Curae (Causes and
    Cures), 61, 117
cave monasteries: overview,
    719–22; advantages of, 727;
    Ajanta, 722–24; Elephanta,
    724–25; Ellora, 726–27;
    Mamallapuram, 725–26
Caves of the Thousand Buddhas,
    990
Celestial Masters movement, 888,
    985
celestial observations: al-Biruni
    (973-1048), 569; astronomy,
    Islamic world, 570–71; Aztec,
    247; European, 61; Indian
    astronomy, 758, 759–60; Mayan,
    245; the Pleiades, 310; Venus,
    338–39
ceramics: Amazonian, 223;
    Barrancoid, 259; Casas Grandes,

270–71; Chinese porcelain, 897,
    906–7, 922–23; Islamic world,
    554; Korean, 899–900, 907–8, 923,
    931; *lapita*, **1095–96**; Moche
    Presentation Theme, 202–3, 222,
    280, 301–2, 316; Polychrome
    Tradition, 295; Salado
    polychrome, 216, 253
cereal and grain crops: African,
    462; European, 34, 56
Chaco Canyon: the arts, 215–16;
    economy, 206; Great Kivas and,
    292–93; historical overview, 191,
    271–72; religion, 198–99; society,
    228
Chahamans, 819
chain drive, 921
Chalukya dynasty, 682–84, 819
Chamorros, 1089
Champagne Fairs, 36, **90–92**,
    156–57
Chan Buddhism, 876, 893, **940**,
    1006
Chan Chan, 212, 274
chandalas (untouchables), 674–75,
    740–41, 785, 790, 840–41
Chandra Gupta I, 661
Chandra Gupta II Vikramaditya
    (r. c. 375-c. 415), 661, 665, 672,
    786–87, 843
Changan, 874, 905
chanson de geste (songs of deed),
    43, 96
Charlemagne (742-814):
    Carolingian Renaissance and
    education reform, 17, 25, 105,
    155–56; chapel at Aachen, 82;
    interactions with Muslim world,
    70–71; life of, **92–94**; marriage
    and, 131; *Song of Roland*, 43;
    unification of western Europe,
    3, 17
Charles the Great, *see* Charlemagne
Charles V (r. 1364-1380), 118
chastity, Islamic world, 634–35
Chaturanga, **787**
Chaucer, Geoffrey (c. 1342-1400),
    44, 86, **94–95**
Chavín de Huantar, 181, 194,
    222–23, 319
Chengzu (r. 1403-1425), 879, 972
Chichén Itzá, 182, 201, 209, 234–35,
    272–73
Chichimecs, 263–64
chickens: Africa, 453; Polynesia/
    South America link, 1065
chiefs, Oceania: overview, 1043–44,
    1072–74; burial, 1036; Hawaiian
    chiefdoms, 1038, 1073; kava,
    1092; Maori, 1039, 1073;

Melanesian chiefdoms, 1033,
    1056; Murik Lakes, 1056; New
    Caledonia, 1087–88; Samoan,
    1073–74; *tapu*, 1120–21; Tongan
    chiefdoms, 1037, 1073
chiefs, Southeast Asian chieftains,
    771–72
chihilganis (Corps of Forty), 782
children: Africa, 408; Chinese
    society, 912–13, 999–1000;
    Europe, 166; North Africa and
    the Middle East, **591–92**, 598–99,
    601
Children's Crusade, 72, 101
Chimor: the arts, 223; economy,
    211–12; global ties, 256;
    historical overview, 194, **274**;
    religion, 203; science and
    technology, 248; society, 236–37
China: Arab trade, 898; the arts,
    903–7; Buddhism and, 833;
    dynasties, 1021; economy, 895–
    99; education, 948–49; Europe
    and, 929–30; family names, 975;
    food, 957–58; global ties, 925–30;
    historical overview, 871–79;
    India and, 710–11, 773, 927;
    inventions, 1024; Japan and, 927,
    932; Jurchen conquest of, 877;
    Korea and, 900, 926, 930–31,
    1019; lineages, 937, 949, **969–70**;
    Mongols and, 812, 877–78, 898,
    928–29; Muslim world and, 928;
    Oceania trade and, 1063; Persia
    and, 927; Roman Empire and,
    929; science and technology,
    918–23, 925; society, 911–18;
    Three Teachings, 888
chinampas, **274–75**
Chinese writing in Japan, 863
Chinggis (Gengis) Khan, 797, 812,
    864, 877, 974–75, 997
Chisti Sufis, 701
chivalry, 55, **95–96**
Chochin, Nestorians and, 661
chocolate, *see* cacao
Chola Empire, 662, 684, 702–3, 707,
    809, 823
Chotona, 304
Christianity in Africa: the arts and,
    404; Coptic Church, 382–83,
    449–50; currency and, 450;
    dynasties, 455–56; Ethiopian,
    383–84, 404, 431, 440; global ties
    and, 430–31; Nubian, 479;
    overview, 370, 382–84, **448–49**
Christianity in Europe: banking
    and, 37; Catholic Church,
    religious life, 24–27; conversion
    of Kievan Rus to, 3; conversion

of Roman Empire to, 16; dramatic performances and, 43; Great Schism and unification, 22–23; heresies and, 31–33, 114–16; Inquisition and, 120–21; marriage and, 131–33; Military Orders and, 28–29; monasticism and, 27–29; reconquest of Spain and, 20, 72; religious criticism and, 31–33

Christianity, South Asia, 697, 698–99

Christians: in China, 929; circumcision and, 592–93; in India and Iran, 698–99; Nestorians, 31, 114–15, 661, 698, 929; relations with Muslim society, 558–62

Christological controversies, 114–15

The Chronicle of Prophets and Kings (al-Tabari), 643–44

chronology, American culture areas, 189–90

church architecture, 46–48, 82, 404, 440, 448

church law, *see* canon law

church leadership, European popes and patriarchs, 29–31

circumcision, **592–94**

Cistercians (White Monks), 28, 85

cities, African: Hausa city-states, 465; Swahili architecture, 402–3, 411, 422–23, 474, 488; Urban Complex clustered cities, 470

cities, European: growth of, 38–40, 112–13; Italian city-states, 20; population declines and, 41; social structure, 57–58; women and, 148

cities, North Africa and the Middle East, 550

clan (*uji*), **940–41**, 971, 998

Clare of Assisi, 29, 112

class hierarchy, Confucian, 914–15, 939

Clement V, Pope (r. 1304-1314), 22, 30, 56, 97

Clement VII, Pope (r. 1378-1394), 22, 31, 97

cliff dwellings, American southwest, 191

climate: African ecological zones, 370, 411, 440, **456–57**; African weather systems and zones, 372, 373; agricultural effects, 41, 462; El Niño/La Niña, 1034, **1078–79**; Inter-Tropical Convergence Zone, 373, 1097–98; Little Climatic Optimum, 1034, 1036;

Little Ice Age, 190, 205, 286, 287–88, 304; ocean travel and, 1061; Oceania religion and, 1044–45; Syria, 542

clock, mechanical, 921

clothing and modesty, North Africa and the Middle East, 591, **594–95**, 635

clothing, Oceania, **1076–78**

clothmaking: in Africa, 390, 422, 465; in Europe, 67–68; Indian states, 704, 714; Islamic world, 543, 545, 548, 554–55; tapa, 1050, 1053, 1075, **1119–20**

clouds, navigation and, 1060–61

Clovis I, King (481-511), 3, 17, 151–52

Cluniacs, monastic reform and, 28

Cluny monastery, 47, 50

clustered villages, manorialism and, 33

codex, 219, **275–76**, 283–84, 350

coinage, *see* money and coinage

Colocasia esculenta (true taro), **1121–22**

color, navigation and, 1060

Columbus, Christopher, 76–77, 344–45

commerce, *see* trade

communes, 40

Comnena, Anna, 71, 99

Comnenus, Alexius I, Emperor (r. 1081-1118), 4, 21, 71, 99

compass: magnetic, 68–69, 919, 929; star, 1059

compurgation, 127

Conciliar Movement, 22, 31, 57, **96–97**

conciliarists, 22

Concordat of Worms, 122

Confessions (Augustine), 149–50

Confucian leaders, merchant class restrictions, 879

Confucianism: overview, 863, 876, 889–92, **941–44**; Chinese society and, 911–12, 918; denunciation of Buddhism, 1013–14; in Japan, 892, 915, 939; in Korea, 881, 892, 914–15; *Zhuangzi* and, 887

Congo, 484

conquest, expansion, and migration, Africa and global ties, 425–26

Constantinople, 4, 16, 21, 58–59

constitutional law, Magna Carta and, 19, 54

continental islands, 1068

Cook, Captain James, 1033, 1038, 1087, 1122, 1124, 1127, 1137–40

Cook Islands, 1027, 1090

Copan, 209, 230, 260, **276–78**, 310–11

Copper Belt, Africa, 370, 416

Coptic Church, 382–83, **449–50**, 459

coral, *see* atolls

Corpus Juris Civilis (The Body of Civil Law), 18, 59, 125

Cortés, Hernan, 183, 193, 289, 333–34

corvée labor, **278**, 872, 873, 874, **944**, 1019

cosmology, Indian, 762–63

cotton, 898

Cotzumalhuapa, **278–79**

Council of Chalcedon, 31

Council of Constance, 4, 22, 31, 97, 174

Council of Pisa, 22, 31, 97

courtly love, 43–44, 55, **97–99**, 166–67

cows, sacred, 745

craft production: Africa, 390, 422; Indian states, 703–5, 714–15

Craig Mound, 318

creation myths, Americas: Popol Vuh, **311–12**; Quetzalcoatl, 312

crime: in China, 967–68; Hindu states, 804; wheat prices and, 56

crops: African farming and, 420–21, 437–38, 461, 462–63; Oceania root-crop production, 1068

Crow Creek, **279–80**

The Crusades: !overview, **99–101**, 518; (1096-1204) map, 9; (1218-1270) map, 10; Anna Comnena describes the First Crusade, 161–62; besieging a tower, 169–70; Byzantine Empire and, 59; castle architecture, 48–49; church leaders and, 19; European interactions with Muslim world, 71–72; Jerusalem and, 4; Military Orders and, 28–29, **135–36**; trade and, 36

cultivation techniques: Africa, 420; Europe, 34–35, 79–80

cultural unification, early Middle Ages, 17

curaca, 202, 210, 262, **280**

currency: African, 419, 423–24, 432–33, **450–51**, 474, 475; European, 36–37, 91, **136–38**, 392; India, pre-Islamic and Islamic, 809–11. *see also* money and coinage

Cuzco, 212, 249, **280–81**, 322

cyclical time, **281–82**, 298–99

Cyril (missionary), 3, 18

Cyrillic alphabet, 3, 18

daimyo, 864

Dalutabad, 686

Damascus, 517, 542–43, 550–51, 616, 657

dance: Bora Bora, 1145–46; Oceania, 1051, **1074–76**, 1078; Siva and, 693–94; war dances, 1122, 1129

Dandanqan, Battle of, 662

Danelaw, 3, 81

Dante Alighieri (1265-1321), 44, 98, **102–3**, 111

Dao De Jing, 886–87, 945, 1009–10

Daoism: overview, 886–89, **944–46**; in China, 921, 922; in Japan, 889, 946; in Korea, 888–89, 946

Dark Ages, 15

Darwin, Charles (1809-1882), 1069

Dauphin, 118–19

death and afterlife, North Africa and the Middle East, **595–97**

The Decameron (Giovanni), 86–87, 172–73

Deccan, **787–88**; Chalukya dynasty, 662, 680

decimals, 755, 756

Decretum, 56, 129

Delhi: account of holy man, 853–54; concubines and slave girls in, 854–55; description of, 848; iron pillar of, 763; pre-Muslim story of, 852; sacking by Timur, 663, 687, 789, 791, 828, 856–57; uprising in, 855–56

Delhi sultanate: overview, 622, **788–89**, 859; 1236 map, 667; 1325 map, 668; Aybak and, 778; Babur's defeat of, 780; Bengal and, 784; economy, 715–16; Firuz Shah Tughluq (d. 1388), 663, 687, 751–52, 789, 790–91, 800; *iqta* and, 797–98; Islam and, 700; Khilij dynasty, 685–86; military households, 713; Mongols and, 812; Muhammad bin Tughluq (d.1351), 663, 685–86, 716, 788, 789, *813–14*

democracies, acephalous societies, 413–14

descent: African descent groups, 406–7; Melanesian, 1055–56; Micronesian, 1054; Polynesian, 1057

deserts, African, 457

Devi Chandra Gupta, 672

devotio moderna, 139

devotio moderna (modern devotion), 27

Dharmachakra Mudra, 688

dhimma, 558–62, 803

Dhramasastra texts, 803–4, 805, 807

dialectic, 142

Diamond, Jared, 70

Dias, Bartolomeu, 368

Dictatus Papae, 160–61

didjeridu, 1108

diet: Ayurvedic medicine and, 777; European, 34–35, 67, 79, **109–11**, 134–35; Hindu beef taboo, 745; Islamic, 583–84, 603–4

dinars, 433, 450–51, 485, 548, 616

Dionysius, 84

Dioscorea alata (great yam), 1133

Dioscorea exculenta (yam), 1133

disease, Africa: overview, **451–52**; child-rearing and, 408; effects of, 373–74; farming and, 420; livestock and, 453–54; traditional religions and, 380

dispersed pattern settlements, in-fields and out-fields, 33

The Divine Comedy (Dante), 44, 103, 111

divine kingship, Americas, **282–83**

diviners, African traditional religions, 379

divorce: Europe, 132–33; Islamic world, 637

Doldrums, 1097

Dome of the Rock, 517, 534, 542, 553, 581, 644–45, 648–50

domestic work, Africa, 390

domesticated animals: African, 370, 432; African economy and, 388–89; African history of, **452–54**; land cultivation and, 34–35. *see also* herding

Dominicans (Black Friars), 29, 120–21

Donatism, 32, 383, 448

Dorset culture: the arts, 216–17; economy, 207; global ties, 253; historical overview, 192, **283**; religion, 199; science and technology, 242; society, 229

drama, Chinese, 864

dramatic performance, 43, **103–4**

Dream Time, 1083–84

dress, Oceania (clothing), **1076–78**

Du Fu (712-770), 904

dualism, 115

Dumont, Louis, 743–44, 745

dynasties: Africa, 383, 412, **454–56**; China, 1021; Indian dynastic turmoil, 681; medieval Europe, 177–78; Turkic, 530

early Middle Ages (476-1000), historical overview, 16–18

earth, flat or round, 77

East Asia: the arts, **903–11**; economy, **895–902**; global ties, **925–33**; historical overview, **871–85**, 1023; philosophies and religion overview, 885–86; religion, **885–94**; science and technology, **918–25**; society, **911–18**

Easter Island (Rapa Nui), 1027, 1028, 1031, 1038, 1053, 1091

Eastern Orthodox Church, 31–32, 139

Eastern Woodlands and the Great Plains: the arts, 214–15; bow and arrow and, 262; economy, 205; global ties, 251–52; historical overview, 190; religion, 196–97; science and technology, 240; society, 225–26

Eastern Zhou Period (771-256 B.C.E.), 885–86

ecclesiastical art, Ethiopian and Nubian, 359, 396, 404, 431, 448, 461, 479, 480

Ecclesiastical History of the English People (Bede), 84, 153–54

Eckhart, Meister (c. 1260-1327), 139

ecological zones, Africa, 370, 411, 440, **456–57**

economy: Africa, **386–95**, 454, 485–86; Americas, **204–13**; East Asia, **895–902**; Europe, **33–42**, 136–38, 148; Gupta Empire, 673–74; North Africa and the Middle East, **541–49**; Oceania, **1046–50**; South Asia, **702–19**. *see also* marketplaces; trade

Edessa, 71, 86, 100

education: African religions and, 378; Aztec schools, 269; Charlemagne's reform of, 105, 155–56; Chinese society and, 913; East Asia, **948–49**; Europe, 60, 93, **104–6**, 166; Muslim India, 751; North Africa and the Middle East, **597–601**. *see also* Islamic scholars; mathematics; universities

education, Oceania, **1078**

Edward I, King (r. 1272-1307), 19–20, 58, 89, 140

Edward III, King (r. 1327-1377), 4, 23, 94, 117

Egypt: cattle and, 453; Christianity and, 382, 384, 430, 448, 449–50; cloth production, 422; dynasties and, 454–55; economy overview, 545–48; farming and, 387; Fatimids and, 447; history, **458–59**; Indian Ocean trade, 393; Islam and, 384, 412; Nubia and, 499–500; Roman Empire and, 368

Ehecatl, 200
Eight Deer Jaguar Claw
   (1063-1115), **283–85**
Eightfold Noble Path, 892
El Niño/La Niña, 1034, **1078–79**
Eleanor of Aquitaine (c. 1122-1204),
   19, 98, 100, **106–7**, 132, 146–47
Elephanta, 724
elephants, 830–31
Ellora, 726–27
Emperor Illustrious August
   (Xuanzong), 863
enfranchisement, Africa, 414
England: Norman and Plantagenet
   dynasties, 3, 19; Parliament,
   19–20, 140; peasant revolts, 141
enlightenment, 892–93
entertainment: North Africa and
   the Middle East, 551, **601–2**;
   Oceania, **1079–81**
environment, Africa, human
   effects, 372–73
equal field system: overview, 872,
   873, 874, **951**; in Japan, 901, 1002;
   Southern Song dynasty and, 936;
   Tang dynasty and, 947–48;
   Tuoba and, 980–81
Erikson, Leif (the Lucky), 75–76,
   159–60, 182, 341–43
estampie, 46
Ethiopian Highlands: overview,
   461; Christianity and, 383–84,
   404, 431, 440, 448, 455–56, **459–61**;
   farming and, 387, 437; global ties
   425, 426; Indian Ocean trade, 393;
   Judaism and, 370; Zagwe and
   Solomnid Dynasties, 360, 412,
   430, 455–56, 460, 503–4, 513–14
ethnicity, Africa, 406, 436
The Etymologies, 133–34
eunuchs, 789, 875–76, 916, **952–53**,
   972
Euphrates River, 544–45
Europe: the arts, **42–51**; dynasties
   of medieval Europe, 177–78;
   economy, **33–42**; Europe and the
   Mediterranean c. 1200 map, 8;
   global ties, **69–77**; historical
   overview, early Middle Ages
   (467-1000), 16–18; historical
   overview, fourteenth century,
   21–24; historical overview, high
   Middle Ages (1000-3000), 18–21;
   religion, **24–33**; science and
   technology, **60–69**; society, **51–60**
Everyman, 104
examination system, East Asia,
   871, 876, 880, 915–16, 943, 948–
   49; overview, **953–55**; Mongols
   and, 1005; Song dynasty and,

979–80; Tang Governance and,
   996
exogamy, 407, 408
exploration: great sea migrations
   (Oceania), 1031–33, 1058, 1061;
   Marco Polo and, 75. *see also*
   Vikings
Ezana, King, 359, 383, 440

fabliaux (poetic compositions), 44
faith, 534–35, 562, 634
falconry, 602
falefa, Tu'i Tonga governance, 1037
famine, Europe, 21, 22, 41, 80, 111
Fan Kuan (d.c. 1023), 903
fans, Japanese, 924
farming, *see* agriculture
fasting, *sawm*, 537–39
Fathers of the Church, 24, 42–43,
   107–9, 131–32, 142
Fatimids (909-1171): Africa, 360,
   412, 413, 447, 455; Ismaili
   Caliphs, 658; North Africa and
   the Middle East, 518, 532, 541,
   545–46, 552, 576, **602–3**
Faxian (d. c. 422), **789–90**; Buddhist
   literature and, 661; on chandalas
   (outcasts), 740–41, 840–41; on
   cremation, 839–40; on Gupta
   society, 674–76
Feathered Serpent, *see* Quetzalcoatl
feminine deities, 679
feng shui, 929, **955–56**
fertilizer, 33–34, 80, 420, 936, 958,
   1068
Festival of Lanterns, 905
feudal law, 18, 53–54, 66, **126–27**,
   154–55
feudal system, Europe, 19
Fibonacci sequence, 62–63
fief, 19, 126
Fiji Islands, 1088, 1143–44
Firuz Shah Tughluq (d. 1388), 663,
   687, 751–52, 789, **790–91**, 800
"Five Classics" of Confucius, 889,
   941
Five Dynasties, Era of, 863
Five Pillars of Islam: overview,
   385, 469, 533–34; *hajj*
   (pilgrimage), 539–41; *salat* (ritual
   prayer), 535–37; *sawm* (fasting),
   537–39; *shahada* (statement of
   faith), 534–35, 562, 634; *zakat*
   (giving of alms), 537
Five Relationships of
   Confucianism, 911, 913, 942, 971
floating gardens, 275
flower squires, 880, **956–57**, 991
"flowery wars," **285–86**
flying buttresses, 47, 83

food, Africa: overview, **462–63**;
   hunting and gathering, **466–67**;
   Iron Age production effects, 370;
   livestock and, 454; spread of
   ideas and technologies, 432;
   traditional religions and, 379
food, Americas: cacao, 208, 209,
   266–67; maize, 205, 287; pulque,
   312
food, East Asia, 935–36, **957–59**
food, Europe, 33, 41, 56, **109**
food, North Africa and the Middle
   East: overview, **603–4**;
   agriculture and, 583–85; Islamic
   recipes, 654–55; Syrian and
   Palestinian, 543
food, Oceania: overview, 1067–68,
   1081–83, 1144–45; breadfruit,
   1027, **1071–72**; climate and, 1045;
   taro, **1121–22**; yams, **1133–34**
food, South Asia: Hinduism and,
   775–76; Islamic, 776–77; Jainism
   and, 799
footbinding, 877, 892, **959–60**, 978,
   991, 1000
Forbidden City, 864, 972
fortification, defensive castles,
   47–48, 55, 89
"Four Books" of Confucius, 889,
   941
Four Noble Truths, 892
fourteenth century, historical
   overview, 21–24
Fourth Lateran Council, 25–26, 123,
   140
France: Capetian dynasty, 20;
   Parliament, 140–41; peasant
   revolts, 141
Francis of Assisi (c. 1182-1226), 26,
   29, **111–12**, 138–39
Francis Xavier, 663
Franciscan Order (Grey Friars), 29,
   112, 139, 143
frankincense, 393, 412, 427, 461,
   498–99
Franks, 16, 17, 531–32, 614
Frederick II, Emperor (r.1215-1250),
   20–21, 73, 101
Fremont Culture: economy, 206;
   global ties, 252; historical
   overview, 191, **286**; religion, 198;
   science and technology, 241;
   society, 226
French Polynesia, 1090
frescoes, 49
Froissart, Jean, 173
Fujiwara family, 882, 883, 963–64,
   987, 989, 1002
Funan, 772–73
Fustat, 546–48, 605

Galen (131-201), 60–61, 134, 543, 571
Gama, Vasco de, 368
garbhagriha, 825
gardens, European peasant
    households and, 34, 80
gargoyles, 50
Garlake, Peter, 398, 399
gender, Africa, political authority
    and, 413, 414
genealogy, Oceania, 1034–35
Genghis Khan, 797, 812, 864, 877,
    974–75
Geniza (Cairo), 561, **605**
geomancy, 955–56
Germanic folk wisdom, medicine
    and, 133
Germanic law, 17, **127–28**
Germanic tribes, 16–17, 35, 43
Germany, peasant revolts, 141
gerontocracy: Africa, 409, 414;
    New Guinea, 1056
Ghadir Khumm, 586–87, 621–23
Ghana: overview, 359, 360, **463–64**;
    Al-Bakri's account of, 501–2;
    Almoravid Movement and, 442;
    political structure, 410;
    Portuguese explorers and, 368;
    trans-Saharan trade, 391; written
    history of, 441
Ghaurids, 778, **791–92**, 802, 817
Ghaznavid principality, 662
Ghaznin, 662
Ghor, 662
The Gift (Mauss), 1046–48
gifts, Polynesian economy and,
    1046–50, 1093–94
Gilbert Islands, 1089, 1148–49
Gita Govinda, 731
glass, 863
global ties: Africa, **425–33**, 467;
    Americas, **251–58**, 270–71; East
    Asia, **925–33**; Europe, **69–77**;
    North Africa and the Middle
    East, **573–79**; Oceania, **1062–66**;
    South Asia, **766–73**
Gnosticism, 114
Go-Daigo, Emperor, 937
God: history and, 526; Muslim
    death and afterlife, 596–97;
    mysticism and, 138–40; proofs of
    existence, 142, 143, 569; *shahada*
    and, 534–35, 562, 634
goddess worship, Hinduism and,
    694–95
Godrick, merchant saint, 164–65
gods: Aztec, 289–90; Eastern
    Polynesian, 1038; Mayan, 201;
    Mesoamérican, 200; Pachacamac,
    307–8; Quetzalcoatl, **312–14**;
    Shinto, 987–88; Staff God, 194,

222–23, **319**, 320; Tlaloc, **330–31**;
    Venus and, 338–39; Wari, 339
gods and goddesses, Oceania,
    1083–85
gold: overview, **464–65**; African
    exports, 368, 392; Bure
    goldfields, 476–77; Indian trade
    and, 768; Korean mines, 900;
    Songhai economy, 485–86;
    trans-Saharan trade, 391, 410,
    427, 439, 443
gold fields, Africa (maps), 363, 364,
    365
gold-for-salt transactions, 391
Golden Age of Byzantine Empire, 18
Golden Era of India, 661, 673
Golden Horde, 614
The Golden Legend, 85
goods, diffusion of, 73–75
Gosala Makkhaliputra, 691–92
Gothic cathedrals, 47, 50, 82–83, 85
government: African acephalous
    (stateless) societies, 413–15, 468;
    African centralized states, 409–
    13; *Book of Government or Rules
    for Kings* (Nizam al-Mulk), 617,
    651–53; Danelaw, 81; East Asian
    examination system and, 871,
    876, 880, 915–16, 943, 948–49,
    953–55; eastern European cities,
    58–59; Gupta Empire, 793;
    Harsha's administration, 679–81;
    Kamakura Period, **963–64**;
    Korea, 880–81; Mali empire,
    476–77; Oceania chiefs, 1043–44,
    1072–74; popol nah (council
    house), **310–11**; South Indian
    agrarian assemblies, 712;
    western European cities and
    towns, 57–58, 112–13. *see also*
    feudal law; manorialism;
    Parliament; Tang governance
Grand Canal, 873, 878, **960–61**, 993,
    1004, 1005
Great Basin, *see* American
    Southwest and the Great Basin
Great Plains, *see* Eastern
    Woodlands and the Great Plains
Great Schism, 3, 22–23, 31, 57, 97
Great Wall, 873, 950, **961–62**, 979,
    993–94
Great Zimbabwe, 360, 401–2, 423,
    451
Greek language, 18
Greek Orthodox Church,
    formation, 3, 18
Greenland Saga, 159–60
Gregorian chant, 45
Gregorian Christian calendar, 539,
    588–89

Gregory II, Pope (r. 715-731), 120
Gregory VII, Pope (r. 1073-1085),
    28, 30, 122, 160–61
Gregory IX, Pope (r. 1227-1241), 120
Gregory XI, Pope (r. 1370-1378), 22,
    30–31, 56–57, 97
Grosseteste, Robert, 64
Gu Kaizhi (344-c. 406), 903
Guacanagari, 344–45
Guibert of Nogent, 166
Guide to Pilgrimage Places (Ibn al-
    Hawrani), 578–79
Guido of Arezzo, 46
guilds: Europe, 40, 57–58, **112–13**;
    Indian states, 704–5, 711–14
guinea worm disease, 452
Gujara-Pritihara dynasty, 681–82
Gujars, 682
gunpowder: China, 922, 929;
    Europe, 16, 23, 49, 55, 67, 90,
    118, 145
Guns, Germs, and Steel (Diamond),
    70
Gupta Empire (320-550): overview,
    792–94, 859; Brahminical
    Hinduism, 675–77; end of, 662;
    Faxian's descriptions of, 789–90;
    historical overview, 671–74;
    inscriptions of Gupta kings,
    843–44; North India expansion,
    661; rulers, 661; society and
    religion, 674–77; under Chandra
    Gupta II, 665, 786–87
Guru Nanak, 663
gynecomorphism, 418

hadith literature: alms, 537; fasting,
    538; on Jews and Christians, 560;
    ritual prayer, 535; *shari'a* and,
    619–21
Hagia Sophia, 47–48, 82
hajj (pilgrimage): overview, 539–41;
    African global ties and, 430–31;
    Almoravid Movement and, 442;
    of Mansa Musa to Mecca, 385,
    431, 477–78, 504–5
al-Hakim, Caliph (r. 996-1021), 560
al-Hallaj (857-922), 625–27
Han dynasty (202 B.C.E.-220 C.E.),
    863, 888, 891, 943, 969
handguns, 145–46
handwriting, Carolingian
    miniscule, 93
Hangzhou, 896, 898, 992
Hanseatic League, 36
haraj, 716, 779, 800, **803**
Haram mosque, 539–40
Harihara I (r. 1336-1356), 828–29
Harsacarita (Banabhatta), 782–83,
    794, 845–46

Harsha (590-647), **794–95**; accounts of, 677–79, 845–47; administration of, 679–80; Bengal and, 783; rule of, 662, 680–81, 802

Harsha Carita (Banabhatta), 662, 677, 678–79

Harun al-Rashid (d. 809), 517, 530, **605–6**

Hasan ibn Ali ibn Abi Talib (d. 669), **606**

hatha yoga, 834

Hattin, Battle of, 4

haus tambaran, 1051, 1087

Hausa: overview, **465–66**; centralized government, 411; development of language, 371; farming and, 388

Hawaii: clothing, 1077; food, 1083; *heiau*, 1100; historical overview, 1038; island chain, 1091; organized society and, 1027; Pele, 1083, 1085; surfing, 1080

healers, African traditional religions, 380

Heian Period (794-1185): overview, 863, **962–63**; aesthetics, 883, 909, 962, 995; food, 958–59; *uji* and, 941; warfare and, 998–99; women and, 999

Henry I, 19

Henry II, King (r. 1154-1189), 19, 30, 107, 122, 132, 146

Henry IV, Emperor, (r.1056-1106), 30, 122

Henry V (r. 1413-1422), 4, 5, 118

herding: African economy and, 388–89; African technology, 421–22, 453–54; rearing methods, 421–22. *see also* domesticated animals

heresies, 31–33, **114–16**, 174–75

hesychasm, 139

high Middle Ages (1000-3000), historical overview, 18–21

Hijaz, 527–28

hijra, 435, 517, 527, **606**

Hildegard of Bingen (1098-1179), 45, 61, **116–17**, 134, 147, 165–66

Hindu, imperial ideology, 674

Hindu architecture, *see* cave monasteries

Hindu iconography, 683

Hindu numerals, 568, 755, 793

Hindu states: crime, 804; justice, 804–6; legal texts, 803–4; punishments, 806–7

Hinduism: *Bhagavad Gita*, 661, 696, 739, 818, 834, 837–38; Brahmin, 675–76; devotional *bhakti*, 679,

683, 695–98; four stages of Hindu life, 743; goddess worship, 694–95; *Kama Sutra*, 746; Muslim account of, 847–48; ritual changes, 697–98; sacred cows, 745; South Asia overview, 692–94; style of worship, 733; temples, 825–27; transformation of, 695; women and, 746–50; yoga and, **833–35**

historical overview: Africa, **367–77**; Americas, **189–96**; East Asia, **871–85**, 1023; Europe, **15–24**; North Africa and the Middle East, **525–33**; Oceania, **1031–40**; South Asia, **671–88**

history and historians, European views of African history, 374

The History of the Franks (Gregory), 151–52

History of the Mongols (Carpini), 74

The Hohokam (750-1450): the arts, 215; economy, 206; global ties, 252; historical overview, 191; religion, 198; science and technology, 241; society, 182, 226–27

Hojoki, 1020

Holy Land, 71–72, 86, 99, 101

Holy Roman Empire: Frederick II and, 20–21, 73; Habsburg dynasty, 21; map, 11; Otto I and, 20

Homo Hierarchicus: Essai sur le système des castes (Dumont), 744

Hopewell culture, 181, 196, 205, 214, 321, 332

Hore-ta-te-Taniwha, 1138–40

horses: Africa, 453, 473, 492; Europe, 34–35; warfare and, 630–31, 716–17, 830

Hospitalers, 135–36

hospitals, Indian, 766

hotels and inns, 574–75

households, Chinese society and, 912–14

housing: Maori *kainga*, 1039–40; North Africa and the Middle East, 551–52, **606–9**

Hrotswitha of Gandersheim, 43, 103–4

huaca, 202, **286–87**

human sacrifice: Abraham's son, 540; Aztecs and, 201-2, 289–90; Moche and, 203, 222; Quetzalcoatl and, 313

humors, medicine and, 60–61

"Hundred Schools," 886

The Hundred Years' War, 4, 13, 16, 23, 67, 94, **117–19**

hunger, *see* famine

Huns, 661, 677, 682, **795**, 819

hunting: African hunting and gathering societies, 409, **466–67**; Islamic world, 601–2; tools, atlatl, 219, **261–62**

Hus, John, 174–75

Husayn ibn Ali ibn Abi Talib (d. 680), 517, **609–10**, 623

hymns, 44–45

Ibn al-Hawrani (d. 1592), 578–79

Ibn al-Haytham (965-1039), 571

Ibn Battuta (1304-1368/1377): overview, **467–68**, **610–11**, **795–96**; on Delhi holy man, 853–54; on Hindu homes, 742; as magistrate in Delhi, 808; Mali description, 506-8; on the pepper tree, 852–53; Swahili coast description, 505–6; on Swahili hospitality, 409; town descriptions, 394, 474; world travel and, 361, 362, 375, 429, 796

Ibn Hawqal, 502, 565

Ibn Jubayr (1145-1217), 550–51, 555, **611–12**

Ibn Khaldun, 566–67

Ibn Sina (980-1037), 569–70

iconoclasm, 26, 49, **119–20**

ideas, diffusion of, 69–70, 432–33

Igbo: overview, **468–69**; Igbo-Ukwu sculptures, 359, 389, 397; social stratification and, 371; trade and, 428

illuminations, Islamic manuscripts, 556

Iltutmish, Shams al-Din (d. 1236), 662, 778, 788, **796–97**, 821, 848

imam/imamate, *see* caliph; Shi'ism

The Imitation of Christ (Kempis), 27, 139

imperial court, Japan, 863

The Inca Empire: the arts, 223; ayllus and, 262–63; economy, 212, 314, 351; global ties, 256–57; historical overview, 194; map, 188; religion, 203, 282–83; rulers, 355; science and technology, 248–49; society, 237, 350–51, 352–53; Tawantinsuyu, **322–23**, 349–50

India: Babur's description of, 857–58; c. 1500 (map), 669; Christians in, 698–99; dynastic turmoil, 681; female seclusion, 748; global ties with Southeast Asia, 766–67; Islam in, 684–87, 699–702; Jews in, 699; joint family and Hindu life stages, 743; pre-Muslim

c. 1200 (map), 666; sexuality, 745–46, 748–49, 751; trade with China, 710–11; transmission of culture to Southeast Asia, 770–73. *see also* North India; South India

Indian Ocean trade, 392–94, 411, 427–28, 497–98, 1063

The Indianized States of South East Asia (Coedes), 768

infallibility, papal, 160–61

inheritance, Islamic world, 637–38

initiation (Melanesia), 1051, 1078, **1085–86**, 1123, 1125–26

Innocent III, Pope (r. 1198-1216), 25–26, 30, 56, 112, 123

Inquisition, 24, 32, **120–21**

Intermediate Area, 193

Intertropical Convergence Zone (ITCZ), 373, 1097–98

Investiture Controversy, 28, 30, 56, **121–23**, 129, 160

Ipomoea batatas (sweet potato), 1039, 1065

iqta, 715, 790, **797–98**

Iran, 553, 698, 699

Iraq, economy, 543–45

iron: African Iron Age and, 369–70, 415, 418; availability and importance, 35; China and, 919; iron pillar of Delhi, 763; iron smelting, African economy and, 389–90, 417–19, 470; iron technology, African economy and, 389–90, 437; technology and, 66

Iroquois, **287–88**

irrigation: Hawaiian Islands, 1027; Islamic world, 584–85

Isidore of Seville, 133–34

Islam in Africa: overview, 370, 384–86, **469–70**; the arts and, 404–5; Berbers and, 384, 441–42; dynasties, 412, **454–56**, 459; mosque architecture, 404, 423; orthodox practice, 435–36; scholarship and education, 385, 412–13, 431, 443, 458, 478; spread of and global ties, 426

Islam in Europe, 3, 16, 35

Islam in India, 684–87, 699–702, 742–43

Islam in North Africa and the Middle East: overview, 525–26; early conquests (632-750), 528–29; expansion of Islam 624-c. 750 (map), 521; Islamic world in 1500 (map), 524

Islamic calendar, 517, 538–39, 570–71, **588–90**, 5127

Islamic scholars: al-Azhar University, 412–13, 431; *jihad* and, 613; Mansa Musa and, 478; *shari'a* and, 619–21; in Timbuktu, 385, 443, 458

island groups, Oceania, **1086–87**

Island of Onogoro, 1012

Israelite identity, Ethiopian Highlands, 361

Italy: city-state sovereignty, 20; merchants and business management, 41–42; Muslim invasion of, 72–73

Itzcoatl (d. 1440), 182, **288–89**, 306

ixiptla, **289–90**

Jacquerie, 141, 173–74

jade, 217, 276–77

jade cycle, New Caledonia, 1032

Jagannatha temple, 730

al-Jahiz (777-869), 560, 593, 646–47

Jainism, 683, 690–91, 731–32, 762–63, **798–99**

James the Elder, Saint, 163–64

Japan: the arts, 908–11; Buddhism and, 882, 917–18, 940; bushi military class, 884; China and, 932; Confucianism and, 892, 915, 944, 978; Daoism and, 889, 946; economy, 901–2; education and, 949; equal field system and, 951; family names, 976; food, 958–59; geographic isolation, 931–32; geomancy and, 956; global ties, 931–33; historical overview, 881–85; Korea and, 931, 932; science and technology, 924–25; secular leaders, 1022; Shinto and, 894; society, 915, 917–18; Taiho code, 955; Tomb Period, 881; warfare and, 998–99; women leaders, 1001

Jasaw Chan K'awiil I (d. 734), 192, 268–69, **290–91**, 329

jati, caste system and, 740, 786

Jawhar, 545–46

Jenné-jeno: overview, 360, **470–71**; Middle Niger figurines, 399; political structure, 410, 468; social complexity and, 371; trade and, 428, 439

Jerusalem, 4, 431, 460, 517, 518, 531, 543, 578, 643

jewelry: Korean, 900, 907; wealth and, 419

Jewish calendar, 588

Jews and Judaism: in Africa, 370, 429–30, 446, 459, 460, 461, **471–72**; dietary laws, 603–4; in Europe, 5, 37, **123–24**, 156,

170–71; in Malabar, 699; in North Africa and the Middle East, **471–72**, 508–9, 558–62

jihad, 534, **612–13**

jinns, 385

jiziya, 559–62, 700, 789, 791, **799–800**, 803

jnana yoga, 834

Joan of Arc (c. 1412-1431), 5, 23, 118–19, 121

Joei Code, 964

John I, King (r. 1199-1216), 4, 140

The Journey of the Mind to God, 139

judges, *shari'a* and, 621

Jurchen conquest of China, 877, 980, 991

justice: Africa, 413; Hindu states, 804–6; Islamic world and women, 637–38

Justinian, Emperor (c. 483-565): codification of Roman law, 18, 59–60, 125, 129; Hagia Sophia church construction, 47–48, 82, 125; life of, **124–25**; rule of Byzantine Empire, 3

Kaaba, 539, 555

Kabul, 662, 663

Kadambari (Banabhatta), 783

Kafur Hazardinari, Malik (d. 1316), 684–85, 779, **800–801**

kainga, 1039–40

Kalabhras, 683

Kalidasa (fl. fourth/fifth centuries C.E.), 661, 673, 787, **801–2**, 841–43

Kalpa cycles, 762

Kama Sutra, 1044

Kamakura Period (1185-1333), 883, 941, 959, **963–64**, 989

Kamo no Chomei, 1020

Kanauj, 662, 677, 794, **802**

Kanchi, 661, 683–84

Kanem-Bornu, 360, 384–85, 411, **472–73**

Kapilavasta, 675

Karle, 721, 722

Karlsefni, Thorfinn, 343–44

karma, 691–92

karma yoga, 834

kava, 1045, **1092**

Kebra Negast, 455–56, 503–4

Kemmu Restoration, Japan, 884, 937

Kempe, Margery (1373-1438), 27, 139, 175–76

Kempis, Thomas à (1380-1471), 27, 139

Khadija, 527, 592

Khanbaliq, 171–72, 864

kharaj, 716, 779, 800, **803**
Kharijis, **614**
Khilij dynasty, 685–86
al-Khwarazmi (c. 800-847), 568
K'ichee kingdom, 193, 254, **311–12**, 337–38, 347–49
Kiev, 3
Kilwa, 360, 371, 392, 404, 451, **473–74**, 510
King Arthur, 166–67
Kings' Crusade, 4, 519
kingship, divine, Americas, **282–83**, 294
K'inich Janaab' Pakal (d. 683), 182, 192, 260, 268–69, **291–92**, 309
kinship and descent: African society, 406, 408–9; Muslim society, 563, 634–35
Kiribati, Republic of, 1089
kiswah, 555
Kitab al-Buldan (Book of Countries), 645–46
Kitab al-manazir (The Book of Optics), 571
kivas, 191, 198, 206, 227, **292–93**, 297
knights, 55, 95–96, 135–36, 144–46, 162–63
Koguryo, 880
Kojiki, 1011–13
Kongo, 360, **474–75**
Koran, 458, 469
Korea: agriculture and, 936; the arts, 907–8; Buddhism and, 880, 917, 940; ceramics, 899–900, 907–8, 923, 931; China and, 900, 930–31; Confucianism and, 881, 892, 914–15, 944, 955; corvée labor in, 1019; Daoism and, 888–89, 946; economy, 899–900; education and, 949; family names, 975–76; food, 958; geomancy and, 956; global ties, 930–31; historical overview, 879–81; Japan and, 931, 932; lineages, 970, 1000; Mongols and, 881; science and technology, 923; slavery and, 1020; society, 915, 917; Tang dynasty and, 880; warfare and, 998
Koryo (Korea) (935-1254), 907, 908, 923, 949, 955, **964–65**
Kosrae dynasty, 1035, 1055
Krak des Chevaliers (Citadel of the Knights), 48–49
Krisha Deva Raya (r. 1509-1529), 829
Krishna, 693, 837–38
Kshatriya caste, 738, 739, 785
Kshatriya theory, 770
Kublai (Khubilai) Khan: Europe and, 74, 130, 170–72; in Japan,

884, 964, 975; Yuan dynasty, 812, 816, 864, 877–78, 1004–5
k'uhul ajaw (holy lord), 218, 220, 232, 282, 290
Kukai, 932, 933, 963
Kukulkan, the Feathered Serpent (Quetzalcoatl), 201
kula, 1032, 1046, 1047–48, 1051, 1087, **1093–94**
Kumara Gupta, 661, 673

Lahore, 662
lakes, African, 372
lamps, fuel oil, 920
land cultivation, manors, 79–80
land revenue, Indian states, 703
landscape painting, Chinese, 864
Landsdowne Bank, 1069
languages, Oceania, **1094–95**
L'Anse aux Meadows, 207, 253, **293**, 342
Laozi, 886
lapita, 1031, 1050, 1063, **1095–96**
Late Woodland (400-1000), 190, 225
Latin literature, 41–42
law: Chinese households and, 913–14; Delhi Sultanate and, 789, 797–98; East Asia, **967–68**; feudal, 18, 53–54, 66, **126–27**, 154–55; Germanic, **127–28**, 150–51; Hindu inheritance, 747–48; Indian guilds and, 704–5; Islamic children and, 592; Legalism, 886, 891, 943, **968–69**; Magna Carta, 4, 19, 54, 127, 140; manorialism and, 53; Oceania, **1096–97**; Roman and canon, 18, 26, 56–57, **128–30**; rule of, 60; Sanskrit codes, 673; South Asia overview, **803–8**; Yajnavalkya law code compilation, 661. *see also* shari'a (Islamic law)
lay (lyric poem), 44
Le Champion des Dames (Champion of Women) (Le Franc), 148
Le Franc, Martin, 148
leeward and windward, **1097–98**
Legalism, 886, 891, 943, **968–69**
Legazpi, López de (1564-1572), 1064–65
legumes, European dietary importance, 35, 79, 111
Leo III, Pope (717-741), 3, 31–32, 119–20
libraries, 458, 815
light, Gothic architecture and, 50
lineages: Americas, **293–94**; East Asia, 937, 949, **969–70**
Lingayats, 697

literature: European, 42–44, 97–99, 166–67, 556; *hadith*, 535; Kalidasa, 661, 673, 787, **801–2**; *Mahabharata*, 661, 675, 696, 725–26, 762, 802, 806, **808–9**, 837–38; Muslim, 426, 458; Nubian, 480; *Ramayana*, 673, 693, 696, 818, **820–21**, 838–39; religion and, 377–78; Sanskrit, 673, 678, 782–83; *Sindhind*, 758–59; *Tale of Genji*, 883, 909, **995**; *Thousand and One Nights*, 605; translation of classical texts into Arabic, 566, 567–68
Little Climatic Optimum, 1034, 1036
Little Ice Age: European societal effects, 190; Fremont culture and, 286; Iroquois and, 287–88; Mississippian chiefdoms and, 205; Moundville and, 304; Oceania and, 1034, 1036, 1039, 1061
liturgical drama, 45
livestock, 388, 421, 454, 777
locks and river travel, 920
Lodi dynasty, 663
Lombard laws, 128
long-distance trade, *see* trade, Africa; trade, Americas; trade, European
longbows, 117, 118, 145
Los Buchillones, 257, **294–95**
Louis IX, King (r. 1226-1270), 20, 72, 101, 124
Lower Central America and the Andes: Andean periods, 193–94; the arts, 221–23; economy, 210–12; global ties, 256–57; historical overview, 193–94; metallurgy, 299–300; religion, 202–3, 286–87; science and technology, 247–49; society, 235–37
Luba, 360, **475–76**
Lydenburg heads, 399–400

Maabar, 849–50
Machu Picchu, 249
Madhava, 697
madrasa, 599–600
Magada, 671, 675, 793
Magellan, Ferdinand, 1028
al-maghrah, 543
Maghrib Christians, 383, 384, 430, 446, 448
Magna Carta, 4, 19, 54, 127, 140
magnetic compass, 68–69, 919, 929
Mahabharata, 661, 673, 696, 725–26, 762, 802, 806, **808–9**, 837–38
Mahavira, 798–99

Mahayana Buddhism, 893, 938–39, 940

Mahmud of Ghazni, 662

mahu, 1141

Maimonides (1135-1204), 143

maize, 205, 287

malangan, 1051

malaria, 374, 408, 451, 452

Mali: overview, 360, **476–77**; 14th Century Mali Empire (map), 364; as described by Ibn Battuta, 506–8; Islam and, 385; oral traditions, 480; political structure, 410–11; rulers, 513; Sundjata and, 487

Malinowski, Bronislaw, 1047, 1093

Mamallapuram, 725–26

Mamluk military, 564–65, 631–32

Mamluk Sultanate (1250-1517), 455, 518, 530, 532–33, **614**, 633

al-Ma'mun ibn Harun al-Rashid (d. 833), 530, **615**

mana, 1039, 1043, 1053, 1057, 1073, **1098–99**, 1112

mandalas, 909–10

mandate of heaven, 871, 890, 916, 941, **970–71**, 996, 1004

Manichaeans, 32

Manigramam guild, 707, 708, 712, 713

manorialism, 21, 33, 52–53

Mansa Musa, 361, 385, 428–29, 431, **477–79**, 504–5

al-Mansur (d. 775), 530, 544, 551–52, 567–68, **615**

Manua Dhrama Sastra, 804, 805

manufacturing: Africa, 422; Indian states, 703–5; Syrian goods, 543

Manzikert, Battle of, 518, 531, 632

Maoris: Captain James Cook and, 1137–40; chiefs, 1120; clothing, 1077; culture, 1039; dance, 1076; gods, 1085; island group, 1091; nose flutes, 1108; settlement, 1027, 1028, 1039; tattoos, 1053, 1122–23

maps: Catalan Atlas, 361, 429; errors in, 76–77; ocean charts, 1028

Mapungubwe, 360, 412, 495–96

al-Maqqari, 502–3

marae, 1038, 1045, 1053, **1099–1101**

Marajó Island, 212–13, 223

Marajóara, 204, 237, **295–96**

Mariana Islands, 1089

marketplaces, Europe, 36, 39, 90–92, 156–57

marketplaces, Islamic world: Egypt and Cairo, 545–48; Iraq and Baghdad, 543–45; money and, 548–49; *muhtasib* and, 549,

557–58, 559–61; Syria and Damascus, 542–43

Marquesas Islands, 1028, 1053, 1123, 1141–42

marriage: Africa, 407–8; caste-based taboos, 743; China, 999–1000; Europe, 54–55, **131–33**, 165–66; Gilbert Islands, 1148–49; Hindu women and, 747; Islamic world, 563–64, 592, 636–37; Marquesas Islands, 1141–42; Murik Lakes (Melanesia), 1056

Marshall Islands, 1060, 1089, 1123

Martel, Charles (the Hammer), 3, 17, 517

Martin V, Cardinal (r. 1417-1431), 22, 31, 57, 97

masalai, 1041, 1052

mashrabiyya, 554, 608

masks, Melanesian, 1051–52

mathematics: in Africa, 423–24; Brahmagupta, 784–85; China, 919; in Europe, 62–63; Hindu and Arabic numerals, 568; India, 754–59

matrilineal societies: Africa, 407; Americas, 293–94; Micronesia, 1054

Mauryan Empire (320-200 B.C.E.), 671–72

Mauss, Marcel, 1046–48

Mawa, 661

The Maya (Classic and Postclassic periods): the arts, 218–20, 277; collapse, 192–93, 201, 234–35, **296**, 309; economy, 182, 208–9; global ties, 254–55; maps, 187; overkings, 306–7; religion, 201, **311–12**, 347–49; science and technology, 243–45; society, 231–35, 290–91, 350–51

Mayapán, 182, 183, 234, 245

Mayor of the Palace, 17

Mecca, 536, 550, 606

medicine, Chinese, 921–22

medicine, Europe, 60–61, 88, 117, **133–35**

medicine, Indian, 764–66, 777

medicine, Islamic world: *al-maghrah*, 543; al-Rhazi (865-925), 568–69; Greek foundations, 571; Ibn Sina (980-1037), 569–70; Jewish and Christian physicians, 561–62

medieval period in Africa, European context, 367–69

Medieval Warm Period, 1034

Medina, 527–28, 535, 606

Mehmed II, 23

Melanesia: overview, **1087–88**, **1101–4**; the arts, 1050–52; betel, 1070; bigman, **1070–71**, 1074; chiefdoms, 1033; dance, 1075; gods and goddesses, 1084; historical overview, 1032–33; initiation, **1085–86**; island groups, 1087–88, 1151; justice, 1097; kava, 1092; languages, 1094; *lapita*, 1095–96; religion and myths, 1041–43; society, 1055–56; status of women, 1132; trade, 1062–64

Melinde, 511

men, role and status in Islamic society, 562–64

Mencius (Meng Ke), 890, 943

merchants: Chinese, 1014–15; Indian, 705, 706–7, 770–71; Jewish, 156; Saint Godric, 164–65

Merovingian dynasty, 17, 151

Mesa Verde, 191, 228, 292–93, **297**

Mesoamérica: the arts, 217–21; atlatl and, 261; cacao and, 266–67; calendar, 219, 232, 242, 243–44, 278, **297–99**; Classic period chronology, 181, 182; economy, 207–10; Eight Deer Jaguar Claw (1063-1115), 283–85; global ties, 253–56; historical overview, 192–93, 355; map, 185; metallurgy and, 193, 246, 255–56; religion, 200–202; science and technology, 242–47; society, 230–35; stelae, 320

metallurgy, Africa: development of, 416; mining, 416–17; sculpture, cast metal, 397–401, 445, 468; shaping, 419–20; smelting, 389–90, 417–19

metallurgy, India, 763

metallurgy, the Americas: Andean, 221; historical overview, **299–300**; Hohokam, 252; Mesoamérican, 193, 246, 255–56; Moche, 211; tumbaga alloys, **335–36**

metalwork, 419, 553

Methodious, 3, 18

Micronesia: overview, **1088–89**, **1104–5**; the arts, 1053; betel, 1070; breadfruit and social change, 1035–36; family groups, 1105; food, 1067, 1144–45; global ties, 1064–65, 1069; gods and goddesses, 1084; historical overview, 1033; island groups, 1088–89, 1151; kava, 1092; languages, 1104; quarrying technology, 1058; religion and myths, 1043; sailing and trade, 1104–5; society, 1054–55, 1105

Middle Ages, described, 15–16

Middle East: European interactions with, 70–73; eve of Muslim Era (map), 520; late eleventh century (map), 522

Middle Woodland (200 B.C.E.-400 C.E.), 190

military households, South India economy and, 713–14

Military Orders: banking and, 37; castle architecture and, 48–49; European, 135–36; St. Bernard and, 86; The Crusades and, 28–29, 72, 101, 169–70

Mina, 539–41

Minamoto family, 883, 901, 963–64, 989

Ming Dynasty (1368-1644), 864, 878–79, 881, 952, 954–55, 968, 971–73, 1022

mining, Africa, 416–17, 507–8

missionaries, Greek Orthodox Church, 18

Mississippian Period: chiefdoms, 205; global ties, 251–52; science and technology, 240; society, 182, 225–26; Southern Cult and, 197, 317–18; Spiro settlement, 318–19

misunderstandings, global, European world views, 76–77

Mitla, 300–301

Mixtecs, 283–85

moai (Easter Island), 1039, 1053, 1105-7

Moche: the arts, 221–22; economy, 210–11; global ties, 256; historical overview, 194, 301–2; religion, 202–3; science and technology, 248; society, 235–36

Model Parliament, 19–20, 58, 140

modesty, see clothing and modesty

moka, New Guinea economy, 1048–49

Moluccas (Spice Islands), 1063–64

Mombasa, 510–11

monasteries, Buddhist, 678

monastery churches, 82

monastery education, 457

monasticism: Buddhist, 721; Christian, 27–29; Coptic Church and, 448, 449–50, 460; in Europe, 27–29

money and coinage: Africa, 419, 423–24, 432–33, 450–51, 474, 475; East Asia, 896, 897, 922, 973–74; Europe, 36–37, 91, 136–38, 392; North Africa and the

Middle East, 548–49, 615–16; Oceania economy and, 1046–50; South Asia, 672, 674, 686, 702, 786, 809–11, 813; Yap stone money, 1034, 1045, 1118–19

Mongols: Balban and, 781–82; conquer of Persia, 518, 864; conquests 1206-1259 (map), 867; defeat by Allauddin, 778, 788–89; East Asia, 974–75; Europe and, 4, 38, 74, 130, 170–72; in Japan, 902; Korea and, 881; Mamluk Sultanate and, 614; South Asia, 662, 811–13; Yuan dynasty, 816, 864, 869, 877–78, 898, 928–29

monophonic Gregorian chant, 45

monophysites, 31, 114, 382–83, 448, 450

monsoon: African weather and, 373; trade and, 393, 709, 768

Monte Albán, 231, 302–3

Montezuma, 288

Monumenta Germaniae, 154–55

Moorea Island, 1027

mortuary customs, see burial practices

mosaics, Byzantine, 49

mosque architecture, 404, 423, 431, 550–51, 647–48, 734–35

motets, 45

mound building, 190, 196–97, 202, 204, 267–68, 295

Moundville, 190, 205, 225, 252, 267, 303–4

mountains and mountain ranges, African, 372–73

movable type, 922, 923

movement of people, European overview, 69–70

Mu'a ceremonial center, 1027

Mu'awiya ibn Abi Sufyan (d. 680), 529, 542, 616

Mughal Empire, 663, 780

Muhammad bin Tughluq (d. 1351), 663, 685–86, 716, 788, 789, 813–14

Muhammad Ghauri, see Ghaurids

Muhammed ibn Qasim, 662

Muhammed Kasim Firishta (c. 1560-c. 1620), 847

Muhammed of Ghor, 662

Muhammed, Prophet (c. 570-632): 'Aisha bint Abi Bakr (wife), 585–86; 'Ali ibn Abi Talib (cousin), 586–87; artistic depiction of, 549; hijra, 435; life of, 517, 526–28; as messenger of God, 534–35; missions and campaigns to 632(map), 519; raids and warfare, 629

muhtasib, 549, 557–58, 559–61

Mu'izz al-Din, see Ghaurids

multilingualism, African, 371

al-Muqaddasi (c. 945-c. 1000): overview, 616–17; on Aksâ Mosque, 647–48; on Dome of the Rock construction, 648–50; on Egypt and Cairo, 546–48; on Iraq and Baghdad, 544–45; on the Nile, 548; on Syria and Damascus, 542–43

Muqaddima (Ibn Khaldun), 566–67

Murasaki, Lady, 883, 909, 962–63, 995, 1016

Murik Lakes, 1056

music: European, 44–46; Incan, 352–53; musical instruments, Oceania, 1107-9; musical staff, 46

music of the spheres, 44

Muslim world, European interactions with, 70–73

Muslims: Almoravid and Almohad Movements, 412, 426, 430–31, 441–42; banking and, 37, 123; conquering of Iberian Peninsula, 3, 517; conquering of northern Africa, 359, 383–84, 450, 517; Crusades and, 71–72, 99–101; dynasties, 454–55; holidays, 589–90; Judaism and, 471–72, 471–72, 508–9, 558–62; Muslim women in India, 750–52; relations with non-Muslims, 558–62; in Sicily and Italy, 72–73

Mwenemutapa c. 1550 (map), 366

mysticism: overview, 138–40; Bernard of Clairvaux and, 26, 85–86; popular religion and, 26–27; scholasticism and, 63; Sufism, 442, 469, 566, 604, 613, 624-27; visions and, 175–76

Nadaraja, 693

Nagarjuna (150-250 C.E.), 753–54

Nagas, 683, 725

Nalanda University, 673, 678, 753–54, 814-15

names, East Asia, 975–76

Nan Madol, 1027, 1035, 1055, 1109-10

Nara Period (710-794), 863, 882, 976-977, 994

Narayana, 693

Naser-e Khosraw (fl. eleventh century), 547, 617, 650

Nasiriah College, 848–49

nationalism, European emergence, 23, 119

natural disasters, Americas, 211, 234, 265–66, 282

naturalism, African arts, 398
The Nature of Things (Bede), 84
navigation: leeward and
    windward, **1097–98**; technology,
    68–69; voyaging/ancient
    navigation, 1058–62, **1126–28**
Naymlap, 265, **304–5**
Nazca: the arts, 222; economy, 211;
    global ties, 256; Nazca lines, 194,
    203, 222, 248, **305**; religion, 203;
    science and technology, 248;
    society, 236
Nderic (Santa Cruz), 1028
Neo-Confucianism, 876, 881, 891–
    92, 944, 949, 954, **977–78**, 1006–7
Nestorians, 31, 114–15, 661, 698,
    929
New Caledonia, 1032, 1087–88
New Guinea: canoes, 1146;
    clothing, 1077; fauna, 1102–3,
    1110–11; flora, 1102, **1111–12**;
    food, 1067, 1133–34;
    gerontocracy, 1056; initiation,
    1086; island group, 1087; Kiwai
    myths, 1041; *kula*, 1032, 1046,
    1047–48, 1051, 1087, **1093–94**;
    languages, 1094–95; *moka* and,
    1048–49; Portuguese exploration,
    1028; taro, 1032–33; trade, 1062–
    64; warfare, 1128, 1129, 1130
New Zealand, 1039–40, 1077, 1091
Nezahualcoyotl (1402-1472), **305–6**
NguzuNguzu, 1050–51, **1112–13**
Niebelungenlied, 43
Niger Delta, 390, 399, 437, 462, 483
night soil, 34, 80, 936, 958
Nika Riot of 532, 125
Nile River, 372, 385, 387, 437–38,
    462, 483–84
nirvana, 892–93
Nizam al-Mulk (d. 1092), 531,
    537–38, **617**, 651–53
nobility, Americas, 233
nobility, Europe: castles as homes,
    90; daily life, 55; marriage,
    54–55; peasant revolts and,
    173–74; titles, 54
noh theater, 910, 936, **978–79**, 1006
nominalism, 50–51, 63, 143
Norman dynasty (England), 19
North Africa and the Middle East:
    the arts, **549–56**; economy, **541–49**;
    global ties, **573–79**; historical
    overview, **525–33**; religion,
    533–41; science and technology,
    566–73; society, **556–66**
North Africa, European
    interactions with, 70–73
North America: L'Anse aux
    Meadows settlement, 293;

Viking exploration of, 75–76,
    341–44; Viking trade with
    natives, 159–60
North India, historical overview,
    681–82
Northern Song Dynasty (960-1126),
    876, 950, **979–80**, 998, 1014–15,
    1022
Northern Wei (386-534), 872, 888,
    980–81, 985
nose flutes, 1108
Notre-Dame, 47
Nubia: overview, **479–80**; the arts
    and, 404; Christianity and, 359,
    383, 384, 430, 448–49; Egypt and,
    499–500; metallurgy and, 416
numbers: Arabic numerals, 568,
    755, 793; decimal, 755; negative,
    784–85

oases, 391, 584
oba (king), 444–45
Oceania: agriculture, 1067–68; the
    Arts, **1050–54**; breadfruit,
    1071–72; economy, **1046–50**;
    entertainment, **1079–81**; food,
    1081–83; genealogy, 1034–35;
    global ties, **1062–66**; historical
    overview, **1031–40**; island
    environment diversity, 1038;
    island groups, 1151–52; religion,
    1040–46; science and technology,
    1058–62; societies (map), 1029;
    society, **1054–58**
Ockham's razor, 143–44
Olmec, 181, 200
oni (king), 397–98
opera, Chinese, 906
oral traditions: overview, **480–81**;
    African history, 375, 376–77, 409;
    education and, 458; Germanic
    law, 17; Mali, 410; New Guinea,
    1064; Ponapean, 1109; Rapa Nui,
    1039
Oranmiyan, 444
ordeal, trial by, 127–28, 150–51
orders, societal organization
    and, 51
Ordo virtutum (Play of Virtues), 116
ores, mining, 416–17
original sin, 149
Ostrogoths, 16
Otto I, 20
Ottoman Turks, 23, 518
overking, **306–7**
Oxford University, 63–64
Ozette, 199, 216

Pachacamac, **307–8**
Pachomius, 27–28

Pacific Coast: the arts, 216;
    economy, 207; global ties, 253;
    historical overview, 191;
    religion, 199; science and
    technology, 242; society, 229
Pacific islands, Autronesian
    migrations, 1027
Pact of Umar (c. 637), 643–44
paddle wheel boat, 920
Paekche, 880, 1001
pagodas, 905
painting, Chinese, 864, 903–4
Pala dynasty, 662, 681–82
palaces, Islamic world, 551–52
Palenque, 181, 192, 260, 268, **308–9**
Pallava dynasty, 661, 682–84, 707
palm products, 776, 1067, 1070,
    1111–12
Panca-Siddhantitaka
    (Varahamihara), 760
Panipat, Battle of, 663, 780
panpipe, 1108
paper money, 137, 863, 897
paper production: China, 919;
    Indian, 715; Islamic world, 543,
    545, 548, 556
Papua New Guinea, *see* New
    Guinea
parish churches, architecture, 46
Parliament, 19–20, 53–54, 58, **140–41**
pastoralism, Africa, 454
patolli, **309–10**
patrilineal societies: Africa, 407,
    409; Americas, 293–94; Islamic
    world, 563, 634–35; Oceania,
    1055–57
patterns, visual arts and, 49
Pavement Period, 397–98, 494
peasants: diet, **109–11**; manorialism
    and, 52–53; revolts, 41, **141–42**,
    173–74; women, 147–48
Pelagians, 32
Pele, 1083, 1085
pepper trees, South India, 852–53
Period of Disunity (220-589), 872,
    980, **981–83**, 985
The Periplus of the Erythraen Sea, 393
Persia, China and, 927
Persian Gulf, Indian Ocean trade,
    393
personal power, Africa, 409
Peshawar, Battle of, 832
Petrarch (1304-1374), 4, 22, 56, 97
Philip IV (r. 1285-1314), 30, 56,
    96–97, 136, 140–41
Philip VI of Valois (r. 1328-1350),
    23, 117–18
Philippines, Oceania trade,
    1064–65
Phoenicians, Africa and, 425–26

phosphorescence, navigation and, 1060

physical geography, Africa overview, 371–74

physics, 61–62, 760–62

pigs, Oceania, 1041, 1046, 1048–49, 1061, 1070, 1074, **1113**

pilgrimage: African global ties and, 430–31; Andean, 287; European, 163–64; Islamic world, 576–79. *see also* hajj

pirates, Japanese, 902, 933

Pitcairn Island, 1027

Pizan, Christine de (1365–c. 1430), 99, 148

Pizarro, Francisco, 349–50

plague, *see* bubonic plague

plainsong, 45

Plantagenet dynasty, 19

Pleiades, **310**

Plumes from Paradise (Swadling), 1062

Poem of the Cid, 43, 96

poetry: Chinese, 904, 1015–16; Dante, 102–3; Islamic, 555–56, 601; Japanese, 863, 1016; Kalidasa, 661, 673, 787, **801–2**; *Mahabharata*, 661, 673, 696, 725–26, 762, 802, 806, **808–9**; mathematical texts, 784; oral, Germanic tribes, 43; troubadour, 97–98

Pohnpei dynasty, 1035, 1055, 1144–45

political power: African women, 492–93; Investiture Controversy, 28, 30, 56, **121–23**

political structures and authority, Africa, 409–15

Polo, Marco (c. 1254-1324): overview, **130–31**; on the Brahmins of Lar, 850–51; coal usage in China, 77, 897; on customs of Maabar, 849–50; description of Mongol capital, 170–72; on Hangzhou, 898; in India, **816–17**; route (map), 868; travels, 4, 38, 75; on yogis, 851–52; on Yuan dynasty, 929

polygyny, 407–8

Polynesia: overview, 1027, **1089–91, 1114–15**; the arts, 1053; atolls, 1069; canoes, 1037, 1058, 1060, 1065, 1126–27; contact with Lower Central America and the Andes, 257; dance, 1075–76; global ties, 1065–66; gods and goddesses, 1084–85; historical overview, 1031–32; island groups, 1089–91, 1151–52; kava,

1092; *lapita*, 1096; *mana*, **1098–99**; *marae*, 1099–1100; nose flutes, 1108; society, 1056–57

polyphony, 45

polytheism, Africa, 378–79, 436

Ponape, 1144–45

Poor Clares, 29, 112

popol nah, **310–11**

Popol Vuh, **311–12**, 347–49

popular religion, Europe, 26–27

population: African growth, 439; China, 897–98, 899, 918; European decline, 41; European growth, 35

porcelain, Chinese, 863, 897, 906–7

ports, Indian, 717–18

Portuguese explorers, 368, 475, 1027

Portuguese forts and colonies, Africa (map), 366

pottery, *see* ceramics

powers, special and unseen, African traditional religions, 380–81, 436–37

prayer, ritual (*salat*), 535–37

pre-Muslim India c. 1200 (map), 666

Presentation Theme ceramics, 202–3, 222, 280, 301–2, 316

Prester John myth, 73

priests: African priests and priestesses, 379; Catholic Church structure, 24–25; Oceania, 1044

printing press, 898–99, 929

Prithviraj Chauhan, 662

Prithviraja III (d. 1192), 778, 792, **817**

processing of food, Europe, 110

Procopius (c. 500-565), 152–53

proportionality, sacred music and, 44

psaltery, 46

Pseudo-Dionysian texts, 138

Ptolemy's map, 76

Pueblo, *see* Ancestral Pueblo

Pueblo periods, 191

puja, 697–98

Pulakasin II, King (609-642), 684

Pulemelei mound, 1031, **1115–16**

pulque, **312**

Puranas, 671, 696, 793, **817–19**

Pure Land Buddhism, 873, 876, 880, 893, 916–17, 939, 948; overview, **984–85**; Kamakura Period, 964; Late Tang Dynasty, 966; Silla Korea and, 991

Pyramid of the Moon, 325, 326

Pyramid of the Sun, 218, 326

al-Qanun al-Masudi (al-Biruni), 569

Qin dynasty, 886, 890–91, 943, 968–69

Quanzhou, 897

quarrying technology, Micronesia, 1058

Queen of Sheba, 455–56, 460, 503–4

Quetzalcoatl, 200–201, 220, 235, 272, **312-14**

quipu, 249, **314**

Qur'an: ablutions and, 582; on 'Aisha bint Abi Bakr, 585; calligraphy and, 552–53; on clothing and modesty, 594–95; on death and afterlife, 596–97; education and, 458, 597–98; excerpts from, 641–43; on food and alcohol, 604; on Islamic conquests and, 528; on Jews and Christians, 559; on *jihad*, 612; on role and status of men and women, 562–64, 633–39, 750; *salat* and, 535, 536; *sawm* and Ramadan, 538; *shari'a* and, 619–21; *zakat* and, 537

Qutb-ud-din Aybak, 662

Radegund (nun), 16

Ra'iatea, 1100–1101

rainforest, 456, 1102, 1111

Raja Raja Chola I (r. 985-1014), 684

raja yoga, 834–35

Rajputs, 749–50, 817, **819**, 822, 831

Ramadan, 538–39, 590

Ramanuja, 696

Ramayana, 673, 693, 696, 818, **820–21**, 838–39

Rapa Nui, 1038–39, 1053, 1091

Rarotonga, 1027

Rashidun caliphs, 528, 583, 587, **618**, 622, 657

ratha religious festival, 676

Raziya Sultana (d. 1240), 662, 782, 788, **821**, 848

rebec, 46

recipes, Islamic, 654–55

reciprocal trade, Polynesian economy, 1046–50

Reconquest, Spain, 20

Record of the Buddhistic Kingdoms (Faxian), 839–41

Red Sea trade, 393, 412, 425, 440, 459, 461, 709

redistributive economy, Oceania, 1046

Reformation, 115–16, 139, 174

The Refutation of Christianity (al-Jahiz), 560

regional trade, Africa, 390–92

regions, Africa, 370, 432, 437–38, **481–82**

religion: Africa, **377–86**, 429–31, 436–37, 459, 473; Ajita school,

692; Ajivakas, 691–92; Americas, **196–204**, 262–63; Brahminical Hinduism, 675–77; Buddhism, 688–90; canon law, 55–56; East Asia, **885–94**; East Asian philosophies and religion, 885; Europe, **24–33**; Hinduism, 692–98; "Islamic science" and, 566–70; Jainism, 690–91; mysticism, 138–40; North Africa and the Middle East, **533–41**; Oceania, **1040–46**; South Asia, **688–702**; syncretism, 436–37, 441–42, 460, 493; women and, 147–48. *see also* Buddhism; Christianity; Hinduism; Islam; Jews and Judaism

religious architecture, Gothic cathedrals, 26

religious criticism, Christianity and, 31–33

Religious Daoism, 872, 946, 955, 982, **985–86**, 1010–11

religious life, Europe, 24–27

religious observance: African traditional religions and, 381–82; Almoravid Movement and, 442; Five Pillars of Islam, 385, 469, 533–34

religious specialists, African traditional religions, 379–80

Renaissance, 15–16

al-Rhazi (865-925), 568–69

Ribiero, Diego, 1028

rice-growing, 879, 936

Ridda Wars (Wars of Apostasy), 529, 551, 583

Rihla (Ibn Battuta), 795–96

rituals: Hindu, 697–98; marriage, European, 132; pilgrimage, Islamic, 576–79, 587; prayer, 535–37. *see also* hajj

Rivas, 202, 221, **314–15**

rivers: African, 372, **482–84**; African traditional religions and, 379, 436; disease and, 374, 451–52

rock art, Africa, 403

Roman Empire: Africa and, 367–68, 425; Byzantine Empire and, 59–60; education and, 104–5; fall of, 3, 15–16; Indian trade balance, 710; Roman numerals, 756–57

Roman law, 18, 26, 56–57, 128–29

Roman numerals, 62

Romance of the Rose, 43, 98–99

The Romance of the Western Chamber, 906

Romanesque churches, 47, 82, 163

romantic literature, 98–99

Roymata (Roy Mata) (fl. c. 1265), 1032, **1116**

Rudolph of Habsburg, 21

rugs, Islamic world, 554–55

Rus, conversion to Christianity, 3

Russia, 4

Sabuktgin, 662

sacraments, 26, 132

sacred music, 44–45

Saharan agriculture, 437–38

Saharan desert, 457

sahel, 457

Saicho, 962–63

sail technology, 68, 768–69

Saladin (1137-1193), 4, 71, 95, 100–101, 431, 455, 518, **618–19**; rule of Egypt and Syria, 532

Salado polychrome, 216, 253

Salamäsina (fl. late fifteenth century), **1117**

salat (ritual prayer), 535–37, 582

salt: manufacture, 422; scarcity, 464; trans-Saharan trade, 391, 443

Samantha government system, 680

Samarra, 517, 551, 577, 631

Samoa, 1073–74, 1090, 1117, 1123

Samudra Gupta (c. 330- c. 375), 661, 672, 674, 792, 843

samurai, 910

samurai swords, 925, **986–87**

Sangitaratnakara (Sharngdeva), 662

Sankoré Mosque, 360, 396, 423, 490

Sanskrit literature and language, 673, 771–73, 782–83

Santa Cruz Islands, 1088

Santarem, 204, 250, 327

Santiago de Compostella, 163

Sapa Inca (divine king), 282–83

sati, 749–50, **821–22**

Saudeleur dynasty, 1027, 1035, 1055

savannahs, 462

sawm (fasting), 537–39

Saxon dynasty, 20

sayrafi, 548–49, 616

scarification, 403–4

scholasticism: overview, **142–44**; critique of, 63–64, 167–68; spread of, 72; Thomas Aquinas and, 63; visual expression of, 50

schools and scholarship, *see* education

science, *see* science and technology

science and technology: Africa, **415–24**, 432–33; Americas, **238–51**; East Asia, **918–25**; Europe, **60–69**; "Islamic science," 566–70; Muslim military, 572; North Africa and the Middle East, **566–73**; Oceania, **1058–62**;

South Asia, **752–66**. *see also* individual nations, peoples, and topics

scientific method, 63–64

Scivias (Hildegard of Bingen), 116

sculptures: cast metal, 359, 397–401, 445, 468, 495; Chinese Buddhas, 904–5; copper Buddha icon, 763; Hindu iconography, 683

sea migrations and explorations, Oceania, 1031–33, 1126–28

sea, origin myths, 1040

Second Battle of Tarain, 662

Secret History (Procopius), 152–53

secular architecture, 48–49

secular life, 19, 57

secular music, 45–46

Seljuk Turks, 71, 99, 518, 530, 651, 662

Sena dynasty, 662

Sena dynasty, Bengal, 662

Sepik River, 1051–52, 1094–95, 1125–26

seppuku, 884, 964, 986, 999

serfs, 39–40, 52–53, 158–59

settlement of Oceania, historical overview, 1031–33

Seven Divine Generations, 1012

Seventeen Point Constitution, 944, 983, **987**, 1001–2

sexuality, India, 745–46, 748–49, 751

Shabik'eshche, 271, **315–16**

shahada (statement of faith), 534–35, 562, 634

Shahnameh (Book of Kings), 555–56

Shaivism, 696–97

Shajar al-Durr, Sultana, 532

al-Sham (Syria), 542

shari'a (Islamic law), 534, 562, **619–21**, 790–91, 807–8

Shashanka, 783

al-Shayzari (d. c. 1193), 559, 561, 598, 599, 653–54

shell valuables: *kula* ring, 1032, 1046, 1047–48, 1051, **1093–94**; Oceania overview, 1074, 1103, **1117–18**

Shi'ism, 576–77, 586, 597, 606, 614, **621–24**, 627, 657

Shintoism, 894, 941, **987–88**, 994, 1011

ships: Chinese junks, 895–96; Chinese ocean-going vessels, 923; construction, 768–69; Indian trade and, 709–10, 718; Korean, 900; New Guinea canoes, 1146; Polynesian canoes, 1037, 1058, 1060, 1065, 1126–27; Tahitian war canoes, 1140, 1142

shogun, **988–89**
shogunate: overview, 883–84; Ashikaga, **937–38**, 959, 978, 989; establishment of, 864
Shotoku, Prince (d. 621), 882, **983–84**, 987, 1001–2
Sicily, 72–73
Siddhanta-Siromani (Bhaskara), 759
Siddhartha Gautama, Prince (Buddha), 893–94
Siffin, Battle of, 614
Sijilmasa, 359, 371, 394, 433, 442, 450, **484–85**, 502–3
Sikhism, 663
silk, 710, 714, 895, 906, 919, 935–36
Silk Road, 674, 677, 708, 895, 928, 947, **989–90**
Silla Korea (674–892), 880, 907, 908, 931, 940, 948, 956, **990–91**
Sinbad, Indian Ocean trade and, 705–6
Sind, 662
Sindhind astronomy text, 758–59
Sipán, 203, **316**
Siva, 693–94, 724–25
Skanda Gupta, 661, 677
skraelings, 159–60, 253, 343
slavery: concubines and slave girls in Delhi, 854–55; Delhi Sultanate economy and, 715; in Korea, 1020; Muslim society and, 564–65, 631, 637, 751–52; slave trade, 368, 473, 475
sleeping sickness, 374, 388, 420, 438, 451, 453–54
slit gongs, 1107–8
smelting, African life, 389–90, 417–20, 470
Snaketown, 206, **316–17**
Sobokht, Severus, 756
society: Africa, 371, **405–15**, 468; Americas, **224–38**; China's economy and, 899; East Asia, **911–18**; European, **51–60**, **146–48**, 158–59; North Africa and the Middle East, **556–66**; Oceania, **1054–58**; South Asia, **736–52**
Socotra, 709
Sofala, 509–10
Soga family, 1001
Solomnid dynasty, 360, 412, 430, 455–56, 460, 503–4, 513–14
Solomon Islands, 1088, 1108, 1112, 1118
Song Dynasty, *see* Northern Song Dynasty; Southern Song Dynasty
Song of Hildebrand, 43
Song of Roland, 43, 96
Songhai, 359, 365, 411, 443, **485–86**, 513

Soninke, 463
Sonni Ali (r. 1464-1492), 443, 485, **486–87**
South America (map), 185
South India, historical overview, 682–84
Southeast Asia: global ties with India, 766–67; land and people, 767–70; transmission of Indian culture to, 770–73
Southern Cross, 1059
Southern Cult (Southeastern Ceremonial Complex), 197, 214, 225, 267, **317–18**
Southern Song Dynasty (1127-1279): overview, **991–92**; emperors, 1022; eunuchs and, 952; Huai River, 980; Neo-Confucianism and, 954; taxation and, 936, 944; trade and, 896–97; Zhu Xi (1130-1200), 1006–7
Southwest Cult, 199, 253
soybeans, 936
Spain: Christian reconquest, 20, 72; peasant revolts, 141; Spanish in the Americas chronology, 183; Visigoths, 16–17
spear thrower (atlatl), 219, **261–62**
special and unseen powers, African traditional religions, 380–81, 436–37
spices: Indian trade and, 705–6; Spice Islands (Moluccas), 1063–64; trade and, 73–74
spinning wheel, 920
spirit mediums, African traditional religions, 379–80
spirits: African traditional religions, 379, 436; Oceania, 1041–43, 1044, 1051, 1052, 1084, 1088, 1112–13, 1133
Spiro, **318–19**
Spread of the Bubonic Plague (map), 12
St. Albans, Battle of, 5
St. Denis cathedral, 82–83
Staff God, 194, 222–23, **319**, 320
star compass and courses, 1059
state societies, Africa: influence of trade on, 394; map, 363; political structures, 409–15; Takrur, 384–85, 411, **489–90**
steel manufacturing, 920
stelae: Aksum, 359, 396, 404, 423, 440; Europe, 218, 277, **319–20**
stone money (Yap), 1034, 1045, **1118–19**
stone structures, 1027, 1036, 1045, 1053, 1115
storytelling, 1081

string figures, 1079–80
stupas, 675, 679, **823–25**
stylized depictions, African arts, 396
Sudra caste, 738, 739–40, 785
The Sufi Orders in Islam (Trimingham), 624
Sufism (Islamic mysticism), 442, 469, 566, 604, 613, **624–27**, 700–701
sugar, 776
Suger, Abbot, 47, 50, 82–83, 85
Suhrawardiyya Sufis, 701
Sui Dynasty (589-617): overview, 863, **992–94**; Confucianism and, 943–44; emperors, 873, 953, 1021; Grand Canal, 960; Prince Shotoku and, 983; Seventeen Point Constitution, 987; warfare and, 998
Sultanganj Buddha (copper icon), 763
Sulva-Sutras, 754
Summa Theologiae (Summary of Theology) (Aquinas), 63, 143
sumo wrestling, 894, 936, 988, **994**, 1070
Sun Temple at Konarak, 730–31
Sundjata (c. 1205-c. 1255), 360, 409, 476–77, **487**
Sunnis, 576, 587, 614, 618, 622, **627**
sun's rays, navigation and, 1061
surfing, 1080
Swadling, Pamela, 1062–64
Swahili: overview, 359, 360, **488–89**; architecture, 402–3, 411, 422–23, 474, 488; cities as described by Duarte Barbosa, 509–11; city-states (map), 366; coast as described by Ibn Battuta, 505–6; coins, 451, 474; global ties, 426; Indian Ocean trade merchants, 392–93; Islam and, 385; Kilwa (city), 360, 371, 392, 404, 451, **473–74**, 489; language origins, 371, 489
sweat bath or lodge, 233, **320–21**
sweet potato, 1039, 1065
swords, Japanese, 925, **986–87**
Syria, 542–43, 578
Syrian Christianity, 697, 698–99

T-O maps, 76–77
Tacuba, 332–33
Tahiti: chiefdoms, 1037–38; *mahu*, 1141; war canoes, 1140, 1142
Taiho Code, 955, 976
Taika reforms, 863, 901, 1002
Taino, 195, 294–95
Taizong, Emperor, 874, 947, 953, 967, 996

Taizu, Emperor (d. 976), 876, 878–79, **949–50**, 954–55, 968, 971–72, 979

Takrur, 360, 384–85, 411, **489–90**

Talas River, Battle of, 863

Tale of Genji, 883, 909, 962, **995**, 1016–18

talud-tablero, 217–18, **321–22**

Tamil country, 683–84, 695–96, **823**

Tanakh, 526, 528

Tang dynasty: education and, 948–49; emperors, 1021; eunuchs and, 952; examination system and, 953–54; golden age, 863; Korea and, 880, 990–91; poetry on old age, 1015–16

Tang Dynasty, early (618-751): overview, **946–48**; c. 645-700 (map), 866; Taizong, Emperor, 874

Tang Dynasty, late (751-907), **965–66**, 997

Tang governance, 874, 879, 915–16, 972, **996–97**

Tanjore, 662, 684

tanka, 811

Tantrism, 662, 679, 689, 698, 731, 746, 835

tapa, 1050, 1053, 1075, **1119–20**

tapu, 1039, 1043, 1057, 1096, 1098, **1120–21**

Tarain, Second Battle of, 662

Tarascan Empire, 336

taro, 1027, 1032–33, 1070, **1121–22**

Tataga Matau, 1036

tattoos, 403–4, 1053, **1122–24**

Tawantinsuyu, 322–23. *See also* The Inca Empire

taxation: Chinese agriculture and, 936; *corvée* system and, 874; Indian states, 703, 715–16, 717; in Japan, 901; land tax (*kharaj*), 716, 779, 800, **803**; Magna Carta and, 127; papacy and, 30, 56; under Edward I, 58

Tayasal, **323**

tea, 898

technology, *see* science and technology

Telegus, 713–14

Templars, 135–36, 137–38, 162–63

temple-pyramids, Moche and Nazca, 222

temples, South Asia: bhakti Hinduism and, 698; Buddhist *stupas*, 675, 679, **823–25**; Hindu temples overview, 728–29, **825–27**; Jain, 731–32; Khajuraho complex, 729–30; Orissa, 730–31; style and construction, 732–33

Ten Abominations, 967

Tenochtitlán, 182, 202, 207, 235, 242, 275, 288, **324**, 345–47

Teotihuacán, 192, 200, 207, **325–26**; the arts, 217–18; chronology, 181, 182; economy, 207, 208; global ties, 254; historical overview, 192; science and technology, 242–43; society, 230–31; Tikal and, 328–29

Teresa of Avila, 108, 139

terra-cotta sculptures, 398–400

terra preta, 250, 259, **326–27**

Texcoco, 333

textiles, *see* clothmaking

Theodora, 3, 124–25, 152–53

Three Kingdoms 264 (map), 865

Three Kingdoms Era, 863

Three Teachings, 888

Thule: the arts, 216–17; economy, 207; global ties, 253; historical overview, 192, **327–28**; religion, 199; science and technology, 242; society, 229–30

Tibetan Buddhism, 682, 815

Tigris River, 544–45

Tikal, 181, 182, 192, 230, 268–69, 290–91, **328–29**

Timbuktu: overview, 360, **490–91**; Islamic scholarship and, 385, 412–13, 431, 443, 458, 478; Sankoré Mosque, 360, 423, 458, 490; social complexity and, 371; Songhai-era description, 511–12; Sonni Ali and, 486; trans-Saharan trade, 391

time, cyclical, **281–82**

Timur/Tamerlane (1336-1405), 663, 687, 700, **827–28**, 856–57

Tiwanaku: the arts, 222–23; economy, 211–12; global ties, 256; historical overview, 194, **329–30**; religion, 203; science and technology, 248; society, 236–37

Tlaloc, 200, 219, 289, **330–31**

tlatoani, 182, 183, 288, **331**

Toghril Beg, 530–31

Tokelau, 1091

toleration, religious, 17, 170–71

Toltec: arts, 220; Chichén Itzá and, 272–73; economy, 209–10; global ties, 255; historical overview, 190, 193, **331–32**; religion, 197, 201–2; science and technology, 245–46; society, 182, 225, 235

Tomb Period Japan, 881

tombs, *see* burial practices

Tondai Mandalam, 683

Tongan Empire (c. 1250-1450), 1036–38, 1073, 1080, 1090, **1124–25**, 1133

Tongatapu Group, 1027

Topkapi Palace, 552

Toramana, 661

totems Hawaii, 1042

tournaments, 96

Tours, Battle of, 3, 517

trade, Africa: the arts and, 405; with Europe, 368; intercontinental trade and global connections, 426–29; intra-African networks, 371; regional and long-distance, 390–94, 465–66, 470; spread of Christianity and, 430–31; spread of Islam and, 384–85; trade route maps, 363, 364, 366. *see also* slave trade; trans-Saharan trade

trade, Americas: Amazonian, 259; American Southwest and the Great Basin, 205–6; Chichén Itzá and, 273; long-distance, 190, 245–46, 254–55; Mayan, 276

trade, European: disruption of networks, 35; growth, 35–38; international percentage of, 74–75; long-distance, 38, 74, 90–91, 137; revival, 36–37; spices and, 73–74; Vikings in North America, 159–60; zones, 36, 91

trade, South Asia: overview, 705–8, 716–17; China and, 895–99; crafts and manufacturing, North India, 714–15; Delhi Sultanate economy, 715–16; routes and balance of trade, 708–11, 717–19; South Indian trade guild and agrarianism, 711–14; Southeast Asia and, 769–70

trade winds, 1097

traditional religion, African: human condition and, 385; Islam and, 487; polytheism, 378–79; regional similarities and differences, 378

trans-Saharan trade: African economy and, 391–92, 439; African global ties and, 427; African urbanization and, 471; Ghana and, 463; gold and, 464–65; spread of Christianity and, 430–31; spread of Islam and, 384–85

travel: Chinese junks, 895–96; difficulties, 91; globalization and, 428–29, 467; Indian sailing vessels, 675; overland, Europe, 70; purposes, 573, 576–79; South Asia trade routes, 708–11, 717–19; transport methods, 573–75. *see also* Ibn Battuta; Ibn Jubayr; *jihad*; pilgrimage

The Travels of Marco Polo, 131
Travels of Sir John Mandeville, 76–77
Treatise on Dramaturgy (Bharata), 661
Treaty of Verdun, 3
tree cultivation, Oceania, 1067–68, 1071–72
tributes, Yap Empire, 1033
Triple Alliance (Aztec Empire), 288–89, 306, 323, **332–34**
trobaritz (women poets), 98
Trobriand Islands, 1041
trope, 45
troubadour poetry, 97–98
Troyes pound, 91
Troyes, Treaty of, 4
trypanosomiasis, 374, 388, 420, 438, 451, 453–54
tsetse fly, 374, 388, 420, 421, 451, 453–54, 492, 495
Tu'i Konokupolu dynasty, 1028
Tu'i Tonga dynasty, 1027, 1028, 1037–38, 1090
Tula, 209, 220, 235, 272, **334–35**
tumbaga, 300, **335–36**
Tuoba, 872, 951, 980–81, 982
Tupiguarani speakers, 195, 204, 257
Turks: China and, 928; Mamluk, 646–47; Seljuk, 71, 99, 530, 651; Turkish slaves, 565, 631
Tuvalu, 1091
Tzintzuntzan, **336**

uji (clan), **940–41**
Umar ibn al-Khattab (d. 644), 529, 622, **627–28**, 643–44
Umayyad caliphate (661-750), 455, 517, 528, 529, 534, 542, 544, **628**, 657
Umayyad Mosque, 517, 550–51, 609, 628
uncles, Oceania, 1085, **1125–26**
Underworld: Mayan, 201, 347–49; Mesoamérican, 264
unilineal descent, Africa, 407
universities: African, 360, 412–13, 431, 458; European, 105, 135, 143; Nalanda University, 673, 678, 753–54, **814–15**
untouchables, 674–75, 740–41, 785, 790
Upper Xingu, **336–37**
Urban II, Pope (r. 1088-1099), 4, 71, 99, 531, 632
Urban VI, Pope (r. 1378-1389), 22, 31, 97
urbanism, Africa: population estimates, 411; West African Urban Complexes, 470–71; Zimbabwe Plateau, 495–96

urbanism, Americas: Amazonian, 195; Eastern Woodlands, 190
urbanism, Europe, 39
Utatlán, **337–38**
Uthman ibn Affan (d. 656), 529, **628–29**

Vaishya theory, 770–71
Vaisya caste, 738, 739, 785
Vanuatu, 1040, 1041, 1042–43, 1088, 1116
varnas, 738–40, 785–86
vassals, 19, 126, 674
Vasudeva, 693
Vatsyanana, 661
Vedic period, Indian mathematics, 754–55
Vedic texts, 817, 822
veils, 591, 594–95
Vellalas, 711–12
veneration of ancestors, **260–61**
Venus, **338–39**
via moderna, 144
"victory coins," 811
Vietnam: Battle of Bach Dang, 863; China and, 928; Funan state, 772–73
Vijayanager Empire, 663, 712–14, 788, 822, **828–29**, 859–60
Vikings: L'Anse aux Meadows settlement, 293; navigation by, 68; North American exploration, 75–76, 341–44; raids on northern and western Europe, 3, 18; settlements in Kiev, 3; trade disruptions, 35; Vikings in the North (map), 7
villages: Chinese society and, 914; Micronesian, 1054–55
Vinland, 75, 159–60, 341–43
vira valanjiar, 705
Virgin Mary, 26, 43, 85–86, 98, 104, 119, 148
Visakhadatta, 672, 844–45
Vishnu, 693
Visigoths, 16–17
visions, 175–76
visual arts, 49–51
volcanic islands, 1068
voyaging/ancient navigation, 1058–62, **1126–28**

Wa'ab island, 1034
Wairau Bar, 1027, 1039
Waldensians, 32
Walter of Henley, 168
Wang An-shih, 863
warfare, Africa, 370, **491–92**
warfare, Americas, 190, 233–34
warfare, East Asia, **997–99**

warfare, Europe: overview, **144–46**; challenges to Germanic kingdoms and, 16–17; crusaders and, 169–70; defensive castles, 47–48, 55, 89–90; Hundred Years' War, 13, 16, 23, 67, 94, **117–19**; importance of iron, 66–67; Wars of the Roses, 5
warfare, North Africa and the Middle East: overview, **629–33**; Battle of the Camel, 585–86; Islamic military technology, 572; *Ridda* Wars (Wars of Apostasy), 529, 551, 583
warfare, Oceania, 1036, 1088, **1128–30**, 1140, 1142
warfare, South Asia, **829–32**
Wari, 194, 211–12, 222, 256, **339–40**
Warring States Period (453-221 B.C.E.), 885–86, 937, 982
Wars of the Roses, 5
water: agriculture and, 584–85, 1067; uninhabited islands and, 1069
water power, Europe, 65–66
waves and swells, navigation and, 1060
Waxaklajuun Ub'aah K'awiil (18 Rabbit), 276–77
the Way (Daoism), 886–87, 945
wealth, Africa: cattle, 388, 421, 454; jewelry and, 419, 465
weapons, 145–46, 262, 864, 1129–30
weather, *see* climate
weights and measures, Japanese, 924
Wen, Emperor (589-604), 873, 983, 992–93
wergeld, 128
wheat prices and crime in England, 56
White Monks (Cistercians), 28
William I (William the Conqueror), 19
William of Normandy, 3
William of Ockham (c. 1300-1349), 63, 143–44
William of Tyre, 162
wind, navigation and, 1059
women, Africa: overview, **492–94**; craft production and domestic work, 390; farming and, 388; gold jewelry, 465; hunting and gathering, 466–67; Luba kingdom, 475; marriage and, 407, 408; Swahili architecture and, 402–3
women, East Asia, **999–1001**; Chinese society, 913, 1011; footbinding and, 877, 892,

959–60, 978, 992, 1000; Heian
Period and, 999
women, Europe: overview, **146–48**;
clothmaking, 67–68; education
and, 116; gardens and, 34; guilds
and, 113; iron and diet, 35, 134;
medicine and, 133, 134–35;
mysticism and, 27, 175–76;
orders and, 51; poets (trobaritz),
98; religious roles, 25, 27, 29,
108; urban life roles, 58; in
Western literature, 43–44
women, North Africa and the
Middle East: overview, **633–39**;
'Aisha bint Abi Bakr (d. c. 678),
585–86; clothing and modesty,
591, **594–95**; education and, 599–
600; food production, 603; home
life, 607–8, 635–36; role and
status in Islamic society, 562–64
women, Oceania: overview,
1130–32; clothing, 1077; dance
and, 1075; economy and, 1048;
food and, 1082; languages, 1094;
mana, 1098–99; New Guinea,
1086; New Zealand *Tapiru*, 1073;
society and, 1054, 1078; tapa,
1119; *tapu*, 1120; weaving, 1105
women, South Asia: Hindu
women, 746–49; Muslim women,
750–52; *sati* and, 749–50, **821–22**
woodblock printing, 863
woodwork, Islamic world, 554, 608–9
world views: Canticle of the Sun
(Francis of Assisi), 112; cyclical
time (Mesoamérica), 253–54,
281–82, 298–99; European, 76–77

writing systems: Aztec, 246–47;
calligraphy, 404–5, 552–53;
codices, 219, **275–76**, 283–84, 350;
Incan quipu, 314; Japan, 909;
Mayan, 245; Mesoamérican
development of, 181
written records, African history
and, 374–75
Wu, Empress (d. 705), 875, 948,
950–51, 954, 996
wu wei, 887, 945

Xuanzang (602-664): overview,
832–33; on Buddhism, 688–89;
on Harsha, 846–47; on Indian
punishments, 806–7; Silk Road
and, 989; visit to India, 662, 673,
678, 736–37
Xuanzong (Emperor Illustrious
August), 863, 875, 965–66

Yajnavalkya, law code compilation,
661
Yamato Period (c. 400-710), 881,
1001–2
Yamato state, 863
yams, Oceania, 1044, 1052, 1082,
1133–34
Yang, Emperor, 873–74, 993–94
Yangzi River, 935, 991–92, **1002–3**
Yap Empire, 1033–35, 1089,
1134–35
al-Ya'qubi (d. 897), 644–46
Yasodharman, 661, 795, 843–44
Yellow River, 920, 935, 947, **1003–4**
Yes and No (Sic et Non) (Abelard),
142–43

Yesong, 900
Yi dynasty, 881, 892, 926, 944, 955,
970, 978
yields, agricultural, 34, 40–41
yoga and yogis, **833–35**, 851–52
Yongle, Emperor (1405-1425), 711
Yoruba, 360, 388, 397–98, 444,
494–95
Yuan (Mongol) dynasty (1279-
1368), 816; overview, **1004–6**;
China and, 864, 869, 877–78, 898,
960–61, 975; emperors, 1022;
warfare and, 997–98

Zagwe dynasty, 360, 412, 430, 455
zakat (giving of alms), 537
Zapotec, 302–3
Zen Buddhism: overview, 864, 876,
893–94, 917–18, 940, **1006**;
Ashikaga shogunate and, 884,
938; noh theater and, 910, 938,
979, 1006
zero numeric concept, 755,
757–58
Zheng He/Cheng Ho, 864
Zhu Xi (1130-1200), 877, 891–92,
949, 954, 977–78, **1006–7**
Zhuangzi, 887, 945–46
zhyza (poll tax), 687
Zimbabwe Plateau: overview, 360,
495–96; the arts and, 400; city
states, 412; Indian Ocean trade,
392, 428; mining and, 417; social
stratification and, 371. *see also*
Great Zimbabwe
Zoroastrians, 698, 699
zuihitsu, 1020

About the Editor, Authors, and Contributors

General Editor

Joyce E. Salisbury is Frankenthal Professor Emerita of History at the University of Wisconsin—Green Bay. She has a doctorate in medieval history from Rutgers University, and throughout her career has won many teaching awards. Professor Salisbury is also a respected scholar who has written and edited more than 10 books, including the award-winning reference work, *The Greenwood Encyclopedia of Daily Life: A Tour Through History from Ancient Times to the Present, Perpetua's Passion: Death and Memory of a Young Roman Woman*, and *The Blood of Martyrs: Unintended Consequences of Ancient Violence*. She has recently taught medieval history while traveling around the world with the University of Virginia's Semester at Sea.

Chapter Authors

William B. Ashbaugh teaches Asian history and American foreign relations at SUNY Oneonta, where he is a tenured assistant professor of history. His work appears in *Reviews in American History, Peace & Change*, and *Film & History*'s CD-ROM collection "War in Film, Television, and History," and he has presented papers at conferences ranging from the Society for Historians of American Foreign Relations to Comic Arts and the Association for Asian Studies.

James L. Fitzsimmons is Assistant Professor in the Department of Sociology and Anthropology, Middlebury College, and Director of the Jaguar Hill Archaeological Project in Guatemala. He received his Ph.D. from Harvard University and has worked at several archaeological sites in Mesoamerica, including Piedras Negras and Copan.

James E. Lindsay is Associate Professor of history at Colorado State University, where he teaches courses on Ancient Israel, Sacred History in the Bible and the Qur'an, the Middle East, and the Crusades. His research and publications focus on medieval Islamic history. He is the author of *Daily Life in the Medieval Islamic World* (2005), the editor of *Ibn Asakir and Early Islamic History* (2001), and co-editor of *Historical Dimensions of Islam: Essays in Honor of R. Stephen Humphreys* (2008). He is the author of numerous articles on the twelfth-century historian Ibn Asakir and his *History of Damacus* as well as several articles on the Fatimids in North Africa. His most recent article, "David son of Jesse and Muhammad son of Abd Allah: Warlords, Statebuilders, Pietists," examines the depiction of religion and violence in the Hebrew Bible and the Qur'an.

Raman N. Seylon is Assistant Professor of South Asian and African Studies at Bridgewater State College in Bridgewater, Massachusetts. He received his Ph.D. at the University of Toronto, Center for South Asian Studies. His dissertation, "Making of a Tamil Hero," focuses on the Poligar Rebellion of 1799. His most recent article, "The Remembered Palayam," which will be published by *Asian Perspectives*, is an archeological study of the Poligar fort at Panjalamkurinchi in Tamil Nadu, South India.

Nancy Sullivan is a Ph.D anthropologist living and working in Papua New Guinea, where she runs a consulting company with former students of hers from the local Divine Word University. In 2007, she and her team won a Guggenheim for their work with the Awim and Inyai people and their mortuary caves at the headwaters of the Karawari River in Papua New Guinea's East Sepik Province.

Victoria B. Tashjian is Associate Professor of History at St. Norbert College in De Pere, Wisconsin. She received her B.A. from William Smith College and her Ph.D. in African History from Northwestern University. She is co-author, with Jean Allman, of *"I Will Not Eat Stone": A Women's History of Colonial Asante* (2000) and has written book chapters and articles addressing gender, cash cropping, and social change in Ghana, women's rights in Nigeria, and "customary law" in West Africa. Victoria dedicates the Africa portion of volume 2 to her daughter, Allegra.

Contributors

Robert D. Craig is Emeritus Professor of history at Alaska Pacific University (APU) in Anchorage. After 35 years of research, writing, and teaching in the Pacific, he has retired to Sarasota, Florida, where he continues his work but on a much reduced scale. He was named Alaska Professor of the year in 1992 by the National Council for Advancement and Support of Education (CASE) and has garnered numerous other teaching and research awards. His major publications include the *Historical Dictionary of Polynesia* (3rd ed.), *Dictionary of Polynesian Mythology*, *Historical Dictionary of Oceania*, and others, as well as being the founder of two scholarly journals — *Pacific Studies* in Hawaii and *Pacifica* in Anchorage.

John A. Wagner has taught history at Phoenix College and at Arizona State University, from which he received his Ph.D. in 1995. He is the author of various reference volumes, including the award-winning *Historical Dictionary of the Elizabethan World* (1999), which was a History Book Club selection, and the *Encyclopedia of the Hundred Years War* (2006).